COOKING
AND
KITCHEN
SKILLS

Editor: Barbara Croxford
Designer: Jo Tapper
Indexer: Alison Leach
Illustrations by Joyce Tuhill
Cover Illustration by Nicola Gregory

Special thanks are extended by author and publisher to Professor David Southgate,
Catherine Reynolds, Julie Loughridge, Dr Terry Roberts and Dr Roger Fenwick of the
AFRC Institute of Food Research for checking and contributing to the text.

Produced by Complete Editions

ISBN 0 11 701624 1

COOKING
AND
KITCHEN
SKILLS

BRIDGET JONES

London: HMSO

CONTENTS

Symbols

The following symbols are used throughout the book.

* This indicates that the item is included as a separate, main A–Z entry.

[X] This highlights distinct dangers related to hygiene and food safety. Points made under this symbol must be observed to avoid risk of food contamination. Certain aspects of general kitchen safety may also be included.

[X] This information also relates to dangers and bad habits in the preparation of food; however, they are less hazardous than those under the previous symbol.

[X] Warnings about potential problem areas.

[✓] Comments on positive practice and important points that relate to good standards of food safety.

[✓] Positive points to remember and to look for when buying, preparing and serving food.

[✓] Comments worth noting and general hints.

Good Food and Balanced Eating

Current nutritional advice on choosing the appropriate diet is based on a large volume of research on the relation between diet and health, also the role of diet in protecting against a range of chronic diseases. The scientific evidence shows that it is possible to give dietary advice that is appropriate for protection against many diet-related diseases. For example, a diet that reduces the risk of heart disease has the same features as one that offers protection against cancer.

This advice concerns the overall diet – the types and amounts of foods consumed over a period of time – not every food, every meal or every day. This means that it is possible to include practically every type of food within the dietary mixture and that there are no good (healthy) or bad (unhealthy) foods. However, there are healthy and unhealthy patterns of consumption, which, if continued, will reduce or increase your risk of acquiring a diet-related chronic disease at some time in the future.

Recommended intakes of protein, fat, carbohydrates, minerals and vitamins (called variously Recommended Dietary Allowances or Amounts (RDA) or Intakes) produced by governments or other authoritative sources are recommendations for populations and cannot be used to judge the adequacy of an individual's diet except in very general terms, because the requirements of an individual vary over a wide range. The new recommendations from the Department of Health provide ranges for most essential nutrients which give a more realistic idea but these Reference Nutrient Intakes also apply to the population as a whole.

From the practical point of view, nutritional advice has to be applicable at the individual level and the best way to judge this relates to the amount of energy you need to maintain your body weight within the appropriate range. This part of the dietary advice requires the individual to make a judgement that concerns him or herself.

The second general piece of dietary advice is to choose a variety of foods and to adopt various ways of cooking and preparing them. So, for example, the way in which potatoes are prepared should be varied throughout the week. This part of dietary advice serves to reduce the possibility of nutrient deficiency.

The third element is to eat regularly a variety of fruit and vegetables. The National Research Council of the USA and the World Health Organisation suggest a target of five servings a day. For most nutritional purposes fresh and frozen vegetables are virtually indistinguishable – if possible include both green and orange/yellow foods. If you do not have access to this variety the servings can be from canned products.

Foods rich in starch – cereal and potato-based foods, breakfast cereals, pasta and rice – should form with vegetables the largest part of main meals. Meats should be chosen from lean cuts of red meats, with poultry and fish (particularly oily fish such as herring, tuna and mackerel) being part of the weekly menu. Meat products should be selected on the basis of fat content and should not be major or frequent items in the diet.

Dairy products are important sources of calcium and vitamins but you should try to use ingredients with reduced fat on a regular basis and to see the high fat products (such as cream) as exceptional items used on special occasions. Try replacing cream with fromage frais or yogurt, for example.

In terms of cooking methods, grilling rather than frying (especially in deep fat) should be chosen as the usual method and wherever possible oils which are low in saturates (for example olive oil) should be used in cooking. If sauces made with butter are essential for the recipe, then this should be a 'special occasion' rather than an 'everyday' dish.

By choosing combinations of a variety of foods you can ensure that a healthy diet isn't a dull diet! It is, in fact, easy to ensure that such a diet is appetising, satisfying and attractive in appearance. Providing that the general principles of healthy eating are followed, the occasional, special occasion, use of food ingredients that seem to breech the more puritanical interpretations of current dietary advice is not likely to compromise an individual's health.

Professor David Southgate
Head of Nutrition, Diet and Health, AFRC Institute of Food Research

---

Six Golden Rules for a Healthy Diet

1 Eat a variety of foods.
2 Choose foods that are rich in complex carbohydrates, such as bread, pasta, rice and potatoes.
3 Use reduced-fat dairy foods.
4 Eat several servings of fruit and vegetables on a regular daily basis.
5 Eat lean cuts of meat, poultry and fish (especially oily fish).
6 Grill rather than fry, and use oils for cooking where possible.

USING THIS BOOK

The essence of good cooking and balanced eating lies in an appreciation of a few facts about food and an understanding of basic techniques. This book explains the essential details needed for safe, successful home cooking, with the emphasis on adopting practical rules for shopping and food preparation along side mastering simple methods which can be used as a basis for more complicated techniques.

Guidelines on adopting a sensible approach to diet are given as appropriate; however a concise, expert view of balanced eating is presented by Professor Southgate in Good Food and Balanced Eating (page 5).

All the information is given in alphabetical order and, so that you know exactly where you are, the first and last entries on each left and right hand page are clearly displayed. Along the bottom of the pages, useful cross references provide helpful information on other entries. A list of related entries is also given under each main A–Z heading. To complement the main section, a glossary of terms, techniques and selected classic recipes, is included at the back of the book.

Throughout the book, in addition to step-by-step methods and principles of selecting, handling and cooking individual foods, detailed recipes provide an essential base for one or more classic dishes. A recipe index means you can quickly find a favourite dish and the main index is the place to look up particular topics of interest.

Whether your quest is to learn the elementary aspects of cooking or to broaden your kitchen repertoire, the information on the pages that follow will impart a culinary confidence to ensure that all aspects of food preparation and eating are as enjoyable as they are essential.

Following the Recipes

• All recipes have been tested using metric measures. When using the recipes, follow one set of measures only, either metric or Imperial.

• All spoon measures refer to standard measuring spoons **not table cutlery**. Use a set of measuring spoons as other cutlery varies in capacity.

• Where necessary, use the size and shape of baking tin suggested in the recipe. If a suitable tin is not available remember that the cooking time may vary if a different tin is used.

• Unless otherwise stated, size 3 eggs have been used for testing the recipes. When a recipe calls for large eggs, size 1 should be used.

• Can sizes are taken from typical products. When cans or packets are used in recipes, the weight or volume listed is as stated on the can. However, sizes vary slightly according to manufacturer, so the nearest equivalent size should be used.

Microwave Information

Microwave tips are included occasionally within the text or to accompany recipes. Always read and follow the appliance manufacturer's instructions and suggested cooking times.

• All suggested cooking times are intended as a guide when using a 650 watt cooker.

• If your microwave has an output of less than 650 watts, then the cooking times will be the longest in the range suggested or slightly longer.

• If your microwave has an output higher than 650 watts, then the cooking times will be shorter than those suggested. Set the timer for a shorter period and check the cooking progress.

Metric/Imperial Equivalents

• The Imperial ounce is equal to 28.35 grams, the pint is equal to 591.48 millilitres and the inch is equal to 2.54 centimetres. The following tables outline adjusted metric and Imperial equivalents for use when weighing or measuring ingredients.

• Throughout the text, measures are expressed in metric first followed by Imperial; for example 25 g/1 oz, 600 ml/1 pint and 2.5 cm/1 inch.

Weights

25 g	1 oz
50 g	2 oz
75 g	3 oz
100 g	4 oz
150 g	5 oz
175 g	6 oz
200 g	7 oz
225 g	8 oz
350 g	12 oz
450 g	1 lb (16 oz)
550 g	1¼ lb
675 g	1½ lb
800 g	1¾ lb
900 g	2 lb

The following conversions are useful when considering the weight of large items, for example when shopping for meat or vegetables.

1 kg	2 lb 3 oz (about 2¼ lb)
1.25 kg	2½ lb
1.4 kg	3 lb
1.5 kg	3 lb 5 oz
1.75 kg	3 lb 13 oz
1.8 kg	3 lb 15 oz (4 lb)
2 kg	4 lb 6 oz (about 4½ lb)
2.25 kg	5 lb
2.5 kg	5½ lb
2.75 kg	6 lb
3 kg	6 lb 9 oz (about 6½ lb)

(**Note:** where the weight of ingredients is not critical, for example as when using large quantities of vegetables, the conversion 1 kg – 2 lb may be used.)

Ovens and Oven Settings

All baking and roasting tests have been carried out in an ordinary oven. Some baking recipes have been tested in both gas and electric appliances.

• If a forced convection oven is used, the manufacturer's instructions should be followed for adjusting the cooking time or temperature, as this type of appliance does not necessarily need preheating (except for delicate items such as soufflés) and the cooking temperature may be reduced. As a guide, either select a setting 10–20°C lower than suggested or reduce the cooking time accordingly. With delicate baked items, refer to the manufacturer's suggested settings for similar recipes or select a lower temperature setting rather than the shorter cooking time.

• All recipes have been tested in a preheated oven. Instructions are given for setting the oven at the appropriate stage in the recipe. However, many new ovens reach the temperature setting quickly and for long-cooked dishes (stews, cottage pie, layered pasta dishes) it is not essential to preheat the oven. If the oven is not preheated for cooking times under 40 minutes, the overall cooking time may have to be lengthened slightly but the result need not be inferior.

• Always preheat for soufflés, puff pastry and light cakes.

Using the Hob and Grill

As far as possible, guidance is given by using cooking terms, such as boil or simmer. In some recipes guidance on the level of setting is also given: for example 'over low/medium heat or setting', 'under a hot grill' or 'heat the grill on a medium setting'. When a guide to the setting is given, allowance must be made for differences between appliances. Many gas hobs have selected burners that are adjusted for faster cooking, even on a low setting.

Abbreviations

The following abbreviations are used throughout this book.

Useful Temperatures

Always use the right thermometer for the task: refrigerator and freezer thermometers for low temperatures, a sugar thermometer or thermometer for frying for high temperatures and a meat thermometer for roasting.

Never expose a thermometer to drastic or sudden changes in temperature. Have a plate ready to hold a thermometer after use. Heat a meat thermometer slowly in the oven from cold.

Acetic Acid

An acid which is used commercially in a diluted form to preserve foods, for example in pickles. This gives the pickles the tang associated with vinegar but without the flavour, which is why some commercial pickles taste harsh yet weak.

Acetic acid in vinegar is produced when wine, or other alcohol, is oxidised by bacteria.

When buying pickles, check whether acetic acid or vinegar are listed in the ingredients.

Additives

An additive is an ingredient which is not a food on its own but it is added to food during its preparation or manufacture.

Much confusing information has been produced about additives, what they are, why they are used, and the good or bad consequences of their use. Many publications concentrate on the topic (see Bibliography, page 288); however there are some general points worth remembering.

The Role of Additives

Additives serve different purposes in the manufacture of food, some functions are important in ensuring that the food reaches the consumer in good condition, others are more 'cosmetic'. The types and uses of additives are controlled by law, as are the rules about the way in which food is labelled. Up-to-

date comprehensive lists and details are published by government departments, food bodies and in a wide variety of books on food. The following are a few examples.

Preservatives These prevent the food from deteriorating in safety and quality, for example by attack from bacteria and moulds, between the time it is prepared, sold and eaten.

Antioxidants These help to prevent the process of oxidation which causes fat to go rancid.

Emulsifiers and Stabilisers These are binding ingredients, used to prevent oils and fats separating from water-based ingredients.

Colours Used to improve the appearance of food.

Flavour Enhancers Used to emphasise flavours already present in food.

Sweeteners Sugar is a food in its own right, therefore it is not considered to be an additive; however artificial sweeteners are additives.

Acids, Buffers and Bases These are used to control the acidity or alkalinity of food.

Humectants These absorb water to prevent certain foods from drying out.

Firming and Crisping Agents Used to keep canned and bottled vegetables crisp.

Flour Improvers and Bleachers To improve the strength of dough, helping out the natural gluten content, giving a lighter dough. Also giving whiter flour.

Identifying Additives

Labels on food have to list the ingredients used in the product. Additives have to be included. The ingredients must be listed in order according to the quantity in which they are used, the first in the list being the ones used in the greatest quantity. Since additives are used in comparatively small amounts, they usually appear towards the end of the list of ingredients.

Permitted additives have been given a number. Some numbers

have 'E' in front of them and this indicates that the additive is permitted by the European authorities as well as in Britain. Additives must be listed by type and by their chemical name or number. For example – setting agent: pectin; or antioxidant: E300. By checking with a list of numbers you will find that E300 is L-ascorbic acid (or vitamin C).

Natural or Synthetic

Condemning all additives as bad is nonsense; making an informed personal decision about the ones you want to eat or not – and why – is sensible.

Natural Additives Many additives are natural. Pectin, found in some fruit, is an additive in sweet preserves – it makes them set properly.

Additives Manufactured Identical to Natural Substances Some manufactured additives are identical to natural substances in their chemical composition. Potassium nitrate (E252) is identical to saltpetre.

Other Manufactured Additives Other manufactured additives are not based on naturally occurring ingredients – they are created to fulfil a specific role in food manufacture, for example azodicarbonamide (927) is a flour improver which has been laboratory created but an equivalent is not found in nature.

Good or Bad?

The obvious question to follow on from asking whether something is natural or synthetic must be to query whether it is good or bad, and whether natural is related to good, or synthetic to bad.

The term 'natural' is often emphasised on products and related to goodness. Yet natural does not always mean good. For instance, there are many examples of foods which contain natural toxins, including red kidney beans, cassava (see vegetables*, exotic) and bitter almonds.

Similarly, synthetic is not necessarily bad. The use of additives

SEE ALSO **Acidulated Water:** Glossary; **Aduki Beans:** Beans and Pulses, Dried; **Aigrette:** Choux Pastry; **Al Dente:** Glossary;

is strictly controlled and continually assessed. Many additives play an important role in ensuring that manufactured food is both safe and of high quality – they have been used for years to improve the standard of canned and packet foods as well as chilled items. Others are not essential by any means but they are used to create products that many people enjoy.

Additives and Allergies

Just as some people produce a negative reaction to some foods (for example to dairy products or chocolate), a few (in fact, a very small proportion of the population) react to certain additives. Naturally, we do not all react in the same way to the food we eat – if something does not agree with us, then we avoid it. The same is true of additives – if a particular item produces a bad reaction then it can be avoided by checking the ingredients list on a label before buying food.

Agar Agar

This is a setting agent made from seaweed. Available in a powder form from wholefood shops, it is used in place of gelatine* for vegetarian dishes. Agar agar dissolves and sets at higher temperatures than gelatine, and it has stronger setting powers. When working with agar agar, for example folding whipped cream into a mousse mixture, it is important to remember that it sets quickly as it cools.

Unlike gelatine, agar agar will set uncooked pineapple and papaya more successfully. The enzymes present in these fruit act on gelatine to prevent it from setting.

Mixtures set with agar agar tend to be more rubbery and chewy when eaten because they do not melt quickly in the mouth.

Albumin

See Eggs*.
Albumin is a protein which makes up a large part of egg white. It is also present in milk. Dried albumin powder is available from cake decorating suppliers for making icing. It may also be used to make meringues.

The dry powder should be stored in an airtight container in a cool place. It is reconstituted by stirring into cold, or barely warm, water. Albumin powder has a slightly unpleasant smell – this does not mean it is bad.

Alfalfa

See Beansprouts*.
Alfalfa sprouts are the fine sprouts of tiny seeds of Mediterranean origin which may be purchased for sprouting at home. The sprouted seeds have a mild taste and a crunchy texture. Wash and drain well before using in salads; good in sandwiches too.

Nutritional Value

Alfalfa seeds are pulses and a source of vegetable protein, making them a useful food for vegetarian salads.

Almonds

See Marzipan* and Nuts*.
Almonds are an important flavouring ingredient in cooking, both sweet and savoury. There

---

ALMOND MACAROONS

These light biscuits are quick and easy to make.

INGREDIENTS
- **2 egg whites**
- **175 g/6 oz caster sugar**
- **100 g/4 oz ground almonds**
- **1.25 ml/¼ teaspoon oil of bitter almonds or natural almond essence**
- **10 blanched almonds, split in half**

FOOD VALUES:
TOTAL • PER MACAROON
kcals: 1366 • 68
kJ: 5740 • 287
protein: 24 g • 1 g
fat: 62 g • 3 g
carbohydrate: 189 g • 9 g
fibre: 16 g • 1 g
Makes 20

Set the oven at 180°C, 350°F, gas 4. Line two baking trays with rice paper or non-stick baking parchment.

Whisk the egg whites in a bowl until they stand in firm, soft peaks. Using an electric beater, gradually add the sugar, whisking all the time. Continue whisking until the mixture is glossy. If using a hand whisk, add the sugar in small portions and whisk well after each addition.

Add the almonds and use a metal spoon to fold them into the egg whites. Add the almond oil or essence when the nuts are half folded in and continue folding until well combined.

Use a dessertspoon to drop 20 small rounds of mixture well apart on the prepared baking trays. Place a piece of almond on top of each and bake for 15–20 minutes, or until the macaroons are pale gold.

Leave the macaroons to cool on the trays for 2 minutes, then transfer them to a wire rack to cool completely. Tear the rice paper (if used) around the edges of the macaroons. Store in an airtight container when cold – the macaroons will keep for about a week.

are two main types of flavouring, both are very strong and should be used with care.

Almond Essence

Synthetic almond essence has a very strong taste that does not compare well with natural flavouring. Look for natural almond essence.

Oil of Bitter Almonds A strong essence that gives a good flavour. Bitter almonds are small almonds which are heat treated and used in small quantities in cooking as a flavouring, typically in macaroons or in natural vanilla essence. However, in their natural state they can be highly poisonous since they contain a substance which reacts with water to create a poisonous acid. When heated the nuts are quite safe and they provide a useful, natural flavouring.

Anchovies

See Fish*.
Small fish, found fresh in Mediterranean countries where they are preserved by salting. Available filleted and canned in oil (some in olive oil).

Use

Canned anchovies are salty, so do not season any dish to which they are added until after they are incorporated and you have tasted it. To remove excess salt, soak the drained anchovy fillets in a little milk for 5 minutes, then drain again before use: however, this is not an economical way of using them. Generally, it is better to chop them finely and add them in smaller quantities to taste.

• Chopped canned anchovies may be tossed with freshly cooked pasta, diced fresh tomatoes and chopped parsley to make a tasty supper dish. Serve with grated Parmesan cheese.

• Use to top pizza.

• Chop and sprinkle over quartered hard-boiled eggs served on a salad.

• Mash and cream with butter, then shape into pats to top grilled beef steak, swordfish or fresh tuna steaks.

Anchovy Essence

A beige-coloured bottled sauce which is used as a flavouring ingredient. It is strong and salty so always use with care and avoid adding too much seasoning.

Apples

See Fruit* for seasonal home-grown apples, Pies* and Flans*.
In Britain apples are divided into two main groups – eaters (or dessert apples) and cooking apples (cookers). Cooking apples are not as sweet as eating apples, and some are quite sour, but the main reason for separating them is that cookers soften quickly on cooking whereas eaters stay in whole pieces even though they become tender. Full-flavoured eating apples may be poached until tender, baked slowly in flans or used to make an upside-down tart French-style (known as tarte tatin).

Buying

Look for firm, unblemished fruit with a good natural sheen. In the supermarket, selecting fruit often makes better sense than buying pre-packed apples, partly because they are usually cheaper unpacked but mainly because you can inspect each apple and avoid bruised fruit. Avoid any fruit that looks slightly wrinkled. The following is a list of the main types that are widely available.

Bramley's Seedling These make up the vast majority of cooking apples sold and they are mainly UK grown. Available all year. These have a good tangy flavour, soften quickly when cooked and are ideal for making pies, apple

sauce or purée. They also bake well whole with peel on.

Cox's Orange Pippin Available from October through to March or April, these are among the best-known eating apples. They are green and orange-red in colour with crisp, sweet, juicy and full-flavoured flesh. At their best up until Christmas and the New Year, by early spring they may become slightly woolly.

Cox's are also good cooked: try peeling, coring and quartering the fruit, then poaching it in a light syrup* with a strip of orange rind and a cinnamon stick. Serve either hot or cold. Also good in apple flan or upside-down tart.

Discovery These are early apples so they do not keep well and are only available during August and September. They are pale yellow flushed with bright red. Their flesh is firm with a refreshing flavour which is accentuated if the apples are chilled before eating.

Egremont Russet These brown-coloured, slightly rough-skinned apples have a red-orange blush in patches. Available during September and October, they have a good, distinct flavour which may be described as slightly nutty. When first available they have a crisp texture but they tend to become woolly as they age. Excellent for adding to salads and really good with a mature Cheddar cheese.

Golden Delicious Yellow-green skinned apples, mainly imported and available for most of the year. At their best, these have a light flavour and slightly crisp texture; however they are mainly weak in flavour and they can be very woolly, when their skin seems tough by comparison. Avoid any that are pale yellow rather than yellow-green.

Granny Smiths Bright green apples with crisp, white juicy flesh and a good slightly tart flavour. They should feel firm and the small to medium apples usually have the best flavour. If their colour has become a dull green they tend to be less crisp in texture; if they are green-yellow they may

SEE ALSO **Almond Paste:** Marzipan; **Angelica:** Glossary; **Angler Fish:** Fish; **Aniseed:** Spices be slightly woolly and lacking in flavour. Good in salads.

Worcester Pearmain Bright-red skin and crisp white flesh are characteristic of this apple which is available during September and October. They have a sweet flavour and are juicy early in the season.

Crab Apples

Small hard wild apples with a bitter taste that leaves a dryness in the mouth. They make a bright, full-flavoured jelly.

Pick-Your-Own

Apples are often available at pick-your-own farms, grown on low-growing trees for easy picking. If you intend picking apples for storing over winter months, take great care not to bruise them and be sure to pick a late variety (harvesting in October).

Storing

Only the late varieties of apples may be stored and each fruit should be perfect as any blemishes result in rotting. Storing apples is only practical if you have a dark, airy, frost free place which is cool. Ideally, apples should be stored in a moist atmosphere, so a shed or unheated cellar are suitable. Each apple should be wrapped in paper (pieces of newspaper) and placed in a tray or box. Single layers in trays are best, otherwise separate layers in a box with cardboard trays or plenty of newspaper. Do not put more than three layers in a box. This packing prevents any minor deterioration from spreading and ruining the whole crop.

Preparation

Always wash apples under cold running water and dry them before use. Bought apples may be eaten whole but unless home-grown fruit is perfect it is a good idea to cut it to make sure the core is free from any small insects or maggots.

APPLE SAUCE

The traditional accompaniment for roast pork.

INGREDIENTS
**450 g/1 lb cooking apples, peeled, cored and sliced
75–100 g/3–4 oz sugar
juice of ½ lemon
25 g/1 oz butter**

Serves 4

FOOD VALUES:
TOTAL • PER PORTION
(Using 90 g/3¼ oz sugar)
kcals: 707 • 177
kJ: 2991 • 748
protein: 2 g • 0.5 g
fat: 21 g • 5 g
carbohydrate: 138 g • 35 g
fibre: 11 g • 3 g

Place the apples in a saucepan. Add the sugar and sprinkle in the lemon juice. Heat gently, stirring often, until the sugar dissolves and the apples soften. Continue cooking over medium heat for about 15–20 minutes, or until the fruit is pulpy. Stir occasionally to prevent the apples sticking.

Off the heat, beat in the butter. Transfer the sauce to a dish and lay a piece of greaseproof paper on its surface, then leave to cool.

VARIATIONS

Apple Mint Sauce Add 60 ml/4 tablespoons chopped fresh mint to the cooled sauce. Serve with grilled lamb chops or steaks or roast lamb.
Lemon Apple Sauce Add the grated rind of 1 lemon when cooking the apples. Serve hot with grilled mackerel.

Baked Apples

Set the oven at 190°C, 375°F, gas 5. Wash, dry and core the whole apples. Score the peel around the middle of each fruit, then stand the apples in a greased baking dish. Fill the hole left by the core with light or dark soft brown sugar and place a small knob of butter or margarine on top. Cover the dish and bake the apples for 40–50 minutes, depending on size.

Filling Ideas
• Raisins, grated orange rind and demerara sugar.
• Mincemeat.
• Chopped walnuts, honey and chopped mixed peel with a little ground cinnamon.
• A soft paste of ground almonds, sugar and orange rind with chocolate hazelnut spread.

Apple Purée

Place the peeled, cored and sliced cooking apples in a saucepan with 100 g/4 oz sugar for each 450 g/1 lb fruit and 30 ml/2 tablespoons water. Heat gently until the sugar dissolves, then continue to cook, uncovered, stirring often, until the apples are reduced to a pulp. The time depends on the type of apple but it is likely to take about 15 minutes. Rub the purée through a sieve or process until smooth in a food processor. Alternatively, beat well until smooth.

The purée may be made without added sugar, in which case a lid should be placed on the pan until the apples have softened to prevent them from drying out and burning. Eating apples make sweet purée.

Peeling and Coring The way in which apples are peeled and cored depends on what they are used for. The easiest way of preparing apples for pies, purées or when a recipe calls for apple slices is to quarter the fruit. Then, using a small, sharp knife, begin at the stalk end and cut out the core leaving a scoop shape, then carry on peeling the outside of the piece of fruit. With practice, it is easy to cut away the core and first strip of peel in one go, then to carry on peeling the fruit. The apple quarter may be left in one piece for poaching, cut into moon-shaped slices or cut across into wedge-shaped slices.

Chopping Apples To chop an apple, hold the quarter, cored side down, on a board and cut it into slices lengthways, holding all the pieces firmly together. Without letting go of the slices, cut across them to make small pieces of apple. The thinner the slices, the smaller the pieces. They are not neat, squared dice but quite good enough for adding to stuffing or salad.

Coring Whole Apples To do this neatly, use an apple corer or a vegetable peeler designed to core apples. Stand the washed and dried fruit firmly on a board. Push the corer down through the centre of the apple and take out the main part of the core. Use the corer or a fine, pointed knife to remove any remaining pieces of core.

Cutting Apple Rings First core the whole apple. If the rings are to be peeled, use a vegetable peeler and cut off the peel from around the outside of the whole fruit. Then slice the fruit. Apple rings may be quickly fried in a little butter or margarine and sprinkled with brown sugar, honey and nuts to make a delicious dessert.

Freezing

Apples freeze well for up to a year. Cooking apples should be peeled, cored and sliced, then blanched in boiling water with lemon juice (acidulated water) added to prevent discoloration, allowing the juice of 1 lemon to every 900 ml/1½ pints water. The fruit may be packed with or without sugar.

Both eating and cooking apples may be cooked and puréed, then frozen. Also a wide variety of prepared apple dishes freeze well – pies, tarts and charlottes, for example.

Apples may be cooked from frozen or thawed in a covered dish at room temperature for a few hours or overnight in the refrigerator.

Nutritional Value

Although apples are not an excellent source of vitamin C, they are eaten raw and, being one of the less expensive fresh fruits, they may be eaten daily or frequently so providing a useful supply of vitamin C.

APPLE CHUTNEY

INGREDIENTS
1.5 kg/3 lb cooking apples, peeled, cored and sliced
450 g/1 lb onions, chopped
75 g/3 oz fresh root ginger
2 cloves garlic, crushed
5 ml/1 teaspoon turmeric
15 ml/1 tablespoon ground coriander
5 ml/1 teaspoon ground cinnamon
2.5 ml/½ teaspoon ground cloves
75 g/3 oz raisins
300 ml/½ pint malt vinegar
225–275 g/8–10 oz soft brown sugar
Makes about 2.25 kg/5 lb

FOOD VALUES:
TOTAL • PER 15 ML/ 1 TABLESPOON
(Using 275 g/10 oz sugar)
kcals: 1904 • 13
kJ: 8087 • 54
protein: 16 g • 0.1 g
fat: 2 g • 0 g
carbohydrate: 483 g • 3 g
fibre: 39 g • 0.3 g

Have ready thoroughly cleaned and dried jars placed on a folded clean tea-towel in a roasting tin. Prepare wax discs, airtight lids and labels.

Place the apples and onions in a large saucepan (do not use an aluminium pan). Wash the ginger, trim off any very tough ends, then coarsely grate the rest of the root and add it to the pan. There is no need to peel the ginger when it is grated but the last piece left should be discarded.

Add all the remaining ingredients, with the smaller quantity of sugar if you prefer a tangy chutney or the larger amount for a sweet chutney. Heat gently, stirring frequently, until the sugar dissolves, then increase the heat and bring the mixture to the boil. Regulate the heat so that the chutney simmers and cover the pan. Leave to cook for about 1 hour, stirring occasionally to prevent the chutney sticking to the pan.

About 20 minutes before the chutney is cooked, place the jars in the oven on the lowest setting to warm. The cooked chutney should be thick and the apples reduced to a pulp. Pot it at once in the jars and place waxed discs, waxed sides down, and airtight lids on immediately. Label and allow to cool before storing for at least a week before sampling. If kept in a cool, dark, dry place, the chutney will keep for up to 9 months.

Stewed or Poached Apples

Stewed apples are not the same as apple purée or sauce. They should be tender but in separate pieces when cooked, not fallen to a pulp. Cooking or eating apples may be stewed or poached in syrup or lightly sweetened fruit juice. Large fruit and cooking apples should be quartered, medium fruit or small cooking apples may be halved and smaller eating apples are good whole. If very large pieces of cooking apple are stewed, the outside tends to break up before the middle is tender.

Syrup A medium syrup* should be used for cooking apples, a light one for sweeter eating apples. About 175 g/6 oz sugar to 250 ml/8 fluid oz water with the juice of ½ lemon may be used to cook up to 1 kg/2 lb cooking apples. Spices such as cinnamon stick and whole cloves (2–4) may be added. Part of the liquid may be made up with fresh orange juice, dry cider or white wine.

Method Add the prepared apples to the syrup which is barely simmering. Turn the fruit in the syrup, then cook it gently with the syrup still barely simmering, until the apples are just tender. This takes about 5 minutes for cooking apples, 15–20 for eating apples, the longer time if they are left whole.
   Cook 675 g/1½ lb cooking apples or 4–6 eating apples to serve four.

Microwave Method Place the prepared apples, sugar and liquid in a suitable covered dish and cook in the microwave on High for 6–7 minutes (for cooking apples) or 8–9 minutes (for eating apples). Leave to stand for 2–3 minutes before serving. Timings are for 675 g/1½ lb.

Using Apple Purée

The cooled purée may be frozen – remember to note the quantity of fruit and sugar used (if any) on the label.

● Apple fool – mix the purée with cold custard, whipped cream or fromage frais*. A little grated lemon rind or vanilla essence may be added. Chill before serving.

● Use sweetened apple purée as a filling for pancakes. Add a few raisins and orange rind if liked. Roll up the pancakes and place in an ovenproof dish. Dot with butter or margarine and sprinkle with chopped toasted hazelnuts. Cover with foil and heat in the oven at 180°C, 350°F, gas 4 for about 20 minutes, or until piping hot. Serve with fromage frais*, yogurt or hot custard*.

● Fry 225 g/8 oz fresh breadcrumbs in 75 g/3 oz margarine or butter until crisp and golden. Stir in 5 ml/1 teaspoon ground mixed spice and 50 g/2 oz demerara sugar. Layer the breadcrumb mixture in a dish with sweetened apple purée. Cool and chill well.

Microwave Tip
Apple purée and apple sauce both cook well in the microwave. Use a deep covered dish to prevent the apples from boiling over and allow 6–9 minutes on High for 450 g/1 lb apples.

Apricots

*See Fruit**
Apricots may be purchased fresh or dried.

Buying

Fresh Fresh apricots should be smooth, slightly furry, evenly coloured and firm but not hard. When over-ripe they tend to be soft and/or dark in colour, and their flavour will be dull.

Use fresh apricots soon after purchase. Depending on how firm they are, they may be stored for up to a couple of days in a shallow dish at room temperature. If they are ripe for using they should be stored in a bag in the salad drawer in the refrigerator.
Dried There are two main types of dried apricots: those that have to be soaked in cold water to cover for several hours (or overnight) before use and others (more common) that are ready to eat. A third variety, available from wholefood shops, is small, dark whole fruit which has to be soaked overnight before use.

Preparing Fresh Apricots

Wash the fruit and dry it gently on absorbent kitchen paper. Cut around each apricot into the stone, then twist the two halves apart. The stone will be left in one half.
   The cut fruit discolours if left exposed to the air, therefore sprinkle it with a little lemon juice and place in a covered container or use at once.
   Small kernels inside the apricot stones are traditionally used for flavouring jams and poached fruit. They contribute an almond-like flavour. Add only a few as too many make the preserve bitter. Kernels **must** be cooked as they are poisonous eaten raw in significant numbers.

Cooking

Poaching Both fresh and dried fruit may be poached (the dried fruit should be soaked first if necessary). Fresh fruit should be poached in a light syrup*, dried fruit is best cooked in unsweetened liquid (water, wine or cider), then sweetened to taste after cooking.
   Add fresh fruit to barely simmering syrup and continue to simmer gently for about 5 minutes. Overcooked fresh apricots tend to be dominated by the skin,

so remove them from the heat when they are just tender.

Dried apricots should be simmered in just enough liquid to cover for about 15 minutes. If the fruit has been soaked, then the soaking liquid should be used for cooking. Dried apricots are good poached with spices – a cinnamon stick, 3–4 cloves or 2–4 split green cardamom pods. Plain poached dried apricots may be puréed, adding enough cooking liquid to give the purée the required consistency.

Puréed Fruit Place fresh apricots in a saucepan and sprinkle with a little fresh lemon juice. Cook the fruit gently, stirring occasionally, for about 20 minutes, until very soft. Rub the apricots through a sieve or purée them in a food processor. Cool and use as required.

● Sweeten to taste with runny honey and serve as a sauce with ice cream or other desserts.

● Sweeten to taste, then swirl into fromage frais or natural yogurt in individual glass dishes and chill before serving.

Ideas for Using Apricots

Apricots are a versatile fruit for use in both savoury and sweet dishes.

● Fill halved fresh apricots with low-fat soft cheese flavoured with chives. Sprinkle with crumbled crisp-cooked bacon or diced cooked ham and serve as a starter.

● Use fresh or ready-to-eat dried apricots in Breadcrumb Stuffing (page 254).

● Both dried and fresh apricots make good chutney. Dried apricots may be chopped and added to a basic Apple Chutney (page 12) or combined with less flavoursome ingredients such as marrow and green tomatoes.

● Pickle halved and stoned apricots in sweetened, spiced distilled white vinegar or cider vinegar. Serve with cooked meats or hot baked ham.

● Arrange poached fresh apricots in a cooked flan case. A base of Confectioner's Custard (page 101) or low-fat soft cheese beaten with a little sugar may be spread in a pastry flan first. Glaze the fruit with the cooking syrup thickened with arrowroot*.

Nutritional Value

Both fresh and dried apricots contain a useful amount of vitamin A and the fresh fruit provides some vitamin C; since apricots are not likely to be eaten in quantity they are not a main source of this nutrient. Dried apricots also provide carbohydrate in the form of fruit sugar.

Aprons

Generally, the apron is seen as a means of keeping clothes clean but one that fits well also works the other way to protect the food. Before handling food you may have popped something in the outdoor bin, had the cat sitting on your lap, made a fuss of the dog or carried out numerous other tasks that leave minute deposits on clothes. As well, a firmly tied apron keeps loose clothing out of the way – a plus from the safety angle.

A practical apron for cooking should cover the front of your clothes from just below the neck down to about knee level; it should also wrap around the sides at the waist. This way it keeps any splashes off clothes and prevents fluff and fibres (along with any other microscopic particles or bacteria) from being transferred off garments to the food.

Wipe-clean plastic aprons may seem a good choice but one that can be washed is better because you can be sure it is clean. If you buy an apron, then try it on first – some can be uncomfortable.

Lastly, remember that a grubby, stained, damp apron is a breeding ground for bacteria, so put it in the wash after cooking.

Arrowroot

A white powdered plant starch. Obtainable in small tubs from delicatessens or chemists, it is used as a thickener.

Unlike cornflour, arrowroot is completely tasteless and it clears when it thickens, making it ideal for glazing fruit or for thickening fruit sauces.

Use

Blend arrowroot to a paste with a little cold liquid before adding the bulk of the hot liquid. Return the mixture to a saucepan and heat, stirring all the time, until the mixture just boils. Remove the pan from the heat as soon as the mixture boils. This is important because arrowroot mixtures will become thinner in consistency if they are allowed to cook beyond boiling point.

Quantities to Use

● To slightly thicken a thin fruit purée, allow 5 ml/1 teaspoon arrowroot for each 300 ml/½ pint.

● To thicken fruit juice to a thin pouring consistency, use 15 ml/1 tablespoon arrowroot to each 300 ml/½ pint.

● To thicken juice or syrup which is to set cold as a glaze, allow 25 ml/5 teaspoons arrowroot to each 300 ml/½ pint.

Artichokes, globe

These are the flower buds of a plant related to the thistle.

Buying

Available from late winter through to early spring with some British produce available in summer. Artichokes have a dull green colour which should be even with a slight bloom. They should be firm and unblemished. The leaves (not true leaves but they are known as such) should be firmly closed together.

Preparation

Wash the vegetables well in salted water.

Cut off the stalk just below the artichoke. Remove the large outer leaves around the base (they tend to be slightly loosely packed). Use a vegetable peeler to peel off the remains of the tough stalk level with the base of the tender leaves. Cut the pointed top off the artichoke, then use a pair of kitchen scissors to snip off the points from all the leaves.

Cooking

Boiling Drop the artichokes into a large saucepan of boiling salted water. Bring back to the boil, reduce the heat so that the water boils steadily, then cover the pan. Cook for 30–45 minutes. Small artichokes take about 30 minutes, larger ones require longer cooking.

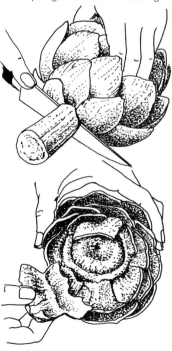

Preparing an artichoke for cooking.

Removing central pack of soft leaves from a cooked artichoke.

To test if the vegetables are cooked, pull off one of the larger leaves around the base. It should come off easily.

Drain the vegetables well. If they are to be served cold, have a bowl of iced water with the juice of a lemon added and put the artichokes in this to prevent them from discolouring.

Steaming Steam prepared artichokes over boiling water for about 25–35 minutes. Test as above.

Microwave Cooking Artichokes cook well in the microwave. Place them in a roasting bag with 30 ml/2 tablespoons lemon juice and 30 ml/2 tablespoons water. Close the bag loosely with a microwave-proof tie or twist the end and fold it under. Place the bag on a plate. Allow 20–25 minutes on High for 4 medium vegetables. The cooking time for 2 artichokes is about 15 minutes on High. When cooking the larger number, they should be rearranged halfway through to ensure even results. Leave to stand for 5 minutes after cooking.

Removing the Choke

In the centre of the leaves there is a hairy, inedible choke. Carefully push out the leaves surrounding the centre of the vegetable, pulling out some of the thinner middle ones. Right in the middle there is a tight, pale-coloured pack of soft leaves – hold these firmly and pull them out in one piece. Part or all of the choke may come out at the same time. If not a soft, hairy down will remain.

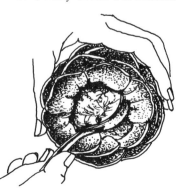

Scooping out the choke.

Use a teaspoon to scoop this out, gently scraping all the hairs off the pale flesh below.

Completing the Preparation Once the choke is removed the vegetable is ready for serving: at the base of each leaf there is a small area of edible flesh. All the leaves are attached to a pale round base, the best part of the vegetable, known as the bottom or fond which may be served in a salad, with a stuffing or coated in sauce.

Cook's Tip
The leaves are very fibrous and they can block a waste disposal unit in a sink.

Serving

Serve one per person. The simplest way is to make a good vinaigrette dressing (see salad and salad dressings*), then to spoon a small amount into the middle of the artichoke. Provide a small dish of dressing with each.

Alternatively, the middle of the vegetable may be stuffed – chopped hard-boiled egg with diced tomato, soft cheese and chives is good or a Breadcrumb Stuffing (page 254) may be used and the stuffed vegetable baked, then served hot.

Always give each person a side dish for the discarded leaves.

Eating Globe Artichokes

Dip the small area of pale flesh cupped in the leaf base in dressing. Eat this area of flesh off the leaf. Discard the rest. When all the leaves are removed the artichoke bottom should be eaten with a knife and fork.

X *Cooked artichokes should be cooled quickly and used promptly. They may be stored in a covered container in the refrigerator overnight but must be used within 24 hours. Mild toxins can develop in cooked artichokes that are left for longer periods before eating. The same applies to unused canned artichokes – use within 24 hours.*

Canned Artichokes

Prepared bottoms (bases, fonds) are available canned in brine.
Artichoke Hearts These are the pale, tender group of leaves taken from the middle of young artichokes which have not developed chokes. They may be used as a topping for pizzas, added to salads, or used in casseroles and sauced dishes.

Freezing

Wash and blanch* for 5–7 minutes according to size. Cool and drain well. Pack in polythene bags and store for up to 9 months. Freshly cooked and cooled bottoms may be frozen for up to 3 months.

Artichokes, Jerusalem

These are not related to globe artichokes. Jerusalem artichokes are root vegetables which are easy to grow. They are knobbly and have a pale brown-beige coloured skin.

Buying

Available from October through to spring, the vegetables should be firm and not too dirty. Avoid limp, wrinkled vegetables and any that look as though they have been nibbled at by pests (evident from small holes). If you want to peel the vegetables, then it is quite hard work with very knobbly specimens.

Preparation

Like potatoes, artichokes may be eaten with or without their peel. Scrub them thoroughly and trim off any blemished areas, then rinse in fresh water if cooking with peel on.

If peeling, first pour some cold water into a saucepan and add the juice of half a lemon. Peel the artichokes and rinse them under clean water before putting in the pan.

Cooking

Boiling Cover with cold water, adding a little lemon juice as before with peeled artichokes, and add a little salt. Bring just to boiling point, then reduce the heat so that the water only just bubbles. If Jerusalem artichokes are boiled rapidly they disintegrate. Cover the pan and cook for about 15 minutes. Small, peeled vegetables are tender after about 10 minutes, larger ones take up to 20 minutes. Peeled artichokes cook more quickly than vegetables with peel on, they also overcook quickly.
Steaming Peeled vegetables should be placed in cold water with lemon juice added until they are all ready for cooking. Steam over boiling water for 15–20 minutes, the longer time for large artichokes with peel on.
Microwave Cooking The prepared artichokes should be fairly even in size. Place in a covered dish with 30 ml/2 tablespoons water and 30 ml/2 tablespoons lemon juice. Do not add salt. Allow 9–10 minutes on High for 450 g/1 lb vegetables, stirring to rearrange them once. Leave to stand, with the lid on, for 3–5 minutes before serving.

Serving Ideas

• Plain cooked, topped with butter. Snipped chives or chopped parsley may be added.

• Mashed with a little butter and pepper.

• Coated with Savoury White Sauce (page 234) or Cheese Sauce (page 234) and topped with breadcrumbs and cheese, they may be baked until golden.

• Jerusalem artichokes make good soup. They must be peeled and cooked in stock with a chopped and lightly fried onion. The puréed cooked vegetables should be thinned with milk and seasoned, then heated before serving.

Freezing

Jerusalem artichokes do not freeze well raw or plain cooked but they can be frozen mashed or in soup for 3–6 months.

Ascorbic Acid (Vitamin C)

See Vitamins.*
Vitamin C is not produced in the human body so it is essential that adequate amounts are eaten. This vitamin is important for good health, particularly for maintaining connective tissue which supports the cell structure of the human body. Deficiency results in poor health, slow recovery from illness and poor wound healing.

 Never add bicarbonate of soda to cooking water as it is an alkali which neutralises ascorbic acid.

Sources

Fruit and vegetables are the main sources of vitamin C, particularly cabbage, Brussels sprouts and spinach. Green peppers have a high vitamin C content. Potatoes, because they are eaten in significant quantities, also provide a major supply. Sprouted seeds (bean sprouts) also provide vitamin C.

Among the fruit, blackcurrants are outstanding in the amount of vitamin C they contain, also citrus fruits and fruit juices are important. Many commercial fruit juices and other products have added vitamin C.

Explaining the vitamin C content of food is only part of the story. There is good reason for the fuss which is made about this vitamin – it is water soluble and destroyed by heating, oxidation and by alkaline substances. Food that may have a high content when it is growing in the field does not necessarily remain as rich a source when it reaches the plate.

Retaining Vitamin C in Food

The choice and handling of fruit and vegetables are important.

Freshness The fresher the produce, the more vitamin C it contains. As soon as fruit and vegetables are harvested their vitamin C content begins to fall. Most commercially frozen vegetables that are processed very rapidly after harvesting contain more vitamin C than their fresh equivalents which have been transported and stored before sale (peas are a good example).

So it is important to eat fruit and vegetables that are as fresh as possible. Buy often and use straightaway is the rule to remember. Frozen vegetables are better than stale 'fresh' vegetables, both for flavour and food value.

Preparation Cutting up fruit and vegetables can cause some loss of vitamin C. To minimise this, a stainless steel knife should always be used (never carbon steel). With vegetables, the more they are cut up before cooking, the larger the surface area for loss of the vitamin.

Cooking Vegetables should be cooked in the minimum of water for the shortest time. This applies particularly to green beans, peas, cabbage and so on.

If possible the cooking liquid should be used to make sauces (for example when preparing cauliflower cheese) or gravy.

Raw vegetables are an important part of the diet. Include them in interesting salads, as sandwich fillers or as snacks.

Asparagus

*See Vegetables.**
Asparagus is one of the more expensive, luxury vegetables.

Buying

British-grown asparagus has a short season, from mid-April or May towards the end of June; however imported vegetables are on offer almost all the year.

Look for firm, bright green spears. Check the ends of the spears – if a good portion of the length looks thick and woody it will be wasted other than for flavouring soup. So slim, firm asparagus is best.

Preparation

Trim off the tough, woody ends. If the spears are slim and tender, then simply peeling the ends to remove any stringy outside is enough. Wash and drain well, taking care not to damage the tips of the spears. Tie the asparagus in neat bundles.

Cooking

A special asparagus cooker consists of a tall, narrow saucepan with a circular metal rack inside it and a lid. This is tall enough for the asparagus to stand upright, with the stalks in the cooking water and the tips supported by the rack, cooking in the steam above. A very specialised item which is rarely found in the average kitchen.

Improvise by standing the bundles of spears upright in a pan of water, with the ends of the spears cooking by boiling and the tips steaming above. Use a tent of foil to cover the pan, crumpling it around the rim to keep in the steam.

Boil the asparagus for 10–15 minutes, the thinner the spears the shorter the cooking time.

Serving

Serve asparagus just as it is, with some melted butter poured over, a good grind of black pepper and a squeeze of lemon. Grated Parmesan cheese may be sprinkled over.

Using Tough Spear Ends

These can be made into soup. Depending on how tough they are, they may be boiled for flavour then sieved out of the soup if very fibrous or, if they are not too stringy, then they may be chopped and served in the soup.

Frozen and Canned

Frozen is better than canned but it tends to be rather soft. Good for dishes containing asparagus rather than serving as a vegetable. All white asparagus spears available in cans are completely blanched (in the horticultural sense, being grown in the dark, rather than in the culinary sense) and they may be used alongside green asparagus for appearance.

Use

• Add cooked and cut up to Savoury White Sauce (page 234) to serve with fish or chicken.

• Wrap in cooked ham, coat in cheese sauce, top with breadcrumbs and grill to make a delicious first course.

• Use as a filling for a savoury flan*. Arrange short spears like the spokes of a wheel, add grated cheese and an egg and milk mixture, then bake.

Freezing

Freeze when very fresh. If asparagus is to be frozen for up to 2 weeks, there is no need to blanch it. Otherwise, prepare as for cooking and blanch for 2–4 minutes, the thinner the spears the shorter the time. Store carefully as the rigid frozen spears are brittle. Freeze for up to 9 months. Cook from frozen.

Aspic

See Clarifying and Stock*.*
This is a clear savoury jelly which may be made from fish, poultry, meat or vegetable stock.

Use

Aspic is used for coating cold savoury foods such as dressed salmon or pâtés. Set in a shallow container, then chopped, it makes a sparkling garnish for cold platters. It may also be combined with Savoury White Sauce (page 234) or mayonnaise to make a chaudfroid coating for chicken or other poultry.

Aubergines

See Vegetables*.

The American for these purple-skinned vegetables which vary in size is eggplant. Very small oval or round aubergines about the size of tomatoes (or smaller) are sometimes available from ethnic grocers. They are more commonly long and thin or plump and oval, varying in size. White-skinned aubergines are also occasionally available (rare but it is worth knowing of their existence).

Buying

Look for shiny, firm aubergines. Avoid any that are wrinkled, bruised or with soft brown patches. Always inspect each aubergine well because it is easy to miss brown patches, particularly if they are hidden near the stalk.

Preparation

Aubergines have a slightly bitter taste which is removed by salting, a process known as degorging.

Trim off the stalk and rounded end of the aubergine. Unless a recipe specifically requests that the vegetables are peeled, there is no reason to do so. Cut up the aubergine as required, in slices, cubes or fingers.

For stuffing, cut each one in half lengthways. To remove the flesh from the shell, make criss-cross cuts down into each half, taking care not to cut right through the skin underneath. Make a neat cut around the inside of the shell, then scoop out the pieces of flesh.

MOUSSAKA

INGREDIENTS
450 g/1 lb aubergines
salt and pepper
450 g/1 lb lean minced lamb
90 ml/6 tablespoons olive oil
1 large onion, chopped
1–2 cloves garlic, crushed
1 (400 g/14 oz) can chopped tomatoes
30 ml/2 tablespoons concentrated tomato purée
10 ml/2 teaspoons dried oregano or marjoram
10 ml/2 teaspoons ground coriander (optional)
150 ml/¼ pint water

30 ml/2 tablespoons chopped fresh mint (when available)
Topping
10 ml/2 teaspoons plain flour
2 eggs
300 ml/½ pint natural yogurt
a little grated nutmeg

FOOD VALUES:
TOTAL • PER PORTION
kcals: 2502 • 626
kJ: 10402 • 2601
protein: 167 g • 42 g
fat: 176 g • 44 g
carbohydrate: 67 g • 17 g
fibre: 17 g • 4 g

Serves 4

Cut the stalk and ends off the aubergines, then slice and salt them. Meanwhile, heat a frying pan gently and add the minced lamb. Dry fry the meat, stirring, over medium to high heat until it is evenly and lightly browned. It will give up its fat as it cooks. Use a draining spoon to transfer the meat to a basin. Pour off excess fat from the frying pan and set the pan aside – you need it later to cook the aubergines.

Heat a little of the oil in a saucepan, then add the onion and garlic. Cook the onion gently, stirring occasionally, until it is soft but not browned. This will take about 15 minutes or longer but it is important for the finished flavour. Cooking onion over too high a heat, too quickly, results in crunchy bits of onion in cooked meat sauces.

Return the meat to the pan with the onion, then stir in the tomatoes, tomato purée, oregano, coriander (if used) and the water. Stir until the mixture just comes to the boil. Cover the pan and leave the mixture over low to medium heat to simmer gently for 30 minutes, stirring occasionally.

Add some of the remaining oil to the frying pan. Heat it briefly – take care not to overheat olive oil – then add as many of the aubergine slices as you can lay in the pan. Cook until just beginning to brown on one side, then turn the slices and cook the second side. Do this over a medium to high heat so that the slices seal quickly without becoming too soft. They should be tender.

Remove the aubergines from the pan as they are cooked (they may be set aside in the basin used to hold the cooked mince) and cook the remaining slices in the same way, adding more olive oil as necessary.

Set the oven at 190°C, 375°F, gas 5 and have ready a large ovenproof dish. Taste the meat sauce for seasoning, then add the mint (if used). Layer the aubergines and meat sauce in the dish, starting with aubergines and ending with meat sauce.

For the topping, whisk the flour and eggs together until smooth, then gradually whisk in the yogurt. Mix in a little seasoning and pour the mixture over the layered meat and aubergines. Sprinkle with a little nutmeg. Bake the moussaka for 40 minutes, until set and golden.

Layer the prepared aubergines in a colander and sprinkle each layer generously with salt. Sprinkle the shells with salt. Place over a bowl and leave to stand for 30 minutes. Rinse well and dry on absorbent kitchen paper, then use as required.

Use

• Slices may be coated in egg and breadcrumbs, then fried until crisp and served with soured cream and chives.

• Slices may be quickly fried in hot oil (olive oil or other), layered with tomatoes, sliced mozzarella cheese and chopped parsley, then baked.

• Cubes may be cooked with onions, green pepper, garlic, courgettes and tomatoes in olive oil to make ratatouille (page 252).

Freezing

Although aubergines may be frozen in made-up dishes, they do not freeze well on their own. On thawing they are unpleasantly slimy.

Avocado

The avocado is a versatile, delicately flavoured fruit with pale green or creamy coloured flesh that has a buttery texture when ripe.

Buying

There are many types, from small elongated oval shapes to huge almost round fruit. The colour of the skin ranges from bright green to black and it may be smooth or rough in texture.

Under-ripe avocados are hard, slightly bitter and lacking flavour. They may be ripened in a warm room at home but if they are to be eaten soon, check for ripeness before buying. Feel the avocado in your hand, pressing it gently near the stalk end with your thumb. The fruit should feel tender but not squashy. (Take care when checking avocados not to bruise them.) If they feel very firm, they are not ripe. Avocados that are really hard and offered at a bargain price are best avoided for serving plain as they tend never to ripen.

Avoid avocados that are bruised or obviously over-ripe. Look carefully at dark-skinned fruit – if there are any wrinkles the flesh will be very soft, possibly black.

> **Cook's Tip**
> Placing an avocado in a brown paper bag with a ripe banana in a warm place speeds up the ripening.

Preparation

Never prepare avocados too far in advance as their flesh discolours badly once it is exposed to air. This applies to pâtés, dips and any other dishes with avocado (except ice creams). Cut the fruit in half, then ease the pieces apart. With luck the stone may come out easily. If not, taking great care, stab the stone with the point of an old knife, then pull it free.

Sprinkle the cut flesh with lemon juice or fill and serve it immediately.

Peeling The easiest way is to cut the stoned avocado into quarters. Starting at the narrow end, slip a knife between the flesh and skin, then gradually pull back the skin. It comes off easily in one piece from perfectly ripe fruit. Use the point of a knife to separate flesh and skin if the fruit is either under or over-ripe.

Serving

Serve one half per person as a starter. The simplest way is to place the avocado in a scoop-shaped avocado dish, then fill the cavity left by the stone with vinaigrette dressing (see salads and salad dressings*).

Crumpled foil on a plate, or kitchen paper in a cereal bowl, may be used to support the avocado half instead of using a special dish.

Use

• Fill with breadcrumbs, chopped spring onion and grated cheese, then grill.

• Dice or slice in salad or to fill baked potatoes.

• Mash to make delicious dips – guacamole is a Mexican dip of avocado, garlic, chopped green chilli, diced peeled tomato and a little soured cream.

• Purée avocado flesh with chicken stock, milk or cream, season and flavour with chives, to make a delicate chilled soup.

• Mashed avocado also makes a rich ice cream.

• Use in sweet dishes such as cheesecakes.

Freezing

Whole avocados should not be frozen as they discolour. However, avocado flesh mashed with plenty of lemon juice may be frozen for short periods (2–4 weeks), which is useful when the fruit is cheap.

Place the avocado in an airtight rigid container and cover the surface with freezer film to minimise contact with air, which causes browning. Put an airtight lid on the container.

Thaw at room temperature for a few hours – the time depends on the size of the pack.

Nutritional Value

Although avocado is not a main food it requires a note on nutrition. Contrary to its light appearance and taste, avocado flesh is rich in fat and therefore has a high calorific value. It is also an excellent source of vitamin A. It provides some protein which makes a valuable addition to a vegetarian meal (although it must not be compared to beans and pulses which are the main sources of vegetable protein).

Bacillus cereus

See Bacteria* and Micro-organisms*.
A type of bacteria carried in food. The bacteria are destroyed during cooking but they produce spores that are highly resistant to heating and may survive cooking. However, these will only germinate if the food remains warm for some time or if it is inadequately warmed through after cooking and cooling. If the spores germinate, the food contains bacteria that are likely to cause food poisoning.

Susceptible foods include rice, cereals and pulses. Food poisoning caused by these bacteria is relatively rare and not often fatal, but it is unpleasant.

Serving Rice

Cooked rice should be served hot or it should be covered closely when cooked and drained, then cooled quickly. When cool, it must be chilled immediately. If the rice is to be served cold (for example in a salad), it should be tossed with other cold ingredients and dressing, then kept refrigerated until it is served. Rice salad is a useful buffet food but it is important to avoid leaving it standing in a warm room for any length of time as the warmth will provide ideal conditions for the spores to germinate. Chill the salad until ready to eat. Afterwards, cover any leftovers and chill them promptly.

Apply these rules to other cereals and grains such as wheat, buckwheat and millet.

Eating Out

Rice salads should be kept covered and in a refrigerator or chiller cabinet. Cooked rice should be very hot not warm. Take note of these standards when ordering from buffet-style establishments.

Bacon and Ham

See Meat* and Pork*.
Bacon and ham are both pork cured by salting. Originally, the curing process was a necessary method of preserving meat. The majority of bacon and ham is cured by salting with brine, which is both injected into the meat and used as a soaking solution. Some pork is still cured by dry salting, mainly for regional hams that are not widely available in all supermarkets.

Unsmoked and Smoked

Both ham and bacon are available plain or smoked. The meat is smoked after it has been cured. Another term for unsmoked is green (green bacon) or pale may also be used.

Buying

Bacon and ham are sold vacuum packed or loose, in a variety of cuts, including sliced cooked ham, joints of cooked ham, bacon rashers, gammon steaks and joints of bacon or gammon for cooking.
Packed As with any other packed food, check details on the label before buying. With uncooked bacon or ham, note the curing method: some bacon is cured by traditional methods (containing less water, more salt and providing a good, traditional flavour). Other packs may be labelled 'tender sweet' or 'sweet cure' which indicates that additional ingredients may have been used to flavour or tenderise the meat. For example, sugar, molasses or fruit, such as pineapple or papaya, may have been used to give the bacon a slightly sweet taste and tender texture.

Check whether bacon rashers have the rind on or removed as this may save preparation time.

There is a wide choice of cooked ham, from the cut to the type of curing and cooking method, also the thickness of slices. Much of the information is shown clearly on the main 'heading' or title of the ham. The ingredients list will provide information on the percentage of water which the cooked ham contains – those types with a high water content tend to be soft and moist, while ham with little or no added water is firmer, more meaty and full-flavoured.
Loose The bacon and ham should be chilled, including ham on the bone ready for hand slicing. Do not be shy about suggesting that perishable food should be kept chilled.

Sliced bacon and ham should look fresh. The fat should look firm and pale white to cream in colour, not tinged yellow or soft-looking. The look of the ham varies according to type: some pressed shoulder should be quite moist and pale pink, other hams may be slightly less moist and nominally darker pink.

Bacon should be an even-coloured red-pink. The lean flesh should not be dark red and dried around the edges.

Raw Cured Ham

Raw cured air dried ham is ready to eat. Italian *prosciutto crudo* is raw cured ham of which the best known is Parma ham. French Bayonne ham and German Westphalian (a full-flavoured smoked variety) ham are also examples. Cumberland ham is an example of a British equivalent but it is not as readily available in supermarkets.

Storing

All types of bacon and ham should be kept chilled in the

refrigerator as soon as possible after purchase.

Packed bacon and ham should be stored according to the instructions on the label and eaten before the 'use by' date. Once the packet is opened, the contents should be treated as loose meat.

Bacon and ham bought loose should be placed in a closed polythene bag. Any greaseproof paper wrapping should be removed before the meat is wrapped and chilled.

Loose cooked ham may be kept for up to 2 days after purchase. Uncooked rashers and joints may be kept chilled for about a week (or according to packet instructions).

Cuts

Streaky Inexpensive, narrow rashers with lines of fat running along the length between the lean meat. Taken from the belly (equivalent fresh cut is belly pork). May be grilled or fried. Streaky is ideal for cutting up (dicing or chopping), for rolling and for wrapping around foods that are skewered (traditionally prunes, scallops, also good around chunks of courgette).

Back Taken from the back of the animal, this has a main eye of lean thinning to a narrow strip, with a thin band of fat running across the top of the rasher. Some back is very lean. Ideal for grilling and frying but also useful for cutting up when a lean result is required.

Middle or Throughcut This is the streaky and back in one piece, usually curved around.

Collar Lean, economical rashers that tend to be wide and short. The fat content varies slightly. Nominally tougher than streaky and back. Ideal for lean diced bacon.

Collar joints are excellent for boiling, providing plenty of lean meat that slices easily. Also good cubed and casseroled.

Gammon Steaks and half steaks are succulent grilled or fried. Joints may be boiled or baked. The gammon is taken from the rear leg of the pig. Middle gammon is the main, evenly shaped, round cut of meat and corner gammon is a small piece of lean, triangular shaped meat from the end of the gammon. Steaks are taken from the middle cut. A large joint on the bone, including the corner, makes an impressive centrepiece for a buffet or for a celebration meal.

Forehock For boiling as a joint or cubing and stewing.

Gammon Hock The knuckle end of the joint, taken from just above the trotter. The boiled meat is well flavoured and tender, and good for soups and stews. The meat may be served hot or cold.

Bacon Chops You may find these in some supermarkets. They are thick cut back bacon for grilling or frying.

Offcuts Small irregular bits of bacon and gammon that are left after slicing, these are usually inexpensive and they are ideal for dicing or chopping. Use to flavour rice and pasta dishes. Finely chopped or minced, they may be combined with breadcrumbs, chopped onion and beaten egg, then shaped into burgers.

Preparation

Remove the rind from rashers before cooking, if liked. The easiest way to do this is to snip it off with a pair of kitchen scissors. Snip out any small areas of bone. Wash the scissors afterwards in hot soapy water.

The fat on gammon steaks, back and middle or throughcut rashers should be snipped at intervals to prevent it curling during cooking.

Soaking Some bacon joints may need soaking before cooking but this depends on the curing method and salt content. Many vacuum packed joints are ready for cooking in their packs – always read and follow the instructions on the pack. Check with the butcher who will give advice on the particular joint. If in doubt do not soak gammon but soak bacon joints (for example collar or hock) for 2–4 hours.

Meat which is to be soaked should be placed in a large bowl with cold water to cover, and covered, then placed in the refrigerator. If space does not allow and the room is warm, then add ice cubes to the soaking water occasionally to keep the meat cool. Drain off the soaking water before cooking the bacon.

Cooking

The following information applies to bacon, gammon and uncooked ham.

Grilling For bacon rashers or chops and gammon steaks. Bacon rashers cook quickly so the grill should be preheated on high. Lay the rashers on a rack over the grill pan and cook for about 3 minutes on each side, or until as crisp as preferred.

Bacon chops should be cooked for 5–7 minutes on each side.

Thicker gammon steaks take longer to cook, so the grill should be heated on a medium setting. Lay the steaks on a rack over the grill pan. Cook for 5–7 minutes on each side, depending on thickness and heat setting.

Grilling is the best way to keep the fat content of cooked bacon to a minimum.

Frying If the bacon is very lean, then trickle a little cooking oil into the frying pan and wipe it around with a piece of absorbent kitchen paper. Most bacon does not need extra fat.

Lay the rashers in the pan, overlapping the fat side of one with the lean of the next, and place it over moderate heat. Cook for 3–5 minutes on each side until the rashers are cooked to your liking. The time depends on the particular bacon – some bacon rashers yield more liquid than others. To crisp wet bacon, the liquid must first be evaporated over high heat.

Boiling For joints. The joint should be weighed and tied like a parcel to keep it in shape during cooking. Place it in a large saucepan and add a thickly sliced onion, sliced carrot, a couple of parsley sprigs, a bay leaf, blade of mace and 4 cloves. A sliced celery stick (with leaves) may also be added. Pour in cold water to cover the meat and put the pan over moderate heat. As the water begins to simmer a foamy scum may rise to the surface: skim this off using a large spoon or draining spoon. Once the water is boiling, reduce the heat so that it simmers steadily and put a lid on the pan. Cook for 20 minutes per 450 g/1 lb plus 20 minutes once boiling.

Lift the joint from the cooking liquid and remove the string. The rind may be removed easily from a hot joint. Use a sharp pointed knife and slide it under the rind at one end of the joint. When a flap of rind is free, lift it in one hand and cut it off the fat, working close to the rind and pulling it back as you cut.

Alternatively the rind may be left on the joint, then cut off individual slices as the meat is served.

Glazing A boiled joint may be glazed in the oven. Remove the rind from the freshly cooked meat. Score the fat in a diamond pattern, if liked, and brush it with clear honey. A mixture of demerara or soft brown sugar combined with a good pinch each of ground cloves and cinnamon makes a good glaze. Press the sugar mixture on the hot fat. Bake the joint at 220°C, 425°F, gas 7 for 10–15 minutes, or until golden.

Baking Suitable for gammon joints but not for tougher bacon cuts. Weigh the tied joint and calculate the cooking time at 20 minutes per 450 g/1 lb plus 20 minutes for joints up to 4.5 kg/10 lb. Larger joints should be cooked for 15 minutes per 450 g/1 lb plus 15 minutes. Place the joint in a large saucepan with cold water to cover and bring to the boil. Skim off any scum, then reduce the heat and cover the pan. Cook the joint for half the calculated time, then drain it and remove the skin if required.

Set the oven at 180°C, 350°F, gas 4. Place the joint in a covered ovenproof dish or wrap in foil and place it in a roasting tin. Bake for the remainder of the time. Unwrap for the final 10–15 minutes to brown the fat, which may be glazed with honey or sugar.

Smaller gammon joints may be baked completely, although it is best to soak the joint in cold water for 1–2 hours beforehand as the baked meat may be rather salty.

Braising and Stewing Cubes of gammon and bacon may be braised or stewed with vegetables in water, cider, beer or wine. The tender cuts of gammon take about 40–50 minutes, while the slightly tougher bacon cuts require 1¼–1½ hours.

Freezing

Bacon and cooked ham may be frozen but the keeping quality varies considerably. Salt and air both promote rancidity in frozen food, so the less salt in the food and the less air in a pack the better. Since bacon and ham are cured meats, with comparatively high salt contents, they do not keep as long as fresh meats. Commercially vacuum packed products keep longer than others. Look out for ready frozen bacon and ham and follow the manufacturer's instructions. Uncooked bacon rashers and joints packed at home may be frozen for about a month. Vacuum packed uncooked products may be frozen for between 3–6 months, the shorter time for joints.

Cooked ham is not an ideal freezer candidate; however diced leftovers from a large joint may be frozen for 3–4 weeks, then used for adding to cooked dishes. Ham sandwiches freeze well for 3–4 weeks. Commercially vacuum packed cooked ham keeps reasonably well for 3 months. Prepared dishes which contain bacon or ham should be stored for about a month, very much longer and they will taste rancid*.

Nutritional Value

Bacon and ham are protein foods. They also provide thiamin (vitamin B1), riboflavin, vitamin B12, nicotinic acid and iron. The fat content varies but it is worth noting that there is a good choice of bacon cuts that are trimmed of excess fat and that the majority of pork meat is fairly lean.

Bacteria

See Bacillus cereus*, Botulism*, Hygiene*, Listeria*, Salmonella* and Staphylococcus*.

Bacteria are micro-organisms, or microscopic living cells. When we speak of 'germs' we usually mean bacteria. Some bacteria cause food poisoning if they are present in large numbers, others have only to be present in small numbers to cause problems. In some cases, the bacteria are not themselves poisonous but they produce toxins which infect the food and cause the upset. Even though the bacteria may be killed by cooking, some are capable of producing spores (rather like seeds) which are resistant to heat. The spores may survive in cooked food, ready to come to life when the conditions are right.

Bacteria are not visible to the human eye but they are all around us – they live in the air, on our bodies, in the home, garden and so on. In acceptable quantities in the right places, bacteria serve useful purposes, for instance in the manufacture of cheese and yogurt. There will be some bacteria on the food we eat but our bodies are used to dealing with the 'normal' amounts.

Conditions for Bacterial Growth

Food poisoning usually results because an insignificant number of bacteria (or their spores) have been allowed to multiply. The conditions must be right for the organisms to grow.

SEE ALSO **Bain Marie:** Glossary; **Bake Blind:** Flans and Glossary; **Bakewell Tart:** Glossary

Air Many bacteria require oxygen from the air in order that they may grow – these are *aerobic* bacteria. This is not always the case and certain particularly dangerous bacteria only multiply in sealed cans, jars or other containers which exclude air – they are *anaerobic*. ·

Moisture Bacteria require water or moisture to grow.

Warmth This is the important requirement and it is the one that can be most easily controlled. Most bacteria multiply at the fastest rate at temperatures of about 37°C/98.6°F (human body heat). Below and above this temperature they are not as active. During freezing the bacteria are dormant. If wet food or dishes are cooked until 'too hot to touch' and the temperature maintained for 10–15 minutes, most of the vegetative pathogens are killed. For example, salmonella bacteria are killed at 70°C/158°F. However, spores may survive.

Food Our food also provides the ideal food for bacteria to grow.

Preventing Bacteria from Multiplying

Keeping food cold is the most important way of preventing the small numbers of bacteria present from multiplying to dangerously high levels or producing toxin.

Chilling Fresh Food Fresh foods should be chilled as soon as possible after purchase. They should not be allowed to warm up in the car after shopping.

Cooling Cooked Food Food which is cooked to be served cold, or leftovers, should be cooled as quickly as possible. It should be kept covered (with some baking exceptions) while cooling, then chilled as soon as it is cool.

Excluding Air Although this in itself will not effectively stop the bacteria from growing (only commercially sterilised vacuum packs can do this), it does help in preventing growth and, more

important, it is essential to stop more bacteria landing on food.

Reducing Bacterial Contamination

Food must be handled properly to reduce the risk of it being contaminated. The notes under hygiene* should always be observed.

As well, remember that food should be kept covered and never left exposed to the air except when it is actually being prepared.

All utensils should be clean before preparing food and washed up immediately after use.

Work surfaces and other areas in the kitchen should be kept spotlessly clean – bacteria will thrive in barely noticeable crevices that are not cleaned out, then they will pass on to utensils and in turn to the food.

Cross Contamination*.

X *A separate entry deals with this in more detail. Never prepare raw and cooked foods using the same set of utensils. Always wash and dry all equipment used for preparing raw food straight after use.*

Washing

The simple process of washing can dispose of much of the bacteria on some food. For example washing vegetables will get rid of some bacteria that first found their way on to the food from the soil. Even though fruit and vegetables may look clean, they should be washed.

Useful Bacteria

✓ *Some bacteria are put to good use in food production. For example, in making yogurt and cheese.*

Baking

This is a method of cooking by dry heat in the oven. During cooking, a certain amount of steam is produced by the moisture content of the food.

Use

A wide variety of food is baked, from breads, cakes, biscuits and pastries to savoury dishes (gratins, cottage pie, meat loaves, pâtés and layered pasta dishes), batters (such as Toad-in-the-Hole, page 238), soufflés and milk puddings.

Effects of Baking

As a rule, baked mixtures have to be carefully balanced so that they rise, set, turn brown or crisp during the cooking process. Raising agents* that react on the application of heat are used and a glaze (such as milk or beaten egg) may be added to improve the browning process.

Browning This can be the result of caramelising of any sugar content. It may also be due to the fat increasing the heat of the surface of the food (for example in pastry) – rather like frying. The process of browning not only provides colour but it also results in the characteristic flavour that is associated with baking.

Crusting Some foods that are baked uncovered, breads and some pastries, form crusts. In some cases the crust may take the form of a skin – for example on a milk pudding. Breadcrumb and cheese toppings form a crust on gratins.

Steam Baking

Professional bakers use steam ovens to make baked goods rise well. Placing a roasting tin or ovenproof dish of boiling water in the base of the oven provides steam which causes items such as choux pastry to rise well. The moisture from the water means that it takes slightly longer for the crust to set, so the pastry has more time to puff up.

A tent of foil may be placed over some baked goods for part of the cooking time to trap some of the steam produced by the moisture content of the food, therefore giving a good rise to the baked items.

Baking in a Bain Marie

A bain marie (see Glossary, page 275) is a container of hot water. The dish or tin of food to be cooked is placed in this container of water, then placed in the oven (although a bain marie may also be used on the hob). The water reduces the temperature of the outside of the dish. This is used for delicate foods (custards and smooth pâtés) which tend to curdle if they become very hot around the side of the container.

Covering Food

Some foods may be covered for all or part of the baking time to retain moisture and prevent over-browning.

Baking Powder

See Raising Agents*.

Baking powder is made up of an acid and an alkali, mixed in the right proportions to react and produce carbon dioxide gas when moistened and heated. The bubbles of gas are trapped in the food as it sets firm during baking. This makes the mixture rise and produce a light result.

Use

Self-raising flour is used more often than baking powder and plain flour. As a general guide, more baking powder is needed for dry mixtures such as scones than for moist cakes.

Storing

Baking powder should be kept in an airtight container in a dry place. Check for the 'best before' date on the container. Baking powder does have a long shelf life but it is the sort of ingredient that may be used only occasionally, so forgotten for many months, if not years.

Baking Tins and Bakeware

There is an enormous variety of tins available, in many different shapes and sizes, with various coatings.

Materials

Aluminium This is lightweight, cheap and it conducts heat well; however aluminium reacts with acids. It may be coated with tin, a non-stick finish may be applied or the aluminium may be uncoated.

Tin Tin may be used as a coating for aluminium, copper or for steel.

Stainless Steel This is a mixture of metals, including nickel and chromium which prevent rusting.

Non-Stick Coatings There are different types of non-stick coatings and price is a good guide to quality.

Enamel Enamel coatings are sometimes used on roasting tins. This does not react with acids or other substances but it must not be chipped or damaged as any exposed metal underneath the enamel will corrode or react with the food.

Glassware Ovenproof glass designed for baking may be plain or it may have a non-stick coating. These dishes may be used in the microwave as well as for conventional cooking, and they are useful for combination cookers.

Buying

The choice of baking tins depends entirely on how often you intend baking and what sorts of foods you plan to cook.

As a general rule, the heavier baking tins that are slightly more expensive last longer; indeed good quality, heavy tins will last for many years. Cheaper, lightweight tins tend to warp more easily and food sticks to them or burns readily. Non-stick coatings vary enormously but even the

most expensive of these will not outlive a sturdy tin.

Shapes and Sizes If you intend roasting meat or poultry regularly, a roasting tin or dish is a necessity. If you only cook a roast occasionally, then it is worth looking beyond a basic metal roasting tin and considering a dish which will double as a baking container for pasta specialities (such as lasagne) or for making casseroles, pies and so on.

A heavy baking tray (or sheet) is one basic item that will give years of service. Either buy a large square tray with a lip along one side or look for a tray with shallow sides which will double as a baking tin for making Swiss rolls.

A pair of sandwich tins and a deep round tin are two basic items of cake-making equipment. A tray of patty tins (or bun tins) doubles for making individual pies as well as for baking small cakes.

Loaf tins and dishes may be used for making meat loaves and pâtés as well as for baking breads and cakes.

The first items to buy are one or two versatile containers, then extend the range as necessary. Bakeware sets that include a number of different tins or dishes look interesting but it is worth thinking about how valuable each individual piece will be in your kitchen.

Quality and Finish As well as using price and the manufacturer's reputation as a guide to quality, look at the finish on bakeware, particularly on tins. Look for smooth edges and rims, neat seams, square corners and a good neat inside edge all around the base of a tin. Always check the inside of baking tins for shape and quality since it is this area that gives the baked food its finished form. Avoid dented items with sharp rims, rough seams and uneven bases. Larger tins and baking trays should not flex easily otherwise they are likely to warp quickly – heavy items are the best buy.

SEE ALSO **Baking Beans:** Glossary; **Baking Soda:** Bicarbonate of Soda

1. Sandwich tins
2. Sponge flan tin
3. Deep cake tins
4. Patty tin
5. Muffin tin (pan)
6. Yorkshire pudding tin
7. Swiss roll tin
8. Dariole moulds
9. Loaf tin
10. Bread tin
11. Barmoral tin
12. Ring tins
13. Spring form tin
14. Loose-bottomed flan tins
15. Raised pie mould

Loose-bottomed Tins and Spring Form Tins Tins that have loose bottoms or sides that are held in place with clips allow for easy removal of baked goods. Spring form tins that are circular with a spring clip and expanding sides usually have a choice of bases, including a ring tin base.

Care of Bakeware

Always read and follow the manufacturer's instructions, particularly with non-stick materials. Remember these general guidelines too.

● Avoid scratching metals with knives or sharp implements. Never use metal utensils on non-stick surfaces.

● Never subject bakeware to sudden dramatic changes in temperature – for example, do not place tins straight from a red hot oven in cold water as they warp.

● Wash bakeware in hot soapy water when it has cooled slightly, then dry it thoroughly. Tins may be returned to the oven to dry in any residual heat.

● Soak off baked-on food rather than using scourers.

● Do not store tins in a damp place where they are likely to become rusty.

Preparing Baking Tins

Greasing Some non-stick bakeware does not require greasing before use (follow the manufacturer's instructions) but the ma- jority of tins and dishes should be greased. When baking plain pastry items with a high fat content there is no need to grease the baking tins; however some enriched pastries may stick. Use light flavourless oil for greasing. Keep a pastry brush for the purpose (washing it in hot soapy water and drying it after use) and brush the oil all over the inside of the tin, especially in fluted edges or corners where food is likely to stick.

Do not use butter or margarine for greasing as they tend to burn; low-fat spreads are unsuitable. Lard or other white cooking fat may be used, in which case it may be smeared on the tin using absorbent kitchen paper or melted, then brushed on.

Greasing and Flouring This is a method used when making light sponge mixtures. The tin is first greased, then dusted with flour to provide an even coating. Once the tin is greased, place a spoonful of flour in it, then tilt and tap the sides of the tin until the whole of the inside is thinly dusted with flour. Shake excess out (or into a second tin to be coated). Light cake mixture clings slightly to the coating as it cooks, helping to give a well-risen, even cake.

Base Lining and Greasing Cut a piece of greaseproof paper to the same shape as the base of the tin. Grease the inside of the tin, then place the paper in the base and grease the paper.

Lining Tins The method depends on the shape of tin.

Round Tin Stand the tin on paper and draw around the outside. Cut the paper slightly inside the drawn circle. Measure the circumference of the tin by holding a piece of string around it and cutting it to length. Cut a strip of paper about 5 cm/2 inches deeper than the side of the tin and slightly longer than the piece of string.

Grease the inside of the tin (this prevents the paper from slipping). Make a 2.5 cm/1 inch fold along the length of the strip of paper, then snip into the fold

Lining Baking Tins

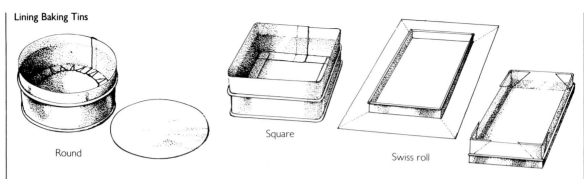

Round

Square

Swiss roll

at 2.5–5 cm/1–2 inch intervals. Place this strip in the tin, pressing it neatly against the side and overlapping the slits in the fold around the base. Lightly grease the paper before placing the circle of paper in the base to cover the overlap around the bottom edge. Grease the paper base.

Square Tin Follow the same method as for lining a round tin, cutting a strip long enough to fit around the sides and a base. Make a fold but do not cut slits in it. Fit the strip of paper against the sides of the tin and make a cut into the fold at each corner. Overlap the cut paper in each corner of the base, then grease it well before putting the base lining paper in place. Grease the base.

Loaf Tin Stand the tin in the middle of a sheet of paper large enough to come up above the edge by about 2.5 cm/1 inch on each side of the tin. Draw around the base of the tin. Cut from the corner of the paper into the corner of the drawn shape. Grease the tin, then place the paper in it, overlapping the cut corners neatly.

Swiss Roll Tin Use the same method as for a loaf tin, allowing about 5 cm/2 inches extra paper all around so that it stands above the rim of the tin.

Measuring Bakeware Capacity

If you want to use a different size or shape of tin from the one given in a recipe, then you have to compare the volume of the substitute tin with the suggested one. If the substitute tin is larger or smaller,

then ingredients in the recipe have to be changed in proportion.

Place the recommended tin on a flat work surface and pour water in it to within 1 cm/½ inch below the rim. Measure the quantity of water. Do the same with the substitute tin. Compare the quantities of water and adjust the ingredients as necessary.

If using loose-bottomed tins, then use a water-tight plastic bag to line them, then pour in the water.

Balanced Diet

See Calories*, Carbohydrates*, Fat*, Fibre*, Minerals*, Protein*, Vitamins* and Good Food and Balanced Eating (page 5).

The term 'diet' refers to food intake over a long period. It is also used in association with short-term eating plans and changes or restrictions to eating habits.

In a scientific sense we have to eat to sustain our bodies. A balanced diet quite simply provides all the food and nutrients a body needs at any time, in adequate amounts and proportions but not in excessive quantities. Although it is possible and useful to generalise about nutritional requirements, clearly these vary according to individual circumstances. The most obvious differences are between growing children and adults or specific groups, including pregnant women and people with certain medical conditions.

Individual Energy Requirements

Apart from specific nutritional needs, energy requirements relate to the body's metabolism (or the rate at which it breaks down and uses food), weight and the level of physical activity.

Food is digested into a form in which it can be used to provide energy and from which nutrients may be extracted and absorbed. Excess energy supplies are stored in the body in the form of fat and some nutrients may also be stored for future needs. The body's minimum fat stores are important but excessive deposits, causing overweight or in extreme cases obesity, should be avoided. Being overweight is a sign of eating more than you need or of eating the wrong balance of food.

Different Foods in the Diet

In addition to the energy value of food eaten, a balanced diet must include a selection of different foods in order to provide all the essential nutrients in the quantities required. Protein foods (fish, meat, poultry, beans and pulses), vegetables and fruit, carbohydrates (including fibre) and fat should feature in proportion.

In the majority of cases, the concern is not so much for eating all the right nutrients but for obtaining them from the right balance of foods. Meeting the suggested recommended daily intakes is one key aspect of diet planning and including the right levels of fibre and starch as energy sources alongside sugar and fat is another. The diet must

---

SEE ALSO **Balmoral Tin:** Baking Tins and Bakeware (illustration)

be assessed over a period of a week or more, not daily.

Indulgences: An Acceptable Extra

Eating is not simply a scientific necessity, it is also a pleasurable and social activity. Therefore a balanced diet allows for indulgences as well as necessities. The foods to set aside as treats are those that have a high fat content or are very sweet, for example rich, buttery sauces, cream cakes, fatty snacks and confectionery. There is nothing wrong with including these in a balanced diet but they must not be eaten frequently and regularly.

The whole concept of a balanced diet is not one of excluding certain foods but of eating a wide variety of different foods and eating the high-fat and sweet items in moderation. Balancing means considering single meals, dishes or snacks in the context of all other foods that are eaten.

Bananas

See Fruit*.
In their native countries of the Far East, India, Africa and the Caribbean, there are many varieties of banana. The common type imported to Britain is shipped while green and under-ripe. **Plantain** Firm, green bananas that are not sweet. They do not ripen in the same way as yellow bananas and they are often used for cooking (deep fried they make banana chips).
Apple Bananas Very small bananas that are sweet and well flavoured. Good for serving whole as a dessert, for example baked or grilled.
Red Bananas Plump and red-skinned, these have slightly dry pinkish flesh.

Buying

Bananas are ripe when they are yellow and lightly speckled with brown. When they are pale yellow or tinged with green the flesh is firm and less sweet; by the time they are deep yellow or even black on the outside the flesh is very soft, sweet and may be browning slightly as the fruit is over-ripe.

Storing

Keep bananas at room temperature. Buy firm, pale yellow fruit if it is to be kept for a few days. Once ripe, bananas should be eaten within 1–2 days. Do not chill or freeze bananas as their flesh blackens and becomes mushy.

Use

● Because they are easy to peel and eat, bananas are ideal picnic and lunch-box food.

● Good sliced with hot or cold custard (and jam), cream, yogurt or fromage frais. Also in trifle.

● Slice in sandwiches.

● Mash with a little milk, cream, yogurt or fromage frais.

● Serve with ice cream and chocolate sauce to make a banana split.

● Wrap chunks in bacon and grill until cooked.

● Quickly fry whole or halved bananas, then serve with bacon.

● Mashed banana and whipped cream or custard makes good ice cream.

Nutritional values

Bananas contain vitamins C and A, some B group vitamins and potassium. They also provide fibre.

Cook's Tip
Prepare bananas just before they are to be served otherwise they discolour. Toss them in a little lemon juice to delay discoloration.

Barbecuing

See Grilling*.
This is a method of cooking food over burning charcoal. The result is similar to that achieved by grilling but the food is flavoured by the burning charcoal. Herbs and wood chips may be burnt under the food to flavour or smoke it.

Equipment

There is a wide variety of equipment on sale and many specialist cookbooks. The simplest form of barbecue is a hibachi grill, a small cast iron container with a rack which is positioned over the burning charcoal. The most sophisticated barbecues include gas or electric powered appliances built into trolleys with cupboards, utensil holders, serving boards and burners for heating sauces or other foods.

Use

For cooking fish, poultry, tender meats, joints, vegetables and fruit.

Hygiene

Pay special attention to food hygiene when barbecuing. Fish, meat and poultry should be kept covered and well chilled until cooked. Never use dishes which have been used for holding raw food for serving cooked food without washing and drying in between. Never leave food outside in the warm for any length of time. When eating outside, keep food covered and replace it in the refrigerator immediately after the meal.

Safety

Barbecues are hot and they can be dangerous. Make sure the barbecue is stable and sited away from any combustible material – hedges, doors and so on. Always use a commercial product for lighting the fuel (or paper and kindling). Barbecue parties are fun but children and animals should be restrained to avoid accidents.

X *When cooking poultry on a barbecue, always make sure the flesh is cooked through. If the coals are too hot, or the rack too close to them, the outside will burn before the middle of the meat is cooked. If this is the case, wrap the food in foil and continue grilling until it is thoroughly cooked. When barbecuing for a significant number of people, it is a good idea to part roast or microwave poultry, then transfer it straight to the barbecue to finish cooking.*

X *Never pour paraffin, methylated spirits or petrol on a barbecue that is difficult to light. Even though it may look as though it has gone out, the heat of the coals may ignite the fuel and cause it to flash back.*

Barley

A grain which is grown in Britain and used mainly for making malt, in turn used for brewing beer and distilling whisky.

Malt Extract

Malt extract is obtained from barley by soaking, sprouting and

---

Barley Water

An old-fashioned drink which is still considered valuable for certain medical conditions.

Place 25 g/1 oz pearl barley in a saucepan with enough cold water to cover and bring to the boil. Drain, then replace the barley in the pan and add 1.1 litres/2 pints water with the pared rind of 1 lemon. Bring to the boil, reduce the heat and cover the pan. Simmer for 20 minutes, then leave to cool. Strain the liquid and add the juice of 2 lemons with sugar to taste. Serve chilled.

THIN BATTER

Deep frying in oil will increase the fat content of batter and the food value of ingredients cooked in the batter must be considered.

INGREDIENTS	FOOD VALUES:
100 g/4 oz plain flour	TOTAL
pinch of salt	kcals: 692
2 eggs	kJ: 2921
300 ml/½ pint milk	protein: 32 g
	fat: 23 g
	carbohydrate: 95 g
Makes about 600 ml/1 pint	fibre: 3 g

Place the flour and salt in a bowl and make a well in the middle. Add both eggs, placing them in the well in the flour, and a little milk. Gently beat the eggs and milk together, allowing a little of the flour to mix in.

Gradually work in more of the flour to make a thick batter, adding a little extra milk occasionally. Continue beating until all the flour is beaten in and about half the milk is incorporated. At this stage the batter should be thick and smooth. It is easier to make a smooth batter and to beat out lumps if the mixture is thick – if all the milk is beaten in too soon, then the flour tends to form lumps that are difficult to remove by beating.

When the batter is smooth, gradually beat in the rest of the milk. At this stage, the batter should be left to stand for about 15–30 minutes so that the grains of flour have time to swell slightly. However this is not essential. If the batter is used for making pancakes and cooked gradually, it may thicken on standing so a little extra milk or water should be added.

USE

Yorkshire pudding* and clafoutis (see cherries*). For pancakes* add an extra 30 ml/2 tablespoons cold water to make thin, light pancakes. Beat in 30 ml/2 tablespoons oil just before cooking the pancakes as this helps to prevent them from sticking to the pan during cooking.

COATING BATTER

INGREDIENTS	FOOD VALUES:
100 g/4 oz plain flour	TOTAL
pinch of salt	kcals: 424
1 egg	kJ: 1799
150 ml/¼ pint water	protein: 16 g
	fat: 7 g
Makes about 350 ml/	carbohydrate: 80 g
12 fluid oz	fibre: 3 g

The method is the same as for Thin Batter but the resulting batter should be thick, smooth and light. Do not leave the batter to stand.

USE

For coating food before deep frying – fish fillets, fruit and so on. The above quantity is enough to coat 6–8 plaice fillets.

SEE ALSO **Bard:** Glossary; **Basil:** Herbs; **Basmati Rice:** Rice; **Bass:** Fish; **Baste:** Glossary

drying the grain, then mashing it with hot water. The starch is converted to sugar which gives malt extract its characteristic sweetness.

Culinary Uses

Two types of barley are available.

Pearl Barley

This has been polished after removing the outer husk. Traditionally, pearl barley is added to soups and stews, then simmered for an hour or so until the grain is very soft. Cooked this way, the barley gives up its starch to thicken the liquid.

Pot Barley

This has had the inedible outer husk removed but the grain is not polished. Pot barley is available from wholefood shops either on its own or as part of mixed grain packs.

Boiled Barley

Both types of barley may be boiled until tender but not soft, then served instead of rice.

Allow 225 g/8 oz barley for four servings. Place the grain in a large saucepan and rinse it with cold water, then drain. Add 900 ml/1½ pints cold water for pearl barley or 1.1 litres/2 pints for pot barley and a little salt. Bring to the boil, reduce the heat and cover the pan, then simmer the grain very gently until tender but not broken. When cooked the barley should have a bit of bite. Pearl barley cooks in about 30 minutes, pot barley takes about 1 hour. Check pot barley halfway through cooking to make sure there is plenty of water left. At the end of the cooking time most of the liquid should be absorbed but the grain should still need draining.

LIGHT BATTER

This very light batter is well puffed, crisp and thin when cooked. It is used for coating foods such as cubed pork used to make Oriental-style sweet and sour pork. A few drops of sesame oil may be beaten in with the egg yolks if the batter is used for sweet and sour pork.

INGREDIENTS
100 g/4 oz plain flour
pinch of salt
2 eggs, separated
100 ml/4 fluid oz water

Makes about 450 ml/¾ pint

FOOD VALUES:
TOTAL
kcals: 497
kJ: 2105
protein: 22 g
fat: 12 g
carbohydrate: 80 g
fibre: 3 g

Place the flour and salt in a bowl, then make a well in the middle. Add the egg yolks to the well in the flour, then gradually stir the water into them. Slowly beat in the flour to make a smooth, thick batter.

The next stage should not be carried out until just before the batter is to be used. In a perfectly clean bowl, whisk the egg whites until they stand in stiff peaks. Add a spoonful of the whites to the batter and beat them in well, then use a spatula to scrape all the batter off the spoon used for beating.

Use a metal spoon to fold the remaining egg whites into the batter, taking care not to knock out the air. The batter should be very light and slightly elastic. Do not overmix the egg whites or the batter will become flat. Use at once.

USE

For coating food before deep frying – fish and seafood (good on squid rings – calamari), cubes of poultry or meat, or fruit. The above quantity is enough to coat 6 small fish fillets or 450 g/1 lb cubed meat or poultry.

Nutritional Value

Barley is mainly carbohydrate and pot barley provides fibre. Pot barley also contains iron, calcium, potassium and protein, all of which are present in less significant amounts in pearl barley.

Batter

See also Fritters*, Pancakes* and Yorkshire Pudding*.
A batter is a pouring mixture of flour and liquid. The batter may be thin and pour easily or it may be thick and used for coating food. A thick batter should still be loose enough to pour from one container to another.

Varying Batter Mixtures

● Any of the batter recipes may be flavoured with herbs (chopped fresh or dried).

● A little vanilla essence may be added to batters used to coat fruit for making sweet fritters.

● Wholemeal flour may be used to make batter but it requires a little additional liquid as it tends to be thicker. A slightly lighter mixture may be achieved using half and half wholemeal and plain flour.

● Half buckwheat flour (from wholefood shops) and plain flour may be used to make a thin batter. The batter may be used to make small pancakes known as blinis – serve them Russian style with soured cream and caviar (or lumpfish roe).

• Beer may be used instead of water in the coating batter recipe. The gas in the beer (lager is lightest in flavour) makes the batter light and crisp.

Bean Curd

Also known as tofu, bean curd is smooth, white and sold in blocks. It is made from soya beans that are soaked and ground to yield a milky liquid that sets into the curd. Although bean curd is flavourless, it readily absorbs the flavour of foods with which it is cooked, therefore it is very versatile.

Buying

Bean curd may be bought ready made in which case it is stored in water to keep it moist and packed in lidded plastic containers or in sealed packets. It is usually displayed in chiller cabinets in supermarkets.

It is also available in the form of a powder mix. The advantage of a packet mix is that it has a longer shelf life.

As well as plain bean curd, other varieties available include smoked bean curd. Creamy dressings, sauces and dips are also available, usually in jars.

Storing

Prepared bean curd in water is a perishable food and it should be consumed by the 'use by' date on the packet. It should be stored in the refrigerator and used within a day of opening.

Use

Bean curd is widely used in Chinese and Japanese cooking. It is also a popular vegetarian food, particularly for vegans. It breaks up easily so it should be handled carefully during cooking.

• Steam or stir fry slices or chunks with soy sauce, strips of vegetables (spring onion, carrot, celery and so on), shredded fresh root ginger and garlic.

• Coat with Tomato Sauce (page 263), top with cheese and bake.

• Coat with egg and breadcrumbs mixed with herbs and fry. Delicious with garlic mayonnaise.

• Mash and use in sweet or savoury recipes such as dips, vegetable pâtés and cheesecakes.

Nutritional Value

Being a soya bean product, bean curd has a high protein value and a low fat content.

Beans, Broad

See Vegetables*.

Buying

Available fresh from May to July, look for firm plump pods but avoid very large hard ones that may well contain old, tough beans. The pods should be unbroken and they should look moist and fresh. They should not be badly speckled with black patches or discoloured. Pods that are mature but not too large will yield about 175 g/6 oz beans for each 450 g/1 lb. About 675 g/1½ lb pods provide 2 portions of beans. Frozen broad beans are available all year.

Preparation

Very young pods (freshly picked before they mature to contain beans) may be cooked whole. More usually, the pods should be popped by bending them in the middle and the beans removed. Discard any blackened beans, then wash the remainder.

Cooking

Cook broad beans soon after removing from their pods. Add

them to boiling salted water, bring back to the boil and reduce the heat slightly so that the beans do not froth over. Boil young beans for 5 minutes, older ones for 10–12 minutes, until tender. Drain and serve at once, tossed with a little butter or margarine and freshly ground black pepper.

Serving Ideas

• Lightly cook and drain the beans, then mix with chopped cooked ham and chopped spring onions – delicious with cooked pasta or rice.

• Cook some chopped bacon with a crushed clove of garlic until crisp, add cooked broad beans and a can of chopped tomatoes, then heat until boiling. Season and serve with spaghetti or baked potatoes. Top with grated cheese.

Freezing

Broad beans freeze well for up to a year. They must be freshly picked. Remove from pods and blanch for 2–3 minutes (depending on size). Unblanched broad beans do not freeze successfully for more than a couple of weeks.

Nutritional Value

Broad beans are a good source of protein, fibre, vitamin C and iron.

Beans, French

See Vegetables*.
Rounded green beans that vary in thickness from being very fine to pencil-thick. Available June to September when they are reasonably priced; however imported beans are available all year.

Buying

Look for firm, bright beans that snap crisply to reveal a moist, bright inside. Since it is not always possible to snap beans before buying, take a good look at them and avoid any that are wrinkled and damaged. Feel them for firmness – a good sign of freshness.

Frozen whole or cut French beans are available all year.

Preparation

French beans do not need stringing; simply trim off their ends and wash them thoroughly. Most French beans may be cooked whole, although larger ones may be cut in half or into shorter lengths.

Cooking

Cooking times are a matter for personal taste; however French beans have the best flavour if they are cooked quickly in the minimum of boiling water (with just a little salt added, if liked) until they are very bright in colour. This takes about 3 minutes once the water has returned to the boil, then the beans will be crisp when served. Larger beans take up to 5 minutes. Always cook French beans just before they are to be served and drain them well.

Serving Ideas

• Top the beans with plenty of chopped parsley and black pepper, adding a squeeze of lemon juice if liked.

• Separate the yolk from the white of a hard-boiled egg. Sieve the yolk and chop the white. Sprinkle the white over the cooked beans, then top with a neat garnish of sieved yolk.

• Toss freshly cooked beans with an oil and vinegar salad dressing (see salads and salad dressings*), then cool. Serve on a bed of shredded lettuce.

• Combine with flaked canned tuna, sliced onion, quartered hard-boiled egg, stoned black olives, roughly chopped canned

anchovy fillets and an oil and vinegar dressing to make salad Niçoise.

Freezing

Blanch* prepared beans for 2 minutes. They keep well for up to a year. Cook from frozen – allow about 3 minutes in boiling water, or to taste.

Nutritional Value

Fresh beans provide some vitamin C and A, and fibre.

Beans, Runner

See Vegetables.*
Available from July through to September or October, these are flat and a strong green in colour.

Buying

Bought runner beans are inferior to home-grown crops as they tend to become limp soon after picking. Look for medium-sized beans that are a good colour, firm and fairly straight. Avoid very large beans (often curled) that may well be too tough and stringy to eat. Also, pale or wrinkled and soft beans are not worth buying.

Preparation

The majority of runner beans have to be strung before cooking. This means removing a tough, stringy strip from both sides of the bean.

Using a small, sharp knife, cut from just underneath the hooked end of the bean and remove a thin strip all down one side to the stalk end. Cut off the stalk end, then remove a strip along the other side.

Wash the beans well at this stage. The beans should be sliced at an angle into thin strips measuring about 5–7.5 cm/ 2–3 inches long. Lightly rinse the beans and cook them soon after they are sliced. Gadgets may be

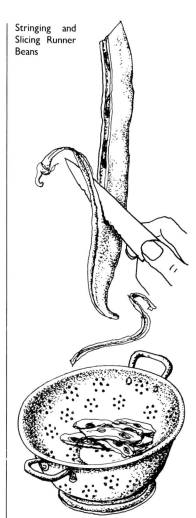

Stringing and Slicing Runner Beans

purchased for slicing beans, they usually cut the bean lengthways into long strips ready for slicing across into lengths.

Cooking

Plunge the prepared beans into boiling, lightly salted water and bring back to the boil. Cook for about 3–5 minutes, until the beans are bright green and slightly crisp. Drain and serve.

Serving Ideas

• Top with low-fat soft cheese (quark or curd cheese) and some chopped walnuts.

• Delicious tossed with cooked diced smoked sausage or bacon and canned chick peas (see beans and pulses, dried*).

• A good accompaniment for boiled bacon or ham, grilled sausages or grilled pork chops.

Freezing

Prepare, slice and blanch* for 2 minutes. Store for up to a year.

Nutritional Value

Runner beans provide some protein, fibre and vitamin A and C (especially when freshly picked).

Beans and Pulses, Dried

Most supermarkets offer a good variety and wholefood shops sell most types.

Buying

Most major brands and supermarket own brands are good quality and ready for cooking. Cheaper and bulk packs are a good buy but they should be sifted through first for any tiny stones and broken beans, then well rinsed.

Since dried beans and pulses keep well for long periods they may be purchased in large packs.

Storing

Keep in airtight packs or jars in a dry, dark cupboard.

Cooking

Depending on type, the beans may need soaking for several hours or overnight before cooking. After soaking, drain and place the beans in a large saucepan with plenty of cold water. (Red lentils are not cooked in vast quantities of water: see separate instructions.) Do not add salt as it prevents the beans from becoming tender. Add 2.5 ml/½ teaspoon bicarbonate of soda, if liked, as it will help to soften the pulses during cooking but it is not essential.

Bring the beans to the boil and boil them rapidly for 10 minutes (this is particularly important in the case of red kidney beans). Reduce the heat, cover the pan and simmer the beans until they are tender – cooking times are listed for the types (opposite page). During long cooking, check that the water is not absorbed.

Drain the beans after cooking and serve or use as required.

Pressure Cooking The pressure cooker may be used for beans that have not been soaked and it reduces the cooking time by half or two-thirds the boiling time. It is important never to have the pressure cooker more than two-thirds full when cooking beans (including the water) as they froth up and can clog the safety valve. Always read and follow the manufacturer's instructions for the pressure cooker.

Butter beans, chick peas and red kidney beans cook in about 10–15 minutes at high pressure or 15 lb in a pressure cooker. Black-eye beans, aduki beans and other beans that take less boiling time are cooked in about 7 minutes in the pressure cooker.

Canned Pulses

Canned beans and pulses, such as kidney beans, butter beans, chick peas and haricot beans, are cooked and ready to use. They are an excellent storecupboard standby. Some types and brands are better quality than others with firm, whole beans rather than broken, slightly mushy ones. They are more popular and practical because they do not require soaking, but dried beans do absorb more flavour if they are cooked for a longer period.

BUTTER BEANS WITH TOMATOES

INGREDIENTS
225 g/8 oz dried butter beans, soaked overnight
60 ml/4 tablespoons olive oil
2 cloves garlic, crushed
2 large onions, sliced
I bay leaf
15 ml/I tablespoon dried marjoram
2 (400 g/14 oz) cans chopped tomatoes
300 ml/½ pint red wine
salt and pepper

FOOD VALUES:
TOTAL • PER PORTION
kcals: 1139 • 285
kJ: 4746 • 1187
protein: 29 g • 7 g
fat: 62 g • 16 g
carbohydrate: 71 g • 18 g
fibre: 21 g • 5 g

Serves 4

Cook the drained butter beans in a saucepan of boiling water for 15 minutes, then drain them.

Heat the oil over medium heat in a large heavy-based saucepan. Add the garlic and onions, then stir well. Put a lid on the pan and cook for 15 minutes. Add the bay leaf, marjoram, tomatoes and butter beans. Pour in the wine, stir well and bring to the boil. Reduce the heat so that the mixture simmers gently, then cover the pan and cook for 30 minutes.

Uncover the pan, stir the bean mixture and continue to cook gently for about 15 minutes, or until the beans are well cooked and the liquid reduced slightly. Add seasoning to taste and serve piping hot.

If the mixture is to be served warm, leave the pan covered off the heat. To serve cold, transfer the mixture to a clean container, cover and cool. Chill until ready to serve.

Glossary of Beans and Pulses

Aduki Beans Small red beans that have a slightly sweet, nutty taste. Soak overnight and cook for about 30 minutes.

Black Beans Also known as black kidney beans, these are similar in size and shape to red kidney beans. Soak overnight and cook for about 50 minutes.

Black-eye Beans Sometimes referred to by their American name of black-eyed peas, these are small and white with a small black spot. They have a pleasant nutty flavour. Soak overnight and cook for about 30 minutes.

Borlotti Beans Also known as pinto beans. Speckled brown beans, readily available canned as well as dried and frequently used in Italian cooking, these have a slightly nutty flavour that goes well in most dishes, including soups and salads. Soak overnight and cook for about 45 minutes.

Broad Beans Dried broad beans are a light brown colour. They have a good flavour but their skins are tough and should be removed after cooking. Soak overnight and cook for about 50 minutes.

Brown Beans Also known as Egyptian brown beans or ful medames, these are small, round and pale brown in colour. Soak overnight and cook for 30 minutes. Tasty hot with olive oil, garlic, lemon and parsley or cold in salad.

Brown Lentils Small flat lentils, similar to green lentils but brown in colour. Sometimes known as Egyptian lentils. These do not require soaking before cooking and they are usually tender after 35–40 minutes cooking. They remain whole rather than falling to a mush and are good hot or cold in salad. Serve instead of rice or make them into a tasty sauce for topping pasta, with onions, garlic, marjoram, mushrooms and tomatoes.

Butter Beans Large, white, kidney-shaped beans. Also known as lima beans (an Ameri-

CHILLI CON CARNE

INGREDIENTS
225 g/8 oz dried red kidney beans, soaked overnight, or 2 (425 g/15 oz) cans red kidney beans, drained
30 ml/2 tablespoons oil
2 onions, chopped
1 green pepper, deseeded and chopped
2 cloves garlic, crushed
225 g/8 oz streaky bacon, rinds removed, chopped
450 g/1 lb minced beef
15 ml/1 tablespoon chilli powder
30 ml/2 tablespoons ground coriander
15 ml/1 tablespoon ground cumin
1 bay leaf
10 ml/2 teaspoons dried marjoram
1 (400 g/14 oz) can chopped tomatoes
30 ml/2 tablespoons tomato purée
600 ml/1 pint water
salt and pepper
plenty of chopped fresh parsley

FOOD VALUES:
TOTAL • PER PORTION
kcals: 2391 • 598
kJ: 9970 • 2493
protein: 198 g • 50 g
fat: 152 g • 38 g
carbohydrate: 60 g • 15 g
fibre: 8 g • 2 g

Serves 4

Place the drained red kidney beans in a large saucepan with plenty of cold water and bring to a full boil. Boil for 10 minutes. Reduce heat so that the water is just boiling steadily and cover the pan, then cook the beans for 30 minutes.

Meanwhile, heat the oil in a flameproof casserole or heavy-based saucepan. Add the onions, green pepper, garlic and bacon and cook over medium heat, stirring occasionally, until the bacon is just cooked and the onions slightly softened – this takes about 15 minutes.

Stir in the mince and cook for about 10 minutes, until it darkens in colour. It will not brown with the other ingredients. Stir in the chilli, coriander and cumin. The amount of chilli may be varied to suit individual taste. Cook, stirring for a few minutes, then add the bay leaf, marjoram, tomatoes and tomato purée. Pour in the water (use 300 ml/½ pint water for canned kidney beans) and heat gently until boiling.

Add the drained beans to the meat mixture, make sure that it is simmering and cover the pan. Cook, stirring occasionally, for 1 hour, until the beans and meat are tender and the flavours are well combined. If using canned beans, leave the meat mixture to cook for 30 minutes before adding them. Season and cook for a final 30 minutes. This is the stage at which to season the mixture.

Stir in plenty of chopped parsley to give the chilli a fresh flavour and serve piping hot.

can term), these readily absorb the flavour of other ingredients. Soak overnight and cook for about 40 minutes, until just tender when their flesh is slightly starchy and rather like potatoes. Traditionally served mashed or puréed, butter beans make a sim-ple vegetable dish tossed with fried onions and parsley. Canned butter beans are generally rather mushy and inferior to the dried type.

Cannellini Beans Oval white beans, these are a member of the haricot family. Soak overnight and cook for about 40 minutes. They are mild and firm, and they readily absorb the flavour of other ingredients. Used in Italian cooking, in both hot and cold dishes. Particularly good cold with flaked canned tuna and thinly sliced onion, dressed with olive oil, lemon and garlic.

Chick Peas Small round beige-coloured peas that are slightly dimpled around the sides. Soak overnight and cook for about 1 hour. They have a delicious nutty flavour and they are good to eat very simply, with cooked onion and herbs (either hot or cold).

Puréed with olive oil, garlic and onion they make a creamy dip known as hummus. Canned chick peas are good quality, firm and flavoursome.

Flageolet Beans Small, oval beans that are pale green in colour with a delicate flavour. Soak overnight and cook for about 30 minutes. Excellent in stews or served as a vegetable with roast lamb. Canned vary in quality and can sometimes be mushy.

Green Lentils Small, flat lentils that do not require soaking before cooking. Cook for about 30 minutes, or until tender. They remain whole and are good hot or cold. Very similar to brown lentils.

Haricot Beans Small oval white beans. Soak overnight and cook for 30 minutes. They absorb flavours well as they are fairly plain on their own. They are the beans found in cans of baked beans. Good in soups and stews, or cold salads.

Mung Beans Small round green beans that are sprouted and sold as bean sprouts*. They may also be soaked overnight and cooked for about 30 minutes. They are usually included as part of a mixed pulses pack or they may be served with rice (cook them with brown rice).

Peas, Dried Soak overnight, then cook for about 40 minutes. Alternatively, they can be cooked for about 1½ hours until soft enough to mash.

Red Kidney Beans The raw beans contain a natural toxin which is destroyed by boiling but not by gentle cooking. Soak overnight, boil rapidly for 10 minutes, then cook for about 50 minutes.

Red Lentils These do not require soaking before cooking and they cook quickly to a soft, creamy consistency. Pour 600 ml/1 pint cold water over 225 g/8 oz red lentils and bring to the boil. Reduce the heat to a low setting and put a tight-fitting lid on the pan, then cook very gently for 20–25 minutes, or until the lentils are soft and all the water has been absorbed. Check after 15 minutes and add up to 100 ml/4 fluid oz water if necessary. Beat the lentils well until creamy, season, add a little butter or margarine and serve.

A few whole green cardamoms, a bay leaf and cinnamon stick may be cooked with the lentils. Topped with fried onions and cumin seeds they make a delicious Indian-style dal. See also pâtés and terrines*.

Soya Beans Soak for at least 24 hours, preferably with the water changed once. Boil for 45 minutes and cook gently, topping up the water as necessary, for another 1½–2 hours.

Split Peas Yellow split peas do not have to be soaked before cooking. If soaked, they cook in about 20 minutes; if not they require about 40–50 minutes cooking. The peas should be soft when cooked, so that they can be creamed with a little butter or margarine.

Cook's Tip
Cooked beans freeze well and they may be added to soups, casseroles or other dishes from frozen. Soak, cook and cool the beans, reducing the cooking time slightly so that the beans remain whole during thawing and reheating. Open freeze, then pack the beans so that small amounts may be removed as required.

Nutritional Value

The main value of dried beans and pulses is as a source of protein, particularly in a vegetarian* or vegan* diet. They also provide a good supply of fibre.

Beansprouts

These are dried beans that are soaked, then allowed to grow sprouts. Mung beans are usually sprouted although other dried beans such as aduki beans and chick peas may be used. Seeds such as alfalfa* and fenugreek (see spices*) may also be sprouted.

Sprouting Dried Beans

Soak a handful of mung beans overnight, then drain them and place in a clean jar. The jar should be no more than one third full. The beans should be moist. Cover with a piece of clean, scalded muslin or a piece of scalded stocking. Put an elastic band around the neck of the jar to keep the fabric in place. Leave in a warm, dark place for about 3–5 days.

Every day, rinse the beans well with plenty of cold water, draining off excess. When the beans have long, white shoots, they should be used. Do not leave them until the first leaf buds develop or they will taste bitter.

Preparation and Cooking

Rinse the beansprouts well and rub off most of the green skins. They require very little cooking and are best quickly stir fried in a little oil.

Use

Beansprouts may be added to other ingredients, such as stir-fried chicken or vegetables, or stirred into braised dishes just before the end of the cooking time. They are a key ingredient in chop suey and part of the

---

SEE ALSO **Béarnaise Sauce:** Sauces – Hollandaise; **Beating:** Glossary

traditional filling for Chinese spring rolls.

Washed and drained bean-sprouts add texture and flavour to salads.

Béchamel Sauce

See Sauces*.
A savoury white sauce, fla-voured with bay, mace and onion. Named after Louis de Béchameil, Marquis of Nointel, to whom the sauce was probably dedicated.

Use

Serve with fish, eggs and veg-etables or use in a variety of baked dishes.

Microwave Cooking

Heat the milk and flavouring in-gredients in a suitable jug on High for 5 minutes, then leave to stand for 30 minutes.

In a suitable large jug or basin, whisk the strained milk into the flour, then add the butter. Cook on High for 3 minutes, then whisk the sauce thoroughly until smooth. Continue cooking for a further 3–5 minutes, until the sauce is boiling and thickened. Whisk well and season to taste.

Cook's Tip
When cooking the sauce con-ventionally, whisking it all the time instead of stirring ensures a smooth result. However, a wire whisk should not be used in a non-stick saucepan.

Beef

See Meat*.
The illustration shows the car-cass and the traditional cuts. In addition, many larger super-markets and good butchers sell prepared items such as kebabs,

BECHAMEL SAUCE

INGREDIENTS	FOOD VALUES:
1 onion, quartered	TOTAL
1 blade of mace	kcals: 732
1 bay leaf	kJ: 3060
1 parsley sprig	protein: 25 g
600 ml/1 pint milk	fat: 44 g
25 g/1 oz butter	carbohydrate: 64 g
40 g/1 ½ oz plain flour	fibre: 3 g
salt and white pepper	**Makes 600 ml/1 pint**

Place the onion, mace, bay leaf and parsley in a saucepan. Pour in the milk and heat very gently until just boiling. Remove the pan from the heat and leave to stand for 15 minutes. This process is known as infusing, and it allows the onion, herbs and mace to impart their flavour to the milk.

Strain the milk into a jug. Heat the butter in the saucepan, then stir in the flour. Cook, stirring, over medium heat for 1 minute. Stirring all the time, slowly pour in the milk. Bring the mixture to the boil, stirring continuously, until the sauce is thickened and smooth. Season to taste.

Reduce the heat and simmer the sauce for 3 minutes. The process of cooking the flour and butter (the mixture is known as a roux), then simmering the sauce, ensures that the flour is cooked properly, otherwise the sauce may have a taste of raw flour when served. However, if the sauce is used as a coating before baking, this simmering is not necessary as the flour will have time to cook in the oven.

---

beef olives, steak strips for stir frying or other portions that are trimmed of all fat. Numbers in the following cuts relate to illustration (below).

Neck A tough stewing cut which may also be minced. This needs long slow cooking. **(1)**
Brisket Usually sold boned and rolled, this is breast meat taken from underneath the ribs. Tra-ditionally a fatty cut but the ma-jority of meat is now leaner. Brisket may be braised as a joint or baked slowly in a covered con-tainer. At one time salted brisket was sold for boiling. Some butchers still prepare salt beef by 'pickling' it in brine – this is excellent boiled. **(2)**
Shin A stewing cut for long slow cooking. **(3)**
Chuck A braising cut which may also be baked slowly in a covered container. Chuck may be cubed, sliced or cooked in a large piece. It also makes prime mince (minced steak). **(4)**

Cuts of Beef

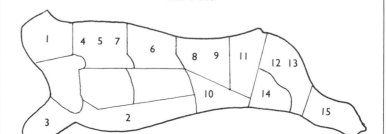

Blade From the shoulder, the boned meat is suitable for braising. **(5)**

Forerib A large tender, flavoursome roasting joint, cooked on the bone. **(6)**

Back Rib The rib section nearer the shoulder, may be roasted on bone or boned and rolled. **(7)**

Ribs (American) Meaty rib bones which are seasoned and cooked in the same way as pork spareribs, by boiling then grilling.

Sirloin One of the most expensive of roasting joints. Sirloin is noted for being a tender cut, ideal for roasting at high temperatures. This section may also be cut into steaks (below). **(8)**

Fillet The fillet of beef is tucked underneath the ribs. It is a long, slender, fine-grained cut which tapers at one end. It may be cut into steaks or roasted whole to give extremely tender results. **(9)**

Skirt Lean coarse-grained from inside the flank, it may be braised or pot roasted. **(10)**

Rump Sold as a large slice of steak or cut into portions for frying or grilling. **(11)**

Topside A lean fine-grained roasting joint, sold boned and rolled. **(12)**

Silverside A lean, rolled joint for braising or roasting, taken from the area behind the topside. **(13)**

Top Rump or Thick Flank This is taken from the area below the rump and silverside. It is boned and rolled for slow baking or braising. **(14)**

Leg A tough cut that requires long slow stewing. **(15)**

Steaks

Fillet Slices cut from the thicker end of the fillet, these are small, usually cut thick, and succulent. They do not have any fat.

Châteaubriand This is the centre section of the fillet. It is cooked in one or two pieces by roasting or grilling, then sliced thickly for serving.

Tournedos or Filet Mignon This is a small round of meat from the thin end of the fillet.

Sirloin The sirloin steak is cut off the bone from above the ribs.

Porterhouse This is a rib steak cut on the bone. It includes the sirloin meat but not the fillet.

'T' Bone This includes the rib bone, sirloin and fillet.

Rump A slice of boneless meat, marbled with a little fat and edged with fat.

Minute Steak Good quality steak, cut thin and beaten out so that it cooks particularly quickly to give tender results.

Buying

The information included on meat* should be followed. In addition, remember that well-hung beef is dark red in colour not bright. Finding a good butcher who hangs beef is worth the effort as the meat will be tender and full flavoured.

Look for creamy-white coloured fat on beef. Stewing and braising cuts that are trimmed and cubed ready for cooking save time. Check that the meat is neatly trimmed of gristle as well as excess fat.

Storing

Unpack the beef and put it in the refrigerator as soon as possible after shopping.

Sealed packs should be left unopened in the refrigerator and consumed by the 'use by' date on the label.

Unwrap loose meat and place it in a covered dish. Make sure that the dish is large enough to hold all meat juices and place it on a low shelf in the refrigerator. Cook joints of beef within 3 days unless otherwise stated on the pack. Cook mince within 1 day.

Cooking

See meat* for methods and cooking times, and for notes on handling cooked meat and meat dishes.

Accompaniments

Yorkshire Pudding* Traditionally the pudding is cooked in a tin under the beef which is placed on a rack, then the pudding is served first (with gravy) as a starter before the meat and vegetables.

Horseradish* Sauce, (page 153). Bought horseradish sauce or creamed horseradish (milder than the sauce) may be served.

Mustard* A wide variety is available – from hot English mustard in powder form to slightly sweet, mild Swedish mustard.

Freezing

Beef freezes well for up to 9 months. General information on freezing meat and using frozen meat should be followed.

Beetroot

See Vegetables.*

Beetroot is most often served cooked and cooled as a salad or pickle; however it also tastes good hot in savoury bakes or it may be used to make soup.

Buying

Check that the beets are firm and that they are not cut. Avoid wrinkled or soft beets.

Ready-cooked Beetroot This is more readily available than the raw vegetable. Before buying make sure that the beetroot is moist with its skin still on. Avoid any that looks dry or that has had areas of skin rubbed off. On most market stalls the cooked beetroot is usually piled alongside other raw, earthy vegetables – if you do buy it ready cooked, then always rub off the peel under running cold water to clean the beetroot at the same time. It is best to buy the raw vegetable and cook it at home, both for flavour and hygiene purposes.

Vacuum Packed Beetroot Cooked and packed without vinegar or acetic acid, this is the best alternative to fresh beetroot. It is available all through the year and the unopened pack usually has a long shelf life. Always check the 'use by' date.

SEE ALSO **Beefburger:** Hamburger; **Beignet:** Glossary; **Bel Paese:** Cheese; **Beurre Manié:** Glossary

BORSCHT

If fresh beetroot is not available, 675 g/1 ½ lb freshly boiled or vacuum packed vegetables may be used instead. Borscht is a slightly sweet-sour, light soup which is low calorie and contains very little fat.

INGREDIENTS
450 g/1 lb raw beetroot
30 ml/2 tablespoons oil
1 onion, chopped
1 celery stick, sliced
1 carrot, diced
100 g/4 oz cabbage, shredded
**1 litre/1¾ pints chicken
    stock**
1 bay leaf
salt and pepper
**5–10 ml/1–2 teaspoons cider
    vinegar**

FOOD VALUES:
TOTAL • PER PORTION
kcals: 752 • 188
kJ: 3162 • 791
protein: 22 g • 6 g
fat: 42 g • 11 g
carbohydrate: 77 g • 19 g
fibre: 17 g • 4 g

Serves 4

Wash the beetroot, then cut off the root and leaves. Peel the beet and grate it coarsely into a bowl. Set aside.

Heat the oil in a large saucepan. Add the onion, celery and carrot and cook gently, stirring occasionally, for about 15 minutes, or until the onion is softened but not browned. Add the beetroot, stir well, then add the cabbage and pour in the stock. Add the bay leaf and a little seasoning.

Bring the soup to the boil, reduce the heat and cover the pan, then simmer the soup gently for 45 minutes. Taste the soup and adjust the seasoning, before adding vinegar to taste to give the soup a slightly sweet-sour flavour. Serve piping hot.

Alternatively, the soup may be strained and all the liquid pressed out of the vegetables.

Cooked Beetroot with Vinegar
Whole, peeled beetroot sold alongside the salad vegetables in supermarkets, and usually packed in trays, is preserved with vinegar or acetic acid. It has the tang of pickled beetroot.
Pickled Beetroot Jars of baby beets or sliced beetroot in vinegar are readily available, some sweetened. Store in the refrigerator if recommended by the manufacturer.

Beetroot is one of the easiest vegetables to pickle at home. See Pickles*.

Preparation

Twist off the leaves just above the beetroot. Do not cut into the beetroot or it will 'bleed', that is lose its colour as it cooks. Wash the beetroot well, then cook it with its peel on.

Cooking

Boiling This is the most popular method of cooking beetroot. Place the trimmed, washed beetroot in a pan with cold water to cover. Bring to the boil, then reduce the heat so that the water is just simmering. Cover and cook until the beets are tender. Small beets take about 20 minutes, medium sized require 35–40 minutes and larger vegetables will take about 50 minutes.
Steaming Place the washed beets in a steamer and cook over boiling water. Allow 20–45 minutes depending on the size.

Pressure Cooking Cook at High pressure with 1 litre/1¾ pints water. Place in the trivet and allow 10 minutes for small beets, 20 for medium and 30 minutes for large vegetables.
Microwave Cooking Place 450 g/1 lb evenly sliced, small to medium beetroot in a suitable covered dish with 100 ml/4 fluid oz boiling water. Cook on High for 7–10 minutes. Leave to stand for 5 minutes.

Peeling

Drain the beetroot, if necessary, and pour cold running water over it. Rub off the peel under cold water. The peel slips off easily when the vegetable is cooked.

Serving Ideas

The traditional British way of dealing with beetroot is to serve it in vinegar but there are other more interesting possibilities.

• Dice or slice with soured cream, fromage frais or natural yogurt. Top with snipped chives.

• Grate and mix with grated dessert apple and a little chopped onion. Dress with soured cream or yogurt and add some horseradish sauce.

• Serve diced beetroot and cut French beans in an oil and vinegar dressing.

• In baked dishes – good with tuna, cauliflower and onions, topped with cheese and breadcrumbs.

• Beetroot makes good chutney, especially with orange rind and juice.

Bicarbonate of Soda

Bicarbonate of soda is an alkali, used in cooking as a raising agent. When mixed with water, bicarbonate of soda effervesces (or fizzes) and gives off carbon dioxide. Acid increases the rate of this reaction, so soured milk or lemon juice is often used with bicarbonate of soda.

Cream of tartar is an acid, therefore it is combined with bicarbonate of soda to make a powerful raising agent for mixtures which do not contain a lot of liquid. This is the traditional raising agent for scones* and, although rather old-fashioned and far less popular than simply using self-raising flour, it gives a superior result.

Other uses for bicarbonate of soda as a raising agent are in cakes made by the melted method, for example gingerbread, and in Irish soda bread. See cakes* and bread*.

It is also added to the cooking water for dried beans to tenderise their skins.

> [X] *Do not add bicarbonate of soda to water when boiling vegetables. An out-dated practice to preserve colour in overcooked vegetables, it destroys their vitamin C content.*

Bins

One of the essential items of kitchen equipment that we tend to take for granted. Here are a few reminders.

● Don't be tempted to buy a huge kitchen bin. A small one which has to be emptied often is more hygienic.

● Buy a bin with a neatly fitting lid to keep all the rubbish in and unwanted attention out (for example, flies and wasps).

● Do not tuck the kitchen bin away in a corner where it is out of sight (and out of mind). Put it in a place where you can easily clean all around it.

● Use some form of waterproof bin liner – old plastic carrier bags are ideal. When emptying the bin, tie the top of the bag before putting it in the outdoor bin.

● Empty used rubbish bins daily and wash them out often with disinfectant. Leave to drain and dry (outside if possible) or wipe dry with absorbent kitchen paper.

● Never leave trimmings from meat, fish or poultry in the indoor bin. Wrap them in plenty of paper and place them directly in the outdoor bin.

● If possible, use plastic rubbish sacks in the outdoor bin. Site this bin away from the kitchen door and windows, in a place where you can move it easily for brushing underneath and around it.

● If possible, wash out the outdoor bin regularly, using disinfectant. Leave the bin to drain upside down until it is dry before putting a new bag in it.

● Always close rubbish sacks that are put out for collection, either by gathering up opposite sides of the bag and knotting them together or by tying the bag with string or a large wire tie.

● Remember that all food rubbish provides a breeding ground for bacteria, so it must be kept away from areas used for food preparation.

● Exposed rubbish attracts flies and other pests, so always keep it covered.

● Consider safety aspects too and make sure that any sharp edges on cans are not left where anyone can cut themselves. Always pack broken glass in a box or bag, then label it clearly.

PLAIN BISCUITS

INGREDIENTS
225 g/8 oz plain flour
175 g/6 oz margarine or butter
50 g/2 oz caster sugar
1 egg
5 ml/1 tsp vanilla essence
grated rind of 1 lemon
a little extra flour
milk for brushing

FOOD VALUES:
TOTAL ● PER BISCUIT
kcals: 2355 ● 49
kJ: 9837 ● 205
protein: 29 g ● 0.5 g
fat: 152 g ● 3 g
carbohydrate: 233 g ● 5 g
fibre: 8 g ● 0 g

Makes about 48

Place the flour in a bowl. Add the margarine or butter, then use a knife to cut the fat into the flour. Wash and dry your hands, then rub the fat into the flour. Stir in the sugar. Lightly beat the egg with the vanilla essence and lemon rind, add it to the mixture and use a round-bladed knife to lightly mix the ingredients. When the mixture clumps together, gather it into a ball and knead very lightly until smooth.

Cut the dough in half. Lightly flour a clean work surface. Shape both portions into rolls measuring about 3–5 cm/1½–2 inches in diameter. Cover the rolls of dough and chill for about 30 minutes. The dough may be wrapped and frozen at this stage or it may be stored in the refrigerator for up to a week.

Set the oven at 180°C, 350°F, gas 4. Grease two or more baking trays. Cut 5 mm/¼ inch thick slices off the rolls of dough and place them on the baking trays, setting them apart to allow for spreading during cooking. Brush the biscuits with a little milk and bake for 12–15 minutes, or until they are crisp and golden. Transfer them to a wire rack to cool.

When cold, pack the biscuits in an airtight container. They will keep for at least 2 weeks in a cool dry place.

SEE ALSO **Bisque:** Glossary; **Bivalves:** Glossary; **Black Beans:** Beans and Pulses, Dried

LACY BISCUITS

The knack to master is not the preparation of the mixture but the timing and technique for removing the cooked biscuits from the baking tray. Use a good, flat palette knife or a blunt, round-bladed table knife.

INGREDIENTS	FOOD VALUES:
40 g/1½ oz plain flour	TOTAL • PER BISCUIT
40 g/1½ oz butter	kcals: 718 • 48
40 g/1½ oz sugar	kJ: 3016 • 201
30 ml/2 tablespoons golden	protein: 5 g • 0 g
syrup	fat: 33 g • 2 g
	carbohydrate: 106 g • 7 g
Makes about 15	fibre: 2 g • 0 g

Set the oven at 190°C, 375°F, gas 5. Grease two baking trays. If food tends to stick to your trays, then it is a good idea to line them with non-stick baking parchment. Have ready a rolling pin, covered with a piece of foil and lightly brushed with oil.

Sift the flour into a small basin. Place the butter, sugar and syrup in a small saucepan and heat gently until the fat melts and the ingredients are well combined. Remove the pan from the heat and stir in the flour.

Using a teaspoon, place four teaspoonfuls of the mixture well apart on one prepared baking tray. Bake the biscuits for 5–8 minutes. While they are cooking, place another four teaspoonfuls of mixture on the second tray.

The biscuits are cooked when the mixture is well spread, golden brown and evenly thin. It should be bubbling very slightly on the tray. Remove from the oven and leave the biscuits for 1 minute. Test one biscuit to see if the mixture has set enough to lift: use a palette knife to lift the edge of a biscuit very slightly. If the mixture lifts easily and looks as though it will stay together, then slide the knife firmly under the middle of the biscuit and lift it off quickly. Place it over the foil-covered rolling pin.

Once the mixture has set enough to lift, work quickly as the other biscuits will harden and become too crisp to remove from the tray. If this happens, do not try to scrape the biscuits off as they will break. Instead, replace the baking tray of biscuits in the oven for 30 seconds, to warm the mixture and soften it again.

When the biscuits have cooled, carefully slide them off the rolling pin – they will be crisp enough after a few minutes. When cold, store the lacy biscuits in an airtight tin for up to a week.

VARIATIONS

Brandy Snaps Instead of shaping the biscuits over a rolling pin, wrap them around greased mixing spoon handles.

Biscuit Cups Shape the biscuits over oranges, upside-down cups or patty tins. They may be filled with scoops of ice cream or strawberries for dessert.

Florentines Add 25 g/1 oz each of chopped glacé cherries, chopped blanched almonds and raisins to the mixture with the flour. The biscuits are not as thin when baked and they should be cooled flat, on a wire rack. When cold, coat the smooth side in melted chocolate and mark it in wavy lines with a fork.

Biscuits

See Almonds*.
Homemade biscuits are quite different from the bought varieties and they can be superior both in flavour and in their contribution to the diet.

Varying Plain Biscuits

The basic recipe may be varied to make different biscuits. The following ideas may be combined.

Wholemeal Biscuits Use half wholemeal flour and add the grated rind of 1 orange.

Nuts Add 100 g/4 oz finely chopped walnuts, hazelnuts or mixed nuts to the dry ingredients. For almond biscuits, add 100 g/4 oz ground almonds and reduce the quantity of flour to 200 g/7 oz. Mix in a few drops of almond essence.

Fruit Add 75 g/3 oz mixed dried fruit or 50 g/2 oz currants with 25 g/1 oz chopped mixed peel.

Chocolate Add 100 g/4 oz chocolate cooking chips.

Freezing

Freeze the uncooked dough. Rolls of dough are ideal freezer candidates as the required number of slices may be cut off easily using a sharp serrated knife without thawing the mixture first. Pack and label the dough rolls, then store them for 3–4 months.

Blackberries

See Fruit*
As well as popular wild blackberries, cultivated fruit is available from late July through to early October.

Types of Blackberries

Wild Blackberries Choose a good patch, where the fruit is easy to pick and good quality. It is not a good idea to pick off roadside brambles that are exposed to traffic dirt. Pick on a dry day, early in the day. Avoid picking very small, hard berries as they tend to be seedy and flavourless. Take several small or medium containers to hold fruit rather than large ones in which fruit underneath becomes squashed. **Cultivated Blackberries** Still a relatively small crop but they are available occasionally from large supermarkets and greengrocers. The cultivated fruit are more reliable for serving uncooked and they need less attention since they tend to be free from pests and dirt.

Buying

When buying blackberries, look for large plump berries that are black but not squashy. Buy small punnets or cartons and try to make sure that fruit in the bottom of the cartons is not squashed – lots of juice stains indicate that the fruit underneath may be mushy.

Preparation

Make sure the fruit is trimmed of all stalks. Briefly rinse cultivated berries in small quantities under cold water, then drain well.

Wild berries should be washed in cold water with a good shake of salt added to draw out any maggots and insects. Do not be tempted to dump a large batch of fruit in a huge bowl otherwise the berries may be badly damaged during washing. Wash small quantities at a time, gently swirling them with your fingers. Drain off the water along with any dirt, then rinse the berries.

Storing

The fruit is best freshly picked or bought. It will usually keep in the refrigerator overnight.

Use

● In pies, crumbles, cobblers and baked puddings topped with sponge.

● Use large juicy fruit to fill meringue cases or sponge flans, or use in fruit salads (good with banana and eating apple).

● Cook and purée to make mousses, ice creams and fools.

● To complement rich savoury dishes such as roast duck, lamb or pork. Poach the berries in a wine sauce and sweeten very slightly for a sweet-sour taste.

Freezing

Freeze prime fruit that is cleaned and dry. Open freeze, then pack in polythene bags when firm. Store for up to a year.

Cooked, puréed and sieved fruit freezes well ready for making fools and mousses. Remember to label the pack with the quantity of sugar (if any) added to the purée.

Nutritional Value

Blackberries provide vitamin C, particularly when fresh and eaten uncooked. They also provide potassium.

Blackcurrants

See Fruit*.
These are available for a short period only, from July to August. They have a strong, sharp flavour.

Buying

Look for firm, bright and glossy currants. Avoid any wrinkled or very soft fruit.

Preparation

Stringing Currants grow in small bunches. The process of removing fruit from these is known as stringing. Hold the bunch by its stalk in one hand and slide a fork down the stalks to push the currants off the end.

Rinse the fruit under cold water after stringing, then drain before cooking.

Cooking

The currants may be stewed with sugar until very soft. Place the fruit in a saucepan and add sugar – about 175 g/6 oz sugar to each 450 g/1 lb currants, or to taste. Heat gently until the sugar dissolves and the fruit gives up its juice. Stir occasionally to mix the sugar and fruit. When the sugar has dissolved, the heat may be increased slightly so that the fruit simmers. Cook, uncovered, for between 5–10 minutes, depending on how soft a result is required.

Microwave Cooking Place the prepared currants and sugar in a suitable large dish – a casserole is ideal – allowing plenty of space for the juices to bubble up. Cover the dish and cook on High, allowing between 5–10 minutes for 450 g/1 lb fruit. Stir halfway through cooking. The shorter time should be used for lightly poached currants, the longer time for fruit which is to be puréed.

Use

● For pies, crumbles and other baked puddings.

● Cooled, lightly poached fruit may be used to fill flans or top cheesecakes. Thicken juices with arrowroot* so that they set on cooling.

● Puréed fruit makes delicious mousse*, soufflé*, ice cream* or fool*.

● Blackcurrants may also be used to flavour savoury sauces for serving with rich meat and poultry, such as lamb, venison or duck.

Freezing

Since the fresh season is short and blackcurrants are not readily available commercially frozen, they are ideal for home freezing.

Open freeze the well drained, prepared fruit. Pack the currants in polythene bags when hard. Store for up to a year.

Cooked fruit may also be

frozen when cooled. Pack it in rigid containers allowing head-space. Puréed fruit freezes well. Remember to label with the quantity of fruit and sugar used in cooking.

Nutritional Value

Blackcurrants have a high vit-amin C content. Frozen fruit or fruit syrup provides a valuable winter supply of the vitamin. Many commercial blackcurrant drinks also provide plenty of vitamin C.

Black Pudding

A sausage made from pigs' blood, cereals, seasonings and spices. Some are studded with pork fat. Black and traditionally horse-shoe shaped, the pudding is sliced, then fried. The slices should be turned once so that both sides are browned and slightly crisp. Black pudding may be served with cooked British breakfast.

The best black puddings are flavoursome and delicious but the bland, stodgy types lack character. Small butchers who take pride in making excellent black puddings usually offer the best of this type of sausage.

Use

• Slice and fry, then serve with bacon or a full breakfast.

• Slice and fry, then serve with fried onion and apple rings.

Blanching

See Freezing*.
Blanching is the term used for submerging food in boiling water for a certain length of time. The technique is used for different reasons.

• Before freezing, certain foods are blanched to destroy enzymes that are naturally present and which would otherwise cause the food to deteriorate during freezer storage.

• Blanching is used for loosen-ing the peel or shell on some food. For example, tomatoes and almonds are blanched to loosen their peel. Sometimes chestnuts may be blanched to free their shells.

• Blanching may be used for barely cooking some foods. For example, some vegetables may be blanched before adding to salads – they are not cooked or even part cooked but the process of blanching takes the raw edge off the vegetables; it also high-lights their flavour and colour. Sliced celery, cauliflower florets and French beans may be blanched before adding to salads.

• Some meats or offal may be blanched to make them firm or to whiten the flesh, before slicing or continuing their preparation and cooking.

Technique

For Freezing Have ready a large saucepan of boiling water, a basket to submerge the veg-etables, the freshly prepared vegetables and a large bowl of iced water for cooling the food. Also, use an accurate timer to check the blanching period.

Blanch food in small batches – this allows the water to return to the boil rapidly. It is also more practical to process food in small quantities than to have a bulk that is difficult to submerge in iced water or to drain and dry easily.

Submerge the food in the water and bring it back to the boil rapidly. Time the blanching from the moment the water returns to the boil, then lift the food out of the water promptly.

Submerge the food in iced water immediately, to cool it and prevent further cooking.

Drain well and dry the food on absorbent kitchen paper, then pack or open freeze it at once.

FRUIT BLANCMANGE

INGREDIENTS
300 ml / ½ pint unsweetened fruit purée (strawberry, raspberry, blackcurrant, peach, apricot or apple)
25 g / 1 oz cornflour
50 g / 2 oz sugar (or extra, to taste)
300 ml / ½ pint milk
fresh fruit to decorate (optional)

FOOD VALUES:
TOTAL • PER PORTION
(Using raspberries)
kcals: 559 • 140
kJ: 2363 • 591
protein: 13 g • 3 g
fat: 12 g • 3 g
carbohydrate: 107 g • 27 g
fibre: 24 g • 6 g

Serves 4

Rinse a 750 ml / 1 ¼ pint mould under cold water. Sieve the fruit purée, if necessary, to remove any seeds. Blend the cornflour and sugar with a little of the milk to make a thin paste.

Pour the remaining milk into a saucepan and heat it until boiling. Pour the milk on to the cornflour mixture, stirring all the time, then return it to the saucepan. Bring to the boil, stirring continuously, then reduce the heat and simmer the sauce gently for 3 minutes. Stir in the fruit purée.

Pour the mixture into the mould and cover the surface with a piece of wetted greaseproof paper. Leave until cold, then chill for several hours or overnight. Unmould as for Blancmange (overleaf).

For Peeling Fruit – Tomatoes, Peaches, Nectarines or Apricots Place the fruit in a bowl, then pour on freshly boiling water to cover it. Leave for between 30–60 seconds; ripe tomatoes will soften quickly, very firm fruit require longer. Drain and slit the skins, which will slide off easily.
For Peeling Nuts Place shelled almonds in a saucepan and pour in cold water to cover. Bring slowly to the boil, then blanch for 2 minutes. Drain and place in cold water. The peel will slip off easily.
For Salads Drop prepared pieces of vegetable into boiling water. Bring back to the boil and blanch for 30–60 seconds, then drain and rinse under cold water. Drain well before use. Alternatively, the hot vegetables may be tossed with dressing and other ingredients, then served at once.

Blancmange

Traditionally a cold, set, white milk pudding thickened with cornflour and flavoured with almond. Rum, spices, rose water or cream may be added to enrich blancmange.

Blancmange is now thought of as a cold set milk sauce, made from flavoured packet mixes. It is worth making a traditional-style blancmange as it makes a special, light dessert.

Boiling

This is a method of cooking food in boiling liquid, usually water (although stock or milk may be used). The water is boiling when it is bubbling rapidly in the pan, the same is true of stock; when milk boils it forms a skin on the surface. The bubbles are trapped under the skin and they rise rapidly causing the milk to boil over.

BLANCMANGE

INGREDIENTS
100 g/4 oz shelled almonds
600 ml/1 pint milk
1 cinnamon stick
25 g/1 oz cornflour
50 g/2 oz sugar
30 ml/2 tablespoons rose water
30 ml/2 tablespoons white rum (optional)
few drops of natural almond essence

FOOD VALUES:
TOTAL • PER PORTION
kcals: 1307 • 327
kJ: 5461 • 1365
protein: 37 g • 9 g
fat: 77 g • 19 g
carbohydrate: 108 g • 27 g
fibre: 15 g • 4 g

Serves 4

Place the almonds in a saucepan with the milk and cinnamon stick. Heat very gently until the milk just boils, then cover the pan and set the milk aside for an hour. Prepare a 750 ml/1 ¼ pint mould by rinsing it under cold water.

Strain the milk, then discard the cinnamon stick. Rub the skins off the almonds, then roughly chop the nuts or split them in half and cut each half into thin slivers. Cutting slivers is best but more time consuming than chopping the nuts. Set the nuts aside.

In a basin or jug, blend the cornflour and sugar to a thin paste with the rose water, rum and a little of the strained milk. Heat the remaining milk until it just boils, then pour it into the cornflour mixture, stirring all the time. Return the mixture to the pan and heat gently, stirring continuously, until the sauce boils. Reduce the heat and simmer the mixture for 3 minutes. Stir in a little almond essence at this stage, tasting the blancmange for flavour as you do so.

Pour the blancmange into the rinsed mould. Cover the surface of the sauce with a piece of wetted greaseproof paper. Leave until cold, then chill the blancmange for several hours or overnight.

Sprinkle the reserved almonds on a sheet of foil and toast them under the grill until golden. Watch them all the time and turn them occasionally for an even result. Leave to cool, then place in a covered container until required.

To unmould the blancmange, have ready a flat serving plate or dish. Rinse it under cold water and leave it damp. Place the plate on top of the mould, then invert the mould and plate. Before lifting off the mould, make sure the blancmange is in the middle. If not, slide it on the damp plate. Lift off the mould and mop any dampness on the plate with absorbent kitchen paper. Sprinkle the blancmange with the toasted almonds. Serve the blancmange on its own or with fresh fruit, such as strawberries.

It is important to distinguish between rapidly boiling water, when the liquid is bubbling fast and producing a lot of steam, and water that is boiling steadily, when it should bubble evenly without evaporating rapidly. Boiling must not be confused with simmering, which is more gentle.

Boiling Techniques

Adding to Boiling Water The food to be cooked may be added to boiling water. This method is

SEE ALSO **Blanquette:** Glossary; **Blend:** Glossary; **Blini:** Pancakes; **Bolognese:** Meat – Meat Sauce; **Bombe:** Glossary;

used for vegetables such as green beans, cauliflower and cabbage; it is also used for pasta* and eggs*. The water should be boiling rapidly when the food is added and the temperature should be maintained until the liquid comes back to the boil. Then the heat may be reduced to prevent the liquid from boiling over. At this stage the food may be boiled or the heat may be reduced until the liquid is barely bubbling in which case the food is simmered.

For vegetables that taste best lightly cooked in the minimum of boiling water, the heat should be reduced only slightly so that the water continues to boil.

> [X] *When adding bulky vegetables to boiling water, it is important to have a large pan no more than a quarter filled with boiling water. If the pan is too full, tipping the vegetables into it will cause the water to boil over. Use a mixing spoon or draining spoon to press the vegetables down into the pan.*

To retain the maximum amount of vitamins and other nutrients, vegetables are added to the minimum amount of water and they are cooked rapidly and briefly. A lid is placed on the pan to keep in the heat and speed up the cooking time, also to prevent evaporation of the comparatively small amount of water.

Adding to Cold Water Some foods are covered with cold water, then heated until boiling. Then heat is reduced so that the food may boil or simmer.

This method is used for potatoes, carrots, pulses, cereals, rice and meat or other foods that must be covered with liquid during boiling and which benefit from being heated slowly rather than being plunged into boiling liquid.

The food should be just covered with water – too much liquid increases the cooking time. The pan should be left uncovered or partly covered until the temperature is controlled so that the liquid boils steadily, then the lid may be placed on the pan. In some cases, the lid should be vented or a small space allowed for steam to escape and to prevent the liquid from boiling over.

The water is usually brought to the boil over moderate heat rather than too rapidly.

Sometimes the water may be changed once it has boiled and fresh water used for cooking (salted meat, such as bacon, is treated this way to dispose of excess salt). Sometimes scum may rise to the surface of the liquid and this should be skimmed off before the heat is reduced and the food allowed to cook (for example, when boiling meat).

Reducing by Boiling Boiling may be used to reduce the quantity of liquid and to concentrate its flavour. This is used for cooking liquid which is to be served as a sauce or for making stock. The liquid should be boiled rapidly in the uncovered saucepan or container, which must be large to prevent boiling over. This method is also used for preserves such as jam*.

Saucepan Size

Usually, saucepans should be about three-quarters full when boiling foods that are covered with cold water. If they are filled to just below the rim, the liquid boils over easily and the saucepan is difficult to lift.

When vegetables (such as cabbage) are added to a small amount of boiling water, they may, at first, fill the saucepan to the brim but they should be pressed down as they reduce rapidly in volume during the first stages of cooking.

Foods that froth up should always be cooked in large saucepans, with space allowed for the liquid to rise.

Draining Boiled Food

Care must be taken when handling saucepans full of boiling liquid as they are both heavy and hot; the steam which is given off can also cause scalding.

A colander or sieve should be prepared, either placed in a clean sink if the liquid is to be discarded or in a large clean bowl if it is to be saved. An oven glove should be used to protect the hand and forearm from the steam, then the contents of the pan may be tipped into the colander. Allow boiled food to drain well.

Alternatively, if the liquid from the pan is added to a sauce or stew, a lid may be placed over the pan and held in place leaving a small gap for liquid to pour out. The arm should be protected and this method should only be used when handling saucepans and quantities of a manageable size.

Advantages of Boiling

Boiling is an easy cooking method but it can be used badly. The main advantage of boiling is that it is speedy. If the cooking liquid is saved, some of the nutrients lost from the food may be retained in a sauce or gravy; others are destroyed by heating. Boiling does not need any extra fat during cooking but this benefit is lost when cooked food is smothered in butter or margarine.

Points to Avoid

• Overcooking by boiling food too rapidly or for too long.

• Adding green vegetables to cold water and bringing to the boil.

• Using too much water when boiling green vegetables – ideally, the vegetables should be cooked partly by rapid boiling and partly by steaming in the water vapour.

• Using too small a saucepan, resulting in liquid boiling over.

• Not controlling the heat properly so that food either soaks in liquid that is not boiling or the food boils too rapidly and breaks up during cooking.

Borlotti Beans: Beans and Pulses, Dried; **Borscht:** Beetroot

Bottling

This is a method of preserving food which involves sterilising it in jars and producing an airtight seal to prevent contamination from bacteria or moulds.

Before home freezing became popular, bottling was widely used for preserving fruit and vegetables. The method is still used for preserving fruit, such as peaches, in syrup or in fruit juice but it is used mainly for the preparation of luxury preserves rather than for keeping fruit in its natural state, as by freezing.

Bottling is not recommended as a preserving method for vegetables: freezing is more successful and safer.

Equipment and Techniques

The right equipment is essential, including suitable jars which may be sealed, new sealing rings, a large saucepan and thermometer. The jars of food may be sterilised and sealed in the oven.

The techniques of preparing, packing and sterilising the fruit must be carried out following reliable instructions in an authoritative book on preserving (see Bibliography, page 288).

X *Never store jars with suspect seals and never eat food from stored jars which appear to have broken or inadequate seals. The food may appear to be edible but it may be contaminated with bacteria that thrive in airless conditions, and they can cause fatal food poisoning.*

Checking the Seal

The seal must be checked once the bottled fruit has cooled and before storing. The jar should be picked up by the lid, without any clips in place. If a suitable vacuum has been formed the lid will be sealed. If the lid is not sealed securely enough for the jar to be lifted by it, then the food must be treated as fresh: it should be chilled and used within about 2 days.

Botulism

See Bacteria*, Hygiene* and Microorganisms*.

Botulism is a dangerous but rare form of food poisoning caused by eating food in which the bacterium known as *Clostridium botulinum* has grown and produced toxin.

The bacteria are found in the soil, therefore they are present on vegetables, and they may be found in some fish and meat. They will not grow in the presence of air but the spores will grow between the folds of muscle in fish flesh or in other areas not directly exposed to air. They are potentially dangerous when they contaminate food before it is sealed in containers, for example, in food that is bottled but not adequately sterilised.

Home-canning was popular at one time; however, it is not an advisable way of preserving vegetables. The vegetables may be contaminated with *Clostridium botulinum* from the soil and heat processing by home canning (or bottling) is usually inadequate assurance of food safety. Spores of the bacteria may survive to germinate and multiply in warm conditions when all air is excluded. They produce a toxin which is highly dangerous – eating only a small amount can be fatal. The toxin is inactivated by proper cooking but it is dangerous since bottled or canned food is often eaten without further cooking.

It is worth emphasising that food manufacturers are aware of even the slightest danger of contamination by *Clostridium botulinum* and canning factories work to the highest standards. There is no danger in purchasing canned foods.

X *Never buy or eat canned food that is blown – bulging due to gas which has been produced by bacteria. Always attract such cans to the shop owner or supermarket manager's attention.*

Bouquet Garni

See Herbs*.

A bunch of herbs used to flavour cooked dishes. The usual bunch of fresh herbs includes a bay leaf, sprig each of thyme and parsley and a small piece of celery (usually from the leaf end). However, the combination of herbs may be varied to suit the dish – rosemary, sage, marjoram, savory, mint or other herbs may be used. A cinnamon stick or strip of orange or lemon peel may be added. The flavourings should be tied together securely using kitchen string. A long end on the string may be tied to a saucepan handle. The bouquet garni is removed before serving.

Freezing

Freeze home-made bouquets garnis in polythene bags ready to add to food that is being cooked. They keep well for 4–6 months.

Buying

Dried bouquets garnis are available in small sachets or pouches. They are not as good as fresh or frozen herb mixtures.

Use

Add a bouquet garni to stock, soup, sauces (tomato or meat), stews and braised dishes. Here are two alternatives to the standard parsley and celery combination.

- Parsley, thyme, bay and lemon – with fish, seafood, chicken or lentils

- Marjoram, thyme, bay and rosemary – with lamb, game or beef stews, soups or vegetable sauces for pasta.

- Sage, celery leaves, thyme and bay – with pork, duck, turkey or chicken.

- Bay, orange rind, thyme and rosemary – with duck, game or lamb.

SEE ALSO **Boudin Blanc/Noir:** Sausages; **Bourguignonne:** Glossary; **Boursin:** Cheese; **Bran:** Glossary; **Bratwurst:** Sausages;

Braising

Braising is a moist cooking method in which food is part baked and part poached. The food is placed in a covered ovenproof dish, usually on a bed of vegetables or other flavouring ingredients, with enough liquid to form a shallow layer in the base of the dish and to produce steam during cooking. The food is then baked and basted with liquid during cooking.

Although the technique is correctly and mainly associated with oven cooking, when food is cooked on a bed of vegetables in a covered container on the hob it is sometimes referred to as braised.

Braising differs from stewing in that it uses less liquid. Pot roasting* is a similar technique but it may use less liquid than braising and rely more on the moisture from vegetables than on added liquid.

Techniques

Meat should be sealed by quickly frying on all sides. This may be done in a flameproof dish then used for braising. All juices from browning should be simmered into the liquid for braising (see deglazing, Glossary page 275). Diced vegetables may be added for flavour.

Whole vegetables for braising may be blanched or browned first (as for braised fennel*) or placed raw in a baking dish (stuffed peppers) with liquid.

The dish should be covered and the food baked or cooked gently on the hob. During cooking the food should be basted. The cooking liquid is served as a sauce, either sieved or with pieces of vegetables in it.

Bread

See Flour*, Gluten* and Yeast*.
Bread is easy to make but the dough must be kneaded properly and sufficient time must be allowed for proving.

Buying

White, Brown and Wholemeal There are three basic types, depending on the flour used in the dough – white, brown and wholemeal. White bread is made of flour containing about 75 per cent of the grain; brown bread is made from flour containing 85 per cent of the grain and wholemeal is made from flour containing 100 per cent of the grain.
Stoneground This refers to the way in which the wheat is milled.
Sliced or Unsliced There is such a wide choice of both types.
Freshness When buying packets of bread always check the 'best before' date. Baker's shops and fresh bake counters in supermarkets offer bread which is baked on the same day as it is sold. Some small shops, late-night shops and delicatessens buy in bread: make sure it is fresh before buying.

Storing

Bread sold in packets should be stored in them until used. Otherwise, bread should be kept in an airtight container in a cool, dry place. A polythene bag, plastic container or tin is suitable. However, bread stored in polythene bags and plastic containers should not be allowed to sweat in a warm room.

The rule for bread is the fresher the better. Most bread will stay fresh for 2–3 days; some types baked by traditional methods or other continental loaves are best eaten within 2 days.

☒ *Bread bins should not be used as a dumping ground for bread of different types and ages. If you do use a bread bin, then empty it twice a week, wash and dry it out well.*

Making Bread

There are three separate stages in making dough before baking.
Kneading When the ingredients are mixed they must be kneaded until the dough becomes smooth and elastic in texture. This stage is vital to develop the gluten* in the flour and form a tough structure in which to capture the gas which is produced by the fermenting yeast, causing the bread to rise.

Wash your hands in hot water and dry them. Turn the very stiff, rather dry dough out on a clean work surface. Press it down and forward with your knuckles, then stretch the front of the dough slightly and fold it back. Press it down and forward again with your knuckles. Turn the dough around occasionally as you knead it so that it is all worked into a smooth, even ball.

Press your finger into the middle of the dough – when it has been kneaded sufficiently the dough will bounce back barely leaving an impression.
Proving or Rising Wash and dry the mixing bowl, then dust it with a little flour. Place the dough in it, cover with lightly oiled polythene and leave in a warm room until the dough has doubled in size. This will take about 2 hours. Near a warm radiator the time is shortened but never put the dough in a very hot place where the yeast may be killed and the dough will not rise.

The dough may be left in a cool place for many hours or in the refrigerator for up to 24 hours.
Knocking Back or Second Kneading Turn out the dough on the work surface and knead it quickly and very lightly to knock out the gas. Then shape the dough and place it in or on the greased baking tins.
Second Proving or Rising Cover the dough loosely with lightly oiled polythene. Leave it in a warm place until doubled in size – this takes between 45–60 minutes. Again, this proving may be done slowly in the refrigerator. Once risen, the dough is ready.

Bread Tins

True bread tins should not be confused with loaf tins. A bread tin is deeper and not as long as a loaf tin. This makes a loaf which gives good-sized slices.

Other tins may be used, including round, deep cake tins. The tin should be just over half full when the knocked-back dough is placed in it. This allows room for the dough to rise to double its size when it should be just above the rim of the tin.

Shaping Dough

Oval Loaves Halve the dough in the recipe, then shape each portion into a roll about 20 cm/ 8 inches long. Cut a few slits across the top of the dough before baking, if liked.

Cob Shape the dough into one or two rounds. Cut a cross in the top of the risen dough before baking.

Cottage Loaf Shape two-thirds of the dough into a large round and place it on a baking tray. Make a deep dent in the middle of the round with your fist. Shape the remaining dough into a ball, moisten its base with water, then place it in the dent. Push the handle of a mixing spoon down through the middle of the loaf. Cut a few vertical slits around the loaf when risen.

Plait Divide the dough into 3 equal portions and roll them into long, thin sausage shapes. Pinch the strips together at one end on a greased baking tray. Plait the strips together neatly on the tray, then pinch the ends together to prevent the dough unrolling. Fold the ends of the plait under neatly.

Rolls The dough in the basic recipe may be used to make 12 rolls. Shape the dough into a roll and cut it into 12 equal slices. Lightly knead each piece into a ball, then place the rolls on a greased baking tray, slightly apart. When risen they should join together.

Alternatively, make individual rolls and place them well apart so that they do not join. Cut a cross

BREAD

INGREDIENTS
**25 g/1 oz fresh yeast or 15 g/
½ oz dried yeast (see
note, right)**
5 ml/1 teaspoon sugar
**250 ml/8 fl oz lukewarm
water**
450 g/1 lb strong plain flour
5 ml/1 teaspoon salt
**50 g/2 oz margarine, lard or
white cooking fat**

FOOD VALUES:
TOTAL WHITE • ALL WHOLEMEAL
(Using dried yeast)
kcals: 1923 • 1838
kJ: 8126 • 7757
protein: 56 g • 64 g
fat: 46 g • 50 g
carbohydrate: 342 g • 302 g
fibre: 16 g • 46 g

Makes 2 loaves

Cream the fresh yeast with the sugar and a little of the water, then add about a third of the water and set the mixture aside in a warm place until it is frothy.

Place the flour and salt in a bowl. Add the fat, then rub it into the flour. Make a well in the middle of the ingredients. Pour in the yeast liquid and the remaining water. Use a mixing spoon to mix in the flour. Wash and dry your hands, then gather the ingredients together into a stiff dough.

Turn out the dough on to clean work surface and knead it into a ball. Sprinkle the surface with a little flour if necessary, then knead the dough until it is smooth and elastic – this takes about 10 minutes.

Wash and dry the bowl, then dust it inside with a little flour. Place the dough in the bowl, cover it with oiled polythene and leave in a warm place for about 2 hours, or until doubled in size.

Thoroughly grease two 450 g/1 lb bread tins. Turn out the dough and knock it back, then divide it in half and press one portion into each of the tins. Cover loosely with oiled polythene and leave in a warm place until the dough has risen just over the tops of the tins – about 45 minutes.

Set the oven at 220°C, 425°F, gas 7. Brush the tops of the loaves with lukewarm water. Bake them for about 40 minutes, or until risen, well

in the top of each risen roll, if liked.

Other shapes for rolls include ovals, knots (made by forming a thin sausage shape and knotting it), small cottage loaves (made as for a large one) or twists (made by dividing each portion of dough in half and rolling these into thin sausage shapes, then twisting them together).

Baking Rolls As for bread, allowing 20–25 minutes.

Toppings for Breads

Glazing Brushing bread with lukewarm water gives it a good crust when baked. Milk may be brushed over for a well browned crust. Beaten egg, thinned with a little water may be used to give a golden glaze. Beaten egg yolk with a little water and a pinch of salt produces a deep golden, shiny glaze. Use the glaze on the risen dough.

Toppings Cracked wheat, sesame seeds, poppy seeds, chopped nuts, caraway or fennel seeds. Sprinkle these over after glazing. Some loaves may be dusted with flour.

Sweet Breads

The following may be made as variations on the basic dough. Enriched doughs often require longer proving.

browned and crisp. Brushing with water gives the bread a good, crisp crust.

Use an oven glove and clean tea-towel to protect your hand and forearm, then turn out one loaf and tap its base: when cooked the bread sounds hollow. If the bread sounds dense, then it is not cooked and should be returned to the oven for a few minutes longer.

Cool the loaves on a wire rack before storing in an airtight container.

Note: Dried yeast should be used according to the manufacturer's instructions. It should either be sprinkled over lukewarm water, stirred, then left until dissolved and frothy, or the easy blend type should be stirred with the dry ingredients once the fat has been rubbed in. If using the easy blend type, only one rising is necessary and the dough may be placed immediately in the prepared baking tins once it is kneaded.

VARIATIONS

Wholemeal Bread Use all wholemeal flour, half and half wholemeal and strong white flour, or two-thirds wholemeal to one-third strong white flour. Add a little extra water to mix the ingredients to a stiff dough – about 50 ml/2 fluid oz with all wholemeal or 25 ml/1 fluid oz with two-thirds wholemeal.

Granary Bread Granary flour contains malted wheat grain. It may be used in place of the strong white flour in the main recipe. Slightly extra water may be added – about 30 ml/2 tablespoons.

Rye Bread Use half and half rye flour and strong white flour. Add 30 ml/2 tablespoons caraway seeds to the dry ingredients. Increase the water by about 50 ml/2 fluid oz, as necessary to make a firm dough. The dough is heavy and it needs a lot of kneading to make it smooth. Keep it warm all the time, then leave to rise for about 3 hours in a warm place or longer – do not rush the proving stages as they are important to make the dough light. The dough should be shaped into two ovals or rounds. The bread is close textured and fine. It cuts well into thin slices.

Milk Bread Use lukewarm milk instead of water in the basic recipe.

Currant Loaf

Add 30 ml/2 tablespoons caster sugar to the flour and mix in 100 g/4 oz currants before adding the liquid. Shape and bake as in the basic recipe.

Currant Buns

Make the dough as for the currant loaf, above, then shape it into 10 buns and bake as for bread rolls. Make a sugar glaze while the buns are baking and brush this over them immediately they are removed from the oven, then cool on a wire rack.

Hot Cross Buns

Add 30 ml/2 tablespoons caster sugar, 15 ml/1 tablespoon ground mixed spice and 100 g/4 oz dried mixed fruit to the flour before adding the liquid. Shape into 10 buns and leave to prove on greased baking trays. Just before baking cut a cross in the top of each bun. Brush with sugar glaze immediately after removing from the oven, then cool on a wire rack.

Chelsea Buns

1 Make the basic dough, increasing the fat to 75 g/3 oz and using butter. Add 30 ml/2 tablespoons caster sugar to the flour before the liquid.

2 Knead and prove the dough for the first time. Thoroughly grease a 23 cm/9 inch square tin.

3 Roll out the dough into a 23 cm/9 inch square. Sprinkle 100 g/4 oz mixed dried fruit, 50 g/2 oz caster sugar and 5 ml/1 teaspoon ground mixed spice over the dough, leaving a 1 cm/½ inch margin all around the edge.

4 Roll up the dough like a Swiss roll, enclosing the fruit filling. Use a sharp knife to cut the dough into 9 equal slices and arrange them, cut sides up, in the tin.

5 Cover with oiled polythene and leave in a warm place until well risen. Set the oven at 220°C, 425°F, gas 7.

6 Bake the buns for about 30 minutes. They may be brushed with sugar glaze immediately they are removed from the oven. Leave in the tin to cool for 5 minutes, then transfer the buns to a wire rack to cool completely.

Sugar Glaze

Place 75 g/3 oz sugar in a saucepan with 100 ml/4 fluid oz water. Heat gently until the sugar dissolves, then bring the syrup to the boil. Boil it hard for 3 minutes. Remove from the heat. Just before the bread is removed from the oven, bring the syrup to the boil. Remove the pan from the heat and brush syrup over the hot bread.

Freezing

Some supermarkets sell bread in polythene bags ready for freezing. Otherwise pack loaves or other breads in polythene bags, expel as much air as possible, then seal the bags. Store for 1–3 months, the longer time for traditional-style close textured loaves, the shorter for light burger rolls. Most types keep well for at least 2 months if properly packed. If the wrapping is not airtight, then the bread tends to become stale very quickly.

Overwrap packets of bread, particularly perforated plastic bags. Open freeze buns or delicate breads, then pack them when firm.

Nutritional Value

All bread provides calcium, iron, thiamin (vitamin B1) and niacin. By law, white and brown breads are fortified to contain the same nutrients as 80 per cent extraction flour.

However, the fibre content of bread is important: white contains 2.7 per cent compared with 5.7 per cent in brown and 8.5 per cent in wholemeal.

Other types of bread, for example with added oatmeal or multi-grain loaves, are available and information on their nutritional value is provided on the packet.

Breadcrumbs

Types: Making and Using

Fresh White Made from fresh white bread, usually with crusts removed. Stand a coarse grater in a large bowl. Rub a chunk of fresh bread on the grater to reduce it to breadcrumbs. Alternatively, process the bread in a liquidiser or food processor.

Use for stuffings, to bind meatloaves and meatballs, or fry in butter or margarine and mix with sugar to layer in a charlotte.

Usually, whenever fresh white breadcrumbs are needed wholemeal or brown breadcrumbs may be substituted – sometimes the colour may be less acceptable.

Dry White Make fresh white crumbs and bake them in a very low oven (or residual heat from cooking) without browning. Reduce them to fine crumbs by

---

Cook's Tip

If ever you have leftover crusts or pieces of bread but no time to crumb them, then freeze them. If they are cut in small pieces before freezing, they may be reduced to fine crumbs from frozen in a food processor or liquidiser.

SODA BREAD

This is good made with wholemeal or malted wheat flour

INGREDIENTS	FOOD VALUES:
450 g/1 lb plain flour	PER LOAF
2.5 ml/½ teaspoon salt	kcals: 798
5 ml/1 teaspoon bicarbonate	kJ: 3402
of soda	protein: 23 g
300 ml/½ pint milk	fat: 4 g
15 ml/1 tablespoon lemon	carbohydrate: 181 g
juice	fibre: 8 g

Makes 2 loaves

Set the oven at 190°C, 375°F, gas 5. Grease two baking trays. Mix the flour, salt and bicarbonate of soda in a bowl. Add the milk and lemon juice, then mix well to make a soft dough.

Wash and dry your hands. Gather the dough into a ball and turn it out on the lightly floured, clean surface. Knead the dough briefly into a smooth ball, then cut it in half. Lightly knead each portion into a round loaf and flatten each one slightly. Place on the prepared baking trays, then cut a large cross in the top of each loaf.

Bake the soda bread for 40–45 minutes, until risen and browned. Transfer to a wire rack to cool. Cut into wedges to serve.

---

processing in a liquidiser or food processor. Stale bread may be used to make dry white crumbs or chunks of bread may be baked in a cool oven until dry but not browned.

Use for coating foods before frying, to give a good golden colour, particularly when the food requires fairly lengthy cooking during which time browned crumbs may become too dark.

Also used as a gratin topping.

Browned Breadcrumbs Either toast slices of bread, leave to cool, then process to crumbs in a liquidiser or food processor; or make fresh breadcrumbs and toast or bake them until golden.

Use for coating food before frying, for example thin fish fillets that cook quickly. Press browned breadcrumbs on the outside of freshly boiled ham which has had its skin removed.

Storing

Fresh breadcrumbs may be kept in a covered container in the refrigerator for about 2 days. Dry breadcrumbs may be stored in an airtight container in a dry place for about 2 weeks. Crumbs must be absolutely dry for storing in this way otherwise they will become mouldy.

Freezing

The best method of keeping all types. Put the crumbs in a sealed polythene bag. Use from frozen – a good freezer item.

Broccoli

See Vegetables*.

There are two types – calabrese has large heads and short thick stalks, and sprouting broccoli has long, thin stalks and smaller heads. Sprouting broccoli may be tinged purple.

Sprouting is available from March to May. Large broccoli is best during the summer and early autumn but it is usually available all year, although sometimes expensive.

SEE ALSO **Brie:** Cheese; **Brill:** Fish; **Brisket:** Beef; **Broiling:** Grilling; **Brown Beans:** Beans and Pulses, Dried

BREAD SAUCE

INGREDIENTS
4 cloves
I onion
I bay leaf
I blade of mace
600 ml/ I pint milk
100 g/4 oz fresh white
   breadcrumbs
salt and pepper
grated nutmeg

FOOD VALUES:
TOTAL • PER PORTION
kcals: 764 • 191
kJ: 3223 • 806
protein: 32 g • 8 g
fat: 25 g • 6 g
carbohydrate: 109 g • 27 g
fibre: 5 g • I g

Serves 4

Stick the cloves into the peeled onion, then place it in a saucepan with the bay leaf and mace. Pour in the milk, then heat the mixture very gently until the milk is just boiling. Continue cooking, stirring to prevent the milk from frothing over, for 5 minutes. Remove the pan from the heat, cover and set it aside for I hour, so that the milk is infused with the flavouring ingredients.

Strain the milk into a jug, then return it to the pan. Whisk in the breadcrumbs and heat the sauce, whisking or stirring all the time, until it boils. Reduce the heat, then simmer the sauce for 3 minutes, stirring occasionally. Add seasoning and a little grated nutmeg to taste.

Use
Serve bread sauce with roast chicken or turkey. It is also good with grilled fish steaks.

Microwave Cooking
Put the studded onion, bay, mace and milk in a large bowl and heat on High for 3 minutes. Stir well, cover and cook for a further 3–5 minutes on High, or until the milk is boiling and the onion sizzling slightly. Leave for 5 minutes, then strain the milk and stir in the breadcrumbs. Cook on High for 2–4 minutes, stirring once, until the sauce is boiling and thickened.

Buying

Look for firm, bright stalks. Avoid any sprouting broccoli with really long, wide stalks that look woody and tough towards their base. Broccoli that looks faded green or, worse, tinged with yellow is old.

Frozen broccoli is good quality and useful for using in baked dishes; however it is not as good as fresh for serving as a vegetable.

Preparation

Trim off spear ends and thoroughly wash the heads. Very large heads may be halved.

Cooking

Add the broccoli to lightly salted boiling water, with the stalks down and heads just out of the water if possible. Bring back to the boil and cover the pan. Young sprouting broccoli cooks quickly – about 5 minutes, or less if preferred very crisp. Larger heads should be cooked for about 10 minutes, or until the stalks are tender.

Use

• Makes delicious soup*.

• Top with white sauce, cheese sauce or egg sauce and breadcrumbs with cheese, then brown under the grill.

• Cut up small and toss with pasta and crispy bacon or cheese.

Freezing

Blanch* for 3–5 minutes, depending on size of spears. Open freeze, then pack. Cook from frozen for about 5 minutes in boiling salted water.

Nutritional Value

Broccoli provides vitamins A and C as well as being a useful source of fibre.

Brushes

Kitchen brushes have different uses. It is important to keep separate brushes for different purposes and to ensure they are thoroughly cleaned.

Use brushes for cleaning difficult corners and crevices, for scrubbing boards, sinks and around taps.

Pastry Brushes Used to brush food or they may be used for greasing tins. Wash the bristles in very hot soapy water – boiling water from a kettle poured into a clean basin is ideal. Rinse under hot water, shake and dry in the air. Store in a closed polythene bag.

Vegetable Brushes For scrubbing potatoes and other vegetables. Always wash these well after use, in hot soapy water, rinse and dry. Never hang them up dirty next to damp dish cloths.

Washing Up Brushes Useful for cleaning difficult items of equipment; however if they are not thoroughly cleaned they provide a breeding ground for bacteria. After use the brush should be thoroughly rinsed in hot water. Clean the brush regularly by soaking it in hot, preferably boiling water with detergent or bleach. Rinse well and dry by hanging up.

Nail Brushes Ideally, these should be kept in the bathroom or cloakroom; however, since they are useful for cleaning the hands after preparing pastry and similar tasks, they are sometimes kept in the kitchen. Wash a nail brush thoroughly after use, rinse and dry it. Keep it dry and separate from cleaning brushes, brushes used for scrubbing food and washing up cloths.

Floor Brushes Keep these away from food preparation areas, preferably out of the kitchen. Wash and dry floor brushes occasionally as they pick up dirt and bacteria from the kitchen floor.

Brussels Sprouts

Available from August or September to April but best during the winter months.

Buying

Look for evenly sized, tight sprouts that are firm and a good green in colour. Avoid loose, soft, pale green or green-yellow sprouts and any that have brown patches.

Preparation

Discard damaged outer leaves and trim bases. Cut a cross in the stalks of any large sprouts – this allows the stalks to cook evenly. Wash the prepared sprouts really well and drain.

Cooking

Add the sprouts to boiling salted water, bring back to the boil and cook for 5–12 minutes, according to taste and size. For very tender results with large sprouts, it is necessary to cook them for about 15 minutes. Soft, overcooked sprouts lack flavour and they have an unpleasant texture.

Serving Ideas

- With boiled chestnuts as an accompaniment to roast turkey.

- With split blanched almonds browned in butter or olive oil.

- With chopped onion and garlic cooked in olive oil and some chopped cooked ham. Good with baked potatoes.

- Wrap lightly cooked sprouts in bacon, thread on skewers and grill until browned.

Freezing

Blanching* is essential. Allow 2–4 minutes, depending on size. Store for up to a year. Cook from frozen by adding the sprouts to boiling water and bring back to the boil, then cooking for 3–5 minutes.

Nutritional Value

Fresh, raw sprouts contain vitamin C and A, also some protein and riboflavin. The vitamin C content can be lost by overcooking.

Buckwheat

Roasted buckwheat is available from wholefood shops. The grain is small, dark and pyramid-like in shape. When cooked it has a nutty flavour. Buckwheat is served in the same way as rice.

Do not confuse buckwheat with bulgur* or cracked wheat* which is a different grain.

Cooking

Place 225 g/8 oz buckwheat in a sieve and rinse it under cold running water. Transfer the grain to a saucepan and pour in 600 ml/ 1 pint water. Add a little salt. Bring to the boil over medium heat. As soon as the water boils, remove the pan from the heat (or turn gas off) and put a close-fitting lid on the pan.

Leave for 30 minutes, by which time the buckwheat will have absorbed the water. Fork the grains and serve at once. Overcooked buckwheat is starchy, soft and tasteless.

Serving Ideas

- Fork in fried chopped onion and diced eating apple with a little chopped sage or marjoram.

- Add to cooked minced lamb with garlic, onions and oregano. Serve topped with yogurt or soured cream.

Bulgur

Also known as bulghar or pourgouri, this is lightly cooked and crushed wheat. Not to be confused with cracked wheat which is the broken, uncooked grain.

Tabbouleh

Place 225 g/8 oz bulgur in a bowl and cover with plenty of cold water. Cover and leave to soak for 30 minutes. Drain well in a fine sieve.

Mix the juice of ½ lemon, 1 crushed clove garlic, seasoning and 5 ml/1 teaspoon sugar in a basin. Add 60 ml/4 tablespoons olive oil, 30 ml/2 tablespoons chopped fresh mint, 60 ml/4 tablespoons chopped fresh parsley, 2 finely chopped tomatoes (peeled if liked) and a finely chopped small onion. Add the drained bulgur and mix well, then leave to stand for a further 15 minutes before serving with crisp lettuce leaves. The tabbouleh is scooped up in the lettuce leaves and eaten with crusty bread.

Butter

See Fat*.

There are two main types of butter: sweet cream butter, which is usually salted, and lactic butter, which is unsalted or slightly salted and referred to as continental butter.

Concentrated Butter This is similar to ghee or clarified butter. It has had the milk solids and water content removed to make a product that contains 96 per cent butter fat. Use for cooking, according to the manufacturer's instructions. May be used instead of ghee in Indian cooking.

Ghee An Indian product, this is clarified butter which has had all the water and other products removed, leaving butter fat. Ghee made from vegetable oils is now available.

Half-fat Butter A product that combines butter with milk protein to give a flavour and texture which is comparable to butter but with a lower fat content. Useful for spreading but this may not be substituted in recipes that use butter for baking and frying. Recipes produced by individual manufacturers should be followed.

Butter Spreads Other spreads based on butter combined with vegetable fats are available under various brand names. These are not necessarily low in fat but they contain a combination of saturated and polyunsaturated fats.

Buying

Butter is packed in foil, paper or rigid containers. Always check the 'use by' date – this should allow plenty of time for you to use the butter at home (at least 3 weeks). Salted butter keeps better than the unsalted type. Butter in foil keeps longer than butter packed in paper.

Storing

Keep butter cool during and after purchase and put it in the refrigerator as soon as possible. Never leave butter to become warm or hot in a car after shopping.

Butter in the Diet

Following a balanced diet does not mean excluding butter. There is nothing wrong with eating butter in moderation. Consuming large amounts of butter (or other fats in the form of margarine and oils) is not recommended.

The use of butter in the diet must be considered alongside all other fats that are eaten regularly, so that a balanced assessment may be made. The rule to remember is not to spread butter lavishly every day, not to smother vegetables, pasta or rice with butter at every meal and not to make a frequent habit of serving sauces that are rich with butter.

Freezing

Place packs of butter in freezer bags and keep airtight, excluding as much air as possible.

Unsalted butter may be frozen for up to 6 months. Salted butter will keep for up to 3 months.

If you use small quantities of butter, it makes sense to cut freshly purchased packs in half and freeze one half. Also, having slightly less butter at hand for use tends to result in less lavish spreading – a plus in promoting a lean approach to everyday eating.

Thaw butter in the refrigerator overnight or for several hours. In an emergency, unwrap the butter and thaw it in the microwave on defrost setting. A 250 g/9 oz pack thaws in 6–8 minutes and softens after 10 minutes.

Nutritional Value

Butter is a saturated fat; in addition it provides vitamins A and D, and traces of protein.

Flavoured Butters
Cream the following with 100 g/4 oz softened butter.
Brandy (Hard Sauce) 100 g/4 oz icing sugar, 45 ml/3 tablespoons brandy.
Garlic 1–2 crushed garlic cloves.
Herb 45–60 ml/3–4 tablespoons chopped fresh herbs.
Maître d'Hôtel 30 ml/2 tablespoons each chopped parsley and lemon juice.

Cabbage

See Vegetables*.

Types of Cabbage

Spring Greens Loose, young dark leaves for boiling, steaming or stuffing.

Winter (Green) Cabbage Green, tight headed cabbage with a few loose outer leaves. The larger leaves may be stuffed, the heart may be shredded and braised, boiled, stir-fried or used raw.

Savoy Cabbage Dark green, curly leaves that are fairly loose are typical of this cabbage. Ideal for stuffed cabbage leaves, boiling or steaming.

White Cabbage This is hard, tightly packed and white. Use raw in salads, white cabbage is also ideal for braising or stir-frying.

Red Cabbage Hard and tightly packed like white cabbage but with dark red-purple leaves. Red cabbage may be pickled in vinegar, served raw in salads, stir-fried or braised.

Chinese Cabbage A cross between a cabbage and a lettuce in terms of flavour and texture. Ideal for salads, this requires little cooking. It may be stir-fried or braised. The leaves may also be blanched and stuffed.

Buying

Whatever type, cabbages should have a good colour with firm unblemished leaves. Some cabbages are overwrapped in supermarkets to prevent loss of moisture. Inspect Chinese cabbages in polythene bags for any signs of moisture and possible softness at the stalk end.

Storing

Eat as fresh as possible. Store in the salad drawer of the refrigerator if the cabbage is not to be used on the same day as purchase. Pack all types in polythene bags. Although fresh white and red cabbage keeps well for up to a week in the refrigerator, looser types should be used within 2 days. Chinese cabbage keeps slightly longer – up to 4 days after which time it deteriorates significantly in quality.

Preparation

Trim off tough and damaged outer leaves and tough stalk ends. Break loose cabbages into leaves. Trim tough stalks by cutting a 'V' shape into the leaves, then wash these well under running water – do not cut up before boiling or steaming as the greater surface area exposed to water the greater the loss of nutrients.

Cut the required portion of white or red cabbage in wedges ready for shredding. Shred the cabbage, then rinse it well in a colander under cold water.

Chinese cabbage may be shredded and rinsed or individual leaves may be removed according to use. Wash well and drain.

Cooking

Boiling For loose, green cabbages. Bring a small amount of lightly salted water to the boil in a large saucepan. (Do not add bicarbonate of soda as this destroys vitamin C.)

Add all the cabbage leaves when the water is boiling rapidly, pushing them into the pan. Put a tight fitting lid on the pan and bring the water back to the boil. Boil the cabbage for about 5 minutes, until just tender. Drain well and transfer to a warmed serving dish. Use a sharp stainless steel knife to cut up the cabbage, then season with

RED CABBAGE WITH APPLE

This is one recipe in which the cabbage benefits flavourwise from long cooking. It is delicious with roast pork, grilled chops, gammon, bacon or sausages.

INGREDIENTS	FOOD VALUES:
30 ml/2 tablespoons oil	TOTAL • PER PORTION
1 onion, chopped	kcals: 1198 • 300
10 ml/2 teaspoons caraway seeds	kJ: 4988 • 1247
675 g/1½ lb red cabbage, shredded	protein: 11 g • 3 g
salt and pepper	fat: 78 g • 19 g
30 ml/2 tablespoons water	carbohydrate: 120 g • 30 g
1 large cooking apple	fibre: 27 g • 7 g
45 ml/3 tablespoons demerara sugar	
15–30 ml/1–2 tablespoons cider vinegar	**Serves 4**

Heat the oil in a flameproof casserole or heavy-based saucepan. Add the onion and caraway seeds and cook gently, stirring occasionally, until the onion is softened – about 10 minutes. Stir in the cabbage, coating it in oil and mixing with the onion and caraway. Cook, stirring occasionally, for 5 minutes, then add a little seasoning and sprinkle the water over the cabbage. Cover the pan and braise the cabbage gently for 20 minutes.

Quarter, peel and core the apple, then cut the quarters across into thin pieces. Stir the sugar and 15 ml/1 tablespoon of the vinegar into the cabbage. Mix in the apple, then re-cover the pan and braise the mixture gently for a further 15 minutes.

Taste a little of the mixture: the sweet-sour flavours of sugar and vinegar should be balanced and the apple should be soft. Add the additional vinegar, if liked, with seasoning to taste, then stir and cook, stirring often, for another 3–5 minutes so that the cabbage is well glazed with cooking juices. Serve piping hot.

Variation

White cabbage may be used instead of the red cabbage. For extra sweetness and more body to the flavour, add 25 g/1 oz raisins with the cabbage, then sprinkle the cooked cabbage mixture with 50 g/2 oz toasted split blanched almonds or roughly chopped walnuts.

freshly ground black pepper and add a knob of butter or margarine. If the cabbage is to be served with a main dish with gravy or sauce, then omit the butter or margarine.

Steaming For loose, green cabbage, wedges of Savoy cabbage or coarsely shredded white cabbage. Place leaves or coarsely shredded white cabbage in a steamer. Wedges or shredded cabbage may be placed in a covered dish, roasting bag or they may be wrapped in foil and placed in the steamer. A knob of butter may be added.

Steam over rapidly boiling water for 7 minutes. Dishes and packs, particularly with wedges, take longer – 10–15 minutes.

The better method is to steam

SEE ALSO **Caerphilly:** Cheese; **Cafetière:** Coffee; **Caffeine:** Coffee

cabbage over a casserole or other simmering main dish, to catch some of the nutrients that seep from the vegetables. The cabbage should be steamed for slightly longer – about 10 minutes.

Stir Frying An excellent method for cabbage heart, white, red and Chinese types. Heat a little olive oil (or other oil) in a large frying pan, heavy-based saucepan or wok. Cook a chopped or sliced onion first for about 10 minutes, or until softened. Add the cabbage and cook it over fairly high heat, stirring continuously, until very hot, bright and slightly tender (for white and red types). Season and serve.

Braising For shredded cabbage (white, red, Chinese or green hearts) or tight wedges of Savoy or other heart. Use a large, heavy-based saucepan, frying pan with a lid or flameproof casserole. First cook a chopped onion in a little oil, then toss shredded cabbage in the oil before adding a little stock, dry cider, unsweetened apple juice or wine to the pan. Add seasoning, stir well or arrange wedges neatly and cover. For a crisp result, braise Chinese cabbage for about 2 minutes; shredded green cabbage heart for 5 minutes; shredded white or red cabbage for 8–10 minutes.

For tender wedges allow 15–20 minutes. For soft cooked red or white cabbage, allow about 40 minutes in a covered pan.

Freezing

Cabbage is not suitable for home freezing as results are very inferior both in texture and flavour.

Nutritional Value

Fresh cabbage provides vitamin C, some vitamin A, calcium and some fibre.

X *Avoid overcooking cabbage in large quantities of water as this destroys its vitamin C content. Using a carbon steel knife to cut cabbage and adding bicarbonate of soda also destroys vitamin C.*

Cakes

Cakes are classified by the way they are mixed: creamed, whisked, rubbed in and melted. These four methods are the bases for developing many recipes.

Steps for Successful Cake Making

● First read the recipe and check that you have enough of all the right ingredients. Make sure you understand the method.

● Check that you have the right baking tin or work out whether you can use an alternative.

● Make sure you have enough time to prepare and bake the cake – you cannot half make a cake, or leave it to bake unattended.

● Before launching into weighing and mixing, make sure there is a clear, clean work surface in the kitchen with enough space for weighing ingredients and preparing tins, also for putting out a wire cooling rack.

● Assemble all equipment needed.

● Weigh and measure the ingredients accurately. This is important when making cakes.

● Prepare the tin or tins in advance unless this is included as a stage within the recipe.

● Check that the oven is empty (no clean roasting tins or wire racks left in there) and set it at the right temperature. If you have an oven which does not require preheating, then follow the manufacturer's instructions.

● Follow the recipe closely when mixing the ingredients. Never shorten beating and whisking times and always check that you have achieved the required result at each stage before adding the next ingredient.

● When the mixture is in the tin or tins ready to bake, place it in the oven at once and check the cooking time. Set a timer immediately for the shortest time.

● Wash utensils and put away leftover ingredients. Clean the work surface and put out a cooling rack or other equipment required for turning out the cake. Have ready an oven glove and a heatproof mat.

● Check the cake at the first recommended time. Try to work speedily, opening the oven door gently and keeping it open for the minimum time.

Is the Cake Cooked?
To check if a creamed mixture or rich fruit cake is cooked, insert a clean metal skewer in the centre: it should be free of mixture. Sponge cakes should be golden and feel springy. Whisked mixtures should be slightly shrunk from the side of the tin.

● Remove the cake from the oven and place the tin on the prepared mat. Use a blunt knife to loosen the cake from the tin.

● To remove a cake from a tin, place the wire rack over the top of the cake. Hold the tin and rack, then invert the tin on the rack. Carefully lift off the tin, leaving the cake on the rack.

● To turn the cake the right way up, cover it with a second rack and invert it. Alternatively, invert the cake on the baking tin base, then slide it on the rack, or cover one hand and forearm with double-thick clean tea-towel and invert the cake on the towel.

Cooling Cakes

If a light cake is left to cool in the tin, then the moisture it gives off will make it slightly soggy underneath. These cakes should be turned out of their tins and allowed to cool on wire racks so that air circulates around them.

Very light whisked sponges can be damaged by wire racks. Cover the rack with a single or double thickness of absorbent kitchen paper or a clean tea-towel to prevent this and to absorb moisture at the same time.

Rich fruit cakes are left to cool in the tin to prevent them from drying out on the surface and forming a crust.

Techniques

Creaming Soften hard margarine by creaming it with a mixing spoon in a bowl. Add the sugar. Cream the margarine and sugar together until they form a soft, light-coloured mixture. To prevent the bowl from slipping on the work surface, place a damp cloth underneath it. Use a strong mixing spoon and try to keep the ingredients down in the base of the bowl as you work. Use a plastic spatula to scrape the mixture down the sides of the bowl occasionally.

> **Microwave Tip**
> Soften hard fat in the microwave, allowing about 5–15 seconds on High.

Rubbing In Place the flour in a bowl, then add the fat. Use a knife to cut the fat into small pieces. As you cut through the fat, the pieces will become coated in flour. Wash your hands under cold water, then dry them quickly. Using the fingertips only, pick up a few pieces of fat and a little flour. Rub the fat and flour together two or three times, then let it fall back into the bowl. Lift the flour and fat above the mixture, slightly higher than the rim of the bowl. This way it stays cool and the resulting crumbs are not clumped together.

The mixture is ready when all the fat is evenly distributed. It is usually compared to fine breadcrumbs – which is about right when there is half fat to flour. In mixtures which contain less fat, the crumb should be very fine; larger if more fat is used.

It is important to keep your hands cool when rubbing in. If

BASIC CREAMED MIXTURE

The proportions for a basic creamed mixture are equal weights of fat, sugar, flour and eggs. For larger cakes the weight of flour is increased by half otherwise the mixture will be too light to rise and set successfully.

INGREDIENTS	FOOD VALUES:
100 g/4 oz margarine	TOTAL • PER SMALL CAKE
100 g/4 oz caster sugar	kcals: 2197 • 183
2 eggs	kJ: 9242 • 770
100 g/4 oz self-raising flour	protein: 23 g • 2 g
Sandwich Cake	fat: 93 g • 8 g
225 g/8 oz jam	carbohydrate: 338 g • 28 g
caster sugar to dust	fibre: 6 g • 0.5 g

Makes 1 sandwich cake or 12 small cakes

Ideally, remove the fat and eggs from the refrigerator 30–40 minutes before making the cake and leave them at room temperature. Prepare the tins: either 2 × 15 cm/6 inch sandwich tins or 12 patty tins. Grease and flour sandwich tins; grease patty tins or line them with paper cake cases. Set the oven at 160°C, 325°F, gas 3 for a sandwich cake or 180°C, 350°F, gas 4 for small cakes.

Cream the margarine and sugar in a bowl until soft and pale. Crack an egg into a small basin. Wash and dry your hands, then tip the egg into the mixture and beat it in, working slowly at first. As soon as the egg is mixed with the creamed ingredients, stop beating. Add the second egg in the same way.

Breaking the egg into a basin first means that you can remove any small bits of broken shell easily. Traditionally this also provided an opportunity for checking that the egg was not off.

Begin beating in the second egg, then add a spoonful of the weighed flour and continue beating. Adding a little flour prevents the mixture from curdling. It is not a disaster if the mixture curdles but it holds less air, so the cake will not be as light. Tip the flour into the mixture. Use a large metal spoon to fold the flour into the mixture.

Divide the mixture between the two tins or patty tins. Spread it out evenly in the sandwich tins. Bake the sandwich cakes for 25–30 minutes or small cakes for 20–25 minutes.

When cooked the small cakes should be risen, golden and feel springy to the touch. Sandwich cakes should be golden, risen, slightly shrunk away from the tins around the top edges and springy to the touch. A good sandwich cake should have an evenly coloured top that is almost level, not peaked in the middle. Very slight doming in the middle is acceptable. Cool the cakes on a wire rack.

To finish the sandwich cake, spread jam on one layer and top with the second. Dust with caster sugar. This is the classic Victoria sandwich.

MADEIRA CAKE

Use softened butter, large eggs and increase the quantity of flour to 175 g/6 oz. Lightly stir in 30 ml/2 tablespoons milk after the flour. Turn into a lined and greased 15 cm/6 inch round tin and place a strip of candied peel on top. Bake at 180°C, 350°F, gas 4 for about 1 – 1 1/4 hours, until risen, firm and cracked across the top.

RUBBED-IN CAKES

These are easy to make and the basic mixture is quite versatile. Light cakes are the result of a good rubbing in technique.

INGREDIENTS
225 g/8 oz self-raising flour
100 g/4 oz margarine, chilled
75 g/3 oz caster sugar
grated rind of 1 lemon
2 eggs

Makes 12 cakes

FOOD VALUES:
TOTAL • PER CAKE
kcals: 1938 • 162
kJ: 8129 • 677
protein: 33 g • 3 g
fat: 95 g • 8 g
carbohydrate: 254 g • 21 g
fibre: 9 g • 1 g

Grease 12 patty tins or line them with paper cake cases. Set the oven at 200°C, 400°F, gas 6. Place the flour in a bowl which is large enough for both hands to fit in comfortably. Add the margarine, then cut it into small pieces and rub it in until the mixture resembles fine breadcrumbs.

Stir in the sugar and lemon rind, then make a well in the middle of the mixture. Crack the eggs into a basin, then wash and dry your hands. Lightly beat the eggs and pour them into the well in the mixture. Use a metal spoon to stir the eggs into the dry ingredients.

Divide the mixture between the patty tins. Bake the cakes for abut 20 minutes, or until they are risen, slightly cracked on top and golden. Cool on a wire rack.

your hands become hot, the fat will begin to melt and the mixture will become heavy and sticky.

Whisking Have ready a saucepan of hot water, placed over very low heat, and a large bowl which fits neatly on top of the saucepan. An electric beater is a real plus. If you do use an electric beater, the mixture may be whisked without hot water. The volume may not be quite as good but if the mixture is pale and thick the cake will be a success.

Crack the eggs into a basin, then place them in the bowl. Wash and dry your hands. Add the sugar to the eggs, then whisk them until they are very thick and pale. The eggs are whisked sufficiently when the mixture holds the trail of the whisk for at least 30 seconds. Remove the bowl from over the hot water and continue to whisk the mixture until it cools.

Folding In This is an important technique – if flour or other ingredients are mixed into whisked

mixtures instead of being folded in, the air is knocked out and the cake will not rise.

Draw the spoon sideways through the mixture to cut through it and the flour. Turn the spoon over so that its bowl is uppermost and lift the mixture over the flour. At the same time, move the spoon back and at an angle across the bowl so that it ends up just to the right of the first position. Repeat this figure-of-eight movement until all the flour is folded in evenly.

Folding in

The same technique is used for folding in melted fat. Add melted fat or other liquids after the flour.
Preparing Fruit Dried fruit may be prepared in two ways for adding to cakes. Some recipes soak the fruit in juice or liquor well in advance. If this is not the case, then toss a little of the **weighed** flour with the fruit. This helps to separate fruit that is clumped together and it helps the fruit to hold itself up in light mixtures.
Preparing Cherries Wash glacé cherries in a sieve under running water. It is best to rinse them with a little boiling water from the kettle. This washes away the heavy syrup coating. Drain the cherries well, then mop them dry on absorbent kitchen paper. Halve, quarter or chop the cherries according to the recipe requirements, then toss them with a little of the measured flour. If the cherries are not prepared in this way, they sink to the bottom of the cake.

Storing

Cakes should be stored in airtight containers once cooled. Plain cakes made by the creamed method keep well for about a week; light fruit cakes keep for 10–14 days and rich fruit cakes will keep for many months.

Whisked sponges become stale quickly as they are very light. Those without any fat should be eaten within 24 hours of baking or frozen. Whisked sponges with some fat added remain fresh for about 2 days.
Wrapping Leave lining paper on fruit cakes before placing them in airtight polythene bags. Wrap cakes in fresh greaseproof paper and place them in an airtight tin.

Never wrap fruit cakes directly in foil as the acid from the fruit reacts with the foil which disintegrates during long storage, leaving a fine dusting of powdered foil on the surface of the cake. If this happens, then scrape off the surface or cut off a thin sliver. Cakes may be wrapped in greaseproof paper, then foil.

Keep cakes in a cool place. Any with creamy fillings or topping should be chilled in a covered container as the cream is perishable. The cake should be eaten quickly, as for using fresh cream.

Other cakes should be kept in a cool place. For long term storage of rich fruit cakes, make sure the container is stored in a cool, dry place away from any likely contamination by vermin.

Freezing

The majority of cakes freeze well, particularly whisked sponges. Pack them in polythene bags and place in a safe place in the freezer to prevent damage. Alternatively, pack the cakes in rigid, airtight containers.

Fatless sponges keep, if well packed, for up to a year. Creamed mixtures may be stored for up to 6 months.

Rich Fruit Cakes There is no point in freezing these as they mature and keep well for months in dry, airtight conditions. However, if you have any doubts about finding a suitable dry cupboard that is not too hot, then the cake will not suffer by being frozen.

Decorated Cakes Do not freeze cakes covered with royal or glacé icing. Cakes covered with plain sugarpaste may be frozen but colours run on thawing so avoid any with decorations.

Gâteaux and other cakes covered with fresh cream may be open frozen, then loosely packed in foil or placed in a rigid container. Decorations should be added after thawing overnight or for several hours in the refrigerator. Keep only for 2–4 weeks.

Uncooked Cake Mixture The basic creamed mixture freezes very well in sandwich tins. Line the tins with freezer film and place the mixture in as usual. Freeze until hard, then lift the mixture out of the tin and pack it in polythene bags. To cook, simply remove the film and place the block of mixture in the tins. Cook from frozen, allowing an extra 5 minutes – the results are really

DATE AND WALNUT LOAF

A wonderful cake that illustrates the melted method. Gingerbread (see Glossary, page 275) is the other classic made by melting the ingredients.

INGREDIENTS
225 g/8 oz plain flour
5 ml/1 teaspoon bicarbonate of soda
225 g/8 oz cooking dates, chopped
100 g/4 oz walnuts, roughly chopped
75 g/3 oz golden syrup
75 g/3 oz soft brown sugar
75 g/3 oz margarine or butter
grated rind and juice of 1 orange
1 egg

FOOD VALUES:
TOTAL
kcals: 3043
kJ: 12806
protein: 45 g
fat: 121 g
carbohydrate: 473 g
fibre: 34 g

Makes a 900 g/2 lb loaf

Line and grease a 900 g/2 lb loaf tin. Set the oven at 160°C, 325°F, gas 3. Place the flour, bicarbonate of soda, dates and walnuts in a bowl and mix well.

Place the syrup, sugar, margarine or butter, orange rind and juice in a saucepan and heat gently, stirring occasionally, until the fat and sugar have melted and dissolved. Take the pan off the heat and cool slightly.

Crack the egg into a basin. Wash and dry your hands, then beat the egg lightly. Make a well in the dry ingredients and pour the egg into it. Pour in the melted mixture and use a plastic spatula to scrape all mixture off the pan into the bowl. Use a sturdy mixing spoon to stir the dry ingredients into the melted mixture. Beat well to make a soft batter.

Turn the batter into the prepared tin. Bake the loaf for 1¼–1½ hours, until risen, browned and firm to the touch. Turn the loaf out on a wire rack to cool.

WHISKED SPONGE

INGREDIENTS
3 eggs
75 g/3 oz caster sugar
75 g/3 oz plain flour
Filling
225 g/8 oz jam
caster sugar to dust

FOOD VALUES:
TOTAL
kcals: 1366
kJ: 5804
protein: 27 g
fat: 17 g
carbohydrate: 294 g
fibre: 5 g

Makes an 18 cm/7 inch sandwich cake or 1 Swiss roll

The eggs should be removed from the refrigerator at least 30 minutes before use, preferably an hour in advance. Prepare the tins: either grease and flour two 18 cm/7 inch sandwich tins or line and grease a 23 × 33 cm/9 × 13 inch Swiss roll tin. Set the oven at 190°C, 375°F, gas 5 for a sandwich cake or 220°C, 425°F, gas 7 for a Swiss roll.

Whisk the eggs and sugar in a bowl over a saucepan of hot water (not simmering) until pale, thick and creamy. Remove the bowl from over the pan and continue to whisk the eggs until cool. Sift the flour over the mixture. Use a large metal spoon to fold the flour into the mixture. Take care not to knock out the air from the mixture.

Divide the mixture between the sandwich tins or turn it into the Swiss roll tin. Spread the mixture very lightly. Bake the sandwich cakes for 20–25 minutes and the Swiss roll for 8–10 minutes.

Have a wire rack covered with absorbent kitchen paper ready for the sandwich cakes. Place the jam in a small saucepan and warm it over low heat until just melted. Remove from the heat.

For the Swiss roll, dampen a clean tea-towel and lay it on a clean work surface. Lay a sheet of greaseproof paper on top and dust the paper with a little caster sugar.

The cakes are cooked when they are browned, risen and slightly shrunk at the sides. The middle of the cakes should feel set and slightly springy to the touch – not as bouncy as a creamed sandwich cake but not soft enough to sink back.

Turn out the sandwich cakes on the absorbent kitchen paper and leave to cool. Turn the Swiss roll out on the greaseproof paper. Work quickly, remove the lining paper from the Swiss roll. Use a sharp knife to cut the crisp edges off the sponge. Make a cut into the cake but not right through across one end. Spread the jam over the cake, then roll it up from the end with the cut. Tuck the end of the cake into a tight first fold – the cut makes this possible – then use the damp tea-towel and greaseproof paper as a guide to roll up the cake. Leave the rolled cake in the damp tea-towel for about 3 minutes, then uncover and transfer it to a wire rack to cool. The damp tea-towel prevents the sponge from cracking as it is rolled.

Dust the top of the Swiss roll with a little extra caster sugar while it is still warm. Spread one of the cooled sandwich cakes with softened jam and place the second one on top. Dust with caster sugar.

excellent. The mixture may be stored for 2–3 months.

Storing the mixture rather than the cooked cakes takes up far less freezer space and the mixture is not easily damaged. It also makes sense to prepare a large batch of mixture and to freeze.

Do not freeze whisked mixtures or melted mixtures. Rubbed in mixtures may be frozen dry, ready for adding the eggs. Store for 3–4 months.

Faults: What Went Wrong?

It is encouraging to remember that even the best cooks have the occasional disaster. If something does go wrong, don't give up in despair – try to decide why the cake is a flop so that you can avoid making the same mistake

again. First re-read the recipe to check that you followed it properly – it can be easy to miss a step or ingredient and this could solve the problem.

If you are certain that you followed the recipe properly, check your oven. Check the setting and try to make sure you timed the baking properly. If you have had other problems with baked items, perhaps the oven needs checking to make sure the thermostat is working properly, ensuring the temperature is correct. In the first instance you can buy an oven thermometer to check the temperature yourself.

Sunken Cake
● Too much liquid used.
● Not enough flour or dry ingredients.

● Far too much sugar – in which case the cake will be dark with white spots on the crust.
● Too much raising agent used – usually the cake looks dark. Melted method cakes become too dark and may sink with too much bicarbonate of soda.
● Oven door opened too soon.
● Too light a mixture (not enough flour) in a large, deep tin.

Shallow Cake – Poor Rise
● Not enough raising agent or very stale self-raising flour.
● Insufficient sugar.
● Too much liquid (added milk, fruit juice) or too little egg.
● Tin too large, therefore too thin a layer of mixture.
● In whisked mixtures, insufficient whisking or flour over-mixed instead of being folded in.
● Far too much sugar or fat in whisked mixtures. Cooked cake will be very moist and heavy.
● Creamed mixtures overmixed after the flour is added.

Peaked Sponge Cakes
● Tin too small for mixture.
● Too much raising agent.
● Oven slightly too hot.

Large Holes in Mixture
● Fat and sugar not well creamed.
● Overmixing of flour in creamed mixtures.
● Flour not folded in sufficiently in whisked mixtures.

Spotted Surface with Dark Crust Cracking Slightly
● Too much sugar.

Very Dark Cake – Melted Mixture
● Too much bicarbonate of soda.

Dry Rubbed-In Cake with Fine Crumbs
● Too little fat.
● Too little sugar.
● Too little liquid.
● Oven temperature too low and cooking time too long.

Fruit Sunk
● Mixture too wet or too light.
● Fruit wet.
● Cherries not washed and dried.

VARIATIONS ON BASIC CAKES

Quantities are for adding to the basic recipes: see below for notes.
Abbreviations: tbsp = tablespoons, tsp = teaspoons.

	Cocoa	Instant Coffee	Dried Mixed Fruit	Desiccated Coconut	Lemon/ Orange Rind (grated)	Glacé Cherries	Nuts
Basic Creamed Mixture Chocolate Cake (sandwich with chocolate spread, whipped cream or chocolate butter cream)	45–60 ml/ 3–4 tbsp (to taste)						
Coffee Cake (walnuts optional, sandwich with coffee buttercream)		30 ml/ 2 tbsp					100 g/4 oz (walnuts)
Orange/Lemon Cake (sandwich with sieved warmed marmalade or lemon curd)					1		
Madeira Type Light Fruit Cake			100 g/4 oz		1 orange	50 g/2 oz	
Coconut Loaf Cake				50 g/2 oz			
Cherry Cake						225 g/8 oz	
Fruit and Nut Cake			175 g/6 oz				100 g/4 oz
Rubbed In Cakes Fruit Buns			75 g/3 oz				
Coconut Buns				75 g/3 oz			
Chocolate Nut Buns	45 ml/3 tbsp						75 g/3 oz
Whisked Sponge Cake Chocolate Sponge (For Black Forest Gâteau. Sandwich with whipped cream or cheese frosting)	30 ml/2 tbsp						
Coffee Sponge (sandwich with whipped cream)		30 ml/2 tbsp					
Lemon/Orange Sponge (sandwich with whipped cream flavoured with lemon curd)					1		

Cocoa Replace an equal volume of the measured flour with the suggested amount. Sift these dry ingredients together.
Coffee Dissolve instant coffee in 30 ml/2 tablespoons boiling water and cool. Fold in last.
Mixed Dried Fruit Add with flour to creamed mixtures; after rubbing in fat to rubbed in mixtures.
Coconut As above. Add 15–30 ml/1–2 tablespoons milk after mixing in coconut.
Cherries Wash, drain and dry. Chop or halve. Dust with a little of the measured flour.
Nuts Walnuts, Brazils, almonds or hazelnuts. In pieces for chunky cakes, chopped for lighter cakes, very finely chopped for whisked cakes.

RICH FRUIT CAKE

Cake sizes are for square cakes; use a 2.5 cm/1 inch smaller round tin.
Abbreviations: tbsp = tablespoons, tsp = teaspoons.

	15 cm/6 inch	18 cm/7 inch	20 cm/8 inch	23 cm/9 inch	25 cm/10 inch	30 cm/12 inch
Glacé cherries	50 g/2 oz	75 g/3 oz	100 g/4 oz	175 g/6 oz	225 g/8 oz	350 g/12 oz
Chopped candied peel	40 g/1½ oz	50 g/2 oz	75 g/3 oz	100 g/4 oz	175 g/6 oz	300 g/10 oz
Raisins	150 g/5 oz	175 g/6 oz	200 g/7 oz	225 g/8 oz	300 g/10 oz	450 g/1 lb
Sultanas	100 g/4 oz	175 g/6 oz	200 g/7 oz	225 g/8 oz	300 g/10 oz	450 g/1 lb
Currants	150 g/5 oz	175 g/6 oz	225 g/8 oz	350 g/12 oz	450 g/1 lb	600 g/1 lb 5 oz
Ready-to-eat dried apricots (chopped)	100 g/4 oz	150 g/5 oz	175 g/6 oz	225 g/8 oz	225 g/8 oz	225 g/8 oz
Crystallised or drained preserved ginger, chopped	25 g/1 oz	25 g/1 oz	40 g/1½ oz	50 g/2 oz	75 g/3 oz	100 g/4 oz
Blanched almonds, chopped	50 g/2 oz	50 g/2 oz	75 g/3 oz	100 g/4 oz	175 g/6 oz	300 g/10 oz
Ground almonds	25 g/1 oz	40 g/1½ oz	50 g/2 oz	100 g/4 oz	175 g/6 oz	300 g/10 oz
Plain flour	175 g/6 oz	200 g/7 oz	225 g/8 oz	350 g/12 oz	450 g/1 lb	750 g/1 lb 10 oz
Ground mixed spice	2.5 ml/½ tsp	3.75 ml/¾ tsp	5 ml/1 tsp	7.5 ml/1½ tsp	10 ml/2 tsp	20 ml/4 tsp
Ground cinnamon	2.5 ml/½ tsp	3.75 ml/¾ tsp	5 ml/1 tsp	7.5 ml/1½ tsp	10 ml/2 tsp	15 ml/1 tbsp
Grated nutmeg	1.25 ml/¼ tsp	1.25 ml/¼ tsp	2.5 ml/½ tsp	3.75 ml/¾ tsp	5 ml/1 tsp	5 ml/1 tsp
Butter	100 g/4 oz	150 g/5 oz	175 g/6 oz	250 g/9 oz	350 g/12 oz	550 g/1¼ lb
Soft brown sugar	100 g/4 oz	150 g/5 oz	175 g/6 oz	250 g/9 oz	350 g/12 oz	550 g/1¼ lb
Grated orange rind	½	1	1	1	2	3
Treacle	15 ml/1 tbsp	30 ml/2 tbsp	45 ml/3 tbsp	60 ml/4 tbsp	75 ml/5 tbsp	75 ml/5 tbsp
Eggs	2 (size 2)	3 (size 3)	4 (size 3)	6 (size 3)	8 (size 3)	11 (size 2)
Orange juice	30 ml/2 tbsp	30 ml/2 tbsp	30 ml/2 tbsp	45 ml/3 tbsp	60 ml/4 tbsp	90 ml/6 tbsp
Brandy or rum	15 ml/1 tbsp	15 ml/1 tbsp	30 ml/2 tbsp	45 ml/3 tbsp	45 ml/3 tbsp	105 ml/7 tbsp

1 Line and grease the tin. Wrap a thick band of brown paper around the outside of the tin, to stand 2.5–5 cm/1–2 inches above the rim. Tie the paper securely in place with string. Set the oven at 150°C, 300°F, gas 2.

2 Wash, dry and halve the cherries. Mix the cherries, candied peel, all dried fruit, ginger, chopped and ground nuts. Mix in a little of the plain flour.

3 Sift the remaining flour and spices.

4 Cream the butter, sugar, orange rind and treacle until very soft.

5 Beat in the eggs, adding a little flour to prevent curdling.

6 Stir in the flour, fruit and nuts. Lastly stir in the orange juice and brandy or rum.

7 Turn the mixture into the tin and press it down well into the corners of a square tin. Smooth the top with the back of a wetted spoon. For a flat top (suitable for royal icing) hollow out the middle slightly.

8 The 15 cm/6 inch cake takes about 2 hours. Check after 1¾ hours. For 18–20 cm/7–8 inch cakes, allow 2½–3 hours. For larger cakes, lower the oven temperature to 140°C, 275°F, gas 1 after 30 minutes baking. For 23–25 cm/9–10 inch cakes, allow about 3½ hours (total); a 30 cm/12 inch cake requires about 4½–5 hours (total).

Calcium

A mineral that plays a vital role in the diet, from childhood through to old age. The main function of calcium is to build and maintain strong bones and teeth. The importance of calcium for children, adolescents and young adults is obvious but it is also vital throughout life as it is required for maintaining the calcium content of bones.

Calcium is also important for blood clotting and the proper functioning of muscles and nerves.

Sources of Calcium

Milk and milk products are the main sources. Fish that are eaten with their bones – canned salmon, sardines and whitebait – also provide a useful supply.

Certain foods that are eaten regularly or in quantity also provide a small but useful source of calcium, for example bread (which contains added calcium in both white and brown or wholemeal varieties) and vegetables.

An adequate supply of vitamin D is essential so that the body can absorb calcium efficiently.

High extraction cereal foods, such as products with bran and wholemeal products, contain phytic acid which can reduce the availability of calcium. This means that a good supply of calcium is essential in a high-fibre diet.

Some vegetables, notably spinach, sorrel, chard and cabbage, contain oxalic acid and this actively inhibits calcium absorption. The oxalic acid reacts with the calcium to 'bind' it in a compound which cannot be absorbed through the cells in the body.

Cook's Tip

Some types and brands of milk are enriched with calcium (in addition to their natural content).

Calories and Joules

Anyone who has followed a diet to lose weight will be familiar with the term 'calories' and most dieters have come across 'joules' as the alternative. Kilocalories is also a widely used term.

Calorie

The calorie is a measure of heat used in physics. Heat is a form of energy which is produced by the body as a side effect of activity. All activity – from breathing through to exercising – produces heat.

The calorie is a minute measure which is too small to be of value when measuring heat produced by the body. Instead the Calorie (capital 'C') or kilocalorie is used and this is equal to 1000 times the value of the calorie used in other areas of science. The terms Kcal, Cal and Calorie are all used in relation to food.

Joule

The kilojoule, kjoule, Joule or kJ is equivalent to 1000 joules and the explanation is the same as for calories and Calories. However, the kilojoule is a scientific measure of energy, not heat.

Recommended Calorie Intakes

There are all sorts of charts and recommendations. As a rough guide, a fully grown, moderately active woman requires 2,150–2,500 Calories/9,000–10,500 Joules per day, depending on activity. A moderately active man requires 2,750–2,900 Calories/11,500–12,000 Joules per day. The important point to remember is that the number of Calories we need depends on the amount of energy we use up, how active we are or on our age.

Counting Calories

If you do have to count the Calories in your food, the best way is to make a list of everything you eat, then add up the Calories at the end of the day. Carry a notebook and pencil and jot down every single nibble of food – a few days of totting up the amount eaten soon reveals any over-indulgence.

The chart on page 273 lists the Calorie contents of some common foods.

Campden Tablets

These are used for sterilising equipment and bottles for home wine making and brewing. Available from chemists, the small tablets (sodium metabisulphite) must be crushed and dissolved in boiling water. A solution made as directed by the manufacturers may be used for sterilising pots and jars for jams and pickles.

Canned Food

See Convenience Foods*.
Canned foods are excellent storecupboard standbys. Frozen foods have replaced certain canned foods but others have retained their popularity.

Buying

Avoid cans that are damaged, dented or rusty. Never buy a can which is blown or bulging. Show blown cans to the shop owner or supermarket manager. The presence of gas in the can means that it has somehow not been sterilised properly or is damaged and dangerous anaerobic bacteria* could be present in the food.

When shopping, buy canned food on a regular basis if you keep it as a storecupboard item. For example, canned tomatoes, tuna fish, baked beans, fruit, chick peas and red kidney beans are just a few versatile items.

Nutritional Know How

Canned vegetables and fruit do not offer the same food value as

SEE ALSO **Calabrese:** Broccoli; **Camembert:** Cheese; **Camomile:** Herbs; **Candied, Candied Peel:** Dried and Candied Fruit and Glossary;

fresh and frozen foods, since some of the vitamins are destroyed during the canning process.

Get into the habit of reading the label on the can and assessing the type and nutritional value of the contents.

Storing

Keep canned foods in a cool, dry cupboard. Most canned foods will keep for years but as a general rule it is a good idea to consume the food within 2 years.

Canned cream, condensed milk, milk puddings, blackberries, blackcurrants, gooseberries, plums, prunes, rhubarb, raspberries and strawberries are best consumed within 1½–2 years.

Baked beans, pasta products, soups, fish in sauce or anchovies in oil, ready meals and hot meat products (stews and so on) should be used within 2 years.

Solid pack cold meat products and fish in oil will keep for up to 5 years.

These suggested shelf lives are a guide – canned food will not suddenly go off or become hazardous to health. However, after prolonged storage the taste and texture of the food will slowly deteriorate, although very slightly at first.

Using Canned Food

As well as for emergencies, consider some canned items as part of a regular labour-saving part of proper cooking. Canned tomatoes and tuna fish are the obvious examples; as well, consider beans and pulses, consommé (as a base for many classy soups and sauces), anchovies and fruit (try lychees, green figs and cherry apples as well as the usual types) in natural juice or syrup.

Opened Cans

Once a can is opened, remove the food from it and treat as you would perishable fresh food. Keep the food in a covered container in the refrigerator.

Remember to dispose of the can sensibly – put the lid back in it and squash the can flat, then place it in the outdoor bin away from pets, animals and vermin.

> **Cook's Tip**
> Keep a rota system for stored canned foods, always putting new cans to the back of the cupboard and bringing others to the front.

Can Openers

Choice depends on personal preference: models range from a simple metal hand-held opener to an electric can opener.

Care

Read and follow the manufacturer's instructions; remember, too, that the mechanism for cutting through the can comes in contact with the contents, so the opener must be washed after use. Many hand-held openers may be submerged in hot soapy water and cleaned with a washing up brush. Always dry the opener thoroughly to prevent it from rusting.

Caramel

Caramel is made by heating sugar until it browns. The sugar may be heated on its own or dissolved in water to make a syrup, then boiled until it caramelises.

Use

● To make praline: stir in 100 g/4 oz toasted blanched almonds as soon as the syrup reaches a dark caramel. Turn out the mixture on to a lightly oiled tin and leave to cool. Crush the praline when cold and hard, and use to decorate cakes or to flavour desserts.

> **Making Caramel**
> Use a stainless steel, non-stick or enamel saucepan. A fireproof glass pan may also be used. Avoid uncoated aluminium saucepans as the metal can react slightly.
>
> Place 225 g/8 oz sugar and 120 ml/8 tablespoons water in a saucepan. Heat the mixture gently, stirring all the time, until the sugar dissolves. Do not allow the syrup to boil until all the sugar has dissolved. Stir the mixture gently to avoid splashing syrup on the sides of the pan. As soon as the sugar has dissolved stop stirring.
>
> Bring the syrup to the boil and continue to cook until it begins to change colour. Never leave the syrup unattended as it overcooks quickly once it begins to brown. Never stir the boiling syrup as this will cause it to form crystals.
>
> As soon as the syrup begins to turn pale gold, be ready to remove the pan from the heat. Watch the cooking closely until the caramel is as dark as required, then remove the pan from the heat and place its base in cold water. If the pan is not cooled, the caramel will continue to cook from the residual heat. Use the caramel at once, before it hardens.
>
> If you want the caramel to stay runny, then add a little boiling water to it as soon as it is removed from the heat. This will prevent it from cooking and from setting hard (no need to dip the bottom of the pan in water). Take great care when adding boiling water to the caramel as it will spit. Protect your hand and wrist holding the saucepan handle with a tea-towel. Stand back slightly as you add the water – never look down into the pan in case the caramel spits in your face. Stir in the water then cool or use.

Cannellini Beans: Beans and Pulses, Dried; **Capers:** Glossary; **Cappuccino:** Coffee; **Capsicum/Capiscum:** Peppers

● For coating the inside of moulds and dishes, for example before adding custard* for making crème caramel. The caramel should be allowed to set hard. It becomes runny after cooling and standing overnight.

● To coat fruit. Pour over peeled and sliced oranges, then cool and chill. Runny caramel may be poured over a variety of prepared fruit.

● Use runny caramel as a dessert sauce, either cooled until just hot or cold. Stir 150 ml/¼ pint single cream into cold caramel to make a rich dessert sauce.

Other Caramels

Caramel may be made by heating sugar gently until it melts, then browns.

Brown sugar may be sprinkled over desserts (notably a rich set custard* in crème brûlée) and placed under a hot grill until it melts and caramelises. Fruit topped with whipped cream or thick yogurt is good topped in this way. It is best to chill the sugar-topped dessert well before grilling so that the ingredients underneath do not overheat.

Storing

Runny caramel keeps well in an airtight jar for several months in a cool place. It may be poured over prepared fruit, cream-filled choux buns or ice cream to make a quick dessert.

Carbohydrates

See Balanced Diet.*
There are three main groups of carbohydrate foods. Sugar and starch make up carbohydrates which are directly digested and absorbed, and fibre is a carbohydrate which comes from the cell walls of edible plants.

Sugars and starch are comparatively easy to digest and they are classed as the energy-giving foods.

Sugars

See sugar* for more information on the culinary types of sugar. Chemically, sugars are grouped according to their structure into monosaccharides or disaccharides.

Monosaccharides

These are simple sugars.
Glucose Found in fruit and plants. Starch and sugars are broken down into glucose by digestion, and the glucose is absorbed into the blood.
Fructose This is the sugar found in honey and fruit, it is sometimes referred to as the 'fruit sugar'. Fructose is also part of sucrose.
Galactose This is a part of lactose but it also occurs in small amounts in fermented foods such as yogurt.

Disaccharides

These are made of two monosaccharides, joined together chemically.
Sucrose Sugar as we know it. This is made up of glucose and fructose.
Maltose This is made up of two glucose units and it is formed when starch is digested or when grain, such as barley*, is germinated to make malt. Liquid glucose contains some maltose.
Lactose This is found in milk. It is made up of glucose and galactose but it is not as sweet as sucrose or glucose.

Starch

Starch is made up of many glucose molecules, linked in a more complex polymer (structure) known as a polysaccharide. The first stage in the digestion of starch is to break it down into maltose. This begins to take place in the mouth where enzymes start to work on the food as it is chewed. This is why well-chewed starchy food begins to taste sweet – generally food is not chewed this long but it is a good 'trick' of simple science for children to try.

Cellulose

Cellulose is a polysaccharide which plays a role in maintaining the structure of plant cells. It is made up of glucose molecules but its structure makes it indigestible in the human body. It is one of the key sources of fibre.

Sources

Sugars are found in honey, fruit and some vegetables and plants (cane and beet used for producing culinary sugar is not eaten, therefore it is not a direct source of dietary sugar).

Starch is found in cereals and grains (and their products), some vegetables and bananas.

Carob

The Mediterranean carob tree produces pods that look rather like large broad beans but they are brown in colour. The beans are processed to make carob bars and powder as alternatives to chocolate. Available from wholefood shops, carob powder and bars may be used instead of cocoa powder or chocolate for cooking, making desserts and confectionery. Useful for those allergic to dairy produce.

Carrots

See Vegetables.*
Carrots are inexpensive, versatile and available fresh all year.

Buying

In spring and early summer look for young carrots sold in bunches with leaves on. Carrots should always be firm, bright and moist-looking. Avoid dry, wrinkled or damaged vegetables. Check plastic packs to make sure that all the carrots are in good condition and reject any that are sweating or with vegetables that look as though they may have soft areas.

SEE ALSO **Caraway:** Spices; **Carbonade:** Glossary; **Cardamom:** Spices

Storing

Keep carrots in a polythene bag in the salad drawer in the refrigerator. Use within 3–4 days, although they will usually keep for up to a week if in good condition when purchased. Remember, though, the fresher the better is the rule for all vegetables.

Preparation

Whether you peel carrots is up to you. The traditional rule is to scrape new vegetables and to peel old ones. Whether they are scraped or peeled, always wash carrots well and trim off their ends. If the carrots are not scraped or peeled, they should be thoroughly scrubbed. Older carrots do benefit flavourwise from being peeled.

Small and medium carrots may be left whole; larger ones should be halved or quartered. Depending on the cooking and serving method, they may be sliced, cut into thin strips, cut into chunks or diced.

Cooking

Boiling Place the prepared carrots in a saucepan with just enough water to cover. Add a pinch of salt, if liked, then bring to the boil. Reduce the heat so that the water boils steadily, cover the pan and cook for about 5–15 minutes, depending on size and age.

Steaming Place the prepared carrots in a steamer and cook over boiling water for 7–15 minutes.

Glazed Carrots This is the best method of preparing and cooking carrots that are to be served as a main vegetable with a formal main course. Cut the prepared carrots into 5 cm/2 inch lengths, then slice lengthways. Cut the slices into matchstick strips. Place these strips (or julienne) in a saucepan with a knob of butter or margarine, a pinch of salt and some freshly ground black pepper. Add just a little water – about 30 ml/2 tablespoons – and put over medium to high heat. Stir the carrots occasionally until

CARROT CAKE

Known as passion cake, this American favourite may be covered with a frosting of cream cheese beaten with icing sugar and lemon juice to taste.

INGREDIENTS

225 g/8 oz grated carrots (see method)
175 g/6 oz margarine
175 g/6 oz light soft brown sugar
grated rind and juice of 1 orange
3 eggs
225 g/8 oz self-raising flour
5 ml/1 teaspoon baking powder
10 ml/2 teaspoons ground cinnamon
100 g/4 oz raisins or sultanas
100 g/4 oz walnuts, chopped

FOOD VALUES:

TOTAL
kcals: 3823
kJ: 15998
protein: 55 g
fat: 213 g
carbohydrate: 450 g
fibre: 29 g

Makes 1 (20 cm/8 inch) round cake

The carrots should be grated and drained of excess juice before they are weighed. Set them aside in a covered bowl. Line and grease a 20 cm/8 inch round tin. Set the oven at 160°C, 325°F, gas 3.

Cream the margarine and sugar together in a bowl until pale and very soft. Beat in the orange rind. One by one, crack the eggs into a basin and beat them into the creamed mixture. Wash your hands after cracking the eggs. Add a little of the measured flour with the second and third eggs to prevent the mixture from curdling.

Add the flour, baking powder and cinnamon to the mixture and fold it in using a metal spoon. Add the carrots, raisins or sultanas and walnuts, then fold all these ingredients in until they are thoroughly mixed. Lastly lightly stir in the orange juice. Spoon the mixture into the prepared tin and spread it out evenly.

Bake the cake for about 1½ hours, or until risen, set and golden. To test if it is cooked, insert a clean metal skewer into the middle. If the cake is cooked, the skewer should not have any signs of sticky mixture on it. If there is mixture on the skewer, then return the cake to the oven and test it again (with a clean skewer) after a further 10 minutes.

Have ready a wire rack, then turn out the cake on to it to cool and remove the lining paper. Store in an airtight container when cold. The cake will keep well for 2 weeks or it may be frozen for 3 months.

the fat melts and the water boils. The fine strips of carrot cook in about 3–5 minutes. During cooking they give up some liquid. The heat should be regulated so that the liquid bubbles rapidly and evaporates to leave the carrots moist and glazed with cooking juices. Sprinkle with snipped chives or chopped parsley.

Use

● Grated raw carrot tossed with a little chopped spring onion, olive oil and a squeeze of orange or lemon juice makes a delicious salad.

● Use grated raw carrot in a variety of salads, including coleslaw.

- Add diced, sliced or cubed carrot to casseroles and vegetable curries.

- To make soup – good with orange and tarragon.

- Use finely grated carrot with grated potato and onion to make tasty vegetable burgers.

Carving

The majority of joints of meat are boned and trussed ready for easy slicing, including beef, pork and lamb. However, it is useful to know how to tackle cuts on the bone, such as leg or shoulder of lamb, and poultry.

Unless you are a confident carver, it is far better and less messy to carve a joint in the kitchen. Either transfer the meat to individual plates and pour a little gravy or sauce over each portion or arrange the slices overlapping on a serving platter. Any small offcuts can be arranged in a neat line down one side of the platter.

Utensils

A two-pronged carving fork is useful but not essential as any sturdy fork may be used. A sharp knife is essential – if not a special

carving knife, then a sharp bread knife or large serrated kitchen knife.

General Points

- When meat is cut across the grain, it is easier to chew, therefore it seems more tender.

- Leave meat to stand, covered, for about 10–20 minutes after cooking and before carving.

- Always have the meat on a stable plate, on a strong surface where it will not slip. A spiked carving platter is ideal for joints.

- Have warm plates ready to receive the meat.

- Loosen meat around a bone, if possible before carving it. This applies to joints such as rib of beef or loin of pork.

- As a rule meat is carved at right angles to a bone, sometimes the angle is reduced, depending on the shape of the joint.

Carving Boned Joints

First remove any skewers or string. Slice the meat across the grain and across any outer wrapping or coating of fat so that the fat is distributed evenly between the slices.

Whether the meat is cut thick or thin is a matter for personal taste, although traditionally beef and lamb are cut thin whereas pork is cut into thicker slices.

Carving Meat on the Bone

As a general rule, cut down through the meat, across the grain and towards the bone. This applies to rib of beef, leg joints (pork or lamb), loin (of lamb or pork) and shoulder of lamb. Cut into thick areas of meat first.

Leg of Lamb The joint should be placed firmly on a dish with the thicker area of meat uppermost. Hold the bone end in one hand, then cut a wedge-shaped slice from the beginning of the main portion of meat. Continue to slice the meat across the grain, down towards the bone, working at a slight angle, along towards the end of the leg. When all the meat is removed from one side, turn the joint over and carve the thinner meat. To make larger slices, carve at a more acute angle on the thinner side. When the majority of meat is carved in neat slices, any small remaining areas should be cut off as neatly as possible.

Shoulder of Lamb Place the joint on a serving platter with the thick side of meat uppermost. Hold

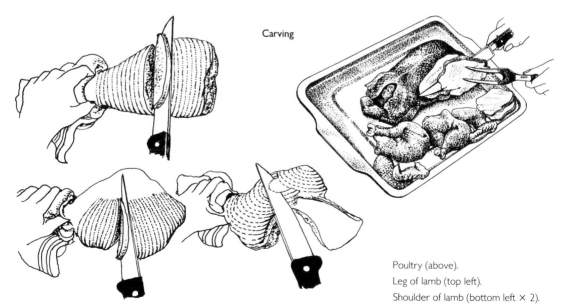

Carving

Poultry (above).

Leg of lamb (top left).

Shoulder of lamb (bottom left × 2).

SEE ALSO **Cashew Nuts:** Nuts; **Cassava:** Vegetables – exotic

the bone end in one hand or stab the meat firmly with a sturdy fork near the bone end. Cut a wedge-shaped slice down towards the bone at the narrow end, then slice downwards working along the largest portion of meat towards the wide end of the joint. Cut the slices at a very slight angle.

Cut sideways into the remaining areas of meat, carving small but neat slices in towards the bone.

Carving Poultry

For chicken, duck, a small turkey or pheasant, cut off the wings and legs before carving the breast meat. In the case of duck or pheasant, the birds may be jointed into four instead of being carved.

When the four joints are removed, carve the breast meat. Take off the first slice at an angle towards the wing and one side of the breast. Continue slicing until all the breast meat has been removed from one side. Carve the meat off the second side in the same way.

After the top slice of skin has been removed, each slice should be bordered with skin, unless the skin is removed before carving. The size of the slices depends on the size of the bird. Turkey breast yields large slices, while duck or pheasant gives small slices.

$\boxed{\text{X}}$ *Wooden boards are not suitable for holding meat or poultry for carving. There is a severe danger of cross contamination. A warmed metal or china platter is far more sensible since it will catch juices which seep from the joint.*

Casein

See Milk*.
A protein found in milk. When treated with an acid and rennet, the casein coagulates, or becomes firm, and separates out to form curds which are processed to make cheese.

Cauliflower

See Vegetables*.
Green and purple cauliflowers are available as well as white ones.

Buying

Whole cauliflowers should be firm, surrounded by some fresh-looking green leaves and free from any blemishes or spots. The head should be rounded and tight – tall, loose headed cauliflowers are overgrown and their florets are leggy. Slightly yellow-looking cauliflowers are not necessarily a poor buy as long as they are firm and otherwise unblemished. Spots and trimmed areas may indicate that the vegetable is beginning to rot at the core. Reject soft or rubbery vegetables.

Packs of separated florets should be closely inspected for any signs of inferior quality or spotting and softening.

Storing

Trim any unwanted outer damaged leaves, then place the unwashed vegetable in a sealed polythene bag in the bottom of the refrigerator. Keep for a day or up to 2 days if bought in prime condition. Sealed packs should be left unopened until use.

Preparation

Trim off outer leaves and tough stalk – these do not have to be discarded as they may be cut up and cooked slightly longer than the tender florets (or reserve them for a separate dish).

Either separate the head into florets or leave it whole. Wash the cauliflower thoroughly under running cold water, then leave it to drain well before cooking.

Cooking

Boiling Add the whole cauliflower (stalk end down) or florets to a pan containing a small amount of rapidly boiling water (with a little salt added if liked) and bring back to the boil. There should be enough water to cover the stalk but the florets should not be submerged. Reduce the heat slightly if necessary but keep the water boiling. Cook florets for 5–7 minutes or a whole cauliflower for about 10 minutes. The cauliflower should be tender but not soft. Drain well.

Steaming Place the cauliflower in a steamer over boiling water and cook florets for about 7–10 minutes, whole cauliflowers for about 15 minutes.

Microwave Cooking Place the prepared cauliflower in a large suitable dish with about 150 ml/¼ pint boiling water. Do not add any salt. Whole cauliflowers cook well this way. Florets should be arranged with the stalks placed together in the middle of the dish and the heads towards the outside. Cover and cook on High, allowing about 7–9 minutes for 450 g/1 lb florets or 12–14 minutes for a whole cauliflower of the same weight. Leave to stand for about 3 minutes, then drain and serve.

Stir Frying Break the cauliflower into small florets, trimmed of tough stalk. Toss these in hot oil with other vegetables, such as leek and carrot, until glazed, hot and slightly tender. The cauliflower is cooked when it begins to look translucent, and is still crunchy. Leeks, onions and carrots should be part cooked before adding cauliflower.

Use

• Raw in salad – break the cauliflower into small florets and combine them with apple, celery and walnuts. If preferred, the cauliflower may be blanched in boiling water for 1 minute, then drained and rinsed under cold water. Drain well.

• Cauliflower makes delicious soup – cook with light stock and potato, then purée the soup until smooth and thin with milk.

• Stir fry cauliflower with diced bacon and leek, then stir in a can of chopped tomatoes and bring to the boil. Serve with rice.

Freezing

Prepare and separate into florets. Blanch for 3 minutes, then cool and drain. Open freeze before packing. Store for 6 months.

Nutritional Value

Cauliflower has a high water content. It provides potassium, calcium and vitamin C.

Celeriac

See Vegetables*.
A root vegetable, similar in size to a swede, with creamy-beige skin and a celery-like flavour. Use raw or cooked.

Buying and Storing

Look for firm vegetables which are not too small. Keep in a polythene bag in the refrigerator for up to a week.

Preparation and Cooking

Peel thickly and place in water with lemon juice added as the flesh discolours quickly. Cut in strips or cubes, or grate to serve in salad. Boil and mash as for swede*.
Stir Frying Toss thin strips with other vegetables over high heat for a crunchy result.

Use

• Mash or purée celeriac to serve hot.
• Add to casseroles or soups.
• Stir fry with strips of chicken, leek or pepper.

Freezing

Do not freeze raw or plain cooked, but may be frozen puréed. Store for up to 6 months, depending on added ingredients.

BRAISED CELERY

INGREDIENTS
1 head celery
30 ml/2 tablespoons oil
1 onion, chopped
1 small carrot, diced
1 bay leaf
salt and pepper
150 ml/¼ pint water, light stock or dry white wine
15 ml/1 tablespoon plain flour
small knob of butter or margarine

FOOD VALUES:
TOTAL • PER PORTION
kcals: 533 • 133
kJ: 2210 • 553
protein: 6 g • 1.5 g
fat: 37 g • 9 g
carbohydrate: 22 g • 6 g
fibre: 16 g • 4 g

Serves 4

Set the oven at 180°C, 350°F, gas 4. Separate the celery into stalks and wash them well. Trim off the leaves – these may be chopped and reserved for garnish. Cut the stalks into 5–7.5 cm/2–3 inch lengths.

Heat the oil in a frying pan, then add the onion and carrot. Cook, stirring occasionally, for 10 minutes, then add the celery and turn the stalks in the oil. Cook for a minute or so, then arrange the celery, onion, carrot and all cooking juices in an ovenproof dish. Add the bay leaf and sprinkle with a little seasoning. Pour in the water, stock or wine and cover the dish.

Bake the celery for about 50 minutes, or until the stalks are tender. Use a slotted spoon to transfer the celery to a serving dish and keep hot (or drain off the cooking juices). Pour the cooking juices into a saucepan. Beat the flour and butter or margarine together until smooth. Bring the cooking juices to the boil, then whisk in knobs of the flour mixture. Continue whisking until the liquid boils. Cook for 3 minutes, then taste for seasoning and pour the thickened juices over the celery.

Celery

See Vegetables*.

Buying

Look for firm, unbroken stalks with bright, fresh leaves if any. Avoid any with badly split, yellowing or limp stalks.

Storing

Keep celery in an open polythene bag in the salad drawer of the refrigerator. It will stay fresh for up to a week.

Another method of keeping celery is to stand it root end down in a bowl or jug of cold water by a window away from direct sunlight. The water should be changed every day.

Preparation

Separate the stalks and trim their ends. There is no need to discard the thin ends and leaves as these may be used in cooked dishes, salads or a bouquet garni*.

Thoroughly scrub or wash the stalks. Scrape away any tough strings and rinse well.

Cutting Celery

Slicing Trim and rinse the whole head, then hold it firmly and cut slices. Wash well in a colander.
Slicing Diagonally Slice washed stalks one at a time. Cut off the end diagonally, then continue to cut thin diagonal slices.
Strips Cut the stalks lengthways into thin strips, then cut these into lengths. For very fine strips, cut stalks into 5 cm/2 inch lengths, then cut fine shreds.

SEE ALSO **Cayenne Pepper:** Chilli; **Ceps:** Mushrooms; **Cervelat:** Sausages; **Chanterelles:** Mushrooms;

Cooking

Braising Whole hearts or lengths of stalks may be braised.
Stir Frying Cut the stalks across into thin slices or cut them diagonally into thin slices for an Oriental-style dish. The stalks may also be cut lengthways into fine strips, then across into short lengths. Stir fry celery in oil with onion, leek and carrot.

Use

• For celery soup, in stews and braised dishes (poultry, meat and fish).

• Raw in salads – with apple and walnut or in green salads.

• Dice finely and cook with chopped onion and garlic in olive oil. When tender (20–30 minutes), toss with cooked pasta and serve with lots of grated cheese.

Microwave Cooking

Celery does not cook well in the microwave as the outsides of the stalks remain tough. Diced and thinly sliced celery may be cooked in the same way as onion, as part of a dish.

Freezing

Celery does not freeze well. Although small pieces may be frozen in cooked casseroles, the raw vegetable becomes limp and tough on thawing. Celery soup may be frozen.

Nutritional Value

Celery provides vitamin C and minerals; including a high sodium content.

Cheese

Cheese is made by treating milk with rennet (see Glossary, page 275), or another agent to cause curdling or separation, which makes the casein* clump together in curds. The majority of the fat content of the milk coagulates with the protein in the curds. The curds are then pressed to squeeze out the whey and they are treated with salt which acts as a preservative, then they are shaped and ripened.

The process involves a number of carefully controlled stages at which specific bacteria are used to sour the milk and ripen the cheese. The conditions in which the cheese is stored and matured are also closely monitored.

As well as cows' milk, cheese may be made from goats' or sheeps' milk and both give a distinct flavour.

Most cheese is made from pasteurised milk. Unpasteurised cheese is made from untreated milk.

Buying

Buy from a reputable supplier. In shops and supermarkets, the cheese should be chilled or kept cool. If it is not cut and packed, it should be covered.
Packed Cheese Always inspect packs of cheese closely and check the date by which it should be eaten. The cheese should look fresh and even in texture and colour, except along any rind. Reject any packs that look as though they are sweating or if any undue mould is growing.
Ripeness Some cheeses darken as they mature, either along a line inside the rind or along veining in blue cheeses: there is nothing wrong with this but some people prefer cheese that is not as well matured.

Cheeses with a soft rind, such as camembert or brie, tend to darken on the outside as they ripen. A cheese that is beige, or forming beige patches, will be ripe whereas a very pale one will be firm and under-ripe.

Texture is a good indication of ripeness. For example a firm, pale, dry-looking blue Stilton will be slightly tangy and not as ripe, or strongly flavoured, as a creamy-coloured, softer cheese which is darkening just inside the rind. A cut piece of brie which looks stark white, very firm and crumbly is not ripe – it will become smooth and creamy, ready to flow slightly, when ripe. The extent to which brie and similar cheeses soften and 'flow' depends on their type.

Storing

At home, the most hygienic place to store cheese is in the refrigerator. Cheese should be individually wrapped and placed towards the top of the refrigerator. Allow the cheese to come to room temperature if it is to be served plain with bread or biscuits. Cheese used for cooking should be kept in the refrigerator until it is to be used.

Any leftovers should be packed promptly and returned to the refrigerator.

If a cheese is firm and it requires ripening before serving, it should be left packed in a cool room for about a day. It is worth noting that some cheeses which are not ripe when sold may well not improve in condition. For example, very firm wedges of brie with a chalky appearance are unlikely to mature to a soft texture. They may become dry or mouldy and less palatable if left at room temperature.

As a general guide, when purchasing from a supermarket look for cheese which is ready to eat to your liking. In a specialist shop – delicatessen, cheese shop or cheese seller on a market – ask for guidance on specific cheeses.

Types of Cheese

There are various means of classifying cheese, one of the most popular methods is according to texture.

Soft Cheese Also known as fresh cheese, since the types in this group are not matured. This includes cottage, cream and curd cheeses as well as fromage frais*.

Semi-soft Cheese This group may also be classed as soft cheese (if the term 'fresh' is used for the above category). Camembert, brie and similar cheeses are termed semi-soft.

Semi-hard Cheese These are the firm types that have a pliable texture – Gouda, Jarlsberg and Edam.

Hard Cheese Cheddar, Red Leicester, Cheshire, Parmesan.

Blue or Veined Cheese These cheeses are treated with specific micro-organisms which are allowed to grow at a certain point in the ripening process by the introduction of air. Blue cheeses include Stilton, Wensleydale, Cheshire, Roquefort, Danish blue, Dolcelatte and Gorgonzola.

Vegetarian Cheese This is made using a vegetable-based curdling agent instead of rennet.

Whey Cheese Most cheese is made from the curds; however, Italian ricotta cheese is made from whey.

Flavouring Ingredients

Herbs, spices or other ingredients may be added to the curds to flavour cheese. A few examples are sage Derby (a hard cheese, veined with ground sage), Windsor red (another hard cheese, veined with red wine) and Edam with cumin seeds.

Processed Cheese

Processed cheese is made from true cheese but the natural maturing is halted to give a mild product that has a consistent flavour and texture. Processed cheese spreads, slices and soft-textured slicing cheeses are all available. Many types are flavoured.

Glossary of Cheese

The following is a summary of some readily available cheeses, with brief notes on what to expect of each type.

Bel Paese An Italian cheese, with a mild, creamy flavour and semi-soft texture.

Boursin French cream cheese, best known flavoured with garlic and herbs.

Brie Shallow, large wheel of semi-soft French cheese, with a soft white rind. Just as there are different Cheddars, brie varies. Some brie ripens to a runny texture and creamy-yellow colour; others soften but do not flow. Although the majority of brie is mild in flavour with a soft texture, farmhouse brie (usually unpasteurised) can be quite strong and very soft when fully ripe.

Caerphilly A firm, white, crumbly, slightly tangy cheese with a mild flavour. Similar to Cheshire.

Camembert Small to medium-sized round, shallow cheeses, originally from Normandy in France. A white, soft rind covers creamy-coloured cheese that is semi-soft and flows when ripe. Ripe camembert has a rich, slightly earthy flavour. When the rind and inside have darkened the cheese smells and tastes very strong.

Chaumes A creamy, semi-soft French cheese with a mild, rich flavour and yellow rind.

Cheddar Many types are produced, from blocks of mild, slightly rubbery-textured cheese to farmhouse cheese with a firm texture and distinct strong flavour. Mature Cheddar has the strongest flavour and the mild cheese can be very weak by comparison. Price is a good indication of quality.

Cheshire Hard, crumbly white cheese with a mild flavour. Cheshire is said to be one of Britain's oldest cheeses, available in red, white or blue. The blue cheese is quite different from the other types – it is soft, golden in colour and creamy with deep-blue veins running through it. Its flavour is rich and powerful.

Cottage Cheese Soft, mild curds of fresh cheese. The fat content varies according to the milk used, some cottage cheese contains small amounts of fat. Long-life cartons of cottage cheese have an inferior flavour. Used in salads or in made up dishes, both sweet and savoury. Cottage cheese is often sieved for making cheesecakes – if you have one, a food processor produces a smoother texture. Mashed with a fork, cottage cheese may be used in dips or as a spread for sandwiches.

Cream Cheese Soft cheese with varying fat contents, but all types are richer than curd cheese or quark that are made with semi-skimmed or skimmed milk.

Curd Cheese Low-fat soft cheese; may be used instead of cream cheese.

Danish Blue An inexpensive blue cheese. A semi-soft texture with blue veining and a strong, slightly tangy flavour.

Derby A hard cheese which is similar to Cheddar. Sage Derby is veined with ground sage, giving it its characteristic green veining.

Double Gloucester A hard, mature cheese which is known for its smooth, full flavour.

Edam Red-rinded Dutch cheese with a rounded shape. A mild, buttery flavour and slightly rubbery texture are characteristic. When melted, Edam is very stringy. A semi-hard cheese with a comparatively low fat content, Edam is sold in wedges or in small whole cheeses. Look out for Edam with herbs or spices.

Feta White, firm, crumbly goats' cheese from Greece. Feta is stored in water to prevent it drying out and usually purchased in small sealed packets. Good in salads, although it may also be mashed and used as a filling for pasties and pies – it complements spinach well as a pie filling. Feta has a low calorie content compared to other firm cheeses.

Fromage Frais* A soft fresh cheese which is more like yogurt or cream than cheese. It is a good substitute for cream. See separate entry.

Gorgonzola An Italian blue cheese which is semi-soft with a creamy texture. It has a mild, tangy and slightly salty taste.

Gruyère A hard, smooth-textured Swiss cheese with a mild, distinct, nutty flavour. Often used in cooking, for example for making fondue.

Jarlsberg A semi-hard, smooth cheese from Norway, with holes and a mild nutty flavour.

Lancashire A hard, mild white cheese with a crumbly texture. Similar to Cheshire and Caerphilly.

Leicester or Red Leicester A mild red-coloured cheese with a firm texture and mellow flavour.

Mascarpone Italian cream cheese, very rich – more like clotted cream than a cheese. Used for making rich desserts, with liqueurs, fruit and Almond Macaroons (page 9).

Mozzarella Small gourd-shaped or round Italian cheeses, made from buffalo milk or cows' milk (or a mixture). Kept in water or whey, look for the small round cheeses in water in sealed plastic packets. Mozzarella has a milky flavour and firm texture. It can be sliced for making a salad with tomatoes and onions or cut into chunks or sliced for topping pizza. Avoid large blocks of so-called mozzarella that are creamy-yellow in colour and rubbery in texture.

Parmesan A very hard Italian cheese. There are different types of Parmesan and the dry, ready grated cheese in tubs is a poor representative. Fresh Parmesan is not too hard to grate and it has a sweet, full flavour. Reggiano Parmesan is long matured and strongly flavoured. Freshly grated Parmesan freezes well and it may be used from frozen.

Port Salut Orange-rinded French processed cheese with a creamy texture and mild flavour.

Quark Low-fat soft cheese, very similar to curd cheese.

Red Windsor Cheddar flavoured with red wine which gives the cheese a red-veined appearance. A modern cheese, sometimes prepared with a black wax rind.

Ricotta Made from whey, this white, soft, light cheese from Italy is unsalted and it has a distinct texture and light taste.

Roquefort A sheeps' cheese from France with green-blue veins. Semi-soft and white with a salty crust, Roquefort has a strong flavour.

Smoked Cheese Various types are available, including regional British cheeses that are smoked. Sausage-shaped smoked processed cheese is the most common in supermarkets.

Stilton Blue Stilton is probably one of the best known of British cheeses. When ripe, Stilton is semi-hard and creamy. Under-ripe Stilton is crumbly, pale and tangy. White Stilton has a hint of the same distinct flavour but it is mild and crumbly.

Wensleydale A firm, white cheese with a mild flavour. This looks similar to white Stilton but it is a milder, slightly tangy cheese.

Blue Wensleydale is a veined cheese with a mild flavour.

Cooking and Serving Cheese

There are many uses of cheese in cooking, from savoury bakes to desserts made with soft cheese. It is important not to overcook cheese, particularly in the microwave.

● Small amounts of cheese may be potted by grating them, then mashing with a little butter, soft cheese, milk, cider or wine. A mixture of cheeses, including blue cheese may be used. When creamy, press the cheese into a pot and serve it with biscuits or as a spread for sandwiches.

● Mature Cheddar gives a good flavour to sauces but other hard cheeses may be used. Edam makes the sauce stringy if used in quantity and the white, slightly tangy, cheeses make slightly piquant sauce (Caerphilly, Cheshire and so on). Grated Parmesan is useful in small amounts for flavouring low-calorie dishes as a little provides plenty of flavour. Measure the grated Parmesan by the tablespoon.

● Cream and curd cheeses melt during cooking. Ricotta tends to stay firm. Recipes which suggest using spinach and ricotta cheese for stuffing pasta should be followed closely – if another soft cheese is substituted for the ricotta, then add some fresh breadcrumbs to keep the mixture firm as it cooks.

● Cheddar melts well when grilled. Red Leicester makes a colourful topping on toast or with breadcrumbs on gratins.

● Some cheeses do not become runny when cooked. Greek halloumi, available from larger supermarkets, forms a golden crust when grilled. It softens inside but does not melt. When marinated in oil, garlic and herbs, then grilled on the barbecue this cheese is delicious with crusty bread or salad.

Freezing

Grated hard cheese, such as Cheddar or Parmesan, freezes well and may be used from frozen in sauces and other cooking. Sliced or cubed mozzarella cheese also freezes well, ready for topping pizza or other bakes.

Portions of cheese may be frozen. They taste acceptable when thawed but are not of prime quality.

Cherries

Sweet cherries (for example, the black cherry, Rivers or Early Rivers which are dark red to brown-red in colour) are suitable for eating raw, including in fruit salads or poaching. Sour cherries (almost black Morello cherries or light red amarelles) are only suitable for cooking as they are too tart to eat raw. They have a good flavour when sweetened and cooked.

Buying

Look for firm, ripe unblemished fruit. Avoid pecked or over-ripe and soft fruit. The majority of fruit should be on the stalk.

Frozen cherries are available from some freezer centres. When buying frozen or canned fruit check whether it is stoned.

Storing

Place the cherries in a shallow container, cover loosely and chill until ready for use. Use within 1–2 days of purchase, depending on ripeness.

Preparation

Remove the stalks and thoroughly wash the fruit. For the majority of uses it is best to stone the cherries. This may be done by using a small, sharp knife to slit the flesh, then carefully scraping out the stone using the point of the knife. As this is a tedious process, it is a good idea to purchase a cherry stoner, an inexpensive gadget that is easy to use. This consists of a small, cherry-sized cup with a large hole in the base. The cherry is placed in the 'cup' and a hinged arm with a single prong is closed on the fruit. The prong pokes out the stone, leaving the hollow cherry in the cup. The process of stoning is also known as pitting.

Cooking

Cherries should be poached gently in syrup for a short period only. For sour cherries, heat 100 g/4 oz sugar and 150 ml/¼ pint water until the sugar dissolves, then bring the syrup to the boil. Lower the heat so that the syrup barely simmers and add the cherries. Poach the fruit gently for 5 minutes, then remove from the heat and use as required. Cherries are also good poached in port.

Use

● Poached cherries flavoured with a cinnamon stick or with some brandy, port or kirsch added make a delicious compote (see Glossary, page 275).

● Poached cherries, cooled and thickened with arrowroot* may be used to top cheesecake or to fill sweet flans*.

● Cherries may be used to fill gâteaux. Poached sour cherries, cooled in syrup, then drained, are used in the classic Black Forest gâteau – a chocolate-flavoured whisked sponge (see cakes*) filled with whipped cream.

● Sweet or sour cherries may be used in pies, combined with other fruit, such as apples, redcurrants, peaches or pears.

● Preserve sweet or sour cherries by placing in a clean jar and covering with spirit – brandy or vodka may be used. Sweeten the spirit to taste with sugar.

Clafoutis

A cherry batter pudding: place 450 g/1 lb stoned sweet cherries in a buttered, shallow ovenproof dish. Sprinkle with 25 g/1 oz caster sugar. Pour in 1 quantity Thin Batter (page 28). Bake at 180°C, 350°F, gas 4 for 1–1¼ hours, until the batter is set, risen and golden. Dredge with icing sugar and serve hot or warm.

Freezing

Prepare and stone cherries before freezing, then use from frozen. They may be stored for up to a year. They are soft on thawing, therefore not ideal for fruit salads or compotes but they are useful for made-up dishes.

Nutritional Value

Cherries provide some vitamin A and C but they are not usually eaten in quantities that make a significant contribution to the diet.

Chestnuts

Available fresh during the winter months, chestnuts are also sold canned in water or syrup, puréed (sweetened or unsweetened – always check the label) or candied (known as *marron glacé*).

Buying

Buy shiny, firm-looking, large chestnuts that do not feel hollow or look dull and dry.

Dried chestnuts are available in most wholefood shops. They are shelled, smaller than fresh nuts, hard and pale. They should be soaked overnight, then drained and simmered in water for about 15 minutes before use.

Storing

They keep well for several weeks in a dish at room temperature.

Preparation

Wash and dry the nuts, then make a lengthways slit through the shell.

Cooking

Boiling For culinary purposes, chestnuts are boiled and peeled before use. Place the split nuts in a saucepan and cover with water. Bring to the boil, reduce the heat and simmer the nuts for 10–15 minutes, depending on size, until they are tender. Drain and rinse under cold water, then drain again. Peel the nuts and use as required.

Roasting The traditional way of roasting chestnuts is to place them on a perforated iron utensil and hold them over an open fire until the shells blacken.

They may be grilled until blackened on the outside. Cool them slightly before peeling.

Use

● Chop or purée the nuts and use in stuffing, with onion, sage, sausagemeat or breadcrumbs.

CHESTNUT STUFFING

INGREDIENTS
450 g/1 lb chestnuts
30 ml/2 tablespoons olive oil
1 clove garlic, crushed
(optional)
1 large onion, chopped
2 celery sticks, diced
25 g/1 oz raisins
1 eating apple, peeled, cored
and chopped
50 g/2 oz fresh breadcrumbs
30 ml/2 tablespoons chopped
fresh parsley
10 ml/2 teaspoons fresh
thyme leaves or
5 ml/1 teaspoon dried
thyme
salt and pepper
milk to bind (optional)

FOOD VALUES:
TOTAL • PER PORTION
kcals: 1417 • 177
kJ: 5968 • 746
protein: 23 g • 3 g
fat: 44 g • 6 g
carbohydrate: 246 g • 31 g
fibre: 38 g • 5 g

Serves 8 as stuffing (food values apply to this portion size)
Serves 4 in a main course dish

Prepare, cook and peel the chestnuts, then roughly chop them and set aside.

Heat the oil in a saucepan over medium heat. Add the garlic (if used), onion and celery. Stir well, then put a lid on the pan and leave the vegetables to cook gently for about 15 minutes. Add the raisins and apple, then re-cover the pan and leave to cook for a further 15 minutes.

Remove the pan from the heat, then stir in the chestnuts, breadcrumbs, herbs and seasoning to taste. Milk may be added to bind the mixture.

USE

• Spoon the stuffing under the skin of turkey or chicken.

• Moisten with milk, then press the mixture into a 450 g/1 lb loaf tin. Bake at 180°C, 350°F, gas 4 for 40–50 minutes, until firm and golden. Serve sliced with Tomato Sauce (page 263).

• Use as a pie filling, topping with cheese wholemeal pastry (see short crust pastry*). Bake at 190°C, 375°F, gas 5 for 40–45 minutes. Good with mushroom sauce.

• Add chopped chestnuts to a rice stuffing.

• Cooked chestnuts and sliced leeks sautéed in olive oil make a tasty pie filling. Add a crushed clove of garlic, sliced mushrooms and a pinch of dried marjoram.

• Add to beef casseroles or pies. Dried chestnuts should be soaked and simmered first.

• Chestnut purée may be sweetened and softened with whipped cream or fromage frais*, then chilled for dessert. The creamy purée may be used to fill meringues or spread in a chocolate gâteau.

Freezing

Freeze the whole uncooked nuts in their shells, then cook them from frozen in boiling water. Peeled cooked chestnuts and chestnut purée both freeze well for up to 6 months.

Nutritional Value

Chestnuts provide plenty of carbohydrate but they are not a rich source of protein, oils or B vitamins. They are useful in vegetarian cooking but their food value must not be overestimated.

Chicken

See Poultry.*
Chicken is readily available in many forms, both fresh and frozen.

Whole Birds

These are available both fresh or frozen, with or without giblets.
Free-range Birds Reared in open fields, free-range chickens are now available both fresh and frozen. Read the label for details relating to production – some confined birds are fed fresh food.
Corn-fed Birds These are fed on a mixture of maize grains which gives the flesh a yellow colour and distinctive flavour.
Boiling Fowl Occasionally available, these are old birds that have reached the end of their laying life. In order to give tender flesh, a boiler must be simmered in water to cover for 2–3 hours. It yields excellent soup and the flesh is usually good served in a flavoursome sauce or for making a pie.
Poussins These young birds of about 4–6 weeks old are tender and delicately flavoured. They are served as individual portions, grilled or roasted whole, or they may be spatchcocked (see poultry*).

Chicken Portions

Quarter This is the largest portion, made up of the wing and most of the breast meat or the drumstick and thigh. A quarter is usually served as a substantial single portion.
Part-boned Breast This consists of the wing bone and the breast meat. The breast bone is

removed from the main portion of meat. This is served as a large single portion.

Boneless Breast Sometimes known as the supreme, this consists of the meat from one side of the whole bird. The boneless meat may be served as one portion, small or large depending on its size. It is ideal for cutting into strips or cubes, in which case it may be combined with other ingredients to make it go further.

Drumstick The leg end up to the thigh. Two or more drumsticks may be served as a single portion.

Thigh Small neat portion, with a rounded neat area of meat and small central bone. Two thighs make up a good single portion.

Chicken Wing This does not have much meat on the bone. Used with flavoursome marinades and seasonings, then roast, grilled or fried until very crisp. Two to four make a single portion.

Buying

Always buy from a reputable source and make sure you are aware of the standards of cleanliness in the store. Chicken that is chilled or frozen should be displayed neatly, below the recommended storage line in the display cabinets and at the correct temperature. Avoid buying from a freezer which is stacked high with food or overfilled refrigerators.

Look for the Quality British Chicken mark on packed birds. This mark of quality is used by members of the British Chicken Association. It indicates that the bird is of grade 'A' and that it has been reared and produced according to standards set down for all stages of handling.

Check that the bird looks plump for its size and that the skin is undamaged and not bruised. Check before buying whether the bird is sold with or without giblets.

Inspect frozen chicken to make sure that it is adequately packed and look for any signs of freezer burn. This makes the surface of the chicken look dehydrated.

Always check the date by which fresh chicken should be used.

Storing

See Shopping* and Refrigerators*.
It is important that chicken is kept cool, so add it to your shopping basket or trolley as late as possible on your journey around the supermarket and keep it cool, preferably in a chiller bag. Avoid allowing frozen chicken to thaw. Place fresh chicken in the refrigerator, in its wrapping, on a low shelf as soon as you arrive home. Frozen chicken should be placed in the freezer immediately.

Chicken bought loose and placed in a polythene bag by the butcher, should be unwrapped and placed in a large dish and covered, then placed in the refrigerator.

Use fresh chicken before the date suggested on the wrapping. Loose chicken should be used with 2–3 days.

Bought frozen chicken should be used within 3 months.

Cooked chicken should be used within 3 days, 2 days if stuffed.

X *If possible avoid using a wooden board for preparing chicken. Also, where necessary, use a plastic mixing spoon instead of a wooden one.*
If a wooden board is used, thoroughly scrub and rinse it after use, then allow it to dry well to avoid encouraging the growth of food poisoning or spoilage bacteria in slivers of meat left behind in the crevices in the wood.

Preparation

Trim off the leg and wing ends from a whole bird. Remove any giblets from the body cavity. Cut off any obvious lumps of fat. Rinse the chicken under cold water and wash the body cavity of a whole bird, then drain it well. Dry the chicken on absor-

bent kitchen paper and place it in the cooking container or on a clean plate. Discard the paper, wash the work surface, sink and all utensils.

Stuffing

Stuffing is intended to flavour the meat.

Stuffing the Body Cavity There are reservations about this method as it takes some time for stuffing to heat through to the centre. For this reason, it is not recommended that larger birds are stuffed by this method.

The bird must be well rinsed and dried. The stuffing should only be placed in the cavity (using a metal spoon) immediately before cooking. The bird and the stuffing must be cooked through thoroughly. Never leave a stuffed chicken to cook very slowly in a low oven as the stuffing may not heat through adequately.

Stuffing Under the Breast Skin This is the preferred method of stuffing the bird. Details of the technique are explained under poultry*. The skin over the breast meat is loosened. The stuffing is spooned into the pocket between the loose skin and breast meat. The skin is kept in place by inserting a skewer. The stuffing over the breast flavours the meat and keeps it moist in cooking.

Cooking Stuffing Separately Small balls of stuffing may be cooked around the bird as it is roasting. The stuffing may be placed in a greased dish and baked.

Trussing

See Poultry*.

Cooking

It is important to make sure that chicken is cooked through. **Roasting** Set the oven at 200°C, 400°F, gas 6. Weigh the oven-ready bird and calculate the cooking time at 20 minutes per 450 g/1 lb, plus an extra 20 minutes. Check the bird halfway through cooking, baste it well and cover the top loosely with foil to prevent overbrowning.

X *Never stuff a chicken in advance of cooking. Any bacteria in the bird and stuffing will thrive in the warmth of any part-cooked stuffing. Keep the stuffed bird chilled until it is placed in the oven.*

Spit Roasting The bird cooks slightly quicker than by ordinary roasting. The same timing should be followed but the bird should be checked about three-quarters of the way through cooking.

Grilling The grill should be set on a medium to medium-high setting for larger portions so that they cook through at the same time as browning on the outside. Allow 15–20 minutes on each side. Brush with marinade* or oil occasionally during cooking to prevent the outside from drying.

Shallow Frying Ideal for small portions and boneless breasts.

Coat the chicken with flour or egg and breadcrumbs. Heat a little oil or a combination of oil and butter (butter alone tends to overcook). Add the chicken to the pan and cook over fairly high heat initially to seal the outside. Reduce the heat to medium and continue to cook until the chicken is cooked through. Turn the pieces about twice and baste often to ensure even cooking.

Breasts take about 15 minutes on each side. Thighs cook slightly quicker – about 10–12 minutes on each side.

Larger portions (for example quarters) may be shallow fried if coated in flour but not when coated in crumbs. They should be browned, then the heat lowered and a lid put on the pan (crumb coating tends to soften). Turn the portions once more so that they are thoroughly cooked.

Cook's Tip
Enclose a pat of garlic butter in a boneless breast and coat twice with egg and breadcrumbs. Deep fry slowly.

Deep Frying Avoid very large quarters that take a long time to cook through. Protect the chicken by coating it in egg and breadcrumbs or in flour. Cook over medium heat so that the chicken has time to cook through before becoming too brown.

Best for small portions, chunks or strips.

Stir Frying Fine strips of chicken meat are ideal for stir frying. They cook quickly and the meat is cooked by the time the outside is well browned. Cook the chicken first, then add vegetables and continue stir frying – this ensures that the chicken is cooked through and browned.

Braising Use a large flameproof casserole or wok with a lid. Brown the chicken portions or a whole bird in oil, then remove it from the pan and add chopped onion, diced carrot, sliced celery and a bay leaf. Toss the vegetables over high heat for about 1 minute, then reduce the heat and replace the chicken.

Pour in enough stock, wine or water to cover the vegetables. Cover the pan and simmer steadily, allowing about 45–50 minutes for portions, turning them once. A whole bird will take about 1½–1¾ hours, depending on size. When cooking a whole bird, check the liquid in the pan and top it up occasionally, bringing it back to simmering point each time.

Casseroling There should be enough liquid to almost cover portions, or to two-thirds cover a whole bird. On the hob, allow 40–45 minutes at a steady simmer for portions; 1¼–1½ hours for a whole bird.

For oven cooking, set the temperature at 180°C, 350°F, gas 4 and allow 45–50 minutes for portions; 1½–1¾ hours for a whole bird.

In both cases, the chicken should be browned first in hot oil and the casserole should be kept covered during cooking. These cooking times may be used for other sauced chicken dishes.

Steaming Always remove the skin from chicken before steam-

ing. Boneless breasts or thighs are the best portions for this cooking method. Oriental seasonings (fresh root ginger, spring onion, salted black beans and soy sauce) give steamed chicken an excellent flavour. Citrus rind and juice, and a combination of finely cut vegetables (celery, carrot, mushrooms, celeriac and so on) may be used with fresh herbs. Use dried herbs sparingly, if at all, when steaming as their flavour can be very pronounced.

Slow Cooking Chicken does not benefit from slow cooking and without careful preparation and pre-cooking, the raw areas of chicken (notably in a whole bird) provide ideal conditions for bacteria to multiply. Although slow cookers may have advantages in other areas of cookery, they are not recommended for chicken.

Microwave Cooking

Skinned chicken portions in sauce cook well in the microwave. The following times are a guide – exact timing depends on the added ingredients and quantity of sauce as well as the wattage of the oven.

Boneless Chicken Breasts These are the best as they cook evenly. On High, allow 12–15 minutes for 4 portions, 9–11 minutes for 3 portions, 6–8 for 2 portions, 2–4 minutes for 1 portion.

Quarters These should be turned twice and rearranged, if necessary, for even cooking. On High, allow 20–25 minutes for 4 portions, 15–20 minutes for 3 portions, 10–12 minutes for 2 portions and about 5–7 minutes for 1 portion.

Whole Chickens The best way to use the microwave for cooking a whole bird is to three-quarters cook it in the microwave, then finish cooking it in the conventional oven at 220°C, 425°F, gas 7, until golden, crisp and cooked through. Allow 5 minutes per 450 g/1 lb in the microwave on High, then transfer the bird to the oven for about 10–15 minutes.

To cook a whole bird completely in the microwave allow an additional 5 minutes, then leave it to stand for 7 minutes. Check whether it is cooked – if not, cook for a further 2 minutes, stand for 3 minutes and check again.

Roasting bags are useful for cooking whole birds – slit the bag before putting the bird into the conventional oven.

Standing Time At the end of microwave cooking, allow portions to stand for 5 minutes, covered, before serving. A whole chicken will 'stand' while it is finishing in the conventional oven.

> ✓ *Always check that the chicken meat is cooked through. Pierce it at the thickest point with a skewer. On a whole bird, the thickest area of meat is behind the thigh. The juices that run out should be clear – if there is any sign of blood or if the juices are pink, then the chicken is not cooked.*

Accompaniments for Roast Chicken

Gravy or Bread Sauce (page 49), sage and onion or parsley and thyme stuffing, roast potatoes and bacon rolls are the traditional accompaniments.

Fruit sauces, Tomato Sauce (page 263), Curry Sauce (page 100), Parsley Sauce (page 234), Wine Sauce (page 235) or many others may be served with chicken. Depending on the sauce, the chicken may be sautéed until brown, then simmered in the sauce or cooked completely and coated with sauce before serving.

Rice, pasta, couscous and buckwheat are all suitable accompaniments in place of potatoes.

The majority of vegetables taste good with chicken – the selection depends on the sauce and other flavouring ingredients.

Flavouring and Seasoning

Rather than stuffing the body cavity of the bird, place a peeled small onion, halved orange or lemon, bay leaves, herb sprigs, bouquet garni, peeled garlic cloves, herb butter or quartered apple in it.

Handling Cooked Chicken

● Place whole birds on a plate or metal dish for carving – not a wooden board.

● After carving the required amount, cover the remaining chicken and set it aside where it will cool quickly.

● As soon as it has cooled, place the chicken in the refrigerator.

● Cooked chicken may be stored for up to 3 days in the refrigerator. A stuffed chicken should be used within 2 days.

● If there is a lot of meat left on the carcass, then cut it all off before placing in the refrigerator. Remove from the refrigerator only the amount of meat required when it is to be used.

● Do not put a cooked chicken carcass in and out of the refrigerator on many meal occasions, allowing it to warm up to room temperature several times. This allows bacteria to grow. Instead, cut off the meat required swiftly, then replace the carcass in the refrigerator.

● Keep the cooked chicken chilled until just before use.

● Any bones to be used for making stock should be boiled up as soon as the meat is used. Strain the stock promptly, cool it rapidly and chill or freeze.

● When reheating chicken, always make sure it is thoroughly hot all through. Do not reheat food more than once. See reheating food*.

Chicory

See Vegetables.*

Small, oval heads of close-packed pale white and green-yellow tinged leaves. The leaves are boat shaped and crisp. In American cookbooks chicory is referred to as endive. Chicory has a slightly bitter taste.

Buying

Look for firm, crisp leaves and neat, undamaged heads.

Storing

Keep the chicory loosely packed in a polythene bag, in the salad drawer of the refrigerator. It should be used within 1–2 days of purchase.

Preparation

Separate the leaves and wash them well or thoroughly wash whole heads. Drain well.

Use

● Raw in salads, shredded crossways.

● Individual leaves may be used as cups for holding salads (rice salad, potato salad and so on) or creamy pâtés.

● Small leaves may be used as crudités to scoop up dips.

● Whole heads may be braised, either on their own or wrapped in cooked ham.

● Braised chicory may be coated in cheese sauce and grilled until golden for serving as a supper dish.

Freezing

Do not freeze chicory – it becomes limp and brown.

Nutritional Value

Chicory provides vitamin C, potassium, calcium, magnesium and other trace elements.

SEE ALSO **Chick Peas, Chilli con Carne:** Beans and Pulses, Dried; **Chine:** Glossary; **Chinese Leaves:** Cabbage;

Chillies

The spelling using one 'l' is the American name, sometimes the term chili peppers is also used.

Types and Forms of Chilli

Fresh Chillies From medium-sized plump, mild green chillies to long, thin wiry red or green chillies that may be extremely hot; however, size, shape and colour are no guide to heat.

Chillies are not just fiery – they have a distinct peppery flavour which is vaguely similar to sweet green and red peppers but less pronounced and more pungent.

The majority of supermarkets tend to stock small, plump green chillies (about 5 cm/2 inches in length) that are comparatively mild. Sometimes there are very thin ones that may be long and curled, and these are often hot. Check the details on the label – many supermarkets offer advice on the flavour of the chillies.

Dried Chillies Dried red chillies are most common – they are hot and should be used carefully.

Chilli Powder Dried and powdered chillies. There are varying strengths but chilli powder is usually hot. Its use depends on the recipe – some starchy foods tend to counteract the hotness more than light-textured vegetables.

Cayenne Pepper This is made from ground, dried extremely hot chillies. It is hotter than chilli powder.

Paprika Not to be confused with chilli powder, this is ground sweet peppers and it is not hot.

Pickled or Canned Chillies One of the most popular types is the jalepeño chilli. When pickled this has a tangy flavour and, without its seeds, it is not too hot.

X *Never rub your eyes or touch your face when handling chillies. Avoid touching your eyes until you have washed your hands a few times. The juices from the chillies burn the eyes and make them very sore indeed.*

Storing

Keep chillies in a polythene bag (unless they are already wrapped) in the refrigerator and use within 3–5 days.

Dried chillies should be kept in an airtight container in a cool, dark place.

Preparation

The seeds inside the chilli are very hot, so should be removed.

Cut the stalk end off the chilli, then slit it lengthways and cut out the core of pith. Rinse the chilli well to remove all seeds, then chop or slice it, as required.

Wash your hands well after handling chillies as their juices irritate the skin.

Use

• Fresh chillies may be cooked with fish, meat, poultry, vegetables or pulses. They are usually fried with onions or other vegetables in the first stages of cooking.

• Raw chillies are sprinkled over side dishes and used in fresh chutneys. They may also be used in salads.

• Dried red chillies and chilli powder have many uses in cooked dishes and pickles.

> **Cook's Tip**
> Do not be afraid of using chillies but treat them with respect, opting for small quantities until you are familiar with them.

Freezing

Prepared fresh chillies freeze well. They should be seeded and chopped, then spread out on a piece of freezer film to open freeze. When hard they may be wrapped and sealed. They keep well for at least 6 months, and are ready to use from frozen.

Whole chillies also freeze successfully but they tend to be soft and less easy to trim.

Chocolate

Chocolate is made from cocoa fat (butter) from cocoa beans. Roasted beans are ground to make cocoa as well as chocolate. It is the fat content of the chocolate that is important for quality.

The beans are not sweet, so sugar is added during the manufacture of chocolate. Cocoa powder is unsweetened. Drinking chocolate is a sweetened product which should not be compared with cocoa.

Expensive types of chocolate have a high cocoa butter content, whereas some of the cheaper types contain very little. Price is a good guide to quality. Check the label for the cocoa butter or cocoa fat content.

Types of Chocolate

Bitter Dessert Chocolate The least sweet type, this is very dark, shiny and bitter.

Dark or Plain Chocolate Usually semi-sweet and good quality, with a high proportion of cocoa butter.

Milk Chocolate Sweet chocolate with added milk products.

White Chocolate Made from cocoa butter and milk products. White chocolate with a high cocoa butter content is expensive and it has a fine flavour. Cheaper types have a different, sweet flavour.

Chocolate Cake Coverings These vary but they usually contain very little cocoa butter, if any. The term 'chocolate-flavoured' indicates that the product is not a true chocolate.

Chocolate Cooking Chips or Drops These vary in quality and flavour. Useful for adding to cakes and biscuits.

Storing

Chocolate keeps well for several months in an airtight container in a cool place. The refrigerator is best. High quality white chocolate does not keep as well as

CHOCOLATE POTS

Richer, classic chocolate mousses use the same quantity of chocolate as here, melted with 2 egg yolks and 75 g/3 oz butter, then the whisked egg whites are folded in and the mousse chilled until set.

INGREDIENTS	FOOD VALUES:
225 g/8 oz dark plain chocolate	TOTAL • PER PORTION
25 g/1 oz butter	**kcals:** 2273 • 568
30 ml/2 tablespoons brandy	**kJ:** 9444 • 2361
150 ml/¼ pint double cream	**protein:** 23 g • 6 g
150 ml/¼ pint fromage frais	**fat:** 169 g • 42 g
Serves 4	**carbohydrate:** 157 g • 39 g
	fibre: 0 g • 0 g

Break the chocolate into squares and place in a basin with the butter and brandy. Stand the basin over a saucepan of hot water and leave until the chocolate melts, stirring once or twice.

Meanwhile, whip the cream until it stands in soft yet firm peaks. Remove the chocolate from over the hot water. Stir the fromage frais into the melted chocolate mixture. Lastly fold in the whipped cream. Divide the mousse between 4 ramekin dishes and chill until set.

CHOCOLATE SAUCE

For ice cream, waffles, plain steamed sponge puddings, as a topping for profiteroles or for topping poached pears. Any leftovers keep well in a covered container in the refrigerator for 2–3 weeks.

INGREDIENTS	FOOD VALUES:
60 ml/4 tablespoons golden syrup	TOTAL • PER PORTION
100 g/4 oz bitter dessert or dark plain chocolate	**kcals:** 889 • 222
2.5 ml/½ teaspoon natural vanilla essence	**kJ:** 3719 • 930
25 g/1 oz butter	**protein:** 5 g • 1 g
15 ml/1 tablespoon hot water	**fat:** 50 g • 12 g
	carbohydrate: 112 g • 28 g
	fibre: 0 g • 0 g

Place the golden syrup in a basin. Break the chocolate into pieces and add to the syrup with the vanilla and butter. Stand the basin over a saucepan of hot water and stir until melted and glossy. Stir in the water and serve.

MICROWAVE COOKING

On High, stirring twice, the sauce melts in about 2–3 minutes.

other types and it should be used within about 3 months, otherwise it can taste slightly rancid.

Melting Chocolate

Break up a block of chocolate and place it in a basin. Stand the basin over a saucepan of hot, not simmering, water. Stir the chocolate occasionally until it melts. The pan may be left over low heat but the water should not be allowed to simmer or the chocolate will overheat and the fat will separate out.

If any water or steam mixes with the chocolate, it tends to separate. Once chocolate has separated (it has a curdled appearance) there is little that can be done to rescue it. It may be mixed with golden syrup and butter to make a sauce or combined with icing sugar and water to make an icing, but it is not suitable for coating cakes or making a mousse once separated.

Melting Chocolate in the Microwave Place the broken chocolate in a suitable basin and heat on High. If melting a large quantity (over 225 g/8 oz) use Medium setting. Allow 1–2 minutes for 100 g/4 oz, 3–4 minutes for 175 g/6 oz and about 5 minutes for 225 g/8 oz.

The timing will vary according to the type of chocolate. Check often by stirring the chocolate – just because the pieces look whole it does not mean they are hard. Molten chocolate often stays in small soft chunks or squares.

Chopping Boards

See Hygiene.*
A good chopping board is essential. The right choice and care of boards are important, for practical and food hygiene reasons.

Buying

Use Think about the use you intend making of the board and look for one that is large enough. Having too small a board is irritating and leads to bad practice as the food falls on the surrounding surface.

Decide on storage space and about the possibility of having separate boards for different tasks. It is best to have separate boards for cutting bread and preparing raw foods, not only because of size but also for hygiene purposes.

Ideally, have one board for cutting raw meat, chicken and fish and another for vegetables or salads.

SEE ALSO **Cholesterol:** Fat; **Chop:** Glossary; **Chorizos:** Sausages

Material Heavy wooden boards are traditional but they are not as easy to clean as modern plastic boards, therefore they can present a threat to food safety. If you are buying a new board, select a plastic one which is easy to wash and non-absorbent.

Colour-coded Boards Boards of different colours or with coloured handles are used in catering to distinguish which are used for raw foods or for cooked foods. If you do a lot of cooking it is worth considering buying a set.

Care and Storage

Boards should be stored in a clean, dry, airy place.

Plastic Plastic is not absorbent, however after some use, plastic boards do have cut marks that must be washed well. Always immerse the board in hot soapy water and scrub its surface, then rinse it under very hot water. Drain and dry the board well, preferably leaning upright in air.

Wood Wooden boards have been condemned because they are absorbent. Unless properly cleaned, wooden boards retain food particles and moisture allowing bacteria to grow.

If you do use a wooden board, then it is vital to have a strict cleaning routine. A cheap board which splits and breaks up on being washed should be discarded. A board which stands up to scrubbing and washing is essential.

After cutting raw food, place the board in hot soapy water, then scrub it using a scouring cleaner. Scrub the wood with the grain, all over both sides and around the edges. Rinse the board under hot water, then stand it upright to drain and dry thoroughly. Never put a damp wooden board away.

Use

See Cross Contamination*.
Before preparing food, think about the order in which you are going to cut it up.

> **X** *Never cut raw fish, poultry or meat on a board, then use the same board (or utensils) for cutting food that is to be eaten raw. Scrub the board between uses.*

First cut foods that are to be served raw (salad ingredients or garnishes for example).

Next vegetables to be lightly cooked, by stir frying or steaming perhaps. Then cut up vegetables, such as onions or carrots, that form the base for flavouring a dish.

Lastly, cut raw poultry, meat or fish. Transfer the cut up food to a clean plate or dish if it is not placed directly in a cooking pot.

Thoroughly wash the board, surrounding surface and knife immediately.

> **X** *Wash and drain vegetables for salads before cutting them up. If cooked food (cheese, meat and so on) is also used, cut it first on the clean unused board, then cut the raw vegetables.*

Choux Pastry

Unlike other types of pastry, this is a paste rather than a dough; it is also referred to as choux paste.

Technique

Choux pastry is not difficult to make as its success does not just rest upon well-practised skills; however, it is important to measure ingredients accurately and to follow the method closely.

- Measure the volume of water carefully – too much makes a sloppy paste that does not rise and set well.

- Heat the water and fat gently until the fat melts. If the water boils before the fat has melted, some of the liquid content is lost by evaporation by the time the fat has melted.

- Once the fat has melted, bring the liquid to the boil as quickly as possible.

- Tip in all the flour at once, then remove the pan from the heat.

- Do not overbeat the flour paste before the egg is added – this makes the mixture greasy.

- Beat the paste really well once the eggs are added.

- The paste may be left to stand before the eggs are added. Once the eggs are beaten in the paste should be cooked promptly. If it is left to stand for any length of time at this stage, air will be lost and it will not rise well.

- Put a dish of boiling water in the oven while it is preheating and during cooking. The steam from the water keeps the paste soft as it rises, allowing it to rise more before it eventually sets to form a crisp crust.

- Split choux pastry items as soon as they are removed from the oven so that steam can escape. This keeps the paste crisp.

- Do not fill choux pastry items too long before serving as the paste softens.

- Crisp thawed baked items that have been frozen or pastries that have been cooked ahead in the oven for a minute or so before filling.

Use

Profiteroles or Small Buns (Makes 20) Pipe or spoon the choux paste in small mounds on greased baking trays, leaving room for each pastry to rise. Bake as overleaf, then cook for a further 10 minutes. Split and cool on a wire rack.

Fill with whipped cream or flavoured whipped cream and serve with chocolate sauce. Fruit fillings or sauces may be used instead.

Savoury puffs may be served hot with sauce-based fillings, such as tuna, chicken, cooked ham or mushrooms in Savoury White Sauce (page 234), or with cold fillings.

Eclairs (Makes 12) Use a piping bag fitted with a 2 cm/¾ inch plain nozzle and pipe 12 éclairs, slightly apart, on a greased baking tray. Cook as right, then allow 25–30 minutes at the reduced temperature. Split and cool on a wire rack.

Fill with whipped cream (250–300 ml/about ½ pint double cream, whipped) and coat with chocolate (100 g/4 oz). Coffee glacé icing* may be used instead of chocolate.

Large Choux Puffs (Makes 10) Pipe or spoon the choux paste in 10 large mounds on a greased baking tray, leaving plenty of room between each for rising. Bake as right, then allow an extra 25 minutes at the reduced temperature. Split and cool on a wire rack.

Fill with whipped cream (300 ml/½ pint double cream, whipped) and dredge with icing sugar.

Choux Ring (Serves 6) Draw an 18 cm/7 inch circle on grease-proof paper. Turn the paper over, place it on a baking tray and grease it well.

Use a piping bag fitted with a 2 cm/¾ inch plain nozzle and pipe the choux paste in a circle on the marked paper. Sprinkle the paste with 25 g/1 oz finely grated Cheddar cheese, if liked, for a savoury ring. Bake as right, then allow 15–20 minutes at the reduced temperature.

When cooked, split the ring horizontally and place the base on a serving dish. Fill with a hot savoury sauce, such as Meat Sauce (page 176) or Savoury White Sauce (page 234) with chicken, ham or fish, and replace the top of the ring. Serve at once.

Alternatively, split and cool the ring on a wire rack. Fill with savoury or sweet cold filling. Whipped cream and fruit, chocolate grated into cream or soft cheese sweetened with honey and flavoured with a little grated lemon rind make good fillings. Serve chocolate sauce or a fruit sauce with a sweet ring.

Storing

The cooked and cooled pastries may be stored unfilled in an air-

CHOUX PASTRY

INGREDIENTS
50 g/2 oz butter or margarine
100 ml/4 fluid oz water
65 g/2½ oz plain flour
2 eggs

Makes – see below

FOOD VALUES:
TOTAL
kcals: 745
kJ: 3103
protein: 19 g
fat: 53 g
carbohydrate: 52 g
fibre: 2 g

Place the butter or margarine in a medium saucepan and pour in the water. If the pan is too large, the water is more likely to boil before the fat melts; also, when the flour is added it is more likely to form lumps in a shallow liquid.

Sift the flour into a small bowl, or on to a piece of greaseproof paper or plate. Heat the water and fat gently until the fat melts. Turn the heat to the highest setting and bring the mixture to a full, rolling boil. Tip in all the flour at once and remove the pan from the heat (or turn an instant heat source off), stir the flour into the liquid to make a smooth, thick paste. It should come away from the sides of the pan in a clean, soft ball.

If the paste looks very soft at this stage, then return the pan to the heat and cook it gently for a few minutes. If the ingredients are accurately measured, and the liquid boiling, the paste should not be sloppy.

Do not overmix the paste. Set it aside to cool until it is just warm. Meanwhile, grease baking trays and set the oven at 220°C, 425°F, gas 7. If necessary, prepare a large piping bag and nozzle for piping the paste. Lightly beat the eggs.

Gradually beat the eggs into the lukewarm paste, beating well after each addition, then continue beating until the paste is smooth and glossy. An electric beater is useful but not essential.

The paste is now ready for use: pipe or shape it as required. Bake the pastries at once for 10 minutes. Reduce the oven temperature to 190°C, 375°F, gas 5 and continue to cook as follows.

GOUGERE (Serves 4–6)
Make a double quantity of choux paste, then beat in 50 g/2 oz grated Cheddar cheese. Spoon it around the inside edge of a greased, shallow 1.4 litre/2½ pint ovenproof dish. Fill the middle with Meat Sauce (page 176) or Lentil Sauce (page 169). Sprinkle 25 g/1 oz grated Cheddar over the sauce, then bake the gougère as above, allowing 35–45 minutes at the reduced temperature. Serve freshly cooked, with a simple salad as an accompaniment.

CHEESE AIGRETTES (Makes about 20)
Make the choux paste, then beat in 45 ml/3 tablespoons grated Parmesan cheese and 25 g/1 oz grated mature Cheddar cheese. Heat oil for deep frying to 180°C/350°F. Prepare a dish lined with double-thick absorbent kitchen paper.

Drop small spoonfuls of the mixture into the hot oil. The paste puffs up, splits and turns crisp and golden as it cooks. When evenly golden, use a draining spoon to remove the puffs from the oil and drain them well on absorbent kitchen paper. Serve freshly cooked.

SEE ALSO **Chowder**: Glossary; **Christmas Pudding**: Pudding

tight container in a cool place for 1–2 days. If they are to be kept before filling, then do not split the pastries before cooling. Crisp them in a hot oven for about a minute (do not cook them further), then split them at once and leave to cool on a wire rack.

Filled pastries do not store well as they soften. Leftovers with filling should be kept covered and chilled in the refrigerator, then used as soon as possible.

Freezing

The pastry may be frozen prepared before cooking or the baked items may be frozen.

Uncooked Choux Pastry Prepare the paste ready for cooking. Pipe or shape the paste on baking trays lined with freezer film and open freeze immediately. When firm, pack the pastries in polythene bags, label and store for up to 3 months.

Cook the pastry items from frozen as per usual. Larger buns and large items need about 2–5 minutes longer at the end of the cooking time. However, usually the cooking time for frozen items is not a lot longer.

The results are excellent – I prefer this method to freezing cooked choux pastry. The pastries are fresh and they rise exceptionally well. This is probably because a few ice crystals form in the paste during freezing, then they thaw and evaporate on heating to produce steam which makes the pastry puff.

Cooked Choux Pastry Split and cool items before freezing. If they are not split, the soft pastries tend to be more easily damaged in the freezer. Pack large items carefully to avoid crushing them – rigid containers are best.

The cooked pastries may be stored for 3–6 months but they do tend to dry out slightly. This is not necessarily noticeable when the pastries are filled and completed but they are crumbly and dry when first thawed.

Crisp thawed pastries in a hot oven for a minute or so, then cool and fill.

TOMATO CHUTNEY

This fruity chutney is suitable for either red or green tomatoes.

INGREDIENTS
1 kg/2 lb tomatoes
450 g/1 lb apples (cooking, eating or a mixture)
450 g/1 lb onions, chopped
1 green or red pepper, deseeded and chopped
2 fresh green chillies, deseeded and chopped
2 cloves garlic, crushed
25 g/1 oz fresh root ginger
15 ml/1 tablespoon ground cinnamon
15 ml/1 tablespoon ground coriander
225 g/8 oz raisins, sultanas or dates, or a mixture
225 g/8 oz dark soft brown sugar
250 ml/8 fluid oz vinegar

FOOD VALUES:
TOTAL • PER 15 ML/
1 TABLESPOON (APPROXIMATE)
kcals: 2096 • 21
kJ: 8912 • 89
protein: 30 g • 0 g
fat: 4 g • 0 g
carbohydrate: 508 g • 5 g
fibre: 47 g • 0.5 g

Makes about 1.75 kg/6 lb

First prepare the jars, making sure they are thoroughly washed in hot soapy water. If in doubt about their cleanliness (for example if they have been stored away for a long time), then sterilise them using a product for sterilising wine bottles or by immersing them in boiling water for 5 minutes. Drain well and place upside down on a folded tea-towel in a roasting tin. Sterilised jars are best left in the hot water until they are used.

Peel ripe tomatoes: place them in a bowl and pour over boiling water to cover. Leave for 30–60 seconds (the less ripe the fruit, the longer the time needed to loosen the skin), then drain the tomatoes and slit their skins with a sharp knife. The skin should slide off easily. Roughly chop the tomatoes and place them in a large saucepan.

Peel, core and chop the apples. Eating apples should be chopped finely so that they soften during cooking – cooking apples may be left in larger pieces. Add the apples to the tomatoes in the pan, then stir in the onions, pepper, chillies and garlic.

Trim off any coarse ends from the ginger before weighing it, then wash and coarsely grate it – the peel will grate but any last piece of tough peel should be discarded. Add the ginger, cinnamon, coriander and fruit to the ingredients in the pan, then stir in the sugar and vinegar.

Heat, stirring often, until boiling. Reduce the heat so that the chutney just simmers, then cover the pan and leave the mixture to cook for 1¼–1½ hours, or until all the mixture is dark and pulpy. Stir the chutney occasionally during cooking to prevent it from burning on the base of the pan. Uncover the pan and leave the chutney to bubble at a fast simmer for a further 15 minutes, or until any excess liquid has evaporated and the mixture has thickened.

Pot at once, then cover with waxed discs and airtight lids. Label when cool. Store for at least 2 weeks before sampling.

Chutney

See Apples*.

A savoury preserve made of vegetables or fruit, or more usually a combination of both. The prepared ingredients are cooked with spices, vinegar and sugar. The balance of sweet to sour depends on the recipe and individual taste – some chutneys are quite tart, others may be sweet and sour. The concentration of sugar or acid is important as they act, either individually, or together, as preservatives.

Preparation

The ingredients may be cut up small or minced before cooking. Aluminium saucepans are not suitable for making chutney and carbon steel knives should be avoided.

Thoroughly cleaned jars with airtight lids should be warmed in the oven. All lids should be coated with plastic or should be made of glass and sealed with rubber rings. Any exposed metal will react with the vinegar.

Cooking

Chutney should be cooked until the ingredients form a soft pulpy or thickened mixture. The initial cooking may be carried out in a covered pan, then the lid should be removed so that excess moisture evaporates.

As chutney cooks, the liquid reduces, the ingredients soften and the mixture darkens as the sugar caramelises. This results in a dark rich preserve.

Potting

Pot chutney as soon as it is cooked and cover with wax paper discs and airtight lids immediately. When very hot, the mixture is sterile and bacteria or moulds are excluded by an airtight seal which forms on hot jars. When cool, the pots should be labelled with the date and type of chutney.

Storing and Using

Store the chutney in a cool, dry place. Most types benefit from being left for 2–4 weeks for the flavour to mature. Well-sealed chutney keeps for 9–12 months.

Serve chutney with bread and cheese or cold meats. Use it in sandwiches or as an ingredient in some cooked dishes.

Fresh Chutney

Fresh chutneys are side dishes that are not intended for keeping, but they are prepared just before serving. They are served with spiced Eastern-style dishes and are equally good with plain grilled meat or poultry.

Chopped fresh tomatoes with onion, sugar, chopped coriander leaves and garlic is one example of a fresh chutney. A spicy mixture of chopped fresh chillies, coriander leaves, garlic and lime or lemon juice seasoned with salt is another example.

Citric Acid

Found in citrus fruit juice (lemons, limes, oranges) and in other fruit juices. This is also available in the form of crystals from chemists and home wine-making suppliers.

The main use for citric acid (whether in fruit juice or otherwise) is to prevent certain foods from discolouring when cut – for example apples, bananas and avocados.

Clarifying

The term used for clearing liquids or for purifying fat. Different methods are used for different purposes.

Clarifying Preserves

When making jelly preserves, the juice is strained from the fruit through a jelly bag or several layers of muslin. This process of straining the cooked fruit gives a clear jelly when cooked.

Clarifying Stock

The prepared stock should be strained and all fat should be skimmed from it – this is important as fat makes the stock cloudy. Techniques for degreasing are explained under stock*. As well as home-made stock, good purchased stock may be used.

Prepare a thoroughly clean saucepan, whisk, bowl, metal sieve and piece of muslin. Scald the sieve and muslin in boiling water, then set aside. Pour the stock into the pan. Add the required quantity of gelatine, egg white and crushed egg shells. Over low heat, whisk the stock continuously until it forms a thick froth, then stop whisking and allow it to come to the boil. The froth sets in a crust which rises in the pan. As soon as it rises, remove the pan from the heat and let the crust subside. Replace the pan, allow the crust to rise and take it off the heat again. Twice is usually enough to clear the stock but if it is particularly cloudy, repeat again.

Finally, strain the stock through the prepared muslin-lined sieve into the clean bowl. Allow the crust to fall into the sieve first as it acts as an extra filter when straining the liquid. **Quantities of Gelatine** The gelatine is used for setting, although it also helps to clear the liquid. Allow 15 g/½ oz to each 600 ml/1 pint liquid.

Eggs Use 1 egg white and its shell for 300 ml/½ pint liquid; 2 for 600 ml/1 pint; 3 for 1 litre/generous 2 pints.

Flavouring Ingredients Chopped uncooked meat or poultry (or minced meat) and vegetables may be added to stocks as well as the egg white and shell. The liquid should be allowed to simmer gently for 30–40 minutes for the best flavour. The meat and other ingredients help to trap particles which make the liquid cloudy.

SEE ALSO **Cinnamon:** Spices; **Citron:** Dried and Candied Fruit; **Clafoutis:** Cherries; **Clams:** Shellfish

Clarifying Fruit Juice

Fruit juices to be set with gelatine are clarified by the same method of boiling with egg whites and shells as used for clearing stocks.

Adding Gelatine Gelatine may be dissolved in the liquid before clearing or it may be sponged and added to the cleared liquid (see gelatine* for technique).

Clarifying Fat

Lumps of beef or pork fat removed from meat may be clarified to yield cooking fat; however this is an out-dated practise which involves simmering the fat in water until it melts, then cooling and chilling it. The fat separates and sets for lifting off the water which is discarded.

Clarifying Butter Butter may be clarified by simmering it in water, as above, but the more practical method is to heat and strain it. The reason for clarifying butter is to remove salt and other solids, and to evaporate the water it contains.

Melt the butter in a small saucepan over low heat, then allow it to simmer gently for about 5 minutes, until any spitting has stopped and a white sediment gathers in the bottom of the pan. Remove from the heat. Strain the butter through a muslin-lined sieve.

Clarified butter keeps well in the refrigerator or freezer. It is also known as ghee. (Vegetable ghee is made from vegetable fat.)

Cook's Tip
Large coffee filter papers may be used instead of muslin. Double them for straining stocks or liquids.

Cleaning Materials

See Cloths.*
The right choice and use of cleaning materials for the kitchen is important in the prevention of food contamination.

There are many products intended for different uses. Always read the label for details of the contents and the suggested uses. It is also important to follow manufacturer's cleaning guidelines for equipment, work surfaces and so on.

Types of Cleaning Materials

Detergents Including washing powders and washing up liquids. These do not kill bacteria and other micro-organisms but they do clean grease and dirt off dishes and cloths.

Abrasives Powders and some cream cleaners are mild abrasives. These are not suitable for all surfaces as they can cause scratching. However, the abrasive action dislodges food and dirt particles from wood, textured surfaces and difficult corners. Not usually suitable for destroying micro-organisms but very effective for cleaning away particles which encourage contamination.

Cream Cleaners These may be multi-surface cleaners or they may be abrasives.

Liquid Cleaners These vary; some kill micro-organisms, others do not, so check information on the bottle. They may be used on floors, walls and surfaces.

Multi-surface Cleaners These may be liquids, sprays or foams. They are not abrasives and are intended for use on the majority of surfaces. They vary in strength and some kill micro-organisms whereas others do not.

Floor and Wall Cleaners Powders – usually detergents. Some liquid cleaners are stronger and more effective.

Bleach A valuable, comparatively inexpensive cleaner that may be used in most areas of the kitchen for killing micro-organisms. Always use bleach according to the manufacturer's instructions, since many types are very strong. Undiluted bleach may be used for drains and lavatories. In solution, bleach is useful for sterilising

wooden boards, surfaces, dish cloths, floor mops and washing up brushes.

Disinfectant Another strong cleaning agent for killing micro-organisms. This is suitable for drains, sinks, rubbish bins, washing up bowls and floors.

Sterilising Solutions Available from chemists for sterilising babies' bottles and for home brewing. These are usually too expensive to use for general cleaning purposes; however they are suitable for thoroughly cleaning surfaces, sinks, washing up bowls and so on. Always follow the manufacturer's instructions for diluting the product.

Polishing Cleaners These are intended to leave surfaces looking shiny but they are not cleaning agents for removing food and cooking deposits, and they do not kill micro-organisms.

Cleaning Notes

• Pay particular attention to corners, joins in the work surface, crevices and the back of surfaces.

• Use a soft brush for cleaning difficult areas.

• A quick wipe may make the kitchen look better but it does not clean away micro-organisms or food deposits.

• All surfaces and walls behind hobs or food preparation areas should be washed and rinsed to remove grease, food and dirt.

• Sinks, draining boards, draining racks, washing up bowls and areas around taps should be washed daily. They should be rinsed well after each use.

• Work surfaces should be wiped clean after every use – crumbs and spillages should always be cleaned up.

• Separate cloths should be used for cleaning surfaces and for washing up.

• Floors should be brushed often and washed at least once a week.

• Spray cleaners for adding shine should be used after the

area has been washed and dried, not instead of thorough cleaning.

X *Never mix different cleaning materials. Many contain strong chemicals which can react with each other to produce noxious gases.*

Cloths

See Hygiene.*

Different cloths should be set aside for different purposes, for washing up, drying dishes, drying hands, washing floors, cleaning bathrooms and lavatories and so on. The following checklist is useful for anyone setting up home for the first time.

Dish Cloths Disposable cloths that are thrown away after a few weeks are most hygienic. All types should be boiled regularly for about 40 minutes, with detergent, then rinsed and hung out to dry.

Tea-towels Look for heavy cotton tea-towels that dry dishes well. Buy several as they should be washed frequently.

Floor Cloths Never use dish cloths or tea-towels for washing the floor. If they are used in an emergency to mop spills, they should be boiled if they are not disposable. Always rinse floor cloths thoroughly after use and dry them. Discard them often.

Oven Gloves Thin, cheap spongy types do not offer enough protection when handling hot dishes or roasting tins. Choose a thick, heavy pair of mits or a long oven glove – some of the short ones do not reach around a large roasting tin.

Remember that oven gloves tend to get very dirty, absorbing fat and cooking juices. A tough glove will withstand the wear as well as the essential frequent washing and an occasional boil.

Hand Towels Always keep a hand towel in the kitchen and avoid using tea-towels to wipe wet hands. At least two hard-wearing towels are the basics as they should be washed often.

Bathroom and Lavatory Cloths These should be disposable and kept quite separate from any kitchen cloths. They should be thoroughly rinsed and hung to dry after use and discarded often.

Cloths: A Source of Contamination

So, why all the fuss about cloths? Take a dish cloth as an example – it's used to wipe the work surface, clearing up bits of food. Then it is used for wiping dirty dishes in hand-hot soapy water. After washing up, the surface is wiped down. The next stage is crucial – the dish cloth is probably wrung out and set aside on the draining board.

Minute food particles and bacteria mingle in the warm, moist folds of the cloth. The bacteria multiply.

Next time it is used it may be to wipe down a bread board or to wipe the work surface before rolling out pastry. The bacteria from the cloth are transferred to the wiped surface, then to the food.

In a different chain of uses, other cloths are just as vulnerable to being infected with bacteria and they can pass on to food from wiping dishes or handling the cloth before preparing food.

Clean Cloth Code

The following points are worth checking and remembering.

● Rinse dish cloths under hot running water after each use. Wring out and shake loose, then hang on a hook.

X *Never leave unrinsed cloths wrung out and left in a damp heap. In this condition, they rapidly become a hygiene hazard.*

● Hang tea-towels and hand towels separately.

● Hang cloths in an airy place where they will not be brushed by everyone who passes, and away from any passing pets.

● Use disposable cloths and change them regularly.

● Wash tea-towels and hand towels frequently.

● Keep floor cloths and bathroom cloths separate from cloths used for wiping hands, dishes and work surfaces.

Coatings for Food

Food is coated to protect it during cooking. The coating seals in flavour and moisture, prevents the food from breaking up and from absorbing oil during frying. There are three main coatings: flour, egg and breadcrumbs, and batter.

Coating with Flour

Used for fish, poultry, meat or vegetables. The prepared food is dipped in the flour just before cooking. Some patties may be coated with flour. A flour coating is almost always applied before food is fried.

Technique Plain white flour is usually used. Place the flour on a large plate and season it well. Mix the seasoning into the flour.

Hold fish fillets, thin pieces of meat and chops at one end, then turn them two or three times in the flour. Shake off excess coating and place the food straight in the heated cooking fat.

Place patties or other similar shaped food on the flour. Use two palette knives (or rounded, fairly blunt knives) to pat the flour against the sides of the patty, turning it around to coat the base. Turn the patty over to coat the second side. Either place the patty in the hot fat or on a clean plate until the remaining food is coated.

The technique for coating small pieces of food (cubes of meat or poultry, or small whole fish such as whitebait) is different. Place the food in a large bowl and sprinkle the seasoned flour over it, then use two forks to mix well until all the pieces are coated. If the food is moist and it is placed on top of the flour in the bowl, it is more difficult to coat.

An easier method of coating small amounts of pieces is to put the seasoned flour in a polythene bag, then add the food. Hold the bag firmly closed and shake the food until it is well coated. This is not suitable for delicate food but useful for cubes of meat, sliced courgettes and so on.

Choice of Seasoning Salt and pepper are the basic seasonings. Grated nutmeg or ground spices (cumin, coriander, chilli, curry powder or five spice powder) may be added to the flour. Avoid chopped herbs or other ingredients which may overcook and develop a bitter flavour.

Coating with Egg and Breadcrumbs

A versatile coating for fish, poultry, meat, vegetables, patties or croquettes. The thickness of the coating may be varied to suit the food and cooking method. Suitable for baking and grilling as well as frying.

Technique There are three stages: first the food is coated in flour, then it is dipped in egg and finally coated with breadcrumbs.

Set out the coatings. Put the flour and seasoning on a large plate. Place the egg in a small or large dish, depending on the size of the pieces of food. It is easier to coat large fillets if the egg is placed in a wide dish rather than in a small cereal bowl. Beat the egg with a little water so that it is thin enough to coat the food evenly. Pile the breadcrumbs fairly thickly on a plate.

Set out the coatings in order, with a clean plate at the end of the line ready for the food.

Wash and dry your hands. Hold large items of food at one end and dip them in the coatings in turn. Use a fork to encourage the egg over the food, turning the food over as you do so. Allow excess egg to drip off before placing the food on the breadcrumbs. Sprinkle crumbs over the top of the food and press them on well. Turn over the food and press plenty of crumbs all over it. Gently shake off excess crumbs and place the coated food on the clean plate.

Use two forks to turn small items of food in the coating.

Coating Soft Foods Very soft foods, for example sauce-based mixtures used for making croquettes or soft fish cake mixtures, that are likely to flow or become mis-shapen as they heat must be handled carefully and coated twice.

These foods should be well chilled before coating. Once one layer of coating is applied, the food should be turned in beaten egg for a second time and a second layer of breadcrumbs pressed on.

Chilling For best results, allow the coating to set slightly by chilling for 15–30 minutes before cooking. Very soft mixtures benefit from longer chilling.

Breadcrumbs* The choice depends on the food. Fine white crumbs give a fine even coating which goes well with delicate foods (croquettes, thin fish fillets, small pieces of seafood or vegetables such as mushrooms). The fine crumbs are ideal when more than one layer of coating is needed as they do not become thick and uneven. They also fry to a good colour, both by shallow and deep frying. However, they do not bake as well as fresh crumbs.

Fresh breadcrumbs may be used on less delicate food and they are more suitable for foods to be baked or they may be dotted with fat and grilled. If they are fried, the coating should be well chilled and the fat must be properly heated otherwise they tend to be oily. Shallow frying is better than deep frying.

Soft crumbs give a thick, chunky-looking coating which is acceptable on less delicate items, for example lentil burgers, sausagemeat cakes or thick portions of fish.

Browned breadcrumbs can become too dark during cooking if not used carefully. They are fine on small items of food which cook quickly – goujons of fish or single shellfish such as scallops – but they become too dark on chicken or meat which requires longer cooking.

Bought golden breadcrumbs look artificial and they do not have a good texture, therefore they are best avoided. Bought unbrowned types are better.

Other Coatings and Seasonings The breadcrumbs may be seasoned with herbs and spices or they may be mixed with finely chopped nuts. Peanuts or walnuts are tasty and crunchy. Sesame seeds may be mixed with the crumbs but they overcook quickly so avoid using them on food which needs long cooking.

Chopped nuts, crushed savoury or sweet biscuits or plain cake crumbs may be used instead of breadcrumbs. Bought packet stuffing mixes make easy, tasty coatings for savoury foods, particularly chicken or turkey strips or thin slices of meat.

Coating with Batter

See Batter*.
A batter coating is used for food to be deep fried*. The batter is applied immediately before the food is fried, therefore the fat must be hot. The batter should be made just before it is used, so the order of work is important.

Batter is usually used on larger or less delicate items of food. The food must be firm enough to dip and strong enough in texture and/or flavour to take a batter coating.

Batter should be browned, crisp and light when cooked. If it is cooked in oil which is not hot enough, then the result will be greasy. If the batter is too thick, it will be doughy when cooked. If the batter is too thin, it will not cling to the food to form an even coating. The consistency of the batter must complement the food – batter lightened with egg white is ideal for light seafood, whereas pouring batter is more suitable for thick fish fillets.

Technique Prepare the food and coat it with seasoned flour. Prepare the oil for deep frying and place it over very low heat. Next make the batter, leaving any whisked egg white until the oil is part heated. Have ready the absorbent kitchen paper for the fried food and the serving dish.

Keep an eye on the oil to make sure it does not overheat as you finish making the batter, then check that the oil is hot enough.

Dip the food in the batter, allow excess batter to drip off. Fish fillets or large items of food may be held at one end while being turned in the batter. Use a scooping action to coat large pieces of food all over. Give the food a sharp turn as soon as the excess batter has drained off it to catch any drips as part of the coating as you lower the food into the oil.

Once cooked, batter should be served quickly as it softens on cooling. Keep batter-coated food hot in an uncovered dish in a warm oven while all the pieces are being cooked; do not cover the food as any steam will soften the batter.

Coconut

Coconut may be purchased in many forms, all useful for savoury and sweet cooking.

Coconut and Coconut Products

Fresh Coconut Sometimes shrink wrapped in supermarkets. Shake the nut and you should hear the coconut water or juice inside. At the top of the nut there are three round comparatively soft holes in the shell. Pierce two of these then drain the coconut water out before cracking the nut open with a hammer. Scoop out the white flesh which should be moist with a creamy coating. If the nut smells musty it has gone off and the flesh will taste bad.
Coconut Water or Juice The liquid from inside the nut. It may be used in drinks or cooking.

Coconut Milk Coconut milk is made by soaking the grated flesh in boiling water to cover for 30 minutes, then squeezing out all the liquid. Fresh coconut may be soaked twice.

Desiccated coconut may also be soaked in boiling water to cover to extract coconut milk.

Blocks of coconut cream may be dissolved in a little boiling water to make coconut milk. Instructions are usually given on the packet. Powdered coconut milk is also available.
Coconut Cream This is sold in blocks or in cans. When buying a can of coconut cream, check whether it is sweetened or not.
Desiccated Coconut Finely shredded and dried coconut for use in baking.
Long Thread Coconut Long shreds of desiccated coconut that are usually used as a coating for cakes and desserts, often toasted.

Storing

Desiccated and long thread coconut should be stored in an airtight container in a dry, cool cupboard. Blocks of coconut cream are best overwrapped in a polythene bag and kept in the refrigerator. Pieces may be broken off the block as required.

Fresh coconut should be placed in a polythene bag in the refrigerator and used within 5–7 days.

Toasting Coconut

Desiccated and long-thread coconut both overbrown easily. Sprinkle the coconut on foil and toast under the grill, using a fork to turn the nut as it browns.

Use

• Add desiccated coconut to creamed or rubbed-in cake mixtures (see cakes*).

• Desiccated coconut may be mixed with plain biscuit mixtures (see biscuits*).

• Sprinkle toasted long thread coconut over portions of fruit salad (particularly a salad containing exotic fruit) just before serving.

• Coconut milk is used in curries and other Oriental spicy dishes, particularly those of Indonesia and Thailand.

Freezing

Fresh coconut freezes well. Cut the flesh into bite-size pieces or grate it. Pack in polythene bags and freeze for up to 3 months.

Nutritional Value

Coconut flesh has a high fat content. Unlike the majority of other vegetable fats which are mainly unsaturated, coconut fat is saturated (see fat*).

Cod's Roe

See Fish*.
The eggs of the female fish. Usually sold plain boiled, firm and creamy coloured, or smoked, when its outer skin is red in colour. Canned pressed cod's roe is unsmoked.

Buying and Storing

Sold by weight, the fishmonger will cut the boiled or smoked roe for you.

Keep the roe chilled and use it within a day of purchase. Smoked roe will keep for 1–2 days after purchase but it is best used fresh.

Preparation

Use the point of a knife to slit the outer membrane covering the roe, then remove it carefully by pulling it off with your fingers. Try to avoid breaking up the roe. Remove any veins.

Cooking and Using

• Both boiled roe and smoked roe may be served simply, as a spread with toast. Season the

SEE ALSO **Cobbler:** Scones; **Cockles:** Shellfish; **Cod:** Fish prepared roe with freshly ground black pepper and serve with wedges of lemon for their juice.

• Slice plain roe or pressed canned roe and coat the slices in egg and breadcrumbs, then shallow fry until golden. Serve with lemon wedges and salad.

• Sliced roe may be dotted with butter and grilled or spread on toast and grilled.

Taramasalata

Pound 100 g/4 oz boiled or smoked roe with 25 g/1 oz fresh white breadcrumbs, 1 crushed clove garlic, a little lemon juice and a little finely chopped raw onion to a paste. Gradually add olive oil, drop by drop, as when making mayonnaise*, beating all the time until the roe forms a thick creamy paste. The proportions are about 175–250 ml/6–8 fluid oz olive oil to 100 g/4 oz roe.

The paste is pale pink if smoked roe is used, otherwise it is a creamy colour. Taste it and add more lemon juice and seasoning as required. Serve with chunks of bread or raw vegetables.

Coffee

There are many types of coffee, including instant coffee, coffee and chicory mixtures and different beans or blends of beans.

A small electric or hand grinder may be used to grind roasted beans at home. Freshly ground beans have the best flavour.

Making Coffee

To make fresh coffee, place the required amount of ground coffee and water, which is just off the boil, in a jug. Strain the coffee after about 5 minutes. Fine coffee settles quickly when it has brewed and it stays in the bottom of the pot.

Filter Coffee Place finely ground coffee in a filter container lined with a disposable filter paper. Reusable filters may be purchased. Stand the filter over a jug, then pour water which is just off the boil over the coffee and allow it to run through into the jug.

Using a Cafetière A cafetière is a jug which has a push-down filter incorporated in the lid. Place the coffee (medium ground) and water in the jug, then put the lid and push-down filter in place. Leave to brew for about 5–7 minutes before pushing down the filter. This is one of the easiest ways of making fresh coffee.

Percolated Coffee Using an electric or hob-top percolator, the coffee is placed in a perforated container which slots into a pot above the water. A tube links the water to the top of the coffee holder. As the water heats, it rises in the tube and drips back down through the coffee grounds, flavouring the liquid below. It is important to have a percolator with a reliable thermostat or to keep the pot over low to medium heat to prevent the coffee overheating and becoming bitter.

Greek or Turkish Coffee Boil fine ground coffee in a small amount of water in a small saucepan. Traditionally, generous amounts of sugar are added to the coffee before it is heated. Pour the coffee into small cups. The grounds settle in a fine sediment at the base of the cup.

Expresso Coffee Very strong coffee, machine-made by forcing steam through fine grounds.

Cappuccino Expresso coffee diluted with milk. Using two-thirds milk to coffee, the milk is heated by passing steam through it, making it frothy. A little cocoa powder or grated chocolate may be sprinkled over the frothy coffee.

Some of the flavour of the coffee is lost if the water is boiling, leaving the drink less well flavoured and slightly harsh. With prolonged heating or reheating, coffee becomes bitter due to chemical breakdown.

Quantities of Coffee to Water

This is, to a large extent, a matter of personal preference. As a general rule, allow about 60 ml/4 tablespoons medium ground coffee to 900 ml/1½ pints water.

Caffeine

Naturally present in coffee and tea, caffeine is a stimulant which has noticeable effects on the human body, including stimulating the heart. When drunk in large or frequent quantities it is, to some extent, addictive.

Decaffeinated coffee is sold both fresh and in instant form.

Coffee Essence

Strong coffee used as a flavouring in cooking. Commercial liquid coffee and chicory mixtures may be used but this is inferior to home-made essence. Expresso coffee may be used or instant coffee may be made very strong. Fresh ground coffee may be infused in a small amount of water until cool, then strained to make essence.

Freezing

Coffee beans and vacuum packed ground coffee both freeze well. Overwrap in sealed polythene bags and store for 6 months or more. Any leftover, freshly made coffee may be frozen successfully – it is good for making iced coffee (or coffee milk shakes).

Reheating Coffee

Coffee should not be kept hot for long as this causes chemical changes that spoil its flavour.

Instead, cool leftovers quickly, then reheat individual portions as required in the microwave. Do not reheat coffee more than once.

Containers for Food

See Storing Food*.

A container must be suitable for the type of food to be stored and it should have a lid to protect the food.

Types of Containers

Lidded Containers Made of either plastic or glass, these are not necessarily airtight. Suitable for food in packets, for example biscuits or packets of dry ingredients, where the open packet forms a satisfactory, but rather weak, wrapping which may tear.

Airtight Containers With tight fitting lids to prevent moisture or bacteria entering. Use for cakes, dried ingredients and any foods that are likely to absorb moisture from the air.

Waterproof Containers Use these in the refrigerator, freezer and for liquids.

Freezer Containers All bags and containers for use in the freezer must be strong enough to withstand the low temperature as well as waterproof. Always check that a product is freezer-proof before purchase.

Materials

Plastic There are many types of plastic containers in the shops. The majority are washable and some are airtight. Not all are suitable for freezer use.

Glass When buying storage jars, make sure they have lids that fit well and that the jar can be lifted by them. Some glass is not suitable for freezer storage.

Tin Storage tins are fine for foods that are packeted. Look for tins with tight-fitting (airtight) lids and neat joins in the metal. They are only suitable for dry foods and for keeping in dry places.

They should be cleaned regularly and washed in very hot soapy water occasionally, then rinsed in boiling water, drained and thoroughly dried at once to prevent them from rusting.

Stainless Steel Containers Not particularly popular but they are available. They are washable and do not rust. Check lids for a good fit before buying.

Crockery Pots Unglazed earthenware is absorbent, therefore check that the inside of containers are glazed. Cork lids should be sealed unless the pot is used only for packeted foods.

Points to Remember

● When buying, look for containers that are easy to handle, with large openings.

● Buy containers that suit your needs.

● Look for washable containers that are easy to clean.

● Although clear containers (glass) look attractive, they are not necessarily the best for the food as some ingredients, notably herbs and spices, should be kept in the dark.

Packet or Container?

It is best to leave food in unopened, commercially sealed packets when possible. Containers are useful for opened packets. Either the opened packet may be placed in an airtight container or the contents may be tipped into the container.

Convenience Foods

Convenience foods play a valuable role in cooking and they can fit well into a balanced diet. Convenience foods should not be dismissed as ready-prepared dishes that leave nothing to the skills of the cook; it is more practical to think of them as useful short cuts to success. The types, quality and value of these products varies enormously.

Frozen Foods

The range of frozen foods sums up much of the information that applies to convenience food in general: from frozen vegetables that offer as much food value as the fresh produce and excellent quality to other products that bear no resemblance to home cooking. Some of the products may contain a good many useful nutrients but they may have a comparatively high fat content or they may be highly refined, therefore lacking in fibre. Some may not offer much in the way of food value.

Positive Points Many frozen foods are valuable for speed and ease of preparation, for quality when fresh alternatives are not available or too expensive and for providing variety in the diet. The ready-to-cook quick snacks and meals must not be ignored; many are good quality and useful when time is short.

Minus Points Ready-made products are expensive and they should not completely replace freshly prepared foods in the long-term diet. Some frozen vegetables are significantly more expensive than fresh ones in season.

Types of Frozen Foods and Their Role

Prepared and Part-prepared Frozen Ingredients Vegetables, fish, meat, breads, cream, pastries, breads and so on all simplify the process of cooking meals and more complicated dishes. They may not replace home-made and freshly bought foods but they are excellent stand-bys and regular alternatives. Some, such as cream, make good sense since it is easier to make more economical use of frozen than it is to buy a carton which may contain more than is required.

Versatile Prepared Products These are prepared ready for cooking and serving simply; however they lend themselves to other uses. Pre-formed fish steaks in sauce are a good exam-

---

ple – they may be used as a pie filling or for other made up dishes requiring fish in sauce. Various vegetable and rice mixtures also fall into this category. Coated fish and meat products, all types of burgers and other ready-to-cook items may be used imaginatively along with fresh foods.

Heat or Cook and Serve Products These are the type to go from freezer to cooker to plate. They may be a complete meal, a made-up dish for the main part of the meal or a snack. Quality and food value varies; for this reason, each product must be considered individually as part of the diet.

Dried Foods

These include many types of mixes – for sauces, pastry, cakes, bread, biscuits, batter, dips, stuffings, soups and so on – as well as some dried foods, like sliced mushrooms, onions, quick-mix noodles and other snacks.

Assessing Convenience Compare packet mixed with the fresh recipe on three levels: effort, time saving and quality. In some cases, there is some saving in effort and time but the quality of the cooked product is inferior. Some mixes may be acceptable only as 'emergency' foods. Some taste so synthetic that it is worth making do with a simple fresh dish, fruit and cheese, or a snack instead – some packet dips are one example and dried instant snacks (such as cartons of fried noodles or rice mixtures).

Bread mix is one of the really good packet mixes that is useful for making pizza as well as for home-baked loaves and rolls.

However, many of the sauce and soup mixes do taste synthetic. The texture of certain mixes is also significantly inferior to the real thing.

Canned

See Canned Food.
Many canned foods have given way to frozen alternatives, for example vegetables, while others

have grown in popularity. Canned beans and pulses are excellent convenience foods.

Canned foods may be divided into the type that may be used to speed up the preparation of a fresh meal (tomatoes, beans and pulses, fruit, custard and so on), those that may be eaten as they are or used as a basis for making dishes (canned fish, meat, consommé, some vegetables) and others that are ready for heating and serving (baked beans, soups, meat or poultry in sauce, canned pies or puddings, sponge puddings, milk puddings).

Convenience and Versatility Canned foods are convenient – they require little preparation before serving and they have the advantage of being versatile. They are also easy to store and they have a long storage life.

Each product must be assessed on its own merits or disadvantages. The nutritional information on each can should be noted.

Chilled Products

The cook-chill, ready meals and other chilled, part-prepared foods are included in this category. The range of products is always changing and there is a great danger of over-generalising.

Many of these products are expensive and the cheaper ones may not be as good to eat or as nutritious. They are useful because they save time. There is no reason to exclude them from the diet but there is every good reason to balance them with fresh foods – salad accompaniments, fresh cooked meals and some foods with a good fibre content.

☑ **Convenient and Safe**
It is important always to read what the manufacturer says about the product before buying it, before opening the container or packet, before preparing and serving it. Follow the instructions closely for storing, cooking, heating and serving all convenience foods.

Cookers

Two main fuel options: electricity or mains gas. Solid fuel, oil fired and bottled gas cookers are also available.

A cooker may combine one or two ovens, a microwave, grill and hob in one appliance or the hob, oven and gas grill may be separate.

Electric Hobs

Radiant Ring This may be dual circuit, allowing a small area towards the middle of the ring to be heated alone.

Ceramic The cooking area is indicated by a pattern on the surface of the hob. A radiant ring is situated beneath the ceramic cover. Dual circuit rings are available. These have to be cleaned carefully and all spills wiped away immediately. They look pleasing and do not have areas that trap spills. Special cleaning materials should be used according to the manufacturer's instructions. The choice of saucepans is limited to types which have a flat base.

Halogen This uses tungsten halogen filaments instead of elements. This type of hob has the advantage of heating and cooling rapidly, making it very responsive.

Induction This relies on the use of a flat steel pan placed on a magnetic coil to provide heat. The hob itself does not become hot and it is responsive to control changes.

Thermostatically Controlled Hobs Some hobs have rings with a built-in thermostat and sensor to keep food simmering or boiling without attention.

Gas Hobs

Gas hobs do not have as many features as electric appliances. Many have two sizes of burners, for fast boiling or simmering. Gas burners are particularly responsive and offer excellent controllability.

The main choice is in the design of pan supports, surrounds, controls and splash trays.

Many gas hobs have hinged covers which act as splash backs during cooking or allow the top of the hob to be used as a surface, following manufacturer's instructions, when closed. Useful in a small kitchen.

Ceramic Discs Ceramic discs to cover burners. The pan sits on the disc which is heated from below.

Solid Plates

On central heating cookers, solid plates with lids are a particular feature. These are used for toasting or as griddles as well as for all other cooking purposes. The lids are lowered when the plates are not in use to reserve the heat.

Solid plates or griddles are also available on a limited number of gas and electric hobs.

Ovens

The traditional British oven is heated from the sides (electric) or directly from the back (gas).

Continental cookers are heated from below. Electric ovens have heat sources below the oven cavity and some also have elements above. Continental-style gas ovens have the heat source outside of and below the oven cavity.

These ovens give different results from British-style cookers, with more bottom browning and less colouration on the top of the food. This is ideal for pastry flans but some cakes tend to be darker on the bottom than the top.

Fan Assisted These have a fan to circulate the heat. Hot air rises, so in a normal oven the top tends to be hotter than the bottom – this is less pronounced with electric appliances but still a distinct feature of gas ovens. If the oven is fan assisted the heat zones do not exist and the temperature varies only slightly from top to bottom.

Forced Convection This must not be confused with fan assisted. In this type of oven the hot air is recirculated. A high speed fan is fitted near or around the heat source to distribute and recirculate the hot air. This type of oven heats up and cooks more quickly than a conventional oven.

As a guide, the temperature should be set about 20°C/45°F lower in this type of oven or the cooking time should be shortened. Follow individual manufacturer's instructions for use.

Combination Ovens These combine conventional heat with microwave power. They are available in full-size ovens or table-top models.

Automatic Controls Most modern ovens have automatic controls which can be set in advance to start and stop cooking.

Timers Most cookers have reminder timers which operate up to 60 minutes.

Rotisserie Attachment For roasting joints and whole birds, or kebabs. A small motor in the oven casing turns the rack or skewers.

Integral Grill Some ovens have a built-in grill (notably continental types) in the main oven. This means that the grill cannot be operated at the same time as the oven.

Grills

These may have separate compartments, they may be wall-mounted (in the case of gas) or they may be sited in the main oven.

Dual circuit grills can be operated in two parts or as a whole unit.

Gas grills may be heated by a burner from the back or centre, or they may have an even burning area, distributed over the whole grill surface. The latter type is faster and the whole surface is heated evenly.

Central Heating Cookers

Traditionally solid fuel cookers, these are now available fired by gas or electric as well (for example Aga and Rayburn). They pro-vide oven space and cooking plates available for use at all time. They vary in size, from large ranges with several ovens to small units with two ovens. The ovens often operate within different temperature ranges, including a cooler oven for stewing and hotter one for baking.

Follow the manufacturer's instructions and recipes, and guidance on the type of cooking dishes or saucepans to use.

Purchasing Points

● *Space*: free-standing, built under or built-in cookers are all available in different sizes. Table top cookers combining oven, limited hob space and grill are also available.

● *Use:* a second small oven is useful for cooking individual items; a large convection oven for batch baking; a combined grill and oven has limited use.

● *Fuel combinations:* gas hob and electric oven; central heating cookers and gas or electric hob; a combination of electric and gas hob facilities.

Care and Cleaning

● Always read and follow the manufacturer's instructions.

● Always make sure appliances are switched off before cleaning. Remove all parts carefully and make sure they are replaced accurately after cleaning.

● Check for self-cleaning linings or other materials that should not be cleaned.

● Clean the oven interior regularly, using hot soapy water or a product for cleaning ovens.

● Always follow instructions closely when using strong cleaning fluids, creams and sprays. Always wear rubber gloves and use sprays in a ventilated kitchen.

● Wipe up spills immediately or at least before the oven cools. Use hot soapy water and a disposable cloth.

SEE ALSO **Cookies:** Biscuits; **Coq au Vin:** Stewing

- Never wipe a very hot glass door with a wet cloth.

- Clean around oven vents and controls at the same time as cleaning the interior as cooking fumes and grease may collect around them.

- Clean hobs regularly, washing all removable parts according to the instructions. Wipe up spills immediately.

- Clean crumbs and fat from grill pans after use.

 Wiping down after every use saves a lot of hard cleaning later.

Cooking

Food is cooked by applying heat to it or, in the case of microwave cooking, by inducing it to produce heat within itself. Food is cooked for different reasons.

- To make it safe to eat by destroying unwanted bacteria.

- To make it digestible.

- To make it more palatable.

Types of Cooking

Three scientific principles of passing heat are involved.

Conduction This is a process of passing heat through a solid object. For example through a solid pan base. Heat spreads through food by conduction, for example towards the centre of a thick joint of meat.

Convection This is the movement of hot particles of gas or liquid. As an oven is heated the hot air circulates within it and this heats the food. In a liquid, the hot particles rise, circulate and distribute heat throughout the food. An egg is cooked by the convection of heat in the surrounding water when boiled.

Radiation When grilling food the heat is transmitted to the food from a heat source.

In practice, these methods are often combined. When the outside of food is grilled, within the food itself heat is passed by conduction. When food is cooked in a microwave cooker, the waves cause the molecules within the food to move and this creates heat in certain areas. The heat is passed on to other parts of the food by conduction.

The Effects of Cooking

See Vitamins*.
Heating food causes it to change. The changes depend on the cooking method used. For example, compare grilled meat with boiled meat. Different foods react in different ways to heat.
Starch This swells on the application of moist heat. In dry heat (toasting or baking), starch changes colour and browns because near the surface of the food some of the starch molecules are converted to sugars. Starchy foods give off moisture during cooking, becoming crisp and dry.
Sugar Heated gently on its own, sugar melts and caramelises, then it burns. If sugar is exposed to radiant heat it caramelises quickly, then burns.

Sugar also dissolves in water and the rate at which it dissolves may be increased by heating.
Fats Solid fats melt on heating. Water present in the fat evaporates, some solids separate out and eventually, if overheated, the fat breaks down and burns.
Protein Protein coagulates or sets when heated. Meat, poultry and fish become firm and eggs set. This happens at different rates and at different temperatures. With fierce overheating, protein becomes hard and unpalatable.

Nutritional Value

Cooking also affects the nutritional value of the food, particularly the vitamin content, which may be reduced.

The Reasons for Cooking

As well as cooking for the reason mentioned, it enables us to combine foods to make completely different products. Baked goods are an excellent example – breads, pastries, cakes and biscuits.

Cornflour

Known as corn starch in American cookbooks, this is a fine white flour made from maize. Unlike wheat flour, cornflour does not contain any gluten, therefore it acts quite differently in cooking.

Use

Cornflour is used in small proportions in some biscuits and light cakes to produce a fine, light texture. Its main use is a thickener for sauces, particularly in Oriental cooking.

When used as a thickening it makes a gelatinous sauce. This texture is not ideal for gravies and most savoury sauces are better thickened with wheat flour or by other means. However it is used for thickening Oriental sauces. It can be useful when very slight thickening is required, otherwise its use is a matter for personal taste. Many commercial sauce or gravy mixes contain cornflour as a thickening ingredient. It is more successful as a thickener for sweet milk sauces or for making a Blancmange (page 42).

Mix cornflour to a thin smooth paste with a little cold liquid, then pour on the remaining hot liquid to be thickened. Stir well and return the mixture to the pan, then bring the sauce to the boil, stirring all the time to prevent lumps forming. When the mixture boils, lower the heat and simmer for 3 minutes. This is important to ensure that the mixture does not taste uncooked.

Storing

Keep cornflour in an airtight container in a dry cupboard.

Corn-on-the-cob

See Vegetables*.
Available home grown during summer and early autumn, this is a good vegetable for pick-your-own enthusiasts. The slim, oval cobs are about 15–23 cm/6–9 inches long. The sweetcorn kernels are tightly packed around them and covered with a coat of fine silky threads and wide, leaf-like sheaths. The uncooked corn is pale creamy-yellow in colour.

Buying

Look for fresh cobs that feel firm and moist. Avoid those that have very limp and dry outer coverings. Many supermarkets sell the cobs of corn ready trimmed of outer covering. The corn will look pale but the kernels should look plump and moist. If the kernels appear slightly dented and dry, then the corn may be old and tough.

Storing

Keep the cobs in a polythene bag in the bottom of the refrigerator and use within 1–2 days. The fresher the corn, the better the taste.

Preparation

Remove the outer covering and silky threads, then trim the ends off the cobs.

Cooking

Prepare a large pan of unsalted boiling water and drop in the cobs. If salt is added it can toughen the corn kernels. Bring the water back to the boil, reduce the heat slightly to prevent it boiling over, then cover the pan. Cook for about 10–15 minutes, depending on the size, age and freshness of the corn.

To check whether the corn is cooked, remove one cob and cut off one kernel with the point of a knife. The corn should be tender, sweet and juicy. If it tastes slightly tough and floury it is not cooked.

Microwave Cooking Place the prepared cobs of corn in a suitable large dish. Pour in 60 ml/ 4 tablespoons water and cover the dish. Cook on High, allowing 3–5 minutes for 1 cob, 6–8 minutes for 2 cobs and 10–15 minutes for 4 cobs. Turn the cobs, and rearrange them when cooking more than 2 cobs, once or twice during cooking. Leave to stand for 2 minutes or so, then drain and serve.

Serving Ideas

• Top with butter, herb butter or garlic butter.

• Serve with a dressing of chopped peeled tomatoes and chopped spring onions tossed in hot olive oil and season with freshly ground black pepper.

Eating Corn-on-the-cob

Small sturdy two-pronged forks may be purchased to stick in the ends of the cobs. Pick up the cobs and bite the corn off them. It is a messy business.

Removing the Kernels

The kernels may be scraped off the cooked cobs using a sharp kitchen knife.

Freezing

Blanch* the cobs for 4–6 minutes, depending on size and age. Pack singly or in pairs and freeze for up to a year. Cook from frozen, allowing 3–5 minutes extra boiling time, or 2–4 minutes extra in the microwave.

Nutritional Value

Sweet corn kernels contain protein, vitamins A and C, and provide fibre.

Canned and Frozen Sweet Corn

Both are useful; canned creamed corn can be good.

Courgettes

See Vegetables*.
Available all year but home-grown courgettes are best in mid summer and early autumn. In American cookbooks courgettes are known as zucchini.

Buying

Both green and yellow-skinned courgettes should look plump and feel firm. They should have shiny skins and moist-looking ends where they have been cut off the plant.

Avoid soft or slightly wrinkled courgettes and any that are damaged. Very large vegetables tend to be slightly woolly and they may have large seeds, also they become rather watery on cooking and do not have as good a flavour as the younger, smaller vegetables.

Storing

Courgettes should be used as soon as possible after cooking and within a day of purchase. They may be kept in an open polythene bag in the bottom of the refrigerator for up to 2 days but they rapidly deteriorate in texture and flavour.

Preparation

Prepare courgettes just before they are to be cooked. Trim the ends off the courgettes, then wash them thoroughly. They may be peeled or the skin may be eaten. Older courgettes are best peeled. Small to medium vegetables may be very lightly peeled so that they are bright green without the pale white flesh showing. For a striped appearance, the peel may be removed thinly in alternate strips.

Cutting Courgettes

• Slice thinly or thickly.

• Cut in half lengthways, then slice the halves into chunks.

SEE ALSO **Coriander:** Herbs, Spices; **Cotechino:** Sausages; **Coulis:** Glossary; **Court Bouillon:** Fish; **Couscous:** Semolina

- Cut in half lengthways, then across into quarters. Cut each quarter into fine strips.

- Cut lengthways into fingers.

Cooking

Sautéing Sauté the prepared courgettes in hot olive oil or butter over high heat for 2–3 minutes. They should be bright, slightly softened outside and crunchy in the middle. This way they have maximum flavour.

Steaming Wrap the prepared courgettes in foil, dotting them with butter or margarine, or trickle a little olive oil over them. Individual portions dotted with butter and sprinkled with snipped chives are attractive.

Place in a steamer over boiling water and cook for 5–8 minutes.

Microwave Cooking Courgettes are delicious cooked in the microwave. Medium slices are best for even cooking. Put them in a suitable dish. A little butter, margarine or oil may be added, but do not use salt. Cover and cook on High, allowing 2–4 minutes for 225 g/8 oz or 4–5 minutes for 450 g/1 lb. Stir once during cooking, moving the pieces of vegetable from the outside of the dish in towards the middle.

Baking The courgettes may be sliced fairly thickly, halved lengthways or cut into fingers. Place in a greased dish and sprinkle with oil or dot with butter or margarine. Add seasoning and cover the dish. Allow about 25 minutes cooking time at 200°C, 400°F, gas 6. The cooking temperature is not critical and they may be placed in the oven with a main dish.

Alternatively, place small foil packets of courgettes on a baking tray and cook for about 20 minutes at the above temperature.

Use and Serving Ideas

- Slice or grate for salad.

- Brown some flaked almonds in the fat and remove them before adding the courgettes. Sprinkle them over before serving.

- Wrap chunks of courgette in bacon, thread on metal skewers and grill until crisp. Serve as a cocktail snack or as supper kebabs.

- Layer sliced courgettes with chopped spring onion and grated cheese. Top with cheese and bake until golden and bubbling.

- Make courgette fritters by coating medium-thick slices of courgette in batter* and deep frying them until golden.

Freezing

Frozen courgettes are soft and rather miserable when thawed. If you have no choice but to freeze rather than waste the vegetables, toss medium slices in hot oil instead of blanching. Cool rapidly, pack and freeze.

Better still make a courgette chutney*.

Crab

Crabs are available live or cooked from April through to December.

Buying

A crab should feel heavy for its size. Both claws should be intact and the shell should be undamaged on a cooked crab. Shake the crab and avoid any that contain water. Buy from a reputable, clean source and make sure that live shellfish look bright and moist.

Storing

Cook crab on the day it is purchased. Cooked crab meat may be stored in a covered container towards the bottom of the refrigerator for a day.

Canned and Frozen Crab Meat

Canned dressed crab is the brown meat, usually mixed with breadcrumbs and seasonings.

Canned queen crab or white crab meat is packed in paper in the can.

Frozen crab meat is available and it is good quality. Crab sticks are manufactured from other fish products, then flavoured and coloured to resemble crab. They are not a good match for the true flavour and texture of crab.

Killing

The two, more humane, ways are either to freeze the crab by placing it in a polythene carrier bag in the freezer or to place it in a covered pan of cold salted water and bring it to the boil.

Cooking

Weigh the crab (or ask the fishmonger to do this for you and note it on the bag). Bring the crab to the boil and allow 15 minutes for the first 450 g/1 lb, then cook for a further 10 minutes for each additional 450 g/1 lb. Allow an extra 5 minutes for a frozen crab.

Preparing Cooked Crab

Also known as 'dressing', the presented crab meat is known as dressed crab. You will need a heavy knife for cutting the body in half, a teaspoon and a small pointed knife for scooping out the meat.

A rolling pin or large nut crackers are needed to crack the claws. Have a small dish for brown meat and a plate for the white meat. Also, have a polythene bag or some kitchen paper ready for the discarded parts.

1 Turn the crab upside down. First twist off the claws and legs and set them to one side.

2 Lift off the ridged flap which covers the middle of the crab. It lifts easily at the mouth end, then breaks off at the tail end where it is lightly attached.

3 With the mouth part of the crab away from you, grip the shell firmly on top, placing one hand on each side. Push your thumbs behind the body which is in the middle of the shell. Push the body out of the shell – it will come out to reveal a hard, honeycomb-like central section and the stomach.

4 Behind the mouth on the body you will find the stomach: discard this. Pull off the greyish finger shaped lungs from around the body and discard them. Cut the honeycomb main section in half and scoop out all the meat. Place this soft, beige-brown meat in the dish. Discard the empty honeycomb body.

5 Use a teaspoon to scoop the brown meat out of the shell and place it with the other meat from the body. Thoroughly wash the shell if it is to be used and rinse it

in clean boiling water. The opening in the shell may be made larger by cracking off the shell inside the natural curved lines on either side – it will come away easily when tapped with a firm implement.

6 Lastly, crack the claws and legs, then pick out all the meat from inside them. This is the white meat. It is normally presented separately from the brown meat.

Dressing

A medium to large dressed crab will serve 2 people. A small dressed crab makes a main meal portion for 1 or a starter for 2.

Mix the brown meat with about 25 g/1 oz fresh breadcrumbs, seasoning, a little lemon juice and some chopped parsley. Put this back in the shell, towards the sides. Pile the white meat in the middle.
Garnishing Crab Cut a hard-boiled egg in half and separate the egg from the white. Finely chop the white and use a teaspoon to arrange it in a neat line down the middle of the dressed crab. Press the yolk through a sieve, then arrange it in a neat

line down the middle of the egg white. Lastly, add neat lines of chopped fresh parsley and coarsely grated lemon rind.

Serving Ideas

● Offer mayonnaise and thinly sliced bread and butter with the crab. Salad may also be served.

● Serve brown meat as a spread on open sandwiches or with toast triangles.

● White meat may be added to a savoury white sauce, spooned into flameproof dishes, topped with breadcrumbs and grated cheese, then grilled until golden.

Devilled Crab

A good way of serving brown meat (fresh or canned). Mix 100 g/4 oz crab meat with 25 g/1 oz fresh breadcrumbs, 2 chopped spring onions, 1 crushed clove garlic, the grated rind of ½ lemon and a good squeeze of lemon juice. Add 2 chopped peeled tomatoes and 10 ml/2 teaspoons paprika and mix well. Season the mixture with a little salt and cayenne pepper (take care as cayenne is very hot), then taste it and add more cayenne if required.

Divide the mixture between four small ovenproof dishes and place a small knob of butter or margarine on each. Bake at 200°C, 400°F, gas 6 for 15 minutes. Serve with toast.

Freezing

Fresh crab, bought live, may be frozen for up to 6 weeks. The dressed meat is best served in a sauce, ready to be served hot, when it may be stored for 1–2 months.

Nutritional Value

Crab is a low-fat protein food. It provides calcium and niacin (see vitamin B group).

Preparing Cooked Crab
(Numbers relate to text steps)

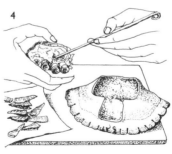

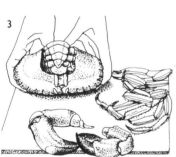

Crab Apples

See Apples*.

Small, hard uncultivated apples. These vary in size and colour, from yellow, blushed red-orange, plum-sized fruit to small, apple-shaped fruit with bright red peel. They are hard and sour. Trim off bad parts, wash, then cut up and cook in water until pulpy. The strained juice is used to make a bright, full-flavoured jelly.

Cracked Wheat

This is wheat which is part crushed but not cooked.

Buying

Do not confuse this with bulgur*, which is part cooked; ordinary wheat, which requires lengthy cooking; or kibbled wheat which is crushed, uncooked grain.

Storing

Keep in an airtight container in a cool cupboard for the time recommended on the packet: the grain does taste rancid if old.

Cooking

Place 225 g/8 oz in a saucepan with 600 ml/1 pint cold water. Bring to the boil, reduce the heat and cover the pan. Simmer for 30 minutes, until tender and all the water is absorbed. Fork a little butter and seasoning into the grain and serve.

Use

Hot or cold, in place of rice. Combined with mince it is a good meat extender.

Cranberries

See Fruit*.

These firm, small red berries are related to blueberries, bilberries and whortle berries. Cranberries have an excellent fruity flavour but they are sour, so they should be sweetened.

Buying

Fresh berries are available from November through to Christmas. Frozen fruit and jars of cranberry sauce are available all year, although many shops do not stock the frozen fruit all year. Look for bright, glossy berries – they are rarely poor quality as they keep very well.

Storing

Keep the berries in their carton in the bottom of the refrigerator. They keep well for several weeks if they are not squashed. Cranberries contain a natural preservative and will keep for long periods in constant cold.

Cooking

Cranberries are usually cooked but may be puréed raw. They need no preparation other than washing.

Place the berries in a saucepan with a little water or other liquid – about 30 ml/2 tablespoons for

Cranberry Sauce

Place 225 g/8 oz cranberries in a saucepan with the juice of 1 orange and 175 g/6 oz sugar. Heat gently, stirring occasionally, until the sugar dissolves and the liquid simmers, then cook for a further 12–15 minutes, or until the cranberries pop and burst. Stir well. Remove the pan from the heat and stir in 45 ml/3 tablespoons port. Transfer to a serving dish and leave to cool.

Serve with roast turkey, goose, duck, pork, gammon or game.

each 100 g/4 oz fruit. Sugar may be added at this stage – about three-quarters the weight of fruit or an equal quantity is usual for sweet recipes or for sauce. Heat the fruit until any sugar dissolves and the liquid simmers, then cook for about 10–15 minutes, or until the cranberries pop and burst. Stir the fruit occasionally. **Microwave Cooking** Place the fruit, liquid and sugar in a suitable covered dish. Cook on High, allowing about 5 minutes for 225 g/8 oz cranberries with an equal weight of sugar. Stir once during cooking.

Use

Use in stuffing*, sweet and savoury sauces, preserves, relishes and desserts.

Freezing

Fresh cranberries freeze well for up to a year. Wash and dry them well before freezing.

Nutritional Value

Fresh and frozen cranberries are rich in vitamin C.

Cream

There are two different types of cream – dairy cream (fresh or 'real' cream) and non-dairy cream (including dessert toppings). Fromage frais is a good substitute for cream.

Dairy Cream

There are many types of dairy cream, categorised according to fat content. Exact regulations are imposed by law on cream production. The following are the main types of fresh cream that are available.

Half Cream Minimum fat content: 12 per cent. It is a thin cream for using in coffee or for pouring over desserts. It may also be used for making set custard instead of milk, or for enriching savoury sauces.

Single Cream Minimum fat content: 18 per cent. For pouring but not suitable for whipping. Single cream may be served with coffee, poured over desserts, used in custards and sauces, or added to savoury dishes.

Whipping Cream Minimum fat content: 35 per cent. Obviously, this cream is suitable for whipping as well as for pouring. When whipped it produces a soft peak; it does not give as firm a result as double cream. It is useful for folding into mousses, for making ice creams and for other recipes that require whipped cream. Whipping cream does not hold its shape well for long periods so it is not suitable for piping decorations on gâteaux. It may be used for filling cakes and pastries that are to be eaten promptly.

Spooning Cream Minimum fat content: 35 per cent or slightly lower. This cream is homogenised to make it thick. It will not whip but it may be spooned over fruit or desserts.

Double Cream Minimum fat content: 48 per cent. For pouring or whipping. Double cream holds well once it is whipped and is suitable for decorating cakes.

Extra Thick Double Cream Minimum fat content: 48 per cent. This is homogenised and it is very thick. It may be spooned over desserts or fruit; some brands are thick enough for serving in place of clotted cream with scones. It will not whip.

Clotted Cream Minimum fat content: 55 per cent. Thick, yellow cream with a rich, buttery flavour. For spreading on scones or serving with fruit. Not for whipping. Not for adding to sauces or for use in cooking.

Soured Cream Minimum fat content: 18 per cent. This is single cream which is treated with a culture of bacteria (the expression 'cultured' cream is also used) which gives the cream a fresh tang and makes it thicken slightly. Used in sweet or savoury cooking. When soured cream is not available, add 15 ml/1 tablespoon lemon juice to 150 ml/¼ pint single cream instead. The texture is not as good and the taste is different but it is a reasonable substitute.

Crème Fraîche French-style equivalent of soured cream. Soured cream may be substituted.

Whipped Cream Minimum fat content: 35 per cent. Ready whipped cream may be sweetened and it may contain stabilisers. Cartons of frozen cream are often whipped. Buying whipping cream and whipping it yourself makes better sense: although a carton of whipped cream may look good value for money, remember that cream increases in volume on whipping.

Aerosol Cream This is UHT cream which is sweetened and packed in aerosol cans. It is foamed rather than whipped and it collapses quickly. Use for topping desserts or drinks.

UHT Cream This ultra heat treated cream is available in single, whipping and double cream form. The cream is heated to at least 140°C/284°F and held at that temperature for not less than 2 seconds to kill bacteria. The cream is also homogenised, then packed under sterile conditions in which state it has a long shelf life. Once the pack is opened the cream must be treated as fresh cream. Because it is homogenised (see milk*), UHT double cream does not whip (it becomes too thick). UHT cream is useful for pouring or for adding to dishes. It has a flavour which is very similar to fresh cream.

Sterilised or Canned Cream Minimum fat content: 23 per cent. To produce sterilised cream, homogenised cream is canned, then heated to at least 108°C/226°F and kept at that temperature for not less than 45 minutes before rapid cooling. This heating process causes the sugar present in the cream (lactose) to caramelise which gives the product its characteristic 'cooked' flavour. Canned cream may be spooned over desserts or used in dips and other recipes but it does not whip. It may be used with care in savoury cooking (for example to enrich sauces) but it should not be added lavishly as its cooked flavour can add an unwanted hint of sweetness.

Frozen Cream Single, whipping, double and whipped cream are all available ready frozen. The cream may be packed in cartons (whipped cream is only available this way) or it may be frozen in pieces (fingers or chips) and packed in bags. Whipped cream may be sweetened.

Free-flow packets are a good buy as small amounts of cream may be removed as required.

Care must be taken to follow the manufacturer's instructions on thawing frozen cream. This is best done in the refrigerator.

Buying and Storing Dairy Cream

Always check the date on the carton to make sure the cream is fresh and use it by the recommended date. Sealed cartons with additional plastic covers are useful if any of the cream is likely to be left over.

Keep cream cool and put it in the refrigerator as soon as possible after purchase.

Once opened, UHT and canned cream should be treated as fresh cream. Transfer the cream to a small basin and keep it covered in the refrigerator.

Use absorbent kitchen paper to wipe the nozzle on aerosol cream after use as any cream remaining on the outside can harden and go off. Always use aerosol cans within the recommended period.

Cream cakes and desserts should be kept covered and chilled. A large upturned container should be used to cover decorated cakes or desserts.

Freezing

Whipped cream (whipping or double) may be frozen successfully but other types are not suitable for home freezing. Place the whipped cream in a covered container, allowing headspace, and freeze for up to 2 months.

Whipping Cream

Chilled cream gives the best volume. Ideally, have the bowl and utensils chilled as well.

Choice of Whisk A hand-held wire whisk is, in theory, the ideal utensil as it incorporates the most air into the cream. It is also hard work if you are whipping anything other than a small amount of cream.

A rotary whisk or hand-held electric beater are the most practical since they make light work of whipping, at the same time giving a good volume.

Avoid using a powerful, large electric whisk unless you are working with catering quantities. This type of machine whips the cream too quickly, giving poor volume or, worse, over-whipping the cream.

Technique: Avoiding Over-whipping Use a basin or bowl which gives a fair depth of cream – if the cream merely forms a small puddle in the bottom of a large bowl it will not whip evenly and will not give good volume.

The aim when whipping cream is to incorporate air. The fat globules in the cream trap the air and this makes the mixture foam and gives it the characteristic texture. Single cream does not contain enough fat to form a foam with air when whipped.

It is easy to see what happens to fat in a warm room – simply compare butter from the refrigerator with butter at room temperature. If the fat in the cream is chilled, and kept cool during whipping, the particles will hold their shape and trap more air. Whipping cream must be chilled in order to give good results. If double cream is too warm, then it quickly forms a buttery mixture.

Whip the cream until it forms a soft thick mixture. If the cream is to be piped, continue whipping it carefully, until it will just stand in soft peaks.

Cream that is firm is over-whipped and as soon as it is spooned from the bowl to use for spreading or topping it will begin to look curdled. This does not affect the taste but the appearance is spoilt. Also, the cream soon becomes watery when used.

Piping Cream

Use a large, cloth piping bag and a metal nozzle. The cream should just hold its shape in soft peaks. It is ready for piping when it looks very slightly too soft. If it is whipped until it looks 'just right' by the time it has been transferred to the piping bag and pushed out it will have a grainy, if not slightly curdled, texture.

Whip cream for piping just before it is to be used. Place the nozzle in the bag, then place the bag in a deep jug, folding the opening back over the jug rim.

Wash your hands under cold water and dry them. Use a spoon to transfer large portions of cream to the bag at a time. Avoid working the cream at all by scraping it down in the bag as this will thicken the cream slightly. The bag should be no more than two-thirds full so that the top may be gathered up in one hand. Never work with a huge bag full of cream that you cannot handle.

Hold the end of the nozzle in position before squeezing any cream out of the bag. Turn or move the bag as you squeeze, then stop squeezing just before you have completed the individual rosette or other decoration.

Cooking with Cream

Cream is added to soups, sauces and casseroles to enrich or thicken them. The cream should be added just before the dish is served. Once the cream is added the dish should not be over-heated and liquids must not boil otherwise the cream will curdle. Cream should not be added to dishes before freezing – it should be stirred in after reheating.

Cream in the Diet

As a high-fat food, cream should not be eaten frequently in lavish quantities. However, there is no reason to avoid it completely. Also, as with all fats, it should be considered as part of the overall amount of fat which is consumed.

Low-fat Alternatives

For everyday use, low-fat yogurt and fromage frais are good substitutes for cream. These may also be used instead of cream by anyone who is following a low-fat or calorie reduced diet. Remember that fromage frais and yogurt curdle more easily than cream when heated.

Non-Dairy Creams

These include dessert toppings and synthetic creams, both prepared and sold chilled or as packet mixes. Usually sweetened, they are useful for sweet cookery. Some unsweetened types have limited use in savouries such as mousses.

Lower Fat Creams These are made from buttermilk and vegetable oils. They may be used instead of single, whipping or double cream for savoury or sweet cooking and are virtually identical in flavour, with good cooking qualities. They have a longer refrigerator life – check the carton for details – and the advantage of containing significantly less fat than ordinary dairy cream. They also tend to be less expensive than dairy cream.

Cream of Tartar

An acid which is used in baking powder. Combined with bicarbonate of soda in the proportions of 10–15 ml/2–3 teaspoons cream of tartar to 5 ml/1 teaspoon bicarbonate of soda, cream of tartar is used as a very effective raising agent for scones.

Crockery and Cutlery

Buying crockery and cutlery is an expensive business and best done gradually, starting with a few basic, essential items.

For Kitchen or Table

Most equipment can be divided into two distinct areas of use: for food preparation in the kitchen or for serving meals. In practice, there is a certain amount of overlap in the domestic kitchen; for example cereal bowls may be used for beating eggs, dinner plates are useful for holding food in preparation and so on.

Kitchen Cutlery

Start with the minimum of equipment, then buy as you need.
Knives Start with one good-quality, medium-sized cook's knife with a thin blade that sharpens well. Specific notes on selecting and using knives* are given separately.
Spoons and Spatulas A sturdy mixing spoon is the second most important basic piece of equipment – you need this if only to stir the baked beans as they heat.

Do not go straight for the wooden type as there are alternatives which are just as strong and more hygienic. Wood is absorbent, so food particles may cling to the surface and, if not completely cleaned off, provide an area on which bacteria can grow. Do not use wooden utensils with raw meat and poultry. Boil

wooden spoons occasionally.

Look for strong plastic utensils that are manufactured to withstand cooking temperatures.
Other Kitchen Cutlery Whisks, sieves, mashers, straining spoons, fish slices and many more items are useful and they make cooking easier but they are not essential in the first instance.

If you are buying, look for good quality equipment with handles that are firmly attached, not loosely stuck in place.

Think about what use each item is likely to have in your kitchen before buying. Handle kitchen cutlery before you buy it to make sure it is comfortable to hold and suits you. This may sound silly but most cooks have a favourite whisk or vegetable peeler. Remember too that if a piece of equipment is intended for a tough task it should be sturdy – a flimsy vegetable masher or dainty whisk may look attractive but will they work? Probably not.

Check Before Buying

Remember these few points before buying kitchen cutlery or use them as a checklist to sort out existing equipment.

- Do I need it and for what use?

- What is it made of? If it's wooden is it likely to be a hygiene risk?

- What sort of handle has it got? Look for secure, well fitted handles.

- Is it dishwasher proof? Is every bit of it washable? How easy is it to clean?

- Is it likely to rust?

- Does it look strong enough to stand up to hard wear?

Kitchen Crockery

A measuring jug, basins, plates and baking dishes come into this category. Strong serving plates, bowls and mugs have many uses in the kitchen but delicate china should be reserved for serving.

Materials Glassware, glazed earthenware and plastic are the three main materials.

Ovenproof glassware is versatile and inexpensive: a good buy as it may be used in the microwave, oven, steamer or for mixing food.

Glazed earthenware bowls and basins may be ovenproof. For food preparation, avoid an unglazed earthenware as it is absorbent and not practical in a food preparation environment. It may be fine for baking or serving purposes but it is not suitable for beating eggs and mixing raw ingredients. Even if the inside is glazed, any spillages and drips will run down the unglazed surface.

There are so many types of plastic containers that it is difficult to generalise. Look for strong, well finished items. Check whether they will withstand boiling water, steaming or using for mixing hot food.

Look for dishes with handles, non-slip bases or lids so that you can maximise their use. Price is a good guide to quality.
Sorting Out Turn out the kitchen equipment occasionally.

Chips and cracks are unhygienic and they can be dangerous. A cracked bowl may well break and cause a nasty accident.

X *Cracks and chips in crockery trap particles of food or dirt and provide a good place for bacteria to multiply. Throw away damaged crockery – or use it for holding plants.*

Multiple-Use Crockery Some items of equipment are designed for storing food in the refrigerator or freezer as well as for microwave cooking or conventional baking. They include measuring jugs, basins and containers. See also baking tins and bakeware*.

Storing Kitchen Crockery

Just three main points to remember here.

SEE ALSO **Crème Brûlée, Crème Caramel:** Custard; **Crêpe:** Glossary; **Cress:** Salads, Watercress;

Cleanliness Some decorative hanging racks are attractive, but unless the items hung up are used very often, they gather grease and dirt.

Safety Some of the most obvious rules of safety are easily forgotten. For example, it's easy to pile up crockery so that taking out the bottom item becomes hazardous. More dangerous is rummaging in a drawer for a utensil among sharp implements. If you do store sharp knives in a drawer, without separating them in a compartment, keep them in plastic sheaths.

Ease of Access Closely linked to safety and making the best of your kitchen. Store the items used most often in places where they can be reached quickly and easily.

Cross Contamination

See Bacteria* and Hygiene*.

This is the term used for transferring bacteria from one food to another, particularly from raw food to cooked dishes or food that is served raw.

For example, uncooked chicken may well contain *Salmonella* bacteria. As the chicken is prepared for cooking, the bacteria may be spread from the flesh to the cutting board, the knife, any plate or other crockery used or the surrounding work surface. If the chicken is properly cooked, the bacteria are destroyed but bacteria transferred to the utensils and surroundings must not be forgotten. Perhaps there is a salad to be served with the chicken. If the raw ingredients for salad are cut on the unwashed board, or using the unwashed knife, the bacteria will be transferred to them. Since the salad ingredients are not cooked, the bacteria will remain alive. Worse, in fact, because there is every chance that those bacteria will multiply between the time

taken to prepare and serve the salad.

Avoiding Cross Contamination

These must be the golden rules of food preparation.

• Never prepare or serve cooked foods or foods to be eaten uncooked with the same utensils used for preparing raw fish, poultry, meat, eggs or unwashed vegetables.

• Always wash all utensils used for preparing raw fish, meat, poultry, unwashed vegetables and eggs after every use.

• Wash the surrounding work surface after every use.

• Wash your hands immediately after handling these uncooked foods and before handling any other equipment or food.

• Take particular care with 'al fresco' cooking – it is remarkably easy to overlook normal hygienic precautions when you are barbecuing. Particularly when there is a crowd to feed too.

Croûtons

These are small pieces of fried bread, usually tiny dice but they may be slightly larger and cut in all sorts of shapes.

Making

Cut slices of bread into dice. Heat a little oil (olive is good) and a knob of butter (if liked) in a frying pan. Add the bread and lightly toss them in the fat at once so that they are evenly coated. Cook over medium heat, stirring often, until the pieces of bread are crisp and golden all over.

Drain the croûtons on absorbent kitchen paper.

Use

To garnish soups and savoury dishes. They are also delicious in

salads – add them at the last minute so they stay crunchy.

Flavouring Croûtons

• Cook a crushed clove garlic in the oil for a few seconds before adding the bread.

• Toss chopped fresh herbs or grated lemon rind with the cooked croûtons – the lemon croûtons are good with fish.

Crumble Toppings

These may be savoury or sweet. Use them for topping fish in sauce, meat mixtures, moist vegetable mixtures or fruit.

Making a Good Crumble

The secret is rubbing the fat into the flour lightly (page 54). The crumble topping should be sprinkled lightly over the base and it must not be too thick. The base should be moist and full flavoured to complement the crumble topping which should be crisp and browned.

Storing

The crumble topping may be rubbed in up to 2 days ahead and stored in a sealed polythene bag or covered container in the refrigerator, then sprinkled over the base just before cooking. If the crumble is sprinkled over several hours before cooking it will absorb moisture from the base ingredients and become heavy and soggy.

Varying Sweet Crumble

The following suggestions may be combined to make exciting toppings. If the crumble is to be frozen they should be added just before it is used, not before freezing the mixture.

• Add grated orange rind and 10 ml/2 teaspoons ground cinnamon.

- Add 100 g/4 oz chopped nuts, such as toasted hazelnuts, walnuts or almonds.

- Add 100 g/4 oz ground almonds.

- Add 50 g/2 oz rolled oats and use 50 g/2 oz demerara or soft brown sugar.

- Add 50 g/2 oz chocolate chips or grated chocolate.

Varying Savoury Crumble

- Add chopped fresh herbs (as well as the parsley suggested) to complement the ingredients used in the base.

- Add 25–50 g/1–2 oz chopped roasted peanuts. Good with meat sauce made with minced pork.

- Add grated lemon rind and use the topping with fish in white sauce.

- Add 50 g/2 oz chopped mushrooms and 50 g/2 oz rolled oats or branflakes.

Cooking Crumbles

Savoury The base ingredients should be cooked before the crumble topping is added. Meats that require long cooking to tenderise them (casseroles, stews or braised meat) should be fully cooked. Poultry should be boneless and cut in bite-size pieces. It should be browned and mixed with a suitable sauce, then it may be allowed to finish cooking under the topping. Fish should be added raw to a cooked sauce and allowed to cook under the topping. The majority of vegetable mixtures, beans and pulses should be cooked before the crumble topping is added.

Set the oven at 190°C, 375°F, gas 5 and allow 30–40 minutes cooking time, until the topping is crisp and golden, and the base cooked through.
Sweet Set the oven at 190°C, 375°F, gas 5 and allow 40–45 minutes cooking, depending on the fruit used. The topping should be golden and crisp.

BASIC SWEET CRUMBLE

The food values given are for the crumble topping only; when calculating the content of a complete dish, remember to add on the values for the base mixture.

INGREDIENTS
175 g/6 oz plain flour
75 g/3 oz margarine
25 g/1 oz sugar

Serves 4

FOOD VALUES:
TOTAL • PER PORTION
kcals: 1259 • 315
kJ: 5283 • 1321
protein: 17 g • 4 g
fat: 63 g • 16 g
carbohydrate: 167 g • 42 g
fibre: 6 g • 1.5 g

Place the flour in a bowl. Add the fat, then use a knife to cut it into small pieces. Wash and dry your hands under cold water. Rub the fat into the flour until the mixture resembles fine breadcrumbs. Stir in the sugar.

The crumble topping is ready to use: it may have other ingredients added if liked. Sprinkle the mixture over a base of prepared fruit – apples, plums, rhubarb or a mixture of fresh fruit. Remember that canned fruit, such as peaches or apricots, go well with fresh fruit. Dried apricots (the ready-to-eat type), figs, raisins or sultanas may also be mixed with fresh fruit.

This mixture is sufficient to top up to 1 kg/2 lb fresh fruit.

BASIC SAVOURY CRUMBLE

An excellent freezer standby for speedy suppers, spoon the frozen mixture thinly over canned baked beans mixed with diced cooked ham and chopped spring onion.

INGREDIENTS
75 g/3 oz plain flour
25 g/1 oz margarine
75 g/3 oz fresh wholemeal breadcrumbs
25 g/1 oz mature Cheddar cheese, grated
30 ml/2 tablespoons grated Parmesan cheese (optional)
salt and pepper
60 ml/4 tablespoons chopped fresh parsley

FOOD VALUES:
TOTAL • PER PORTION
kcals: 997 • 249
kJ: 4181 • 1045
protein: 44 g • 11 g
fat: 43 g • 11 g
carbohydrate: 116 g • 29 g
fibre: 9 g • 2 g

Serves 4

Place the flour in a bowl. Add the fat and cut it into pieces. Wash and dry your hands using cold water. Rub the fat into the flour. Stir in the breadcrumbs, Cheddar and Parmesan (if used). Add seasoning and the parsley, then mix well. The crumble topping is ready for use.

Sprinkle it over savoury sauces – vegetables in sauce, ratatouille, lentils or bean mixtures, fish in sauce, minced meat sauces or braised or stewed meat.

SEE ALSO **Crustaceans, Crystallised:** Glossary; **Cumin:** Spices; **Curd Cheese:** Cheese; **Currants:** Dried and Candied Fruit

Freezing

Plain crumble toppings freeze well for up to 3 months. They may be used from frozen.

Cucumber

Available all year, cucumber is a familiar salad ingredient; however it may also be braised or used to make soup.

Buying

Look for a firm cucumber. Inspect shrink-wrapped vegetables very carefully for any signs of brown spots which indicate that the cucumber is past its prime. Avoid any that are slightly yellowed and soft.

Storing

Unwrap shrink wrapped cucumber. Keep cucumber in the refrigerator. Cover the cut end of a cucumber by sliding the vegetable into a small polythene bag. A fresh cucumber will keep for about a week in the refrigerator.

Ridge Cucumbers

These small, plump, thick-skinned cucumbers are used for pickling. They should be salted, then rinsed and drained before pickling in spiced vinegar. Sprigs of fresh dill and onion slices may be added.

Use

• Cut into long strips. Sauté in butter with onion, then braise in chicken stock for 20–25 minutes. Thicken and season. Serve with lamb, chicken or fish.

• Cut into short thin strips and added to stir fry dishes. Cucumber should be added about a minute before the stir fry is ready otherwise it quickly becomes limp and watery.

CUMBERLAND SAUCE

This fruity sauce is traditionally served with baked or boiled ham or bacon, or grilled gammon. It also complements grilled or roast lamb or pork. Crab apple jelly may be used instead of the redcurrant jelly.

INGREDIENTS
100 g/4 oz redcurrant jelly
coarsely grated rind of
1 orange and juice of
2 oranges
60 ml/4 tablespoons port
5 ml/1 teaspoon arrowroot
(optional)
Serves 4

FOOD VALUES:
TOTAL • PER PORTION
kcals: 415 • 104
kJ: 1763 • 441
protein: 2 g • 0 g
fat: 0 g • 0 g
carbohydrate: 91 g • 23 g
fibre: 4 g • 1 g

Place the redcurrant jelly in a small saucepan. Add the orange rind and juice, then heat the mixture gently, stirring occasionally, until the jelly melts. Add the port and heat through until just boiling. Remove the pan from the heat. The sauce may be served at this stage.

If you would prefer to thicken the sauce slightly, mix the arrowroot with just a little water to make a smooth paste, then stir in a spoonful of the hot sauce. Pour the arrowroot mixture into the sauce, stirring. Return the pan to the heat and bring the sauce back to the boil, stirring all the time. Remove the pan from the heat as soon as the sauce boils.

MICROWAVE COOKING

Place all the ingredients, except the arrowroot, in a suitable jug or basin. Heat, uncovered, on High for about 5 minutes, whisking once, until hot and the jelly has melted. Cook on High for about 1 minute after the arrowroot has been added, until slightly thickened.

• To make soup, peel and dice a cucumber, then sauté it with a chopped onion. Add chicken stock and simmer for 30 minutes. Purée the mixture, thin with cream or milk and season. Serve hot or chilled.

Tsatziki

A Greek dip. Coarsely grate ½ cucumber, then squeeze all the liquid from it. Mix it with 1 crushed clove garlic, 15 ml/ 1 tablespoon finely chopped onion and 300 ml/½ pint Greek yogurt. When in season, a little chopped mint may be added. Season to taste and serve with chunks of crusty bread as a starter.

Curry

The name curry or 'kari' means sauce and the dish is made of food cooked in a curry sauce.

Curry Spices

Curry powder is a Western interpretation of authentic Indian spice mixtures, prepared individually for specific dishes. The quality of the commercial curry powders has improved but vibrant yellow, poorly flavoured ones do still exist. Price is a good guide to quality.

Rather than buying ready mixed spices, have a go at mixing them at home. The main spices used for flavouring curry are fenugreek, cumin, coriander, cinnamon, turmeric, cloves, ginger and chilli powder. They may be mixed in quantities to suit your taste, always considering the food which is to be spiced.

Even if you do not want to keep a variety of spices, a simple combination of ground cumin and coriander (twice the quantity of coriander to cumin), cooked with garlic and a bay leaf, make a delicious base for seasoning all sorts of food, from fish and poultry to vegetables and pulses.

Using Curry Sauce

The basic recipe for curry sauce is mild and full flavoured with sweet spices. It may be used with all foods: fish and seafood, poultry, meat, vegetables and pulses. Depending on the type of food to be curried, the sauce may be used in different ways.

Fish and Seafood Prepare the curry sauce and cook it completely before adding the fish or seafood. Cod steaks or fillet, coley fillet (in large portions or cut into chunks), peeled cooked prawns or squid rings may be added to the sauce. Once the seafood is added, bring the sauce back to a simmer, cover the pan and cook gently for 15–25 minutes, or until the seafood is cooked. Peeled cooked prawns simply need heating through thoroughly. Take care not to overcook fish until it breaks up.

Poultry To give the cooked flesh the best flavour, remove the skin and cut several slashes into large portions. Quarters, thighs or boneless portions may be used. Cubed raw turkey breast is also suitable.

Brown the poultry all over in hot oil (or ghee), then add the curry sauce and bring just to the boil. Reduce the heat, cover the pan and simmer gently until the poultry is cooked through. Allow 45–60 minutes for quarters, slightly less for smaller portions. Slow, longer cooking is best as it allows time for the flavour of the spices to penetrate the meat. Cubes of boneless meat will cook in 20–30 minutes.

CURRY SAUCE

I have used a modest amount of chilli powder in this recipe – it may be adjusted to taste or omitted completely.

INGREDIENTS
25 g/1 oz fresh root ginger
45 ml/3 tablespoons oil
1 large onion, finely chopped
2 cloves garlic, crushed
1 bay leaf
1 cinnamon stick
6 green cardamoms (optional)
4 whole cloves
15 ml/1 tablespoon ground fenugreek
30 ml/2 tablespoons ground cumin
60 ml/4 tablespoons ground coriander
5 ml/1 teaspoon turmeric

5 ml/1 teaspoon chilli powder
30 ml/2 tablespoons tomato purée
750 ml/1¼ pints water
salt and pepper

FOOD VALUES:
TOTAL • PER PORTION
kcals: 703 • 176
kJ: 2911 • 728
protein: 19 g • 5 g
fat: 50 g • 13 g
carbohydrate: 48 g • 12 g
fibre: 1 g • 0 g

Serves 4

Use a heavy based saucepan for making the sauce. First prepare the ginger: the weighed piece should be trimmed of any very coarse ends. Wash the ginger, then grate coarsely, discarding the very last piece of peel that remains.

Heat the oil in a saucepan, then add the onion, ginger, garlic and bay leaf. Cook over low to medium heat, stirring occasionally, for about 10 minutes, or until the onion is soft but not browned. Add the cinnamon stick, cardamoms (if used) and cloves. Cook the whole spices for about 30 seconds before stirring in the ground fenugreek, cumin, coriander, turmeric and chilli. Stir the mixture well and continue to cook for 3 minutes.

Stir in the tomato purée and pour in the water. Add plenty of seasoning and bring the sauce to the boil, stirring all the time. Reduce the heat, cover the pan and simmer the sauce for 45 minutes. Stir the sauce occasionally during cooking. Taste the sauce and adjust the seasoning as necessary.

If the sauce is used for stewing or braising meat or poultry that requires more than 40 minutes cooking, simmer it for just 10 minutes first.

Check occasionally during cooking to make sure the curry does not become too dry and add a little extra water as necessary.

Cubed Meat Brown tough meat which requires long cooking in oil first, then pour in the curry sauce. Cover and simmer very gently until the meat is tender. Alternatively, stew the meat in the oven. If the meat is cooked on the hob, check occasionally to make sure the sauce does not

become too thick and add a little extra water.

Minced Meat Brown the mince over low to medium heat in a heavy pan without any extra fat. Drain off excess fat before adding the curry sauce. Bring to the boil, then reduce the heat and cover the pan. Simmer gently for 1 hour.

Vegetables Toss the vegetables in hot oil first, then pour in the sauce and bring to the boil. Reduce the heat, cover the pan and simmer gently for about 40 minutes, or until all the vegetables are tender.

Potatoes make a delicious curry on their own and a few frozen peas may be added half way through cooking.

For a mixed vegetable curry, use cubes of parsnip, carrot, potato and pumpkin or marrow (if available). Add cauliflower florets after 10 minutes cooking. Frozen cut green beans or peas may be added about 10 minutes before the end of cooking.

A variety of other vegetables may be used, including cubes of aubergine*, green or red peppers*, okra or spinach*. Spinach is delicious curried: cook and drain, then stir it into the sauce and serve topped with chopped hard-boiled eggs.

Pulses Dried or canned beans make good curries as they readily absorb the flavour of the spices. Since they are starchy, they also take quite a hot sauce.

Soak and cook dried pulses until they are only just tender, then drain them before adding to the sauce. Simmer the pulses very gently in the sauce for a further 30 minutes before serving.

Add drained canned pulses to the sauce – chick peas and red kidney beans taste terrific.

Eggs These may be curried in two ways: add hard-boiled eggs to the cooked sauce and heat them gently for 15 minutes.

Alternatively, pour the sauce into a fairly deep frying pan and heat until it is simmering. Break eggs individually into a mug, then slide them into the sauce and poach for about 5 minutes or until they are cooked to taste.

Curried Cooked Meats Cold cooked poultry or meat may be curried and this is a good way of using up leftover roasts. Cut the meat into pieces and add to the sauce. Simmer very gently, covered, for about 15–20 minutes, or until the leftovers are thoroughly reheated.

Use canned beans or parboiled potatoes to make a small amount of meat go further.

Freezing

Make and cool the sauce, then pack it in a rigid container allowing a little headspace. Freeze for up to 6 months.

Curtains

There are two reasons for including a note about curtains.

If the window is anywhere near a cooker it is probably best to avoid curtains. Have a blind that rolls up away from the heat source to avoid danger of fire.

Secondly, curtains must be washable because they attract dust and grease. For hygiene purposes, make sure curtains are short enough to sit neatly away from any food preparation areas.

Custard

A custard is a liquid which is set or thickened with egg. Some custards have flour as a thickening as well as the egg.

Curdling: What and Why?

A custard sets or thickens when the protein in the egg is part coagulated (or part cooked). In this

CONFECTIONER'S CUSTARD

INGREDIENTS
25 g/1 oz plain flour
5 ml/1 teaspoon natural vanilla essence
3 egg yolks
30 ml/2 tablespoons caster sugar
300 ml/½ pint milk
150 ml/¼ pint whipping or double cream, or fromage frais

FOOD VALUES: TOTAL
(Using whipping cream)
kcals: 1082
kJ: 4501
protein: 24 g
fat: 81 g
carbohydrate: 69 g
fibre: 1 g

Makes about 600 ml/1 pint

Place the flour in a basin. Add the vanilla essence, egg yolks and sugar, then pour in a little of the milk, stirring to make a smooth paste. Gradually pour in the remaining milk. Pour the smooth mixture into a saucepan and heat gently, stirring all the time, until it begins to thicken.

As some of the flour cooks it will form lumps so stir the custard vigorously. Carry on stirring until the custard comes to the boil by which time it will be very thick. Beat it well and all the lumps will break down. Reduce the heat so that the mixture is just bubbling and continue to cook for 3–4 minutes, stirring most of the time. This is important otherwise the custard will taste of raw flour.

Remove the pan from the heat. Dampen a piece of greaseproof paper and press it on the surface of the custard, then set aside to cool. When cool, transfer the custard to a bowl and cover it, then chill for several hours or overnight.

Whip the cream until it stands in soft peaks. Beat the thick custard thoroughly until it is smooth. An electric beater may be used for this. Fold the cream or fromage frais into the thick custard, then use as required.

USE

To fill pastries, flans or cakes, pipe on gâteaux or top a trifle: use double the quantity of cream or fromage frais.

state, the egg remains mixed with the liquid. If the mixture is overcooked or heated to too high a temperature, the protein in the egg hardens. Once this stage is reached the egg separates from the liquid, forming small lumps or curds. This is when the mixture is said to be curdled.

Curdled custards are disastrous because they cannot be rescued. When the egg cooks with the liquid it combines with any fat present (for example in milk or cream) and this separates out with the solid egg, leaving a thin whey. Both taste and texture are unpleasant.

Avoiding Curdling
Do not heat custards too fiercely and do not heat them for too long as both will cause the egg to cook completely and curdle.

There are exceptions to this rule. For example, confectioner's custard is thickened with a significant amount of flour as well as egg yolks. The flour stabilises the yolks. The fact that egg whites are not used also makes the custard more stable because whites harden at a lower temperature than yolks.

• Custard sauces made without significant amounts of flour should be cooked in a bowl over hot water or double saucepan.

• Do not allow the water under the custard to boil: it should be kept over low heat.

• Stir or whisk the custard sauce all the time to prevent any areas from becoming too hot against the side of the bowl.

• In the oven, always stand the dish in a bain marie (see Glossary, page 275).

• In the microwave check custards frequently – every 30 seconds after the first half of the cooking time.

Types of Custard

Pouring or Custard Sauce This is made by cooking eggs and milk in a bowl over hot water or in a

SET CUSTARD

INGREDIENTS
600 ml/1 pint milk
2 size 1/large eggs
2 size 1/large egg yolks
30 ml/2 tablespoons caster sugar
2.5–5 ml/½–1 teaspoon natural vanilla essence
Serves 4

FOOD VALUES:
TOTAL • PER PORTION
kcals: 956 • 239
kJ: 3992 • 998
protein: 47 g • 12 g
fat: 60 g • 15 g
carbohydrate: 60 g • 15 g
fibre: 0 g • 0 g

Set the oven at 150°C, 300°F, gas 2. Prepare a bain marie: have a roasting tin and boiling water ready for holding the dish of custard. Grease a 900 ml/1½ pint ovenproof dish with a little butter. Heat the milk in a saucepan until it is just about to boil.

Beat the eggs, egg yolks and sugar with the vanilla essence in a bowl. Allow the milk to cool for a few seconds, then pour it into the eggs, stirring all the time. Strain the custard through a fine sieve into the prepared dish (this removes any stringy parts from the egg whites). Stand the dish in the roasting tin and pour in boiling water around the dish to come almost up to the rim of the roasting tin. Lay a piece of greaseproof paper over the top of the dish of custard.

Bake the custard in the bain marie for 1–1¼ hours, or until it is set. When set, the top of the custard will feel wobbly. Serve the custard hot or allow it to cool in the bain marie, then chill.

VARIATIONS
Individual Custards Divide the custard between 4 small ovenproof dishes and bake them in a bain marie, as above, allowing 45 minutes, or until the custard is set.
Crème Caramel or Caramel Custard Line the dish with caramel* first. Half and half single cream and milk may be used to make the custard. Cool and chill the custard overnight, then invert it on to a serving dish. Individual dishes may be used instead of the large one.
Crème Brûlée Use half and half double cream and milk (or all double cream for a really rich pudding). Cool and chill the custard. Cover the top of the custard with a thick layer of soft brown sugar, then chill it again for 30 minutes or more. Just before serving, put the custard under a preheated hot grill until the sugar melts and caramelises – this is very quick so stand and watch the sugar, removing it as soon as it is bubbling.
Baked Custard Tart Use an extra egg and omit 1 yolk, then pour the custard into a cooked pastry case. Bake as above, without the bain marie as the pastry protects the sides of the custard from overheating.
Other Puddings The basic custard mixture may be poured over bread and butter, left to soak for at least 30 minutes, then baked to make a bread and butter pudding. Dried fruit may be added to the basic pudding. Sponge cake may be soaked in custard and baked. When cooled and chilled, the unmoulded pudding may be decorated with whipped cream.
Savoury Custard Omit the sugar and vanilla. Season the custard with salt and pepper. Pour it over flaked drained canned tuna fish mixed with 30 ml/2 tablespoons snipped chives. This is best made in 4 individual ramekin dishes. Serve from the dishes.

POURING CUSTARD

INGREDIENTS
4 size 1/large egg yolks
45 ml/3 tablespoons caster
sugar
2.5 ml/½ teaspoon natural
vanilla essence
600 ml/1 pint milk

FOOD VALUES:
TOTAL • PER PORTION
kcals: 839 • 300
kJ: 3510 • 878
protein: 33 g • 8 g
fat: 47 g • 12 g
carbohydrate: 76 g • 19 g
fibre: 0 g • 0 g

Serves 4

Place the egg yolks, sugar and vanilla in a heatproof bowl. Prepare a saucepan of hot water on which to stand the bowl. Heat the milk in a saucepan until it is just about to boil.

Whisk the yolk mixture in a bowl until it is pale, thick and creamy. Remove the milk from the heat just before it boils up and leave to cool for a few seconds. Pour the milk over the yolks, whisking lightly all the time. Stand the bowl over the pan of hot water and cook the custard until it forms a milky coating on the back of a mixing spoon. Remember this custard will not resemble a custard made from custard powder – it is far thinner and more delicate in colour. If you continue cooking the mixture, expecting it to thicken as when made with flour, it will curdle.

Keep the pan of water over medium or low heat all the time but do not allow it to come to a simmer.

VARIATIONS
Chocolate Custard Gradually stir the cooked custard into 175 g/6 oz melted plain chocolate. Instead of melted chocolate, blend 15 ml/ 1 tablespoon cocoa with 30 ml/2 tablespoons boiling water until smooth, then slowly stir it into the custard.

Coffee Custard Blend 10 ml/2 teaspoons instant coffee with 30 ml/ 2 tablespoons boiling water and stir it into the custard. Alternatively, use 300 ml/½ pint strong fresh coffee and 300 ml/½ pint single cream instead of the milk.

double saucepan. Lightly whisk or stir the custard continuously. With practice, you will recognise when the custard is cooked.

Pouring custard may be served hot with puddings or it may be cooled and chilled. Depending on the ratio of eggs to milk used, the custard may set when cooled and chilled. Therefore it may be used as a topping for trifle.

Set Custard The eggs and milk are combined and placed in a dish. The dish may be placed in a bain marie and cooked in the oven at a low to moderate temperature or it may be cooked by steaming or pressure cooking.

Set custard may be served hot and baked with a topping of grated nutmeg or as an accompaniment to cooked fruit. The cooked custard may be cooled, chilled and turned out for serving; when prepared in a caramel-coated dish it is known as caramel custard. When serving cold, the mixture may be enriched with single or double cream instead of or as well as milk. Cold set custard made with cream and topped with brown sugar is grilled to make crème brûlée.

Confectioner's Custard This is thickened with flour and egg yolks. The flour stabilises the yolks and the mixture may be boiled. Whipped cream and/or whisked egg whites may be folded in.

Confectioner's custard is used as a filling for flans, cakes and pastries. It may also be used as a topping for trifle or as a base for making ice cream.

Savoury Custard Savoury sauces thickened with eggs are forms of custards but they are not usually referred to as such. However, set custards may be made without sugar and flavoured with cheese, fish or other delicate ingredients such as asparagus.

Convenient Custards

Custard Powder This is a mixture of cornflour, vanilla and egg powder or flavouring. It should be brought to the boil, stirring, then simmered for 3 minutes before serving so that the flour has time to cook.

Canned and Other Prepared Custards Chilled and canned custards are available for heating or serving cold, as well as for using in recipes.

Cook's Tip
Whip 150 ml/¼ pint double cream with 15 ml/1 tablespoon icing sugar and 5 ml/ 1 teaspoon natural vanilla essence. Fold it into canned custard and use on trifle.

X *Since the eggs in custard are not completely cooked, only those from a reputable source should be used. The elderly, young children and frail are usually advised to avoid eating custards set with egg alone to avoid any risk of food poisoning.*

Freezing

Do not freeze custards as they curdle. Confectioner's custard may be used as a base for making ice cream.

Damsons

See Fruit*.
Dark coloured, purple-blue fruit that can appear almost black when ripe. Looking like small plums, damsons have tart, golden flesh under the dark skin. They are ready for picking in the autumn, about September and October time.

Buying

They are cultivated only in small quantities, so are not widely available. Look for dark, firm, but not hard, undamaged fruit.

Preparation

Wash the fruit under cold running water. Damsons are not usually stoned before cooking as they are small and firm. The stones may be removed by sieving the cooked fruit to a purée.

Cooking

Poach the damsons with a little water and sugar, allowing about 75–100 g/3–4 oz sugar per 450 g/ 1 lb of fruit. The amount of sugar may be varied to taste, also depending on how sour the fruit are, since this can vary considerably if they are slightly underripe or well ripened. Cook the damsons gently in a covered pan for about 15–20 minutes once the sugar has dissolved.

Use

• Uncooked fruit may be used to make fruit pies, on their own or with apples or pears.

• Sieve the fruit to make a purée without any stones, then use it to make fool, mousse, soufflé or other desserts.

• Damsons make excellent jam, jelly or fruit cheese.

Freezing

Either freeze the washed and dried fruit or the cooled cooked purée. Both will keep for a year. Remember to label packs of purée with the quantity of fruit and sugar used.

Dates

Dates are available dried or candied all year, or fresh during late autumn and winter.

Fresh Dates

Fresh dates are moist and sweet with a crisp skin which slides off easily. The flesh is firm.
Buying Look for plump, medium-brown coloured fruit. The skins are usually very slightly 'dented' or loose but they should not be wrinkled. If the fruit is very dark and soft it will probably be over-ripe.
Storing Fresh dates keep well in a covered container in the refrigerator for a week or so.
Use Fresh dates are delicious with cheese. Their skin slides off easily, then they may be split and the long thin stone removed.

Once stoned the dates may be sliced and included in a tropical fruit salad – good with pineapple or kiwi fruit. Sliced fresh dates also make a pleasing addition to savoury salads – for example, with crisp lettuce, crispy bacon and spring onion.

Either peeled or with peel on and stoned, the dates may be stuffed with soft cheese mixtures and served as a savoury.

Dried Dates

These come either as a block (often known as cooking dates)

or chopped into small pieces and sold in packets. Dried dates are sweeter than fresh dates.
Buying Blocks of dates are stoned dates, pressed together. Packets may be sweetened with extra sugar.
Use Dried dates may be used in cakes, breads, chutneys or for adding to stuffing.

Blocks of dates are usually chopped before cooking. To chop a block, hold it firmly at one end on a sturdy board, then cut across it into thin slices. The slices break into small pieces as the pressed fruit separates.

Candied Dates

Packed in boxes, these are sweet and sticky. Some brands are ready stoned.
Use Usually eaten as a sweetmeat. These may be stoned and stuffed with marzipan, then rolled in caster sugar for serving as petits fours or with a selection of home-made sweets and chocolates.

Dishwasher

Dishwashers use water at far higher temperatures than for hand washing. They are hygienic as the dishes do not have to be dried with a cloth. Read and follow the manufacturer's instructions for using the appliance. The following are a few general reminders.

• Do not put crystal glass or your best glasses in the dishwasher. Glass can develop a bluish bloom.

• Keep different types of metal in separate compartments. Do not put silver or bronze cutlery in the dishwasher.

• Do not put knives with bone or wooden handles in the dishwasher.

• Always check that crockery and kitchen utensils are dishwasher proof before buying them.

- Before loading the dishwasher, remove all scraps of food from the dishes and drain off dregs from cups or mugs.

- Baking dishes and saucepans may be cleaned in the dishwasher and some appliances have intensive programmes for such dirty dishes. Baked-on food and residues should be soaked off before the dish or pot is put in the dishwasher.

Care and Cleaning

Clean all the filters and around the door seal and hinges.

Filters should be emptied and thoroughly washed in hot soapy water, then rinsed.

Special degreasing liquid cleaner is available for dishwashers. For cleaning specific areas this may be used on a dishcloth. For cleaning all the inside of the dishwasher the carton of fluid is designed for placing in the cutlery holder, then the empty machine should be put through a normal washing cycle.

Other liquid smooth-surface cleaning products may be used but abrasive materials must be avoided. Never put a foaming product (ordinary washing up liquid or soap powder) in the dishwasher.

About once every 4–6 weeks is often enough for cleaning out the dishwasher, depending on use.

Take particular care to thoroughly clean the dishwasher if it is to be left unused for any length of time. Leave the door ajar.

Drains

The majority of drains need little attention to keep them running smoothly. The fact that they usually operate well tends to mean they are neglected until they cause a problem. The following notes apply to the drains from the kitchen sink.

- As well as cleaning the sink thoroughly, use a brush to clean as far down and around the plug

hole as possible. Even if the sink may not be cleaned using bleach, squirt some carefully down around the inside of the drain exit to clean it thoroughly.

- When straining cooking liquids down the sink always wash them away with clean water. If they remain in the 'U' bend they can smell.

- Never pour neat melted fat down the drain, as this can block it. Allow it to set, then scrape it on to paper and put it in the bin.

- If any oil or small quantities of fat are placed down the drain they should be mixed with plenty of detergent, such as washing up liquid. This will ensure that the fat is washed away.

- Disinfect drains regularly, about once a week, in addition to everyday cleaning.

- Keep the outside drain clear. It is best to have a cover over it to prevent it from becoming clogged with leaves or dirt. Clean and disinfect it occasionally.

- If the drain appears to be slightly clogged (for example, if water runs out slowly), wait until the sink is completely empty. Pour a kettle of boiling water down the plug hole. Look for cleaning products manufactured for clearing drains – you are more likely to find them in a hardware shop than in a supermarket.

- Always read and carefully follow any instructions on strong cleaning products. Remember they can be corrosive and dangerous.

- If you are still concerned that the drain is not running properly after attempting to clear it yourself, then call in professional drain cleaners.

Waste Disposal Units

A waste disposal unit provides a hygienic way of disposing of foods waste, such as vegetable trimmings. It operates out of sight, so it can be ignored when other areas are cleaned.

Read and follow the manufacturer's instructions for the type of waste which may be put down the unit and for cleaning instructions.

Remember to disconnect the power supply before cleaning the waste disposal unit. Clean down around inside the opening using bleach, an abrasive cream cleaner or other suitable cleaner and a brush. Squirt cleaner or bleach down into the grinding chamber and operate the disposal unit, then wash it through with hot water. Disinfect the disposal unit often.

Dried and Candied Fruit

Currants, raisins, sultanas, apricots, apples, peaches, pears and prunes are all dried. As well as citron peel, a variety of fruit are candied – known as glacé fruits (see next page).

Dried Fruit

Buying Reputable brands are cleaned and ready for use. Raisins and sultanas should look plump. Good currants are black and shiny. Apricots, apples and prunes are available ready to eat (with stones removed) but most other dried fruit (such as peaches and pears) need soaking. Avoid dull or dusty looking dried fruit.

Packets of mixed dried fruit contain chopped mixed peel as well as a mixture of dried fruit. **Storing** Keep fruit in unopened packets. Once the packet is opened the fruit should be kept in an airtight container. Either close the packet with a wire tie or transfer the fruit to a lidded container. Check the packet for any indication as to when the fruit should be used. Otherwise most dried fruit keeps well for at least 6 months in a dark, cool, dry place.

The ready-to-eat types should be used within the manufacturer's recommended time and used quickly once the packet is opened.

Use In baked cakes, breads and biscuits. In muesli or combined with other breakfast cereal such as wheat flakes; also in desserts. Many dried fruits are added to savoury sauces, salads, stuffings and casseroles.

Candied Fruit

This is fruit preserved by being impregnated with sugar syrup. Candied peel of oranges, lemon and citron are most common. Fruit and peel may be preserved by this method at home but it is a long process (taking up to 14 days) and detailed instructions must be followed closely for success. The fruit is submerged in sugar syrup daily and the sugar concentration is increased on each occasion.

Buying Candied fruits are very expensive. Look for delicatessens that sell them loose as they are slightly cheaper than boxed fruit.

Candied peel is also expensive but this is available in two forms. Chopped mixed peel is the less expensive version. Pieces of candied peel are sold single or in pairs in packets or they may be purchased loose. The pieces of peel have a far better flavour than chopped mixed peel.

Use Candied fruits may be served as confections with coffee or they may be used in making cakes and desserts.

Candied peel is used in fruit cakes. A strip of candied peel is the traditional topping for a Madeira cake.

Storing Keep candied fruit in a box in a clean, dry place. Peel should be kept in an airtight container. Both will keep for several months.

Dripping

Dripping is the combination of fat and juices that meat yields as it roasts. Potatoes fried in dripping are particularly flavour-

DROP SCONES

These are sometimes referred to as pikelets. They are delicious eaten fresh off the griddle, brushed with melted butter and sprinkled with caster sugar. Although drop scones may be eaten cold, or can be frozen, they are not at their best except when piping hot.

INGREDIENTS	FOOD VALUES:
225 g/8 oz plain flour	TOTAL • PER DROP SCONE
25 g/1 oz margarine	(APPROXIMATE)
25 g/1 oz caster sugar	kcals: 1411 • 31
5 ml/1 teaspoon cream of tartar	kJ: 5957 • 132
2.5 ml/½ teaspoon bicarbonate of soda	protein: 44 g • 1 g
	fat: 45 g • 1 g
2 eggs	carbohydrate: 221 g • 5 g
about 300 ml/½ pint milk	fibre: 8 g • 0 g
	Makes about 45

You will need a griddle or heavy-based frying pan to cook the drop scones. Have a small amount of cooking oil ready to grease the griddle and an old pastry brush or pad of absorbent kitchen paper. Lay a clean tea-towel on a wire rack.

Place the flour in a bowl. Add the margarine and cut it into small pieces. Wash and dry your hands, then rub the fat into the flour until it is evenly dispersed. Stir in the sugar, cream of tartar and bicarbonate of soda. Make a well in the middle of the dry ingredients and add the eggs. Pour in a little milk. Beat the eggs and milk together, then gradually beat in the dry ingredients to make a smooth thick batter. Add the milk, a little at a time, beating well after each addition and working in the dry ingredients until the batter is smooth and very thick.

Heat the griddle and grease it with a little oil. Use a metal serving spoon to drop the batter on the hot griddle. Hold the spoon of batter well above the griddle and pour the batter from the point of the spoon. This will make neat, round drop scones. Cook about 4–6 at a time, depending on the size of the griddle.

Keep the heat regulated so that the drop scones bubble and begin to set on top after about 2 minutes cooking. The underneath should be golden brown. When the bubbles burst on the top of the scones, slide a palette knife or slice under them and flip them over to cook the second side until golden.

Transfer the scones to the covered wire rack and fold the tea-towel over them to keep hot. Serve with butter and sprinkle with a little extra sugar, if liked. Drop scones are also good with jam, honey, thick yogurt, fromage frais or thick cream.

some. Bread and dripping are chunks of bread spread with the meat juices and jelly from under the set dripping, along with some of the fat.

Meat now tends to be leaner so it yields far less fat. Also, with more sensible emphasis on reducing the amount of fat we eat and greater use of vegetable oil for cooking, dripping is rarely saved. Beef dripping (clarified) is sold for cooking.

SEE ALSO **Duck – wild:** Game; **Dumplings:** Suet Pastry, Glossary; **Duxelle:** Glossary

Drying Food

Before the advent of the freezer, drying was one of the more important methods of preserving food. Dehydrators are now available for drying food but this is more for the culinary value of the dried product than as an essential method of preservation. It is a useful way of preserving large quantities of apples, for adding to home-made muesli; or for drying some vegetables, particularly mushrooms, or herbs.

Electric Dehydrator

This consists of a sturdy electric heater base with perforated trays which stack on top. The trays are designed as separate shallow compartments to hold prepared and cut up fruit and vegetables (up to 1 kg/2 lb a layer, depending on the produce). After an initial short preheating period, the dehydrator uses little energy during the drying period which may be from 4 to 12 hours or longer, depending on the food.

Duck

See Poultry.
Frozen and fresh duck, both whole or in portions, are readily available.

Portions

Quarters Fresh or frozen, these include part of the breast meat and the thigh or wing joint. Serve one portion per person.
Boneless Breast The breast meat is sold with or without the skin. Serve one per person, although a large fillet may be made to serve two, depending on the presentation and accompaniments.

Buying and Storing

Select larger birds as small ducks yield little meat. A reputable brand bird is likely to be good quality and less fatty than the cheaper options.

Frozen duck should be bought and transferred to the home freezer quickly to prevent it thawing on route. Fresh duck should be kept cool and chilled as soon as it is unpacked after shopping.

Preparation

Remove the giblets from the body cavity and trim wing ends. Cut off and discard any lumps of fat from just inside the body cavity. Rinse the bird under cold water, then drain it well and dry it on absorbent kitchen paper. Remember to wash the sink and work surface afterwards.

Cooking

Roasting Weigh the bird. Prick the skin all over to allow the fat to run out as it melts – this ensures that the bird remains moist during cooking. Rub some salt into the skin, then place the duck on a wire rack in a roasting tin. The fat will drip away from the duck as it cooks.

Allow 30 minutes per 450 g/1 lb at 180°C, 350°F, gas 4. Increase the oven temperature to 200°C, 400°F, gas 6 about 30 minutes before the end of cooking to crisp the skin.
Grilling Duck breasts and portions may be grilled. Prick the skin and cook the portions under a moderately hot grill, turning once or twice, until well browned and cooked through.
Braising and Casseroling Portions may be cooked in a sauce. First brown the duck on all sides over moderate heat, allowing plenty of time for the fat to run and for the skin to become crisp and golden. Remove the portions from the pan, then drain off excess fat before cooking the onion or other ingredients. Return the duck portions to the pan when the flavouring ingredients and liquid (stock made from the giblets or red wine) are added. Cover and simmer gently for about 1 hour.

Microwave Cooking Combine microwave cooking with conventional methods for exceptionally good results. Cook the duck in the microwave on High for 5 minutes per 450 g/1 lb, then drain off the fat and transfer the duck to a preheated oven at 220°C, 425°F, gas 7 and cook for a further 20 minutes, until golden, crisp and cooked. The result is superb – tender and crisp.
Combination Microwave Cooking Duck is ideal for combination microwave cooking. Follow the instructions supplied with the microwave. As a guide, allow 7–8 minutes per 450 g/1 lb on Medium and at 250°C.

Seasoning for Duck

- Cut an orange in half and stud it with 6 cloves, then place it in the body cavity of the bird before roasting. Serve with Savoury Orange Sauce (page 194).

- Roast a whole duck or duck portions on a rack in a tin. Just before increasing the oven temperature, remove the duck and drain off all the fat from the tin below, leaving just the sediment. Replace the duck in the tin, then pour 600 ml/1 pint dry cider over the bird. Brush the skin with 30 ml/2 tablespoons clear honey and sprinkle it with a little ground cinnamon. Finish roasting.

Transfer the duck to a heated serving platter and keep hot. Boil the cooking liquor, stirring all the time, until reduced by two-thirds and thickened slightly. Taste the sauce and season, then serve it with the duck.

- Sprinkle 60 ml/4 tablespoons coarsely crushed coriander seeds and 30 ml/2 tablespoons chopped fresh sage over the duck two-thirds of the way through roasting.

Accompaniments for Duck

Redcurrant or crab apple jelly, apple sauce, grilled apple slices or roasted halved eating apples are all excellent.

Eggs

Eggs are nutritious, versatile and essential for making a wide variety of dishes, from custards to sponge cakes. Bad publicity in the late 1980's, when eggs were at the centre of salmonella scares, and concern about egg production resulted in greater public awareness about shopping, using and eating eggs.

The information here relates to hen eggs; however quail and duck eggs are also relatively easy to purchase and they may be used as for hen eggs.

Buying

Always buy from a reputable source: this means going to a busy supermarket or shop, or buying directly from a reputable local producer with hens.

As for all food shopping, be aware of the general standards of cleanliness in the shop and hygiene of the personnel. This applies equally to larger supermarkets as to small shops.

Check the carton before buying eggs. Do not buy dirty eggs or any that are damaged.

Sources to Avoid Avoid shops that sell few eggs and tend to overstock, so that the packs are always just reaching their 'best before' dates.

Brown or White? The colour of the egg shell is not an indication of quality but it depends on the species of hen which laid it.

The Lion Mark

The lion mark is now stamped on all packs of eggs from registered British producers. All egg production in the UK is subject to strict regulations. However, the larger reputable registered producers are subject to unplanned inspections to ensure they maintain the highest standards at all levels of production. Eggs from these sources are packed and stamped. This is not to say that a small, local producer may not be reliable but look for the lion mark as a guide to quality at all major outlets.

Checking the Carton

Eggs sold directly by a small producer – from the farm gate, at a local produce market or through a small local shop such as a butcher – should have an indication of their size and the name of the producer (this is obvious if you buy from the farm) but they do not have to be packed. However packs of eggs must be clearly labelled with certain information and this is what you should check before you buy.

Size and Number of Eggs All cartons should indicate the size of the eggs (see grading, right) and the number in the pack.

Quality of Eggs They may be class A or B, as explained.

Best Before Date All cartons should have a date by which time the eggs should be used. Check this and make sure that you have between 7–14 days to use the eggs. Remember the eggs will not suddenly go off if you have them in the refrigerator for a day longer than recommended, but you should certainly not purchase any with an expired shelf life.

Name and Location of Producer All packs should have the name and location of the producer on the pack. The producer will also have a code number which will not mean much to you but it is worth quoting in case of any complaint.

Packing Date This has to be indicated but it is often given as a week number which is meaningless to the shopper. Again, it is there if you should have cause for complaint.

Egg Sizes

Size 1 – 70 g
Size 2 – 65 g and under 70 g
Size 3 – 60 g and under 65 g
Size 4 – 55 g and under 60 g
Size 5 – 50 g and under 55 g
Size 6 – 45 g and under 50 g
Size 7 – under 45 g

Sizes 3 and 4 are the most commonly used and the majority of recipes are based on size 3 eggs; although size 4 may usually be substituted without any cause for failure except in delicate dishes.

Cook's Tip
The following spoon measures are a useful rough guide to the volume of egg, whole and separated.
1 beaten egg = 45 ml/3 tablespoons
1 yolk = 15 ml/1 tablespoon
1 white = 30 ml/2 tablespoons (size 3–4).

Egg Quality

Freshness is one of the key points for determining quality. An egg is made up of the white and yolk, both surrounded by membranes, two small linking 'chords' which keep the yolk in place (they are the stringy bits in the white) and an air sac in the rounded end of the egg.

Egg shells are porous, allowing air in and carbon dioxide out. A newly laid egg has a small amount of air in the air sac (it is likely to be about 2.5 mm/⅛ inch

SEE ALSO **Eccles Cakes:** Glossary; **Eclair:** Choux Pastry; **Edam:** Cheese; **Edoes:** Vegetables – exotic; **Eggplant:** Aubergine

in depth at this stage) but as it ages more air enters, making the sac bigger.

Fresh eggs have thick whites which support the yolks firmly in place. As the egg ages, the white becomes more runny, therefore the yolk moves more within the shell.

The eggs are tested by a process known as 'candling'. A light is shone through the eggs, allowing the position of the yolks and the size of the air sac to be examined.

Class A These are fresh, clean eggs which have not been cleaned or refrigerated below 8°C/46.4°F. Their air sacs are no more than 6 mm/generous ¼ inch in depth and the whites are gelatinous and translucent. When the egg is rotated the yolk should not be seen to move.

These eggs should be free of any tiny blood spots caused by minor blood vessels damaged within the chicken during egg production. They are harmless but unpleasant and spoil the appearance of the egg.

Class B These have larger air sacs but they must not exceed 9 mm/generous ⅓ inch in depth. These eggs may have been cleaned or refrigerated below 8°C/46.6°F. The eggs must be individually stamped to tell whether they have been refrigerated or preserved in any way.

Class C These are not sold to retailers but they are eggs which are fit for human consumption. They are sold to food manufacturers.

Production Terms

The majority of boxed eggs do not mention the way in which the eggs were produced. Terms such as 'free range' or 'barn' are used on some packs.

Free Range The birds must have open-air runs which are mainly covered with vegetation.

Barn or Perchery This is a term used for a production method which is a compromise between free range and battery farming.

Storing

Store eggs in their cartons in the refrigerator. Remember that eggs are porous so they absorb flavours and they are easily spoiled by cross contamination by bacteria from other sources.

Remove the required number of eggs from the refrigerator about 30 minutes before they are used.

Using Eggs

Observe these general food safety guidelines when cooking with eggs.

• Rinse eggs under cold water and dry them on absorbent kitchen paper before cracking them. Make sure your hands are clean.

• After cracking an egg, put the shell straight in the rubbish bin, then wash your hands.

• Wash utensils and work surfaces which have been in contact with raw egg before doing any other cooking. This is important to avoid cross contamination*.

• Avoid cracked or dirty eggs.

• Dishes containing raw or lightly cooked egg should only be made with absolutely fresh eggs, from a sound source. Government recommendations that raw or part cooked eggs should be avoided by the elderly, infirm, pregnant women and young children have been made.

• Dishes containing eggs or cooked eggs (for example, boiled) should be eaten as soon as possible after preparation. Cold dishes should be refrigerated without delay if not served at once.

X *Do not pass mixing bowls used for cake making to children to clean out and to eat up the scrapings – remember the mixture contains raw egg.*

Testing Eggs for Freshness

Fresh eggs sink on their side; eggs that are off float with the

rounded end on the surface of the water. This is because as the egg ages it absorbs air, and air is lighter than water. Most eggs will not sink but they should not float.

Another guide to freshness is the appearance of the egg white: a gelatinous, firm white which stays in a neat ring around the yolk is fresh. As it ages, egg white becomes runny.

Preparation Techniques

Cracking an Egg Both the egg and your hands should be washed and dried. It is best to crack an egg into a small basin before adding it to a cooking pan or other ingredients. Tap the side of the egg firmly on the side of the basin. Use your thumbs to part the halves of the shell at the crack. Hold the egg over the basin as you do this, then allow all the egg to run from the shell halves. Place the shell halves in the bin or on a plate if you are cracking any more eggs. Put the shells in the bin. Wash your hands.

Separating Have two containers ready. Crack the egg as above. Part the shell with your thumbs, working over a basin, then scoop the yolk into one piece of shell and let all the white drain into the basin. Carefully slip the yolk into the second portion of shell, allowing as much white as possible to drop into the basin as you do so. Continue until virtually all the white has been separated from the yolk. Put the yolk in the second container.

Beating Eggs Whole eggs are beaten. This may be done using a mixing spoon or a whisk.

Whole eggs are beaten with sugar until they form a thick, creamy mixture. In this case an electric beater or rotary whisk is used. The process is speeded up and a better volume achieved by standing the bowl over hot water.

Whisking Egg Whites As egg whites are whisked, they form a structure which traps air to make a stiff white foam. The smallest hint of fat prevents the whites from forming the strong structure to trap air and they will not whisk successfully. Egg whites may be whisked to four stages, depending on the recipe.

Lightly Whisked The whites are broken down slightly and frothy on the surface. This is the stage to reach for making royal icing or if the whites are used as a glaze.

Soft Peak Stage The whites have formed a white foam which can be drawn into soft peaks which fall over and do not quite hold a sharp shape. The whites are suitable for folding into some firm mixtures, for example baked soufflés.

Firm Peak Stage The foam can be drawn into peaks that hold their shape well and stand up in peaks. The whites should still look moist and shiny. This is the stage for folding in whites to soft mixtures.

Stiff and Dry Stage The whites should be very stiff and dry in appearance. If the bowl is inverted sharply the whites will stay in place. At this stage a knife should make a clean cut through the whites. This is the stage for meringues.

• All utensils must be spotlessly clean and free of any grease.

• Any fat (for example from the yolk) in the white will prevent it from forming a foam.

• Fresh eggs give a good volume and dry peaks. Stale eggs do not form as good a volume or as stable a foam as fresh ones.

• Whisk egg whites just before they are to be used, if left to stand they will begin to collapse or weep.

• Know how firm a foam you require: if the egg whites are to be folded into a soft mixture, the peaks should be soft but not floppy. If the eggs are whisked for meringues they should be dry – this is the stage when you can invert the bowl and the eggs will not fall out. Take care though, hold the bowl at an angle and the whites will slide out as one whole portion of mixture.

• Egg whites whisk better at room temperature.

Creaming Egg Yolks Egg yolks may be creamed with sugar until they become thick and pale. A mixing spoon is used and the mixture may be placed over a bowl of hot water to speed up the process.

Cooking

Boiling

There are two ways: either the eggs are brought to room temperature, then lowered gently on a spoon into a saucepan of just boiling water or eggs from the refrigerator are covered with cold water and brought to the boil. For soft boiled eggs, lower them into boiling water to ensure the yolks become hot during cooking.

The cooking should be timed as soon as the water boils. The time depends on the size of the eggs and the texture required.

Soft Boiled 3 minutes (size 1–3); 2 minutes (size 4–7)

The above eggs will have runny yolks and soft whites.

Firm White, Part-set Yolks 5 minutes (size 1–3); 4 minutes (size 4–7)

Hard Boiled 10 minutes (size 1–3); 8–9 minutes (size 4–7)

The above eggs will be firm, with floury yolks rather than overcooked, hard yolks.

Once the eggs are cooked, use a draining spoon to lift soft ones from the water and put them into egg cups.

Hard-boiled eggs should be drained at once, cracked and placed in cold water. This prevents the black ring which forms around the yolk as the egg is cooling.

For serving hot, shell the eggs in the cold water, then place them at once on a plate – the eggs will still be steaming hot. Otherwise, leave the eggs to cool under cold water. Shell them and place in a covered container in the refrigerator until required.

Scrambling

Have hot toast and/or a heated serving plate ready for the eggs.

Beat the required number of eggs with a little seasoning and 15 ml/1 tablespoon milk for each egg. Put a knob of butter or margarine in a saucepan over moderate heat. Allow the fat to part melt and coat the bottom of the pan before pouring in the eggs.

Cook, stirring all the time, until the eggs begin to set. Pay special attention once the sides and bottom of the eggs are setting and stir them vigorously. Scrambled eggs are cooked when they are creamy. Do not overcook them until they are hard and curdled when a watery whey separates from the lumps of egg. Serve the eggs at once.

Poaching

Poached eggs are cooked in a wide pan of simmering water. A deep frying pan is ideal. The water should be up to 5 cm/2 inches deep but no deeper. Add 10 ml/2 teaspoons vinegar to the water and heat it until just simmering.

Crack the egg into a small basin. Swirl the water gently, then slide the egg into the middle of the swirl of water. Cook the egg in the barely simmering water for between 3–5 minutes. By gently part-raising the egg on a draining spoon you will be able to tell how firm it is: the whole egg appears and feels quite floppy when both white and yolk are soft. It is usually fairly easy to distinguish an egg with a firm white and soft thin covering of white over a soft yolk.

See the notes on using an egg poacher, (page 112).

Fried Eggs

Heat a thin covering of oil in a frying pan. Crack the eggs and slide them into the pan one at a time. Baste the edges of the eggs with fat at once to firm the white into a neat shape.

There are various options at this stage.

Basting The eggs may be cooked in an open pan over medium to high heat. They should be basted all the time with fat so that they cook fairly quickly on top, particularly around the white, before the underneath is hard.

Turned Eggs Cook the eggs fairly quickly, over medium to high heat, until they are set underneath and part set on top. Use a large slice to turn the eggs over, placing them down gently to avoid breaking the yolks. Cook for about a minute, or slightly less on the second side, until the yolk is set to your liking. Lift them out of the pan firmly but carefully and flip them over on to a heated serving plate.

Covering the Pan Once the edges of the eggs are beginning to set, reduce the heat and place a lid on the pan, then let the eggs cook gently for 2–3 minutes, or until they are cooked to your liking. This is a good method as the whites stay tender but firm and the yolks remain runny.

Deep Fried Eggs Take care when deep frying eggs as they spit when added to the hot oil. The oil must be hot (about 190°C/375°F). Have the egg in a small basin and stand back slightly. Turn the heat down under the pan. When cooking just 1–2 eggs, the heat may be turned off as they cook quickly in the hot fat.

The eggs splutter and sink in the pan. After about 30 seconds they rise to the surface of the oil in a crisp-edged bubble. Baste the middle of the egg and continue cooking for about 30 seconds to a minute at the most. Use a draining spoon to scoop up the egg and allow the oil to drain away before serving.

Baked Eggs
Set the oven at 180°C, 350°F, gas 4. Grease the required number of ramekin dishes or other ovenproof dish or dishes with butter. Crack the eggs one at a time into a small basin, then slide them into the dishes. Season and dot with butter. Trickle a little single cream over the eggs. Bake for about 10 minutes, or until the white is set but the yolk is still soft.

Eggs may be baked with other ingredients, such as cooked spinach, crumbled blue cheese, chopped, peeled tomatoes and chives or diced cooked potatoes. The other ingredients may lengthen the cooking time slightly by protecting the egg from the heat.

Making an Omelette

1. Have ready a heated plate and any accompaniments – a crisp green salad and thin slices of wholemeal bread and butter are delicious with a simple herb or cheese omelette.

2. Next prepare any filling ingredients or herbs. Allow 2 eggs per omelette. Beat the eggs with 30 ml/2 tablespoons water until they are really frothy. Add a little seasoning. Herbs, such as chopped fresh parsley, chervil, dill or tarragon and snipped chives may be added to the eggs.

3. Heat a little olive oil (about 15 ml/1 tablespoon) or a knob of butter in an omelette pan with curved sides. Have a slice ready to turn the omelette and keep the heat high under the pan. Remember that olive oil heats and burns quickly.

4. When the fat is almost smoking hot, pour the eggs into the pan, beating them as you do so. They should sizzle and bubble at once. Cook the eggs for a few seconds over high heat. As the edges begin to set, lift the edge of the omelette and tilt the pan to allow the raw egg to run on the hot base. Continue cooking over high heat, lifting the omelette and tilting the pan.

5. When the underneath of the omelette is golden and the top creamy it is ready for the filling. Sprinkle the filling on one side, then push the slice firmly under the opposite side of the omelette and flip it over the filling. Slide the semi-circular omelette on to the plate and serve it at once.

6. The whole cooking process takes about 1–2 minutes, any longer and the omelette is cooked too slowly and it will be flat, tough and miserable.

Soufflé Omelette

1. Have a heated plate, filling and accompaniments ready. Hot creamy fillings in sauce are wonderful with soufflé omelette (smoked haddock is superb) or good quality jam and a sprinkling of caster sugar may be used.

2. Separate 2 eggs. Beat the yolks well with seasoning and 15 ml/1 tablespoon milk, until creamy. Whisk the whites until they form soft peaks – if they are too dry they will not fold into the yolks. Heat the grill to the hottest setting and make sure that there is enough space to slide the omelette pan underneath it.

3. Heat a little oil or butter in the omelette pan. Use a metal spoon to fold the whites into the yolks, then turn the mixture into the pan at once. Scrape all the egg from the basin and very gently spread it out in the pan. Reduce the heat to moderate and cook the omelette until the base is golden.

4. Use a slice to lift the edge of the omelette and check that the base is cooked, then place the omelette under the grill. It will puff up and set. When pale golden in colour, spoon the filling quickly over one half, fold the other half and slide the thick, light omelette on the plate. Serve at once.

Omelette Fillings
The following may be combined to taste.

Savoury fillings
● Grated cheese.
● Diced cooked ham or chicken.
● Flaked, drained canned tuna fish mixed with chopped spring onion and seasoning.
● Roughly chopped peeled and seasoned tomatoes.
● Sliced mushrooms tossed in a little melted butter or hot oil over high heat for 30 seconds.
● Savoury white sauce with flaked poached haddock (an omelette with this filling is known as omelette Arnold Bennett, after the man who first ate it at the Savoy Hotel).

- Hot diced cooked chicken and mushrooms in savoury white sauce.
- Drained cooked spinach in savoury white sauce.

Sweet Fillings
- Jam or conserve.
- Lightly poached or stewed fruit.
- Soft cheese sweetened with honey and mixed with chopped peaches.
- Grated chocolate and whipped cream.
- Pieces of fresh fruit with just a little sugar sprinkled over the top of the omelette – orange segments, seedless grapes, kiwi fruit, cherries and so on.

Coddled Eggs

These are cooked in small lidded containers known as coddlers (available from specialist cookshops). The egg is cracked into the greased container and the lid is put on top. The coddler is placed in a saucepan of boiling water. The cooked eggs are like boiled eggs without their shells.

Microwave Cooking*

Although 'poached' eggs and the equivalent of baked eggs may be cooked in the microwave the results are usually inferior, therefore not to be recommended unless the eggs are cooked as part of a dish, such as ratatouille with eggs.

Although recipes exist, a good omelette cannot be made in the microwave even using a brown-ing dish.

> **X** *Do not attempt to cook a whole egg in its shell in the micro-wave. Heat builds up inside the shell causing the egg to explode and making a terrific mess.*

Microwave Scrambled Eggs These are excellent. Crack the required number of eggs into a suitable basin. Add a little seasoning and beat them well, then add a small knob of butter or margarine.

Cook the eggs on High for 45–60 seconds at first, then for bursts of 30–60 seconds depend-ing on the number of eggs. On each occasion the eggs should be cooked until they are just begin-ning to set and rise slightly around the top edge, then whisk them well.

They are cooked when they appear to be slightly too runny. Allow them to stand for 1 minute, then whisk again until creamy. They stay hotter than eggs scrambled conventionally. The following is a guide to cooking times.

2 eggs – 2–3 minutes
4 eggs – 3–4 minutes
6 eggs – 6–7 minutes

Egg Poachers and Steamers

Perforated egg poachers These are available as individual stands or in the form of a tray to hold up the 4, or more, eggs. The tray has legs and a handle, with per-forated cups to hold the cracked egg. The perforations are not large enough to allow the egg to run through but they allow the water to reach the egg. The poacher is placed in simmering water and the eggs are dropped into the cups. The eggs are covered in water and cooked just as for poaching (above) but they have a good shape when cooked and are easily drained.

Egg steamers These are most often referred to as poachers but they consist of a stand with cups that are not perforated. The eggs are dropped into the greased cups and the stand is placed in shallow boiling water. The eggs are above the water level and they cook in the steam. They are not true poached eggs.

Egg Separators

These are gadgets for separating the yolk from the white of an egg. Shaped like a large measuring spoon, the separator has slots in its side to allow the white to run out while the yolk stays in the base.

Hold the separator over a basin, then pour the egg into it. When all the white has run through, place the yolk in another container.

Egg Timers

Traditional hour-glass shaped timers have a small quantity of sand which runs from one glass chamber to another through a narrow passage in 3 minutes.

More versatile clockwork or digital timers may be set to the required time and they ring or ping when this is reached.

Freezing

Whole Eggs Do not freeze whole eggs in shells. Well beaten whole eggs may be frozen for 6–9 months. Add about 2.5 ml/½ tea-spoon salt or 10 ml/2 teaspoons sugar to every 4 eggs to prevent the yolk thickening during freez-ing. Label the carton with the number of beaten eggs and the quantity of salt or sugar.
Whites These freeze very well for up to a year. Simply place them in a rigid container and label with the number of whites.
Yolks Cream the yolks very lightly with salt or sugar other-wise they harden during freez-ing. Allow 2.5–5 ml/½–1 tea-spoon salt or 30 ml/2 tablespoons sugar to every 4 yolks. Label the carton with the number of yolks and the quantity of salt or sugar.
Packing Use rigid cartons for containing the eggs. Allow a little headspace in the cartons for the eggs to expand on freezing.
Thawing Thaw the eggs in the refrigerator or in a cool room. Use on the same day as they are thawed.

Enzymes

Enzymes are natural substances, organic catalysts, that are pres-ent in all living organisms. Plants, animals and fish all have them – life depends on their existence.

Enzymes play an important role in ripening fruit but they also continue working after the fruit has ripened and carry on encouraging the process until the food rots.

Destroying Enzymes

Enzymes are not destroyed by chilling or by freezing. They are destroyed by cooking – the exact length of time depends on the food.

If fresh fruit and vegetables are frozen without being blanched, the enzymes carry on working slowly and, over prolonged periods of time, they can cause the quality of the frozen food to deteriorate.

Therefore food, such as fruit and vegetables, is blanched before being frozen to destroy the enzymes and ensure that it stays in good quality over many months in the freezer.

Equipment

See Baking Tins and Bakeware*, Containers for Food*, Crockery and Cutlery*, Knives* and Saucepans and Cooking Pans*.

The Necessities

There are just a few essential items for the most basic cooking: a can opener; a knife to cut, peel and carry out all food preparation; a pan in which to cook; a mixing spoon; a small and large plate, bowl and mug for serving food or drinking from; a knife, fork, dessertspoon and teaspoon. Other basic items of equipment include a cutting board, whisk, fish slice and basin.

As well, have at least two heavy, white cotton tea-towels. These will last for years even if they are boiled once a week. Disposable washing cloths are a must.

Knife Make your first choice of knife one with a 12.5 cm/5 inch blade. It should sharpen well so that you can use it for most cutting and chopping. This is not

large enough for major chopping jobs but it is small enough for peeling vegetables, although opting for a peeler or simply giving them a good scrub and wash is better under the circumstances.

Cooking Pan The most versatile cooking pan is a skillet. This is a deep frying pan with a tall lid that fits well. With sides about 7.5 cm/3 inches tall and measuring about 25 cm/10 inches across, it may be used for cooking anything from omelettes or bacon and eggs to risotto, bolognaise sauce, boiled potatoes, stewed apples or rice pudding.

Because of the different use it will get, it is worth going for a good quality, non-stick finish.

Mixing Spoon Buy a heatproof plastic spoon. A flattened, spatula shape is more versatile as it may be used for turning as well as stirring food.

> **X** *Avoid wooden utensils which are not hygienic in the best environment and, although acceptable when set aside for specific use in a well-equipped kitchen, they are not practical when facilities are minimal.*

Dishes and Cutlery These will have to double up for a number of uses in food preparation as well as serving, so buy sensible, plain, sturdy crockery and plain stainless steel cutlery.

Cutting Board A medium-sized plastic cutting board, preferably with a handle so that it may be hung on a hook somewhere.

Whisk Useful but not essential. One with a coating suitable for use with non-stick pans may be used for whisking sauces.

Basin Buy one which will be just as handy for tossing a salad as for beating eggs for omelettes. If it is heatproof and just fits into the cooking pan with the lid on, you have an ideal container for cooking as well as preparing food.

Basic, Versatile Equipment

Moving on from a camp-style kitchen, the basic items of equipment must include containers for

use in the oven as well as on the hob. With more storage space, there is scope for useful items such as a colander, a choice of knives and more than one cutting board.

Cutting Boards Ideally, keep one for meat, fish and poultry; another for salad ingredients and vegetables. Both should be washable plastic.

Knives The one basic knife may be enough, plus a serrated salad knife for tomatoes. Most cooks tend to rely very heavily on just one or two favourite knives for most food preparation. An array of knives is only useful if you intend boning meat, skinning fish and so on. One or two good quality knives are infinitely better than half a dozen inexpensive ones.

Steel or Knife Sharpener Better than a second knife, buy a good steel to sharpen the one good quality knife: with proper use and care both will last for very many years, if not a lifetime.

Saucepans and Casseroles Add to the all-in-one pan a small pan for heating small amounts of food and milk or for making sauces. Again, select one small and/or medium sized pan of reasonable quality, to go in the oven as well as on the hob, rather than a battery of incredibly cheap pans that warp, stick and burn easily.

Colander A colander is useful for washing and draining raw fruit and vegetables as well as for boiled food.

Basins, Bowls and Jugs Look for ovenproof glass which are sturdy, versatile and they last forever if you manage not to break them! They are hygienic and easy to wash and they have the advantage of being useful cooking containers too.

Gadgets Avoid filling up valuable cupboard space with gadgets that rarely see the light of day. A vegetable peeler, garlic crusher (if you like garlic), grater and citrus juice squeezer are useful basics.

Pick them carefully and you will never want to abandon

them. Look for a peeler that is comfortable to hold, with a fine sharp blade. The tough-looking, thick ones can be difficult to use.

Opt for a grater that has a choice of grating surfaces, with a good firm handle and large wide base that will stand on a board.

The better citrus squeezers have a good sized glass base with pouring lip and a top that screws on. The top should keep the pips away from the juice.

Linen Have a **thick**, plain, oven glove.

The Better Equipped Kitchen

At this level, the choice depends on the type of cooking that goes on, personal preferences and the type of storage space.

Pots and Pans For everyday meals, it may be time to improve or extend the range of cooking pans to include an omelette pan, several saucepans, a steamer or even a wok.

Weighing and Measuring Equipment Preparation equipment should at this stage include weighing scales, a standard set of measuring spoons and a measuring jug.

For Baking Baking tins and dishes are necessary for cake making and for pies and gratins.

Cooling, Cutting and Serving A wire cooling rack, carving knife, bread knife, draining spoon, ladle and large serving spoon are all useful. A fish slice and palette knife, possibly a pair of food tongs, are all versatile.

Electric Appliances A small electric food mixer, preferably with a liquidiser is useful. If cake making is not a priority, then the better bet is a hand-held liquidiser which may be used for puréeing food and mixing light ingredients.

Specialist Equipment

Adopt a business-like approach to buying specialist equipment. Here the term specialist is used for items ranging from food processors or pressure cookers to a wok, piping equipment, griddles, salad spinners, double saucepans and so on.

If you intend spending a significant amount of money, start by listing the reasons for wanting the equipment.

As you look around at the variety of products, make notes about the functions and prices.

Food Processors There are many types performing different functions, some combined with liquidisers. This may seem strange but a liquidiser produces a smoother liquid.

Food Mixers and Liquidisers They may be combined or separate. Whether you need both and a food processor depends on what you cook. Larger food mixers are better for mixing large cakes. Think about storage space, either on the work surface or in a cupboard.

Deep Fryers and Work-Top Cookers Such as contact grills, sandwich makers, electric cook pans and so on. As well as thinking about the type of cooking you do, consider the available work surface. These appliances are only really beneficial when they are kept out on the surface, ready to use at a moment's notice.

Assessing Requirements

- Think about space and storage.

- Badly stored equipment may be damaged, dirty and/or unhygienic.

- Think about what you eat already and what you would like to cook.

- List the use you have for any item of equipment before buying it.

- When the budget is small, look for good quality at a moderate price and buy fewer, more versatile items: they will last and you will be able to add to them.

- Shop in genuine sales at reputable stores, buying known brands of equipment – you can save a lot of money. Only buy items you know you want.

Faggot

A small meatball made of pork offal, mainly liver, breadcrumbs, onion, herbs and spices. Traditionally wrapped in caul fat, baked and coated with rich gravy, then served with 'mushy' or processed peas.

Well made, flavoursome faggots are delicious but many poor substitutes have done nothing for the faggot's reputation.

Buy faggots from high quality butchers or make them yourself.

Fat

See Butter*, Margarine* Dripping*, Lard* and Oil*.

Many types of fats are found naturally in different foods – in fish, poultry, meat, vegetables, nuts and seeds. Fat is very rich in calories and therefore it provides one of the best means of storing energy.

Most of us are aware of the excess fat that we store in our bodies and often it is a result of eating more than the amount of energy that we expend. However, the minimal fat stores in the body are important for maintaining hormone status, insulation and protection of internal structures.

Fat provides an energy store that is used whenever food energy intake is inadequate to meet expenditure. Hormone changes associated with pregnancy also encourage the deposition of extra fat to meet the demands imposed by the growing child and the lactation period after birth.

SEE ALSO **Escalope, Espagnole:** Glossary

Home-made Faggots

Rinse 225 g/8 oz pig's liver under cold running water, then dry it on absorbent kitchen paper. You can, if you prefer, use lamb's liver. Trim any membrane from the outside of the liver and slice it through horizontally. Cut out any sinews – it is best to do this using kitchen scissors (wash them straightaway afterwards).

Cut the liver into 4 pieces. Heat just a little oil in a frying pan and brown the liver on all sides – do not cook it through. Drain the pieces on absorbent kitchen paper and set aside to cool slightly.

Meanwhile, finely chop a large onion and mix it with 100 g/4 oz fresh wholemeal breadcrumbs. Add 30 ml/2 tablespoons chopped fresh sage, 15 ml/1 tablespoon fresh thyme or savory leaves (or 5 ml/1 teaspoon dried thyme), 30 ml/2 tablespoons chopped fresh parsley and plenty of seasoning. Add 15 ml/1 tablespoon ground coriander and 5 ml/1 teaspoon ground mace.

Next, finely chop the liver. If you have a food processor, then it makes the process easier, less messy and more hygienic. Mix the liver with the breadcrumb mixture.

Adding a small amount of chopped bacon or pork gives the faggots a good flavour. Use bacon offcuts or streaky bacon; belly or sparerib of pork may be used. Trim off any rind and bone from 175 g/6 oz bacon and chop finely, then add it to the faggot mixture. Add an egg (no need to beat it first), then mix all the ingredients really well until they are thoroughly bound together.

Have ready a lightly oiled ovenproof dish and set the oven at 200°C, 400°F, gas 6. Wash and dry your hands, then shape the mixture into 10–12 balls. Place them in the dish. Top each faggot with a dot of margarine, then cover the dish and bake them for 30 minutes. Uncover the dish, turn the faggots and continue to cook them for a further 20 minutes, or until they are browned and cooked through. Use the cooking juices to make gravy.

Plants store fat in their seeds. When the seeds germinate and grow, the stored fat provides energy for the new plant to grow until it is large enough to manufacture its own food.

It is possible to generalise and separate animal and vegetable fats into separate groups according to their chemical structure.

Saturated/Unsaturated Fats

These terms are widely used in food chemistry. They refer to the chemical composition of the fat.

Fat is made up of chains of carbon and hydrogen atoms. Saturated fats have two hydrogen atoms attached to each carbon atom in the chain. This does not leave any 'links' free for the carbon atom to attach itself to any other available atoms.

Unsaturated fats do not have all the available links on the carbon atoms attached to hydrogen. Spare carbon atoms link to each other.

Polyunsaturated Fats The term polyunsaturated is used for fats that have more than one carbon link available within each of group of atoms (or molecule).

Monounsaturated Fats This term is used for fats which have only one carbon to carbon link unsaturated within the molecule.

Characteristics of Fats Saturated fats are usually solid at room temperature whereas unsaturated fats are liquid (or oil) at the same temperature. In other words, saturated fats usually have a higher melting point than unsaturated fats.

Unsaturated fats break down more easily than saturated ones. For example, when deep frying oil will overheat and smoke at a lower temperature than lard. The oil begins to smoke when its chemical structure is breaking, causing it to change from the oil which was in the bottle into different chemical substances, including unpleasant smelling gas.

Unsaturated fats react more readily especially with oxygen. When this happens and oxygen atoms link up with the available carbon atoms in the fat, the process is known as oxidation. These oxidised fats readily break down to give rancid flavours.

Animal and Vegetable Fats The fat in beef and lamb, milk and milk products, is mainly saturated. Other animal fats may be less saturated depending on the diet fed to the animals.

Vegetable oils are generally more unsaturated but there are exceptions; for example palm and coconut oils are saturated. Others, such as sunflower and corn oil, are highly unsaturated.

Many food products contain a mixture of fats, including some that are saturated and others that are unsaturated. This is why some products are 'high in polyunsaturated fats'.

Cholesterol

Cholesterol is a substance found in animal fat. Animals (including humans) manufacture cholesterol in their bodies. It is not found in vegetable fats.

It must be remembered that the cholesterol we eat does not necessarily affect the levels of cholesterol in our blood.

Confusion and concern about cholesterol in food can be misleading. It is more important to think about the overall amount of fat eaten and the balance of unsaturated to saturated fats.

Uses of Fat in Cooking

● As a cooking medium, fat reaches a very high temperature

causing food cooked in it to become brown and crisp. The cooking temperature and the fat give fried foods their characteristic flavour.

● In cake making, fat is creamed to incorporate air.

● Fat is used as a 'shortening'. It is rubbed into flour in pastry making. It gives short crust pastry and similar doughs their characteristic texture and richness.

● Fat is used to enrich a wide variety of foods, from baked breads and pastries to mashed potatoes.

● Fat makes starchy food more palatable and easier to eat. For example, butter or margarine is spread on bread or crackers.

● Fat is also used to make sauces and dressings by using it to form an emulsion with vinegar, egg yolks or other liquids that do not readily combine with it.

Fat in the Diet: A Balanced Approach

Fat plays an important role in the diet as a source of energy and it provides the fat soluble vitamins* which are commonly found with fat in food. For example, animal fats provide vitamin D and some vitamin A, and vegetable fats provide vitamin E and carotenes, which are converted into vitamin A.

Everyday Foods and Fat

The main function of fat is to supply energy. However, it is recommended that the amount of energy from fat should be no more than 35 per cent of total energy intake. The recommended upper limit for saturated fat is 10 per cent. The upper limit for polyunsaturated is about 8 per cent, with the remainder of the 35 per cent coming from monounsaturated sources.

To put these figures in the context of the daily diet: the energy-giving foods are the carbohydrates and fats. In a diet which provides the right level of energy foods for an individual, 65 per cent of the energy should be taken from foods other than fat.

X *The fat intake of children under 5 years old should not be restricted. These recommendations apply to adults.*

Sources of Fat

Many fats are easy to spot, for example butter, margarine, cooking oils and fat on meat. Other sources include whole milk, cheese, poultry skin, nuts, some fish and manufactured products such as biscuits, cakes, pastries, pies, sausages and ready meals.

In some cases the fat content of a meal is not in the food itself but it is added during cooking. The most obvious example must be chips. Other shallow fried or deep fried foods have fat added to them. Sauces may also be enriched with fat.

Eating Moderate Amounts

Making detailed calculations about what we eat each day is neither practical nor sensible. Becoming neurotic about each meal takes the pleasure out of eating and cooking.

Be Aware of What You Eat

Assessing your shopping can be easier than thinking about meals. For example, do you buy biscuits every week (what sort?); do you buy significant amounts of margarine or butter every week; do you often buy cooking oil; do you get through a lot of cheese, bacon, sausages and meat? Assessing meals alone does not allow for the occasional in-between meal snack of biscuits, cheese and crackers, a packet of crisps, some nuts and so on, whereas taking stock of all food purchased does.

Cutting Down on Fat Eating less fat does not mean forfeiting flavour. Try to make a habit of keeping daily meals fairly low fat as this allows room for indulgence on other occasions, for example, a chunk of creamy gâteau occasionally, some fish and chips, fried breakfast with fried bread. These types of foods or meals should be treats.

● Use skimmed or semi-skimmed milk.

● Spread margarine or butter thinly. Try eating fresh crusty bread continental style, without any butter (for example with soup or salad).

● If sandwiches are eaten daily, try using low-fat cheese as a spread instead of butter. Use low-fat fillings or cut whole fat cheese thinly. Grated cheese goes a lot further.

● Add lettuce, cucumber, sliced celery, tomatoes and spring onions to sandwiches for bulk, crunch and flavour.

● Avoid eating lots of rich biscuits, cakes and puddings, except as treats.

● Have low-fat yogurt or fresh fruit instead of puddings or as a snack.

● Try half-fat cream, yogurt or low-fat fromage frais on desserts and when cooking special meals.

✓ *The best way to balance all aspects of your diet, particularly the fat content, is to be aware of the nutritional value of the food you buy. This is far easier than trying not to eat too much of the goodies in the refrigerator. Remember these tips.*
● *Find out about nutrition and read food labels.*
● *Buy lower fat foods and less fat.*
● *Buy smaller amounts of high-fat foods.*
● *Every now and then check your shopping habits just to be sure you are buying for a balanced diet.*

SEE ALSO **Fennel:** Herbs, Spices; **Fenugreek:** Spices; **Feta:** Cheese

Fennel

See Herbs*.
Also known as Florence fennel, this is a bulbous vegetable about the size of a closed fist. It is similar in texture to celery and has a slight aniseed flavour.

Buying

Look for small to medium, firm bulbs. They may have two or more short stems and a hint of feathery leaves.

Avoid limp-looking bulbs with loosely wrapped stalks. Any bruised or browning fennel is not worth buying. Also, if the fennel looks coarse and fibrous it may well be stringy.

Preparation

Trim off any remains of the root end and trim off the stems. Stems and leaves may be chopped fine for use in cooked dishes or salads; leaves may be reserved for garnish.

Wash well, scrubbing the outside with a vegetable brush if necessary.

Cutting

Fennel becomes brown on cut surfaces and it dries out quickly, so do not cut it far ahead of use. The bulb may be cut in half or quartered lengthways.

To slice fennel, hold the bulb firmly by the root end, then slice across working from stem downwards. This is easier if the bulb is halved first.

Use

• Raw in salads.

• Braised: select small to medium bulbs and follow the recipe for Braised Celery (page 66). Cook the bulbs whole or halved and allow about 1¼–1½ hours cooking.

• Slice and add to stir fry dishes or casseroles. Fennel is delicious braised with chicken or turkey.

Fermentation

See Yeast*.
This is the term used for the action of yeast that is 'working'. The fermentation process is used to make wine, beer, bread and other yeast products. In cooking and other uses of fermentation, the yeast is added to the food and the process is carefully controlled so that yeasts naturally present in the food do not spoil the process. In cooking, fermentation is used to produce carbon dioxide gas in food, making it rise.

Bacterial food fermentations are also important in food production. For example, lactic acid bacteria in the manufacture of cheese and yogurt. A similar form of fermentation is used to give olives, gherkins and salami their characteristic tangy flavour.

Unwanted Fermentation This takes place when unwanted yeasts attack food. For example, jams or similar preserves may ferment if they contain too little sugar to prevent yeasts from growing in them.

Open cartons of fresh fruit juice which are kept for too long become fizzy due to the fermentation of yeasts that are naturally present.

Fibre

See Balanced Diet*.
Also referred to as dietary fibre and roughage (an old-fashioned term). When plant foods are eaten and digested, the nutrients are broken down and absorbed. Fibre is provided by the plant cell walls in foods which are not digested. Most fibre present simply passes on through and out of the body as a waste product, although some is broken down by bacteria in the bowel.

Importance of Fibre

Fibre absorbs moisture and keeps food moving easily through the intestine, then it forms an efficient, moist carrier for taking other waste products out of the body easily. Food takes between one to three days to pass through the body, allowing for nutrients to be absorbed and for waste products to be carried away. If there is insufficient fibre in the diet, this process can take up to a week or longer.

In addition to its main, vital function, some types of fibre may well play a positive role in slowing down the rate at which the human body absorbs carbohydrates, and uses the cholesterol which it produces.

Fibre and its Sources

Fibre is made up of complex carbohydrate particles that cannot be fully digested. The usefulness of the fibre varies and some foods are a better source of fibre than others. Fibre may be insoluble (but it will absorb moisture) or it may be soluble. Both types are important in the diet.

The best recognised sources of fibre are whole cereals but fibre is present in all plant foods. For example, wholemeal flour and foods made from it, including bread, crackers, biscuits and pastry. Beans, both fresh and dried, and other pulses such as lentils are excellent sources of fibre. Bran taken from wheat grain and used in cereals and other food products is a rich source of fibre.

Oats are now known to be a particularly valuable source of soluble fibre. Pectin*, found in the skin of fruit, is a soluble fibre with similar properties to oat fibre.

Fresh vegetables and fruit contain less fibre than cereals, grains and pulses on a weight basis. Although they play an essential role in the diet, on their own fresh fruit and vegetables (with peel or skin) are not an adequate source of fibre unless they are eaten in large amounts. Fruit and vegetables have a high water content which dilutes the fibre.

It is best to eat a range of foods containing fibre so that the diet includes a mixture of soluble and insoluble types.

Figs

See Fruit*.
Figs are small fruit about the size of large plums. They may be green or purple skinned, with pale pink to deep red flesh speckled with lots of edible seeds. Ripe, red-fleshed figs with purple skin are sold individually. They are sweet and juicy.

Buying

The skin has a faint bloom. The figs should be just firm not squashy, not hard. Avoid any that have brown or dark blotches or patches as they are bruised or over-ripe and they will be tasteless.

Look for figs that are displayed in shallow cartons, each wrapped in tissue. Inspect figs individually before buying.

Preparation

Wash fresh figs and dry them on absorbent kitchen paper. Trim off the stalk end and cut out any small mouldy areas. Usually fruit that has any sign of mould will be tainted with an unpleasant flavour and therefore must be discarded.

Use a sharp vegetable peeler to thinly peel off the outer skin, then halve or quarter the fruit.

Use

• Serve with ham (cooked or dried ham) or cheese. Figs are delicious with Parma ham or goats' cheese.

• Include as part of a fruit salad, adding the quartered figs at the last minute or using them as a decoration.

• Serve quartered figs in individual dishes with a little ice cream or sorbet.

Dried Figs

Readily available from supermarkets as well as wholefood shops, these are very sweet and good to eat as they are. They may be soaked and cooked with other dried fruits.

☒ *Check dried figs and discard any that look slightly mouldy or which have a slightly mouldy taste.*

Canned Figs

Green or golden figs in syrup are ready to serve for dessert. Combine them with other fresh green fruit to make an exotic salad. Try mixing sliced kiwi fruit, grapes, melon and canned figs then adding a topping of roughly chopped pistachio nuts.

Filo Pastry

See Pastry*.
Very thin Greek pastry, also spelt 'phyllo'. Strudel and Turkish pastries are similar. Tunisian malsouqua is another thin pastry, made from a thick batter.

Filo is made with flour, water and egg but it does not contain much fat. It cooks in crisp layers and may be used with savoury or sweet ingredients.

Buying

Large supermarkets sell filo, either frozen or chilled. The sheets measure about 35 × 20 cm/14 × 8 inches. They are rolled and packed in a sealed polythene bag, in a box.

Use

Thaw the pastry in its pack in the refrigerator or in a cool room. Prepare any fillings or other ingredients before unwrapping the pastry. Here are a few tips.

• The work surface must be clean and absolutely dry – the pastry will stick to damp patches, become soggy and break.

• Keep the pastry covered with a split polythene bag except when working with it, otherwise it will dry out and crumple.

• The sheets of pastry are usually used at least double or they may be kept in layers up to 4–6 sheets thick.

• Brush the sheets with a little oil or melted butter as you layer them. Brush with fat as you fold or roll the pastry. The fat seals the pastry together around filling, prevents it from drying out and gives crisp, separate layers when cooked.

Folding and Filling

Strudel To make a large strudel, overlap the edges of the sheets by about 5 cm/2 inches to give a large area of pastry. Have the pastry about 3 sheets thick.

Fillings such as sliced cooked apples with sugar, lemon and raisins, or chopped cooked ham with chopped spring onion, cooked green lentils and cheese may be used. Spread the filling evenly over the pastry, leaving a 2.5 cm/1 inch space all around the edge. Roll up the dough and filling, then place it on a greased baking tray – it may be curved if the tray is too small. Brush with melted butter. Bake at 180°C, 350°F, gas 4 for about 40 minutes, until golden. Dredge a sweet strudel with icing sugar and serve hot, warm or cold.
Triangular Pasties Use double thick sheets of pastry. Cut strips down the width of the dough from 5–10 cm/2–4 inches wide, depending on the size triangles required. Fill with mashed feta cheese and chopped spring onion, cooked chopped spinach with a little cooked onion and a little nutmeg or diced cooked mixed vegetables (potatoes, carrots, peas, onion) with a pinch of curry spices (see curry*). Place a little filling on the left side of the end of one strip and fold the corner of the strip over it. Brush the pastry with oil or melted butter, then fold the pastry and filling over and over from side to side to

make a triangular pasty. Bake at 200°C, 400°F, gas 6 for about 20–30 minutes.

Pies and Layered Dishes Layer the pastry in a greased dish or flan tin. Start with 3 layers of pastry, then add topping – some chopped walnuts, a sprinkling of ground mixed spice and a little honey is ideal – then add more pastry. Work up about 4 layers of filling and pastry sheets. Leave the edges of the pastry overhanging the side of the dish until all the layers are finished, then brush the top with melted butter and fold over the dough. Brush with more melted butter. Bake at 190°C, 375°F, gas 5 for about 50–60 minutes, until crisp and golden.

Savoury fillings may be used and the number of layers may be reduced.

Cook's Tip
Most packets contain a good number of sheets of filo. Any leftover should be filled promptly with a mixture that will freeze (for example, cheese and herbs), then shaped into small pasties and open frozen. Pack when hard. Bake from frozen as required, allowing a few minutes extra cooking time.

Fish

See Shellfish*.

There are two separate groups of fish: seafish and freshwater fish. The chart groups the different types in recognised categories, in addition separate notes are included on less familiar species.

Buying

Buy from a reputable fishmonger or seller. Note the standard of cleanliness and the way in which the fish is handled. The shop or stall should smell fresh; any establishments with a lingering odour, stale smell or very strong 'fishy' smell are best avoided.

Signs of Freshness

All fresh fish should look moist. Whole fish should look firm with bright eyes and markings. The skin should be bright and undamaged.

Cuts of fish – fillets or steaks – should be firm looking and moist. White fish should be a good white, salmon flesh should be bright and red, salmon trout or pink trout fillets should be a fresh pink colour.

The fish should be displayed on refrigerated counters or it should be laid on well-packed ice.

Any live seafood – lobsters, crabs or eels – should look lively. Live mussels in shells should be shut, cold and bright. Other seafood or shellfish, such as prawns, scallops or squid, should be bright and moist not sad, pale and dry.

Seafish Quality Award

This award is given by the Sea Fish Industry Authority to fishmongers who achieve a high standard in all aspects of handling, displaying and selling fish.

The award is given to fishmongers who offer quality fish and good service on premises of a high standard.

Preparation

A good fishmonger will prepare the fish to your requirements (see below). Not only does this save time and effort but it is more hygienic to allow the fishmonger to prepare the fish, than to have the mess in your own kitchen.

Gutting

Always ask the fishmonger to gut fish. If you have to gut fish at home (for example, mackerel, salmon or trout), then follow these guidelines.

1 Gut the fish as soon as possible after it is caught. Have ready a large clear area of work surface. Lay two or three thicknesses of newspaper on the surface.

2 Lay the package of fish on the newspaper or put a sheet of greaseproof paper under the fish. Cut the fish along the belly from head to tail, then scrape out all the innards on the paper. Make sure all the intestines are removed. As each fish is gutted place it on a large clean plate.

3 When all the fish are gutted, fold the paper around the innards and wrap them thoroughly before placing in the outside bin. Wash and dry your hands, then thoroughly wash each fish under cold running water.

4 Pat the fish dry on absorbent kitchen paper and place in a clean covered dish in the refrigerator until it is to be cooked.

5 Wash down all work surfaces, the sink and all utensils.

Trimming Whole Fish

Use a pair of kitchen scissors to cut off all fins. The head and tail may be left on the fish or removed: ask the fishmonger to remove the head and tail. To cut off the head yourself, place the fish on a clean board and use a heavy, sharp knife to cut off the head just below the gills. Tap the knife with a rolling pin or meat mallet if necessary. Pack all trimmings in paper and place in the outside bin. Rinse the fish under cold water and wash all surfaces and utensils well.

Scaling or Descaling

Some fish are covered with scales which should be removed before cooking. Again, ask the fishmonger to do this as it is a very messy task.

If you do have to scrape off the scales, hold the fish in a clean sink and have the tap running slowly. Hold the fish by its tail and use a sharp knife to scrape off all the scales, working from the tail towards the head. Keep the water running all the time to wash away the scales and rinse the fish occasionally.

Boning Round Fish

This technique is useful for mackerel or herring.

1. Gut the fish and remove the head, then split down the belly.

Make sure that the split goes right the way along to the edge of the tail.

2. Turn the fish on the board so that it has the skin side up. Press firmly down the middle of the fish, along its length, from the head end to the tail.

3. Turn the fish over and the back bone should lift off easily, bringing most of the smaller bones with it. Use a pair of kitchen scissors or a sharp knife to cut the bone off at the tail. Pick off any remaining bones.

Skinning Fish Fillets

Lay the fish fillet on a clean cutting board, skin down. Rub a little salt on your finger tips and hold the tail end of the fillet – the salt gives a bit of grip.

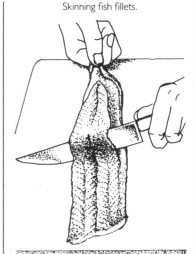
Skinning fish fillets.

Using a sharp knife, cut the flesh off the skin at the tail end. Once a small piece of flesh is separated from the skin, carry on cutting from side to side using a sawing action. Hold the knife at an acute angle to the skin so as not to cut through it.

As you cut, the fish flesh will fold back naturally. Keep it well folded back so that you can easily see where to cut between the next part of the flesh and the skin.

Rolling Fillets

Fine fillets from plaice, sole, trout, herring, mackerel or other small fish may be rolled up neatly for baking. Depending on the fish, the fillets should be skinned first.

Stuffing or seasoning ingredients (herbs, grated lemon rind, a little mustard on herring or mackerel) may be spread over the fillets or placed at the head end.

Start from the head end of the fillet and roll it up towards the tail end. Secure the roll with a wooden cocktail stick, then place the fish roll in a dish.

Cutting Goujons

Goujons are fine strips of fish. They may be cut from fillets of plaice, sole, whiting or mackerel.

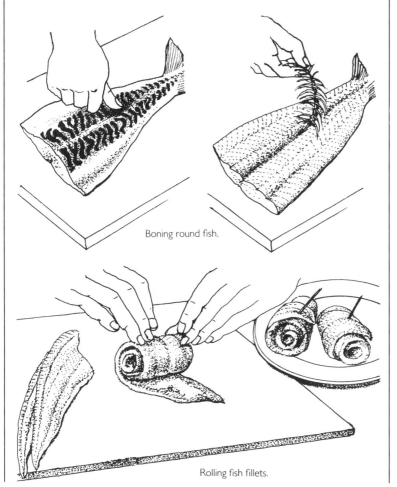
Boning round fish.

Rolling fish fillets.

SEE ALSO **Different Types of Fish and Cooking Methods** (pages 126–127)

Cutting goujons.

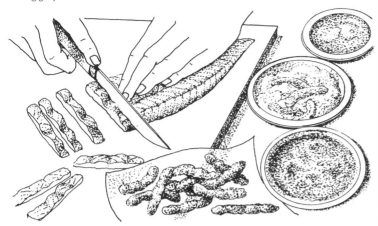

Larger fish, such as cod, haddock or coley, have flakes that are too large for cutting goujons. Plaice, whiting and sole fillets should be skinned. Cut across the fillets, making the strips about 1–2 cm/½–¾ inch wide.

Coat the strips in seasoned flour, egg and breadcrumbs. They may be deep or shallow fried or baked.

Filleting Fish

Filleting is a technique that is perfected with practice. All fishmongers will fillet fish for you at no extra cost, with speed and success. However, the following background information is useful so that you know what to expect.

Round Fish The fish should be gutted with head and tail on. Using a sharp, fine-bladed knife, cut from the head towards the tail, working along the backbone. Cut around the gills at the head end, then cut the flesh off the bones. Turn the flesh back as it is removed from the bones. Work close to the bones all down the length of the fish to the tail. Cut the fillet off at the tail end. Turn the fish over and repeat the process on the second side. This yields 2 fish fillets.

Flat Fish Cut the flesh to the bone around the head. Cut down the middle of the fish, into the back bone, from head to tail. Starting at the head end, slide the knife between the fish flesh and the

bones. Fold back the flesh so that you can see the bones and continue cutting the flesh off the bones all the way down to the tail. Work as close to the bones as possible. Cut the flesh off the opposite side: these are two quarter cut fillets. Turn the fish over and remove two quarter cut fillets from the other side.

Fishmongers usually sell two fillets from each fish such as plaice or lemon sole. If you ask for a whole fish to be filleted into quarter fillets, the flesh will be removed as described.

Cooking Methods

Fish cooks quickly and it is most important to avoid overcooking it. The main exception to this rule is freshwater eel which requires longer stewing. Overcooked fish is dry, the flakes break apart easily and it lacks taste.

Testing if Fish is Cooked Fish is cooked when the flesh is just firm and opaque. Look at raw white fish and notice that the flakes have a translucent appearance. When they are cooked they will turn opaque – a sort of hazy white for want of a better description. The fish should still be moist and the flakes should stay together easily.

Gently push the point of a knife between the flakes at the thickest part of the fish to check whether it is cooked. If the flakes are not quite ready, then cook for a further brief period.

The fish chart indicates the cooking methods that may be used.

Poaching

A moist cooking method for all types of fish. Fine fillets (for example plaice) should be rolled. The liquid used may be dry white wine or cider, fish stock, milk or a mixture of milk and stock, wine or cider and water. The cooking liquor should be reserved to make a sauce.

Larger whole fish may be poached in court bouillon (page 128). Court bouillon is discarded after cooking.

The best cooking pan is a large skillet, or deep, lidded frying pan. The cooking liquid should be about 2.5–3.5 cm/1–1½ inches deep in the pan so that the fish is half to two-thirds covered as it cooks.

Add a bay leaf, seasoning and a sprig of parsley to the liquid and heat it gently until simmering. Add the fish to the liquid, then regulate the heat so that the liquid is not quite simmering. Cover the pan and cook the fish gently for 5–15 minutes. Small portions of fillets will cook in about 5 minutes. Small whole fish take up to 15 minutes.

Have ready a heated serving dish and thickening ingredients for the sauce. Either prepare a roux (a mixture of flour cooked in a little fat) in a saucepan, ready to take the cooking liquor or make some beurre manié (flour creamed with fat: see Glossary, page 275) to whisk into boiling liquor.

Poaching Large Whole Fish

A fish kettle is required for large salmon, sea bass, grey mullet or carp. Fish kettles are expensive to buy but better cookshops do hire them out. Instead, a large roasting tin may be used and the fish may be curved into it on its belly, rather than lying on its side.

The fish should be gutted and trimmed, with head and tail on.

Note the weight of the fish to calculate the cooking time. Tie the body in two or three places to prevent it gaping during cooking and tie the mouth shut. If you have difficulty tying the mouth use a wooden cocktail stick.

Lay the fish on the trivet of a fish kettle or wrap two 5 cm/2 inch wide bands of thick foil under the fish to lift it easily. Put the bands under the main part of the body to prevent it breaking when cooked.

Have enough court bouillon in the pan to two-thirds cover the fish. The court bouillon should be cool or cold, not simmering. Lower the fish into the liquid and heat it very gently until it is just beginning to simmer. When you see the first couple of bubbles, reduce the heat and cover the pan. Cook the fish for 4–5 minutes per 450 g/1 lb.

To serve hot, lift the fish from the liquid. Have someone to help if you do not have a trivet, and use two fish slices as well as the bands of foil. Allow the fish to drain, then place it on a large serving platter.

Skinning and Garnishing Use kitchen scissors to snip the string around the fish. Use a small pointed knife and carefully cut the skin around the tail end, then pull it off gently towards the head end. Garnish the fish with parsley and lemon, then serve at once with a hot sauce, such as Hollandaise, Tomato Sauce or a white Wine Sauce (pages 236, 263 and 235).

To serve cold, leave the fish to cool in the cooking liquor. As soon as it is cool, lift it out of the liquor and remove the skin as above.

Boning Cooked Whole Fish This is fiddly but worth the effort. Use a sharp knife and cut around the head and tail into the bone. Slit the flesh down the middle, along the line of the bone. Use a palette knife and slide it horizontally between the fish flesh and the bone along the line of the back bone. Keep the knife close to the bone and loosen the fillet of fish. On a large fish it is easier if the fillet is

FISH IN SAUCE

This is a useful basic recipe: with canned fish extra milk or wine may be used instead of cooking liquor.

INGREDIENTS
675 g/1½ lb white fish fillets
175 ml/6 fluid oz water
1 parsley sprig
1 bay leaf
Sauce
25 g/1 oz margarine or butter
1 small onion, finely chopped
40 g/1½ oz plain flour
450 ml/¾ pint milk
grated rind of 1 lemon
30 ml/2 tablespoons chopped
    fresh parsley

FOOD VALUES:
TOTAL • PER PORTION
kcals: 1270 • 317
kJ: 5324 • 1331
protein: 162 g • 41 g
fat: 46 g • 11 g
carbohydrate: 55 g • 14 g
fibre: 6 g • 1 g

Serves 4

Place the fish in a large frying pan or saucepan and pour in the water. Add the parsley and bay leaf, then heat gently until the water is only just beginning to simmer. Reduce the heat slightly to prevent the water from simmering and continue to cook the fish for about 5 minutes, or until the flesh is just firm.

Have a large plate ready to hold the fish. Use a fish slice to lift the fillets from the cooking liquor, allow them to drain and place them on the plate. Reserve the cooking liquor.

Use two forks to push the fish flesh off the skin, picking out and discarding any bones as you work. Do this by holding the fillets in place with one fork and pushing the flakes off by separating them with the other fork. Transfer the fish flesh to a dish and discard the skin.

Melt the margarine or butter in a medium saucepan. Add the onion and cook gently until it is soft but not browned, stirring occasionally. Stir in the flour and cook, still stirring, over medium heat for 2 minutes. Slowly pour in the milk, stirring all the time, and increase the heat slightly to bring the sauce to the boil. As it boils, the mixture will thicken and it must be stirred well to prevent lumps forming. It will be very thick until the reserved cooking liquor is added.

Strain the liquor into the sauce and stir well, then allow it to simmer very gently (so that it is just bubbling) for 3 minutes. Stir in the lemon rind, parsley and a little seasoning. Add the flaked fish and mix it very lightly into the sauce. Heat gently for about a minute, then check the seasoning and remove the pan from the heat. Serve at once with rice, pasta or mashed potatoes or use as required.

USE

- Top with grated cheese and breadcrumbs and brown under the grill.
- Top with a savoury crumble* mixture and bake.
- Use as a filling for gougère (see choux pastry*).
- Pour into a baking dish, top with mashed potato and bake at 200°C, 400°F, gas 6 for 20–30 minutes, until golden.
- Use to fill pancakes*, then top with grated cheese and grill until golden.

SEE ALSO **Different Types of Fish and Cooking Methods** (pages 126–127)

cut in two across the middle. Lift the fillet off and lay it on a board.

Slide the point of a knife between the bones and remaining fillet, then remove it in the same way.

Now, snip the backbone at the head and tail, then carefully lift it off the fish, leaving the bottom fillets in place. Remove any stray bones before replacing the fillets.

Garnish with thin cucumber slices, piped mayonnaise, lemon and parsley. The garnish may be used to disguise any untidy areas.

Steaming

Place the prepared fish in a greased heatproof dish with lid or wrap it in greased cooking foil. The dish or pack should fit into a steamer or the dish may be placed directly over a saucepan of boiling water.

Add seasoning, herbs and other flavouring ingredients to the fish.

Have a large saucepan of boiling water and put the steamer with the fish or the dish over the water. Cover and cook for about 15–20 minutes.

Individual packages of steamed fish may be mopped dry on a clean tea-towel and transferred to plates ready to be opened at the table.

Casseroling

Fish casseroles can be delicious. To avoid overcooking the fish, it is important that other ingredients and sauce that requires long cooking are cooked before the fish.

Begin by cooking onion (with any celery, carrot, green or red pepper, fennel and garlic) in a little olive oil, butter or margarine until well softened but not browned. This takes at least 10 minutes, stirring occasionally, or up to 20 minutes.

Next add the liquid – canned tomatoes, stock, wine or cider – and bring the mixture to the boil. Curry sauce may be used instead of liquid. Add seasoning and any

FISH PIE

INGREDIENTS
1 quantity Fish in Sauce, made using smoked haddock or cod fillet
4 eggs, hard-boiled
50 g/2 oz frozen peas, thawed
225 g/8 oz puff pastry, thawed if frozen
beaten egg or milk to glaze

FOOD VALUES:
TOTAL • PER PORTION
kcals: 2854 • 714
kJ: 11936 • 2984
protein: 203 g • 51 g
fat: 159 g • 40 g
carbohydrate: 164 g • 41 g
fibre: 16 g • 4 g
Serves 4

Prepare the fish in sauce, removing the pan from the heat when the sauce is cooked and adding the fish off the heat. Do not cook the mixture any further. Shell and roughly chop the eggs, then add them to the fish in sauce. Drain the peas well and stir them into the mixture.

Set the oven at 220°C, 425°F, gas 7. Have ready a 1.7 litre/3 pint pie dish. Wash and dry your hands, then lightly flour a clean work surface. Roll out the pastry large enough to cover the top of the pie dish, plus about 2.5 cm/1 inch larger all around. Trim off a narrow strip of pastry (about 1 cm/½ inch wide) from the edge. Brush the rim of the pie dish with a little water and press the pastry strip on it.

Turn the fish mixture into the pie dish. Brush the pastry rim with a little water, then lift the rolled-out pastry over the top. Press the pastry all around the edge to seal in the filling. Holding the pie dish up at about shoulder level in one hand, use a sharp knife to trim off the excess pastry – see pies*.

Knock up the edge and pinch it neatly or mark into scallops. Cut a small hole in the middle of the pastry lid for steam to escape during cooking. Brush the top of the pastry with a little beaten egg or milk. Stand the pie on a baking tray. Bake for about 20 minutes, or until the pastry top is risen and golden. Serve freshly cooked.

vegetables that take a while to cook and simmer the sauce for about 10–15 minutes before adding the fish.

The fish may be cubed, rolled, in steaks or portions of fillets. Small whole fish may be casseroled (for example mullet). Nestle the fish into the sauce and regulate the heat so that the liquid is barely simmering. Cover the pan and cook for 10–25 minutes, depending on the fish. Do not overcook.

Serve with pasta, rice, baked potatoes or just have the casserole with crusty bread.

Shallow Frying

The prepared fish should be coated to protect the outside

during cooking (see coatings for food*). Seasoned flour or egg and breadcrumbs may be used. Batter is not suitable for shallow frying.

Have a frying pan large enough to hold the fish, a heated plate and absorbent kitchen paper to drain it, unless the cooking fat is to be used as a base for a sauce.

Heat a little oil or melt a little butter or margarine in the pan. Tilt the pan so that it is evenly coated with a thin layer of fat. Heat the fat until it is just below smoking hot, then add the fish to the pan and reduce the heat slightly. Cook the fish on one side for about 2–3 minutes, depending on thickness.

Use a fish slice and palette

knife to turn the fish over and cook the second side.

Fish with an egg and bread-crumb coating should be drained on absorbent kitchen paper.

If you like, add a squeeze of lemon juice, some parsley and a little freshly ground black pepper to the pan, then heat the juices and serve them with the fish. This is the usual way of serving any cooking butter or oil such as olive oil. Flaked almonds may be browned in the butter for trout.

Deep Frying

See Frying*.
Have the fish ready and coated or with the batter to hand. Have a large platter covered with double-thick absorbent kitchen paper.

Heat the oil to 180°C/350°F. Lower the pieces of fish into the oil and cook for between 3–5 minutes, depending on the thickness and size of the pieces. Small goujons cook in 1–2 minutes.

Drain the fish well on the absorbent kitchen paper. Serve at once.

Stir Frying

Pieces of firm white fish and other seafood may be added to stir fried vegetables. Vegetables such as celery, carrots, mange tout and spring onions make a delicious base. They should be two-thirds cooked before the fish is added.

Clear a space in the vegetables and add the pieces of fish. Cook over medium to high heat for 2–3 minutes, turning the fish once or twice but do not toss the ingredients vigorously. Gently mix the fish and vegetables just before serving.

Grilling

Place the rack in the grill pan. Heat the grill to high for thin cuts, to medium for whole fish. Have a little oil, melted butter or margarine for basting the fish. A little lemon juice and seasoning

may be added to the fat for basting.

Brush the underside of the fish with a little oil to prevent it sticking to the rack. Brush the top with the basting mixture.

Cook for about 4–5 minutes on the first side, until the fish is lightly browned and cooked. Turn and cook the second side in the same way. Use a large flat fish slice for turning the portions. Thin fillets do not need turning.

Kebabs: Firm portions of white fish, or fish wrapped in strips of bacon, may be threaded on metal skewers, then grilled as above. Small steaks of mackerel may be skewered sideways but they must be turned carefully to avoid breaking them.

Baking

Set the oven at 180°C, 350°F, gas 4. The prepared fish may be placed in a greased ovenproof dish or individual portions may be wrapped in greased cooking foil. Season the fish, add any flavouring ingredients and dot with butter, margarine or oil. Sprinkle with a little lemon juice, if liked, and cover the dish.

Bake the fish for 20–30 minutes. Thin rolls and finer portions cook quickly. Small whole fish will be cooked in about 30 minutes. Medium whole fish may require an extra 5–10 minutes.

Baking with a Topping Fish cutlets or steaks may have their central bones cut out and a stuffing or topping (breadcrumbs with grated cheese) added. In this case, set the oven at 190°C, 375°F, gas 5.

Arrange the topping or stuffing on the fish and dot it with a little fat, if liked. Bake the fish uncovered for about 20–30 minutes, or until the topping is browned and the fish flesh is cooked through.

Microwave Cooking

Fish cooks well in the microwave. Arrange thin parts towards the middle of the cooking

dish or overlap any thin tail ends. Arrange small whole fish head to tail in the dish. Cover the dish.

The following are a guide to timing; as well, check the microwave manufacturer's instructions and recipe book.

Turn and rearrange the fish once or twice during cooking – fillets may not need rearranging or turning but steaks and whole fish do unless single items are cooked. Leave the fish covered for 2 minutes before serving.
Fillet
225 g/8 oz 4–6 minutes
450 g/1 lb 7–10 minutes
Steaks (evenly sized, medium)
1   2–3 minutes
2   4–7 minutes
4   8–10 minutes
Small Whole Fish (trout or mackerel)
1   5–6 minutes
2   7–10 minutes
4   15–20 minutes

Flavouring and Garnishing Fish

Here are just a few ideas.
Carrots Cut them finely, by slicing, dicing or cutting in strips. Strips may be rolled in fine fillets. Use with baked or steamed fish.
Celery Slice thinly, dice or cut in fine strips. Ideal with steamed, poached or casseroled fish.
Fresh Root Ginger Excellent in fine shreds with steamed fish. Add soy sauce and spring onions.
Herbs Parsley, tarragon, dill, chervil and other delicate herbs go well with fish in most cooking methods. Good for garnishing as well. Rosemary and thyme may be used with stronger fish, such as mackerel.
Lemon or Lime Shredded or grated rind and the juice are all suitable for the moist cooking methods. Serve wedges with fried or grilled fish so that the juice may be squeezed over just before the fish is eaten.
Onions Cut onions finely and part cook them in a little oil or butter before adding to fish. Spring onions may be added to most fish, particularly steamed or baked fish.

SEE ALSO **Different Types of Fish** and **Cooking Methods** (pages 126–127)

FISH CAKES

INGREDIENTS
450 g/1 lb white fish fillets
150 ml/¼ pint milk
**1 kg/2 lb potatoes, boiled and
   mashed without any milk
   or butter**
**45 ml/3 tablespoons chopped
   fresh parsley**
salt and pepper
flour for shaping
50 g/2 oz margarine or butter

FOOD VALUES:
TOTAL • PER PORTION
kcals: 1693 • 141
kJ: 7149 • 596
protein: 114 g • 9 g
fat: 53 g • 4 g
carbohydrate: 204 g • 17 g
fibre: 11 g • 0 g

Makes 12

Place the fish in a frying pan or large saucepan and pour in the milk. Heat gently until the milk is just about to simmer, then lower the heat and cook the fish for about 5 minutes or until it is just firm. Leave to cool in the cooking liquid, then use a fish slice to remove the fillets from the pan and transfer them to a large plate. Reserve the cooking liquor. Flake the fish as in the recipe for Fish in Sauce (page 122).

Set the oven at 220°C, 425°F, gas 7. Thoroughly grease a large baking tray. Beat the mashed potato well to make sure it is smooth – it should be stiff at this stage. Beat in the reserved cooking liquor from the fish to soften it and mix in the parsley. Stir in the flaked fish and season the mixture well. Mark the mixture into 4, then into 8 portions.

Wash and dry your hands and flour a clean work surface. Spoon out a portion of the mixture on to the flour. Sprinkle a little extra flour on top of the fish mixture, then pat it down firmly with a palette knife or spatula. Use the knife and your other hand to shape the mixture into a neat, thick round cake, about 7.5 cm/3 inches across. Transfer it to the baking tray. Shape the remaining cakes and place them on the tray.

Dot the tops of the fish cakes with butter or margarine and bake them for 30 minutes until light golden. Use a fish slice to transfer them to plates and serve piping hot.

VARIATION

Canned tuna, pilchards, sardines or salmon may be used instead of white fish. Mash sardines with tomato sauce from the can. Add a little milk to the mixture if necessary to soften it.

Soy Sauce Sprinkle a little over fish before steaming. Add fresh root ginger and spring onions.

Some Less Familiar Fish

The range of fish on sale according to season and, to some extent, fashion or trends.
Redfish Available all year, this is a large golden red fish with white flesh and a good flavour. It may be baked whole or you can have the fish filleted.

Red Mullet Small, red-skinned fish with white flesh. Available from May to November, they are cooked whole by baking, casseroling, grilling or frying. Red mullet may also be steamed. They do not have a lot of flesh on them but they have a fine flavour.
Snappers Red snapper is one of the most common but others are available throughout the year. Another medium white fish that may be baked whole or filleted.

Swordfish Sold in steaks and available all year. The flesh is firm and meaty. Swordfish steak is ideal for grilling, baking, shallow frying and barbecuing. It is best to marinate the steaks first in a moist and slightly oily mixture as the flesh can be dry. Baste often during cooking.
Shark Sold all year, as steaks, the skin is removed before serving. The flesh is firm, meaty and dry. It should be marinated and basted during cooking. May be casseroled as well as grilling or frying. The flesh can be rather cartilaginous and the texture is not to everyone's liking.
Tuna Fresh tuna steaks, available all year, are dark red-brown in colour with distinct flakes. It is a dry fish which should be marinated and basted during cooking. Good barbecued, grilled, baked or casseroled.

Fish for Convenience

Frozen Fish This is usually good quality and offers excellent food value.

Thaw frozen fish overnight or for several hours in the refrigerator. If time does not allow for this, then cook the fish from frozen, making sure the process is very gentle and allowing extra time until the fish is cooked through.

X *Do not thaw fish by holding it in cold or running water. This results in fish with a poor texture and lack of flavour.*

Canned Fish There is a wide variety of canned fish which is ideal for making fish cakes, pies and other sauced dishes. It may also be used for sandwiches, pâtés, salads and serving on toast as a snack. Top pizza with canned fish or toss the flaked fish with freshly cooked pasta.

Read the label to check whether the fish is canned in oil, water, brine or some type of sauce. Brine, water or oil may be added to sauces; oil may be used as a dressing for salads. Alternatively, the contents may be drained.

DIFFERENT TYPES OF FISH AND COOKING METHODS

Key to Chart: **P** = Poaching **S** = Steaming **C** = Casseroling **SF** = Shallow Frying **DF** = Deep Frying **STF** = Stir Frying **G** = Grilling **B** = Baking

FISH	P	S	C	SF	DF	STF	G	B
Seafish – Flat White Fish **Brill** (fillets) June to February	•	•	•	•		•	•	•
Dab (fillets or whole) September to May	•			•	•	•	•	•
Flounder (fillets) March to November	•		•	•	•	•	•	•
Halibut^ (fillets, steaks or chunks) June to March	•		•	•		•	•	•
Megrim (fillets) May to March	•			•	•	•	•	•
Plaice (fillets or whole) May to February	•	•		•	•	•	•	•
Skate^ ('wings') May to February	•			•			•	•
Sole, Dover^ (whole or small fillets) May to February	•	•		•			•	•
Sole, Lemon^ (fillets or whole) May to March	•	•		•	•	•	•	•
Turbot^ (fillets or steaks) April to February	•		•	•		•	•	•
Seafish – Round White Fish **Bass** (whole or fillets) August to March	•	•		•			•	•
Catfish/Rockfish (fillets) February to July	•	•	•	•		•	•	•
Cod (fillets, steaks or chunks) June to February	•	•	•	•				
Coley/Saithe/Coalfish (fillets) August to February			•	•	•	•	•	•

Notes on Specific Fish (^)

Halibut Halibut has firm, delicately flavoured white flesh with a meaty texture.

Skate Skate, or ray as it is sometimes known, is a cartilaginous fish. The edible parts are the large wings, sold whole or in portions. Skate can smell very slightly of ammonia. It should be cooked on the same day as purchase. Fish that is kept has a more distinct smell of ammonia which can spoil its flavour. The skate may be blanched in simmering water with a little vinegar or lemon juice added for a minute, before being drained and grilled or fried in butter. Discard the blanching liquid.

Sole: Lemon and Dover These are not to be confused. Lemon sole is not a true sole but it is a fine-textured fish which has a distinct lemon hint to its flavour. Dover sole is considered the more superior, with an excellent flavour and firm, fine texture. Dover sole is always skinned as it has tough skin – the fishmonger will pull the skin off for you – and since the fillets are very often slim and small, Dover sole is most often cooked whole.

Turbot A large, firm, flat white fish with a good flavour. Expensive and meaty. Turbot can be poached whole – turbot kettles are available for this.

Monkfish Usually displayed prepared as monkfish have huge ugly heads. Only the tail meat is used for its fine flavour and firm texture.

DIFFERENT TYPES OF FISH AND COOKING METHODS

Key to Chart: **P** = Poaching **S** = Steaming **C** = Casseroling **SF** = Shallow Frying **DF** = Deep Frying
STF = Stir Frying **G** = Grilling **B** = Baking

FISH	P	S	C	SF	DF	STF	G	B
Conger Eel (steaks) March to October	●		●	●				●
Haddock (fillets or steaks) May to February	●	●	●	●	●	●	●	●
Hake (steaks) June to March	●	●	●	●	●	●	●	●
Huss/Dogfish/Flake/Rigg (fillets) All year			●	●	●		●	●
Monkfish^/Anglerfish (fillets) All year	●	●	●	●		●	●	●
Mullet, Grey (whole or fillets) September to February	●	●	●	●			●	●
Mullet, Red (whole) May to November		●	●	●			●	●
Whiting (fillets or whole) June to February			●	●	●	●	●	●
Seafish – Oily Fish **Herring** (whole or fillets) May to December				●			●	●
Mackerel (whole or fillets) All year		●		●	●	●	●	●
Sardine (whole) Jan, Feb, April, Nov and Dec				●			●	●
Tuna (steaks) All year			●	●		●	●	●
Freshwater Fish **Salmon** (whole, steaks or fillets) All year	●	●	●	●			●	●
Salmon Trout (whole or fillets) All year	●	●		●			●	●
Trout (whole or fillets) All year	●	●		●			●	●

Accompaniments for Fish

● Potatoes – boiled, new, mashed, sautéed, chips or baked. With all sorts of fish.

● Salads – tomato, mixed, green or salad of cooked vegetables, such as potatoes, all go well with grilled or shallow fried fish.

● Pasta or rice – both delicious with fish in sauce or casseroled fish. Also good with moist steamed or baked fish.

● Sauces to serve with fish include tartare sauce, with fried or grilled fish; parsley sauce, with steamed or baked fish; cheese sauce, with poached or steamed fish; Hollandaise sauce, with poached, steamed or baked fish; tomato sauce, with poached, steamed, grilled, shallow fried or baked fish.

● Other accompaniments include lemon wedges for their juice, deep fried parsley and croûtons* with poached or sauced fish.

Stuffing Fish

See Stuffings.
Whole fish such as trout or mackerel may be stuffed. Thin fillets (plaice or sole) may be stuffed before rolling. Steaks and cutlets may have the central bone removed and they may be stuffed before baking.

Fish Stock

Fish stock cubes may be purchased, some are salty and too strong in flavour, others are good. Also look for chilled fish stock. Use trimmings from white fish for making stock. Heads, bones and skin may be used. Ask the fishmonger for trimmings for stock – those from plaice or sole are ideal. If you have only a small quantity of trimmings, then add some inexpensive fish fillet, such as coley, but do not use more than about 225 g/8 oz when making 600–750 ml/1–1¼ pints stock or the flavour will be too strong.

Place the trimmings in a saucepan. Add a sliced onion, carrot, celery stick, bay leaf, parsley sprig and 4 black peppercorns. Pour in plenty of cold water to cover and heat gently until just boiling. Reduce the heat and cover the pan, then leave the stock to simmer very gently for about 45–60 minutes. Strain the stock and use as required.

Court Bouillon

Place a sliced onion, carrot, celery stick and bay leaf in a saucepan. Add 8 black peppercorns and pour in 1.1 litres/2 pints water. Bring to the boil, reduce the heat and cover the pan. Simmer the mixture for 15 minutes. Add 100 ml/4 fluid oz white wine vinegar or cider vinegar and leave the court bouillon to cool slightly before using.

Storing and Freezing

Keep fresh fish as cool as possible from the time of purchase until it is unwrapped and placed in a covered dish in the refrigerator. It is best to use the fish on the day it is purchased but it may be kept in the refrigerator for 24 hours.

Bought frozen fish is prepared and frozen soon after it is caught to ensure high quality. Unless it is bought from a fisherman, at the quayside, most wet fish is not suitable for long term freezing. Freshly caught fish should be gutted, rinsed, dried (prepared as for cooking), then frozen. However, it is possible to buy fresh wet fish from a fishmonger and freeze it immediately, in which case it may be stored in the freezer for up to 3 months. Always pack the fish in airtight polythene bags and freeze it promptly after purchase.

Do not refreeze fish that has been thawed.

Prepared fish cakes freeze well but most forms of cooked fish become dry and weak in flavour if frozen, so it is not worth freezing cooked fish.

Nutritional Value

Fish is a protein food and it also provides calcium, iodine and fluorine. All fish contains riboflavin, niacin, vitamins B6 and B12; in addition, the oily fish are a source of vitamins A and D.

The majority of fish has a low fat content; however oily fish are rich in polyunsaturated fats. There is some indication that the fat contained in fish may make a positive contribution towards preventing heart disease.

Flaky Pastry

This is a rich, light-textured pastry which puffs into layers when cooked. It does not rise as well as puff pastry but it is easier to make.

Use

• As a sweet or savoury pie covering.

• For mince pies, sausage rolls, pastry horns or other small pastries.

• Instead of puff pastry, except for vols-au-vent that require the depth of puff pastry.

Technique

1. Mix both types of fat in a basin, cutting them together with a knife. When reasonably well mixed, press the fat down in the basin and divide it into quarters, then chill it.

2. Sift the flour into a bowl. Add a quarter of the fat and cut it into the flour. Wash and dry your hands under cold water. Rub the fat into the flour until it is thoroughly mixed and fine.

3. Using a palette knife, or blunt knife, mix in about 100 ml/4 fluid oz cold water (about 105–120 ml/7–8 tablespoons). Gather the dough together with your fingertips – it should be fairly soft. Press gently together into a ball.

4. Lightly flour a clean surface. Place the dough on it and knead gently two or three times so that it is just smooth. Do not handle the dough roughly. Roll out into an oblong measuring 15 × 35 cm/6 × 14 inches. Mark the oblong into thirds, by drawing the blunt edge of a knife across it in two places.

5. Dot one of the remaining quarters of the fat over the top two-thirds of the pastry. Leave the fat in chunks, do not be tempted to flatten them. Leave a neat space around the edge of the pastry so that you can seal the fat in at the next stage.

6. Fold the bottom third of pastry over the middle third, then fold the top third down over the top. Press the edges of the dough together well to seal in the fat.

7. Give the block of pastry a quarter turn clockwise so that the right edge is facing you. Using the rolling pin, press several ridges in the pastry, then roll it out lightly to an oblong about the same size as before.

8. Mark into thirds, dot with fat and fold the pastry as before. Place the pastry on a plate and cover with a polythene bag.'Chill for 20–30 minutes. Chill the remaining fat too.

SEE ALSO **Flageolet:** Beans and Pulses, Dried; **Flambé:** Glossary; **Flapjack:** Oats

Flaky Pastry
(Numbers relate to text steps)

9. Roll the pastry once more to use the last portion of fat, then chill again. Roll and fold it once more without using any fat. The pastry is now ready for use.

Cook's Tip
Instead of chilling the pastry in the refrigerator, place it in the freezer for 5–10 minutes.

If the pastry begins to feel greasy at any time, then stop working on it, place it in a polythene bag and chill.

Quantities

Use three-quarters fat to flour. For example use 225 g/8 oz plain flour and 175 g/6 oz fat. The most satisfactory fat is a combination of 75 g/3 oz lard with 75 g/3 oz block margarine (or butter). If preferred, all margarine may be used. Soft spreading margarine is not suitable.

FOOD VALUES: TOTAL
kcals: 2003
kJ: 8357
protein: 22 g
fat: 138 g
carbohydrate: 180 g
fibre: 8 g

Although these food values look very high in fat, remember that they are for the total batch of pastry made with 225 g/8 oz flour as here. The value of individual portions depends on the amount of pastry eaten, for example whether the pastry is used to make a pie to serve 6 or to make 24 sausage rolls. Remember to add on the value of fillings used with the pastry. Rich pastry of this type is something of a treat and it should be an occasional indulgence.

Storing

Keep the made pastry in a sealed polythene bag in the refrigerator for up to 2 days.

It may be frozen for 3–4 months.

Cooking

Cook flaky pastry at 220°C, 425°F, gas 7. The pastry cooks in about 15–20 minutes after which time the oven temperature should be reduced if any filling requires lengthy cooking.

Flans

A flan is a filled case. The case may be made from pastry, sponge or crushed biscuits and the filling can be sweet or savoury, cooked or cold.

Flan Tins, Rings and Dishes

Flan Tins Two types: the first has a raised middle and a deeper moat around the edge. This is for baking sponge mixture. When cooked and turned out the middle may be filled.

The second type is for lining with pastry or a biscuit crust and it may be one piece or it may have a loose bottom for easy removal of the flan.

The metal type without a loose bottom is not a good buy. Although it is possible to remove a baked empty pastry case, filled flans have to be served in the tin.
Flan Rings These are metal rings which are placed on a baking tray. The ring is lined with pastry and the flan baked. The ring may be lifted off the cooked flan, which can then be transferred to a serving dish using a large slice.
Flan Dishes Ovenproof glass or ceramic, these are used for serving prepared pastry or biscuit crust flans.

Metal tins or rings produce the best pastry case as the base cooks well. Some glass dishes also produce a well cooked base. Thick ceramic dishes do not allow the pastry base to cook as well as in metal tins.

Pastry Flans

See Short Crust Pastry.*
Short crust or any of the variations may be used for making a pastry flan case.

Quantities

Pastry made with 225 g/8 oz flour will yield enough dough to line a 25–30 cm/10–12 inch flan tin or dish. About 175 g/6 oz flour will give enough pastry for a 23 cm/9 inch flan and 100 g/4 oz flour will make enough pastry for a 15 cm/6 inch flan.

The quantity of pastry depends on how thinly and evenly it is rolled. Deep flan dishes require slightly more pastry. A confident pastry cook can roll pastry made with 175 g/6 oz flour to line a 25 cm/10 inch flan tin; this gives a thin pastry case.

Lining the Flan Tin

Place a flan ring on a baking tray. A loose-bottomed flan tin should also be placed on a tray. It is also easier to lift most flan dishes if they are placed on a baking tray.

Roll the prepared pastry into a circle (or oblong, depending on the shape of the tin) which is about 7.5 cm/3 inches larger than the diameter of the tin or dish.

Have the tin next to the pastry on the work surface. Place the rolling pin across the middle of the pastry, then fold half the pastry over the rolling pin. Use the rolling pin to lift the pastry over the flan tin, holding it above the middle of the tin.

Steady the pastry with one hand as you unroll it off the rolling pin over the tin.

Now work fairly speedily before the pastry has time to crack over the rim of the tin. Lift the edge of the pastry with one hand and gently nudge it down into

Lining a Flan Tin

the rim of the dish with the fore-fingers of the other hand. Work around the inside of the dish once, just to prevent the pastry from breaking where it over-hangs the tin.

Then work around the pastry again, this time encouraging the top edge to push downwards slightly, pressing the pastry into any flutes and making sure the base of the dish is lined right up to the edge.

Curve any excess dough out-wards, then roll the rolling pin over the top of the tin to press off the excess.

At this stage, use the trim-mings to patch up any small breaks or cracks in the pastry.

Prick the base all over with a fork, then chill the pastry well.

Baking Blind
Set the oven at 200°C, 400°F, gas 6. Lay a sheet of greaseproof paper in the pastry flan. Sprinkle dried peas or ceramic baking beans over the paper. This pre-vents the pastry from bubbling up in the middle as it cooks.

Bake the case for 15 minutes. At this stage it is part cooked and ready for any baked filling.

To cook the pastry completely, bake for 20 minutes, then remove the paper and baking beans and continue to bake the pastry for another 5–10 minutes, until it is golden and cooked through. Leave to cool before filling as required.

Storing the Pastry Case
The raw, part-baked or cooked pastry case may be wrapped in a polythene bag and kept in the refrigerator for up to 3 days.

The pastry case may be frozen, sealed in a polythene bag, for up to 3 months. Thaw for 2–4 hours at room temperature before use. Crisp the cooked case in the oven for a few minutes.

Sponge Flans

You will need a sponge flan tin. It should be well greased or pre-pared according to the manu-facturer's instructions. Set the oven at 160°C, 325°F, gas 3.

One-stage Mixture
Place 75 g/3 oz soft margarine, 75 g/3 oz caster sugar, 75 g/3 oz self-raising flour, 5 ml/1 tea-spoon baking powder, 1 large egg and the juice of 1 lemon in a mixing bowl. Beat the mixture by hand or using an electric mixer until all the ingredients are thoroughly combined. The mixture should be pale and soft.

Spread the mixture evenly over the prepared tin, making sure that plenty goes down into the deeper rim.

Bake the sponge flan for 30–35 minutes, until it is risen and golden. It should feel springy to the touch. Allow to cool for 2 minutes in the tin, then carefully ease the sponge away from the tin around the edge using a blunt knife. Turn out the flan on to a wire rack to cool.

FOOD VALUES: TOTAL
kcals: 1195
kJ: 5001
protein: 15 g
fat: 68 g
carbohydrate: 139 g
fibre: 3 g

When calculating the food value of the sponge flan, remember to add on the value of the filling before dividing the total into the number of portions. The above flan will serve 6–8.

Biscuit Crumb Cases

These are suitable for sweet fill-ings, for cheesecakes or set fill-ings such as mousse. For a quick dessert, fill a biscuit flan case with fresh fruit and glaze the top with warmed jelly marmalade or any other jelly preserve. Strawberries, plums, peaches, apricots, raspberries or canned fruit may be used.

Quantities

To line the base and sides of a 23 cm/9 inch flan tin or dish, use 350 g/12 oz digestive biscuits and 150 g/5 oz butter or margarine.

Break the biscuits into chunks and place them in a polythene bag. Fold the end of the bag over and use a rolling pin or bottle to crush the biscuits. Take care not to split the bag or the biscuit crumbs will gush out and make a dreadful mess. Set the crushed biscuits aside in their bag.

If you have a food processor, then crush the biscuits in it.

Melt the butter or margarine in a large saucepan. Take the pan off the heat and stir in the crushed biscuits. Mix the crumbs and butter really well until they are thoroughly coated and cling together. Turn the mixture into the flan dish, then use the back of a metal spoon to press it out over the base and up the side of the dish.

Wash and dry your hands, then use a forefinger to press the biscuit mixture into the bottom rim of the dish and tidy up the top edge.

Chill the flan case for at least an hour at this stage so that the biscuits become firm.

Savoury Fillings for Flans

There are two main options: either the part-baked case is filled with prepared ingredients and coated in an egg and milk mixture, then baked or a cooked sauce filling may be use. If a cooked sauce filling is used, the pastry case should be fully cooked, then the top of the filling should be grilled or baked until brown.

Baked Savoury Custard Fillings

For a 23 cm/9 inch flan case, beat 3 eggs, then stir in 300 ml/½ pint milk. This is sufficient to fill a flan which has at least 2–3 of the following ingredients.

Onion Finely chop 1 large onion and cook it in a little oil or butter until soft but not browned.

For an onion flan, finely slice 450 g/1 lb onions and cook them in olive oil or butter in a large frying pan until they are thoroughly softened and just beginning to brown. This will take about 20 minutes over medium heat, with frequent stirring. The result is a delicious flan, particularly if a cheese pastry case is used.

Cheese Use finely grated cheese, between 50–100 g/2–4 oz, depending on the other fillings. Emmenthal, Gruyère, Cheddar, Lancashire or any other hard cheese may be used.

Bacon Diced, rindless, lean bacon should be cooked with onion or on its own, then cooled slightly before placing in the flan. About 100 g/4 oz is sufficient to flavour a flan but up to 225 g/8 oz may be used.

Cooked Ham Diced or shredded cooked ham goes well with onion and cheese. Use 100 g/4 oz.

Mushrooms Thinly slice 225–350 g/8–12 oz button mushrooms and toss them in hot butter or olive oil until they are reduced in volume. Use a draining spoon to transfer them to the flan case. Use the cooking liquor as part of the volume of liquid to eggs. Good with fromage frais instead of milk.

Courgettes Trim and thinly slice 225 g/8 oz young courgettes and sprinkle them over cooked onion. Top with about 50 g/2 oz grated cheese and the egg and milk mixture.

Cooking the Fillings

Pour the well seasoned custard mixture over the other filling ingredients. Bake the flan at 180°C, 350°F, gas 4 (reduce the temperature if necessary after baking blind) for 50–60 minutes, until the filling is golden and set.

Sauce-based Fillings

Cook a finely chopped onion in 25 g/1 oz margarine until soft but not browned. Stir in 40 g/1½ oz plain flour and cook for 1 minute,

stirring. Gradually pour in 600 ml/1 pint milk, stirring all the time, and bring to the boil, still stirring. Simmer for 3 minutes. Add any of the following.

Tuna or Salmon Drain a 200 g/7 oz can tuna or salmon (use the liquor from salmon as part of the measured milk). Flake the fish, removing skin and bones, then add it to the sauce with 30 ml/2 tablespoons chopped fresh parsley and seasoning to taste.

Ham and Cheese Flan Add 100–175 g/4–6 oz diced cooked ham and 75 g/3 oz grated Cheddar cheese.

Chicken Add 225 g/8 oz diced cooked chicken and 50 g/2 oz sliced button mushrooms. A little chopped tarragon may be added.

Topping and Browning

Spread the sauce filling in the flan. Sprinkle 25 g/1 oz fresh breadcrumbs mixed with 25 g/1 oz grated cheese over the top. Bake the flan at 200°C, 400°F, gas 6 for about 15–20 minutes, until golden.

Sweet Fillings for Flans

Cold Fruit Flans

Spread 600 ml/1 pint confectioner's custard (see custard*) in a sweet cooked flan case, either pastry or sponge. Arrange fresh or canned fruit on top – try strawberries, raspberries, sliced peaches or mangoes, halved apricots or cherries.

To glaze the fruit, heat 175 g/6 oz redcurrant jelly, jelly marmalade or apricot jam in a saucepan until melted. Bring the melted preserve to the boil. Sieve jam or marmalade to remove pieces of fruit, then warm again. Brush the warm preserve over the fruit.

Alternatively fruit juice may be thickened with arrowroot* and used to glaze the flan.

Cooked Fruit Flans

Have ready a part-baked pastry flan case, made from plain or rich pastry – do not let the pastry become brown as it bakes blind. While the pastry is baking, prepare any of the following.

Apples Quarter, peel, core and thickly slice 900 g/2 lb cooking apples. Toss the slices in plenty of lemon juice, then arrange them, overlapping, in the flan. Sprinkle with 75 g/3 oz demerara sugar. Bake at 180°C, 350°F, gas 4 for 45–50 minutes.

Plums Halve and stone 675 g/ 1½ lb plums and arrange them in the flan. Brush 100 g/4 oz clear honey over the fruit. Bake at 180°C, 350°F, gas 4 for about 40 minutes.

Other Sweet Fillings

Other fillings which may be used with cooked sponge or pastry flans include sweet mousses*, scoops of ice cream* or sorbet*, fresh or canned fruit coated in part set jelly*, or blancmange* or custard* poured over a base of cooked or fresh fruit.

Flies

An enemy of hygiene. The house fly has a most unsavoury life-cycle during which it visits dung heaps or the excrement of any animals. Flies feed on even the most minute scraps of food but in order to digest them, they first vomit on the food before consuming it. They also lay eggs on food sources, these eggs hatch into maggots which eventually turn into flies.

So, there is every good reason to keep flies out of the kitchen and well away from any food. Take particular care during the summer months.

● Keep kitchen windows shut if possible when preparing food and cooking.

● Use a fly killer or deterrent recommended for kitchen use and follow the manufacturer's instructions closely.

● Never leave food out on the work surface uncovered. When eating outside, keep food covered as far as possible.

Flooring

There is a good choice of kitchen floor coverings, including carpet. You are by far the best judge of the use that your kitchen floor gets but it is a good idea to seek out as much expert advice as is available, at the same time remember the following.

● The covering must be suitable for the type of base, for example many kitchens have concrete floors.

● The covering should be resistant to moisture and spillages.

● The floor covering must be washable or specially recommended for kitchen use.

● The covering should be non-slip.

● Avoid loose mats, turned-up edges and poor joins that can cause bad accidents. The covering should fit well to avoid trapping dirt around the edges.

Flour

There is a wide choice of flour in the shops and the majority is derived from wheat.

Wheat Grain

The wheat grain is made up of the *germ* which is the small part of the seed that will grow. The main part of the grain is the *endosperm* and it is surrounded by seed coats and a tough outer *pericarp*.

Flour is made by milling, or grinding, the grain. The particular type of wheat grain and the climate in which it is grown combine to give the flour certain characteristics. In addition, the percentage of the grain used determines the type of flour.

Types of Flour

There are three basic types of flour and many more varieties.

Wholemeal Flour This is sometimes known as wholewheat flour. This flour contains the whole of the wheat grain. It is known as 100 per cent extraction flour.

Brown Flour Contains about 85 per cent of the grain. This type of flour is often sold under particular brand names.

White Flour This contains about 75 per cent of the grain (sometimes less), with most of the bran and wheatgerm removed.

Flour for Different Uses

The following are also standard types.

Plain Plain flour refers to plain white flour. In American cookbooks you will find all-purpose flour (beware: flours differ according to the type of wheat used and the results in baking can be startlingly different).

Self-raising Flour White, brown and wholemeal types are available. These flours have added raising agent.

Strong Flour This is usually a white flour. It has a high protein or gluten content which makes it ideal for breads and yeasted mixtures.

Soft or Sponge Flour The opposite to a strong flour, this has a low protein or gluten content and it is ideal for light cakes.

Malted Wheat Flour The trade name for this type of flour is 'Granary'. Usually a brown flour with grains of malted wheat added to give a nutty texture and flavour.

81 Per Cent Extraction This flour is usually sold under brand names; check details on the packet.

Stoneground This refers to the milling method, not the composition of the flour.

Storing

It may come as a surprise to learn that flour does go off. Plain white flour keeps for 4–6 months; self-raising for 2–3 months. Wholemeal flour has a higher fat content and it goes rancid quicker

SEE ALSO **Fleurons, Florentine:** Glossary; **Flounder:** Fish; **Fondant:** Icings; **Fondue:** Glossary

than white flour. Always check the 'best before' date on the packet.

Flour is best kept in the bag, in an airtight container, in a cool, dry, dark cupboard.

Never add new flour to the remnants of old flour in containers. Always wash and thoroughly dry containers before putting new flour in them.

Non-wheat Flours

These are not used extensively but they are available from wholefood shops or ethnic stores. Different flours vary in their cooking properties, so they are not necessarily interchangeable.

Rye Flour A heavy, pale grey flour. Use it half and half with wheat flour (strong white) to make delicious rye bread. Used extensively in Eastern European cooking.

Rice Flour Use for making some Oriental noodles and doughs. Also used for making biscuits.

Maize Flour Used for making Mexican tortillas (pancakes) and American corn bread.

Chick Pea Flour Known as *besan* and available from ethnic stores, this is used for Indian pancakes and fritters.

Nutritional Value

Flour contains carbohydrate, protein, thiamin, nicotinic acid and calcium. Wholemeal and brown flours are also useful sources of fibre. Even white flour provides as much fibre as some vegetables (weight for weight).

Food Intolerance

This is a term used to describe abnormal unpleasant reactions (not psychological in origin) to certain foods. There are a number of different types of intolerance. For example, some adults (especially of Asian nationality) cannot digest the carbohydrates in milk, causing colic and pain.

True Allergy

A true allergy occurs when the immune system reacts, just as it does in illness, to protect the body against something foreign.

True food allergy is more common in young children under the age of 3 years, especially to milk protein, eggs and wheat.

Signs of Intolerance

Common symptoms are skin irritation and problems such as diarrhoea, stomach pain and vomiting. Eczema and asthma can also be aggravated by food intolerance.

Which Foods and Why?

Contrary to popular belief, it is mainly natural components of certain foods that cause intolerance rather than additives. Wheat (the gluten content), beans and pulses (particularly soya beans), peanuts, milk, eggs, fish and shellfish are some examples of foods that can cause reactions.

A few individuals show intolerance to some types of additives. For example tartrazine (a yellow colouring) causes reactions in a few people, some people are sensitive to benzoates (used as preservatives) and others to sulphites, also used as preservatives.

The problem of food intolerance has received much publicity – probably because much of the information about is the result of comparatively recent research – but to put it into perspective, only a small percentage of the population suffer from it and then only to a few foods.

Coping with Food Intolerance

Doctors and dietitians diagnose and treat food intolerance. The dietitian or doctor can interrogate an information source known as The Food Intolerance Database to provide the sufferer with a list of manufactured foods free of the problem food ingredient. On a daily basis being a careful shopper is important, taking note of all the information on labels and looking for alternative foods. When a reaction is first confirmed it is worth spending time shopping very carefully and looking at the variety of different foods available, taking note of the ones to avoid and others to buy instead. To some extent the solution is to change shopping, eating and cooking habits.

X *Radical changes in eating habits or diet restrictions should not be undertaken without medical advice as severe dietary inadequacies can result.*

Fools, Fruit

Fruit fools are creamy desserts, made by combining puréed fruit with whipped cream or custard. Fromage frais or thick yogurt may also be used.

Some fruit should be cooked before being puréed – apples, gooseberries, currants and rhubarb – soft fruit may be puréed raw.

Purée the fruit in a liquidiser or food processor, then press it through a sieve, if necessary, to remove pips or traces of skin. For example, both raspberries and blackberries have unpleasant pips.

Sweeten the purée to taste with sugar (use icing sugar with uncooked fruit as it dissolves easily) or honey; some fruits may not need sugar. Grated orange, lemon or lime rind may be added to bland fruit purées, such as apple. Whole spices (cinnamon and cloves) may be cooked with fruit.

Combine 300 ml/½ pint full-flavoured cold fruit purée with 450 ml/¾ pint thick cold custard* or confectioner's custard, whipped double cream, thick yogurt or fromage frais*. If using fromage frais, carefully drain off loose liquid before disturbing it in its tub – this gives a thicker result.

Use a large metal spoon to fold the two mixtures together. Spoon the fool into glass dishes or large wine glasses and chill it for at least an hour.

Fruits for Fools

- Cooked gooseberries with grated lime rind or chopped preserved stem ginger.
- Cooked apples with cinnamon and orange rind.
- Cooked blackcurrants or redcurrants.
- Raw mango, peach, apricot or nectarine.
- Strawberries, raspberries or blackberries.
- Passion fruit with peach or paw paw.

Freezers and Freezing

There are three main types of freezer: chest, upright and fridge-freezers. The choice depends on the size required, use, space available and the position for siting the appliance.

Before Buying

Deciding on the size of freezer is not easy. As well as cost, there are three points to consider. Make a checklist and jot down as much information as possible.
1. Where to site the freezer.
2. What to use it for.
3. Which type of appliance.

Siting a Freezer

The freezer has to be near a 13 amp socket. It should be kept in a dry place, preferably cool, although some types of freezer are more suitable for a warm kitchen. The freezer should not be placed next to a heat source, for example a cooker or boiler.

There should be a small amount of space behind and around the freezer for the air to circulate.

The freezer must be in a reasonably accessible place, with a light for finding food in the dark.

A warm room, cupboard, conservatory or similar buildings that get hot on sunny days are not suitable.

The freezer should not be sited in a damp place as this causes the exterior cabinet to deteriorate and it can adversely affect the unit.

The ideal place for the freezer is a cool utility room, near the kitchen, or a spacious integral garage.

Use

Think about the use you expect to get from a freezer.

- Storing bought frozen food.

- Shopping less frequently for certain foods, buying larger quantities.

- Freezing fresh produce – home grown, pick-your-own or bought from a local producer when inexpensive and good quality.

You may want a freezer for just one reason or all three.

Calculating a certain amount of space for each member of the household is not the best way of deciding on the type of appliance. It is better to list the foods you intend freezing and to jot down some idea of the quantities in which you eat them over a period of a month. Think about the bulk of food you buy when you go shopping and you will get some idea of how much space certain items will take up in the freezer.

Types of Freezer

Chest Freezers

These have a hinged lid and the food is stored in a chest compartment. They vary in size from medium to very large.

Advantages Slightly less expensive than the upright type. This type holds a lot of food for its volume. There is minimal loss of cold air when the lid is opened.

Disadvantages It is more difficult to organise the contents. Shorter people can have distinct problems reaching items at the bottom furthest corner of a large chest freezer. A chest freezer takes up more floor space than an upright freezer. Not suitable for siting in a kitchen, where the lid must be kept clear, also best suited to an unheated site.

Ideal for garages, utility rooms, unheated spare rooms. Good for storing bulk purchases and lots of fresh produce.

Look for a locking lid (particularly if buying secondhand) and an internal light.

Upright Freezers

These have a front opening door with a series of shelves or drawers inside. They vary in height and width; some are designed to fit under the work surface.

Advantages They are usually suitable for siting in a kitchen. It is easy to see the contents and to organise the food. It is easier to remove food items. They take up less floor space. Better for delicate foods as they are less likely to get crushed.

Disadvantages An upright freezer provides slightly less storage space for its size than a chest freezer. Large items of food (such as whole salmon or long French loaves) may not fit in. Slightly more cold air is lost when the door is open – although this varies with the design of the shelf fronts or drawers.

Ideal for kitchens or small utility rooms. An excellent second freezer – have a chest freezer for storing bulk and a small upright (or fridge-freezer) in the kitchen for transferring food to or for delicate items.

Look for drawers or shelf fronts that fit well.

Fridge-Freezers

These combine a refrigerator and freezer in one appliance, with two separate doors. The fridge may be above or below the

---

SEE ALSO **Forcemeat:** Stuffing; **Frankfurters:** Sausages freezer, or the appliance may be wide with doors side by side. The fridge and freezer compartments may be equal in size or either one may be larger than the other.

> ☒ *Do not give up refrigerator space to gain freezer room: the refrigerator is the most important food storage area in the kitchen, it should provide plenty of space for all fresh food and it should not be overcrowded or it will not work efficiently. Loss of refrigerator space can result in bad hygiene.*

Advantages The main advantage of this appliance is that it saves space and provides proper freezer storage for anyone who wants to freeze small amounts of food.
Disadvantages Limited storage room for both freezer and refrigerator.
Ideal for single people, small families and homes where space is at a premium.
Look for an appliance with the right balance of refrigerator to freezer space for your needs.

General Features

Controls Check that the controls are easy to reach and use. You may want controls that are out of the reach of young children.
Fast Freeze Setting This overrides the thermostat on the freezer and keeps the motor running to reduce the internal temperature so that fresh food may be frozen quickly and effectively.
Star Rating Be sure that the freezer has the four star rating as illustrated. This means that it is suitable for long-term food storage and for freezing fresh food. Three star freezers are suitable for storing frozen food for up to 3 months but not for freezing fresh food. Two star freezer compartments run at −12°C/10°F and they may only be used for storing bought frozen foods for up to a month. One star compartments

run at −6°C/21°F and should only be used for keeping bought frozen food for up to a week.
Thermometer Some freezers have thermometers to check the internal temperature.
Drainage Hole In a chest freezer: some have this for draining away water when defrosting.

Temperature

The freezer should run at −18°C/0°F or just below to store food safely and to keep it in good condition for long periods.

If the freezer does not have a thermometer on it, then buy one to check the internal temperature and adjust the controls to maintain the cold setting.

Freezing Food

Always read and follow the manufacturer's instructions.

FISH, POULTRY AND MEAT

Food	Storage Time
Fish	
White Fish	3–4 months
Oily Fish	2–3 months
Poultry and Game	
Chicken	9–12 months
Duck	4–6 months
Game Birds	6–9 months
Goose	3–4 months
Turkey	6–9 months
Venison	9–12 months
Meat	
Bacon	
traditional cure	2–3 weeks
vacuum packed,	
low salt	4–6 weeks
joints, vacuum	
packed	1–2 months

Note The more fat and more salt the lower the storage time. Exclude as much air as possible from packs. Bought vacuum packs keep best.

Beef	9–10 months

Note The leaner cuts keep longer, if well packed and frozen at low temperatures, for up to 12 months.

Lamb	6–9 months
Pork	6–9 months

Choice of Food

The chart provides guidelines for the storage times for different types of food. All food for freezing must be fresh and in the best condition. Freezing will not improve food and any that is not at its best may well deteriorate during freezing and thawing.

Freeze food which you want to use at a later date and in quantities which you are able to use within the recommended storage time.

> ☒ *Do not use the freezer as a dumping ground for unwanted leftovers and rejected food.*

Preparing Food for Freezing

Food should be prepared as for cooking or eating before it is frozen.

Wash, trim and cut vegetables and fruit. Gut and descale fish. Trim poultry and meat, removing excess fat, and truss it neatly in shape.

Blanching*
Vegetables and apples should be blanched before freezing to

FRUIT AND VEGETABLES

Note The following all keep for up to a year if blanched unless otherwise stated. Times are for blanching:

Apples	1–2 minutes
Artichokes, Globe	8 minutes
Asparagus	2 minutes
Beans	
broad	2 minutes
French	2 minutes
runner	2 minutes
Broccoli *(Store up to 9 months)*	3 minutes
Brussels Sprouts	3 minutes
Carrots	2–3 minutes
Cauliflower *(Store 9–12 months)*	3 minutes
Corn-on-the-cob	3–5 minutes
Leeks *(Store 9 months)*	2 minutes
Peas	1–2 minutes

See also information given under individual entries throughout book.

destroy enzymes which cause deterioration in quality over long storage periods.

Information on the technique is given under the separate entry on blanching.* Blanching times are given on the previous page.

Packing

Freezer packages must be water-proof and they must withstand prolonged storage at the cold temperature. Packs must be air-tight.

Packing Materials
The choice of packaging depends on the food. Heavy gauge poly-thene bags are the most versatile.
Polythene Bags Make sure they are suitable for use in the freezer; food storage bags are not thick enough for freezing. The bag should be large enough to hold the food and to allow room for it to be sealed properly with a wire tie.

Look for colour-coded poly-thene bags and bags with inte-gral labels.

Self-sealing polythene bags are more expensive but they can be useful for bulk packing burgers, sausages and so on.
Cook-in Bags Bags suitable for freezing and cooking in boiling water are useful for small por-tions of vegetables and individ-ual portions of cooked food.
Foil Thick foil may be used for wrapping some food but it is not the ideal material as it tends to rip fairly easily and it is difficult to achieve a good, lasting seal. It is useful for protecting food during short-term storage, for example tenting it over a pie or cake.

Rigid foil containers with lids are useful for cooked food. The containers should be sealed and overwrapped in a polythene bag. Several foil packs of the same food may be stored in one large polythene bag.
Interleaving Film This is useful for separating individual food items that may be packed in one bag. Burgers, steaks, fish cakes and so on should be layered with interleaving film.

The Importance of Good Packing
Not only does proper packing keep the food in good condition, it also prevents one type of food from con-taminating other items in the freezer. Smells and flavours can be trans-ferred between badly packed foods.

Rigid Plastic Containers Check that they are recommended for freezer use before buying and follow the manufacturer's in-structions.
Freezer to Ovenware There are many ranges of cooking dishes that are suitable for use in the freezer, on the hob or in the oven, including flameproof glass.

Make sure containers may be put straight from freezer to oven or on the hob otherwise they could shatter.
Freezer Tape Useful for sealing containers, this is a thick sticky tape. Stretch it slightly as you apply it, then it shrinks back to form an excellent airtight seal.

Cook's Tip
Apart from use for freezer packs, this tape is particularly useful for sealing jars of pre-serves too.

Extracting Air
As much air as possible should be excluded from packs before they are sealed. Air reacts with fats to promote rancidity*.
Vacuum Pump This is useful for extracting the air from packs. It looks like a pump for blowing up balloons but works in reverse.

X *Do not use a drinking straw to suck air out of packs – it is not hygienic.*

Another method of extracting air from packed food is to sub-merge the food in the bag in a bowl of cold water, keeping the bag opening above the water. The water surrounding the bag pushes the air out. Gather the bag opening together just below

the water and seal it with a wire tie. Wipe the pack dry on a tea-towel.

Open Freezing
This is a method of freezing food to keep items separate either to preserve a good shape or texture or to allow small amounts to be removed from a large pack.

Lay the food on trays lined with interleaving film and put them in the freezer until hard. Then pack them together in a sealed bag.

Soft fruit, burgers, fish cakes, uncooked piped biscuits and many other items may be open frozen.

Labelling Packs

Label all packs of food with the name and quantity of food, the date when it was frozen and the date to use it by. As well, note any details such as sugar added to fruit or instructions to remem-ber when thawing and using.

Fast Freezing

During freezing, water in food forms crystals. The faster the food freezes, the smaller the crystals. Larger crystals which form when food freezes slowly can puncture the cell walls and this spoils the texture and quality of the food when it thaws.

Always use the fast freeze set-ting according to the manufac-turer's instructions, turning it on well in advance of adding a large quantity of food and leaving it on for several hours after the food is placed in the freezer. This lowers the temperature to freeze the food as quickly as possible.

It helps to have food well chilled before it is placed in the freezer.

Storage Times and Freezer Record

Food should be used within the recommended storage time or promptly after it has expired.
Does Overdue Mean Off? Food does not suddenly go off in the

freezer simply because it has been stored a few days or weeks longer than recommended but it does slowly deteriorate in quality, both texture and taste.

The one real exception to this rule is fatty food, notably foods that are high in both fat and salt. Bacon and ham must be used within recommended times otherwise they become rancid.

Keeping a Record Ideally, every freezer should have a written list of everything it contains, with dates by which the food should be used. Each time an item is removed it should be crossed off the list and whenever you are looking for something you should check the list first to find the oldest food.

In practice, this can be too time consuming a task. However, it is vital that you develop some system of your own for monitoring the freezer contents. One of the best ways is to have a regular sort out, checking all the food and bringing items to be used quickly right to the front, then planning meals around them within a few days. Never neglect packages at the bottom of a chest freezer for more than 4–6 months.

Thawing Food

The best method of thawing most food is by placing it in the refrigerator overnight or for several hours. If time does not allow this, then the food may be thawed in a cool room.

Rules for Thawing Unpack the food and place it in a covered dish in the refrigerator. If it is to be thawed at room temperature, then always make sure it is covered and never leave it unattended in a warm place. Take particular note to chill, cook or use the food as soon as it has thawed.

Microwave Thawing Use a defrost setting or the setting recommended by the manufacturer. Follow the guidelines supplied by the manufacturer. Remember the following points.

● Place the food in a covered dish suitable for use in the microwave, removing all metal.

● If in doubt about timing, set the microwave for short periods and check the food often.

● Turn and rearrange food during thawing for even results.

● Never set the timer, then leave the food unattended for long periods once the microwave has stopped working. The food will warm up and become a breeding ground for bacteria if left in this way.

● Be sure that food is thawed before continuing to reheat or cook it.

Cooking From Frozen

Vegetables and fruit are usually cooked from frozen. Bought frozen foods are sometimes cooked from frozen, in which case always follow the packet instructions closely. Make sure food is well heated throughout.

Otherwise, cooking from frozen is not recommended for two reasons. Firstly, there is a distinct danger that the outside of the food is cooked, or even overcooked, before the middle is properly thawed or cooked. This in turn can result in bacteria surviving, or thriving, in the raw or warm areas of food.

Secondly, some foods are inferior in texture if they are cooked from frozen. They benefit from slow thawing and even cooking.

X *Never cook poultry from frozen unless it is prepared specifically for this purpose – for example, cut into fine strips or tiny pieces in which case it thaws and cooks through successfully. Always check that portions and whole birds are thawed before cooking and make sure that the meat is cooked through before serving.*

Part thawed poultry will warm through allowing bacteria to multiply before cooking. Then any risk of food poisoning from undercooked flesh is far greater.

Using Thawed Food

Use thawed food within a day of removing from the freezer.

Defrosting the Freezer

Read and follow the manufacturer's instructions about defrosting. As a general rule, chest freezers should be defrosted annually and upright freezers every 6 months. In between time, any build up of ice should be scraped off carefully with a plastic scraper.

Plan ahead when to defrost the freezer and put your food into a friend's freezer. Or run the stock down to a minimum, pack it in plenty of newspaper or chiller bags and place it in a cold place on a cold day.

Do not put an artificial heat source in a freezer to defrost the ice as this can ruin the appliance. A bowl of hot water in the base will help.

Clean the ice and water out of the freezer, then wash it out with warm water and washing soda. If there is any odour in the freezer, open freeze a container of lemon juice and water in it.

Dry the freezer well with clean tea-towels before switching it back on. Put the frozen food back in straight away.

Food Safety and the Freezer

● Check the temperature in the freezer and make sure it stays below −18°C/0°F.

● Always pack food properly.

● Always label food and use it within the recommended storage time.

● Never put unwrapped food in the freezer.

● Never put warm or hot food in the freezer – it raises the temperature of the surrounding food.

● Observe strict hygiene rules when preparing food for the freezer and when thawing food.

● Always thaw food properly.

• Always make sure that thawed poultry, fish and meat is cooked properly.

• Food that is to be reheated should be heated right through to the original cooking temperature before serving.

Fritters

See Batter* and Frying*.
Fritters are pieces of food coated in batter and deep fried. Use a light batter with whisked egg white folded in. As the food should all cook quickly, cut it in small pieces (bite size), then coat in flour. Have ready double thick absorbent kitchen paper on a plate for draining and the oil for deep frying heated to 180°C/350°F.

Courgettes, cauliflower, mushrooms, aubergine and pepper make good fritters. Most fruit may be used for sweet fritters.

Fromage Frais

A very lightly fermented, soft, creamy cheese, resembling thick yogurt in texture but it is not as tangy as yogurt. Fat content varies: some is virtually fat free, other types contain 5 per cent or 8 per cent fat. Fruit fromage frais is sweetened.

Plain fromage frais is a versatile ingredient in cooking or it may be served instead of cream with desserts.

Buying and Storing

Sold in tubs, check the fat content and the 'use by' date. Store in the refrigerator.

Use

• Instead of cream in desserts. Fromage frais does not whip but it is thick and may be folded in.

• To make rich-tasting, low-fat set custards*.

• To make delicious salad dressing, add seasoning, herbs, a pinch of sugar and just a little salad oil (walnut, hazelnut or olive) for flavour, if liked.

• Mix fromage frais with mayonnaise to make a dressing or dip.

• Use in sauces and cooked dishes. Fromage frais curdles quickly on heating. Add it to a sauce at the end of cooking, off the heat, then stir well and heat the sauce very gently for a few seconds only.

• Add to smooth soups to enrich them just before serving.

Freezing

Fromage frais freezes reasonably well and it will keep for 1–2 months. It looks slightly separated on thawing but when stirred well it is fine.

Fructose

This is the sugar found naturally in some fruit and honey. It is one of the sweetest of sugars and it forms a part of sucrose.

It may be purchased in fine granular form from wholefood shops and chemists.

Fruit

See Apples*, Apricots*, Bananas*, Blackberries* and so on; also Dried and Candied Fruit*, Freezing*, Jams and Jellies* and Pectin*.
Specific information on using different fruit is given under each type.

Buying

Look for undamaged, bright fruit that is ripe but not squashy and

not overchilled. Some fruit that has been in a cold store overnight may look firm but by the time it reaches room temperature it is soft and sad. Strawberries are a classic example.

Pick-Your-Own and Farm Shops
Both well worth visiting for fruit, particularly if you intend making preserves or freezing. Remember only to pick as much as you can process within 24 hours.

Storing and Using

Fresh fruit should be used as soon as possible for flavour and food value.

Most fruit should be kept cool but not chilled, the exception being soft fruit, such as raspberries and strawberries, that are best stored in the refrigerator until they are used.

Preparation

Before it reaches the shop, fruit has been picked, sorted, packed, transported and displayed. It has probably passed through many hands and a variety of conditions. Yet it is very easy to forget to wash apples, peaches, nectarines, plums and so on before eating them as a snack.

So, when you unpack fruit after shopping or immediately before use, first wash it under cold running water, then dry it on absorbent kitchen paper.

Use

• An excellent snack food – apples, bananas, oranges and other fruit are easy to carry and eat, and far better than savoury alternatives which may be high in fat and salt.

• As a dessert. Served very simply, fresh fruit may be mixed or served alone on a daily basis instead of rich puddings.

• As a first course – melon, grapefruit, figs or exotic fruit may be served on their own or with fine slices of ham. Different fruits may be combined in light first-course cocktails.

SEE ALSO **Fricassee, Fruit Butter, Fruit Cheese:** Glossary

• In salads, both savoury and sweet. A little fruit can cheer up a very simple savoury salad. Add orange segments, diced apple or pear, seedless grapes, sliced star fruit or diced peach to a green salad.

Preserving Methods
Freezing
Jams, Jellies, Marmalades
Chutneys and Pickles
Bottling
Preserving in Spirit
Drying

Fruit Standbys

As well as frozen fruit, canned and bottled fruits (purchased) are excellent storecupboard standbys for instant desserts, sauces or to dress up a salad.

The most versatile canned fruit is packed in natural fruit juice. Commercial bottled fruit is usually significantly more expensive than canned types but it can be excellent quality and ideal for serving as a special dessert, dressed with a little liqueur or spirit. Some fruits are preserved in syrups flavoured with liqueurs or spirit.

Fruit Salads

Fruit salads can be quick and easy for family meals or exotic and special.

Use good quality fresh fruit – it is not worth including produce past its prime. Canned fruit may be combined with fresh fruit to good effect.

Try some of these combinations.

• Sliced banana with chopped up orange, sprinkled with toasted desiccated coconut.

• Diced eating apples with raisins and walnuts in orange juice. Top with yogurt.

• Sliced ripe pears dressed with warmed marmalade and served with cinnamon toast.

• Halved plums with blackberries and a little honey.

• Green fruit salad – seedless grapes, sliced kiwi fruit, melon balls, grapefruit segments and pears.

• Red fruit salad – strawberries, raspberries, redcurrants (poached or raw) and cherries (stoned).

• Orange fruit salad – orange segments with sliced peaches, mango slices and pawpaw slices.

• Gingered fruit salad – toss melon balls, sliced ripe pear and orange segments with chopped preserved stem ginger and a little syrup from the jar. Add grated lime rind if you like.

Sweetening Fruit Salad

The traditional sweetening is a light syrup*; however, there are easier, more interesting options. Many fruits are quite sweet enough on their own or in tangy and sweet combinations.

• Sprinkle a little icing sugar over fruit.

• Trickle a little clear honey or maple syrup over tart fruit – good with blackberries or bland fruit like pears.

• Use fresh fruit juice, either squeezed or from a carton. Try some of the exotic juices with

---

BRITISH FRUIT CALENDAR

JANUARY	FEBRUARY	MARCH	APRIL
Apples – Laxton's Superb and Cox's Orange Pippin; pears – Conference and Comice; and forced rhubarb.	Apples – Cox's Orange Pippin and Crispin; pears – Conference; and forced rhubarb.	Apples – Cox's Orange Pippin; pears – Conference and Comice; and rhubarb.	Apples – Cox's Orange Pippin; pears – Conference; and rhubarb.
MAY	**JUNE**	**JULY**	**AUGUST**
Strawberries and rhubarb.	Gooseberries, strawberries and raspberries.	Blueberries, cherries, currants, gooseberries, loganberries, plums, raspberries and strawberries.	Apples – Discovery; blackberries, blueberries, cherries, currants, gooseberries, loganberries; pears – Williams and Beurre Hardy; plums and strawberries.
SEPTEMBER	**OCTOBER**	**NOVEMBER**	**DECEMBER**
Apples – Howgate Wonder, Discovery and Worcester Pearmain; blackberries, damsons, greengages and plums.	Apples – Howgate Wonder, Crispin, Cox's Orange Pippin, Egremont Russet, Spartan and Worcester Pearmain; pears – Conference and Comice; blackberries and quinces.	Apples – Laxton's, Crispin, Cox's Orange Pippin, Egremont Russet and Spartan; pears – Conference and Comice; and quinces.	Apples – Crispin and Cox's Orange Pippin; and pears – Comice.

Note Bramley's Seedling cooking apples are available all year and various types of eating apples are stored for all year consumption.

simple fruits – passion fruit juice with pears or apples and pears; mango juice with bananas.

Fruit Sauces and Glazes

There are many exciting possibilities for using fruit or fruit juice to make sauces for savoury or sweet dishes. The basic recipe may be used for any full-flavoured fruit juice and it may be served hot or cold.

Serving Ideas

- Hot on apple pie instead of custard.
- Hot with sponge pudding.
- Hot with pancakes or waffles.
- Cold with ice cream or sorbet.
- Cold with set desserts such as mousse or soufflé.

Exotic Fruit

The following are just a few examples of the exotic or unusual fruit.

Cape Gooseberries Cherry-sized, yellow fruit with a yellow covering that looks like a Chinese lantern. The fruit has a central stone. Eat raw or poached. Available with 'lantern' turned back and the fruit dipped in chocolate.

Guavas Pear-shaped, pink-tinged or cream coloured fruit. Scented flesh is pale pink or cream coloured. Quarter, scoop out central seeds and peel. Available canned.

Kiwi Fruit Brown, slightly furry, thin skin covers a green fruit with

BASIC FRUIT SAUCE

Fresh fruit juice (orange, lemon or lime) or unsweetened juice from a carton or bottle is suitable. With sour juice, increase the sugar to taste. Use 15 g/½ oz arrowroot if the sauce is served cold.

INGREDIENTS
450 ml/¾ pint fruit juice
25 g/1 oz arrowroot
25 g/1 oz sugar
25 g/1 oz unsalted butter

Serves 4

FOOD VALUES:
TOTAL • PER PORTION MADE
WITH FRESHLY SQUEEZED
ORANGE JUICE
kcals: 543 • 136
kJ: 2284 • 571
protein: 3 g • 1 g
fat: 21 g • 5 g
carbohydrate: 92 g • 23 g
fibre: 1 g • 0 g

Pour most of the fruit juice into a saucepan and heat it gently until just below boiling point. Meanwhile, in a heatproof jug, blend the arrowroot with the remaining cold juice to a smooth paste, then stir in the sugar.

Pour some of the hot juice into the jug, stirring all the time, then pour all the mixture back into the juice in the pan. Heat gently, stirring all the time, until the sauce just boils. Remove the pan from the heat at once and stir in the butter. Stir well, then serve.

If the sauce is to be served cold, place a sheet of damp greaseproof paper on its surface to prevent a skin forming. Stir well before serving.

FOOD VALUES:
TOTAL • PER PORTION MADE
WITH UNSWEETENED APPLE
JUICE (FROM A CARTON)
kcals: 548 • 137
kJ: 2302 • 576
protein: 0 g • 0 g
fat: 21 g • 5 g
carbohydrate: 96 g • 24 g
fibre: 1 g • 0 g

FOOD VALUES:
TOTAL • PER PORTION MADE
WITH UNSWEETENED
PINEAPPLE JUICE (FROM A
CARTON)
kcals: 611 • 153
kJ: 2572 • 643
protein: 2 g • 0.5 g
fat: 21 g • 5 g
carbohydrate: 110 g • 28 g
fibre: 1 g • 0 g

A selection of exotic fruit.

WHOLE FRUIT SAUCE

This is suitable for serving with savoury dishes as well as sweet, for example apricot, kumquat or cherry sauce may be served with duck or lamb.

INGREDIENTS
450 g/1 lb sour cherries
75 g/3 oz sugar
300 ml/½ pint dry cider
10 ml/2 teaspoons arrowroot
60 ml/4 tablespoons water

Serves 4–6

FOOD VALUES:
TOTAL • PER PORTION
kcals: 615 • 154
kJ: 2610 • 653
protein: 2 g • 0.5 g
fat: 0 g • 0 g
carbohydrate: 140 g • 35 g
fibre: 7 g • 2 g

First wash and dry the fruit well. Stone cherries. For variations, below, halve and stone apricots, halve kumquats lengthways and remove their seeds.

Heat the sugar and cider together in a medium saucepan, stirring until the sugar dissolves. Bring to the boil and boil hard for 3 minutes. At this stage add the kumquats and reduce the heat, then simmer the fruit for 15 minutes, until tender. Poach the cherries or apricots for 5 minutes, until they are tender but not broken.

Blend the arrowroot with the water, then stir it into the sauce and bring to the boil, stirring all the time. Remove from the heat and serve. The sauce may be served cold, in which case cover with a sheet of damp greaseproof paper until cool to prevent a skin forming.

VARIATIONS

The sauce may be made using apricots or kumquats, as above.

FOOD VALUES:
TOTAL • PER PORTION MADE
    WITH APRICOTS
kcals: 565 • 141
kJ: 2394 • 599
protein: 3 g • 1 g
fat: 0 g • 0 g
carbohydrate: 126 g • 32 g
fibre: 10 g • 3 g

FOOD VALUES:
TOTAL • PER PORTION MADE
    WITH KUMQUATS
kcals: 1060 • 265
kJ: 4464 • 1116
protein: 2 g • 0.5 g
fat: 2 g • 0.5 g
carbohydrate: 255 g • 64 g
fibre: 0 g • 0 g

a ring of fine, edible black seeds inside. Peel thinly.

Kumquats Miniature oranges with quite large seeds. May be eaten raw but better poached. Wash and use whole.

Limquats Miniature limes. As for kumquats.

Lychees Firm, reddish skin covers a translucent, white fruit on a large stone. Slit skin on one side and it slips off easily. Slit flesh down one side, then ease out the stone. Use raw.

Mangosteen The size of large tomato, with red-purple skin. Slit the fruit around the middle and take off half the skin to reveal white, juicy segments of fruit with a delicate flavour. Use raw.

Passion Fruit Purple or black-skinned. Cut the crisp shell in halve to reveal yellow, fragrant and full flavoured centre. Scoop out the soft juicy middle and eat with the crunchy, small black seeds. Sieve to use juice only for desserts.

Pawpaw Also known as papaya. Yellow or yellow-green skin covers peach-coloured, sweet flesh. Halve, scoop out black seeds and peel. Use raw. An enzyme in the fruit acts as an effective tenderising agent for meat.

Persimmon Tomato-sized and similar also in texture, this orange fruit has a delicate, rather strange flavour with a hint of tomato to it.

Pineapple Cut off both ends, then peel and cut out all spines. Halve or quarter the fruit lengthways and cut out tough central core. Alternatively, halve small whole fruit and cut out flesh. Use shells to serve.

Pomegranates Tough beige, blushed-red, skin covers dark seeds, each with a juicy, sweet covering. Add to salads.

Prickly Pear Cactus fruit – look for those that have had prickles removed or handle using rubber gloves. Peel thickly, then slice. The middle is refreshing and delicately flavoured but not spectacular. Use raw.

Rambutans Like large lychees.

Star Fruit Pale yellow fruit, also known as carambolas. Slices are star shaped. Wash and dry, then use raw in salads or as decoration. Delicate flavour and crisp texture.

Tamarillo About the size of plum tomatoes, these are oval and dark purple or aubergine coloured. The flesh is lightly flavoured, again rather tomato-like and not very sweet.

Nutritional Value: The Role of Fruit

Fruits are important sources of vitamin C; however, their value varies as some fruits are not especially rich sources. Black-currants are rich in the vitamin whereas apples contain far less, but it is worth considering that apples may well be eaten in considerable quantities so they make a useful contribution.

Fruit also contains sugar and some offer small amounts of other vitamins and minerals.

Frying

See Fat* and Oil*.

Greater awareness about reducing the fat content of the diet has led to frying becoming less popular. Alternative terms are used as often as possible in recipes, with sautéing, browning and stir frying being used in preference to plain 'frying', even when the method does not justify the name.

As for all foods and cooking methods, there is nothing wrong with eating fried food occasionally but there is good reason not to have fried food several times a week.

The quality of fried food and its fat content is affected by the technique used when cooking.

Deep Frying

Equipment

• A deep pan which is fairly wide, with or without a basket, depending on what is cooking.

• A large metal slice or draining spoon for turning food or for draining food if a basket is not used.

• Plenty of absorbent kitchen paper on a large plate for absorbing most of the fat off the cooked food.

• A thermometer to test the temperature (not essential).

Technique

1. The pan should be no more than half full of oil. When the oil heats and food is added, the level rises significantly.

2. Prepare and coat the food before the oil is heated.

3. Test the temperature of the oil with a thermometer. If a thermometer is not available, as a rough guide a small cube of day-old bread should brown in about 45 seconds.

4. Lower the food into the oil and maintain the temperature for a few minutes, then lower the temperature slightly to prevent the oil from becoming too hot.

5. Do not cover the pan while deep frying.

6. Never neglect food that is deep frying, always stand near it and make sure it is not overheating, boiling over or overcooking.

7. Drain the food over the pan and turn the heat off immediately. Transfer the food to absorbent kitchen paper and mop well. Serve at once.

Important Points
• If the fat is not hot enough the food will be greasy.
• The fat must be clean: after cooking and cooling the fat should be strained through a paper coffee filter or absorbent kitchen paper.
• Fat which has overheated and become dark should be discarded.
• Fat should only be used two or three times for deep frying.

Shallow Frying

Equipment

• A heavy, wide pan which sits flat on the hob.

• A metal, or suitable (non-stick) slice and a fork or palette knife to turn food.

• Absorbent kitchen paper for draining the food.

Technique

1. Prepare and coat the food before the pan is heated.

2. Pour oil into the cold pan to a depth of about 5 mm/¼ inch. Alternatively heat margarine, lard or butter in the pan until melted. Heat solid fats gently until melted. A combination of oil and solid fat may be used. Heat the fat until it runs freely and is just shimmering hot, not quite smoking. The fat should move quickly when the pan is tilted. Do not overheat butter or olive oil as they burn quickly.

3. Place the food in the pan and keep the heat fairly high until the underside has browned lightly and crisped. Turn the food over and cook the second side.

4. When the second side is two-thirds browned, the heat may be reduced to cook the food through. By this time the outside of the food is sealed and it will not absorb fat.

5. Use a slice to drain the food, then place it on absorbent kitchen paper to drain.

Important Points
• The fat must be hot when the food is added otherwise the food will become greasy.
• The outside of the food should be sealed quickly before the heat is reduced to cook the food through.

Dry Frying

This is a technique for cooking foods which contain significant amounts of fat, for example bacon, sausages or nuts.

A heavy pan is used and the food is heated over low to medium heat until it gives up its fat, then food is turned and the heat may be increased when the base of the pan is greased.

Nuts and seeds are browned by dry frying (sometimes the term roasting is used) but they should be stirred frequently, if not all the time, during cooking.

Sautéing

This is browning small or thin items of food in a small amount of hot fat over high heat. The food should be turned or stirred often during cooking to prevent it burning. It should be lightly browned outside when cooked, ingredients such as courgettes should retain a crunchy texture. Potatoes should be evenly browned and crisp.

SEE ALSO **Fumet:** Glossary; **Fusilli:** Pasta; **Galantine:** Glossary

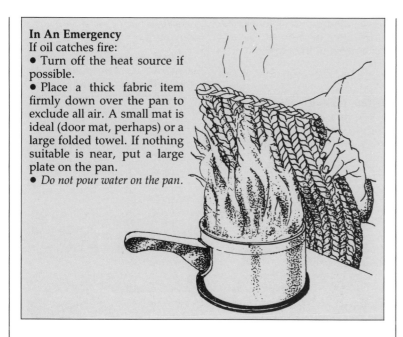

In An Emergency
If oil catches fire:
● Turn off the heat source if possible.
● Place a thick fabric item firmly down over the pan to exclude all air. A small mat is ideal (door mat, perhaps) or a large folded towel. If nothing suitable is near, put a large plate on the pan.
● *Do not pour water on the pan.*

Stir Frying

An Oriental cooking method, now popular for the small amount of fat it uses, speed and the texture of food cooked in this way.

Equipment

● A wok – a large rounded frying pan – or a large frying pan is needed. A large saucepan may be used.

● A scoop, cooking spoon or spatula should be used for stirring the ingredients.

Technique

1. Prepare all the food; cut into small pieces for quick and even cooking. Keep foods that require different cooking times separate so that they may be added at different stages.

2. Pour just a little oil into the pan and heat it over high heat until it is almost smoking hot. Tilt the pan to coat it evenly with the oil.

3. Add the first batch of ingredients – these should be the ones that require the longest cooking. Stir the ingredients and turn them as they cook.

4. Add the next batch of ingredients when the first ones are part cooked and continue stirring.

5. Add foods that simply require quick heating last – bean sprouts or mushrooms – toss them quickly over the high heat.

6. Add any sauce or moistening ingredients (in small quantities) at the end of cooking and toss over high heat until hot.

7. If a complicated mixture is cooked, separate the ingredients by pushing them up the side of the wok while fresh foods are cooked in the middle of the pan.

8. Serve stir-fried foods immediately.

Cook's Tip
To clean a cast iron wok, wipe it out with absorbent kitchen paper after cooking. Sprinkle salt into the pan and add a little oil, then use a pad of paper to scour the inside until it is clean. Heat for a few seconds, then wipe the wok clean. Wipe with a little fresh oil before storing in a large polythene bag.

Game

Game is the term for birds and animals (also fish, although the majority is farmed) hunted or caught in the wild. Strict regulations govern the hunting of game, with separate seasons laid down for different birds and types of deer.

With the exception of duck, most types of game are low in fat but at the same time they have a distinct rich flavour.

Buying

It is against the law to hunt or sell British game more than 10 days outside the specified seasons; although some imported game and 'farmed' game is outside the restrictions.

Buy from a reputable, licensed game dealer. Butchers or fishmongers usually advertise the fact that they are authorised to sell game. This way you know that the game has come from a good source and that it has been correctly prepared.

Most sellers provide the game ready for cooking – hung, drawn, plucked and trussed or jointed.

Preparation

The techniques of hanging, plucking and drawing are specialised and they require the right environment to avoid any risk of spoilage.
Trussing Birds should be tied neatly in shape to prevent the legs and wings falling apart from the body during cooking. The technique is similar to that used for poultry*.

Barding Since game can be dry, strips of fat or fat bacon are wrapped over the breast meat or around joints before cooking. The fat is secured in place with string.

Larding This is a technique of threading strips of pork fat through holes in solid pieces of lean meat. The holes are made with a skewer, then a larding needle is used to pull the fat through the holes. Used for venison in particular.

Duck

There are several types of wild duck, including teal which is the smallest and will only serve one person. The mallard is the most common.

Season Sept 1 to Jan 31.

Cooking Methods Roasting, braising or stewing.

Roast at 200°C, 400°F, gas 6 for about 30 minutes.

Serves Two or three.

Grouse

Young grouse are tender, older ones may be tough and more suitable for braising rather than roasting.

Season Aug 12 to Dec 10.

Cooking Methods Roasting, grilling or braising.

Roast at 190°C, 375°F, gas 5 for about 30 minutes.

Serves One or two.

Partridge

There are two main types: grey or less common and less good red-legged (or French). Mid-season is the best time for these birds.

Season Sept 1 to Feb 1.

Cooking Methods Roasting or casseroling.

Roast at 190°C, 375°F, gas 5 for about 30 minutes.

Serves One.

Pheasant

Most widely available of game birds. A brace of pheasant consists of the bright-feathered male (cock) and female (hen) with light brown plummage. The hen is the most tender.

Season Oct 1 to Feb 1.

Cooking Methods Roasting, braising or stewing.

Roast at 190°C, 375°F, gas 5 for 40–50 minutes, slightly longer for larger birds.

Serves Two to three; four at a pinch if boned out and stuffed.

Pigeon

Dark-fleshed wild wood pigeon has a strong flavour. Useful for pâtés and for potting.

Season All year.

Cooking Methods Braising, casseroling or stewing.

Serves One or split before cooking to make two small portions.

Quail

Now farmed and protected as wild birds but usually still considered as game in culinary terms.

Season All year.

Cooking Methods Roasting, grilling or braising.

Roast at 200°C, 400°F, gas 6 for 10–15 minutes.

Serves One or serve two per portion.

Hare

One of the best known dishes is jugged hare, a casserole thickened with the blood of the hare. Hare is hung, whole, with a dish below to collect its blood. The blood is mixed with a little vinegar to prevent it clotting, then it is covered and chilled. A rich stew of hare may be thickened at the end of cooking by stirring in the reserved blood. It is important that the sauce is not boiled after the blood is added or it will curdle. Jugged hare is usually enriched with port.

Season August 1 to end of Feb.

Cooking Methods The saddle may be roasted or braised; other joints should be braised or stewed.

Roast a whole saddle or trussed hare at 190°C, 375°F, gas 5 for 1¼–1½ hours.

Rabbit

Most rabbit in supermarkets is farmed. Remove all traces of fat from rabbit as it has an unpleasant flavour.

Season All year.

Cooking Methods Grilling, roasting, frying, braising or stewing.

Roast a barded rabbit at 190°C, 375°F, gas 5 for about 1 hour, or longer according to size.

Woodcock

Not a common bird.

Season Oct 1 – Jan 31.

Cooking Methods Roasting or braising.

Roast at 190°C, 375°F, gas 5 for 20–30 minutes.

Serves One.

Venison

The seasons for venison are complicated, relating to different species, age and sex of the animals. Farmed venison is readily available.

Any traces of fat should be removed from venison before cooking as it has a rather unpleasant flavour.

Available All year.

Cooking Methods According to cuts: roasting or grilling (saddle, loin, haunch or shoulder), braising (shoulder or roasting cuts) or stewing (shoulder and cubed meat sold for stewing).

Some like venison roasted very quickly in a hot oven to seal the outside and leave the meat rare, others prefer the meat cooked through but it should never be overcooked as it will be dry. Allow between 15–30 minutes per 450 g/1 lb at 200°C, 400°F, gas 6, according to taste.

Also Available Venison sausages are dark, rich and dry with a firm meaty texture.

Accompaniments for Game

Redcurrant or crab apple jelly or cranberry sauce, fresh breadcrumbs fried in butter until golden, stuffing balls, thin gravy or wine sauce and game chips. Watercress to garnish.

SEE ALSO **Garam Masala**: Spices; **Garnish**: Glossary; **Gazpacho**: Soup; **Gâteau**: Glossary

Game Chips

Peel and thinly slice large potatoes, then wash the slices well and leave in cold water until ready to cook.

Heat oil for deep frying to 180°C/350°F. While the oil is heating, drain the potatoes and pat them dry on absorbent kitchen paper. Sprinkle the slices into the hot fat and cook them until they are crisp and golden.

Drain on absorbent kitchen paper and serve at once.

Storing and Freezing

Prepared, oven-ready game should be kept in the refrigerator and used within 1–2 days of purchase. Well-hung game should be cooked within a day of purchase.

Most game freezes well. It should be prepared as for cooking but it should not be very well hung. Duck may be frozen for up to 6 months; other game birds keep for up to 9 months and trimmed venison will keep for 9–12 months.

Garlic

Garlic is a member of the onion family. Small rounded bulbs with a papery covering, made up of small portions known as cloves. The cloves may be as small as the little finger nail or as large and plump as a Brazil nut.

Buying

Look for firm bulbs with large cloves – if the bulbs look small, thoroughly even in shape and a beige-brown colour they are not the best. Fresh garlic should be quite bright and white, perhaps with a hint of pink skin showing through. Mid-summer to autumn is the best time. A jar of minced garlic is a useful standby.

Storing

Whole strings of garlic may be hung in a cool, dry place. In a damp or warm place they will become either mouldy or shrivelled, or both.

Store bulbs in an earthenware pot with air holes or keep them in the salad drawer of the refrigerator for up to 2 weeks.

Best bought and used within a month or shorter period but most bulbs will keep for at least 2 months.

Crushing Garlic

Using a crusher is by far the best way of crushing garlic cloves.

Pull as many cloves as needed away from the bulb, then peel each clove by cutting off the root end and slipping off the peel. The pointed top usually has to be trimmed too.

Using a Crusher Place one or two cloves in the small perforated scoop of the crusher. Hold the crusher over the dish or pan then close the handles together and the plunger will crush the garlic.

Use a knife to scrape all the garlic flesh off the outside of the crusher. The remains on the inside may also be scraped out and used.

By Hand Put the peeled garlic clove on a board. Using a large cook's knife, press the wide end down on the clove with the heel of your hand. Once crushed, the garlic may be chopped.

Chopping or Slicing Cut a peeled garlic clove lengthways into strips, then across into small pieces. Slice a clove crossways.

These methods give a lighter garlic flavour than crushing.

Freezing

Garlic is not a good freezer candidate for two reasons: it is difficult to pack pure crushed garlic to keep the smell and flavour in; also the flavour seems to become more intense on freezing and can be slightly bitter.

Garlic butter freezes well. Take care when freezing light cooked dishes flavoured with garlic as the garlic can dominate the food. Richer, or heavier, dishes tend to stand up to the garlic better during freezing.

Gelatine

A setting agent derived from animal sources, including beef carcasses and pig skin.

Buying and Storing

Gelatine is available as a powder (most common) or in leaves. Store gelatine in a sealed packet in a dry, cool place.

Setting Qualities

As a general guide, 7 g/¼ oz or 11.25 ml/2¼ teaspoons of powdered gelatine sets 600 ml/1 pint liquid, giving a soft set as required for sweet jellies. For a firmer set, for example in a jelly to hold pieces of food firmly in place and in shape, then use 20 ml/4 teaspoons gelatine. This is also suitable for firm terrines.

The following is an approximate guide, check the manufacturer's instructions for exact details.
1 sachet = 7 g/¼ oz
11.25 ml/2¼ teaspoons = 7 g/¼ oz
3 leaves = 7 g/¼ oz
The above sets 600 ml/1 pint.

Using

Many people have problems with gelatine, yet it is easy to use if the correct steps are followed.

Leaf Gelatine

Softening Leaves Leaves of gelatine must be softened before dissolving. Place them in a basin and cover with cold water. Leave to soak for 15 minutes. Wash your hands, then scoop the soft filmy leaves from the water, draining it away at the same time if you can. Discard the water.

Dissolving Powdered Gelatine

1. Sprinkle the gelatine over the surface of cold liquid.

2. After 15 minutes standing, the gelatine swells and looks spongy in texture.

Dissolving Leaves Add the leaves to hot water – about 45 ml/3 tablespoons for 3 leaves – in a heatproof basin.

Stand the basin over a small saucepan of hot, not boiling, water. Leave the gelatine for about 5 minutes, then use a teaspoon to stir it. Leave the gelatine over the hot water until it has dissolved completely.

Powdered Gelatine
Sponging Powdered Gelatine
Many problems associated with powdered gelatine are due to missing the following stage. Always sponge gelatine, unless you are adding the powder to a large quantity of hot liquid, such as stock (for aspic) or cooked thin fruit juice.

For 7 g/¼ oz gelatine, place 45 ml/3 tablespoons cold water in a small basin. Sprinkle the powdered gelatine evenly over the surface of the water. Do this fairly slowly so that the powder sinks into the water. Some will stay on the surface of the water but do not stir the powder into the water. Leave the gelatine for 15 minutes. During this time it will absorb the water and expand, losing its white appearance and becoming more yellow in colour. It will look spongy, hence the use of the term.

If there are any small areas of powder left it is because it was not sprinkled evenly and slowly enough on the water in the first place. Never mind, leave them where they are.

Dissolving Sponged Gelatine
Place the basin over hot water as before and dissolve it in the same way.

Using Dissolved Gelatine
The gelatine must be clear. If any strings or blobs have formed and they will not dissolve, then rinse a tea strainer with boiling water (to warm it) and strain the gelatine into a warmed mug or basin.

Do not add the small amount of gelatine to chilled liquids or it will begin to set at once, in strings. Quickly stir the liquid into the gelatine.

When adding gelatine to thick mixtures (purées and so on), make sure they are at room temperature and add the gelatine in a slow trickle, whisking vigorously all the time. Do not put the whisk directly under the trickle of gelatine or it may set on the blades.

Setting Problems

An enzyme naturally present in some fruit – particularly pineapple and pawpaw – acts on the chemical structure of gelatine, breaking it down and preventing it from setting or causing it to become runny.

The enzyme is only a problem in fresh fruit or fresh fruit juice – in canned or sterilised fruit or juice the enzyme has been destroyed.

Freezing

Mixtures set with gelatine tend to be far softer on thawing. Anything that relies solely on gelatine for a good set does not freeze well.

Germs

See Bacteria*, Micro-organisms* and Moulds*.
An everyday term for potentially harmful bacteria, moulds and undesirable sources of possible food poisoning.

Glucose

Also known as dextrose, this is a simple sugar which is found naturally in fruit and some plants. When sucrose (ordinary sugar) is digested it is broken down into glucose and fructose. Starch is also reduced to glucose during digestion and this process can be copied commercially.

Glucose syrup or liquid glucose is made from maize. As well as glucose it contains maltose and other carbohydrates. Liquid glucose does not crystallise and it is used to prevent sugar syrups from crystallising easily. It is also added to icing to keep it soft.

Powdered forms of glucose (available from chemists) should not be confused with liquid glucose as they are pure glucose and may not be used instead of the liquid form when making icing.

Gluten

The protein in flour. Some types of flour, known as strong flours, are richer in certain proteins than others.

When kneading bread, made with strong flour, the gluten develops and strengthens the dough to trap carbon dioxide produced by fermenting yeast. This causes the bread to rise and gives it the characteristic texture.

SEE ALSO **Genoese Sponge:** Glossary; **Ghee:** Butter; **Gherkin:** Pickles; **Giblets:** Glossary; **Ginger:** Spices;

Gluten Intolerance

Those with coeliac disease react to gluten as well as to certain other proteins. All wheat flour products have to be avoided by those who are allergic to gluten. **Gluten-free Flours** Other flours, such as cornflour or rice flour, do not have the same gluten content and therefore they have different cooking properties. However, these are useful alternatives in cooking when preparing dishes for people who are allergic to gluten.

Goose

See Poultry*.
Goose was at one time the most popular bird for Christmas dinner, but now turkey has taken over that role.

Buying

Available mainly from September through to December, it is wise to order a goose in advance. Some larger supermarkets and busy butchers stock frozen geese but most prefer to take orders.
 Geese range in weight from about 3–6.75 kg/7–15 lb. At the lower end of the size range, the birds tend to yield very little meat for the carcass size. A bird of at least 4.5 kg/10 lb has a better ratio of meat to bone. A small goose will serve about 4 people; over 3.6 kg/8 lb and the numbers of servings are roughly equal to each 450 g/1 lb.

Storing

Fresh goose must be refrigerated. Unwrap the bird and place it on a rack in a large roasting tin or dish. Cover with foil or polythene and cook within 3 days of purchase.

Preparation

Weigh the goose so that the cooking time may be calculated. Trim leg and wing ends and wash the body cavity under cold running water, then dry it on absorbent kitchen paper. Discard any obvious lumps of fat.
 Truss the bird neatly (see poultry*) and prick the skin all over, then season it well.

Roasting

Stand the goose, breast down, on a rack in a deep roasting tin to catch the fat. Set the oven at 180°C, 350°F, gas 4 and calculate the cooking time at 20 minutes per 450 g/1 lb.
 Roast the goose for half the time, then remove it from the oven. Drain off most of the fat from the tin under the bird, turn the goose over so that the breast is uppermost and continue cooking.
 Check the goose occasionally during cooking and cover the top loosely with foil if the skin is becoming too dark.
 Use a fork to pierce the meat towards one end of the breast to check that it is tender. If it feels at all tough, then continue roasting.

> **Cook's Tip**
> To drain off the fat, have a large piece of foil ready to hold the goose, then remove the rack and drain the fat. Replace the goose rack and continue cooking if necessary.

Carving

The main area of meat is on the breast. This should be carved in thin slices in the same way as the meat on a chicken.

Accompaniments

Sage and onion stuffing, slightly thickened gravy and apple sauce are the usual accompaniments for goose.

Freezing

Goose may be frozen for 3–4 months. Young birds may keep longer as they contain less fat.

Gooseberries

See Fruit*.

Buying

Available from May to August. Later types are larger and sweeter, therefore suitable for eating raw with or without sugar.
 Early gooseberries are fairly small green, firm and sour. The larger varieties for eating raw are softer, with a slight pink glow.

Preparation

Gooseberries have to be topped and tailed before cooking unless they are going to be puréed, in which case the purée may be sieved.
 Pinch both ends off each fruit, then wash the gooseberries well before using.

Cooking

Place the wet fruit in a saucepan and add about 100–175 g/4–6 oz sugar to each 450 g/1 lb sour fruit. Sprinkle in 30 ml/2 tablespoons water.
 Heat gently until the sugar dissolves in the moisture from the fruit, then put a lid on the pan and cook gently for about 15–20 minutes, or until the gooseberries are popped and tender. Stir occasionally during cooking.
 The stewed gooseberries may be served hot, topped with chopped walnuts and a little chopped preserved stem ginger and custard*.

Use

● Use raw gooseberries as a base for amber pudding: place 450–675 g/ 1–1½ lb prepared gooseberries and 175 g/6 oz sugar in a baking dish and top with creamed cake mixture made from 100 g/4 oz margarine and 2 eggs (see cakes*). Bake at 180°C, 350°F, gas 4 for about 1 hour, or until the cake topping is risen, golden and firm. Serve hot, with custard. The combination of tangy fruit and cake is delicious.

- Gooseberries make a tempting fruit sauce for sweet or savoury use and they may also be used to make a stuffing for fish or for rich meat such as lamb.

- Gooseberries combine well with sweet dried fruit (dates, figs or apricots) in chutney.

Grapefruit

See Fruit*.

Buying

As well as the familiar, tart, yellow-skinned variety, look for pink and red grapefruit.
Pink Grapefruit This has a pink blush to the skin. The flesh is tangy but not as tart as yellow fruit and it is tinged with pink.
Red Grapefruit The skin has a red glow and the flesh is distinctly red and far sweeter than the yellow type. Ideal for eating like an orange.
Sweetie A new variety of fruit which is naturally sweet despite its yellow-green skin.

Preparation

The classic, simple way of serving grapefruit is to cut it across in half, then loosen the segments.

A grapefruit knife is useful for this – it has a curved blade which is serrated on both sides.

Cut around the edge of the fruit, between the pith and the flesh, working down the side and just under the flesh. Cut between each segment and remove any white pith from the middle of the fruit.

Serving and Using

- Place the halved fruit in a cereal bowl. Sprinkle halved yellow fruit with brown sugar, or trickle a little honey over the top, and cover with an upturned basin. Leave to stand overnight or for at least an hour. By morning you have a wonderfully juicy breakfast.

- Remove the segments (see orange*), mix all three types in a zesty cocktail.

- Mix grapefruit and orange segments in a classic fruit cocktail.

- Add all types to fruit salads or use the sweeter pink and red types for making ice creams*, sorbets*, mousses* and soufflés*.

- Use grapefruit in savoury cooking in the same way as orange, to accompany grilled meats – lamb or pork chops, or gammon steaks – or in stuffings for meat and poultry.

- Use the grated rind to flavour cakes and desserts.

Other Grapefruit Products

Grapefruit juice is available chilled, long-life or frozen. Canned grapefruit in syrup or in natural juice is a useful standby for a quick, light breakfast; canned grapefruit is inferior to the fresh fruit.

Grapes

See Fruit*.
There are three basic types – black, red and green. Large, juicy dark-skinned fruit with pale flesh and large pips contrasts with small tender-skinned green fruit that is seedless.

Buying

Look for plump, bright fruit. Some types have a natural bloom, particularly the dark-skinned fruit. Boxes of fruit should have separate bunches, packed in tissue. The grapes should be firm and upright on the stalks.

Avoid limp bunches in boxes littered with dropped fruit. Look carefully at green grapes to be sure they are not yellowing and going soft. When over-ripe they can be tasteless.

Avoid any bunches with squashed, brown or very small and wrinkled fruit.

Preparation

Always wash grapes. To do this, hold the bunch firmly on the palm of one hand and wash it under cold running water, then allow the fruit to drain before placing it on double-thick absorbent kitchen paper to dry.

Storing

Display grapes when the washing water has drained off them. Mop them and place them in a dish in a cool room. They will keep for about 3 days.

Otherwise, grapes may be kept in the refrigerator for up to 5 days (if they are in good condition when purchased). The grapes should be protected in a covered rigid container and large bunches should be broken in smaller branches to avoid squashing lower fruit.

Techniques

Removing Pips or Seeds Seedless grapes are more suitable for cooking, otherwise the fruit has to be halved and the pips removed using the point of a knife.
Peeling A tedious, time-consuming task. Use a small, sharp pointed knife and slit the skin on each grape, then pull it off carefully.

Use

- In fruit salad or in savoury salads.

- Add seedless green grapes to Wine Sauce (using white wine, page 235) to serve with chicken or fish such as plaice or sole (known as véronique).

Tempting Grape Ideas

Frosted Place some caster sugar in a basin. Snip seedless green grapes into small bunches, then brush them with lemon juice and turn them in the caster sugar. Serve as a decoration for desserts or with coffee.

Chocolate Dipped Hold individual seedless grapes by their stalks and part dip them in melted dark or white chocolate. Place on wax paper to dry.

Gravy

See Sauces*.

Gravy is a sauce made from meat juices. In its simplest form it may be the juices drained of most fat. More usually, liquid is added and then boiled with the juices. Stock, cooking water from vegetables or wine may be used.

Opinions about thick or thin gravy vary enormously. The old fashioned approach was to lay down rigid rules about when to serve thin or thickened gravy. Thickness is a matter for personal taste; it is more important that gravy has an excellent flavour. Thick or thin, it must be well flavoured and perfectly seasoned. Good gravy makes a meal; bad gravy ruins it.

Thin Reduced Gravy

Add stock, water or wine to the cooking juices. If a joint of meat or whole bird is roasted, drain off most of the fat two-thirds of the way through cooking, then pour some liquid into the cooking pan to form a shallow layer. Keep topping up this liquid for the remaining cooking time. It makes a wonderful gravy which is ready to serve or to thicken.

Alternatively, remove the cooked meat or poultry from the roasting tin or cooking pan, then drain away excess fat and pour liquid into the pan. Bring the liquid to the boil over high heat, stirring all the time to lift any cooking residue off the pan and into the gravy.

The amount of liquid to add depends on the number of servings but enough should be used to allow for the gravy to boil down by at least half. This boiling process, or reducing, is known as deglazing, since it removes all the residue from the cooking pan.

With steaks, chops and smaller cuts of meat and poultry that do not require large quantities of sauce, boil the liquid until it is reduced to a shallow layer in the pan. By this time it will be shiny, rich and delicious.

Light Thickened Gravy

Add cooking liquid to the pan as before, and bring it to the boil. Reduce the heat and simmer the liquid gently for about 5 minutes. Whisk in knobs of beurre manié (see Glossary page 275) to thicken the gravy, whisking all the time until the gravy boils and simmers for 3 minutes. Allow about 20 g/¾ oz each of flour and butter (beaten together) to each 600 ml/1 pint liquid added – this gives a thin, fine gravy. Taste for seasoning before serving.

Dark Thickened Gravy

Pour off excess fat from the cooking pan, leaving a thin layer with all the meat juices in the bottom.

Sprinkle 25–40 g/1–1½ oz plain flour into the pan for each 600 ml/1 pint stock or liquid used. Stir the flour into the cooking juices over medium heat, then continue to cook, stirring most of the time, for about 15 minutes, or until the flour mixture darkens. Regulate the heat so that the flour does not burn but allow the mixture to brown.

Stir vigorously and gradually pour in the liquid, then bring the gravy to the boil, stirring all the time. Simmer the gravy for a few minutes, stirring, then season to taste before serving.

Onion Gravy
Make as for dark thickened gravy but cook a thinly sliced onion in the fat before stirring in the flour. Cook the onion over medium heat, stirring often, for 20–30 minutes, until browned.

> **Cook's Tip**
> Gravy may be pepped up, depending on what it accompanies, by adding a dash of Worcestershire sauce, a little concentrated tomato purée (not more than 15 ml/1 tablespoon to 600 ml/1 pint) or a little mild mustard. A bay leaf simmered in gravy also gives a good flavour.

Greengages

See Fruit* and Plums*.

Small, green hard plums, used mainly for making preserves such as jam*.

Grilling

A method of cooking food under radiant heat, either electric, gas or solid fuel.

Choice of Food

Grilling is a quick cooking method suitable for tender meat, poultry, fish and vegetables that require little cooking. It is not suitable for tough foods that must be tenderised by moist cooking methods.

Small, or thin, portions are best since they cook quickly. Larger items require more attention and the heat source should be carefully controlled to avoid overcooking the outside before the middle is cooked.

Very large items are rarely grilled, the exception being on a covered barbecue.

Techniques

Trimming and Shaping The food must be trimmed and cut or skewered in a neat shape so that it will lie flat on a rack (or in a tin) under or over the grill.

Most foods benefit from being marinated before grilling, to moisten them and promote tender, flavoursome results.

Slitting Thick Foods or Skins Thick portions of poultry that must be cooked through or fish with skin on, such as mackerel, should be slit two or three times. These short slashes into the flesh ensure that the food cooks well and prevents taut skin bursting.

Arranging the Food The food should be arranged on a rack placed in a grill pan. This allows the cooking juices and fat to drip into the pan below. The base of the pan may be lined with foil to catch juices.

Regulating the Heat Heat the grill before putting the food to cook. Set the grill to the highest setting for foods that cook quickly; use a medium or low setting for items such as chicken portions and sausages to allow them to cook through thoroughly. As well as altering the heat setting, the position of the cooking rack or pan may be changed. The further away from the heat, the slower the cooking.

Basting During cooking most foods should be brushed with a little oil or melted fat, or marinade may be used for basting. This keeps the food moist and gives it a good flavour.

Turning A large slice and palette knife or fork should be used for turning food at least once during cooking. Metal tongs are useful for turning less delicate items.

Fragile foods, such as fish, should be cooked completely on one side before they are turned to avoid having to turn them again. However, many foods may be turned several times.

Checking that Food is Cooked

Grilled food should be evenly browned outside. Any areas of fat (for example around a meat cutlet or steak) should be crisp and well browned.

To check if meat is cooked as required, pierce it with a skewer or point of a knife. Beef and lamb may be rare, medium or well cooked. Pierce meat on the bone near the bone to check if it is well cooked. Pork must be cooked through.

Always make sure that poultry is cooked through by piercing the meat with the point of a knife at the thickest part. Look for any signs of blood in the juices or pink flesh and continue cooking if you see either of these.

Safety Rules for Grilling

● When grilling small items of food, heat part of the grill or catch fat and cooking juices in a small foil container under the food. A large area of fat is more likely to spit and catch fire.

● Place fatty food on a rack so that the fat drips away underneath. If the fat surrounds the food in a dish it is likely to spit and it may catch fire.

● Drain off excess fat from the pan, if necessary, during cooking to prevent it from catching fire.

● Never leave food unattended under the grill. Regulate the heat setting and distance of the food from the grill with care.

● Always keep the grill door open so that you can watch the food.

● Remove the grill pan from under the heat source immediately after cooking and leave the grill open, if necessary, until cool.

● Wash the grill pan and rack after use. Never allow fat, crumbs and bits of food to build up in the pan – this is unhygienic and the pan is more likely to catch fire.

Haggis

A Scottish speciality, a cross between a sausage and a faggot. Made from sheep's offal, herbs, spices and onions, then bound with oatmeal, haggis is packed in a skin to make a round 'sausage'. Traditionally, the casing was a sheep's stomach but modern haggis are synthetic wrapped.

Cooking

Place the haggis in a saucepan and cover it with cold water. Bring to the boil over medium heat, then lower the heat slightly and cover the pan so that the water is just boiling. Cook a 450 g/1 lb haggis for 45–50 minutes, or according to any instructions on the wrapper.

When cooked, the haggis should look plump and the mixture should look swollen and dark through the casing.

Lift the haggis from the water using a draining spoon. Transfer it to a heated serving dish and cut the casing open in a cross shape. Scoop out the oatmeal and offal mixture with a large spoon.

Accompaniments

● Buttery mashed swedes.

● Baked or boiled potatoes.

● A personal favourite but not traditional – whisky sauce, made by making a Savoury White Sauce (page 234) with half milk and half light chicken stock. Stir in about 60 ml/4 tablespoons whisky to 600 ml/1 pint sauce and add a good sprinkling of chopped parsley.

SEE ALSO **Grouse:** Game; **Gruyère:** Cheese; **Guacamole:** Avocado; **Guava:** Fruit – exotic; **Haddock, Hake, Halibut:** Fish;

Hamburgers

Good hamburgers are made from minced tender steak and seasoning. Allow 225 g/8 oz lean trimmed braising or frying steak per burger and mince it finely yourself or ask the butcher to do this for you.

Season the steak with salt and freshly ground black pepper, then pound it well with the back of a sturdy mixing spoon. This pounding is important as it makes the meat bind together.

Wash your hands, then rinse them under cold water. Shape the steak into a round burger measuring 7.5–10 cm/3–4 inches across (depending on the weight of meat). If your hands are wet the meat will not stick.

Cooking

Brush the burgers with a little oil, then grill them under a hot grill or over a barbecue until well browned on both sides and cooked through. This takes about 7–10 minutes on each side.

Serving

Serve burgers in split and toasted buns, with salad ingredients such as lettuce, cucumber, spring onions and tomatoes.

Offer mustard, ketchup, chutney, piccalilli or relish with the burgers.

Alternatively, arrange the burgers on a plate with plenty of fresh salad and serve with baked potatoes.

Meat Combinations

- Beef with horseradish sauce.
- Lamb with chopped rosemary and a crushed clove of garlic.
- Pork with sage and grated orange rind.

X *Always thoroughly cook bought burgers and burgers made from bought minced meat. In the commercial preparation of minced meat there is a slight risk of contamination from bacteria which exist in the internal organs of the animal.*

Freezing

Make a large batch of burgers and open freeze them. When hard, pack the burgers in sealed polythene bags. Store for 3–6 months. Cook from frozen by part browning the burgers under a hot grill, then reducing the temperature to moderate and continuing to grill until the burgers are cooked through.

MINCE BURGERS

These may be made with any minced meat, either lean beef, steak, lamb, pork, veal or bacon. They are more economical than true hamburgers.

INGREDIENTS
450 g/1 lb minced meat
1 small onion, finely chopped
50 g/2 oz fresh wholemeal
  breadcrumbs
30 ml/2 tablespoons chopped
  fresh parsley
10 ml/2 teaspoons chopped
  fresh thyme or marjoram,
  or 5 ml/1 teaspoon chosen
  dried herb
salt and pepper
1 egg
oil to cook

FOOD VALUES:
TOTAL • PER PORTION 4/8
kcals: 1422 • 356/178
kJ: 5932 • 1483/742
protein: 94 g • 24 g/12 g
fat: 92 g • 23 g/12 g
carbohydrate: 58 g • 15 g/7 g
fibre: 7 g • 2 g/1 g

Makes 4 or 8

Put the meat in a bowl. First mix in the onion until it is thoroughly combined with the meat. Then add the breadcrumbs, parsley and thyme or marjoram. Pound the ingredients together until they are well mixed – the mixture will be very dry at this stage. Add seasoning and the egg, then mix well until the meat, crumbs and flavourings are well bound together. Mark the mixture into 4 or 8 portions, depending on the size of burgers required.

Heat the grill. Wash and dry your hands, then rinse them under cold water. Shape the meat into burgers and put them on a clean plate as you work.

Brush the burgers with a little oil, then grill them until well browned on both sides and cooked through. Allow about 5–7 minutes on each side for the small burgers; 8–10 minutes for larger ones. Serve at once.

Herbs

Herbs are used to enhance the flavour of food. They should complement the main food, or combination of ingredients, without dominating the finished dish.

A bunch of herbs is known as a bouquet garni*.

Fresh herbs are unmistakably better than dried types, but frozen herbs are an excellent alternative. Fresh herbs are available from supermarkets all year with a few exceptions that are truly seasonal. They are also easy to grow in pots and small gardens.

Some dried herbs are better than others; however their use depends on the recipe and on the individual flavour of the herb.

Ham: Bacon and Ham; **Hare:** Game; **Haricot:** Beans and Pulses, Dried

⊠ *Do not add fresh herbs straight to food without first washing them.*

Herbs and Their Uses

Basil Available fresh only during summer, best bought growing. Dried is a poor substitute. Preserve by creaming shredded leaves with butter and freezing, or by making pesto – a paste of basil, garlic, pine kernels, Parmesan cheese, garlic and olive oil. Made with plenty of olive oil, the paste will keep in an airtight jar in the refrigerator for several months or it may be frozen.

Do not chop basil, instead roughly shred the leaves. Add to salads and at the last minute to cooked dishes as the herb diminishes in flavour during cooking. Good with tomatoes, pasta or any savoury foods.

Bay Leaves Thick, shiny leaves from a member of the laurel family. They have a strong flavour. Fresh available all year. Dried are a good substitute. Use in sauces, with fish, meat, vegetables, pulses and rice.

Camomile Mainly used for making herb tea, this is a delicate leafed plant which has groups of tiny, daisy-like flowers.

Chervil One of the herbs classed as the 'fines herbes' of French cooking. Chervil is a feathery, delicately flavoured herb used for fish, sauces, butters and egg dishes. Particularly good in omelette. Also good with vegetables and in salads (only when fresh). Not one of the easiest of herbs to find fresh. Dried is a reasonable substitute in moist cooked dishes.

Chives This herb resembles fine, bright green grass and it has an onion-like flavour. Purple flowers may be eaten in salads or used as a garnish. Do not chop. Instead, wash and shake dry, then hold the bunch firmly in one hand and use scissors to snip the chives into very short pieces. Referred to as snipped chives.

Coriander Widely used in Indian cooking, coriander resembles flat-leafed parsley but it has a distinct, peppery flavour. Best bought in large bunches nearly always sold with the roots on. The leaves can be chopped and frozen.

Dill A delicate, feathery herb with a light flavour that goes well with fish, eggs (excellent in omelette) and vegetables. Dried is known as dill weed and it is a poor substitute for fresh dill.

Fennel Not to be confused with Florence fennel, the vegetable. Fennel is feathery, tall and it has long thin fronds rather than the short, slightly more dense feathery groups that are characteristic of dill. Also unlike dill, fennel grows very easily into very tall plants. Fennel has an aniseed flavour. Good with fish, poultry, eggs and vegetables. Dried fennel is not a good substitute.

Lemon Balm This grows easily and spreads all over the garden given the chance. Bushes of small, medium-green coloured leaves that have a light lemony aroma when rubbed. Good in drinks, with salads or fish.

Lemon Grass Sold as short lengths of reed-like grass, this has a distinct lemon flavour. Used in cooked dishes, crushing or beating the stalks first helps to bring out the flavour. Not eaten but discarded before serving or left to one side.

Marjoram A full-flavoured herb associated with Mediterranean food. Use with all sorts of savoury foods, particularly tomatoes, olive oil, garlic and meat. Dried may be used instead of fresh.

Mint There are many different types, including apple mint, pineapple mint, cologne mint and spearmint. Cologne mint is very scented, as its name suggests, although ideal for drinks it should be used with caution in savoury cooking.

Use with lamb, vegetables, salads (cucumber or tomato), in sauce, apple jelly (see jams and jellies*) or in drinks.

Dried is a poor substitute. However, chopped mint may be preserved by covering with vinegar or by freezing.

Oregano This is a type of wild marjoram and it has a similar flavour but it is stronger and more aromatic. Good with all sorts of tomato dishes, poultry, meat and vegetables. Dried is a good substitute.

Parsley Flat-leafed parsley is nominally more delicate than the curly-leafed type. This herb goes well in all sorts of dishes, including salads, soups and sauces. Parsley is traditionally used to flavour fish, poultry and egg dishes. Add lots to a green salad for a terrific, fresh flavour.

Rosemary A spiky herb with a distinct flavour. Good with lamb, pork and vegetables. Also tasty with mackerel but too strong for most fish. Evergreen plants are best. Dried is a bit spiky and unpleasant to eat. Chop fresh rosemary and freeze it.

Sage Muted green leaves are characteristic of this full-flavoured, peppery herb. Variegated varieties are decorative to grow. Use with onion in sage and onion stuffing. Also good with pork, ham, cheese and poultry. Dry sage, then rub the leaves to a powder. Dried may be bought as 'rubbed' sage.

Savory Both summer and winter savory are available. This herb has small leaves and a strong flavour which is vaguely similar to thyme. Use with all meats, poultry, vegetables and pulses. Use sparingly with some fish.

Tarragon An aniseed-flavoured herb with soft, long fine green leaves. French tarragon is the one with the flavour; other types that grow easily tend to be flavourless. Good with eggs, fish, poultry and vegetables. Dried is a reasonable substitute. Freeze chopped tarragon creamed with butter.

Thyme A full-flavoured herb of which there are many types, some less aromatic than others. Use with meat, sparingly with fish, poultry, vegetables and other savoury dishes. The small leaves may be used whole.

Look for lemon thyme, a pale, yellow-green herb with a distinct lemon and thyme flavour.

SEE ALSO **Herring:** Fish; **Hobs:** Cookers; **Hollandaise:** Sauces; **Homogenise:** Milk; **Honey, Hotpot:** Glossary

Freezing

• Freeze chopped herbs in small rigid containers, then pack them in polythene bags. Use from frozen.

• Cream butter or margarine and chopped herbs – individual or mixed herbs. Shape into a roll, pack and freeze, or freeze small pats.

• Freeze whole sprigs of sage, parsley, thyme and mint. When frozen the leaves may be crushed off the stalks.

Horseradish

Fresh horseradish root is ready for picking in the autumn. It is worth cultivating.

Preparation

Cut off the leaves and root end, then scrub and peel the horseradish. This is an eye-watering task which is slightly easier under running water.

When you are left with a pale cream coloured root, grate it and use as required. Better, finely chop the root in a food processor or liquidiser.

Use

Serve any of the following with roast beef. The cold horseradish sauces also go well with smoked mackerel. Hot horseradish sauce is delicious with boiled beef or plain poached white fish, served gratin style, browned under the grill.

Horseradish Cream Mix the horseradish with soured cream or fromage frais.

Horseradish Sauce Mix the horseradish with mayonnaise or half and half mayonnaise and soured cream or fromage frais.

Polish-style Horseradish Sauce Make a Béchamel Sauce (page 35) then add about 60–90 ml/4–6 tablespoons freshly grated horseradish, or to taste. Serve hot.

Preserving and Freezing

Preserve grated horseradish by placing it in a jar and covering with distilled white vinegar.

Alternatively, pack it in an airtight container and polythene bag, then freeze the horseradish for up to a year.

Buying

Horseradish sauce is stronger than creamed horseradish. Dried grated horseradish is also available, although it is less common.

Hot Water Crust Pastry

This is a comparatively heavy pastry, used for savoury pies. Although heavy compared to light short crust and layered puff or flaky pastries, hot water crust should not be cloying in texture. It should be close textured, with a crisp, brown outside. On the inside of a pie, the hot water crust pastry absorbs the juices from the filling to become a moist, flavoursome crust.

Technique

Prepare the tin or mould to be lined, the filling ingredients, water for sealing the edges and beaten egg for glazing. Remember these guidelines.

• Have a saucepan of hot water, a basin and a polythene bag ready to keep the pastry warm and moist when not being worked. For example, any pastry for making a pie lid must be kept warm.

• Do not allow the water to boil before the fat has melted.

• Add the boiling liquid to the flour in one go and mix it immediately and vigorously to avoid lumps.

• Before handling the dough your hands should be clean and warm.

• Touch the dough carefully at first unless you are used to handling very hot food. Try to work with the dough as hot as possible.

• When kneading the dough, remember that it should not be kneaded as for bread but simply drawn together and gently patted into a smooth round shape.

• By keeping the dough moving on the surface as you work with it, you will not have to use too much extra flour to prevent sticking.

• When rolling out hot water crust pastry, remember that it stretches easily when hot. If it is rolled too large and thin it will quickly develop holes as it is used to line a tin or moulded over a tin.

• Pastry that is cool is difficult to mould. A poor finish on a raised pie is the result of allowing the pastry to become cool.

Lifting Hot Water Crust Pastry

If the pastry is lifted in the usual manner for other doughs, by folding it over a rolling pin, it will stretch and break. Hot water crust pastry should be lifted on the palms of the hands and wrists or over the back of the hands, whichever is easier.

To do this, fold the rolled pastry in half, then place one hand and forearm flat on the work surface, with palm upwards. Open out the folded pastry dough so that it lies over the hand and wrist. Slip the other hand under the second side of the dough.

Raising a Pie

The quantity of pastry given is sufficient to make a 15 cm/6 inch diameter round raised pie.

Before making the pastry have ready a round baking tin, greased on the outside with a little oil and upside down on the work surface; a greased baking tray and a triple-thick band of greaseproof paper, the same depth as the tin. You also need cooking string to tie the paper in place.

1. Make the pastry. Cut off a quarter of the dough, wrap it in a polythene bag and keep it warm in a basin over a pan of hot water off the heat. If the water is too hot the dough will begin to cook, too cold and it will set.

2. Roll out the main portion of pastry to about 5 cm/2 inches larger than the diameter of the base of the baking tin.

3. Carefully lift the pastry over the middle of the tin. Mould the pastry over the tin, until the tin is completely covered in an even layer of dough. Keep your hands warm as you work.

Raising a Pie
(Numbers refer to text steps)

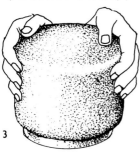

3

5

4. Wrap the band of greaseproof paper around the pastry and tie it in place. Set the covered tin aside in a cool place until set. If you have a cold room, this will take about 20 minutes, otherwise it can take as long as an hour. As soon as it is cool enough, place the pie case in the refrigerator or even in the freezer to speed up the process.

5. The pastry must be firm enough to slip off the tin and stand upright as a case until the

filling is spooned in place. Once the filling is in place and the lid on, the pie is more stable.

6. Set the oven at 180°C, 350°F, gas 4. Invert the pie case on to the greased baking tray and slip the tin out. Now fill the pie and brush the edge with a little water. Roll out the reserved pastry large enough to cover the top. Lift it in place, then pinch the dough in place all around the top edge.

7. Trim off any excess dough before neatening the edge. Smooth the edge of the pastry with a blunt knife and pinch it neatly.

8. Make a hole in the middle of the pie for steam to escape and use the trimmings to mould leaves. Place the leaves on top of the pie, dampening them first. Glaze with beaten egg before baking: the cooking time depends on the filling.

Pouring aspic into a pie.

Lining a Tin

Lining a tin or pie mould with this pastry is not easy. Roll out the pastry to half or two-thirds of the size necessary to line the tin. Lift it into the tin and try to keep the edge of the dough about half way up the side of the mould or tin.

This means that the middle part of the dough will stretch down slightly into the base of the tin and that you can mould the sides and edges of the pastry up to the top edge of the tin.

If the dough is simply placed in the base of the tin, it is difficult to mould it upwards as it requires too much stretching.

If the dough is rolled out large enough to line the tin completely, then it is likely to be too thin to lift successfully while warm.

Use

● Mould individual pies over jam jars and fill with minced lamb, chopped onion, a little chopped rosemary and a little diced cooked potato.

● Use to line a loaf tin or mould, then fill with pâté before baking.

Pork and Apple Pie

Mix 675 g/1½ lb diced lean pork with a finely chopped onion, 5 ml/1 teaspoon dried sage, 1 peeled, cored and roughly chopped cooking apple tossed with 15 ml/1 tablespoon lemon juice and 15 ml/1 tablespoon soft brown sugar. Add plenty of seasoning to the meat mixture and pack it into the pie case. Sprinkle with 30 ml/2 tablespoons water before covering. Bake for 2 hours, then cool before cutting. Aspic* may be added.

Keeping Qualities

Hot water crust pastry does not keep well. It must be made, moulded, filled and covered in one operation. At this stage it may be left before baking; however, remember that this depends entirely on the filling.

The moulded pies may be frozen raw or cooked. The storage time depends on the filling. They should be thawed in the refrigerator before cooking.

SEE ALSO **Hull:** Glossary; **Huss:** Fish

HOT WATER CRUST PASTRY

INGREDIENTS
100 g/4 oz lard
60 ml/4 tablespoons water
60 ml/4 tablespoons milk
350 g/12 oz plain flour
2.5 ml/½ teaspoon salt

FOOD VALUES:
TOTAL
kcals: 2155
kJ: 9052
protein: 36 g
fat: 106 g
carbohydrate: 283 g
fibre: 12 g

Makes one 15 cm/6 inch round, deep pie
4 individual pies, moulded over 450 g/1 lb jam jars
Place the lard, water and milk in a small saucepan. If the pan is too large the liquid is more likely to boil and evaporate before the fat has melted. Heat the mixture very gently until the fat melts.

Meanwhile, place the flour and salt in a bowl and make a well in the middle. As soon as the fat melts, bring the mixture to the boil, then pour it straight into the well in the flour.

Use a mixing spoon to mix the liquid into the flour, stirring well to get rid of any lumps or pockets of flour. Use clean, warm hands to gather the dough into a ball. Knead the dough quickly and lightly until smooth. The kneading action is to smooth the dough, so it must be light, not firm.

The dough is now ready for use. Roll out quickly on a lightly floured surface. At this stage it is easy to mould or shape. As it cools it hardens and eventually becomes difficult to mould with a smooth surface.

Hygiene

See Bacteria*, Cross Contamination*, Germs* and Micro-organisms*.
A high standard of kitchen hygiene is important in preventing food contamination and possible food poisoning. There are two basic areas of hygiene related directly to food preparation and two other general areas to consider.

Personal Hygiene

Good personal hygiene is important to avoid passing bacteria from the body to food.

● Always wear a clean apron to avoid transferring bacteria from clothes to food.

● Always wash hands and wrists thoroughly before preparing food. As well, scrub nails if they are at all grubby.

● Wash hands after visiting the lavatory.

● Wash hands after blowing the nose – bacteria from the nose are transferred to hands.

● Wash hands after putting food in the rubbish bin.

● Wash hands after handling raw fish, poultry, meat and eggs, and before continuing to prepare food.

● Keep long hair tied back.

● Avoid preparing food for other people as far as possible if you have a stomach upset. Keep other members of the family with colds or illness out of the kitchen.

● When preparing food, do not scratch your face or handle hair as bacteria from the skin, hair, nose or ears may be passed on to the food.

● Avoid wearing long sleeves that cannot be rolled up and do not wear jewellery.

Kitchen Hygiene

This is the area of good cooking habits as well as hygiene related to cleaning.

● Never comb or brush hair in the kitchen.

● Never smoke in the kitchen.

● Have liquid soap for washing hands in the kitchen – this is more hygienic than having a tablet of soap. If possible wash hands in a separate area.

● Keep pets out of the kitchen if possible. If this is not practical, then train pets not to jump on to work surfaces. Both cats and dogs can be trained, and dogs can be trained to stay out of the kitchen. If pets cannot be kept out of the kitchen permanently, shut them out when preparing food.

● Keep pets away from towel rails, refrigerator doors, and any other areas which come in contact with food.

● Keep work surfaces, sink, floors and walls thoroughly cleaned.

● Encourage children to use the kitchen and to keep it clean. Make sure everyone who uses the kitchen adopts the same standards of hygiene – washing hands and cleaning up after themselves.

● When preparing food, never dip a finger in to taste or use the same spoon to taste several times. Do not encourage others to dip into food which is being prepared. Every time you take a little taste and return the spoon to the food, bacteria are transferred from your mouth to the food. Although the bacteria may be acceptable in the mouth they are not wanted in the food.

● Never leave food uncovered on the work surface.

● Never leave dirty dishes stacked on the work surface or draining board.

● Always wash dishes in hot soapy water – use water as hot as the hands can stand or wear rubber gloves.

• Always mop up spillages immediately and keep cupboard fronts clean.

• Avoid using sponges and highly absorbent cloths. Instead use cloths that may be rinsed out and dried easily between use.

• Hang tea-towels, spread out, after use.

X *Damp cloths harbour bacteria. Crumpled dish cloths and folded tea-towels take longer to dry than those that hang freely and they are more likely to be contaminated with large numbers of bacteria.*

General Household Hygiene

• Keep cloths for cleaning bathrooms and toilets separate from cloths used in the kitchen.

• Encourage the family to treat the kitchen as a place where food is prepared; discourage them from using it as a general dumping ground, for example, for dirty boots and shoes, old newspapers and so on.

• Dust and dirt in other areas of the house is transferred to the kitchen, so keep up standards.

Outside the Home

Being aware of hygiene standards is important when shopping as well as when eating out.

• Note the personal hygiene and standards of dress of staff at the supermarket or food shops. Do not be shy about commenting to the manager about inadequacies.

• Always watch the way in which staff handle food you are purchasing, whether in a supermarket, small shop, cafe or restaurant. Complain if necessary.

• Take note of the general standards of cleanliness in supermarkets, shops and wherever you eat out. Remember that you do not want to take food home laden with bacteria from other people and buildings.

Ice Cream

See also Sorbet* and Yogurt*.
Ice cream is not difficult to make.

Successful Ice Creams

• The fat and sugar content of the mixture affect the finished texture. The lighter the mixture, the more icy the ice cream.

• Before freezing, the mixture should have a good flavour and be very slightly sweeter than required. When frozen the flavour and sweetness is less pronounced.

• Thorough beating when the mixture is half frozen is important as it breaks down the ice crystals and makes the mixture smooth.

• Beating more than once during freezing gives better results. The exception is mixtures which contain a large proportion of whipped double cream. The fat content gives the ice cream a smooth texture, similar to parfait.

• Have all equipment for beating chilled. A food processor gives best results, particularly if the bowl, blade and lid are well chilled.

• Before serving, many types of ice cream should be placed in the refrigerator to soften slightly. This process is sometimes known as ripening. It allows the ice cream to soften enough to be scooped, also the flavour is more noticeable if the ice cream is not overcold. About 15–30 minutes in the refrigerator is usual.

Ice Cream Makers

Also known as a sorbetière or ice cream churn. There are three types but they all provide one similar function: to constantly stir the mixture as it is freezing. This makes the ice cream smooth and creamy. Electric, battery-operated or clockwork churners are filled and frozen.

Table top models usually consist of a container for the mixture surrounded by ice and salt. The cold of the ice and salt freezes the mixture which is stirred all the time.

The most expensive ice cream makers are large and they have a built-in freezing unit.

Although an ice cream maker is useful it is not essential. A food processor is a great help as it is ideal for processing the part-frozen mixture.

Flavouring Ice Cream

The following may be used with the basic recipe.

Chocolate Before making the custard, break 175 g/6 oz dark plain chocolate into squares. Place this is a saucepan with the milk and heat it gently until the chocolate melts, stirring occasionally. Use the chocolate-flavoured milk for the custard.

Coffee Make 150 ml/¼ pint very strong fresh coffee, by infusing 60 ml/4 tablespoons finely ground coffee in 150 ml/¼ pint just boiled water. Leave until cool, then strain through a filter paper. Make the coffee up to 600 ml/1 pint with milk and use to make the custard.

Fruity Ice Soak 100 g/4 oz chopped glacé cherries, 50 g/2 oz raisins, 25 g/1 oz finely chopped candied peel and the grated rind of 1 orange in the juice of 1 orange for 1 hour. Strain the juice into the custard before cooling. Mix in the fruit after beating the half-frozen ice cream.

Strawberry Sweeten 300 ml/ ½ pint strawberry purée with 30 ml/2 tablespoons icing sugar and fold it into the custard. Beat the ice cream at least twice.

VANILLA ICE CREAM

INGREDIENTS
50 g/2 oz plain flour
4 egg yolks
75 g/3 oz sugar
10 ml/2 teaspoons natural
  vanilla essence
600 ml/1 pint milk
300 ml/½ pint whipping
  cream

FOOD VALUES:
TOTAL • PER PORTION
kcals: 1962 • 245
kJ: 8180 • 1023
protein: 39 g • 5 g
fat: 136 g • 17 g
carbohydrate: 155 g • 19 g
fibre: 2 g • 0 g
Serves 8

Place the flour in a basin. Add the egg yolks, sugar and vanilla essence, then pour in just a little of the milk. Beat this mixture thoroughly until it is smooth, adding enough milk to make a thin paste.

Pour the remaining milk into a saucepan and heat it until just boiling. Stir the hot milk into the flour paste, then pour the mixture back into the pan. Bring this custard slowly to the boil, stirring all the time. It will become quite thick and lumpy just before it boils – mix it vigorously at this stage to beat out all the lumps. Reduce the heat so that the custard just bubbles and cook for 3–5 minutes, stirring often. This is essential.

Remove the pan from the heat. Dampen a piece of greaseproof paper and press it on the surface of the custard, then leave to cool. Beat the cold custard well until it is smooth. Whip the cream until it stands in soft peaks, then fold into the custard.

Transfer the mixture to a rigid freezerproof container, cover the container and freeze the mixture for about 3–4 hours or until it is part frozen. The top and sides should be crusted with frozen mixture.

Beat the mixture well or work it in a food processor. All the ice crystals should be removed. Return it to the container and freeze the ice cream until it is firm. This will take several hours or leave overnight.

VARIATIONS
Low-Fat Ice Cream Use skimmed milk to make the custard. Instead of double cream, fold 450 ml/¾ pint one per cent fat fromage frais into the cooled custard. Continue as above, beating the ice cream twice during freezing to make sure it is smooth and creamy.
FOOD VALUES: TOTAL • PER PORTION
kcals: 1035 • 129
kJ: 4411 • 551
protein: 69 g • 9 g
fat: 10 g • 1 g
carbohydrate: 179 g • 22 g
fibre: 2 g • 0 g

Quick Ice Cream Use a 425 g/15 oz can or 532 g/18 oz pack of custard instead of making the confectioner's custard. Whip the cream with 60 ml/4 tablespoons icing sugar and 5 ml/1 teaspoon natural vanilla essence before folding it into the custard. If using fromage frais, stir the icing sugar and vanilla into it.
FOOD VALUES: TOTAL • PER PORTION WITH CREAM
kcals: 1752 • 219
kJ: 7291 • 911
protein: 22 g • 3 g
fat: 124 g • 16 g
carbohydrate: 144 g • 18 g
fibre: 0 g • 0 g
FOOD VALUES: TOTAL • PER PORTION WITH FROMAGE FRAIS
kcals: 1017 • 127
kJ: 4302 • 538
protein: 51 g • 6 g
fat: 20 g • 3 g
carbohydrate: 168 g • 21 g
fibre: 0 g • 0 g

Icings

See also Marzipan*.
The choice of icing depends on the type of cake: solid cakes can take heavy icing, whereas light cakes need soft icing.

Buttercream

Also known as butter icing.
Preparation Cream the softened butter with sifted icing sugar until pale and creamy. Beat in natural vanilla essence or other flavouring.
Use Use as a filling, topping or coating for light cakes, such as Madeira, Victoria sandwich type cakes and small cakes. May be used with Swiss roll but not often used on light whisked sponges. Not suitable for fruit cake.
For Decorating Spread buttercream in decorative lines or swirls using a palette knife. Pipe buttercream using large or medium size nozzles.
Storing and Freezing Keep buttercream in a covered container in the refrigerator for up to 2 weeks.

Freeze any leftover buttercream in a covered container for up to 3 months. Thaw it in the refrigerator, then soften the icing at room temperature and beat well before using.

Glacé Icing

Preparation Probably the easiest icing to make. Sift the icing sugar into a bowl, then beat in the water to make a thin smooth icing.

The icing should be thin enough to just pour in a thick stream from a spoon. If it is any thinner it will provide only a fine covering on a cake, any thicker and it will not spread easily.
Use On light cakes and small cakes, such as Madeira and Victoria sandwich type cakes, whisked sponge cakes and Swiss roll. It may also be used on biscuits or pastries, such as mille feuille or cream slices (see puff

pastry*). Once it is poured over a cake, glacé icing tends to crust over fairly quickly, so any decoration should be added at once. Colours from decorations run easily into glacé icing.

For Decoration Glacé icing may be coloured but it is not suitable for decorative piping as it is too soft. It may be used for writing on the top of a simple cake.

Feather icing is the decoration usually associated with glacé icing. Parallel lines of coloured glacé icing are piped over an even coat of white or contrasting glacé icing. A fine metal skewer is dragged across the surface, pulling the lines of coloured icing into the base coat. The skewer is pulled in parallel lines in alternate directions to create the feathering effect. The skewer should be wiped with absorbent kitchen paper after each stroke.

Storing and Freezing Glacé icing should be used as soon as it is made.

Royal Icing

Royal icing mix is easy to use and ideal when only small amounts are required. Follow packet instructions which usually involve adding water to the mix and beating well.

Preparation Albumin powder is reconstituted or egg white is used. Lightly whisk the egg until it is just frothy, then gradually beat in the sifted icing sugar. A heavy-duty food mixer is invaluable for making large quantities of royal icing. The icing should be smooth, light and soft to spread after long beating.

A little glycerine is added to prevent the icing from setting too hard.

Use On rich fruit cakes over a base covering of marzipan. The marzipan must be allowed to dry for 1–2 weeks before applying royal icing, otherwise the oil from the almonds can stain the icing when it dries.

Use a palette knife to apply royal icing, spreading it thickly and working it with the knife to burst air bubbles. Rinse a metal

QUICK FROSTING

This is a quick frosting because all the ingredients are whisked together over hot water. The more complicated method is to boil a syrup* to the soft ball stage, then slowly whisk it into the whisked egg whites.

INGREDIENTS
175 g/6 oz icing sugar
2 fresh egg whites
60 ml/4 tablespoons hot water
2.5 ml/½ teaspoon cream of tartar
2.5 ml/½ teaspoon vanilla essence

FOOD VALUES:
TOTAL
kcals: 711
kJ: 3032
protein: 5 g
fat: 0 g
carbohydrate: 184 g
fibre: 0 g

Makes enough to cover a 23 cm/9 inch cake

Have a large saucepan of water on the hob – it should be just simmering. Put all the ingredients, in the order listed, in a large heatproof bowl that fits on the pan. Give the mixture a stir, then use an electric beater to whisk them together.

Stand the bowl over the hot water and whisk the mixture constantly for about 5 minutes, or until it is thick and very glossy. It should stand in soft peaks. Keep the water only just simmering, do not allow it to boil too fast.

Remove the bowl from the hot water and continue to whisk the frosting for 2–3 minutes, until it cools slightly. Use at once, swirling the frosting over the cake. Leave to set for at least 30 minutes before serving.

straight edge or icing rule with hot water, dry it, then pull it evenly across the top of the icing to make it smooth. The sides are smoothed using plastic scrapers.

Several thin coats of royal icing are applied to a formal cake until a smooth, thick coat is built up.

For Decorating Royal icing may be piped using very fine nozzles. It is used for intricate piping on formal cakes.

Storing and Freezing Keep royal icing in an airtight container in a cool place for 3–4 days. Beat it lightly before use.

Fondant Icing

This must not be confused with sugarpaste or the bought roll-out icing. Fondant is made by boiling sugar and water syrup until it reaches the soft ball stage. It is worked until smooth, then pieces are warmed over hot water and poured over cakes.

Preparation Place the sugar, glucose and water in a large saucepan and heat the mixture gently, stirring occasionally, until the sugar dissolves. When the sugar has dissolved, bring the syrup to the boil and boil it hard until it reaches the soft ball stage (see syrup*) or 116°C/240°F on a sugar thermometer. Remove the pan from the heat.

Pour the fondant on to a heatproof surface – a marble slab or board is ideal as it allows the mixture to cool quickly.

Use a palette knife to scrape the sides of the fondant towards the middle, sliding the knife under the icing and folding it over in sheets. As the fondant cools it will become white, smooth and firm.

Knead the fondant into a smooth ball, then wrap it in a polythene bag.

Use Break off pieces of fondant and heat them in a basin over a

INGREDIENTS FOR MAKING DIFFERENT ICINGS

Icing	Sugar	Glucose/ Glycerine	Egg Whites	Butter (unsalted)	Water	Flavouring
Buttercream	75 g/3 oz (icing)	—	—	100 g/4 oz	—	1.25 ml/¼ tsp natural vanilla
Glacé Icing	225 g/8 oz (icing)	—	—	—	30–45 ml/ 2–3 tbsp	—
Royal Icing	675 g/1 ½ lb (icing)	7.5 ml/1 ½ tsp (glycerine)	3	—	—	—
Fondant	450 g/1 lb (granulated or lump)	10 ml/2 tsp glucose	—	—	150 ml/¼ pint	—

Note The quantities given make enough icing to cover the top and sides of a 20 cm/8 inch round cake, except in the case of glacé icing which makes enough to cover the top only. Abbreviations: tbsp = tablespoon, tsp = teaspoon.

pan of hot, not simmering, water. Stir the fondant as it melts and thin it with a little sugar syrup, if necessary. Do not over-heat the fondant, simply melt it.

Pour the fondant over light or rich cakes. For a perfect coating the cakes must be covered in marzipan first. Fondant may be used on small cakes or biscuits.

Sugarpaste

Sugarpaste may be bought from specialist cake decorating sup-pliers. Roll-out icing, which is similar to sugarpaste, is available from most supermarkets.
Use On Madeira type cakes or rich fruit cakes, over a covering of marzipan. The paste is rolled and applied in an even covering. Royal icing decorations may be added.
Storing and Freezing Sugarpaste keeps well if double wrapped in thick polythene bags and sealed. It may be stored in the refriger-ator or a cool dry place for several weeks: follow the manufac-turer's instructions.

Cakes covered in sugarpaste may be frozen undecorated for short periods.

Frosting

An American, soft 'icing' which should be made and used promptly on light cakes. Swirl frosting on cakes at once, before it sets on the surface.

Iron

An important mineral which is an essential part of haemoglobin, the oxygen carrying substance in the blood. Iron is found in the red blood cells and it is also stored in the liver and muscle.

The diet must contain an adequate supply of iron as it is not absorbed easily. Deficiency results in anaemia which causes tiredness and makes the body more susceptible to illness. More pronounced anaemia leads to serious illness. Iron deficiency is usually treated with iron supple-ments that are readily absorbed by the body.

Sources of Iron

Meat, meat products and offal, such as kidneys and liver, all are good sources of iron in a form that is easily absorbed. Bread, cereals, flour and green veg-etables also provide a valuable regular supply.

Irradiation

This is a method of treating fresh food to kill unwanted bacteria and the insect pests that damage stored foods. The ripening of fruit and sprouting of potatoes can also be delayed, reducing loss in transport and storage.

Irradiation is an alternative to chemical treatment of some im-ported foods, such as herbs and spices, to inactivate any con-taminating bacteria.

What is Irradiation?

The technique used is similar to that used for sterilising medical instruments and dressings.

Food is exposed to X-rays or gamma rays for a specific period to give a controlled dose of radi-ation (lower than that used for sterilising medical supplies) that pasteurises it. As they pass through the food, the rays cause minor chemical changes to its structure.

Foods for Irradiation

Not all food responds well to irradiation and many fats in food become rancid during the pro-cess. The use of irradiation as a means of keeping food in good condition has to be selective. Premises wishing to irradiate food will be licensed and subject to inspection. They will be re-quired to meet high standards in process control. By law, clear labelling will be used on ir-radiated food.

The types of foods likely to be irradiated are herbs and spices, poultry, some seafood (such as prawns) and high-value, short shelf-life fruit and vegetables.

Jams and Jellies

See Fruit*.

Jams and jellies are set, sweet fruit preserves. The information given here must also be remembered when making marmalade*.

For a Good Set

Three essential ingredients combine to make jams, jellies and other sweet preserves set.

Pectin Pectin is a gum-like substance which is present in the cell walls of some fruit. Different fruits contain different amounts of pectin.

Under-ripe fruit contains more pectin than ripe fruit, so for best results use a combination of slightly under-ripe and ripe fruit.

Pectin Stock Made by boiling apples to a pulp, then straining the juice. Commercial pectin is obtainable from chemists and it should be used according to the manufacturer's instructions. Sugar with pectin is also available.

Acid Acid, either naturally present in the fruit or added, is essential for a good set. It is also useful in helping to extract the pectin from the fruit. Lemon juice is added to fruits that are not acidic to give the preserve a good colour, to bring out the flavour of the fruit and to ensure that it sets well.

Sugar The right balance of sugar to pectin is essential. When pectin is boiled with sugar in the right proportions, the preserve will set.

The sugar is also a preservative

as yeasts and moulds are unable to grow on mixtures that have a high sugar content.

Equipment

A large stainless steel or heavy enamelled pan is essential. Aluminium and copper preserving pans were once popular but should not be used because the fruit acid reacts with the metal. The pan must be large enough to allow room for the preserve to boil up. It should be no more than half to two-thirds full.

Have ready thoroughly clean jars, waxed discs and airtight lids. Warm the jars on folded tea-towels on a baking tray in the oven.

A jam funnel, oven gloves and several clean tea-towels should be ready for use.

Making Jams and Jellies

There are distinct stages.

Preparing the Fruit Wash the fruit and discard any bad or bruised fruit along with leaves and stalks. When making jelly, no further preparation is necessary, except to cut up large fruit such as apples.

For jam, the fruit must be peeled, cored and cut into small pieces if necessary. Soft fruit may be left whole. Stones should be removed from plums, apricots and peaches.

Cooking the Fruit The fruit must be soft before the sugar is added. Soft fruit for making jam are cooked with the minimum of extra water; other fruit that require slightly longer cooking have some water added. More water is added for making jelly.

Acid may be added at this stage.

Straining the Fruit For jellies and jelly marmalade, the cooked fruit must be strained through a jelly bag for several hours or overnight.

Squeezing the fruit will make the preserve cloudy.

Boiling with Sugar Once the fruit is completely tender, the sugar may be added. When making jelly, the sugar is added to the strained juice. Warming the sugar first makes it dissolve more quickly and this results in a clear preserve with less scum.

Dissolve the sugar completely, stirring occasionally, over low heat. Once the sugar has dissolved, bring the preserve to a full rolling boil and cook at boiling point until it sets.

Testing for Setting

There are three simple ways of testing for setting; in addition, the setting point can be checked by a more complicated weighing process which is explained in specialist books.

Start testing for setting after 3–5 minutes boiling. Remove the

JAM MAKING			
Quantities of Sugar, Water and Acid for 450 g/1 lb Fruit			
Fruit	Sugar	Water	Juice of lemons
Apricot	450 g/1 lb	150 ml/¼ pint	1
Blackberry	450 g/1 lb	30–45 ml/2–3 tablespoons	1
Blackcurrant or redcurrant	575 g/1¼ lb	150 ml/¼ pint	—
Gooseberry	450 g/1 lb	200 ml/7 fl oz	2
Plum	450 g/1 lb	100 ml/4 fl oz	1
Raspberry	450 g/1 lb	30 ml/2 tablespoons	½
Strawberry	350 g/12 oz	30 ml/2 tablespoons	2

SEE ALSO **Jamaican Pepper:** Glossary; **Jarlsberg:** Cheese; **Julienne:** Glossary; **Juniper:** Spices

pan from the heat or turn instant heat off when testing for setting. It is possible to overcook preserves beyond setting point, in which case they never set successfully.

Flake Test Probably the least reliable method. Hold a mixing spoon out of the preserve and allow some of the preserve to drip off it. If the preserve sets in flakes on the end of the spoon it will set. If it runs freely, it will not set.

Saucer Test Have a cold saucer ready. Put a little of the preserve on the saucer and set it aside. A distinct skin should form on the sample of preserve and this should wrinkle when pushed.

Temperature Test The majority of preserves set when they have boiled to a temperature of 104°C/220°F. The mixture boils at this temperature when the correct concentration of sugar is reached for a good set.

Skimming

Stop cooking the preserve when setting point is reached. Skim any scum off the top of the preserve using a large, clean metal spoon.

Stirring a knob of butter into jam disperses scum but it is essential that jelly is skimmed.

Potting and Covering

The preserve should be potted at once and its surface covered with discs of waxed paper. The waxed side should be placed down on the preserve. Cover the pots at once with airtight lids.

Labelling and Storing

Label the preserve with type and date when it was made. Store preserves in a cool, dark, dry place. Most preserves will keep for at least 6 months and up to 12 months.

Some Common Problems

- Overboiling causes jam or jelly to be syrupy and dark in colour rather than set. Once a preserve has boiled beyond setting point it will not set. Usually caused by allowing the preserve to continue boiling while testing for setting.

- Lack of pectin means that the jam will not set. Check the fruit chart for a guide to pectin content. By adding more fruit or fruit juice and commercial pectin, then re-boiling, some preserves may be rescued.

- Too little acid can prevent the pectin from being adequately extracted from the fruit and the preserve will not set.

- If the preserve is not boiled properly or for long enough it will not set.

Jelly

See Agar Agar*, Aspic*, Clarifying* and Gelatine*.

A jelly is a set liquid. Aspic is a savoury jelly but the majority of jellies are sweet and made from fruit juice or from a commercial, flavoured jelly tablet. Gelatine or agar agar may be used for setting.

Jelly Tablets

Break the tablet into pieces and melt it in a small amount of water that is just off the boil, then make it up to the recommended volume using cold water. Ice cubes may be added for a quicker set. Chill until set.

Fresh Fruit Jellies

Make fresh fruit jellies by clarifying fruit juice (page 81), then sweeten it to taste and set with gelatine.

Pineapple, pawpaw and lemon juice contain enzymes that inhibit the setting of gelatine. If the juice is boiled for a few min-

utes first, the enzymes will be destroyed and the juice will set.

Milk and Cream Jellies

Melt a jelly tablet in a small portion of water, then make up the quantity with milk, single cream, yogurt or fromage frais.

When using fresh fruit, remember that pineapple, lemon or orange and other acid fruit juice will make milk curdle. Fruit purées may be combined with cream, yogurt or fromage frais and set.

Unmoulding Jellies

Rinse a flat plate with cold water. Dip the mould into hot water – if using a thick glass jelly mould, dip it into hand hot water as anything hotter may cause it to crack. Leave the mould in the hot water for about 30 seconds. Wipe the outside of the mould with a tea-towel, then place the plate on top of the mould.

Hold the plate and mould together, then invert the mould on the plate. Before removing the mould, slide the jelly into the middle of the plate – if the plate is moist this is easy but it is not possible on a dry plate. Carefully lift the mould off the jelly.

Junket

Similar to yogurt, junket is made by adding rennet (see Glossary, page 275) to milk. The rennet essence is added to warm milk which may be sweetened, then left to stand until set. If stirred or shaken the junket separates into curds and whey.

Kitchen Planning

The kitchen is probably one of the busiest rooms in most homes; often small with space at a premium.

Ease of Cleaning

• All surfaces must be moisture-proof and washable.

• Avoid heavily textured surfaces and intricate mouldings which trap dirt and may become clogged.

Work Surfaces

• Have a space next to the cooker or oven for taking hot or heavy dishes, pots and pans.

• Have one clear area large enough for food preparation.

• If possible, have an area where dishes may be put out ready for serving or where used dishes may be stacked.

• Slide-out or fold-down surfaces are a plus in small kitchens; if not for taking a lot of weight at least as a temporary preparation surface.

Food Storage Space

Make sure that you have adequate cupboard space for dried and packet foods as well as jars, tins, herbs and spices. Avoid shelves and open racks that leave foods exposed to light.

Remember to allow room for a refrigerator that is large enough to suit your needs.

A cool dark place for storing root vegetables, such as potatoes,

is ideal; if you do not have a suitable place, think about the best place to keep them.

For Storing Crockery and Equipment

Have cupboards that close for storing the majority of equipment. Open shelves and hanging hooks allow the equipment to become dusty and dirty.

Have equipment that is used often in accessible positions.

Drawer and Hanging Space

Assess your needs – use drawers for cutlery and small items of equipment, also for tea-towels and other kitchen linen. Do not have too many drawers that can become a dumping ground.

Have separate hanging space for hand and tea towels. Also have a place to hang dish cloths and washing up brushes. Keep cleaning cloths separate.

Pots and Pans

Have a cupboard or rack where pots and pans may be stored, either stacked or hanging. If they cannot be stored in a cupboard, any pans that are not used frequently need washing before use.

Heating and Ventilation

The kitchen should be well ventilated to allow cooking smells to escape and fresh air to enter. If possible, a ventilator which allows fresh air in without allowing flies through is ideal for use in the summer.

The ideal kitchen for cooking is too cool for standing around in but fine when working. A warm room is not ideal for preparing food. If the room is warm, then think about the size of refrigerator you need, going for a larger one to keep most food chilled.

A separate unheated utility room adjoining the kitchen is ideal, allowing for refrigerator, freezer and food cupboards to be kept as cool as possible.

Knives

See Equipment*.

Good knives that are properly treated will last for years and their blades will always sharpen well to give a good cutting edge.

Buying

When buying look for:

• riveted handles which are comfortable to hold;

• fine-edged stainless steel blades that are very sharp;

• knives that feel well balanced when used in a cutting action.

> ☑ *Well-formed laminated or plastic handles are available on good-quality knives and they are dishwasher proof.*

A Basic Knife Set

Cook's Knife A fairly heavy knife with a blade of about 15–20 cm/6–8 inches long. This knife should be bought as one of the main kitchen utensils, so look at all the types that are available and buy one that is most comfortable. Use this for the majority of cutting, from slicing cucumber to cubing meat or chopping an onion.

Small or Medium Serrated Knife A serrated knife is used for cutting tomatoes and other foods that squash easily. Look for one with a blade measuring about 10–12.5 cm/4–5 inches long.

Vegetable Peeler The best peeler is one that has the blade attached to an open handle by a shank through the middle. This allows the blade to move and it will rattle slightly when you pick it up. Do not be put off – when peeling uneven vegetables the blade will move easily over the bumps, allowing a thin layer of peel to be removed.

Small Knife Have a small knife with a good point for poking pips out of fruit or for delicate cutting. Make sure it has a very fine flexible blade that will sharpen to a razor finish or have a serrated blade.

Bread Knife A good-quality, serrated bread knife is essential.

Palette Knife A medium-sized palette knife is most versatile, useful for removing cooked items from baking trays as well as for spreading creamy mixtures or icings.

Steel As well, have a good steel for sharpening knives.

Additional Knives

Add to your knife set as you need more equipment and according to the type of food you prepare or serve.

Carving Knife At one time considered one of the most basic knives but now the importance of a carving knife depends entirely on how many joints of meat you cook. Usually, a thoroughly sharpened large cook's knife may be substituted.

Large Cook's Knife A very heavy knife with a long, wide blade that is flat at the wide end. For chopping significant quantities of ingredients, slicing and dicing larger vegetables or meat.

Boning Knife A knife with a narrow, tapered blade that is firm. This should sharpen well as it is used to cut meat from bone.

Cleaver For chopping poultry and for dicing or finely chopping meat.

Various Small Cook's Knives Two small knives, one serrated and one plain edged, for trimming pastry edges, cutting small food items and garnishes and so on. The choice at this level is very personal – some knives become favourites for certain tasks.

Grapefruit Knife Serrated on both sides of the curved blade; for scooping around segments of halved grapefruit and other citrus fruit.

Corer For removing the core from whole apples.

Paring Knife A short-bladed sharp knife with a fairly wide, rigid blade. For peeling or cutting strips off citrus fruit or vegetables, such as carrots, when holding the food in one hand as opposed to working on a cutting board.

Canelle Knife For removing narrow strips of peel to give fruit or vegetable slices a decorative appearance.

Caring for Knives

Have a solid knife block, rack or compartments in a drawer for storing knives where they will not get damaged or cause an injury.

Unless you buy knives that are dishwasher proof, do not put knives in the dishwasher. Wash knives by hand. Wash wooden handles briefly, without allowing them to soak in water.

Occasionally rub a little fresh cooking oil into wooden handles and rub the handle well with absorbent kitchen paper, then leave overnight before using.

Sharpening a Knife

There are two ways, use the first if you are confident at handling knives but use the second method if you are less used to handling sharp implements.

Method 1 Hold the steel in one hand and the knife in the other hand. Hold the knife blade on the steel, with the handle end of the knife at the handle of the steel. Slide the knife along the steel, down towards the tip of the steel. By the time the knife is at the tip of the steel its point should be on the steel. Always sharpen the full length of the knife in this way, then put the steel on the other side of the blade and repeat. The knife

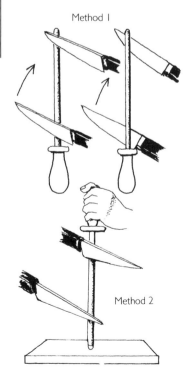

Method 1

Method 2

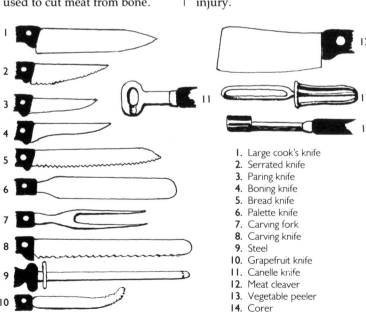

1. Large cook's knife
2. Serrated knife
3. Paring knife
4. Boning knife
5. Bread knife
6. Palette knife
7. Carving fork
8. Carving knife
9. Steel
10. Grapefruit knife
11. Canelle knife
12. Meat cleaver
13. Vegetable peeler
14. Corer

should be pulled across the steel about 4–6 times, depending on how blunt it is.

Method 2 Hold the steel with its point down on a firm surface – a heavy cutting board is ideal. Hold the knife in the other hand and pull it down the length of the steel, working from the handle end of the knife to its tip. Do this several times before sharpening the other side of the blade.

Kohlrabi

See Vegetables*.

A vegetable of the cabbage family, although this is the swollen stem. It looks rather like a small, pale green or purple swede with a few stems emerging from the sides.

Buying and Storing Look for firm vegetables that are unmarked. Avoid those that feel slightly soft or look wrinkled on the surface.

Keep kohlrabi in the refrigerator and use within 2–3 days.

Preparation

Trim the ends of the vegetable, then peel it and cut into chunks for boiling and mashing, or into fine cubes or strips.

Cooking

Place the prepared kohlrabi in a saucepan and cover with cold water. Add a little salt, then bring to the boil. Reduce the heat and simmer large chunks for 10–15 minutes, until tender.

Fine strips or dice should be simmered for 2–5 minutes, until just tender.

Serving Ideas

● Mash with butter and pepper.

● Toss with butter and snipped chives.

● Toss with a little soured cream and chopped spring onion, then sprinkle with grated Gruyère cheese and grill until golden.

Labelling

The law and guidelines that are set out for manufacturers and retailers are constantly under review and therefore subject to change. Details are available from consumer advice centres or local libraries.

Reading Labels

Labels on fresh food give essential, useful information about how to store and handle the food as well as basic details about its type and weight.

However, many food labels are packed with so much detail that they can be confusing. It is important to get used to reading the notes so that you can quickly recognise the ones that are important.

Description of the Food The food must be described well so that you know what you are buying. The description must not be misleading but there are phrases that are worth recognising. For example, if something is 'flavoured' it does not necessarily contain the food item: 'strawberry-flavoured' is not the same as 'with strawberries'. Check the ingredient list to find out exactly what is in the food.

The Ingredients Everything that goes into the food must be listed in the ingredients, including the water content of processed meat and additives. Do not be put off by 'E' numbers – they are a concise way of listing ingredients. If in doubt about any of the ingredients that are listed by number or chemical name, then complete lists of permitted additives are

available for the consumer to check.

Ingredients lists often make interesting reading – you may be surprised at the balance of ingredients. For example, something you consider to be a protein food may contain a significant proportion of starch.

Use By Dates and Storage Instructions Always check the use by date on fresh foods.

Fresh food may be kept at home until the use by date following the instructions on the label. It is important to check this information – it explains whether food must be kept cool or at room temperature, or whether it should be chilled. As well the label will tell you whether packets or jars may be kept at room temperature until opened, then chilled.

Weight, Volume or Number This is important when you are estimating the number of servings that you will get from the food. Many manufacturers give additional information, such as the number of slices of meat as well as weight.

The number, weight or volume must be correct: it is an offence to short sell.

Preparation or Cooking Instructions For food safety always read and follow the manufacturer's advice about how to prepare, heat or cook food products to avoid any risk of undercooking or not reheating food properly.

Name and Address of the Manufacturer This tells you where the food came from and where it was processed, if at all. It is also worth knowing that this information is available so that you can make a complaint or comment if necessary.

Labelling Exceptions

Canned and packeted foods, or other items that keep well, fresh foods that must be eaten quickly and certain cheeses that improve with keeping do not have to carry a date by which they must be eaten. However, many manufacturers mark cans and packets with a guide to when the food should be eaten to be at its best. This may be up to a year ahead and a month is given rather than a date. Food with a long shelf life, unlikely to go off suddenly, may be used when just past the suggested date (by days rather than weeks).

Other labelling exceptions include some small packets that do not have to have a weight or quantity, or items such as a pint milk bottle which is easily recognised without having a volume displayed on it.

Nutrition Information

Information on the nutrients that are provided by the food is important as it allows you to assess the value of the food or product within the diet.

It is usual for the energy (calorie) value, fat, sugar, carbohydrate and protein content to be given as well as details of vitamins and minerals.

The label must tell you:
- what the food is;
- the ingredients that are used, listed in order according to weight giving the ingredients that weigh most first;
- how to store fresh food and for how long;
- the weight, volume or number of items in the pack;
- a guide to preparation and cooking instructions for prepared foods;
- the name and address of the manufacturer.

Lamb

See Meat*.
The illustration shows the carcass and the cuts. Look out for prepared boneless meat portions and joints as well as the traditional cuts.

Scrag and Middle Neck Usually sold on the bone, chopped into pieces. These are the stewing cuts of lamb. **(1)**

Shoulder Sold on the bone or boned and rolled. Part shoulder joints, knuckle and blade end, are also available on the bone. Traditionally, shoulder of lamb has a higher fat content than leg or other roasting joints. Shoulder is a roasting joint; it may also be trimmed and cubed for braising or it may be minced. **(2)**

Best End of Neck This may be bought whole, with six or seven ribs and roasted on the bone. The backbone should be chined, sawn through, to make carving easier. The whole joint may be boned and rolled. Also suitable for barbecuing or grilling as well as for roasting. Individual cutlets may be grilled. **(3)**

Guard of Honour Two best end of neck joints with bone ends interlocked.

Crown Roast Two best end of neck joints with ends trussed together and arranged in a ring, or crown, for stuffing and roasting. The bones are on the outside.

Noisettes The boned loin is trimmed of excess fat and rolled, then sliced to make neat rounds of meat.

Fillet The lean eye of meat from the middle neck chops.

Loin and Chump Both cuts may be roasted as joints or cut into chops for grilling or braising. Loin is usually divided into the loin end and chump end. Chump chops have a small round bone in the centre with a good portion of meat around it. **(4)**

Saddle of Lamb A large roasting joint which consists of the whole loin from both sides of the animal.

Leg A prime roasting joint for cooking on the bone or boned. Sold whole or cut into smaller joints. Fillet off the leg or fillet end joint and shank end are typical smaller joints cut from the leg.

Lamb steaks are cut from the wide end of the leg, with a small central bone or boneless. **(5)**

Breast Sold on the bone or boned and rolled, the breast is streaked with fat and lean. For slow roasting, grilling, braising or pot roasting. The breast may be chopped into separate ribs and roasted or grilled – good with curry spices and lemon. **(6)**

Mince Ready minced lamb varies in fat content. Ask the butcher to mince a whole shoulder for best quality mince.

Buying

The new season's lamb is available from early March when it is at its most succulent. Some specialist suppliers provide milk-fed lamb.

Lamb fat should look firm, dry and white. The meat should be a good red colour. Look for a thin outer covering of fat on joints or around chops.

Storing

Leave packs of meat wrapped and place them in the refrigerator as soon as possible after purchase. Use by the date given on the label. Unwrap meat bought loose and place it in a covered dish. Store meat on a low shelf in the refrigerator for up to 3 days if bought fresh.

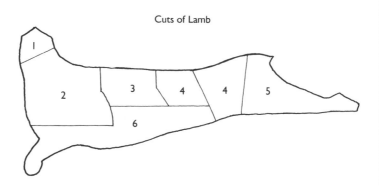

Cuts of Lamb

Cooking Times

See Meat* for cooking times.

Accompaniments for Lamb

Mint Sauce (page 186), red-currant jelly and thin gravy* are the traditional accompaniments for a roast joint.

Herbs that go well with lamb include mint, rosemary, marjoram, fennel and tarragon.

Fruit also goes well with lamb, either in a stuffing or in sauce. Fresh, canned or dried apricots or peaches; apple or orange all complement the flavour of roasted, grilled or braised lamb.

Stuffings based on bread-crumbs, cooked rice or sausage-meat may all be used for boned shoulder, leg or breast of lamb. They may also be used in a crown roast.

Lard

Lard is purified pork fat. Less popular now but at one time used half and half with margarine for making short crust pastry, as well as for shallow and deep frying.

In pastry making lard gives a short texture but little flavour. It is used in hot water crust pastry*.

For frying, lard reaches a higher temperature than vegetable oils, so it tends to make food crisp on the outside. If lard is not heated sufficiently before the food is added the result can be very greasy. Oil is preferred for frying for its polyunsaturated fat content.

Leeks

Available all year but mainly in the autumn and winter, leeks are a versatile vegetable with an onion-like flavour.

Buying

The proportion that is blanched – that is white – varies.

Look for firm, bright leeks – any green part should be a good strong green colour and the white should be bright, not yellowing and soft or wrinkled. Avoid leeks that have only a small white part with a thick, tough and loose green part.

If you intend cooking the leeks whole, then look for small tight vegetables that are clean and mainly white.

Storing

Put the leeks in a large, unsealed polythene bag in the salad drawer of the refrigerator. If the leeks are pre-packed, then leave them wrapped and use them by the date on the label. Leeks usually keep for 3–4 days in the refrigerator if they are really fresh when purchased.

Preparation

Wash the leeks well to remove any outer dirt. Trim off the root ends and any damaged green part or the end. Slice the leeks and place them in a colander, then wash them again under running cold water.

Alternatively, split the leeks lengthways about two-thirds of the way through before removing the root end. Open out each leek and hold it under running water to wash away all dirt.

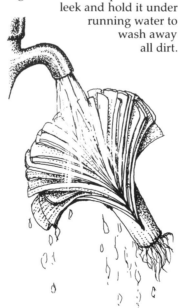

Cooking

Leeks are often cooked in casseroles or soups. They are equally good served as an accompaniment.

Stir frying The leeks should be thinly sliced and separated into rings. Alternatively, cut them into 5 cm/2 inch lengths, then cut each piece in half vertically. Slice each half into thin strips and wash these well.

Add the pieces of leek to hot butter, olive oil or other oil and cook them for about 3–5 minutes. Season to taste.

They are good stir fried with strips of cooked ham or bacon.

Boiling Place thickly sliced leeks in a saucepan and pour in cold water to cover the vegetables. Sprinkle in a little salt, then bring the water to the boil. Reduce the heat, cover the pan and simmer the leeks for about 10 minutes or until they are tender but not soft. Drain well, saving the cooking water for soup or for making a sauce.

Serve coated in savoury white sauce and topped with cheese, then grilled.

Braising Braise thinly sliced leeks with a little marjoram or rosemary and canned tomatoes or chicken stock.

Thickly slice the leeks, then toss them in melted butter over medium heat for a minute or so, until beginning to cook. Add a little chopped herb, if liked, and enough stock to half cover the leeks or a can of chopped tomatoes. Add a little seasoning. Heat until the liquid is simmering, then cover the pan and cook gently for about 30–40 minutes.

Use

● Use in soups, stews, braised dishes or with minced meat in a sauce for pasta (good with lamb).

● Mix with Savoury White Sauce (page 234) and layer with diced cooked ham and lasagne; top with cheese and bake until golden. Leeks may be layered with lasagne and sauce.

- Use with chicken, boiled bacon or gammon as a filling for pie or for savoury crumble*.

Freezing

Leeks do not freeze well as a vegetable for serving alone. Instead they may be sliced and blanched by tossing them in hot oil for 2 minutes, then cooled and packed. This way they freeze well for up to 6 months. Useful in casseroles, soups and other cooked dishes.

Leftover Food

Any cooked leftover food must be handled carefully so that bacteria are not given the opportunity to contaminate it or multiply in it.

- Cool leftovers as quickly as possible to room temperature, then chill them.

- If food is still warm late in the evening or before you are going out, then place it in the refrigerator rather than leaving it in a warm place for many hours.

- Use leftover food promptly, within 1–3 days, depending on the type of food.

- Do not take cooked food out of the refrigerator on several occasions and allow it to warm up.

- When reheating cooked food, make absolutely certain that it is thoroughly heated right through to the original cooking temperature. Do not reheat food more than once.

Lemons

See Fruit.*

Buying

Look for unblemished fruit. Very large lemons tend to have a thick layer of pith under the skin which can make slices look ugly – use smaller fruit for garnishing.

Avoid lemons that are small, slightly dried or wrinkled looking and dark yellow as they are old and will not be juicy.

Waxed Fruit Most citrus fruit is coated in a wax to prevent loss of moisture. Some lemons are labelled unwaxed.

Preparation

Always wash lemons before use.

Grating the Rind Use the fine or medium side of grater. Grate only the rind and not the pith which is bitter.

Squeezing the Juice It is important to remember to remove any rind that is needed before squeezing out the juice. Why not try warming the whole fruit in the microwave for about 30 seconds on High – this tends to give a better yield of juice.

LEMON MERINGUE PIE

INGREDIENTS
175 g/6 oz plain flour
100 g/4 oz margarine
30 ml/2 tablespoons caster sugar
45 ml/3 tablespoons water
Filling
40 g/1½ oz cornflour
grated rind and juice of 3 lemons
175 g/6 oz caster sugar
2 eggs, separated

FOOD VALUES:
TOTAL ● PER PORTION
kcals: 2401 ● 300
kJ: 10111 ● 1264
protein: 31 g ● 4 g
fat: 94 g ● 12 g
carbohydrate: 382 g ● 48 g
fibre: 12 g ● 2 g

Serves 8

Have ready a 23 cm/9 inch flan dish, loose-bottomed flan tin or flan ring on a baking tray. Set the oven at 200°C, 400°F, gas 6. Place the flour in a bowl, then add the margarine. Cut the margarine into the flour in small pieces. Wash and dry your hands, then rub the fat into the flour until the mixture resembles fresh breadcrumbs. Mix in the sugar and water so that the pastry clumps together. Gather the mixture into a ball.

On a lightly floured surface, very gently knead the dough together for a few seconds until it is smooth, then press it flat. Roll out the pastry into a round measuring about 28 cm/11 inches across. Use to line the flan dish, tin or ring. Prick the pastry all over and bake it blind (following the instructions on page 130) for 25 minutes.

Meanwhile, make the filling. Place the cornflour and lemon rind in a basin. Pour the juice into a measuring jug and make it up to 600 ml/1 pint with cold water. Add 50 g/2 oz of the sugar and the egg yolks to the cornflour, then stir in enough of the lemon juice mixture to make a smooth thin paste.

Pour the remaining lemon juice mixture into a saucepan and bring to the boil. Stir some of the hot liquid into the cornflour mixture, then return it all to the pan. Bring the lemon sauce to the boil, stirring all the time.

Pour the sauce into the baked pastry case. Whisk the egg whites until they stand in stiff peaks. Whisking all the time, gradually add the remaining sugar and continue whisking until the mixture is stiff and very glossy.

Pile this meringue over the lemon filling in the pastry case, swirling it over evenly to cover the filling completely. Bake the pie for about 10 minutes, until the meringue topping is lightly browned. Allow to cool, then serve warm or lightly chilled.

LEMON CURD

Remember that lemon curd is not a preserve. Always use very fresh eggs bought from a reputable source and do not cut down on the lemons. Use thoroughly cleaned pots or jars, keep the cooled curd in the refrigerator and use it within 3 weeks.

INGREDIENTS
**3 size 1/large fresh eggs
grated rind and juice of 3
  large lemons
350 g/12 oz caster sugar
100 g/4 oz unsalted butter**

Makes 1 kg/2 lb

FOOD VALUES:
TOTAL • PER
  15 ML/1 TABLESPOON
  (approximate)
kcals: 2399 • 36
kJ: 10088 • 151
protein: 23 g • 0 g
fat: 102 g • 2 g
carbohydrate: 371 g • 6 g
fibre: 5 g • 0 g

Have ready warmed, clean pots, waxed discs and airtight lids. Have a saucepan of hot water on the hob and a large, thoroughly clean mixing bowl and mixing spoon.

Wash the eggs under cold water and dry them with absorbent kitchen paper. Break the eggs into the bowl, then wash and dry your hands. Beat the eggs well. Add the lemon rind and juice, and sugar to the eggs. Cut the butter into small pieces and add it to the mixture.

Place the bowl over the hot water, then stir the mixture all the time until the sugar dissolves and the butter melts. Continue cooking the curd, stirring, until it is thick enough to coat the back of a spoon. Keep the water just below simmering point all the time – you will probably have to keep adjusting the heat slightly, reducing it as the water just begins to simmer, then increasing the heat as the water cools.

It is important that the curd is cooked properly – it should take about 20 minutes – but it must not be overcooked or it will curdle.

At this stage it is traditional to strain the curd, in which case you should have a scalded sieve and warmed clean jug. However, this is not essential and the curd may be poured straight into the prepared pots. Cover at once with waxed discs, wax down, then cover the top of the jars loosely with absorbent kitchen paper and leave the curd to cool completely before putting on airtight lids.

Label the pots with the date before storing the curd in the refrigerator.

Storing

Keep lemons in a dish in a cool room. Place cut fruit in a polythene bag in the refrigerator and use within 2–3 days.

Freezing

Freeze grated lemon rind on its own or with the squeezed juice – they may be combined in ice cube trays. Freeze lemon slices for adding straight to drinks.

Whole fruit may be frozen or the lemons may be prepared ready for making marmalade, then frozen.

Lentils

See Beans and Pulses, Dried*.
Three types of lentils are readily available from whole food shops and supermarkets: red, green and brown.

Lentils do not need soaking before cooking and they all cook fairly quickly.

Preparation

Wash the lentils by placing them in a basin and covering with cold water, then drain off the water and repeat.

Cooking

Red Lentils Place 225 g/8 oz lentils in a saucepan with 450 ml/¾ pint cold water. Add a pinch of salt, if liked, then bring the water to the boil. Reduce the heat, give the lentils a stir and put a lid on the pan.

Simmer the lentils gently for 20–25 minutes, by which time they will have absorbed all the water and be very soft. Keep the heat low and check that the lentils are not too dry after 15 minutes. It is important that the lid fits the pan well to avoid loss of moisture by evaporation.

When cooked, the lentils should have absorbed all the water and they should be dry and very soft.

Green and Brown Lentils Place the lentils in a saucepan with plenty of water to cover. Bring to the boil and reduce the heat, then cover the pan and simmer the lentils for 35–45 minutes. Green lentils are tender after about 35 minutes; brown ones take slightly longer. Check that the lentils do not dry up during cooking. Drain them and serve tossed with a little butter and parsley.

Use

Serve lentils instead of rice or pasta. They may be flavoured with herbs (add a bay leaf when cooking them) or chopped cooked onion. The onion may be added to red lentils before cooking.

All types of lentils are versatile and they combine well with poultry, meat or vegetables in soups, stews, pies or layered pasta dishes.

SEE ALSO **Lemon Balm, Lemon Grass:** Herbs; **Lemon Soufflé:** Soufflés

LENTIL SAUCE

INGREDIENTS
225 g/8 oz green lentils
30 ml/2 tablespoons olive oil
1 onion, chopped
1 clove garlic, crushed
1 stick celery, thinly sliced
1 carrot, diced
**2 (400 g/14 oz) cans chopped
    tomatoes**
1 bay leaf
**5 ml/1 teaspoon dried
    oregano**
salt and pepper

FOOD VALUES:
TOTAL • PER PORTION
kcals: 638 • 160
kJ: 2668 • 667
protein: 28 g • 7 g
fat: 32 g • 8 g
carbohydrate: 64 g • 16 g
fibre: 19 g • 5 g

Serves 4

Cook the lentils as left in plenty of boiling water for 35 minutes. Meanwhile, heat the oil in a saucepan and add the onion, garlic, celery and carrot. Cook over medium to low heat, stirring occasionally, until the vegetables are softened, about 30 minutes. Do not allow to brown.

Add the drained lentils and canned tomatoes, then stir in the bay leaf and oregano with seasoning to taste. Bring just to simmering point, cover the pan and cook the mixture for 15 minutes, allowing time for all the flavours to combine.

Serve the lentil sauce with rice, baked potatoes or pasta. It may be used as a pie filling or to fill pancakes. It is also good layered with lasagne, topped with Béchamel Sauce (page 35) and cheese, then baked until golden.

LENTIL SOUP

INGREDIENTS
25 g/1 oz butter or margarine
1 large onion, chopped
1 large carrot, diced
2 celery sticks, diced
1 medium potato, diced
1 bay leaf
100 g/4 oz red lentils
**1.1 litres/2 pints chicken or
    ham stock**
salt and pepper
**plenty of chopped fresh
    parsley**

FOOD VALUES:
TOTAL • PER PORTION
kcals: 1602 • 267
kJ: 6719 • 1120
protein: 32 g • 5 g
fat: 128 g • 21 g
carbohydrate: 88 g • 15 g
fibre: 9 g • 2 g

Serves 6

Melt the butter or margarine in a large saucepan and add the onion, carrot and celery. Cook the mixture, stirring, for 10 minutes to soften the vegetables slightly. Add the potato, bay leaf and lentils before stirring in the stock.

Sprinkle in a little seasoning and bring the soup to the boil. Give it a good stir, reduce the heat so that the soup simmers, then cover the pan. Simmer the soup gently for 1 hour, stirring occasionally, until the lentils have fallen. Stir in the parsley and taste the soup for seasoning.

Lentil Pâté

Cook the red lentils as left, adding a finely chopped onion and a bay leaf to the cooking water.

When cooked, remove the bay leaf and beat in 50 g/2 oz butter. Beat the lentils well so that they are almost smooth. Mix in 150 g/5 oz low-fat soft cheese with garlic and herbs, and seasoning to taste. Transfer the mixture to a large dish or to 6 small dishes. Cover and allow to cool, then chill well before serving with toast or crusty bread.

Lettuce

See Salads and Salad Dressings.*
Lettuce is mainly used raw in salad but it may also be used to make soup or it may be braised.

Buying and Storing

Lettuce should be crisp with bright leaves.

Cos lettuce will keep for up to 5 days in the salad drawer of the refrigerator if purchased really fresh. Other softer types should be used within 1–2 days of purchase.

Preparation

Separate the leaves and discard any tough base stalk. Wash the leaves well in cold water, then drain and dry them in a salad spinner.

If you do not have a salad spinner, wrap the leaves in a clean tea-towel and swing the tea-towel around your head (outdoors).

Cutting Leaves Break lettuce leaves by hand or cut them using a stainless steel knife.

Types of Lettuce

Batavian This is a large lettuce with curly leaves. It may be tinged red on the outer edges.

Butterhead Also known as round or cabbage lettuce. The familiar lettuce, somewhat uneventful by comparison with other types.

Cos This is tall, with long, oval, dark crisp and well-flavoured leaves.

Iceberg Round, firm, very crisp and sweet-flavoured.

Lamb's Lettuce Small, oval leaves of fresh green. Sold in small heads that resemble immature plants.

Lolla Bionda A pale green lettuce with wavy leaves, similar to lolla rossa.

Lolla Rossa Also known as lolla rosso, this is a red version of endive.

Oak Leaf A dark red leaved small lettuce which wilts easily.

Limes

See Fruit* and Lemon*.
A citrus fruit, smaller than lemon and dark green. Use as for lemon.

Listeria

See Bacteria*, Hygiene*, Cross Contamination* and Micro-organisms*.
Listeria monocytogenes is a bacterium which can contaminate vegetables, dairy produce and chicken. Contamination can result in illness (such as meningitis) although cases are few.

These bacteria are able to grow at low temperatures in refrigerators, therefore particular care is necessary when handling cooked food that is chilled. Salad vegetables that are eaten raw should be thoroughly washed.

Lobster

A crustacean that yields delicately flavoured, firm white flesh tinged pink on the outside.

Buying

Live lobsters are almost black in colour (when cooked they are bright red-pink). Live lobster should be lively and kept in a cool place. Do not buy black lobsters that do not have a lively response and are limp in appearance.

Buy only from a reputable fishmonger.

Killing

Tie the lobster in a plastic carrier bag and freeze it. The method of driving a large knife through the lobster, in the middle of the cross just behind the head, is not a pleasant way of killing it. Leave the lobster in the freezer for 4–6 hours or overnight, then allow a little extra boiling time.

Various other methods of killing and cooking lobster in one operation are suggested and have been recommended at different times, including plunging the crustacean into a huge pan of boiling water or covering it in cold water and heating slowly until boiling.

Cooking

Place the part-frozen or frozen lobster in a large saucepan and cover it with cold water. Bring slowly to the boil, then reduce the heat slightly and simmer for 15–20 minutes, or until the shell has all turned deep red-pink.

Drain the lobster and leave in the covered pan until cool enough to handle.

Cleaning Cooked Lobster
Method 1.

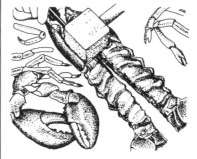
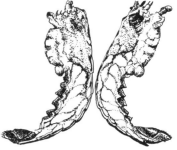

Cleaning Cooked Lobster
Method 2.

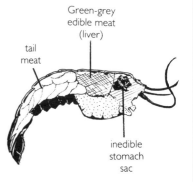

Green-grey edible meat (liver)

tail meat

inedible stomach sac

Cleaning

Break off the claws and legs – twisting them is the best way of removing them. Set these aside.
Method 1 Lay the lobster on its back on a heavy cutting board. Use a heavy cook's knife to cut the lobster in half down through the body – you may need a meat mallet or rolling pin to tap the knife through the shell.

Remove and save any red eggs or coral from near the head end of the lobster. Remove the dark (almost black) intestinal tract that runs down the length of the body. Carefully lift out the tail meat. Clean out the shell and head and reserve the halves for serving the lobster if liked.
Method 2 Turn the lobster on its back. On the underside of the body, a soft shell-like covering runs from head to tail. Use a sharp pointed knife to cut this free from the main shell which overlaps it slightly. Do this down both sides of the tail meat, then lift away the covering and the tail meat may be lifted out in one piece. The shell is discarded if the meat is extracted in this way.

Serving Ideas

- The tail meat may be left in the cleaned halved lobster, then brushed with butter and grilled.

- The meat may be cut into pieces, coated with a wine sauce, then spooned back into the shell halves and topped with breadcrumbs and cheese. Grill the topping until golden.

- Serve lobster meat with mayonnaise and salad.

- Brush halved lobster with garlic butter or herb butter and brown it well on the barbecue.

Storing

Live lobster should be prepared on the same day as purchase. The cooked meat may be kept in a covered dish in the refrigerator overnight.

Freezing

The cooked meat may be frozen for up to 3 months. This is something of a waste as lobster meat is not as succulent when thawed, even when served in a sauce. It is best dressed in a suitable sauce and frozen for no more than 1 month.

The live lobster may be frozen and stored for up to 3 months. Remember to pack it properly in thick polythene bags once it is frozen.

Low-Fat Spreads

These are alternatives to butter or margarine for table use. In general, their usefulness for cooking is limited and the manufacturer's advice should be followed.

There are many different products and their fat content and other ingredients vary. Some very low-fat spreads contain a high water content.

Buying and Storing

Check the nutritional information on the pack. As well, check the use by date to be sure that the product has sufficient shelf life for your use.

Low-fat spreads should be kept in the refrigerator at all times. They spread easily and thinly when chilled.

X *Take particular care when using any spreads from the refrigerator to avoid the possibility of cross contamination from other foods. Always use a clean knife to dip into the spread.*

Freezing

Low-fat spreads are not suitable for freezing.

Mange Tout

See Vegetables*.
Also known as mange tout peas or snow peas (an American term). These are pea pods which are tender and sweet. They do not contain peas and the pods are eaten whole, after trimming.
Sugar Snap Peas These are similar to mange tout but they have small peas in the pods. Again, they are eaten whole and they have an excellent flavour.

Buying and Storing

Mange tout should be bright and firm, not limp and damaged. Keep them in their carton or in a polythene bag in the drawer of the refrigerator for 1–2 days.

Preparation

Trim the stalk ends off the mange tout, then wash them well.

Freezing

Blanch* mange tout for 1 minute, then cool, dry and pack. Store for up to a year.

Cooking

Boiling Blanching is the better term to use as mange tout cook very quickly and they should still be crisp when served.

Have a saucepan no more than half full of boiling water. Add the mange tout and bring the water back to the boil. Boil for 2–3 minutes, then drain well and serve.
Steaming Place the mange tout in a steamer over rapidly boiling water and cook for 3–5 minutes.

Stir Frying This is the best cooking method. Heat some oil or melt a little butter or margarine in a large pan. Add the mange tout and toss them over high heat for 2–3 minutes, until heated through. Serve at once.

They are good stir fried with chopped spring onion and chopped fresh parsley.

Nutritional Value

Fresh mange tout provide vitamin C and some vitamin A.

Margarine

See Fat*.
Margarine consists of at least 80 per cent fat and no more than 16 per cent water. Vitamins A and D, flavouring, emulsifiers and other ingredients are added during the manufacturing process. There are many brands of margarine and they all differ in content. Margarine must not be confused with low-fat spreads*.

Types

There are two types: soft margarine in tubs and block margarine. Both may be used for all cooking purposes, although the firm block margarine gives better results when making pastry. Soft margarine is not suitable for making the rolled and folded pastries as it is too soft.

Soft margarine is more popular than the block type. It has the advantage of spreading straight from the refrigerator, so it is considered better for table use. In the majority of cases, it also has a lighter flavour than block margarine.

Fat in Margarine

Most margarines are made of a mixture of fats, including fish oil and vegetable oil. Some brands also include beef fat. In many cases, the exact mix of oils used varies slightly according to the market availability and price.

Certain types are made from specific oils – vegetable oils, sunflower or safflower oils. This will be made clear on the packet or tub.

Buying and Storing

Make sure that tubs are not opened. Check the 'use by' date on the tub or packet. Margarine has a shelf life of about 13 weeks so the use by date should allow plenty of time for you to use the product.

Transfer the margarine to a refrigerator soon after purchase and keep it chilled.

Use

Both types may be used instead of butter for shallow frying and for cooking vegetables at the first stage in making many cooked dishes and sauces. To a large extent its use in this context is a matter for personal taste.

However, like butter, margarine contains a small percentage of water and it does not heat to as high a temperature as cooking oils that are sold specifically for frying food. Margarine is not suitable for deep frying.
Block Ideal for rubbing into flour, for pastry, scones or crumble toppings. May also be used as a cooking fat for frying or making sauces.

It may be creamed successfully but should be brought to room temperature first and it requires the same amount of beating as butter. Some brands are suitable for spreading.
Soft Tub Margarine Used for most cooking, some soft tub margarine is softer than others. It should be used straight from the refrigerator for rubbing in, although it is not ideal for this. It does not combine well in rich short crust pastry, where significantly more than half fat to flour is used, as it makes the dough sticky.

Soft margarine is ideal for creaming, for example in cake making, and for spreading.

Freezing

Margarine freezes well for up to 6 months. Overwrap packs or tubs in sealed polythene bags. Thaw margarine in the refrigerator.

Marinades

A marinade is a mixture of ingredients with some liquid, used to soak food before cooking. The process is known as marinating.

Food is usually marinated to flavour, moisten and tenderise it. This is reflected by ingredients used in marinades – fruit juices, wine, vinegar, oil, herbs, spices and other seasonings. The choice of ingredients depends on the food and dish. Often food is marinated before being cooked very simply by grilling and the marinade is used for basting the food or for making a sauce.

Marinating Technique

Containers The choice of container may be important. The food must be covered or coated in the marinade. Sometimes it is ideal to have a thin layer of food with the marinade poured over, so a large, shallow container may be best. It is usually best to avoid uncoated metals as these may react with acids or alkaline marinades. Make sure there is room for the container in the refrigerator if the food is left to marinate for any length of time.
Soaking Time This depends on the food, marinade and type of dish. Delicate foods and flavours usually have the shortest marinating time. Vegetables, such as peppers or tomatoes, may be marinated briefly for a salad – about 15–30 minutes. Fish or poultry may be left for 15–30 minutes. The minimum time for meat is usually slightly longer for flavours to be absorbed.

Longer marinating times may be in days rather than minutes or hours. Poultry or meat may be left to soak up the flavour of spices over a period of 2–3 days.

SEE ALSO **Mango**: Fruit – exotic; **Marinate**: Glossary; **Marjoram**: Herbs; **Marmelade**: Glossary

☑ *Buy very fresh meat or poultry for marinating. Tell the butcher what you intend to do with the meat or look for pre-packed meat with a number of days before the use by date expires.*

Preparing the Food For the flavour to be absorbed, poultry should be skinned or cuts should be made into the flesh.

Vegetables, such as tomatoes or peppers, should be skinned so that the fleshy part absorbs the flavour of the marinade ingredients.

Small portions of meat or poultry – thin slices, strips or cubes – absorb more flavour than large cuts, so the marinating time may be reduced.

Turning Food Turn and baste food as often as possible during marinating, particularly when marinating large joints or whole poultry.

Simple Marinating Ideas

● Sprinkle chopped herbs or spice onto meat or poultry. Place the food in a dish and trickle a little oil over it. Cover and chill overnight.

● Crushed garlic, grated fresh root ginger, grated citrus fruit rind, chopped dried fruit (apricots, raisins or apples) or peeled and chopped tomatoes make good flavouring ingredients. Sprinkle them over chicken, duck, lamb or pork.

● Sprinkle flavoursome oils over food. Hazelnut, walnut, sesame or chilli oils may be used sparingly and they may be rubbed into large portions.

● Some chutneys, marmalade or other preserves make good marinades. Plum, damson or cherry jam are all suitable. Warm set preserves to melt them and sharpen sweet preserves with lemon juice or cider vinegar.

☒ *Do not pour hot or warm marinades over meat and poultry which is to be left to marinate for some time. The warmth of the marinade provides conditions for bacteria in the food to multiply. It may also begin to cook the food if it is too hot and this does not give the best flavour or texture.*

Marmalade

See Jams and Jellies* and Oranges*. These are traditional British breakfast preserves, made using citrus fruit, notably bitter oranges, such as Seville.

Stages in Making

The stages for making jams and jellies are relevant but the preparation and softening of the fruit is important.

Preparing the Fruit The method depends on the texture required. For a fine, jelly marmalade, pare the rind off citrus fruit and shred it finely. Squeeze the juice. Save all pith, pips and trimmings and tie them in a piece of muslin to boil with the rind and juice. The trimmings provide a valuable source of pectin.

Coarse Marmalade This may be made by chopping up the whole fruit. Pick out the pips and wrap them in muslin. A semi-coarse marmalade may be made by shredding or chopping the rind, then cutting off all the pith. The pith should be boiled in muslin with the pips. Then chop the fruit.

Boiling the Fruit The fruit is boiled in a significant amount of water until it is absolutely tender. The fruit and peel must be softened at this stage otherwise the peel becomes tough and unpleasant when boiled with sugar.

Boiling with Sugar Add the sugar and boil as for jams and jellies* until setting point is reached.

Potting Marmalade Coarse marmalades may be potted as for jams and jellies.

Fine jelly marmalades must stand for about 15 minutes after boiling. Stir the marmalade before potting it to distribute the shredded rind evenly. If fine marmalade is potted straight after boiling, the rind floats.

Basic Marinades

White Wine Marinade Heat 6 black peppercorns, 1 bay leaf, 2 parsley sprigs, 1 slice onion, 30 ml/2 tablespoons olive oil, 250 ml/8 fluid oz dry white wine gently until just boiling. Remove from the heat and leave to cool.

Use for fish, chicken, turkey, pork or vegetables such as fennel.

Vary by adding lemon, lime or orange rind, thyme, sage, marjoram, tarragon or green cardamoms.

Red Wine Marinade Heat 1 bay leaf, 6 black peppercorns, a blade of mace, a small piece of pared orange rind and 4 juniper berries with 30 ml/2 tablespoons olive oil and 250 ml/8 fluid oz rich, dry red wine. Bring the mixture slowly to the boil, then leave it to cool.

Typical Quantities of Ingredients

Bitter Orange Marmalade To 900 g/2 lb bitter oranges and the juice of 3 lemons, use 2.25 litres/4 pints water and 1.75 kg/4 lb sugar.

Three Fruit Marmalade To 2 each of grapefruit, oranges and lemons, use 1.75 litres/3 pints water and 2.25 kg/5 lb sugar.

Marrow

See Vegetables*.

Marrow is a fairly bland late summer and autumn vegetable, best cooked with flavoursome ingredients or used to make good chutney.

Buying and Storing

Look for small to medium sized, firm, heavy vegetables that are not damaged or bruised. Marrows keep well in a cool, dry place. Ideally they should be hung to prevent any bruising. Either use netting vegetable bags or hang marrows in old stockings or tights. Marrows for keeping should be absolutely perfect. Store in a cool, dry place to stay in good condition for several months.

Place cut marrow in a polythene bag in the refrigerator and use quickly.

Preparation

Cut the marrow in half or into slices. Discard the seeds and pith from the middle. Cut off the peel and cut the marrow flesh into large cubes.

Marrow halves may be stuffed with the peel on, then scooped out to serve. Slices should be peeled before being stuffed.

Cooking

Boiling Cover cubes of marrow with cold water, bring to the boil, then simmer for about 5 minutes. However, this is not the best method as the result can be bland.

Steaming Place the cubed vegetable in a steamer and cook over boiling water for about 5–10 minutes. Serve coated with a sauce, such as cheese sauce.

Braising By far the best way to treat marrow. Cook a chopped onion in a little butter for 10 minutes. Add the marrow cubes, a bay leaf, salt and pepper, some chopped parsley and a 400 g/14 oz can of chopped tomatoes. White wine, cider or chicken stock may be used instead of the tomatoes – add enough to half cover the marrow. Heat gently until the liquid is simmering, cover the pan and cook gently for 10 minutes. Stir once during cooking, turning the pieces of marrow. Taste for seasoning before serving.

STUFFED MARROW

INGREDIENTS

½ quantity Meat Sauce (page 176) or Lentil Sauce (page 169)
4 slices from a small marrow (about 3.5 cm/1½ inches thick, weighing about 675 g/1½ lb)
1 eating apple (Cox's Orange Pippin or a full-flavoured type)
25 g/1 oz raisins
50 g/2 oz fresh wholemeal breadcrumbs

25 g/1 oz mature Cheddar cheese, grated
25 g/1 oz walnuts, chopped

FOOD VALUES:
TOTAL • PER PORTION
(Using lentil sauce)
kcals: 801 • 200
kJ: 3353 • 838
protein: 30 g • 8 g
fat: 39 g • 10 g
carbohydrate: 89 g • 22 g
fibre: 22 g • 6 g

Serves 4

First make the chosen sauce. Scoop the seeds and pith from the middle of the marrow rings and peel them. Place them in a greased ovenproof dish. Set the oven at 190°C, 375°F, gas 5.

Halve, peel, core and dice the apple. Add the apple and raisins to the sauce. Divide the sauce between the marrow rings, spooning it into the holes in the middle of them. Cover the dish and bake the stuffed marrow for 30 minutes, or until they are three-quarters cooked.

Mix the breadcrumbs, cheese and walnuts, then divide this topping between the stuffed marrow rings. Continue to bake, uncovered, for a further 15 minutes, or until the topping is browned and the marrow tender. Serve the stuffed marrow piping hot.

VARIATION

To stuff a halved marrow, use the full quantity of either sauce. Halve the marrow lengthways and trim off just the ends from each half, leaving 2 neat boats. The baking time may be reduced by cooking the halves in boiling water for 10 minutes. Drain them well, then place them in an ovenproof dish and fill with sauce. Cover and bake for 1 hour. Uncover, sprinkle with topping (the quantities given are enough for a thin topping) and bake for a further 20 minutes.

Alternatively, transfer the marrow mixture to an ovenproof dish. Cover and bake in the oven at 180°C, 350°F, gas 4 for about 20 minutes.

The cooking liquor may be thickened with a little beurre manié* or plain flour blended to a paste with milk. Cream or fromage frais may be added to enrich white liquor. Parmesan or grated Cheddar cheese goes well with marrow braised with tomatoes.

Sautéing Toss small cubes of marrow in butter over high heat for about 5–7 minutes. Season with black pepper and sprinkle with a mixture of snipped chives and chopped fresh parsley.

Freezing

Marrow becomes very watery on thawing, therefore it is not recommended for freezing. Use a glut for chutney instead.

Nutritional Value

Marrow provides iron and some vitamin C when fresh, also calcium and vitamin A.

SEE ALSO **Mascarpone:** Cheese

Marzipan

Also known as almond paste. White marzipan purchased from specialist cake decorating suppliers is usually excellent quality.

Buying and Storing

Price is a good indication of quality. Bright yellow marzipan is usually coloured and inferior quality to pale types. Check the ingredients list on the label as this also provides a useful guide to quality.

If it is kept in a sealed packet, marzipan may be stored for 2–3 months. However, always check the manufacturer's advice. If the packet of marzipan feels very hard, then it may be dry.

Cook's Tip
Soften marzipan that has become hard on storage by unwrapping and placing it in a warm grill compartment for a few minutes, then kneading it well. Alternatively, heat the marzipan in the microwave on High for 30–60 seconds.

Do not overwork marzipan as it becomes oily and difficult to manage. Once it is oily, it can stain a top coat of icing.

Making Marzipan

Marzipan can be made by two methods, either using raw egg or boiled syrup. However, bought marzipan can be good enough to make buying the paste an unnecessary task.

Use

• About 1 kg/2 lb marzipan makes sufficient to cover the top and sides of a 23 cm/9 inch round cake.

• For making sweets and petits fours – shape marzipan fruit and vegetables; coat balls of marzipan in caster sugar; coat squares in chocolate.

Mayonnaise

See Sauce*.

Bought Mayonnaise This is not usually made from fresh eggs. The quality of bought types varies from very poor to excellent. Jars of bought mayonnaise may be stored in a cool cupboard until they are opened, then kept in the refrigerator. Mayonnaise displayed chilled should be kept chilled.

Home-made Mayonnaise Ideally, make mayonnaise in quantities which you can use within 24 hours. Leftovers must be used within 3 days, stored in a covered container in the refrigerator. Only use perfectly fresh eggs from a reputable source. A liquidiser or food processor may be used to make mayonnaise.

Use

• As an accompaniment or dressing to cooked, fish, meats and salads.

• In dips or sandwiches.

Flavouring

• Add a crushed garlic clove. Garlic mayonnaise may be seasoned with cayenne pepper and paprika to make rouille, a spicy mayonnaise traditionally served with French fish soup.

• Add chopped fresh herbs or grated lemon.

Rescuing Curdled Mayonnaise

If the mixture curdles as you are adding the oil, stop immediately. Place a fresh egg yolk in a clean basin. Add 15 ml/1 tablespoon of the curdled mixture and whisk until thoroughly combined. Continue whisking, adding the curdled mixture a little at a time, then add the remaining oil and lemon juice.

X *Minimise the risk of salmonella infection by washing the eggs in cold water before cracking them. Wash your hands after breaking and separating the egg.*

MAYONNAISE

INGREDIENTS	FOOD VALUES:
2 egg yolks	TOTAL • PER 15 ML/1
salt and pepper	TABLESPOON
2.5 ml/½ teaspoon sugar	**kcals:** 2391 • 80
2.5 ml/½ teaspoon made mustard	**kJ:** 9835 • 328
juice of 1 lemon	**protein:** 7 g • 0 g
250 ml/8 fluid oz olive oil or other vegetable oil	**fat:** 261 g • 9 g
	carbohydrate: 4 g • 0 g
	fibre: 0 g • 0 g

Makes about 300 ml/½ pint

Bring the eggs out of the refrigerator 30 minutes before making mayonnaise. Place the egg yolks in a basin. Add a good sprinkling of seasoning, then the sugar and mustard. Add about a quarter of the lemon juice and just a little oil (about 15 ml/1 tablespoon). Whisk the egg yolks and other ingredients together until thoroughly combined. An electric beater is best.

Whisking all the time, add the oil in a very slow trickle, allowing it to combine with the egg. As the mixture begins to become pale and thicken slightly, the oil may be added a little faster. When all the oil is added the mayonnaise should be pale and thick.

Stir in the remaining lemon juice to taste and check the seasoning.

Meat

See Carving*, Bacon*, Beef*, Freezing*, Lamb*, Offal*, Pork* and Veal* for cuts and accompaniments.

Buying

Use the information on different cuts as a guide when deciding what to buy. Always buy from a good butcher or supermarket, or from a reputable supplier. This is the best way of ensuring that you are buying good-quality meat.

A good butcher will give advice about cuts and value for money for the type of meals you want to cook. Also, a butcher will prepare meat to your requirements, often at less than supermarket-trimmed cuts.

Minced Meat You can ask a butcher to mince a particular cut. The colour of minced meat can be a useful guide to quality. For example, if it contains a lot of fat it will look very pale. This is particularly true for beef. Pork meat has a paler colour.

Remember to check 'use by' dates on pre-packed meat.

Portion Size As a rough guide, when buying meat off the bone allow 100–225 g/4–8 oz per person. For example, 225 g/8 oz mince will usually serve 2 when cooked with vegetables.

Calculating the size of boneless joints is more difficult as the yield tends to vary. Joints on the bone should be large enough to be worth cooking. The exception is a joint sawn off a leg or rack of lamb.

Storing

Put meat in the refrigerator as soon as possible. If the meat is pre-packed and sealed, leave it wrapped. If sold loose, then placed in a polythene bag, unwrap it and place in a covered dish.

Put meat on a low shelf in the refrigerator as this is the coldest part. Never allow meat juices to drip out of dishes or packs.

MEAT SAUCE

As well as the uses given below, the meat sauce may be served in baked potatoes or it may be used as a filling for pastry-topped pies.

INGREDIENTS
1 large onion, chopped
1 clove garlic, crushed (optional)
100 g/4 oz lean rindless bacon, diced
450 g/1 lb mince
15 ml/1 tablespoon plain flour
225 g/8 oz carrots, diced
225 g/8 oz mushrooms, sliced
300 ml/½ pint stock (beef, chicken or veal)
salt and pepper

1 (400 g/14 oz) can chopped tomatoes
1 bouquet garni

FOOD VALUES:
TOTAL • PER PORTION
kcals: 1723 • 431
kJ: 7190 • 1798
protein: 152 g • 38 g
fat: 105 g • 26 g
carbohydrate: 46 g • 12 g
fibre: 18 g • 5 g

Serves 4

Place the onion, garlic, if used, and bacon in a heavy-based saucepan and cook gently until the fat runs from the bacon. Continue to cook over medium heat, stirring occasionally, for about 10 minutes or until the onion begins to soften.

Add the mince to the pan and break it up well, then continue to cook, stirring occasionally, until lightly browned. At this stage, any excess fat may be drained off. Stir in the flour and continue to cook for a minute or so, then add the carrots and mushrooms before pouring in the stock. Stir in the tomatoes, seasoning and bouquet garni, then bring the mixture to the boil.

Reduce the heat, cover the pan and simmer the sauce for 45 minutes, or until the meat is tender. Stir occasionally during cooking. Remove the bouquet garni. Taste and adjust the seasoning before serving.

USING THE MEAT SAUCE

With Pasta Add a deseeded and chopped green pepper with the onion, if liked, and serve the sauce ladled over cooked spaghetti, noodles or pasta shapes. Offer grated Parmesan cheese with the sauce.

Cottage Pie Omit the garlic and tomatoes. Add an extra 150 ml/¼ pint stock. Cook the sauce as above, then place it in a deep ovenproof dish. Reserve any extra liquid if necessary to serve as a gravy with the pie. Top the meat mixture with mashed potatoes and mark them with a fork. Bake at 200°C, 400°F, gas 6 for 20–30 minutes, until the potato is golden. Alternatively, simmer the meat sauce for just 5 minutes, then top it with potato and bake the pie at 180°C, 350°F, gas 4 for 40–50 minutes.

Lasagne al Forno Layer the meat sauce in a greased ovenproof dish with cooked lasagne and top it with Béchamel Sauce (page 35). Dot 150 g/5 oz sliced mozzarella cheese over the top and sprinkle with a little grated Parmesan cheese. Bake at 190°C, 375°F, gas 5 for about 30 minutes, or until bubbling and golden.

Savoury Pancakes Use the meat sauce to fill 16 large pancakes*, roll them up and place in a greased baking dish. Top with a little Wine Sauce (page 235) or Béchamel Sauce (page 35) and sprinkle with grated Cheddar cheese and a few dry white breadcrumbs. Brown the topping in the oven at 200°C, 400°F, gas 6 for about 20 minutes before serving.

MEATBALLS

Make these with lamb, beef or pork, or use half and half beef and pork. Good with spaghetti, pasta or rice, the meatball mixture may also be pressed into sausage shapes on skewers, then grilled and served with salad.

INGREDIENTS
30 ml/2 tablespoons oil
1 onion, finely chopped
1 clove garlic, crushed
450 g/1 lb minced meat
50 g/2 oz fresh breadcrumbs
1 egg
30 ml/2 tablespoons chopped
    fresh parsley
5 ml/1 teaspoon chopped
    fresh thyme or 2.5 ml/
    ½ teaspoon dried thyme
5 ml/1 teaspoon dried
    marjoram, chopped fresh
    rosemary or
    10 ml/2 teaspoons chopped
    fresh mint (optional)

salt and pepper
1 quantity Tomato Sauce
    (page 263) or Red Wine
    Sauce (page 235)

FOOD VALUES:
TOTAL • PER PORTION
(excluding sauce)
kcals: 1593 • 398
kJ: 6640 • 1660
protein: 117 g • 29 g
fat: 106 g • 27 g
carbohydrate: 46 g • 12 g
fibre: 4 g • 1 g

Serves 4

Heat the oil in a frying pan, then add the onion and garlic. Cook the onion over medium heat, stirring often, for about 10 minutes, or until it is softened but not browned.

Meanwhile, place the meat, breadcrumbs, egg and herbs in a mixing bowl. (Marjoram, rosemary or mint go well with lamb; marjoram or rosemary with pork; or marjoram with beef.) Use a draining spoon to transfer the onion to the mince and reserve any fat remaining in the pan for browning the meatballs. Season, then mix all the ingredients together until thoroughly combined. Mark the mixture into quarters.

Have a clean plate ready to hold the meatballs. Wash your hands well, then rinse them under cold water. Shape each quarter of mixture into 4 meatballs, making 16 in all. To shape the meatballs, press the mixture firmly together in the palm of your hands until it binds well into a smooth ball. Having wet hands prevents the meat from sticking and this makes the meatballs smooth.

Heat the fat remaining from cooking the onion. Add the meatballs to the pan and brown them all over. Use a spoon and fork to roll the meatballs around the pan, keeping them in good shape as well as browning them.

Pour the sauce into the pan with the meatballs and bring it to the boil. Reduce the heat so that the sauce just simmers, cover the pan and cook the meatballs gently for 30 minutes, turning them once. Taste the sauce and adjust the seasoning as necessary before serving.

Storage Times

Check details on a label and follow the use by date. If there is no guide, the following times apply:

Fresh Meat
Beef – 3 days
Pork – 3 days
Lamb – 3 days
Bacon Rashers – 7 days
Mince – 1 day
Offal – 1 day
Sausages – 3 days

Cooked Meat
Casseroles – 2 days
Ham – 2 days
Meat Pies – 1 day
Sliced Meat – 2 days
Pâté – 2 days

Roasting Meat

Personal preference is important. Traditionally pork is cooked until quite dry; however, there is no reason to overcook it. The best results are achieved if the meat is cooked through but still succulent, not dry and falling in shreds.

Cook's Tip
Remember to weigh a joint before cooking so that the cooking can be calculated accurately.

Preparation
Set the oven. Trim off excess fat and any gristle or sinew. The joint should be tied neatly or skewered in shape. Do not prick the joint or make cuts into it unless you are inserting herbs, for example sprigs of rosemary into lamb. Any cuts made into the meat should be small and at an angle, running close under the skin, to keep loss of cooking juices to a minimum.

Rub seasoning all over the meat, then place it on a rack or trivet in a roasting tin. A little fat may be added but this is not essential and it depends on the cut of meat. If the joint is very lean, trickle over a little cooking oil or dot the meat with lard. Add sprigs of herbs, if liked. Foil may be used to cover the joint, if necessary.

Resting Roast Meat
Once the meat is cooked, transfer it to a heated serving platter and cover closely with a piece of foil, then set aside to rest for 15–20 minutes before carving. This allows the meat to soften slightly after cooking, making it slightly more tender.

Beef
Beef may be roasted in a very hot oven or more slowly at a lower temperature. Cooking in a hotter oven is suitable for very tender cuts (such as fillet) or if you prefer a rare result, with meat which is well browned outside but bloody in the middle. Roasting at a high temperature is not suitable for very large joints.

Slow roasting results in a moist joint and less shrinkage. This is a good method for joints that tend to have some fine gristle running through them, such as top rump, or for braising cuts that may be roasted in a covered tin.

One of the best methods is to put the joint into the oven at the higher temperature and cook for 15 minutes. Lower the temperature and continue cooking. This seals the outside and keeps the middle of the joint succulent and moist, at the same time giving it a good flavour. Calculate the total time from the lower temperature but remember that the joint will cook slightly faster.
At 220°C, 425°F, gas 7: 15–20 minutes per 450 g/1 lb plus 15–20 minutes.
At 180°C, 350°F, gas 4: 20–30 minutes per 450 g/1 lb plus 20–30 minutes.
Slow Roasting For slow roasting braising cuts in a covered tin, reduce the temperature to 180°C, 350°F, gas 4 and cook for 25–35 minutes per 450 g/1 lb plus 20–25 minutes. Uncover the joint about 20 minutes before the end of cooking.

Lamb
Lamb may be served pink in the

MEATLOAF

INGREDIENTS
450 g/1 lb minced beef, veal or pork (or a mixture of beef and pork or veal and pork)
1 onion, finely chopped
75 g/3 oz fresh breadcrumbs
10 ml/2 teaspoons chopped fresh sage or
5 ml/1 teaspoon dried sage
5 ml/1 teaspoon ground mace
salt and pepper
15 ml/1 tablespoon Worcestershire sauce

1 egg
2 bay leaves

FOOD VALUES:
TOTAL • PER PORTION
kcals: 1397 • 349
kJ: 5848 • 1462
protein: 120 g • 30 g
fat: 76 g • 19 g
carbohydrate: 63 g • 16 g
fibre: 4 g • 1 g

Serves 4

Grease and base line a 450 g/1 lb loaf tin. Grease the paper well. Set the oven at 180°C, 350°F, gas 4.

Place the meat in a mixing bowl. Add the onion, breadcrumbs, sage, mace, a good sprinkling of seasoning, Worcestershire sauce and the egg. Mix all the ingredients thoroughly.

Arrange the bay leaves in the bottom of the prepared tin. Carefully spoon the meat mixture into the tin, putting 2 spoonfuls on top of the bay leaves first to keep them in place, then filling in the space between. Press the mixture down evenly with a blunt knife. Cover the tin with foil. Bake the meatloaf for 1 ½ hours, or until firm and lightly browned.

Place a plate on top of the meatloaf and tin, then hold both firmly and invert the tin on the plate. Lift off the tin. Serve the meatloaf sliced. To serve the meatloaf cold, leave it covered and allow it to cool in the tin, then chill.

middle or well cooked. Legs may be started in a hot oven at 220°C, 425°F, gas 7 for 15 minutes, then the temperature reduced and the joint cooked as below, allowing slightly less time.

Leg, loin and shoulder cook best at 190°C, 375°F, gas 5. Breast, which tends to be fatty and slightly tough, should be roasted at the lower temperature.
At 190°C, 375°F, gas 5: 20–30 minutes per 450 g/1 lb plus 20–30 minutes.
At 180°C, 350°F, gas 4: 20–35 minutes per 450 g/1 lb plus 20–30 minutes.

Pork
Pork must be cooked through. Have the fat scored and rub it well with salt. Set the oven at

220°C, 425°F, gas 7 and cook the joint for 15 minutes. Alternatively, roll the rind in a hot, heavy-based frying pan until it begins to crackle. Then roast the joint at 180°C, 350°F, gas 4 for 30–35 minutes per 450 g/1 lb, plus an extra 30–35 minutes.

Using a Meat Thermometer

A meat thermometer may be inserted into the centre of a joint. It must not touch any bone and it should be placed into the middle of the eye of meat if the joint is on the bone. The thermometer should be heated cold from in the oven. By checking the temperature you can tell whether the meat is rare, medium or well cooked.

SEE ALSO **Medallion**: Glossary; **Megrim**: Fish; **Meguez**: Sausages; **Melba Sauce**: Raspberries

Beef
Rare – 60°C/140°F
Medium – 70°C/158°F
Well done – 80°C/76°F

Lamb
Medium – 70–75°C/158–167°F
Well done – 75–80°C/167–176°F

Pork
Well done – 80–85°C/176–185°F

Grilling

The following times are for cooking under a hot grill, for one side only. The meat should be turned and cooked on the second side for the same length of time. Baste occasionally during cooking to keep the meat moist.
Beef Steak 2–6 minutes, for rare or well done. The exact time depends on the cut and thickness. About 2–2.5 cm/¾–1 inch is an average thickness. Fillet steaks are usually thicker but they are very tender and cook quickly.
Pork Chops 7–10 minutes.
Lamb Chops 5–8 minutes.
Lamb Cutlets 3–6 minutes.

Stuffing Meat

Both joints and small cuts may be stuffed and slices of meat may be rolled around a stuffing. Do not stuff meat more than 3–4 hours in advance of cooking.

Always make sure the stuffing is cold by allowing any cooked onion, rice or other ingredients to cool completely if the stuffed meat is to be set aside before cooking. Once stuffed, put the meat in a covered dish in the refrigerator until it is cooked.

Minced Meat

Minced beef and steak are the most popular types. Minced lamb, pork and veal are also available.

X *Bought minced meat should always be thoroughly cooked. To make rare or medium-rare burgers, buy good quality steak and mince it at home.*

Degreasing Mince

To remove as much fat as possible from minced meat, brown it in a heavy-based frying pan without any extra fat. Begin over low to medium heat and regulate the heat carefully to prevent the meat from burning. As the meat gives up its fat, the heat may be increased.

When the mince is lightly browned, use a slotted spoon to remove it from the pan, then pour off the fat before cooking the other ingredients and replacing the mince.

Alternatively, cool meat sauces, then chill and remove any fat which has set on the surface.

Nutritional Value

Meat provides high quality protein, iron, minerals such as zinc, and vitamins B6 and B12. The amount of fat obtained from meat varies according to the cut and the cooking method.

The main role for meat in the diet is as a source of protein and vitamin B12.

Melba Toast

Very thin toast to serve with light starters and cheese.

Lightly toast medium-thick slices of bread on both sides. Do not toast more than 4 slices at a time as you have to work quickly before the bread cools. Cut off the crusts, then slice each piece of toast in half horizontally. Toast the second side of the very thin slices, placing the grill pan well away from the heat so that the toast curls.

Cool the melba toast on a rack. It may be stored in an airtight container for up to a week.

Tiny squares of melba toast may be baked in the oven once they are sliced through and cut up. Be sure to very lightly toast the bread before it is cut through, so that it does not become too dark when it is dried out in the oven.

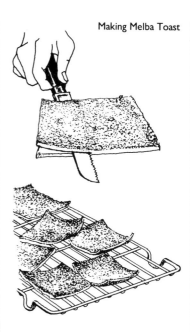
Making Melba Toast

Mini Melba Toast
Make mini melba toast squares for serving with dips, or topping with pâté and serving as a cocktail snack. Toast and slice the bread, then cut each thin piece into 4 small squares. Place these on a baking tray and brown them in a cool oven or under the grill on a low setting until pale golden. Cool on a wire rack, then store in an airtight container. Melba toast keeps well for 2–3 weeks.

Melon

See Fruit*.

Buying

To test whether a melon is ripe or not, press it gently at the stalk end. If ripe it will give slightly; if it feels very hard, then it is not ripe. Watermelon should sound hollow when ripe.

Fruit that looks bruised or a dark colour (particularly honeydew melon) may well be overripe.

Types

Canteloupe Small fragrant melons, including charentais

and ogen. The flesh is peach coloured and sweet. Outside, the melon is covered by a close network of pale markings.

Galia Small round melons with fragrant green flesh. The outside is covered by an open network of pale markings over a golden skin. The skin is a paler yellow before it is ripe.

Honeydew Large, oval melons with a yellow skin and lightly flavoured pale green flesh.

Watermelon Large melons with dark green skin, bright red flesh and black seeds. Usually sold in wedges.

Storing

Keep melons in the refrigerator. Use cut melon within a day, others will keep for up to a week, depending on ripeness. Under-ripe melon may be left in a dish in a cool room until ripe.

Do not freeze melon.

Preparation

Cut small melons across in half, scoop out the seeds and serve one halve per portion.

Cut wedges from larger melons and discard the seeds. Halve a larger melon and scoop out the seeds, then use a melon baller to scoop out the flesh for salads or cocktails.

Menu Planning

See Balanced Diet*.

Planning daily meals within a budget and to provide a balanced diet is not easy without practice. Menu planning is something that has to tie in with individual taste and lifestyle, but there are some basic starting points to consider before organising shopping.

Meal Occasions

Think about the types of meals for the week ahead.

Breakfast This may be very simple yet nutritious and it can be a good opportunity to eat some fibre in the form of cereal, porridge or wholemeal toast. Most weekday breakfasts have to be easy, so remember fresh fruit, yogurt, bread rolls and sandwiches as well as favourites.

Mid-day Meal This may be a light lunch, packed lunch or the main meal of the day.

A snack-type meal should still make a contribution to the nutritional value of the day's diet. Sandwiches or rolls can be very nutritious depending on the filling. Fresh or dried fruit and salads* that last well are good candidates.

The pitfall to avoid is regularly eating snack foods that are high in fat or sugar yet low in nutrients – crisps, sweets, biscuits and cake should be the treats, not the daily snack.

Soup is a great snack meal, particularly when it is home made. Vegetable soup is very easy to make, it may be chilled for up to 2 days and reheats easily for those who are at home. Soup can be filling, nutritious, inexpensive and easy.

Main Meal This must make a significant nutritional contribution.

Usually, the protein content is important, whether it is fish, meat, dairy produce or beans and pulses. The meal is built around the protein, either a traditional meat-and-two-veg menu or a flexible one-pot dish.

Snacks or Light Meals The number of these depends on individuals but they should be included in long term menu planning. Again, an opportunity for fruit, crackers, bread rolls in place of biscuits, crisps and very sweet foods. Hot and cold drinks also make a contribution.

Light meals may consist of something on toast, sandwiches, bread and cheese, salad or soup.

Types of Menus

Most of the minor meals look after themselves and tend to be routine, so the main concern is organising main meals and special occasion meals.

Everyday Meals One course only. Occasional dessert or fresh fruit on a regular basis. Plan along the following lines.

● It is important that these meals are nutritious. They should supply protein, vitamins, minerals and carbohydrate. They must be balanced alongside other meals eaten during the day and over a period of a week or so, particularly in terms of fat and fibre.

● Variety is often a good sign – combining plenty of different fresh and ready prepared foods, as well as using different cooking methods, usually results in a well balanced diet.

● Likes and dislikes of the family; introducing new foods to children.

● Time available for preparing meals.

● Freezer and/or storecupboard supplies.

● Which fresh vegetables, fruit and other fresh foods to include.

Special Meals

These may be informal or formal, consisting of 2 or more courses.

● Since they do not feature often, these meals allow for indulgence and slightly less regard for the overall nutritional balance.

● As well as likes and dislikes, remember any dietary restrictions of guests; vegetarian diets are most common.

● Plan courses that complement each other in flavour, texture and temperature.

Planning Main Courses

● Foods must taste good together. Do not mix lots of strong flavours.

● Do not make 2 sauced dishes; opt for plain vegetables with rich sauced main dishes or vegetables in sauce with grilled or plain cooked main dishes.

- Have a contrast in texture: crisp salad with moist main dishes such as chilli con carne or a moist filling for crisp baked potatoes.

- Food should always look appetising but pay special attention to appearance, including colour and shape, for special meals.

- With good planning and proper attention to food safety, cook ahead dishes are ideal for mid-week meals.

- One-pot meals (mixed casseroles, savoury crumbles, risottos, pasta dishes, pies and cobblers) can be nutritious and delicious, particularly when served with simple salads.

Planning Complementary Courses

Always plan a meal you can cook with reasonable confidence, both in terms of the techniques involved, the amount of work and the cooking equipment needed.

- Think about the flavours and textures: do not start with a strongly flavoured dish, then follow on with a delicate main course.

- The courses should make a satisfying, not overfilling meal. Do not serve a filling starter followed by a stodgy main course and a rich pudding. Balance a rich starter with a light main course, or a light first course with a more filling main course.

- Think about the amount of last minute work involved and try to keep this to a minimum.

- Check that you have enough refrigerator space for chilling prepared food as well as raw ingredients.

- Make sure you have enough oven and hob space for the different foods that need cooking. As well, check the oven temperatures for cooking different foods as you may not be able to put them all in together if one item needs a very hot oven, while others need gentle cooking.

Organising the Cooking

1. Plan and write out the menu.

2. Make a shopping list. Separate foods that have to come from different shops, if necessary, and allow for taking advantage of food that is best value. Vegetables and salads should be flexible so that you can buy best quality.

3. If you are planning well ahead, the shopping list may be split over a period of time. For example, check storecupboard ingredients, seasonings, herbs and spices well ahead to lighten the last-minute shopping.

4. Before you start cooking, make a list of what has to be done and the order intended.

5. Note the dishes or parts of recipe that can be cooked ahead. Make note of whether to freeze or chill them.

6. Make a clear list of all the last minute tasks. If there are too many, then go back over your work plan and try to prepare more in advance.

Meringues

See Eggs*

Use

- Sandwich meringues with whipped cream or chocolate spread.

MERINGUES

INGREDIENTS
4 egg whites
225 g/8 oz caster sugar

Makes 12 individual meringues, 6 pairs or 1 nest

FOOD VALUES:
TOTAL • PER MERINGUE
kcals: 933 • 78
kJ: 3976 • 331
protein: 12 g • 1 g
fat: 0 g • 0 g
carbohydrate: 236 g • 20 g
fibre: 0 g • 0 g

Line a baking tray with non-stick baking parchment. Set the oven at 110°C, 225°F, gas ¼. Prepare a piping bag fitted with a large plain or star nozzle.

Whisk the egg whites until they are stiff and dry. If using a rotary or electric beater, add half the caster sugar and whisk well. Sprinkle in the remaining caster sugar and whisk the whites until they stand in firm, glossy peaks.

If whisking by hand using a balloon or wire whisk, whisk in about a quarter of the sugar. Use a clean metal spoon to fold in the remaining sugar.

Transfer the meringue to the piping bag. Pipe 12 round meringues on the prepared baking tray. To make a meringue nest, pipe or spread one third of the mixture in a 15 cm/6 inch round. Use the remaining mixture to pipe a raised swirl all around the edge of the meringue circle.

Place the meringue in the oven and turn the heat to the lowest setting. If possible, prop the door ajar using a wooden spoon. Leave the meringues to dry out for 3–5 hours, depending on how cool the oven is and whether the door is propped open or not.

The meringues are ready when they feel firm and lift off the baking tray easily. If they are dried out slowly for a long period they will be white and firm. Leave them to cool on a wire rack, then store in an airtight container.

- Fill a large or small meringue nest with whipped cream and top with fresh fruit such as strawberries or raspberries.

- Pile individual meringues in a dish in layers, topping each layer with whipped cream and strawberries. Make a meringue pyramid by layering meringues, cream and fruit to a peak.

- Pipe meringue fingers and dip them in melted chocolate to serve with soft desserts.

Flavouring Meringue

Coffee Dissolve 10 ml/2 teaspoons instant coffee in 15 ml/1 tablespoon boiling water. Whisk this into the meringue after the sugar.

Chocolate Whisk in 30 ml/2 tablespoons sifted cocoa powder after the sugar.

Orange or Lemon Fold in the grated rind of 2 oranges or lemons after whisking in the sugar.

Micro-organisms

See Bacteria*, Cross Contamination*, Hygiene* and Moulds*.

Microscopic organisms live everywhere, except in sterile conditions. Some are utilised in food production; others have to be prevented from causing food spoilage. Bacteria, moulds and yeasts are all micro-organisms.

Firstly, it is important to prevent micro-organisms contaminating food. Covering food, using clean utensils and observing hygiene rules are the ways to minimise contamination. Cross contamination can be a serious problem, often caused by using the same chopping board, dishes, knives and other utensils for preparing cooked and raw food.

In the right conditions, some micro-organisms produce spores which can survive boiling, then germinate and multiply after cooking. Since the food itself often provides them with the moisture and nourishment needed to reproduce, the other conditions needed must be controlled.

Microwave Cooking

Microwave cooking differs from other methods in that it does not use an external heat source to cook the food. The microwaves agitate the molecules that make up the chemical structure of the food and the internal friction produces heat, which in turn cooks the food.

Rules for Microwave Cooking

As when using any appliance or complicated equipment, it is essential to read and follow the manufacturer's instructions. Use the cookbook provided with the microwave or the basic cooking times until you are familiar with the appliance.

- Never use metal containers, dishes with metal trims or decorations, or wire ties in the microwave. Do not leave metal utensils in the microwave.

- Do not operate the microwave empty. The waves spark and they can damage the appliance.

- Use ovenproof glass, glazed earthenware, sturdy china and dishes recommended for microwave use.

- Observe standing times as they allow the internal temperature of the food to equalise throughout. Not only does this ensure the food is cooked evenly (essential in poultry and meat) but it also allows hot spots to cool slightly (practical in foods such as scrambled egg).

X *Although the microwaves may not heat plates and utensils, the hot food does. When cooking or heating food for more than a few seconds, use an ovenglove to lift dishes from the microwave.*

Microwave Cooking: Expectations

This is a moist cooking method, best compared to steaming. A basic microwave cooker will not crisp or brown food. Therefore, it is ideal for foods traditionally cooked by moist methods.

For Good Results

- Fish and fish dishes.

- Poultry, including chicken, duck and turkey. Sauced and moist dishes are good; crisp plain poultry or whole birds under the grill or in a hot oven.

- Vegetables – most are good, giving results that are crisp and full-flavoured.

- Rice and other cereals.

- Scrambled eggs – whisk them often and they are terrific, even without a knob of butter. Add just a little milk, slightly less than for conventional cooking.

- Sauces.

- Poached or stewed fruit.

Disappointing

- Pastry – it does not crisp, brown or cook properly. Choux will not cook successfully. Both short crust and puff are overcooked by the time they are crisp and they retain a raw flour flavour.

- Whisked sponges will not cook.

- Creamed cakes will cook but they have a steamed flavour which is more like pudding. Acceptable if the cake is full-flavoured.

- Roast meat. However, the microwave may be used for part cooking meat before finishing in the conventional oven.

- Stewing or braising tougher meats. These remain tough unless a microwave pressure cooker is used.

- Pasta – unless very small portions are cooked – it must be boiled in plenty of water.

SEE ALSO **Meunière:** Glossary

● Poached or 'baked' eggs. Avoid so called omelettes.

Equipment Tips

Before embarking on a spending spree, check existing equipment and get to know what you cook in the microwave. Buy items you need as and when you need them. Elaborate and expensive items of equipment may rarely emerge from the cupboard once the novelty of using them has worn off.

● Look at dishes which may be used in the conventional cooker as well as the microwave.

● Ovenproof glass measuring jugs, basins and bowls are useful.

● Buy larger dishes than you think you need as they are more versatile. Look for dishes with lids.

● Use plain, heatproof dinner plates to cover dishes which do not have lids.

Specialist Equipment

Browning Dishes There is a wide variety, including browning gadgets for making excellent toasted sandwiches, hamburgers and waffles. To a large extent, the gadgets are more successful than browning dishes but they work on the same basis. A special coating absorbs microwave energy and becomes hot. Always follow the manufacturer's instructions for preheating dishes.

Microwave Pressure Cooker An excellent accessory. This is designed to cook tougher cuts of meat and it tenderises them superbly in a fraction of the time taken in the conventional oven.

The pressure cooker has a domed lid and weight bedded in a thick rubber-like covering. It will hold up to 1 kg/2 lb cubed meat in a stew, or sufficient ingredients to make vegetable dishes to serve 4.

Divided and Shaped Dishes Their usefulness depends entirely on individual requirements. Buy these once you have

had a chance to experiment with using the microwave. Price is a good guide to quality.

Microwave Thermometers For checking the internal temperature of food – useful if you are unsure of when food is cooked or hot by appearance.

Cooking and Reheating Food

● Know the power rating of your microwave cooker. The higher the rating, the quicker the appliance cooks food. For example cooking times in a 700 watt cooker will be shorter than in a 600 watt cooker for identical portions of food. All timings given in this book are a guide for using a 650 watt cooker.

● Cooking times relate to the quantity of food: the more food to be cooked, the longer the time. Small portions cook quickly; larger amounts take longer and require turning or stirring more often during cooking.

● Undercook food, check it, then continue cooking until it is cooked sufficiently. Remember to overcook in one operation is to ruin food.

● Opt for large rather than small dishes. They allow room for spreading out the food and for stirring, turning or rearranging it during cooking.

● Cover food when the recipe, or manufacturer suggests this – it prevents food from drying out and shortens cooking slightly.

● Stir, turn or rearrange food so that it cooks or reheats evenly.

● Check that food is cooked or reheated sufficiently after any recommended standing time.

● Check packets for microwave instructions and follow them. Double check that frozen or chilled food is really hot in the middle before serving.

X *Never serve chicken, turkey, pork or bacon that is undercooked. Always make sure reheated food is hot right to the middle.*

Thawing Food in the Microwave

● Unwrap food and place it in a covered dish.

● Read and follow instructions on packets of bought food.

● Follow the microwave manufacturer's guidance on the setting to use. Usually Defrost, Low or Medium Low.

● Make sure poultry, meat and other bulky items of food are thawed before heating or cooking them.

● Take particular care when thawing and reheating or cooking food in one continuous operation.

Microwave Tips

The microwave has many uses as well as straightforward cooking. Here are a few.

Butter or Other Solid Fat Thaw or soften in the microwave, for bursts of 5–15 seconds on Medium. Remove any foil wrapping first.

Bacon Cook chopped bacon in a basin on High until thoroughly cooked, stirring once or twice. Drain on absorbent kitchen paper and cool until crisp.

Biscuits Crisp softened biscuits by cooking them in the microwave on High for a few seconds.

Breadcrumbs Dry fresh breadcrumbs on High in the microwave. Place them in a dish and cook uncovered, stirring occasionally, until very hot. Allow 30–60 seconds, then continue to cook in bursts of 30 seconds until the crumbs are very hot and beginning to feel dry on the surface. When cool they will be dry.

Chocolate Melt chocolate in the microwave. Break it into small pieces and place them in a basin. Heat on High, allowing about 1–2 minutes for 100–175 g/4–6 oz.

X *The pieces of chocolate often look firm, retaining their shape, even when melted. So stir the chocolate before continuing to cook.*

Citrus Juice Heat citrus fruit on High for 30 seconds before halving and squeezing the juice – this helps to extract the maximum juice from the fruit.

Croûtons Make small croûtons by drying cubes of bread on High. Spread the bread on absorbent kitchen paper and allow about 2–3 minutes for 50 g/2 oz bread. Allow to cool, then store the croûtons in an airtight container for 2–3 weeks. Toss them in hot melted butter with herbs and garlic before use.

Honey or Syrup Warm honey or syrup in the microwave to make it run easily. If warming in a pot, make sure it is free from metal.

Sugar Warm sugar for jam making in the microwave. Place it in a suitable bowl and heat on High for bursts of 30–60 seconds stirring occasionally.

Milk

The vast majority of all milk is heat treated and rapidly cooled to reduce the micro-organism content and to give it better keeping qualities.

Buying

Check the use by date on cartons of milk.

Place fresh milk in the refrigerator as soon as possible after purchase.

Long-life packs of milk do not have to be refrigerated until they are opened but they should be stored in a fairly cool place. Follow the manufacturer's instructions.

Types

Pasteurised The majority of fresh milk is pasteurised, including all supplies from major producers. The milk is heated continuously to at least 71.7°C/161°F for at least 15 seconds. It will keep for 4–5 days in the refrigerator.

Semi-skimmed Milk This has part of the fat layer removed, leaving a 2·3 per cent fat content.

Skimmed Milk This has virtually all the fat layer removed, leaving a 1 per cent fat content.

Homogenised Milk This is warmed and forced through tiny jets to break up the fat particles and mix them with the milk.

Calcium-enriched Milk Milk is naturally rich in calcium. However, some types will have added calcium.

Lactose Reduced Milk Whole and reduced fat milks with reduced lactose (see food intolerance*).

Milk Tops: A Guide to Content

Silver Top Pasteurised whole milk with an average fat content of 3.9 per cent.

Red Top As silver top but homogenised.

Gold Top Pasteurised Guernsey or Jersey milk containing an average of 5.1 per cent fat.

Red and Silver Striped Top Pasteurised semi-skimmed milk. Average fat content, 1.6 per cent.

Blue and Silver Checked Top Pasteurised skimmed milk. Average fat content, 0.1 per cent.

Crown Cap or Blue Foil Sterilised whole milk with an average of 3.9 per cent fat.

Green Top Milk This is untreated whole milk which may only be sold under licence. The milk has not been heated and it may therefore contain harmful micro-organisms.

Storecupboard Milk

UHT Milk Ultra heat treated milk, is homogenised, continuously heated to about 140°C/284°F for 2–4 seconds, then rapidly cooled to 20°C/68°F. It is packed in sterile, airtight cartons and may be stored for long periods at room temperature.

Dried Milk Skimmed milk powder is available ready to be reconstituted with water. It should be stored in its airtight container in a dry cupboard and will keep for several months. Most packs indicate a date by which to use the product.

Evaporated Milk This is unsweetened and sterilised milk with a distinctive flavour. May be used in sweet or savoury cooking, or as a dessert topping.

Condensed Milk This is thick and sweet, and may be purchased sweetened or unsweetened. Sweetened condensed milk is very sweet. Used for making desserts or as a topping.

Goats' Milk

Available from wholefood shops, both fresh and frozen. Goats' milk is whiter than cows' milk and it tastes less creamy than whole milk. It does not have the distinctive 'tang' associated with goats' cheese but there is just a hint of 'freshness' to the flavour. Use as cows' milk.

Sheeps' Milk

This is available fresh or frozen, mainly from wholefood shops. It looks and tastes more creamy than cows' milk but does not have any distinct flavour characteristics. Use as for cows' milk.

Soya Milk

This is a non-dairy milk, obtained from soya beans. It is useful for those who are sensitive to dairy milk. Soya milk looks like creamy cows' milk, it is bland and odourless. It may be used instead of dairy milk in hot and cold drinks, sauces, custards and so on.

☑ *Milk is an important food for young children. Whole milk should be given to children under five years old, unless otherwise advised by your doctor.*

Nutritional Value

Whole milk is highly nutritious, providing protein, calcium, phosphorus, magnesium, potassium and other minerals, vitamin A, riboflavin and sugar in the form of lactose. However, milk does not provide iron.

SEE ALSO **Mince:** Meat

Whole milk is an important food for young children but for adults it can provide an unwanted volume of fat if consumed in large quantities. Semi-skimmed milk is a lower fat alternative and it may be substituted in all cooking as well as for use on cereals and in drinks to reduce the fat content of the diet.

Minerals

See Calcium*, Iron* and Zinc*. Classified either as the major minerals or as trace elements, there are 15 which are essential in significant quantities in the diet and about a further 5 that are necessary in small quantities.

The Role of Minerals

Minerals play a vital role in building and maintaining healthy bones and teeth. As well they are important to the balance of body fluids and they play a role in assisting the body enzymes and proteins to fulfil their functions.

Mincemeat

A preserve that originally included minced meat. It is a traditional preserve for Christmas. Make mincemeat at least a month before it is to be used, ensure the pots are airtight and store in a cool dark place. It will keep for a good year if the lids are sealed with freezer tape.

Making Mince Pies

Have ready 15 deep patty tins and set the oven at 200°C, 400°F, gas 6. Prepare 1 quantity of rich short crust pastry*. Roll out two-thirds of the pastry and cut out 15 rounds to line deep patty tins.

Use about 450 g/1 lb mincemeat to fill the pies fairly generously. Roll out the remaining pastry and cut out lids. Dampen the edges of the pastry lids, then press them on top of the pies. Make a small hole in the middle of each pie to allow the steam to escape. Brush the tops of the pies with a little milk.

Bake the pies for 20–25 minutes, or until they are lightly browned. Leave them in the tins for 5 minutes – this allows the pastry to firm up slightly – then cool them on a wire rack.

Cook's Tip
Ordinary short crust pastry may be used for making mince pies but it is not very exciting. Pep it up by adding the grated rind of 1 orange and 30 ml/2 tablespoons caster sugar if you want to avoid using the rich pastry.

MINCEMEAT

Seal the lids on jars with freezer tape for an airtight fit.

INGREDIENTS
450 g/1 lb cooking apples
225 g/8 oz carrots
225 g/8 oz currants
225 g/8 oz raisins
225 g/8 oz sultanas
100 g/4 oz cooking dates
100 g/4 oz candied peel
grated rind and juice of
  1 orange
grated rind and juice of
  1 lemon
225 g/8 oz dark soft brown
  sugar
5 ml/1 teaspoon ground
  cinnamon
5 ml/1 teaspoon grated
  nutmeg
5 ml/1 teaspoon ground
  mixed spice
200 ml/7 fluid oz brandy
225 g/8 oz shredded suet

FOOD VALUES:
TOTAL • PER
  15 ML/1 TABLESPOON
kcals: 5479 • 47
kJ: 23040 • 197
protein: 17 g • 0 g
fat: 197 g • 2 g
carbohydrate: 851 g • 7 g
fibre: 75 g • 1 g

Makes about 1.75 kg/4 lb

Quarter, core and peel the apples. Peel the carrots and cut them into chunks. Mince or finely chop the apples; mince or finely grate the carrots. A food processor is ideal for making mincemeat. Mince or finely chop the currants, raisins, sultanas, dates and candied peel.

Place all the minced ingredients in a large mixing bowl. Add the orange and lemon rind and juice, sugar and spices. Stir the mixture well, then pour over the brandy and cover the bowl. Leave the mixture to stand for 24 hours, stirring occasionally so that the fruit soaks up the brandy.

Stir in the shredded suet and spoon the mincemeat into clean pots, pressing down well. Cover with waxed discs and airtight lids, then place in a cool, dark, dry cupboard to mature for at least 3 weeks.

VARIATIONS

Vegetarian Mincemeat Omit the suet or use vegetarian suet instead.
Nutty Mincemeat Add 225 g/8 oz chopped mixed almonds, walnuts and Brazil nuts.
Honey Mincemeat Omit the sugar and use 225 g/8 oz clear honey instead.
Chunky Mincemeat This makes an interesting change from the tradiional preserve. Finely grate or chop the apple and finely grate the carrot. Finely chop the dates. Leave the other fruit whole.

Major Minerals

Iron, calcium, phosphorus, magnesium, sodium, chlorine and potassium are the minerals that are required in the largest amounts in the diet. Iron* and calcium* are discussed separately; the other elements are readily available in food and are rarely found to be lacking in the diet.

Trace Elements

These are essential in small quantities: fluorine, zinc, copper, selenium, iodine, manganese, chromium and cobalt. The majority of the trace elements are readily available in foods and not deficient in the diet. Attention should be paid to zinc* as it is not always readily absorbed by the body, therefore it is discussed separately.

Mint Sauce

See Herbs.*

Mint sauce is easy to make. Take a large handful of fresh mint and wash it well. Shake off excess water, then pick off the leaves. Place them on a chopping board, sprinkle with a little sugar and chop finely.

Dissolve 30 ml/2 tablespoons sugar in 30 ml/2 tablespoons boiling water. Add the mint. Top up with white wine vinegar or Balsamic vinegar to taste – about 100 ml/4 fluid oz vinegar makes a good sweet and sour sauce.

Use

● Serve with roast or grilled lamb or add a little to stir fried lamb with vegetables.

● Not traditional but very tasty: mint sauce goes well with boiled bacon or ham, cabbage and baked potatoes.

● Another odd, yet successful, combination: add a spoonful of mint sauce to canned baked beans.

Moulds

See Micro-organisms.*

Like bacteria and yeasts, moulds are present in the air and they can cause food spoilage. Most are destroyed by heating, although there are some which survive prolonged heating.

The characteristic 'mould' which appears on food is the spores of the micro-organisms. Unlike bacteria, moulds rarely cause illness but they spoil the food and make it inedible.

Moulds do not readily grow on strong acid or alkali foods or on foods with a high enough sugar concentration. Their growth is

CHEESE MOUSSE

Set the mousse and serve scoops of it on individual plates. Cheese mousse makes an excellent filling for halved avocados.

INGREDIENTS
7 g/¼ oz gelatine
150 ml/¼ pint dry white wine
225 g/8 oz quark or curd cheese
60 ml/4 tablespoons freshly grated Parmesan cheese
30 ml/2 tablespoons finely snipped chives
salt and pepper
300 ml/½ pint whipping cream

FOOD VALUES:
TOTAL ● PER PORTION
kcals: 1978 ● 495
kJ: 8166 ● 2042
protein: 52 g ● 13 g
fat: 181 g ● 45 g
carbohydrate: 12 g ● 3 g
fibre: 0 g ● 0 g

Serves 4

Have 4 individual dishes or one large dish ready for serving the mousse. A 900 ml/1½ pint soufflé dish or a plain glass dish is suitable. Sprinkle the gelatine over the white wine in a basin, then set aside for 15 minutes. Prepare a saucepan of hot water, place the basin of gelatine over it and leave over low heat to dissolve completely, stirring occasionally.

Beat the quark or curd cheese, Parmesan and chives until thoroughly combined. Stir in the dissolved gelatine mixture and seasoning to taste.

Whip the cream until it stands in soft peaks, then fold into the cheese mixture. Divide the mixture between the individual dishes or place it in one dish and chill until set. This takes about 4–6 hours. Serve the mousse with melba toast* or crackers.

VARIATIONS

Egg Mousse Hard boil, shell and mash 2 eggs, then mix them into the soft cheese. Add a little chopped fresh tarragon, if liked.

Stilton Mousse Mash 75 g/3 oz blue Stilton cheese (weighed without rind), then beat it into the soft cheese. Omit the Parmesan.

Salmon Mousse Drain a 200 g/7 oz can pink or red salmon. Discard all skin and bones, then thoroughly mash or purée the fish with 15 ml/1 tablespoon lemon juice. Mix the fish with the soft cheese. Omit the Parmesan.

Ham Mousse Mince or finely chop 100 g/4 oz lean cooked ham. Mix it with the soft cheese, reducing the Parmesan to 30 ml/2 tablespoons. Serve with tomato salad.

SEE ALSO **Mint:** Herbs; **Mocha, Molluscs:** Glossary; **Monkfish:** Fish; **Mornay:** Glossary; **Mortadella:** Sausages; **Moussaka:** Aubergines;

arrested by freezing but the spores will germinate and grow on thawing.

Although any minor signs of mould on food may be cut off and the remainder of the food eaten (for example small mould spots on the edge of cheese), if there is any significant mould on food the whole piece should be discarded.

Moulds are likely to attack bread stored in a plastic bag in a warm room, cheese or low-fat spreads that have been kept for too long or cross contaminated from other sources. Any food that is mouldy from prolonged storage must be discarded.

Mousse

A mousse is a cold, set mixture which is lightened with whisked egg white and/or whipped cream. Mousses may be savoury and sweet. Vanilla mousse is superb with a fruity sauce.

Mushrooms

See Sauces*.

There are many types of mushrooms and edible wild fungi; specialist publications cover the subject in detail.

Readily Available Types

Large Open Mushrooms or Flat Mushrooms These are dark and well flavoured, ideal for stuffing, grilling or frying but less suitable for adding to sauces or dishes which they will discolour.
Cup Mushrooms These are part open. They are ideal for threading on skewers, for frying whole or for slicing and chopping for use in sauces and cooked dishes. They may also be stuffed with a small amount of breadcrumb stuffing.
Button Mushrooms These are small, white, closed mushrooms which may be cooked whole, halved or sliced. Ideal for delicate

VANILLA MOUSSE

Since the eggs in this mousse are uncooked, it is important that they come from a reputable source and that they are perfectly fresh.

INGREDIENTS	FOOD VALUES:
11.25 ml/2¼ teaspoons gelatine	TOTAL • PER PORTION
60 ml/4 tablespoons medium sherry	kcals: 1462 • 366
2 size 1/large eggs	kJ: 6062 • 1516
50 g/2 oz caster sugar	protein: 31 g • 8 g
10 ml/2 teaspoons natural vanilla essence (half this if using synthetic essence)	fat: 116 g • 29 g
	carbohydrate: 62 g • 16 g
300 ml/½ pint whipping cream	fibre: 0 g • 0 g
	Serves 4

Have 4 glass dishes ready for serving the mousse. Sprinkle the gelatine over the sherry in a small basin, then set aside for 15 minutes. Prepare a saucepan of hot water, place the basin of gelatine over it and leave over low heat to dissolve completely, stirring occasionally. Have a second pan of hot water ready.

Separate the eggs: place the whites in a perfectly clean bowl and set them aside. Place the yolks in a bowl. Wash and dry your hands. Add the sugar and vanilla to the yolks. Stand the bowl over the second pan of water. Cream the yolks with sugar and vanilla until thick and pale. Keep the water under the bowl just below simmering point.

Remove the bowl from over the water, then beat in the dissolved gelatine. Whip the cream until it stands in soft peaks and fold it into the egg yolk mixture. Whisk the egg whites until they stand in firm, but not dry, peaks, then fold them in using a clean metal spoon.

Divide the mousse between the dishes and chill until set – about 4–6 hours. Serve crisp biscuits with the mousse.

VARIATIONS

Lemon Grate the rind and juice of 2 lemons and cream them with the egg yolks instead of the vanilla. Increase the sugar to 100 g/4 oz.
Chocolate Cream 45 ml/3 tablespoons cocoa with 45 ml/3 tablespoons boiling water, then beat the mixture into the creamed yolks instead of adding the vanilla.
Coffee Mousse Add 60 ml/4 tablespoons very strong black coffee to the creamed yolks and omit the vanilla.

sauces, for tossing in garlic butter or for serving marinated and uncooked.
Chestnut Mushrooms Dark beige-brown on the outside and about the size of cup mushrooms, these have slightly more flavour than the paler type.
Oyster Mushrooms These are large and flat with delicate fins and a pale outside. They have a delicate flavour and are best served very lightly cooked in butter or olive oil, or added to the minimum of sauce. Usually used whole or cut into halves and quarters.
Shitake Mushrooms Dark, brown-coloured flavoursome mushrooms that are small and

open. They are full-flavoured and used dried in Oriental cooking. Available fresh from larger supermarkets or dried from Oriental stores and delicatessens. Soak dried shitake in a little hot water for 15 minutes, then discard the woody stalk and slice the cap. Save the soaking liquid for flavouring sauces.

Chanterelles These look similar to oyster mushrooms but they are a pale golden colour and have a fine flavour. Expensive and available fresh or dried from delicatessens and specialist food shops.

Ceps Large, firm caps with pale spongy undersides instead of fins. Available dried from delicatessens.

Morels Brown, closed caps that are pitted all over, these should be split and thoroughly washed as they trap dirt. Available dried from delicatessens.

Black Truffles Rare and expensive, available canned singly from better delicatessens. Use sparingly for special meals and save the liquor from the can to use in cooking. There is also a white variety of truffle.

Buying

Look for firm, undamaged specimens. Avoid damp-looking prepacked mushrooms or any that are squashed by the wrapping.

Preparation

Mushrooms should not be soaked in water as they absorb it.

Trim off the stalk ends, then place closed button mushrooms in a colander and rinse them well under cold running water.

Hold large open mushrooms, caps uppermost, under running water and rub them gently, avoiding wetting the fins.

Cup mushrooms are the most difficult but it is best to rinse them quickly under cold running water, then make sure that they are all turned caps uppermost so that the fins do not soak up water.

Dried Mushrooms

These have to be soaked in water before use. They are best left for at least 15 minutes for small pieces and longer for whole dried mushrooms.

Rub the mushrooms well to rinse any dirt out of them. Strain the soaking water through a sieve lined with absorbent kitchen paper or muslin, or through a coffee filter and save it for flavouring sauces and stews. Freeze it in ice cube trays if not needed immediately.

Cooking

Sautéing Melt some butter, olive oil or a mixture of butter and oil in a large frying pan. Add the mushrooms and cook them quickly over high heat, turning all the time. They are cooked in 2–3 minutes. Season with black pepper and a little salt, sprinkle with plenty of chopped fresh parsley and serve – good on toast.

Grilling Brush the caps of large open mushrooms with melted butter or olive oil and cook them under a hot grill for 2 minutes. Turn the mushrooms over, dot with butter or trickle a little oil over them and cook for a further 2–3 minutes. Serve with grilled bacon, chops or steaks, or on toast.

Poaching Place whole cup mushrooms (about 225 g/8 oz) in a frying pan and pour in just enough milk to cover the bottom of the pan. Season lightly and bring the milk slowly to simmering point, turning the mushrooms often. Simmer for 1 minute, then serve.

Stuffed Mushrooms Meat, rice, lentil or grated vegetable fillings may be used. The easiest stuffing is Breadcrumb Stuffing (page 254). Remove the stalks from the mushrooms and chop them, then add them to the breadcrumb mixture. Place the mushrooms on a greased ovenproof dish. Use a teaspoon to pile the mixture on to the mushrooms. Bake at 200°C, 400°F, gas 6 for about 15 minutes, or until lightly browned.

Mustard

There are many types from which to choose, including powders and ready-made mustard.

English mustard is the hot, yellow type. French or Dijon mustard is brown and mild. Wholegrain mustard has coarsely ground mustard seeds in it. Other types include Swedish mustard which is sweet and mild, horseradish mustard, mustard mixed with beer, mustard flavoured with different herbs or garlic, mustard with apple and very mild, yellow, American-style mustard.

Mustard Sauce

Stir 45–60 ml/3–4 tablespoons English mustard into Savoury White Sauce (page 234). Serve with sausages, hamburgers, grilled herrings or mackerel.

Mustard Cream

Mix 30 ml/2 tablespoons wholegrain mustard with 150 ml/¼ pint soured cream or fromage frais. Good with grilled fish or meat.

Mycoprotein

Known as quorn, this is a cultivated protein, grown from microscopic fungal spores. The fungus is processed to form pieces which resemble chunks of poultry in texture but without any distinct flavour. The protein absorbs the flavour of other ingredients in cooking. It may be frozen or cooked by stir frying or adding to sauces.

Suitable for vegetarians and vegans, as well as for use in meat or poultry dishes, mycoprotein has a low fat content and it is rich in fibre as well as protein.

Available chilled as well as in products such as pies.

SEE ALSO **Mussels:** Shellfish; **Mutton:** Glossary; **Nibbed, Niçoise:** Glossary; **Noisette:** Lamb; **Noodles:** Pasta; **Nut Butter:** Glossary;

Nuts

See Almonds*, Chestnuts*, Coconut* and Oil*.

Buying

The majority of packed shelled nuts are good quality and fairly fresh, except those left over many weeks after Christmas.

> **Cook's Tip**
> Freeze whole nuts in shells when bought fresh and they keep well for up to 6 months.

Techniques

Discard bad or damaged nuts, for example any with split shells, holes or bad spots on them when shelled.

Grinding A food processor is ideal; a liquidiser may be used but the nuts tend to clog below the blades as they form a powder, so they need frequent freeing with a spatula. A rotary grater (mouli grater) may also be used for finely grating the nuts.

Skinning Either soak or blanch in boiling water (for almonds) or toast under the grill, then rub off the skins (for hazelnuts or walnuts).

Chopping A food processor or liquidiser makes this far easier. Otherwise use a large knife and a firm but gentle chopping action to prevent the nuts from flying everywhere as they are cut. Hazelnuts and Brazils are more difficult to chop.

Peeling Place shelled nuts under the grill until the peel is begin-ning to scorch, turning often. Cool slightly, then rub off the peel. Best to do this in a clean tea-towel.

Storing

Keep shelled nuts in an airtight container in a cool, dark cupboard. Nuts in shells should be stored in a cool, dry room or used fairly quickly. If left in a warm room for many weeks, they tend to dry out and become shrivelled. Most nuts keep well in cool conditions for up to 3 months.

Types

Almonds* These are discussed separately. Available in shells, whole, blanched, split, nibbed, flaked or ground. Widely used in cooking, both savoury and sweet. Salted, roasted and spiced almonds are popular snacks.

Brazils Sold in shells, also as whole shelled nuts or pieces (look for them in wholefood shops). Not as widely used in cooking as almonds mainly because they are not as readily available. Unlike almonds and hazelnuts they are not sold ready chopped or ground and they tend to be more expensive. However, they are good in biscuits, cakes and salads.

Cashews Salted or plain, these have a mild, buttery flavour. They are good in salads, curries, risottos, vegetarian burgers and nut roasts, stir fries or in baking.

Coconut* See separate entry.

Hazelnuts Buy these in shells, whole shelled, chopped or roasted. Chopped and roasted nuts are useful for baking – delicious in biscuits or cakes – as well as for salads or burgers.

Macadamia Nuts Either salted or plain, these shelled nuts are expensive. With an excellent buttery flavour, they are pale and round, about the size of a thumb nail. Prized as a snack to serve with drinks, they may also be used in cooking, both savoury and sweet; however, they are too expensive for most baking.

Peanuts Also known as monkey nuts or groundnuts, there are a wide variety of peanut products on sale, including peanut butter, both smooth and crunchy. Peanuts are sold in shells, shelled, roasted and salted or spiced. They are also included in chopped mixed nuts, where their flavour can dominate the other nuts.

Useful in savoury cooking and baking.

Pecans Oval nuts with smooth red shells and dark red skins. These look like elongated walnuts but they have a milder taste. Useful in cooking, for savoury dishes, sweet pies and salads, also baking.

Pine Nuts or Kernels Small pale, oval kernels with a delicate, nutty flavour. These are good in savoury and sweet cooking, or for sprinkling on biscuits or adding to bread dough. Crushed to a paste with fresh basil, garlic, Parmesan cheese and olive oil, they make pesto – a flavoursome Italian sauce for pasta.

Pistachios Small nuts with thin pale shells, they have green skins, tinged red, and a delicate flavour. Sold salted or plain, with or without shells. Use in savoury and sweet cooking, and baking.

Walnuts Sold in shells, as halves or pieces. Walnuts have a distinctive flavour and they are widely used in savoury or sweet cooking and baking.

The quality of shelled nuts varies and some can taste quite bitter. Buy from a shop that has a good stock turnover.

Nutritional Value

The majority of nuts contain valuable amounts of protein and are a good source of B vitamins. Chestnuts are an exception, having a high starch content and offering little protein value. In the majority of diets, nuts play a minor role; however in vegetarian cooking they can be a valuable protein food. Most nuts have a high fat content, in the case of coconut this is saturated fat.

Oats

Types

Groats The oat grain once the husk has been removed. Requires long soaking and cooking to become palatable and digestible.

Jumbo Oats Cut and lightly rolled to make a large rolled oat that requires longer cooking than ordinary rolled oats. They should be simmered for 8–10 minutes to make porridge.

Rolled Oats Hulled, steam-softened and flattened oats.

Porridge

To serve 3–4, place 900 ml/1½ pints water or milk in a saucepan and stir in 175 g/6 oz rolled oats. Add 2.5 ml/½ teaspoon salt and bring the mixture to the boil, stirring all the time. Reduce the heat and simmer the mixture gently for 8–10 minutes. Quick cook oats require less cooking: follow packet instructions. Serve with sugar to taste. If made with water, serve with extra milk.

Microwave Method

Make an individual portion using 50 g/2 oz rolled oats, 300 ml/½ pint water or milk and a good pinch of salt. Allow 4–5 minutes cooking time on High, stirring twice. Make the porridge in a large basin if using milk to prevent it boiling over.

OATCAKES

INGREDIENTS	FOOD VALUES:
25 g/1 oz margarine or butter	TOTAL • PER PORTION
225 g/8 oz medium or fine oatmeal	kcals: 1087 • 91
2.5 ml/½ teaspoon salt	kJ: 4581 • 382
2.5 ml/½ teaspoon bicarbonate of soda	protein: 28 g • 2 g
about 100 ml/4 fluid oz boiling water	fat: 40 g • 3 g
	carbohydrate: 164 g • 14 g
	fibre: 16 g • 1 g
	Makes 12

Set the oven at 160°C, 325°F, gas 3. Grease 2 baking trays. Place the butter in a small saucepan and put it over low heat to melt. Alternatively, place the butter in a small basin and melt it on High in the microwave for 30–60 seconds.

Mix the oatmeal, salt and bicarbonate of soda in a bowl. Add the melted butter and boiling water, then mix well. The mixture will be very sticky but as it is mixed it becomes firmer. Leave to stand for a minute and wash and dry your hands.

Gently knead the dough into a ball and cut it in half. Sprinkle plenty of oatmeal on a clean surface and lightly knead one portion of dough into a smooth ball. Roll out thinly into a round measuring about 20 cm/8 inches in diameter. Transfer the rolled-out dough to a baking tray and mark it into 6 wedges. Repeat with the remaining dough.

Bake the oatcakes for 20–25 minutes, until firm and very lightly browned. Separate the wedges and transfer them to a wire rack to cool. Pack in an airtight container when cold and they will stay fresh for 2–3 weeks. The oatcakes may be frozen for up to 3 months.

LOW-FAT FLAPJACK

INGREDIENTS	FOOD VALUES:
100 g/4 oz low-fat spread (suitable for cooking)	TOTAL • PER PORTION
50 g/2 oz caster sugar	kcals: 1452 • 91
50 g/2 oz golden syrup	kJ: 6077 • 380
200 g/7 oz rolled oats	protein: 29 g • 2 g
	fat: 55 g • 3 g
Makes 16 pieces	carbohydrate: 224 g • 14 g
	fibre: 30 g • 2 g

Set the oven at 200°C, 400°F, gas 6. Base line and grease an 18 cm/7 inch shallow square tin.

Place the low-fat spread, sugar and syrup in a large saucepan over low heat and stir occasionally until the spread has melted. Remove from the heat. Stir in the rolled oats, making sure they are well coated in the syrup.

Turn the mixture into the prepared tin, scraping all the syrup out of the pan using a plastic spatula, then press it down evenly. Bake for about 15 minutes, or until the top is golden and firm.

Leave to cool in the tin. Cut into 16 squares after 10 minutes, then leave until completely cold before removing from the tin. Use a plastic spatula to remove the first piece, from a corner of the tin.

Muesli

Mix 100 g/4 oz jumbo oats or rolled oats, 25 g/1 oz raisins, 25 g/1 oz sultanas, 25 g/1 oz chopped dried apricots (ready-to-eat), 75 g/3 oz chopped nuts (Brazils, hazelnuts, pecans, cashews or walnuts, or a mixture) and 2 cored and chopped eating apples. Add a sliced or diced banana if liked. Divide between 4 dishes and sweeten to taste with demerara sugar or clear honey. Moisten with milk, yogurt or fromage frais.

Make a large batch of muesli without any fresh fruit and store it in an airtight container.

These cook quickly for making porridge or they may be used raw in muesli. Used for making flapjacks and other biscuits.

Oatmeal Hulled and ground oats, either fine, medium or coarse ground. Traditionally used for making porridge, also used for baking, for coating food, such as herring, before frying or for mixing in haggis.

Oatbran The outer coating from the grain.

Storing

Keep oats in an airtight container in a cool, dry cupboard. Since most oatmeal is steam treated it has a long shelf life, although the raw product contains an enzyme that combines with the fat content of the grain to cause rancidity on long storage.

Offal

This includes edible internal organs and minor parts of the carcass remaining after the main sources of meat are removed.

The use of offal varies from country to country and according to eating customs and trends. Less use is made of offal in more affluent countries, where there is a good choice of alternative inexpensive foods.

Types

Feet and Trotters May be boiled for making soup. Pig's trotters are probably the most popular but none are widely available. Order them from a butcher if required.

Heart Lamb's and pig's hearts are available as well as calf's and ox heart. Ox heart is large (weighing up to 2.75 kg/6 lb) and tough, requiring long slow cooking. Both lamb's, pig's and calf's hearts may be braised.

Heart must be thoroughly cleaned; all tubes and blood vessels removed. When cleaned, the offal should be soaked in cold salted water for 1 hour. The smaller hearts make individual portions and they are usually stuffed before cooking.

Kidneys Lamb's kidneys are the most popular and they are tender for grilling or frying. Ox kidney is strong and used for stews or pie filling. Calf's kidney is similar to ox kidney. Pig's kidney may be used for pies or for grilling and frying.

Remove the outer, thin membrane from kidney and cut out the central white core, along with any attached membranes.

Liver Calf's and lamb's liver are the most delicate and may be fried, grilled or braised. Pig's liver is strong and usually used in pâtés. Ox liver is very strong and not popular.

Remove the outer membrane from liver, then slice it or cut into pieces for cooking.

Poultry livers (chicken, duck, turkey and goose) cook quickly and make fine pâté. Goose liver is a delicacy, known as foie gras.

Oxtail This is more meat-like than other offal. The butcher chops the oxtail into chunks. The outer covering of fat should be trimmed off, then the oxtail may be stewed for 2–3 hours or until the meat is very tender.

Sweetbreads These are the thymus gland of either lamb or veal. Preparing them is fairly complicated, involving soaking them in cold water for 30 minutes, then simmering in clean water for 30 minutes. The drained sweetbreads are then trimmed of all membrane and tubes, and pressed. Finally, the sliced sweetbreads are sautéed or coated in egg and breadcrumbs, then fried.

Tongue Available cooked and pressed, usually sold in slices like cooked ham.

Both ox and lamb's tongue may be bought uncooked, either pickled in brine or fresh. Soak fresh tongues for 2–3 hours in cold water; salted for 4–8 hours (the longer for ox). Boil the tongue until very tender – up to 4 hours for ox tongue, topping up the water as necessary. Add sliced onion, carrot, celery, bay leaves, a blade or two of mace, some allspice berries and peppercorns to the cooking water.

Strip the skin off the cooked tongue, cut out the 'root' and all bones or gristle, then roll and press the meat. An ox tongue will fit into a small to large round cake tin. Several lamb's tongues may be pressed together. A heavy weight should be used to press the meat.

Hot tongue may be served with mustard sauce or it may be braised in sauce.

Tripe White and rubbery, tripe is the first or second stomach of an ox. Tripe from the second stomach has a honeycomb texture. Sold ready cleaned and boiled in larger supermarkets. It should be cut up and braised in a flavoursome sauce (there is a wide variety of continental sauces) or stewed with milk and onions. It has a distinct taste which is not to everyone's liking.

Buying and Storing

Buy only from a reputable supplier and always check the use by date on pre-packed offal. Frozen offal should not be allowed to thaw between purchase and being placed in the freezer. All offal should look and smell fresh; do not use any that smells strong.

Offal is highly perishable: chill it as soon as possible after purchased, cook within 24 hours.

Freezing

Offal may be frozen for short periods only, usually between 1–2 months.

Nutritional Value

All offal is highly nutritious and provides protein, vitamin B12, riboflavin, iron and, in the case of liver, vitamins A and D. With the exception of oxtail, offal has a low fat content.

X *Liver may have a high vitamin A content which can be unsuitable for some people. Since vitamin A can be ingested to excess, it is recommended that pregnant women, the elderly and infirm should avoid eating liver and that it should not be eaten more than once a week by others.*

Oil

See Fat*.

Oils have different uses according to type.

Almond Oil Made from sweet almonds, this is expensive and not used for cooking but it is useful for greasing moulds in which special desserts are set. Buy it from chemists.

Cooking Oil A blend of different oils, check the information on the label for details of sources. For frying, greasing baking tins or other cooking but not for salad dressings.

Corn Oil Extracted from maize, this is a yellow oil which is useful for frying as it has a high smoking point; however, corn oil does have a slight taste and it is not as light as sunflower or safflower oil. Not suitable for salad dressing. Corn oil may be heated to smoking point – 221°C/430°F.

Grape Seed Oil Very light and comparatively expensive, this is useful for salad dressings.

Hazelnut Oil This has a strong flavour. Use in small quantities to dress salads or flavour dips (good with low-fat soft cheese and chives, add a little trickle at a time and taste as you go). It is also useful for flavouring sweet cooking, including creamy mixtures and biscuit doughs.

Mustard Oil Available from ethnic shops, it is used in Indian cooking. Mustard oil is usually sold in small bottles and is comparatively expensive.

Olive Oil There are various grades of olive oil and all have the distinctive flavour that contributes to a variety of dishes, both in the cooking or dressing.

Extra virgin olive oil is dark green, full-flavoured and expensive. Keep it for trickling over salads or for special dishes.

Lighter olive oils are not as sweet as extra virgin oil and they have less flavour. They are also less expensive and suitable for salads and cooking. Lighter olive oil is preferred by some who do not like the strong virgin oil.

Olive oil has a smoking point which is lower than other commonly used frying oils, so great care must be taken to avoid overheating it when cooking. Although there are occasional references to deep frying in olive oil, this is not recommended.

Peanut or Groundnut Oil This is a light oil which has a high smoking point (218°C/424°F), therefore it is ideal for cooking and for dressing salads.

Rapeseed Oil Used in blended oils and margarine. Also available as a pure oil. It may be used for cooking but is less popular for salads as it has a distinct flavour when used in quantity.

Safflower Oil May be used for cooking or for dressings. High in polyunsaturated fats.

Sesame Oil The flavour varies according to the quality of the oil. The best place to buy this is in an Oriental supermarket, if possible. It has a strong flavour and some dark brown oils can taste slightly burnt or bitter. It adds a delicious nutty flavour to Oriental dishes. Use sesame oil sparingly, combining it with another light cooking oil. Excellent with pork – rub some into the meat and allow to marinate before stir frying it with vegetables or cooking with sweet and sour sauce.

Soya Oil Often blended with other oils, this is useful for cooking but not for salad dressings.

Sunflower Oil A good general purpose oil.

Walnut Oil Has a distinct, strong flavour; use as for hazelnut oil.

Smoking Point

When water boils it gives off steam as it changes from a liquid to a gas. Fat can be heated to far higher temperatures before its chemical structure begins to change.

The smoking point is the temperature at which the fat or oil begins to change or break down. It gives off a slight smoke, which increases as the fat is heated, and some oils and fats break down to give off smoke that smells strong. At the same time, when fat or oil is overheated it develops unpleasant flavours.

Heating Oils

When heating a little oil in a pan, notice when it runs more easily. Small amounts of oil are usually hot enough for cooking after 1–2 minutes over high heat. Take care not to overheat olive oil or sesame oil.

When deep frying, always use an oil which is recommended for the cooking method. For best results use a thermometer (a sugar thermometer) to check the temperature of the oil. Temperatures between 170–190°C/340–375°F are used for most deep frying.

If you do not have a thermometer, test the temperature of the oil by dropping a small piece of day-old bread into it. It should bubble and rise to the surface, then brown in 30–60 seconds.

Flavoured Oils

Flavour light oil, such as sunflower or grape seed, with sprigs of herbs or spices. Thoroughly

SEE ALSO **Okra**: Vegetables – exotic; **Olives**: Glossary; **Omelettes**: Eggs wash and dry a few sprigs of fresh herbs, such as bay, rosemary, thyme, sage, basil or marjoram, then place them in a clean jar or bottle with an airtight lid. Cover with oil, then leave for at least a month.

Spices such as dried red chilli, coriander, garlic, fresh root ginger or cumin seeds may be added to the oil. Do not add ground spices.

Onions

See Vegetables*.

Buying

Look for onions that have tight, shiny skins. They should be firm and in good condition. Avoid bruised or sprouting onions and any that show signs of being soft or mouldy.

Spring onions should be firm and bright, avoid browning, limp or soft vegetables.

Storing

Keep onions in a brown paper bag or net bag in a cool dry place. Onions that are in good condition will keep for 2–3 weeks but since most kitchens are fairly warm they usually only keep for 7–10 days before beginning to soften, sprout or become mouldy.

Wash and trim spring onions, then keep them in a polythene bag in the refrigerator. They will keep for 4–7 days.

Types

Spanish Onions These are very large and they have a mild flavour. Ideal for boiling or stuffing or for adding in quantity to cooked dishes, for example as a topping for pizzas or a filling for savoury flans. Also used raw.
English Onions These are small and stronger. As a general rule, the smaller onions have a stronger flavour.

Pickling Onions Small onions, about the size of walnuts, with a strong flavour. Ideal for cooking whole or for pickling in vinegar.
Shallots Small onions that grow in clumps. They have a mild flavour and are used in delicate dishes.
Red or White Skinned Onions Mild-flavoured Italian onions. These are ideal for salads as they are quite sweet.
Spring Onions Referred to as scallions in American cookbooks. These are young onions which have not formed bulbs. They have a short white part running down to the roots and long green ends.

Preparation Techniques

Cut off the root end and remainder of the stalk, then slit and remove the peel.

There are all sorts of hints about how to avoid having running eyes and nose when peeling onions. Cutting the root end off first and peeling onions under water is supposed to help.

Persuade the rest of the family to help with the preparation of pickling onions.
Spring Onions Trim off the ends of the green part and the roots.

Slicing
Peel the onion and rub off any fine membrane as this makes it slippery to hold. Use a sharp knife and hold the root end of the onion firmly on the board, then slice it from the stalk end.

Small pronged gadgets are available for holding onions while slicing.

Unless you specifically need complete onion slices or rings, the easiest way to slice an onion is to cut it in half down through the stalk and root, then slice each half in turn.

Chopping
Peel and halve the onion as above. Hold one half cut side down on the board, with your thumb at the root end and fingers holding down the stalk end. Slice the onion under the bridge of

Chopping an Onion

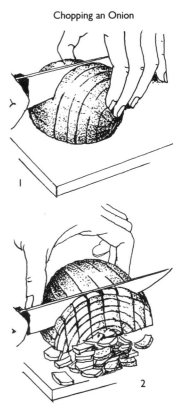

your hand, keeping all the slices neatly in place. The sharper and finer the knife blade, the easier it is to avoid breaking the shape of the onion as you slice it.

Lower your hand to one side of the onion without letting go of it, then cut across the slices to make small pieces.
Chopping Spring Onion For most recipes, simply cutting across the onion gives pieces that are fine enough. However, for finely chopped spring onion, hold the onion flat on the board so that the green leaves are more or less on top of each other. Cut the onion in half lengthways, through the white and green parts. Then cut them across into small pieces.

Grating Onion
Use the coarse side of the grater. The last piece is difficult to grate; however usually grated onion is used in small quantities so grate as much as required, then place the rest of the onion in a sealed polythene bag in the refrigerator and reserve it for another use.

Cooking

Frying Onions may be lightly cooked before other ingredients are added.

The phrase 'cook until soft but not browned' is often used. It takes some time to soften onion in fat – between 10–20 minutes, depending on the quantity, the way in which it is cut and the heat. Never rush this stage.

Browning onions takes considerable time. Slices are usually browned. The onions should be cooked over medium heat so that they soften and gradually brown. If the heat is too fierce, the pieces will burn quickly before being properly cooked.

Use a slice to turn onion slices occasionally as they are cooking. Allow at least 20 minutes, more like 30–40 minutes to brown onions evenly and to a deep golden colour.

Boiling Boiled whole onions are delicious topped with butter and served as a vegetable.

Peel the onions and place them in a saucepan with water to cover. Add a little salt and bring to the boil, then reduce the heat, cover the pan and simmer the onions for 45–60 minutes, until they are tender through. Drain well and serve piping hot.

Small whole pickling onions may be boiled for about 20–30 minutes, then served coated in Cheese Sauce or Savoury White Sauce (page 234).

Braising or Glazing Toss whole pickling onions in a little melted butter over medium to high heat, so that they are just beginning to brown outside without being cooked through. Add a little medium sweet cider, stock, water or unsweetened apple juice to the pan and bring to the boil. There should be enough to cover the bottom of the pan thinly. Reduce the heat and roll the onions in the liquor, then cover the pan and cook the onions gently for 15 minutes. Remove the lid and continue cooking until most of the liquid has evaporated, leaving the onions tender and shiny.

Oranges

See Fruit*.

As well as sweet oranges that are available all year, look for bitter oranges around January and February time for making marmalade.

Bitter oranges, for example Seville oranges, have a high pectin content which makes them suitable for setting the preserve.

Blood oranges are small and tinged with red on the skin and all the way through the fruit. They are sweet but some have lots of pips.

Buying and Storing

Look for bright, firm fruit that feels fairly heavy. Avoid wrinkled, darkened or damaged oranges.

Keep oranges in a cool room. Do not stack the smaller, thin skinned fruit on top of each other in a dish in a warm room as the oranges underneath become mouldy quickly.

Most oranges will keep for 1–2 weeks.

Preparation Techniques

Wash oranges before use. They may have a wax coating on their peel to protect the fruit from loss of moisture.

Grating Rind Grate the rind on the fine blade of the grater. Avoid grating off the pith too as it is bitter.

Paring Rind Use a vegetable peeler and cut off thin strips of rind, working in a circular direction around the fruit if you want to use all the rind. A parer removes narrow strips of rind.

SAVOURY ORANGE SAUCE

Serve this sauce with pork, lamb, duck or pheasant.

INGREDIENTS
2 large oranges
25 g / I oz butter or a little fat
  (see below)
I bay leaf
30 ml/2 tablespoons plain
  flour
300 ml/½ pint stock (made
  by adding water to the
  roasting tin when cooking
  a joint or bird, or from the
  giblets)
salt and pepper
30 ml/2 tablespoons sugar

FOOD VALUES:
TOTAL • PER PORTION
kcals: 885 • 221
kJ: 3729 • 932
protein: 12 g • 3 g
fat: 49 g • 12 g
carbohydrate: 106 g • 27 g
fibre: 9 g • 2 g

Serves 4

Coarsely grate the rind and squeeze the juice from the oranges. Melt the butter in a saucepan. (If the sauce is served with a roast joint or bird, then pour excess fat from the roasting tin, then use the cooking juices and a little fat instead of the butter.) Add the bay leaf and orange rind to the pan and stir well for about 30 seconds. Stir in the flour and cook over medium heat for 3–4 minutes, stirring often.

Gradually pour in the stock and orange juice. Bring the sauce to the boil, stirring all the time. Reduce the heat and simmer the sauce for 5 minutes. Taste and add seasoning along with the sugar. Bring back to the boil, give the sauce a stir and serve hot.

SEE ALSO **Oregano:** Herbs; **Organic:** Glossary; **Oysters:** Shellfish; **Panada:** Glossary

Shredding Rind Pare off the rind, then cut across the pieces to make fine strips.

Peeling Rind and Pith Cut both ends off an orange so that you can just see the flesh. Stand the fruit on a board and use a serrated knife to cut off all peel and pith in strips. Trim off any remaining pith afterwards.

Removing Segments Peel the fruit. Hold the orange over a basin to catch the juice. Use a medium-sized serrated knife to cut into the middle of the fruit, close to one membrane dividing the segments. As you reach the middle of the fruit, twist the knife and cut outwards, scraping the segment off the next membrane. Once the first segment has been removed, it is easier to cut out the remainder. Squeeze all juice from the membranes before discarding them. This is the best way of cutting oranges for salads and sauces.

Peeling an orange.

Removing orange segments.

Pancakes

A good pancake pan or frying pan is essential for success – set aside a heavy, non-stick flat pancake pan with a shallow rim only for making pancakes.

Make up one quantity of Thin Batter (page 28) to make 8 large pancakes or 12–16 small ones.

Technique

1. For fine pancakes, beat 30 ml/2 tablespoons cold water into the batter.

2. Beat in 15 ml/1 tablespoon oil. This helps to prevent the pancakes from sticking as they cook.

3. If possible, cover the bowl and leave the batter to stand for 30 minutes. This is not essential but if the batter is cooked when freshly made, the pancakes tend to bubble slightly rather than being perfectly flat. Pour the batter into a jug or have a ladle ready.

4. Have a plate ready for the cooked pancakes. Sweet pancakes to be eaten freshly cooked should be sprinkled very lightly with caster sugar to prevent them sticking together. Pancakes that are to be cooled and kept (for example for stuffing or if they are made in advance) should be interleaved with paper, either greaseproof or, more practical, absorbent kitchen paper. Separate each piece of kitchen paper into 2 thin layers.

5. Have some oil and a pad of absorbent kitchen paper for greasing the pan. Heating the pan to the right temperature and maintaining it is important. Turn the heat to medium and heat the pan well, then pour a little oil on it and wipe it over with a pad of paper. Heat the pan for another minute or so before cooking any batter.

6. Stir the batter if it has been standing. Hold the pan in one hand and pour on a small amount of batter (about a third of a soup ladle full). At the same time, tilt the pan so that the batter runs evenly all over the surface. Do this quickly before the batter sets.

7. Cook the pancake until it is well set on the surface and browned underneath. When the edges begin to look crisp and they lift slightly off the pan, slide a palette knife or slice under the edge of the pancake and lift it carefully to see whether it is browned underneath.

8. Loosen the pancake all around the edge, then slide a palette knife or slice under the middle of it and turn it over quickly. Cook the second side until lightly browned.

9. To toss a pancake, first loosen it around the edge, then shake the pan back and forth. When the pancake is loose and moving easily, flip the pan sharply away from you and upwards. Lower the pan slightly to catch the flipped pancake. Practice makes perfect.

10. The first pancake is often disappointing but once the pan is well heated and lightly oiled, the pancakes do not stick. Be patient with the first one – it often breaks up because it is too soft and undercooked.

Serving Ideas

Savoury

• Fill with fish, chicken or ham in sauce, roll up and place in a buttered ovenproof dish. Top with Tomato Sauce (page 263), white Wine Sauce (page 235) or Savoury White Sauce (page 234). Sprinkle with grated cheese and bake until bubbling hot through or grill until golden.

• Fill with Meat Sauce (page 176) or Lentil Sauce (page 169) and top with Cheese Sauce (page 234). Bake until golden.

• Fill with spinach (cooked, well drained and seasoned) or Ratatouille (page 252) and coat with Cheese Sauce (page 234).

Sweet

• Sprinkle with a little caster sugar, some currants and a squeeze of lemon juice. Roll and eat.

• Trickle maple syrup or honey over the pancakes and sprinkle with chopped walnuts.

• Cold pancakes are good spread with jam, rolled or folded. They are terrific for picnics like this.

• Fill pancakes with poached fruit or apple sauce, then roll or fold. Serve with fromage frais or cream.

Storing

Interleave the pancakes and pack them in a large polythene bag or foil. They will keep in the refrigerator for 5 days.

Reheating Pancakes

Melt a little butter in a frying pan and heat it until foaming. Add a pancake, press it down well all over, then turn and heat the second side.

Pancakes may be filled when cold, folded or rolled and coated with sauce or topped, then baked.

Freezing

Packed as above, they may be frozen for up to 3 months. Separate the required number of pancakes from a frozen stack by sliding a palette knife between them. Thaw a whole pack in the refrigerator overnight. Individual pancakes thaw quickly at room temperature.

Papers, Wrapping and Packing for Food Use

There is an ever changing choice of products for covering and wrapping food.

Absorbent Kitchen Paper Use for mopping fat from fried foods after draining; for drying herbs and other food that has been washed. Suitable for microwave use, for loosely covering food which gives off moisture.

Boilable Bags These are suitable for use in the freezer and they withstand boiling water. Useful for packing individual portions for reheating in the microwave or in a pan of boiling water.

Cling Film and Plastic Films These are useful for covering bowls and deep basins or other containers of food, for example bowls which contain bread dough while it is proving.

Do not use fine household film directly on foods with a high fat content (cheese, biscuits, cake, sausages and so on). As a general guide, the best advice is not to use film directly on any food on a regular basis. Never use film to line dishes before cooking in the microwave or as a cover to come in contact with food during microwave cooking (or any other method, such as steaming).

Foil Use to cover food during conventional cooking as well as in storage. Wrap fruit, cakes with a high fruit content or other acidic foods in greaseproof paper before overwrapping in foil.

Foil is not the most practical material for freezer use as it can be ripped easily and ordinary (thin) cooking foil does not provide sufficient protection against loss of moisture.

Foil Containers With foil-covered cardboard lids, these are useful for packing portions of cooked dishes for freezing. A variety of shapes and sizes of dishes are produced, including tart dishes, pie dishes and flan dishes, large and small. Overpack in polythene bags.

Greaseproof Paper Use to line baking tins and as a wrapping for food. Greaseproof paper is not moisture proof or airtight but it may be used as a first wrapping under foil or cling film to prevent both from coming into direct contact with the food.

Greaseproof paper bags are useful for wrapping sandwiches and packed lunches.

Interleaving Film For separating foods that are stacked before being overwrapped and frozen.

Micro Crisp Or other brand names, this is a coated paper for use in the microwave, it causes food to become brown and crisp.

Non-stick Baking Sheet Washable, reusable sheet of non-stick material which may be cut to fit baking tins. Also useful for rolling out pastry. May be used in the microwave as well as in conventional ovens.

Non-stick Cooking Parchment For lining baking tins and trays. Ideal for difficult items such as meringues. Also good for wrapping foods that are baked 'en papillotte' (in paper, see Glossary, page 275) as this is tougher than greaseproof paper.

Polythene Bags These vary in thickness: the thicker type must be used for wrapping food to be frozen. Check the manufacturer's recommendations on the packet. As well as plain polythene bags, look for colour coded bags that are useful for quickly identifying different foods in the freezer.

Rice Paper Edible paper used as a base for making macaroons or other very sweet items.

Roasting Bags and Film This is suitable for use in the conventional oven and microwave. Film with a foil strip along one side is not suitable for use in the microwave. Use special plastic ties for microwave use, allowing a small gap for steam to escape during cooking.

Bags are ideal for roasting a joint to be served cold. Simply leave the bag unopened until the meat is cooled (drain off any fat), then chill the food in the bag too. Not suitable for freezing.

SEE ALSO **Paprika:** Spices; **Parboil, Parcook:** Glossary; **Parmesan:** Cheese; **Parsley:** Herbs; **Partridge:** Game;

Wax Paper This is used mainly for cake decorating and icing techniques, such as making icing or chocolate run outs. Ready cut discs of waxed paper are used for covering preserves.

Parsnips

See Vegetables*.
An autumn and winter vegetable, now available from August through to April.

Buying

Parsnips should be firm, plump and unmarked. Brown patches outside usually penetrate through the vegetable. Avoid limp or shrunken vegetables.

Preparation

Cut off the stalk and root ends, then peel the parsnips. They are usually cut up for cooking. Cut them in half lengthways, then across into chunks for boiling. For roasting, leave small vegetables whole or halve or quarter larger parsnips lengthways.

Cooking

Place the prepared parsnips in a saucepan and cover with cold water. Add a pinch of salt, then bring to the boil. Reduce the heat so that the water is just boiling and cover the pan. Cook for 10–15 minutes, or until the parsnips are tender.
Drain and mash with butter and pepper.
Roasting Roast parsnips are a traditional accompaniment for beef. Add the halved or quartered vegetables to the roasting pan and turn them in the fat and cooking juices from the meat. Cook for about 1–1¼ hours, or until the parsnips are browned and tender.

Use

● Mashed parsnips may be served with all meats and poul-

try. Mixed, half and half with mashed potato they make a tempting topping for cottage pie.

● Parsnips are delicious in vegetable curry. Combine them with onions, carrots, cauliflower and potatoes.

● Add cubed or diced parsnips to soups and stews; they are particularly good in pork stews, with some cooking apple added.

● Make parsnip and cheese croquettes: beat some grated mild cheese (Caerphilly or Lancashire) into mashed parsnips, then shape them into cakes and coat with egg and breadcrumbs. Dot with butter or margarine and bake or fry until golden.

Pasta

Fresh and dried pasta is sold in many shapes, colours and flavours. Pasta is also easy to make.

Dried Pasta

Cannelloni These are wide tubes, about 7.5–10 cm/3–4 inches long. They are boiled, drained and dried, then filled with a stuffing, such as meat, soft cheese or spinach and cheese. Stuffed cannelloni are coated with sauce and baked until hot through.
Lasagne Oblong sheets of pasta, plain or flavoured and coloured

PASTA DOUGH

INGREDIENTS
450 g/1 lb strong plain flour
2.5 ml/½ teaspoon salt
4 eggs, beaten
45 ml/3 tablespoons olive oil
30–45 ml/2–3 tablespoons water

FOOD VALUES:
TOTAL ● PER PORTION
kcals: 2215 ● 369
kJ: 9336 ● 1556
protein: 75 g ● 13 g
fat: 72 g ● 12 g
carbohydrate: 337 g ● 56 g
fibre: 14 g ● 2 g

Makes about 675 g/1½ lb Serves 6

Place the flour and salt in a bowl, then make a well in the middle and add the eggs. Stir the oil and smaller quantity of water into the eggs, then gradually work in the flour.

Wash and dry your hands. Gather the mixture together, then knead the dough into a smooth ball. Turn out the dough on to a work surface and knead it firmly until smooth. Wrap the dough in a polythene bag and set aside for 30 minutes.

Roll and shape the dough in 4 batches. You need a large area of clean work surface. Cut the dough into 2 or 4 pieces and work on one portion at a time, wrapping the pieces not in use. Roll out the portion of dough into a thin sheet on a lightly floured surface.

To make tagliatelle, dust the dough with flour, fold it into 4 and use a sharp knife to cut it into strips measuring about 5–10 mm/¼–½ inch wide. Shake out the strips, then place them on a plate dusted with a little flour. Cover the pasta with a large dish, placed upside down, until required.

For lasagne, simply cut the rolled dough into squares or sheets. For cannelloni, cut oblongs measuring about 7.5 × 12.5 cm/3 × 5 inches. Cook these sheets and roll them around a filling instead of pushing the filling into tubes.

green with spinach. Wholemeal lasagne is also readily available. Proper lasagne is difficult to find as most packets are the no pre-cooking type which is unmistakably inferior to ordinary dried or fresh pasta. Look for dried pasta that has to be boiled for 10 minutes before use – Italian delicatessen shops are the usual source.

Lower the sheets individually into a large pan of boiling water, give them a stir and cook according to the packet directions. Drain and rinse lasagne under cold water, then lay the sheets out to dry on clean tea-towels or absorbent kitchen paper.

Macaroni Short cut or elbow macaroni are most common. These thin hollow tubes are used in sweet and savoury dishes. Long macaroni is not as easy to find.

Quick-cook Pasta There are various brands of quick-cook pasta shapes. They are usually tender after 3–5 minutes boiling. Their quality varies, some tend to have a gelatinous texture.

Shapes Between supermarkets, wholefood shops and delicatessens, there is an excellent choice of dried pasta shapes, including novelty pasta for children as well as traditional Italian types.

Shells These range from tiny soup pasta to large shells for stuffing. Medium shells are versatile, for baked dishes, salads or as a side dish with fish.

Soup Pasta These are tiny shapes for adding to soup. They cook quickly, so should be added to the soup about 5 minutes before the end of the cooking time.

Spaghetti Long thin strands of pasta, either plain or wholemeal.

Tagliatelle Ribbon noodles. Fetuccine are very similar to tagliatelle. Available plain, spinach or tomato flavoured.

Twists Plain, wholemeal, green or red twists are versatile.

Fresh Pasta

Tagliatelle, spaghetti, twists and lasagne are among the most

common of unfilled types. Fresh filled pasta include tortellini (semi-circular shapes), ravioli (small squares) and annellini (mitre shapes, made by curving semi-circular pasta and pinching the corners together). Various stuffings include traditional meat, spinach and cheese mixtures.

Pasta: An International Food

Pasta is eaten in many countries, including China and Japan. Wiry, yellow, Chinese egg noodles may be purchased fresh from Oriental stores but are more common dried in small blocks. All types cook quickly in boiling water (1–3 minutes) and are the basis for making chow mein.

Rice sticks in fine and medium strands or ribbon strips are opaque and gelatinous in texture. They are used in both Chinese and Japanese cooking.

Other Oriental pasta include small filled dumplings that are steamed or boiled and served as dim sum (snacks).

Eastern European equivalents include filled polish dumplings, very similar to ravioli or annellini.

Cooking Pasta

1. Have a large saucepan three-quarters full of water. Add a little salt and a little cooking oil. The oil serves two purposes: it helps to prevent the pasta from sticking together and the water from frothing up.

2. Bring the water to the boil, then add the pasta and give it a stir. Bring the water back to the boil and give the pasta another stir. Time the cooking from this point. Reduce the heat slightly to prevent the water from boiling over but keep it boiling. Partly cover the pan during cooking.

3. Most dried pasta cooks in about 10–15 minutes. Wholemeal types take longer, 20–30 minutes. Check the packet instructions. When cooked, pasta should be tender but firm not

---

Quick Pasta Dishes

Each of the following serves 4.

Macaroni Cheese

Cook 350 g/12 oz short-cut macaroni in boiling water, then drain well. Mix it with 600 ml/1 pint Cheese Sauce (page 234) and 2 chopped spring onions, 1 small chopped onion cooked in a little butter or 45 ml/3 tablespoons snipped chives. Turn the mixture into a flameproof dish. Top with 25 g/1 oz fresh breadcrumbs tossed with 50 g/2 oz grated cheese and grill until golden.

Pasta Carbonara

Cut 225 g/8 oz cooked ham into thin shreds (or better, use air-dried ham such as Parma; bacon may also be used). Cook 350 g/12 oz pasta. While the pasta is cooking, melt 50 g/2 oz butter or margarine in a large frying pan. Add the ham and cook gently for a few minutes. If using bacon, cook it gently without browning.

When the pasta is cooked and drained, add 6 beaten eggs to the ham or bacon and stir them over low heat until just beginning to set. Add the pasta, then stir well so that the mixture is creamy. Season with plenty of freshly ground black pepper and serve at once.

---

soft, known as 'al dente'. Use a draining spoon to remove a small piece and taste it. Drain cooked pasta immediately.

4. Unfilled fresh pasta cooks very quickly, in about 2–3 minutes. Filled pasta takes longer and the exact time depends on the filling. Cheese and spinach fillings cook fairly quickly, as do other cooked fillings. Raw meat mixtures require longer boiling, about 15 minutes. Read the label on packets or follow a reputable recipe.

Serving

Drain the pasta in a colander, then turn it into a heated serving dish. Top it with a knob of butter and sprinkle with chopped fresh parsley or shredded basil. Serve at once.

Storing

Dried pasta keeps well for months in an airtight container in a cool, dry cupboard.

Fresh pasta freezes extremely well and it may be cooked straight from frozen, allowing about 2 minutes extra cooking once the water is boiling.

Nutritional Value

Pasta provides carbohydrate and some protein, depending on the ingredients used in its manufacture. Wholemeal pasta is a better source of fibre.

Pasteurisation

Pasteurisation is usually used to rid food of vegetative pathogens and the process varies according to the exact requirements. This often involves heating food to a specific temperature and maintaining the temperature for an exact length of time before rapidly cooling the food. Pasteurisation makes the food safer to eat and improves its keeping qualities. The process is controlled so that changes to the flavour and nutritional value of the food are minimal.

Pasties and Turnovers

These are individual pastries with a sweet or savoury filling, either oval or triangular.

Choice of Pastry

See also Filo Pastry*.
Short crust, flaky, puff and rough puff pastries may be used. A different technique is used for shaping filo pastry.

Technique

Make short crust pastry* using 350 g/12 oz flour or use 1 quantity (450 g/1 lb bought) of puff pastry*.

Pasties

1. To make pasties, divide the dough into 4 and roll each portion out into a 18 cm/7 inch round.

2. Divide the filling into 4 and place a portion in the middle of each piece of pastry.

3. Dampen the pastry edges, then fold both sides over the filling into the middle and to enclose it completely.

4. Knock up and flute the edges, then brush the pastry with a little beaten egg or milk.

Filling and Sealing Pasties

2

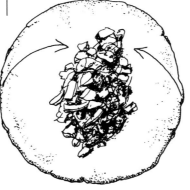

1

Suggested Fillings

Cornish Pasties
Use short crust pastry. Mix 225 g/8 oz diced lean braising steak, 1 diced carrot, 1 chopped onion, 1 diced medium potato, plenty of seasoning, 2.5 ml/½ teaspoon chopped fresh thyme and some chopped fresh parsley. Moisten the mixture with 30 ml/2 tablespoons water.
Bake At 200°C, 400°F, gas 6 for 15 minutes, then reduce the oven temperature to 180°C, 350°F, gas 4 and continue to cook the pasties for 1 hour.

Spiced Chick Pea Pasties
Use wholemeal short crust pastry. Cook ½ finely chopped onion and a crushed clove garlic in 30 ml/2 tablespoons olive oil until soft but not browned. Stir in 15 ml/1 tablespoon cumin seeds and 15 ml/1 tablespoon coarsely crushed coriander seeds. Cook for 5 minutes, stirring often. Add 1 peeled and chopped tomato, 1½ peeled, cored and chopped eating apples and a drained 425 g/15 oz can chick peas. Season the mixture.
Bake At 200°C, 400°F, gas 6 for 30–40 minutes.
Serve Hot or cold. Good with grated cucumber and yogurt.

Almond Apple Turnovers
Use puff pastry. Peel, core and roughly chop 450 g/1 lb cooking apples. Grate 100 g/4 oz bought marzipan on the coarse side of a grater, then mix it with the apples. Add 25 g/1 oz sultanas.
Brush the filled turnovers with a little egg white and sprinkle with flaked almonds.
Bake At 220°C, 425°F, gas 7 for 20–25 minutes. Cool the turnovers on a wire rack and dust with a little icing sugar before serving, either warm or cold.

Turnovers

1. To make turnovers, roll out the dough into a 40 cm/16 inch square, then cut it into four 20 cm/8 inch squares.

2. Place the filling on one side, towards a corner of the pastry. Dampen the pastry edges, then fold the unfilled side over to enclose the filling completely in a triangular pasty.

3. Knock up the edges of the pastry and scallop them or leave them plain. Brush with beaten egg or milk.

Filling and Sealing Turnovers

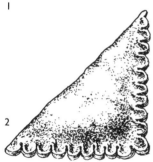

Pastry

See separate entries for types.
Pastry is a dough made from flour and water, usually with added fat. Rich pastries have a higher proportion of fat to flour and added ingredients may include egg, sugar, cheese and nuts.

Comment on Nutrition

Food values are given for each type of pastry. The value of fillings must be added to that of the pastry, then the total should be divided by the number of portions.

The food values for the whole recipes for pastry show a high fat content; however this should be considered in the context of the role that pastry plays in the diet and the food values per portion. For example, puff pastry has a high fat content but it is probably only eaten occasionally.

Preparation Points

● A light touch is important when preparing most pastry. Handle pastry as little as possible. When the term knead is used (for example to make hot water crust dough smooth), the technique must be less vigorous than for bread dough and very brief. Pastry dough is kneaded by using a combination of rolling, pressing and patting, not by pounding with the knuckles.

● For most types, all ingredients, hands and utensils should be kept cool. Hot water crust and choux are exceptions.

● Work quickly when preparing, rolling, shaping and filling pastry. If pastry is uncovered for a long time during its preparation it tends to dry on the surface.

● Short, puff, flaky and rough puff pastries are all better if they are rested. They should be prepared quickly, then covered and chilled. This is essential when folding and rolling rich dough. Short crust and similar types of pastry have a shorter texture if they are rested after mixing and before rolling. Resting shaped items is important to prevent them from shrinking during cooking. Always wrap pastry in a polythene bag or cover items.

Techniques and Finishes

Trimming and Cutting A serrated knife cuts short pastries well but a very sharp, fine bladed knife is better for puff, flaky, rough puff and filo as the serrations tend to drag the dough.

Pastry Techniques

Trimming excess pastry.

Knocking up.

Scalloped edge.

Fluted edge.

Kitchen scissors can be useful for cutting pastry, for example when cutting shapes such as leaves or particularly for trimming the top edge of raised pies.

Knocking Up This is a technique for sealing edges when 2 layers of pastry are pressed together. Use a blunt knife or the blunt edge of a sharp knife. Using the side of your index finger, press down gently but firmly just behind the pastry edge. Tap the knife horizontally against the edge of the pastry, at the same time pushing outwards slightly with your index finger. Do this all along the pastry join, for example around the edge of a pie or turnover.

On pasties or other items that have an upright pastry join, hold the edge firmly between your thumb and forefinger as you tap down gently with the knife.

Scalloped Edge Used on pies and other flat edges. Push downwards and outwards on the edge of the pastry with one finger, then use the blunt end of a pointed knife to drag the pastry in slightly next to the finger. Do this all the way around the edge, making large scallops on savoury items and small ones on sweet pastries.

Fluted Edge For upright edges as well as flat ones. Press the pastry down (or in one direction) with the end of your index finger, at the same time pushing up (or in

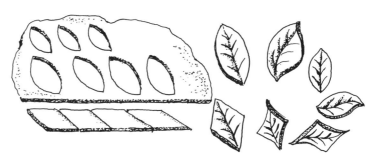

Pastry Leaves
These may be cut out using a cutter or the point of a knife. Alternatively, pastry strips may be cut into diamond shapes, then marked as leaves.

the opposite direction) with your thumb and third finger.

On upright edges, the thumb and third finger should be on the opposite side of the pastry to the index finger. On a flat edge these fingers push the dough inwards causing it to flute upwards.

Forked Edge This is easy but it must be used with care as the pastry becomes thin and it can overbrown or burn easily. Press the prongs of a fork all along a flat pastry edge to make a decorative impression.

Use only on thick pastry where an impression is made without overthinning the dough.

Pastry Leaves Cutters are available for stamping out leaves. They may also be cut from strips of pastry. Cut a strip of rolled-out pastry, then cut the strip diag-

onally into triangular pieces. If you like, trim the side corners off using the point of a knife. Mark veins on the leaves.

The better way to make leaves is to cut the dough freehand into oval shapes, with a sharp point at one end. Pinch the rounded end slightly and mark veins with the point of a knife. Make leaves of similar or various sizes.

Dampen the underneath of leaves with a little water to stick them on the pastry, then curve them slightly as you press them into position.

Cutter Decorations Biscuit cutters and aspic cutters may be used to stamp out shapes – circles, diamonds, triangles and so on. Overlap these around a plain pastry edge or in a central arrangement on pies.

PASTRIES: A QUICK GUIDE (simple – difficult: 1–6)								
	Choux	Filo	Flaky	Hot Water Crust	Puff	Rough Puff	Short Crust	Suet Crust
Difficulty	1	6	2	3	5	4	1	1
Good Bought		●			●			
Savoury	●	●	●	●	●	●	●	●
Sweet	●	●	●		●	●	●	●
Baking	●	●	●	●	●	●	●	●
Grilling					●			
Frying	●	●			●			
Boiling								●
Steaming								●

Pâtes and Terrines

See Meat*, Offal* and Fish*.

Pâtés and terrines may be made from any type of food – fish, meat, liver, vegetables, pulses or fruit (dessert terrines).

They may be smooth, coarse, layered with pieces of food or set in a casing such as bacon or spinach.

A terrine takes its name from the cooking dish, a heavy lidded oblong or oval ovenproof container. Terrines may be earthenware or cast iron but a deep ovenproof dish may be used instead – soufflé dishes are good substitutes (cover with foil). Mixtures known as terrines are served from their cooking dishes whereas pâtés may be turned out. A terrine is usually coarse.

Types of Pâtés and Terrines

Fish These may be uncooked, made from cooked fish, such as smoked mackerel, canned tuna or sardines, or a raw purée of fish may be baked or steamed.

Meat, Game and Poultry Belly pork or minced pork combined with pork or lamb's liver is the usual combination. For a fine, smooth pâté, the raw ingredients should be minced twice or puréed in a food processor.

Part cooking the meats first by sautéeing them in a little oil or butter produces a fairly fine pâté, and the processing is easier and not so messy.

Duck, chicken and turkey livers and meat may be used to make pâtés and terrines. Fine pâté made from poultry liver is inexpensive and delicious. Goose liver is expensive and a good pâté made from it is equally prized (foie gras and pâté de foie gras).

Stewing venison, pheasant and pigeon all make good pâtés. They are best stewed very slowly first until thoroughly tender, then puréed with other ingredients and moistened with the reduced cooking liquor to make richly flavoured pâtés.

VEGETABLE TERRINE

INGREDIENTS
50 g/2 oz butter or margarine
1 onion, finely chopped
50 g/2 oz plain flour
1 bay leaf
600 ml/1 pint milk
50 g/2 oz fresh white breadcrumbs
225 g/8 oz carrots, sliced
225 g/8 oz cauliflower florets
450 g/1 lb fresh spinach or 225 g/8 oz frozen chopped spinach, thawed
100 g/4 oz curd cheese
salt and pepper
3 eggs
50 g/2 oz Lancashire, Cheshire or Caerphilly cheese, finely crumbled
a little grated nutmeg

FOOD VALUES:
TOTAL • PER SLICE
kcals: 2020 • 253
kJ: 8436 • 1055
protein: 99 g • 12 g
fat: 127 g • 16 g
carbohydrate: 129 g • 16 g
fibre: 44 g • 6 g

Makes about 8 slices

Grease a 1 kg/2 lb loaf tin and line the base with a piece of greaseproof paper. Grease the paper well. Set the oven at 180°C, 350°F, gas 4. Have ready a roasting tin and a kettle of boiling water.

Melt the butter in a saucepan, add the onion and cook gently for about 15 minutes, until it is softened but not browned. Stir in the flour and cook for 1 minute, then add the bay leaf and gradually pour in the milk, stirring all the time. Bring to the boil, stirring, and simmer the sauce for 2 minutes. Remove from the heat, then stir in the breadcrumbs. Cover the pan and set the mixture aside to cool.

Place the carrots in a saucepan – add enough cold water to cover them. Bring the water to the boil. Reduce the heat so that the water simmers, cover the pan and cook the carrots for 10 minutes or until they are just tender. Drain and mash the carrots, then press them through a sieve or purée in a food processor or liquidiser.

Bring a small amount of water to the boil in the saucepan used to cook the carrots. Add the cauliflower florets to the water, then bring it back to the boil. Reduce the heat slightly, cover the pan and cook the cauliflower for 5 minutes, then drain thoroughly. It is best to leave the cauliflower to drain for 5 minutes so that all the water runs out of the florets.

Trim the stalks and thoroughly wash fresh spinach, then place the wet leaves in a large saucepan. Put a lid on the pan and put it over high heat. Cook the spinach for 2 minutes, then stir it well. The leaves should be limp. Reduce the heat to medium, re-cover the pan and continue to cook the spinach for another 2 minutes. Drain well and use the back of a spoon to press all the water out of the leaves. Press all the liquid out of thawed frozen spinach.

Mash and sieve the cauliflower or purée it in a food processor or liquidiser. Finely chop or purée the fresh spinach.

Beat the sauce and breadcrumb mixture and discard the bay leaf. Add a third of the sauce to each of the vegetables. Beat the curd cheese into the carrot mixture. Add seasoning to taste, then beat in 1 egg. Place the mixture in the loaf tin and smooth it with the back of a wetted metal spoon.

Beat the crumbled cheese into the cauliflower mixture, then season it to taste before beating in 1 egg. Spread this over the carrot mixture in the tin and smooth the top.

SEE ALSO **Pâte**: Glossary

Finally, add a little grated nutmeg and seasoning to taste to the spinach mixture before beating in an egg. Spread this in the tin. Top with a piece of greased greaseproof paper and cover with foil. Stand the loaf tin in the roasting tin, then pour in boiling water to come just below the rim of the roasting tin. Bake the terrine for 2¼ hours, or until it feels firm in the middle. Uncover the terrine for the final 30–40 minutes. Leave it to stand, covered, for 5 minutes. If serving cold, leave to cool completely, then chill it for at least 2 hours.

Slide a knife around the inside of the tin to loosen the vegetable terrine. Cover the top of the tin with a flat platter and invert the tin on it – hold both plate and tin with a large ovenglove if hot. Carefully lift off the tin, then peel the greaseproof paper off the top of the terrine and serve at once. Use a large serrated knife to slice the terrine and hold a spatula or fish slice against the end of the terrine to catch and lower each slice in turn. This prevents the layers from falling apart in each slice.

CHICKEN LIVER PATE

INGREDIENTS
225 g/8 oz chicken livers
75 g/3 oz unsalted butter
1 large clove garlic, crushed
6 juniper berries, crushed
15 ml/1 tablespoon chopped onion
1.25 ml/¼ teaspoon ground mace
15 ml/1 tablespoon brandy
salt and pepper

FOOD VALUES:

TOTAL • PER PORTION
kcals: 1085 • 271
kJ: 4489 • 1122
protein: 47 g • 12 g
fat: 91 g • 23 g
carbohydrate: 11 g • 3 g
fibre: 1 g • 0g

Serves 2–4

Thaw the chicken livers if they are frozen, then remove any membranes from around them and trim off any sinews. Cut the livers into small pieces. Place them on a clean plate, then thoroughly wash your hands, all utensils and the work surface.

Melt the butter in a frying pan or saucepan. Add the garlic, juniper berries and onion, then cook for about 5 minutes, stirring, or until the onion is beginning to soften. Add the livers and mace, then cook them gently for 15 minutes, or until all the pieces are cooked. Stir occasionally during cooking, then leave the livers to cool slightly.

Blend the liver mixture to a purée in a liquidiser or food processor, scraping all the butter from the pan. Stir in the brandy and seasoning to taste. Divide the mixture between 2 ramekins or 4 small pots (or place in one dish) and smooth the top. Cover and allow to cool, then chill for several hours or overnight.

MICROWAVE METHOD
Place the prepared livers, butter, garlic, onion, juniper and mace in a covered dish and cook on High for 5–6 minutes, stirring once. Leave to stand, covered, for 3 minutes. Check that the livers are cooked, then continue as above.

Coarse meat or poultry terrines or pâtés should be full flavoured. Serve them with crusty bread and a salad for a light meal.

Vegetables and Pulses These can be simple or elaborate. Some vegetables such as carrots, parsnips and cauliflower make delicious pâtés. Cook and mash or purée them, then mix with soft cheese, herbs and garlic. Stronger cheese, such as Stilton or mature Cheddar, may be finely grated and mixed with the vegetables – add the cheese to the hot vegetables and beat well until smooth.

Layered vegetable terrines may be served hot or cold. If served hot, Tomato Sauce (page 263) or Mushroom Sauce (page 234) are good accompaniments.

Lentils and chick peas make nutty pâtés which may be flavoured with herbs and spices.
Fruit Strawberries, orange segments, star fruit, mango, peaches and kiwi fruit may all be used.

Layer the fresh fruit in a loaf tin, setting each layer in clear jelly before adding the next.

Fruit terrines may also be made by setting purées, either with gelatine or by cooking them in a custard.

Storing Pâtés and Terrines

Keep pâtés and terrines in a covered dish on a low shelf in the refrigerator. Use fish and poultry pâtés within 1–2 days of making. Meat and game pâtés should be used within 3 days.

Using and Serving Pâtés and Terrines

• Serve small portions as a first course with hot toast, melba toast*, warmed butter biscuits or Bath Oliver biscuits, thinly sliced wholemeal or rye bread and butter or chunks of crusty bread.

• Serve with salad.

• Use as a filling for sandwiches or spread on open sandwiches and canapés.

Freezing

Pâtés and terrines may be frozen but their texture is inferior on thawing. Rich, fine chicken liver pâté freezes reasonably successfully for short periods (2–3 weeks) but others tend to be watery and grainy when thawed.

Tuna Pâté

Drain a 200 g/7 oz can tuna in brine. Pound the fish to a paste using a mixing spoon or blend it in a liquidiser or food processor. Mix in a crushed clove garlic, the grated rind of ½ lemon, 30 ml/2 tablespoons lemon juice and freshly ground black pepper. Add 30 ml/2 tablespoons chopped spring onion and 225 g/8 oz curd cheese. Mix the ingredients well, then taste the mixture for seasoning and lemon juice – you may have to add a little salt. Press the pâté into a dish. Cover and chill for at least 2 hours. Serve with hot toast or warmed water biscuits.

Canned sardines, smoked mackerel, smoked salmon or smoked trout may be used instead of tuna. Cooked unsmoked mackerel or salmon may also be used to make delicious pâté.

Peaches

See Fruit*.
Peaches and nectarines come from the same family. They are available during the summer, from May to August, sometimes at Christmas.

Buying

Fruit that is green or yellow-green and hard is not ripe. Look for unblemished fruit which has a good colour but is not very dark and soft. When buying cartons of peaches, check that the fruit in the bottom are not squashed.

PORK PATE

INGREDIENTS
4 bay leaves
12 rindless streaky bacon rashers
675 g/1 ½ lb belly of pork
225 g/8 oz pig's or lamb's liver
1 large onion, chopped
3 cloves garlic, crushed
2 thick slices fresh bread
10 ml/2 teaspoons ground coriander
5 ml/1 teaspoon ground mace
5 ml/1 teaspoon chopped fresh thyme or 2.5 ml/ ½ teaspoon dried thyme
10 ml/2 teaspoons chopped fresh sage or 5 ml/ 1 teaspoon dried sage

150 ml/¼ pint red wine
30 ml/2 tablespoons brandy
2.5 ml/½ teaspoon salt
freshly ground black pepper

FOOD VALUES:
TOTAL • PER PORTION
kcals: 5147 • 643
kJ: 21333 • 2667
protein: 260 g • 33 g
fat: 410 g • 51 g
carbohydrate: 66 g • 8 g
fibre: 7 g • 1 g

Serves 8

Set the oven at 160°C, 325°F, gas 3. Prepare a roasting tin and a kettle of boiling water. Lightly grease a 1 kg/2 lb loaf tin and arrange the bay leaves on its base. Stretch 8 bacon rashers by pressing them out firmly using the blade of a kitchen knife. Do this on a board, using a spreading action as you run the knife firmly along the length of the rashers. Line the tin with the rashers, overlapping them neatly, leaving any extra overhanging.

Trim the rind off the pork and remove any bones, then cut the meat into chunks. Trim any sinews and membrane off the liver, then cut it into chunks. Roughly chop the remaining bacon rashers and place them in a large frying pan with the onion and garlic. Cook gently, stirring, until the fat runs from the bacon. Continue cooking until the onion is just beginning to soften – it does not have to be well cooked at this stage. Remove the pan from the heat and allow the onion mixture to cool slightly.

Mince the pork, liver and onion mixture in batches until smooth. Put the mixture through a coarse blade first, then through a fine blade. For a coarse pâté, mince the pork or process it until reduced to a coarse mixture. Finely chop the bacon and liver. The onion mixture may be left chopped.

Mince or process the bread to crumbs last. Mix the coriander, mace, thyme and sage with the pork, liver, bacon, breadcrumbs and onion. Stir in the wine, brandy, salt and plenty of pepper.

Spoon the pâté into the prepared tin, making sure all the corners are filled. Fold any overhanging bacon rashers over the top of the pâté. Cover the top with greased greaseproof paper and foil, then stand the pâté in the roasting tin and pour boiling water into the tin to just below the rim.

Bake the pâté for 2½ hours, topping up the water as necessary. When cooked, the pâté should be firm and darkened. Leave to cool, still covered. When cool, press the pâté under a heavy weight – weights from kitchen scales are ideal. Chill overnight.

Slide a knife between the pâté and the tin, then turn it out. If the pâté does not come out, hold the tin over the hob for a few seconds.

SEE ALSO **Paupiette:** Glossary; **Pawpaw:** Fruit – exotic; **Peanuts:** Nuts; **Pearl Barley:** Barley

Storing

Under-ripe fruit will soften if left in a warm room for a few days. Fresh peaches and nectarines keep for 2–3 days.

Preparation

Wash the fruit under cold water and pat dry with absorbent kitchen paper.
Peeling Place the peaches in a bowl, then pour on freshly boiling water to cover them. Leave for 1 minute, then slit the peel with the point of a knife and it should slide off easily.
Stoning Cut the fruit all around into the stone, then twist the 2 halves and they come apart. Hook the stone out of one half using the point of a knife.
Slicing Wedge-shaped slices may be cut in as far as the stone and removed easily when the fruit is ripe.

Use

● In savoury salads – good with cooked chicken or ham.

● With grilled gammon, cooked ham or roast pork.

● Pickle peeled peaches in sweetened spiced vinegar*. Good with cold cooked meats.

● To make chutney, mix half and half with apples for economy.

● Bottle peaches in neat brandy or vodka, sweetened with honey or sugar.

● In fruit salad.

● Serve with Vanilla Ice Cream (page 157) and Melba Sauce (page 224) to make peach Melba.

● Stuff with crushed almond macaroons mixed with whipped cream.

● Poach peaches in a light syrup mixed in equal quantities with port. Not a dessert for drivers.

● Fill flans, gâteaux or tarts.

● Puré and use to flavour ice cream*, mousse* or soufflé*.

Freezing

Peeled peaches may be frozen in syrup* for up to a year. However, their texture on thawing is not good.

Puréed peaches may be frozen for making soufflés, mousses and other desserts.

Nutritional Value

Both peaches and nectarines contain vitamin A as well as some vitamin C.

Pears

See Fruit.

Buying

Available all year. British fruit is best in autumn months.
Conference These are long and tapering with a yellow-green skin and firm flesh that is tender but coarse. Very juicy and sweet.
Comice Large pears with yellow skin speckled with brown. The creamy-white flesh is tender, aromatic and juicy.
Cooking Pears These are slim, firm pears that soften on cooking.

Preparation and Storage

Wash the fruit and dry it on absorbent kitchen paper. Store pears in a cool dry room. Eat ripe fruit quickly, firm fruit may be kept for 3–5 days.

Peel pears from the stalk end down to the wide end. Either cut them in half and use the point of a knife to cut out the core, or cut out the core from underneath. Removing the core from underneath leaves the fruit looking whole and it may be stuffed before baking. Leave the stalk on the whole fruit for poaching or baking as it improves the appearance.

Pears discolour quickly once cut. Toss them in a little lemon juice to prevent, or delay, discoloration.

Use

● Stuff pear halves with soft cheese and chives.

● Top pear halves with Stilton cheese and grill until bubbling.

● Add diced pears to savoury salads. Good in green salad.

● Poach whole peeled and cored pears in red wine with sugar to taste until just soft. Transfer the pears to a serving dish. Boil the wine and sugar until reduced and syrupy, then pour it over the fruit as a glaze.

● Add poached or ripe uncooked pears to fruit salad.

● Use to make chutney – wonderful with plenty of fresh root ginger. Substitute chopped pears for apples in Apple Chutney (page 12) and add 100 g/4 oz grated fresh root ginger, 1 diced green pepper and a chopped green chilli.

Nutritional Value

Pears provide potassium, vitamins A and C and some fibre.

Peas

See Mange Tout and Vegetables*.* Available from mid-June to October, peas are a good pick-your-own crop.

Buying

Look for bright, plump pods that are firm and juicy. Avoid very large, dull or wrinkled pods.

Storing and Freezing

Use on the same day as purchased or as picking. They may be frozen for up to a year.

Preparation

Hold a pod over a colander or bowl, then bend it to snap it open. Run a finger through the inside of the pod to push out the peas. Wash the peas well.

As a guide, 450 g/1 lb peas in pods yield about 175 g/6 oz shelled peas, enough to serve 2.

Cooking

Boiling Place the peas in a pan and add cold water to cover them. Add a sprig of mint, if liked, and bring to the boil. Reduce the heat, part cover the pan and simmer for about 15 minutes or until the peas are tender.

Steaming Put the shelled peas in a steamer and cook over boiling water for 20–25 minutes.

Using and Serving

- Toss with chopped fresh parsley, chopped spring onion and butter.

- Add to braised duck or duck casserole.

- Mash peas, mix them with seasoning, some chopped fresh parsley and spring onion, then bind with fresh breadcrumbs and soured cream or fromage frais. Shape into small patties, coat in egg and breadcrumbs and bake or fry until golden. A good vegetarian main course.

- Toss peas with freshly cooked pasta and some chopped cooked ham.

- Braise with sautéed onion and canned tomatoes.

Nutritional Value

Peas contain protein, carbohydrate, vitamins A, B1, B2 and folate; fibre and vitamin C when fresh (or good-quality frozen).

Pectin

Pectin is a binding substance found in the cell walls of plants and fruit, particularly in the skin, pips and pith. It is extracted from the fruit by boiling. When combined with the right proportions of sugar and acid, pectin causes sweet preserves to set.

Pectin Content of Fruit

This varies according to type. All fruit trimmings should be tied in scalded muslin and boiled with fruit for making preserves to extract the maximum amount.
Good Sources Apples (particularly cooking and crab apples), citrus fruit, gooseberries, blackcurrants and redcurrants.
Moderate Sources Plums, greengages, raspberries and apricots.
Poor Sources Rhubarb, strawberries, pears, cherries and blackberries.

Pectin Test

The cooked fruit pulp may be tested for pectin content by placing a small spoonful in a jar containing 30 ml/2 tablespoons methylated spirit. Cover and shake well. If the pulp has a good pectin content it will form 1–2 large lumps or clots; a medium content will give several lumps; a poor content will result in lots of small lumps.

Exotic and Unusual Fruit

Many have a low or unknown pectin content; however those with a good flavour may be combined with apples or other high pectin fruit to make jams.

Peppers

See Vegetables*.
Also known as sweet peppers or capsicums, the most common are green or red; however other types include yellow, orange, deep purple (almost black) and white. Bottled or canned red peppers are known as pimento.

Buying

Peppers should be firm, bright and smooth. Avoid soft, wrinkled or bruised specimens.

Storing

Place in the salad drawer of the refrigerator or in a polythene bag on a high shelf. Good peppers keep well for up to a week.

Preparation Techniques

Deseeding Cut the peppers according to their use. For whole peppers, cut a slice off the top or cut around the stalk with the point of a knife. Do the same for pepper rings. For strips or chopped pepper, cut the vegetable in half lengthways, straight through the stalk. Cut out the core and all the white pith, along with the seeds. Wash the pepper well.
Cutting Techniques Slice whole peppers into rings. Cut halved peppers across into short, curved strips or lengthways for long strips.

To chop a pepper, halve it lengthways and cut it into long strips, then hold these together firmly and cut them across into small pieces.
Skinning The fine skin on peppers is removed by burning it off. Put the pepper under a hot grill and cook it until the skin blisters and is covered in blackened spots. Turn the pepper occasionally.

Hold the pepper under cold running water and scrape off the skin using a small kitchen knife.

Peeled peppers make a delicious salad – good enough just on their own with some olive oil, a sprinkling of cider vinegar and some chopped fresh parsley.
Stuffing The usual way is to cut off the tops, leaving the pepper whole, then to trim the base so that it stands firmly.

However, halving peppers vertically (with stalks on) makes boat shapes that are ideal for stuffing and this gives a better balance of pepper flesh to filling. Do not remove the stalk end or the pepper halves collapse on cooking. Carefully cut out all pith and seeds.

Use

- Fry chopped pepper with onion as the base for meat sauce or casseroles.

SEE ALSO **Peperoni:** Sausages; **Pepper:** Spices; **Persimmon:** Fruit – exotic; **Pestle and Mortar, Petits Fours:** Glossary;

- Use in Ratatouille (page 252).

- Add raw to salads.

- Stuff with meat, vegetable or rice filling and bake, covered, with a little stock until tender.

- Add to chutneys and pickles.

- Serve sticks of raw pepper with dips.

Freezing

Chopped peppers freeze very well without blanching for at least 6 months. Since the flesh tends to soften, the texture of the skin becomes more pronounced, therefore slices and rings do not have as good texture on thawing. This is less noticeable when the vegetables are chopped.

They may be used from frozen in cooked dishes but are not good enough for salads.

Nutritional Value

Peppers contain vitamins A and C, the red variety has ten times the amount of vitamin A as the green ones. They also contain traces of vitamins B1 and B2.

Pets and Pet Food

See Hygiene*.
Pets should be kept out of the kitchen. In practice this is not always possible but it is essential that both cats and dogs are trained never to jump on to work surfaces nor to steal food. Keep separate utensils for pet food.

Although a well trained pet may not be dirty, they carry micro-organisms and dirt on their coats and paws. They bring contaminants from the outside – from dustbin areas, the garden compost heap, drains and so on – and they carry bacteria from inside their own bodies from licking themselves. As well as causing contamination by rubbing against surfaces, animals shed hair or fur which causes contamination.

Pickles

See Vinegar*.
There are two main types of pickles. The first are foods preserved in vinegar. The second are chunky versions of chutneys, with distinct pieces of food in a cooked sauce.

Tips for Success

- Only pickle fruit and vegetables in prime condition.

- Salting is important to remove excess water and bitter juices from vegetables. Do not leave vegetables in salt for too long or they become soft.

- Always make sure jars are perfectly clean. If jars have been stored for long periods in dusty, dirty conditions they should be sterilised in a solution suitable for food use (as for wine making) or by boiling for 5 minutes after thorough cleaning.

- Pack pickles so that the jars are well filled but avoid squashing the ingredients.

- Tap the covered jars firmly on the work surface to loosen any air bubbles which may be trapped between the pieces of food – important with cabbage or other finely cut food.

- Check pickles after a day and top up the vinegar to cover them if necessary.

- Airtight covers should be plastic coated as any metal will react with the vinegar.

- Label pickles with the date and any notes about flavourings or sweetening added to the vinegar.

- Store pickles in a cool, dry, dark cupboard. If space allows, it is best to store opened jars in the refrigerator.

Plain Pickles

Apples Quarter, peel and core eating apples, then pickle them in sweetened spiced vinegar.

Beetroot Either pickle small whole beetroot or sliced larger vegetables. Place the hot, freshly cooked beetroot in clean jars, adding a little sliced onion. Top up with spiced vinegar, plain or sweetened. Good with a strip of orange rind added to each bottle. Store for 4–6 months.

Cabbage Use fresh red cabbage. Shred it coarsely and layer it in a bowl, sprinkling each layer with salt. Leave overnight, then rinse and drain the cabbage well. Pack it into clean jars and cover with spiced vinegar, plain or sweetened.

Cucumbers Small ridge cucumbers are available only during the late summer months. Wash and dry them, then trim off their stalks and prick the skins. Place the whole cucumbers in a bowl and sprinkle with salt (about 50 g/2 oz for each 450 g/1 lb). Leave overnight, then drain, rinse and dry them. Pack the cucumbers into clean jars, adding a slice of onion and a few sprigs of dill to each jar. Bring some sweetened spiced vinegar to the boil, then pour it into the jars to cover the cucumbers. Cover the jars at once.

Eggs Hard boil some small eggs and shell them. Place them in clean jars and top up with spiced vinegar to cover.

Eggs are delicious pickled in vinegar flavoured with curry spices. Add 30 ml/2 tablespoons cumin seeds, 15 ml/1 tablespoon ground turmeric, 10 split green cardamoms and 4 peeled cloves garlic to the vinegar with the other spices. Strain the vinegar through muslin or a coffee filter to remove the ground turmeric. Add a bay leaf to each jar of eggs. Allow eggs to spice for at least a week, then use them within 3 months of pickling.

Gherkins These are small ridge cucumbers. Process as for cucumbers above.

PICCALILLI

INGREDIENTS
2 large onions
225 g/8 oz carrots
2 celery sticks
350 g/12 oz cauliflower
  florets
50 g/2 oz salt
225 g/8 oz sugar
5 ml/1 teaspoon ground
  turmeric
15 ml/1 tablespoon English
  mustard powder
2.5 ml/½ teaspoon ground
  ginger
300 ml/½ pint white wine
  vinegar
30 ml/2 tablespoons plain
  flour

FOOD VALUES:
TOTAL • PER 15 ML/
  1 TABLESPOON
kcals: 1197 • 18
kJ: 5091 • 76
protein: 18 g • 0 g
fat: 5 g • 0 g
carbohydrate: 288 g • 4 g
fibre: 18 g • 0 g

Makes about 1 kg/2 lb

Prepare thoroughly cleaned warmed jars with airtight lids. Have a folded tea-towel to hold the jars and a jam funnel if available to fill the pots. You also need a large spoon to put the piccalilli into the pots.

Roughly chop the onions. Quarter the carrots lengthways, then cut them across into chunks. Halve the celery sticks lengthways, then cut them across into small pieces. Trim any leaves from the cauliflower; the florets should be small to medium and fairly even in size. Layer all the vegetables in a bowl, sprinkling them with salt, then cover and leave to stand overnight. Drain the vegetables well, rinse and dry them.

Mix the sugar, turmeric, mustard and ginger in a saucepan. Gradually pour in the vinegar, stirring all the time, and bring to the boil. Add all the vegetables, stir well to coat them in the spiced vinegar, then bring the mixture back to the boil. Reduce the heat to simmering and cook the vegetables uncovered for 7 minutes. They should be just tender.

Blend the flour to a smooth paste with a little water, then add a couple of spoonfuls of the hot liquid and stir well. Stir the flour paste into the piccalilli, bring to the boil and simmer for 5 minutes.

Pot the piccalilli at once, cover and tap the jars firmly to remove air bubbles. Label and leave the pickle to mature for a couple of days, although it may be eaten immediately. Use within 6–9 months.

Mixed Pickles Combine small cauliflower florets, onions, chunks of red pepper and fingers of celeriac. Salt the onions, cauliflower and celeriac together for 5–6 hours, then drain and rinse the vegetables. Dry them well and pack into clean jars with the pepper. Top up with spiced vinegar, sweetened or plain.
Onions Layer peeled pickling onions with salt, allowing about 50 g/2 oz salt to each 450 g/1 lb onions, and leave overnight. Drain, rinse and dry the onions, then pack into clean jars. Top up with spiced vinegar (any of the flavours given) and cover. Leave to mature for at least 2 weeks before eating. Best after about 1 month. Onions keep well for 6–9 months, after which time they tend to lose their crunch but are still acceptable up to a year.

Peaches Peel fresh, firm peaches that are just slightly under-ripe. Halve and stone them, then pack the fruit in clean jars and cover with sweetened spiced vinegar. Leave to mature for 2 weeks, then use within 4 months. Good with cold cooked meats or grilled gammon.

Pies

See Hot Water Crust Pastry*, Pastry*, Puff Pastry*, Short Crust Pastry* and other types of pastry.

A pie consists of a filling and a topping, usually a pastry covering. The term is also used for some dishes with a vegetable topping, typically cottage pie.

Pies differ from tarts in that they are deeper. Most pies do not have a pastry base; however, a double-crust pie is made in a deep dish which is lined with pastry.

Raised pies may be made using hot water crust pastry or short crusty pastry. Hot water crust must be used for pies that are moulded around the outside of a container, set, then filled. Short

Making a Pie
(Numbers refer to text steps)

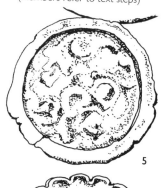

5

6

SEE ALSO **Pigeon:** Game; **Pikelet:** Drop Scones; **Pilaf:** Glossary; **Pilau, Pimento:** Glossary; **Pineapple:** Fruit – exotic;

crust may be substituted if the pastry is used to line a mould.

Making Pies

1. Roll out the pastry about 5 cm/2 inches larger than the top of the dish.

2. Trim off a strip of pastry, about 1–2.5 cm/½–1 inch wide from around the edges.

3. Dampen the rim of the pie dish, then press the strip of pastry on it.

4. Put a pie funnel in the middle of the dish, if necessary, to hold up the pastry if the filling is very moist.

5. Put the filling in the dish, then lift the pastry over the top and press it firmly around the rim to seal in the filling.

6. Trim, knock up and flute the edges. Make a hole in the middle of the pie to allow steam to escape. Use any pastry leftovers and trimmings to cut out leaves or other decorations for the top of the pie.

7. Glaze the top of the pie, using beaten egg for savoury pies or milk for sweet ones. Milk may also be used for savoury pies but it does not give as deep or as shiny a glaze.

Pizza

See Bread*.
True pizza, Italian style, should have a thin, crisp and bubbly base, with a full-flavoured and moist topping.

Making and Shaping a Pizza Base

1. Make up 1 quantity dough for Bread (page 46) and allow it to prove.

2. Grease 4 baking trays. Divide the dough into 4, then roll and stretch each portion into a 23–25 cm/9–10 inch round.

3. Set the oven at 240°C, 475°F, gas 9. Place the dough on the trays, cover with oiled polythene and leave for 5 minutes in a warm room before adding the topping. This allows the dough to rise slightly, giving a light pizza. When the topping is added, leave the dough for another 5 minutes before baking.

4. Bake for 15–20 minutes, until the pizza is crisp, golden and bubbling hot.

Pie Fillings

Almost any food may be covered with pastry and made into a satisfying meal. The following are a few basic suggestions, with quantities for a 1.1 litre/2 pint pie dish (or slightly larger) and to serve 4 people. Use short crust pastry* made with 225 g/8 oz flour.

Steak Filling

1. Heat 15 ml/1 tablespoon oil in a flameproof casserole. Add a chopped large onion and cook gently for 15 minutes, until softened.
2. Add 450 g/1 lb cubed braising steak and cook, stirring occasionally, until it is lightly browned.
3. Stir in 30 ml/2 tablespoons plain flour with a good sprinkling of seasoning. Add a bay leaf and 30 ml/2 tablespoons chopped fresh parsley. Gradually pour in 600 ml/1 pint beef stock and heat the mixture gently, stirring occasionally, until simmering.
4. Stir well, cover the casserole and simmer gently for

1½ hours. Taste for seasoning before cooling. Add 100 g/4 oz small button mushrooms. Use to fill the pie dish and cover with pastry.
5. Bake at 190°C, 375°F, gas 5 for 35–45 minutes.

Vegetable Filling

1. Peel and thickly slice 1 large potato, 2 medium carrots and 2 medium onions.
2. Place the vegetables in a saucepan and cover with cold water. Add a pinch of salt, then bring to the boil. Reduce the heat, cover the pan and simmer for 15 minutes. Drain, reserving the cooking liquid and returning it to the pan.
3. Trim and thickly slice 2 medium courgettes. Bring the liquid back to the boil, then add 100 g/4 oz frozen peas. Bring the peas to the boil, cook for 1 minute at a fast boil, then add the courgettes.
4. Bring the water back to a full boil, cook for 30 seconds, then drain the vegetables and reserve 300 ml/½ pint water.
5. Layer the vegetables in the pie dish. Melt 25 g/1 oz butter

or margarine in a saucepan. Add 25 g/1 oz flour and cook for 1 minute, stirring, then add the reserved cooking water, stirring all the time.
6. Bring the sauce to the boil and cook for 2 minutes, until quite thick. Remove the pan from the heat. Beat in 225 g/8 oz low-fat soft cheese with herbs and garlic, then taste for seasoning. Pour the sauce over the vegetables and cover with pastry.
7. Bake at 190°C, 375°F, gas 5 for 35–45 minutes, or until golden.

Fruit Filling

1. Quarter, peel and core 450 g/1 lb cooking apples, then slice thinly.
2. Layer the apple slices in the pie dish, sprinkling them with 50 g/2 oz sugar and adding 4 cloves and 50 g/2 oz raisins between the layers.
3. Cover with pastry and glaze it with a little milk. Bake at 200°C, 400°F, gas 6 for 15 minutes, then reduce the heat to 180°C, 350°F, gas 4 and cook for a further 30 minutes.

Tomato Topping

Cook a finely chopped onion in 60 ml/4 tablespoons olive oil for 15 minutes, stirring occasionally. Add 2 crushed cloves garlic, 15 ml/1 tablespoon dried marjoram and 30 ml/2 tablespoons tomato purée. Stir in a 400 g/14 oz can chopped tomatoes and a little seasoning, then bring to the boil.

Reduce the heat and simmer for 20 minutes, or until the mixture is thickened slightly. Stir occasionally during cooking, then taste for seasoning before using.

Other Toppings

- Sliced button mushrooms.
- Roughly chopped drained canned anchovy fillets.
- Black olives – stoned are best.
- Drained canned tuna fish.
- Peeled cooked prawns and/or drained canned clams.
- Sliced spicy Italian sausage or peperoni.
- Diced mozzarella cheese – add this at the end as it will become brown and crisp at the same time keeping the topping below moist.

Alternative Bases

Scone Dough (page 240) may be used to make a thicker base. This type of pizza is cut into wedges to serve as it is more filling.

Bought packet bread dough or pizza base mix is good. Bought ready-made bases vary in quality; some are excellent.

Freezing

Part-cooked bases without topping freeze very well. Make them as before and bake the untopped dough for 5–7 minutes, until lightly browned, bubbly and firm. Cool, pack and freeze for up to 6 months.

Use the bases from frozen, adding the topping and baking as for fresh. They thaw rapidly and the topping cooks quickly.

Deep Pan Pizza

An American savoury, consisting of a thicker base and more topping than on an Italian pizza. Use ½ quantity Bread Dough (page 46) to line a 25 cm/10 inch loose-bottomed flan tin. The topping should fill the pizza. Bake at 220°C, 425°F, gas 7 for 30 minutes, until the bread and topping are cooked through. Serve cut into wedges.

Plums

See Fruit*.
There are many varieties of plums on sale most of the year; however UK grown fruit is in season from the end of July until early October. Red and yellow plums are available from August through to March, with Victoria plums coming in about late August to September time. Greengages, firm green plums with a good flavour for cooking and preserving, are usually available from August through to September.

Buying

Plums should be firm and unbruised with a faint bloom on the skin. Avoid soft or wrinkled fruit.

Storing

Under-ripe plums will ripen in 2–3 days in a warm room. Place ripe fruit at the top of the refrigerator for up to 2 days. Best used soon after purchase.

Preparation

Wash plums well and remove their stalks. Cut them in half, then twist the 2 halves apart. Remove the stone by cutting around it with the point of a knife.

Cooking

- Poach halved plums in light syrup for about 3–5 minutes, longer for hard fruit, until just tender but not squashy.

- Stew whole or halved fruit with a little water and a sprinkling of sugar. Cook gently with the lid on the pan for about 15–20 minutes, then sieve the fruit to remove the stones. Use the purée for making mousses and other desserts.

- Use halved plums as a filling for flans (mouthwatering in a pastry case enriched with ground walnuts, then topped with clear honey) or press them cut side down into a base of sweetened bread dough. Plums also make good pies and tarts.

- Sweet, ripe dessert plums are good in meringue cases or in fruit salad.

- Plums go well with rich savoury poultry or meat – for example, duck, pork or lamb.

- Use for jams and chutneys.

Freezing

Halved and stoned fruit may be frozen for up to a year. It is soft when thawed but useful for purées.

Nutritional Value

Some of the sweeter types have a fairly high calorific value. Fresh plums contain vitamin C, carotene and potassium.

Poaching

A moist, gentle cooking method. The food may be completely immersed or part covered in liquid. Poaching must not be confused with boiling which is a harsh cooking method.

Suitable for delicate foods, such as fish, eggs and poultry. The food and liquid may be heated together or the liquid may be brought just to simmering point before the food is added. This depends on the type of food. Eggs are added to the hot

---

SEE ALSO **Plaice:** Fish; **Plantain:** Bananas; **Pomegranate:** Fruit – exotic; **Porridge:** Oats; **Port-Salut:** Cheese

liquid so that they set in a neat shape; fish is heated in cold liquid as the skin tends to shrink and the flesh become mis-shaped if it is added to hot liquid. The cooking time may be short, as for fish, and the food may be allowed to cool in the poaching liquid.

X *When cooling food in poaching liquid, always leave it in the cooking pan with the lid on. As soon as the food is cool enough it must be transferred to the refrigerator.*

Pork

See Bacon and Ham* and Meat*.
The illustration shows the different cuts of meat (numbered) in relation to the carcass. The majority of pork is tender but some cuts require more trimming than others.

Neck End This includes the spare rib and blade, often sold as separate joints. These are economical joints and both may be trimmed, then cut up for stir frying, braising, casseroling or making into dishes such as sweet and sour pork.

Spare rib chops are ideal for grilling, frying or barbecuing. **(1)**
Hand and Spring A large cut from the front of the carcass, this is often separated into hand of pork and shank. Another cut which may be trimmed and used for braising, casseroling or for stir frying with careful preparation. **(2)**
Belly This is streaked with fat and lean. The spare ribs are sold separately for barbecues and grilling. The meat may be roasted, particularly Chinese style with five spice powder (see spices*), or used in pâtés as well as for mincing. **(3)**
Leg The fillet end is a prime roasting joint, while the knuckle or shank end needs more trimming but it is also good roasted. The knuckle end may be cubed and braised. Steaks may be cut off the fillet end. **(4)**

Cuts of Pork

Chump Cut into chops which are large and meaty; ideal for grilling. **(5)**
Loin On the bone or boned and rolled, this is an excellent roasting joint. It may be separated into chops for grilling or frying. **(6)**
Tenderloin This is the fillet of meat which lies under the ribs and backbone, the equivalent of the fillet of beef. A succulent piece of meat which may be sliced into medallions. **(7)**
Boneless Cuts Boneless cubed pork, minced pork, steaks and lean trimmed nuggets of meat are all available prepared for cooking. **(8)**

Buying, Storing and Cooking

See meat* for storing and cooking.

Pork meat is pale pink and it should be firm. The fat should be firm and white and the bone ends should be a pinkish blue colour. The meat itself looks moist when freshly cut.

Pork Crackling

The rind becomes a bubbly, crisp delicacy when roasted correctly. Ask the butcher to score the rind so that the joint is easy to carve. The scoring should take the form of fairly deep parallel cuts, with an occasional cut running in the opposite direction for easy carving.

Before roasting, brush the rind with a little oil and rub salt into it. Place the rind uppermost and cook the joint at a high temperature for the first 15 minutes so

that the rind has a chance to become crisp. For good crackling and a succulent roast, roll the rind on a hot, heavy-based frying pan until it begins to crackle, then roast it at the lower temperature (page 178).

Accompaniments

- Apple Sauce (page 11).

- Sage and Onion Stuffing (page 254).

- Rub caraway, crushed garlic and paprika into joints of pork before roasting (Polish style).

- Fruit such as peaches, plums and pineapple also go well with grilled cuts.

- Cranberry Sauce (page 93) also complements pork.

Potatoes

See Vegetables*.

Buying

Potatoes must be sold by variety rather than being labelled 'reds', 'whites' or 'new' potatoes. There are many varieties of early (new) and main crop (old) potatoes, including small vegetables with an excellent texture and flavour for salads. These tend to be more expensive and they are usually sold in small packs, labelled with cooking information and serving suggestions.

Check loose potatoes or packets for the quality of vegetables. Avoid those that are damaged, badly speckled with 'eyes' and any that are green.

Only buy main crop or old potatoes in bulk as new potatoes do not keep. Buy in bulk only if you have a suitable storage area.

Storing

The best place to store potatoes is a cool, dry out-house, clean garage or utility room. They should be kept in a closed brown paper bag. Larger quantities keep well in a double-thick brown bag, raised off the floor (on a piece of wood on a couple of bricks) to prevent it from getting damp. This way the potatoes will keep for about 4 months or longer. However, in moist, warm conditions they will become mouldy or begin to sprout.

When suitable storage conditions are not available, potatoes should be purchased in small quantities and eaten within a few days. Unless they are to be used within a couple of days, transfer vegetables from a plastic bag to a paper bag (a thick carrier bag or small cardboard box are both suitable).

X *Potatoes become green when they are stored in the light because they produce chlorophyll. Natural toxins, normally present in small, harmless amounts in good potatoes, develop: these toxins are present in and under the skin of green potatoes and they are also concentrated in areas that are sprouting. Proper storage is essential to prevent toxins from developing. Always cut off all green parts, eyes and any sprouts before cooking the potatoes.*

Varieties

New potatoes, or early and second early crops, have a firmer, more waxy texture than main crop vegetables. They also have thinner skins and a distinct flavour. They should be used within 2–3 days of purchase.

The texture of main crop potatoes varies according to their type, some are floury and ideal for baking but they tend to fall, or

break up on the outside, when boiled. Others have firm, waxy flesh that is ideal for boiling but not as 'fluffy' when baked. Larger supermarkets and green-grocers often label potatoes with notes on cooking quality.

Cara Large, white potatoes with a hint of pink around the eyes, these are suitable for baking. They tend to fall apart easily when boiled.

Desiree A red-skinned variety that is useful for all cooking methods.

Jersey New potatoes in the shops from Christmas or before, these are expensive but full flavoured. Scrub, then cook with skins on.

King Edward A good potato for all cooking methods. White skinned with a hint of pink, the flesh is white and quite floury. Particularly useful for boiling and mashing or baking.

Maris Piper A popular white main crop variety, with creamy flesh, that stands up to all cooking methods without discolouring or falling apart.

Pentland Crown Whites that are useful for baking but tend to fall apart on boiling and have a tendency to blacken after cooking.

Pentland Dell Whites for baking or for making chips. These are floury and tend to fall apart when boiled.

Pentland Squire Large potatoes well suited to baking.

Romano Reds suitable for all cooking methods, particularly baking.

Preparation

Wash or scrub well if cooked with peel on. Cut out eyes, blemishes, all green parts and surrounding flesh. Rinse under cold water, then cover with cold water until ready to cook. Best prepared just before cooking to prevent loss of nutrients by seepage into soaking water; however, it is useful to prepare potatoes in advance when cooking a special meal. Add a squeeze of lemon juice to the water to prevent discoloration.

Cooking

Boiling in Skins Place the whole potatoes in a saucepan and cover with cold water. Add a pinch of salt, if liked, then bring to the boil. Lower the heat so that the water is just boiling and cover the pan, allowing a little space for steam to escape (or open the vent in the lid).

Small new potatoes are tender after 10 minutes; medium ones take about 15 minutes.

Main crop potatoes take about 25 minutes when cooked in their skins; longer if they are large.

Boiling Peeled Cut large peeled potatoes in half or into quarters. The pieces should be roughly the same size for even cooking. Cover with cold water and add a pinch of salt if liked. Bring to the boil as above, then cook for about 20 minutes.

Boiling for Mashing If the potatoes are to be mashed, the boiling time may be reduced by cutting the vegetables into chunks (equivalent to 5 cm/2 inch cubes). Cook as above for about 10 minutes.

Baking Set the oven at 200°C, 400°F, gas 6. Prick the scrubbed potatoes several times to prevent the skin from bursting during cooking. Place them on a baking tray and brush very lightly with cooking oil. Small or medium potatoes take about 50 minutes; large potatoes are tender after 1¼–1½ hours.

Potatoes may be baked at other temperatures, for example, they may be cooked at the same time as a casserole, at a lower temperature for longer.

Roasting from Raw Halve medium potatoes or cut very large ones into quarters. Small potatoes should be peeled, then left whole. Add the potatoes to the roasting tin with the meat, turning them in the cooking fat and juices until coated all over. Alternatively, place them in a dish and trickle a little oil or melted fat over them.

At 190°C, 375°F, gas 5, allow about 1½ hours cooking time, turning the potatoes once or

Classic Potato Dishes

Croquettes Add some chopped parsley or snipped chives to very creamy mashed potatoes. Chill well, then shape into small cylindrical croquettes or fingers. Coat in flour, egg and breadcrumbs. Chill again before deep frying until golden.

Dauphinoise Layer thinly sliced potatoes in a shallow gratin dish and dot with butter. Cover and bake until part cooked (about 1 hour at 180°C, 350°F, gas 4, depending on quantity). Trickle single cream over, then continue cooking until the potatoes are tender and golden – another 30 minutes or so.

Duchesse Beat an egg into cold, smooth and creamy mashed potatoes (about 1 kg/2 lb uncooked). Pipe the potatoes in neat swirls on a greased baking tray. Brush lightly with egg yolk beaten with a little water. Bake at 200°C, 400°F, gas 6 for 20 minutes, or until golden. Serve at once.

Latkes Irresistible potato cakes. Peel and grate 675 g/ 1½ lb potatoes. Place in a sieve, rinse under cold water, then squeeze out the moisture. Place in a bowl and add 45 ml/3 tablespoons plain flour, salt and pepper, and 1 egg. Mix thoroughly. Drop spoonfuls into a little hot oil in a heavy-based frying pan and spread thinly into round cakes. Fry until golden, turn the cakes and cook the second sides until golden. Drain on absorbent kitchen paper. These freeze well.

Lyonnaise Cook 2 thinly sliced onions in butter until softened, about 20 minutes. Add 2 large sliced par-boiled potatoes and cook until onions and potatoes are lightly browned.

twice so they brown evenly. This method gives potatoes that are crisp outside and tender through, some may be soft and floury depending on variety.

Roasting Par-boiled This is suitable for waxy potatoes. Floury ones or those that fall easily will begin to disintegrate slightly on the outside during par-boiling.

Boil the peeled potatoes as left, for just 10 minutes. Drain them and dust immediately with a little seasoned plain flour. Add the potatoes to hot fat, straight from the oven. Either place them around a roast or heat the fat in a roasting tin or dish first. Baste the potatoes carefully (do not turn them and risk breaking them), then roast for 1–1¼ hours at 190°C, 375°F, gas 5, turning halfway through cooking.

Roasting New Potatoes Small whole new potatoes roast well in their skins. Boil them first, as left, for about 7 minutes, until they are almost tender. Place the drained potatoes in hot fat around a roast or in a separate dish. They are best cooked at 200°C, 400°F, gas 6 for about 30 minutes, so that their skins become crisp. Allow 40 minutes at a lower temperature. Turn once during cooking.

Chipping The potatoes may be peeled or they may be well scrubbed and cooked with peel on. Large, rounded potatoes are best for cutting into chips. Cut the potatoes into 1–2 cm/½–¾ inch thick slices, then cut these lengthways into chips. Wash the chips, then drain them well and pat them dry on double-thick absorbent kitchen paper.

Heat oil for deep frying to 190°C/375°F. Place the chips in cooking basket and lower them into the hot fat. Leave them for 30 seconds, then give the basket a shake and reduce the heat. Fry the chips for 5 minutes, or until they are tender and forming a skin but not crisp and brown.

Lift the chips from the oil and allow them to drain well. Heat the oil back to the original temperature, then lower the chips into it again and cook for a fur-

ther 5–8 minutes, or until they are crisp and golden. Drain well, then transfer to a dish lined with double-thick absorbent kitchen paper. Shake the paper under the chips to remove excess fat from them.

Chips may be part fried, then allowed to cool and left covered. The oil should be cooled. Fry the chips for the second time just before serving.

This double frying technique makes the chips light and crisp. Removing them from the oil allows it to reheat to the original cooking temperature.

Fried Potatoes Par-boil potatoes in their skins until almost tender – about 20 minutes for large ones. Drain the potatoes and remove their peel under gently running cold water. Cut into chunks or thick slices.

Heat a knob of butter with a little oil in a large, heavy-based or non-stick frying pan. Do this gently at first until the butter melts, then increase the heat until the butter begins to foam. Add the potatoes and cook them until they are crisp underneath, then turn them and cook the second side. Usually the potatoes have to be turned 2–3 times until they are very crisp and golden.

For sautéed potatoes, cut the vegetables into smaller pieces that cook quickly. Cook them in a small amount of fat over high heat, using a slice to turn them often. They should be lightly browned and slightly crisp, not as deep a colour or as crunchy as fried potatoes.

Microwave Cooking

The microwave is ideal for cooking whole potatoes in their skins and for small to medium quantities of unpeeled new potatoes. However, it cannot replace traditional boiling for cooking whole, halved or quartered peeled potatoes.

New Potatoes Place the prepared potatoes in a roasting bag or large dish. Add 60 ml/4 tablespoons water and cover the dish or loosely close the bag. Cook on

High, allowing 7–9 minutes for 675 g/1½ lb and rearranging the potatoes once.

Whole Potatoes The equivalent of baked potatoes. Place the scrubbed and pricked potatoes on double–thick absorbent kitchen paper as far apart as possible in the microwave. Cook on High for the following times, turning and rearranging once or twice.

1 – 7–8 minutes
2 – 12–14 minutes
3 – 15–18 minutes
4 – 20–22 minutes
(timings for 350 g/12 oz potatoes)

Serving Potatoes

Plain boiled potatoes may be topped with a knob of butter or margarine and sprinkled with chopped fresh parsley or mint, or snipped chives. For everyday meals, serve the potatoes plain, without additional fat.

Mashing Drain boiled potatoes, then return to the hot pan and mash them with a fork or potato masher. Add a knob of butter or margarine, plenty of white or black pepper (freshly ground is best for flavour) and beat well. When the butter has melted, add a little milk to soften the potatoes and beat again. The potatoes should be smooth and creamy.

Puréed Potatoes Press mashed potatoes through a sieve or through a food mill. With care, a food processor may be used but it is very easy to overprocess potatoes and end up with a waxy mixture. For a soft purée, add hot milk or warmed cream.

Potato Salad Boil large potatoes in their skins or cook small whole new potatoes in their skins.

Peel and cube old potatoes; leave small new ones whole. The potatoes may be dressed with oil and vinegar or Mayonnaise (page 175). Pour all the oil and vinegar dressing over the hot potatoes and mix well, then cover and cool. If using mayonnaise, toss 15 ml/1 tablespoon light oil (sunflower, safflower or grapeseed) or olive oil over the potatoes and mix well without

breaking them up. Cover and cool, then add the mayonnaise.

Snipped chives, chopped fresh parsley, roughly chopped black olives, toasted flaked almonds or salted cashew nuts all perk up plain potato salad.

Freezing

Uncooked potatoes do not freeze well. Croquettes and latkes freeze successfully.

Nutritional Value

Fresh new potatoes are a good source of vitamin C. Main crop vegetables also provide a valuable supply because of the quantity in which they are eaten. Potatoes also provide iron, calcium, vitamin B1, nicotinic acid and dietary fibre.

Pot Roasting

This is a method of roasting in a covered container. Joints of meat or whole poultry are cooked on a bed of cut vegetables (such as onion, carrot, turnip, leek and swede) in a covered casserole. The meat is dotted with fat and a little water may be sprinkled over the vegetables during cooking to keep them moist. The cooking is long and slow, suitable for braising cuts as well as roasting joints.

The vegetables are used to flavour a sauce or gravy. They may be left in the sauce or, more often, sieved out.

Poultry

See Chicken*, Duck*, Goose* and Turkey*.

The majority of poultry is more tender than meat, the exception being boiling chickens. Chicken and turkey must be cooked throughly before serving; however duck breast is sometimes served pink rather than well done; goose is cooked long and slow for succulent tender results.

The following preparation techniques may be used on all poultry and larger game birds, such as pheasant.

Cuts

Quarters Two leg and thigh joints and 2 wing and breast joints from each bird. Turkey and goose are too large to be treated in this way.

Halves Duck, poussin and pheasant are often served halved, allowing one half per portion.

Part-boned Breast This includes the boneless breast meat with wing joint attached. Mainly chicken.

Drumsticks Chicken or turkey, the latter being large and fairly tough if not slow roasted.

Wings Chicken wings are popular coated in a flavoursome marinade or basting sauce, then grilled until crisp.

Thighs Small, meaty portions of chicken with a small central bone.

Boneless Breast Chicken, turkey and duck breast are all popular. Whole turkey breast makes a substantial roast.

Breast Fillets Of chicken, duck or turkey. These are usually fairly slim slices that are ideal for coating and frying, grilling or cutting into strips and stir frying.

General Preparation

Remove giblets from a whole bird. If they are included they are usually found in a bag in the body cavity.

Trim off wing and leg ends and cut off any obvious lumps off fat from the opening to the body cavity. Rinse the body cavity under cold running water and wash the bird, then drain it well. Dry the bird on absorbent kitchen paper.

Check that all feathers have been removed and singe off any hairs or tiny feathers.

Giblet Stock The giblets may be used for making stock along with trimmed off leg or wing ends. Place these in a saucepan with a

SEE ALSO **Potato, Sweet**: Vegetables – exotic

sliced onion, bay leaf and sliced carrot, cover with water and simmer, covered, for 1 hour. Strain and use for gravy.

Trussing

Fold the flap of neck skin under the bird. Make a small slit into the skin under the body cavity at the tail end, opposite the vent (parson's nose). Push the vent through the slit in the skin to keep the body cavity neatly closed.

Using a Trussing Needle

1. Thread the needle with sufficient string to wrap around the bird and to tie. Insert the needle through the one wing, near the body. Pass the needle into the body and out through the flap of neck skin. Insert the needle again and pull it out through the opposite wing, in the same position as on the first side.

2. Thread the needle back into the end of the wing joint, body and through the end of the first wing. Tie the ends of the string, making sure the wings are held firmly and neatly against the body.

3. Thread the needle again. Hold the drumsticks vertical and insert the needle through one drumstick, at the thick part and close to the body, then push it right through the bird and out through the opposite drumstick.

4. Take the string and wrap one end around each leg, then tie the ends together over the vent.

Tying with String

1. If you do not have a trussing needle, cut a length of string to go around both ends of the bird and to cross underneath. Place the bird breast down and lay the string over the flap of neck skin, with equal lengths on either side. Wrap the ends around the wings, then turn the bird over.

2. Make sure the wings are neatly in place, pull the ends of the string underneath them and

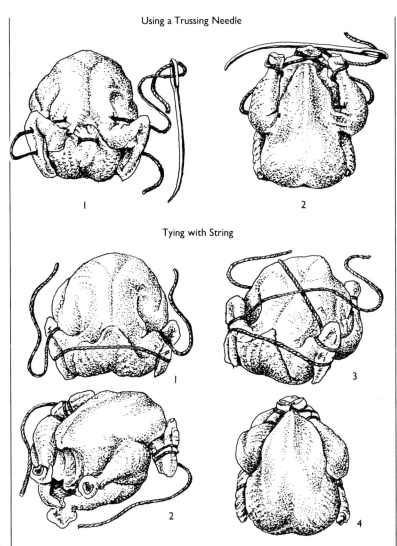

Using a Trussing Needle

Tying with String

turn the bird over. Cross the string under the body and bring it up around the legs.

3. Turn the bird breast uppermost and wrap the string around the leg ends, then tie it firmly.

Spatchcock

1. Place the bird breast down. Using a sharp pointed knife, cut through the flesh and bone along the length of the bird. Do not cut the bird completely in half.

2. Separate the two halves to open out the body of the bird.

3. Turn the bird over, opening the body out flat, then use the

heel of your hand to flatten it firmly along the breast. Thread 2 long skewers horizontally through the bird to keep it flat.

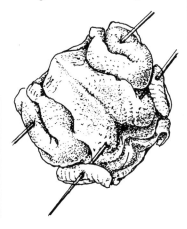

Halving

1. Prepare the bird as for a spatchcock, without flattening it. With breast down, separate the 2 halves, then cut through the breast bone, from the body cavity outwards.

2. Separate the 2 halves, then trim off the back bone and any small pieces of bone.

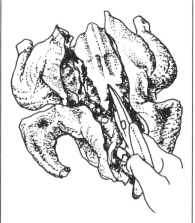

Cutting Quarter Portions

1. Halve the bird. Make sure the back bone and breast bone are removed by cutting them free using scissors and a knife.

2. Take one half and use kitchen scissors or poultry shears to cut through the skin and flesh around the main portion of breast meat. This makes 2 portions – the breast and wing in one portion; the leg and thigh in the second portion. Repeat with the remaining half.

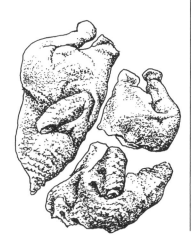

Boning a Bird

You need a sturdy board, a fine-bladed, sharp cook's knife and plenty of time to bone out a whole bird. It is not difficult but a little fiddly until you have practised a couple of times.

It is important to avoid tearing the skin as it must be kept whole to keep the bird in good shape after boning and stuffing.

By far the easier option is to find a good small butcher who will bone out a chicken for you as long as you give advance notice.

1. Place the bird breast down on a board. Cut through the skin and flesh down to the bone from vent to neck end. Cut off the parson's nose.

2. Work on one side first. Gently ease the point of the knife between the flesh and bones, scraping at the bone as you slip the knife under the flesh. As you loosen a piece, hold it away from the carcass as you are cutting.

3. Continue working down the carcass, under the breast flesh and towards the breast bone. Leave the flesh attached to the end of the breast bone.

4. Removing the flesh from the legs and wings is rather like turning the sleeve of a jumper inside

out. First, carefully cut through sinews and scrape the flesh off the joints – a pair of kitchen scissors is useful for this. When the flesh is loosened at the joints, pull the bones out and turn the flesh and skin inside out towards the tip of the bones. Snip the flesh and skin at the ends of the wing and leg if necessary.

5. When all the flesh is removed from one side of the carcass, turn the bird around and do exactly the same on the second side. You should end up with the boneless flesh joined to the carcass along the breast bone.

6. Carefully cut the flesh off the breast bone, taking the finest sliver of bone to avoid breaking the skin.

7. Use the bones for making stock. Turn the joint flesh and skin the right side out. Spread the boned bird out flat and pile or arrange stuffing down the middle over the breast meat. Fold the sides (flesh and skin) over the stuffing, then sew their ends together to seal in the stuffing.

8. Turn the bird over and place it in a roasting tin or foil for cooking. Plump it neatly into shape. The leg flesh may be skewered together at one end to plump up the breast flesh.

Boning a Bird (Numbers relate to text steps)

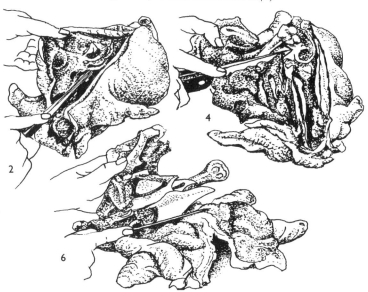

SEE ALSO **Praline:** Caramel

Prawns and Shrimps

Prawns are larger than shrimps; however, the American term 'shrimp' is used for prawns, usually the very large type.

Buying

Large prawns may be known as Mediterranean, king or jumbo prawns.

Shrimps look like small prawns and they are usually sold cooked with their shells. Brown are sometimes available.

Prawns and shrimps are usually cooked immediately after they are caught, the exception being the larger types which are available frozen raw, with or without their shells. Most prawns and shrimps, particularly peeled types, have been frozen.

Use

Use fresh or thawed shellfish on the same day as purchase. Frozen shellfish are usually frozen in a thin coat of ice. Thaw them in a covered dish in the refrigerator, then drain them well and pat dry on absorbent kitchen paper.

Use cooked shellfish in salads, savoury flans, stir fries, risottos, curries and mixed seafood dishes. Uncooked prawns are delicious in cooked dishes. Do not overcook prawns and shrimps as they toughen. Add cooked shellfish to hot dishes towards the end of the cooking time, reheat thoroughly but do not boil.

To Peel Prawns and Shrimps

Hold the head and tail ends, then pull off the head. Remove the shell from underneath, slipping it off sideways, then remove the tail. Remove the black intestinal vein which runs down the back (on larger shellfish).

Pressure Cooking

This cooking method works on the principle that water boils at a higher temperature under pressure.

At sea level, the boiling point of water is 100°C/212°F. At greater altitude (therefore less atmospheric pressure) the boiling point of water is lower. In some countries, in areas of high altitude, foods take longer to cook, notably dried beans. Therefore if the pressure is increased, the boiling point of water is higher and the cooking time is shorter.

A pressure cooker is a sealed cooking pot. The escape of steam produced by water during cooking is carefully controlled by a weight which is attached to a vent in the lid of the cooker. This means that the pressure in the cooker is raised and that the water boils at a higher temperature.

Advantages of Pressure Cooking

● Cooking times are short; for example, some dried beans cook in about 5 minutes after brief pre-soaking, and tougher stewing meat is succulent after 20 minutes rather than 2 hours by traditional methods.

● The saving in cooking time saves fuel.

● The volume of food does not determine the cooking time. The shape and size of the pieces of food alter the cooking time but adding more food does not increase the time. This is useful when cooking for large numbers.

● The pressure cooker may be used for cooking a wide variety of foods, including fish, poultry, meat, vegetables, rice and delicate dishes such as custards.

● It may also be used for making preserves that require long boiling by traditional methods, such as chutney, and for softening fruit rind when making marmalade.

Pressure Options

The majority of modern pressure cookers operate at 15 lb pressure, the equivalent of High in some older models. Some models still have variable pressures and others operate only at low pressure – always check these details before purchase as a cooker which operates at low pressure does not perform well for all types of cooking, for example for tenderising tough meats or cooking pulses quickly.

High Pressure This gives a pressure of 15 lb (per square inch) and a cooking temperature of 121°C/250°F. It is the most popular pressure and most versatile for tenderising food and speed.

Use for meat, poultry, fish, dried beans and pulses (soak for 1 hour first), heavier steamed puddings, chutneys, vegetables, rice, soups and stock. Surprisingly, Set Custard (page 102) cooks well at this pressure. Allow about 5 minutes for a 600 ml/1 pint milk mixture placed in a suitable dish and covered tightly with foil.

Medium Pressure Usually 10 lb with an internal temperature of 115°C/239°F, this is not widely used but it can be useful for softening tender fruit for making jam or for other foods that may overcook easily.

Low An internal temperature of 108°C/227°F and 5 lb pressure make this suitable for light sponge puddings that tend to separate at high pressure. However, this is not used for the majority of cooking.

Safety Points

● Always read and follow the manufacturer's instructions.

● The pressure cooker must contain sufficient water to provide steam during cooking as well as to prevent the pan from boiling dry.

● Never operate the pressure cooker with the lid on with less than 300 ml/½ pint water (or an equivalent liquid to produce steam) for the first 15 minutes. For each additional 15 minutes cooking time make sure there is an extra 150 ml/¼ pint liquid.

● Never overfill the pressure cooker:

It should not be more than two thirds full when cooking solid foods in liquid (large pieces of meat or vegetables).

No more than half full when cooking liquid foods such as soup, stock, stews or rice.

No more than one third full when cooking foods that froth up, such as milky mixtures, cereals and pulses.

● Always make sure that the vents and safety outlets are clean and clear; that the seal is in place and that the lid is fitted correctly.

● Make sure the weight is correctly in place.

● Make sure that any foil or paper covering on food is secured so that it cannot rise and block the vent in the lid during cooking.

Cooking Under Pressure

● Follow the manufacturer's instructions for cooking different foods, taking particular note of the weight or setting to use to ensure success.

● Use suitable containers that withstand the temperature. Ovenproof glassware and dishes, foil containers and tins are all suitable. Containers that are designed for holding boiling water are not necessarily suitable as the temperature in a pressure cooker is higher than normal. As a guide, containers should be able to withstand temperatures up to 130°C/266°F.

● In some cases, a period of pre-steaming may be necessary before the cooker is brought to pressure. Do this with the lid on but without the weight in position. This is used when cooking mixtures containing raising agent, to allow time for the raising agent to work before the other ingredients set.

● When cooking foods that are likely to froth up, bring to pressure over medium heat.

● When the cooker comes to pressure, reduce the heat so that the pressure is just maintained.

● Check whether the pressure should be reduced quickly or slowly for the food being cooked. If the steam is allowed to escape slowly the food continues to cook. In some cases, if the steam is released quickly the food may collapse, froth or burst.

● To reduce pressure slowly, the cooker should be removed from the heat and allowed to stand until the pressure indicator has dropped completely. In some cases, fast pressure release means holding the cooker under cold running water to rapidly reduce the temperature. This normally causes a high-pitched whining noise. Always follow the manufacturer's instructions or a reputable specialist cookbook.

● Automatic pressure cookers have built in timers which allow the steam to escape at the end of the pre-set cooking time. Before beginning to cook, check whether the steam should be allowed to escape quickly or slowly.

Protein

See Balanced Diet*.
Protein is essential for building and maintaining the body. It must be contained in adequate quantity and quality in the diet.

Amino Acids

Proteins are complicated nutrients, made up of amino acids. The quality of any one protein depends on the type and number of amino acids that it contains.

Essential Amino Acids An adult's diet must include 8 essential amino acids; a growing child must have a regular supply of these plus an additional amino

acid. These cannot be manufactured by the body.

Non-essential Amino Acids These are also present in protein foods but they can be manufactured by the body if necessary.

Animal and Vegetable Proteins: Sources of Supply

Proteins can be roughly separated into 2 groups, animal and vegetable.

Animal proteins contain all 8 essential amino acids, whereas a single vegetable protein food may not provide all the amino acids. Animal proteins are found in fish, poultry, meat and dairy produce (eggs, milk, cheese and so on).

Vegetable proteins are acquired mainly from beans and pulses, nuts and cereals).

Combining Proteins

The amino acids lacking in one protein may be obtained from another food. So it is important to combine different protein foods.

Vegetarian Diets* Combining different sources of protein is vital in a vegetarian diet, which does not rely on animal proteins that contain all the necessary amino acids. A regular supply of foods such as rice, nuts, pulses and dairy produce is essential.

Vegan Diet A vegan diet, which totally excludes all animal products and makes very selective use of vegetables and cereals, may well be lacking in essential amino acids. This sort of diet should not be followed without very careful planning and consideration of the problems of obtaining nutrients, not only proteins but vitamins, iron and other nutrients. Such a diet must not be imposed on infants and growing children.

Balancing Animal and Vegetable Proteins Even in a diet which includes animal protein, the presence of a broad variety of vegetable sources ensures that the body obtains a good mixture

SEE ALSO **Prickly Pear:** Fruit – exotic

STEAMED SPONGE PUDDING

INGREDIENTS
**100 g/4 oz margarine or
    butter**
100 g/4 oz caster sugar
2 eggs
175 g/6 oz self-raising flour

Serves 6

FOOD VALUES:
TOTAL • PER PORTION
kcals: 1874 • 312
kJ: 7858 • 1310
protein: 29 g • 5 g
fat: 95 g • 16 g
carbohydrate: 241 g • 40 g
fibre: 7 g • 1 g

Grease a 1.1 litre/2 pint boilable pudding basin. Cut a piece of greaseproof paper and make a wide pleat in the middle of it, then grease it well. It should be large enough to cover the top of the basin when pleated. Cut and pleat a piece of cooking foil. Have ready a large saucepan two-thirds full of water and a steamer to hold the basin. Set the water to boil. Cut a long strip of foil and fold it double – this will be used for lifting the pudding out of the steamer.

Cream the margarine or butter with the sugar in a bowl until pale and soft. Beat in the eggs, then fold in the flour. Turn the mixture into the basin. Cover the top with the greaseproof, then with the foil. Tie the cover securely in place or fold and crumple the foil firmly around the edge of the basin to seal the cover and exclude steam. Stand the basin on the strip of foil, then place it in the steamer and put on the lid.

Steam the pudding over boiling water for 1¾–2 hours, or until it is risen and firm to the touch. Top up the water in the pan under the steamer occasionally, adding boiling water from the kettle.

Uncover the pudding and gently loosen it from the basin by inserting a knife part-way down the side. Put a plate over the top of the basin, then invert the basin on it. Give the basin and plate a firm shake to release the pudding, then lift off the basin. Serve piping hot, with Jam Sauce (page 238), Pouring Custard (page 103), warmed golden syrup or lemon curd.

VARIATIONS
Lemon Pudding Add the grated rind of 1 lemon when creaming the fat and sugar. Fold in the juice of 1 lemon after the flour. Stir 150 ml/¼ pint lemon curd and serve this with the pudding.
Jam Pudding Put 225 g/8 oz jam in the bottom of the basin first.
Fruit Pudding Add 100 g/4 oz mixed dried fruit to the mixture after folding in the flour.
Chocolate Pudding Weigh the flour, then remove 60 ml/4 tablespoons (return this to the packet). Add 60 ml/4 tablespoons cocoa powder to the flour and sift the mixture. Continue as above. Serve the pudding with Chocolate Sauce (page 235) or Brandy Sauce (page 235).

MICROWAVE METHOD
The pudding cooks extremely well in the microwave. The mixture rises rather alarmingly, so make half the above quantity and cook it in the same basin without the foil covering. Use a suitable plate instead. Cook the pudding on High for 3–4 minutes, or until just firm but slightly sticky in appearance on top. Leave to stand for 5 minutes before turning out. The result does not have as good a shape as a conventional pudding but it tastes terrific. It will serve 4, instead of 6.

of the non-essential amino acids, other nutrients and fibre that make up a balanced diet.

Puddings
See Suet Pastry*.
In British cookery the term has two uses, firstly for more substantial desserts, usually hot, secondly for savoury puddings (described under suet crust pastry). When serving a filling pudding, plan a light main course to balance the meal.

Puff Pastry
See Pastry*.
Puff pastry is a rich, layered pastry used for both sweet and savoury dishes. It is readily available frozen or chilled. Bought pastry is good and some high quality brands are excellent. Home-made does have a particularly good flavour and texture but it does take time, effort and practice to get it right.

Quantities

Use butter and plain flour for best results. Strong flour strengthens the pastry layers but it can also toughen it. The lemon juice also strengthens the gluten content of the flour.

Use equal quantities of butter to flour, for example 225 g/8 oz butter and 225 g/8 oz plain flour.

FOOD VALUES: TOTAL
kcals: 2424
kJ: 10071
protein: 26 g
fat: 187 g
carbohydrate: 169 g
fibre: 7 g

These food values are for the whole block of dough. The value of individual portions depends on the number of items of serving cut from the dough. Fillings and other ingredients used must also be taken into consideration.

CHRISTMAS PUDDING

Make the pudding at least a month before it is to be eaten so that it has time to mature. A good pudding will keep for up to a year in a cool, dark, dry place if well laced with brandy or other spirit before storage. Serve with brandy sauce or brandy butter.

INGREDIENTS
100 g/4 oz raisins
100 g/4 oz currants
100 g/4 oz sultanas
50 g/2 oz cooking dates, chopped
50 g/2 oz ready-to-eat dried apricots, chopped
grated rind and juice of 1 orange
30 ml/2 tablespoons brandy or rum
50 g/2 oz dark soft brown sugar
30 ml/2 tablespoons black treacle
5 ml/1 teaspoon ground mixed spice
5 ml/1 teaspoon ground cinnamon

50 g/2 oz shredded suet or vegetarian suet
225 g/8 oz cooking apples, quartered, cored, peeled and grated
1 large carrot, grated
50 g/2 oz ground almonds
100 g/4 oz fresh breadcrumbs
1 egg, beaten

FOOD VALUES:
TOTAL • PER PORTION
kcals: 2574 • 429
kJ: 10865 • 1811
protein: 37 g • 6 g
fat: 79 g • 13 g
carbohydrate: 439 g • 73 g
fibre: 56 g • 9 g

Serves 6

Place the dried fruit in a bowl. Stir in the orange rind and juice and the brandy or rum. Cover and leave the fruit to macerate (soak) well, preferably overnight.

Grease a 1.1 litre/2 pint boilable pudding basin. Grease a piece of greaseproof paper to cover it and cut a large piece of foil. Cut a strip of foil and fold it in half. Prepare a steamer as for the previous recipe, setting the water to boil.

Mix the macerated fruit well, then add all the remaining ingredients and make sure they are all thoroughly combined. There is no great secret to the mixing of Christmas pudding other than plenty of stirring. Spoon the mixture into the basin and press it down well. Cover with greaseproof paper and foil, tying it down well or crumpling and folding the foil.

Place the pudding on the strip of foil and lower it into the steamer. Cook over boiling water for 5 hours, topping up with boiling water regularly. Leave the pudding to cool, then wrap it in clean greaseproof paper and overwrap in foil or seal it in a polythene bag.

Before serving, steam the pudding over boiling water for a further 2 hours. Invert the pudding on to a heated plate and serve with Brandy Sauce (page 235) or Brandy Butter (page 51).

Note If the pudding is to be stored for a long period, pierce it in several places with a clean skewer and trickle 15 ml/1 tablespoon brandy or other spirit over it before wrapping. Check occasionally during storage and moisten the pudding with more brandy if it looks dry. Do not overdo the brandy or the pudding will flow out of the basin; however, it will take up to 45–60 ml/3–4 tablespoons over 6–9 months.

Puff Pastry – Technique

1. Chill 225 g/8 oz butter thoroughly. Put some ice cubes in a small jug of water. Mark the butter into quarters, then cut off one quarter. Shape the remaining butter into a block measuring about 10 cm/4 inches square. Wrap this block and chill it.

2. Place 225 g/8 oz plain flour in a bowl and rub in the quarter portion of butter. Sprinkle over 15 ml/1 tablespoon lemon juice and 90 ml/6 tablespoons ice cold water. Mix to a fairly soft dough, adding an extra 15 ml/1 tablespoon water if necessary.

3. Gather the dough into a ball, then turn out on to a clean, lightly floured work surface and knead it very briefly into a smooth, square shape.

4. Roll out the dough into a 23 cm/9 inch square, dusting the surface with as little flour as necessary.

5. Place the block of butter in the middle of the dough, then fold the sides and ends over to enclose it completely.

6. Press the dough into slight ridges with a rolling pin to seal the folds of dough, then roll out into an oblong, about 25–30 cm/10–12 inches long. Turn the dough over, then fold the bottom third over the middle and fold the top third down.

7. Chill the dough well. Turning the dough over during the last rolling gives a thicker coating around the outside of the butter and makes it easier to roll.

8. Give the chilled dough a quarter turn clockwise, then roll it into an oblong again and fold it as before. Repeat the turning, rolling and folding. Make 3 indentations in the dough with your fingertips (to indicate it has been rolled 3 times) before chilling.

9. Repeat the rolling and folding another 3 times, chilling the dough each time. The dough is now ready for use.

Makes 625 g/1 lb 6oz

Puff Pastry
(Number relates to text steps)

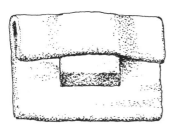

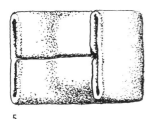

5

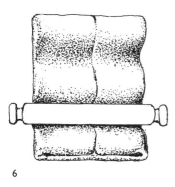

6

General Notes

• There is no need to grease cooking tins for puff pastry as it yields enough fat to prevent sticking.

• Chill the rolled and shaped items before cooking to prevent shrinking.

• Putting a small ovenproof dish of boiling water in the base of the oven creates steam which helps to make the pastry puff.

• Always cook puff pastry in a hot oven. If the filling requires long cooking, then reduce the temperature after the first 15–20 minutes.

Classic Puff Pastry Items

Puff pastry may be used to cover pies or tarts or for pasties.
Pastry Squares The whole quantity may be rolled into four 15 cm/6 inch squares, for making turnovers or for cooking boneless chicken breasts or lamb cutlets en croûte.
Cream Horns Roll out a 30 cm/12 inch square from ½ quantity of dough, then cut 1 cm/½ inch wide strips. Wind these around horn-shaped tins. Bake at 230°C, 450°F, gas 8 for 10–15 minutes. Cool, then fill with jam and whipped cream. Dust with icing sugar. The horns may be filled with a savoury mixture.
Vol-au-vent Halve the pastry and roll out two 20 cm/8 inch rounds. Place one on a baking tray. Cut a 15 cm/6 inch round from the middle of the second round. Dampen the remaining pastry ring and press it lightly on the outside of the round on the baking tray. Prick the middle all over. Put the small round on a separate baking tray. Brush the top of the pastry ring and the smaller round with a little beaten egg. Bake at 230°C, 450°F, gas 8 for 20–25 minutes. Fill the middle of the vol-au-vent with a hot savoury sauce and top with the lid. Serve at once.

Alternatively, the pastry may be cooled and a savoury or sweet filling used.

Storing and Freezing

Place the dough in a sealed polythene bag in the refrigerator and use within 2 days of making. It freezes well for 3–4 months and should be thawed in the refrigerator for several hours before use.

Pumpkin

See Vegetables*.
Pale orange outside, with deep orange-coloured flesh, pumpkin may be used for sweet or savoury cooking. These vegetables grow to enormous size, therefore they are often sold cut into wedges. Medium and smaller vegetables are sold whole.

Preparation

Halve a whole pumpkin. Discard the seeds and woolly surrounding fibre. Use a sharp knife to cut off the thick, tough peel.

Halved small pumpkins may be stuffed, otherwise they should be cut into wedges – best to do this before peeling as wedges are easier to peel. Cut large portions into fine wedges, then across into large chunks.

Cooking

For purée, steam chunks of pumpkin over boiling water for about 15 minutes or until soft. Beat to a purée, then sieve. Alternatively, purée the cooked pumpkin in a food processor.
Frying Cook a chopped onion in a little butter, then add small cubes of pumpkin and seasoning. Cook, stirring occasionally, for about 10–15 minutes, or until the pumpkin is tender but firm.
Braising Add large chunks of pumpkin to cooked onion as above and turn in the hot fat for 2–3 minutes. Add a little water, wine or a can of tomatoes and seasoning. Bring to simmering point, cover and cook gently for about 15–20 minutes.

Serving Ideas

• Pumpkin is delicious with diced bacon, onion, garlic and canned or fresh tomato. Serve with pasta, in baked potatoes or with rice; use as a pie filling, base for savoury crumble or in pancakes (top with cheese sauce).

• Add chunks of pumpkin to meat or vegetable casseroles about 20–30 minutes before the end of cooking. Serve with couscous (see semolina*).

• To make pumpkin soup, simmer the cubed vegetable with onion in stock. Purée, then swirl in cream or fromage frais.

Quince

See Fruit*.

A yellow-skinned fruit about the size of small apples or pears, with a core of seeds and creamy-white flesh which is acidic and firm.

A relative of the apple, the quince is golden and perfumed when ripe, although flavour depends on type.

The quince has a high pectin content and is used for making jams and other preserves. More popular in Mediterranean countries than in Britain, it may be cooked in savoury dishes such as stews.

The fruit should be peeled, cored and all seeds removed before cooking. All trimmings should be wrapped in muslin and boiled to extract pectin.

Rabbit

Wild rabbit is sold by some country butchers but the majority of prepared rabbit meat is farmed, and mainly British or Chinese.

Buying

Prepared rabbit, fresh or frozen, is sold whole by some butchers or ready jointed. Boneless portions and cubed rabbit meat are also available, the latter mainly from freezer centres. The meat should be firm and pale pink in colour, and virtually fat free.

An average domestic rabbit weighs about 1–1.25 kg/2–2¾ lb and it will serve 4 when roasted or 4–6 jointed.

Storing

Leave chilled packed rabbit in its wrapping and place it in the refrigerator (low shelf) as soon as possible after purchase. Check the label for the use by date.

Rabbit bought loose from a butcher should be placed in a covered dish in the refrigerator. Use within a day of purchase.

Cooked rabbit should be eaten with 1–2 days. Pies should be stored in the refrigerator. Cut off slices as required and return the pie to the refrigerator immediately.

Preparation

Cut off any small areas of fat as it has an unpleasant taste. Rinse and dry portions.

Use

Rabbit is tender and lean. It may be braised or cooked in casseroles, made into pies or grilled. Saddle of rabbit (the whole of the back of the animal) or whole rabbits may be roasted. Rabbit portions may be barbecued.

Rabbit meat has a rather bland flavour, so herbs and spices may be used to pep it up. Marinate the meat before cooking and use the marinade to make a sauce. Mustard sauce is a classic accompaniment for rabbit.

Cooking

Braising and Casseroling As a rule, rabbit may be treated as chicken, allowing about 45–60 minutes for braising or casseroling, depending on ingredients.

Grilling Portions may be grilled under medium to high heat, allowing 10–15 minutes on each side. Baste often with fat or a marinade otherwise the meat tends to dry out.

Roasting A trussed whole rabbit or saddle may be roasted. Bard the rabbit to prevent it drying out and cook at 190°C, 375°F, gas 5. Allow about 30 minutes for a saddle, 1–1½ hours for a whole rabbit.

Before roasting a whole rabbit, it is a good idea to part cut through the back bone behind the shoulders and at the rear end of the saddle, to make jointing the cooked carcass easier. The saddle may be part cut into 2–4 portions.

Seasonings and Accompaniments

● Rosemary, thyme and sage all go well with rabbit.

● Bacon or pork fat may be used for barding; diced bacon gives rabbit casserole a good flavour. Raw diced gammon is good in rabbit pie.

● Prunes and apples are traditional ingredients for adding to rabbit casseroles. The portions may be flamed with brandy or rum after browning, before adding the liquid.

● Brush mustard over rabbit towards the end of roasting or grilling. Select a mild wholegrain mustard flavoured with herbs.

Radishes

See Salads and Salad Dressings* and *Vegetables**.

There are 2 types: small red radishes and large white radish, about the size of a large carrot. Both have a similar crunchy texture and slightly hot flavour.

Buying

Look for bright, firm, unblemished radishes. They may be sold with leaves on (in bunches) or trimmed and packed. The bunches are often better quality. Check packets carefully to make sure all the contents look in good condition.

Large white radishes should be firm and the skin should look bright and moist.

Storing

Trim, if necessary, and place in the salad drawer of the refrigerator. Use within 2 days, the fresher the better.

Preparation

Trim off the leaves and stalk end, also the root end. Wash well and cut away any blemishes.

Large white radish should be thinly peeled before use.

Use

Red radishes are used in salads, usually sliced. They may be served whole as part of a selection of crudités with or without dips.

Large white radish may be grated and served as a salad or accompaniment. It may be cut into fine strips and stir fried.

Raising Agents

See Baking Powder*, Bicarbonate of Soda*, Cream of Tartar*, Eggs* and Yeast*.

A raising agent lightens mixtures giving them an open texture. As well as chemical raising agents, air and yeast are also widely used.

Air is incorporated into mixtures by beating or whisking. The air visibly increases the volume of egg whites or whole eggs beaten with sugar. During cooking, the air expands to make the mixture rise before it sets.

In the presence of moisture and food, and in warm conditions, yeast produces carbon dioxide. This gas is trapped in dough, batters and other mixtures making them rise before baking. Heat causes further rising and it sets the mixture.

Rancidity

Fats become rancid during prolonged storage under the wrong conditions. Rancidity is the result of oxidation, that is oxygen molecules from the air forming a chemical link with the fat to change its structure slightly. This produces off flavours as well as a change in texture and colour. Fats become softer, pale cream to distinct yellow in colour.

The presence of salt can also promote rancidity in storage, particularly in frozen food or cooked ham.

Rancidity and Freezing

The main problem of rancidity is in frozen food. During freezing, enzymes that promote rancidity continue to work very slowly; therefore if the food is not packed adequately to exclude air and if there is a high salt content, then the fat can become rancid in comparatively short periods.

Bacon (depending on the curing method and salt content), salted butter, turkey fat and cooked ham are all examples of foods that are prone to turning rancid if stored beyond the recommended time for freezing.

When freezing food with a high fat content, double wrap it in thick polythene bags and exclude as much air as possible from packs. Never freeze large quantities that cannot be eaten within the recommended storage time. Remember that diced bacon or ham in casseroles and stuffings can taint the whole dish.

Other Foods Prone to Rancidity

Coconut is particularly vulnerable, so products such as creamed coconut should be used within the period recommended on the packet. Other nuts have a high fat content and may go rancid after long periods of storage in unsealed packs in warm conditions. Good quality white

chocolate also tends to develop off flavours on prolonged storage (over a period of 4 months or so) even in an airtight packet placed in the refrigerator.

Clarified Fat

Clarified fat that has been cooked to cause evaporation of the water, then strained to get rid of the salt deposits, has a long shelf life if stored in an airtight container. The prolonged heating halts the enzyme action. Ghee, clarified butter, may be stored in an airtight container in the refrigerator for many months. Similarly, clarified duck and goose fat, both of which are used in classic French meat preserves.

Raspberries

See Fruit*.

Available from late June to September and October, although mainly in the early part of summer. Frozen raspberries are available all year.

Buying

The fruit should look bright, firm and juicy. Avoid raspberries that are very soft and dark red as they are slightly over-ripe and past their prime in terms of flavour.

Check that fruit at the bottom of cartons is not squashed and damaged. Bad juice staining in the base of the carton is usually a sign of squashing.

Storing

Best used freshly picked or on the same day as buying. They may be kept in the refrigerator overnight.

Preparation

Pinch out any stalks and discard any fruit that is squashed or mouldy.

Rinse the raspberries under gently running cold water and drain well.

Use

● Serve plain with cream, fromage frais, thick yogurt or ice cream.

Melba Sauce

Purée 225 g/8 oz prepared raspberries in a liquidiser or food processor, then rub them through a sieve to remove seeds. Sweeten with 45–60 ml/3–4 tablespoons icing sugar and stir well. Serve with ice cream, pancakes or waffles, as an accompaniment to Vanilla Mousse (page 187) or Lemon Soufflé (page 244). Serve with vanilla ice cream and fresh peaches to make peach Melba.
Serves 4

● Use to fill gâteaux, meringue cases or flans, or use in trifle.

● Use in pies or compotes.

● Good for making jams or for flavouring vinegar*.

● Purée for flavouring ice cream, making soufflés or mousses, or for Melba Sauce (above).

Freezing

Open freeze raspberries on trays lined with freezer film, then pack them in airtight polythene bags. They keep well for up to a year.

Nutritional Value

Fresh raspberries provide vitamin C, potassium and carotene.

Redcurrants

See Blackcurrants*.
The information on blackcurrants is applicable to redcurrants in terms of preparation and use.
Redcurrants are poached for use in desserts, particularly summer pudding (see Glossary, page 275). They are also used for making jelly (see jams and jellies*).

Refrigerator

Proper use and care of the refrigerator is vital in the prevention of food contamination.

Care and Cleaning

Always read and follow the manufacturer's instructions.
Siting The refrigerator should not be positioned next to a cooker, radiator or other heat source.
Defrosting Many modern refrigerators have an automatic defrost facility, others must be switched off and defrosted regularly. In the absence of user's instructions, defrost the refrigerator every 2–3 months.
Cleaning The refrigerator must be cleaned regularly. Removable racks, salad drawers and compartments should be washed often, at least once a month. Depending on use, the rest of the refrigerator should be washed out every 6–8 weeks.
The refrigerator should be switched off and unplugged, then washed out with hand-hot water with 5 ml/1 teaspoon bicarbonate of soda to every 600 ml/1 pint before use. A solution of sterilising liquid (Milton or equivalent, made up according to the manufacturer's instructions) or a very mild bleach solution (6 ml/generous 1 teaspoon to each 1 litre/1¾ pints) may be used for regular cleaning.
Do not use abrasives, polishes or fragrant cleaning solutions in the refrigerator.
Thoroughly clean door areas, shelf supports and other ridges in the cabinet.

 Any spillages must be cleaned up immediately.

Before Going Away

If the refrigerator is to be left unused, it must first be emptied, washed out and dried. Then the door should be left open. Before using again after long periods, wash the interior thoroughly.

It is usually better to leave the refrigerator switched on but to remove all perishable contents before going away for short periods (a few days).

Use: Arranging Food

Warm air rises, so the lower shelves are the coldest areas. The salad drawer is usually located at the bottom of the cabinet and the ice-making compartment is usually found at the top. A larger refrigerator does not have an ice compartment and this allows more space for storing food.

Covering and Wrapping

● Leave sealed purchased packs unopened, commercial wrapping is applied in hygienic conditions to prevent contamination.

● Always keep food packed or placed in covered containers. Use polythene bags with ties for cheese, prepared pastry, pies and similar solid pieces of dry food.

● Put foods that are likely to drip in covered dishes that are large and deep enough to catch all liquid.

● Airtight rigid containers that stack well are useful for food such as cheese and for leftover cooked items like quiche or vegetables. However if they are re-used often (as for cheese), make sure they are washed and dried regularly – do not add new packs of cheese to the container alongside older portions without cleaning the container first.

From Top to Bottom

● Fruit and vegetables may be placed towards the top of the refrigerator in the absence of a salad drawer.

● Cheese, unopened packs of juice, eggs in cartons and any bottles of drink that do not fit on the door should be placed towards the top of the refrigerator.

● Next shelf down is for cooked meats and vegetables, butter and

---

SEE ALSO **Ratafia Biscuits:** Glossary; **Ratatouille:** Stewing; **Réchauffe, Refresh:** Glossary

other cooking fats. Leftover cooked dishes and desserts should be placed here.

• Raw meat, bacon, sausages, poultry and fish should be placed towards the bottom of the refrigerator.

• Compartments on the door are usually convenient for milk and other drinks. They may be used for packs of butter, opened jars of preserves that need refrigeration, items such as chocolate, peanut butter, bought mayonnaise and so on.

All-important Temperature Check

Refrigerator thermometers are inexpensive. The internal temperature must be 5°C/41°F or lower. Select the setting to ensure that the temperature is maintained at this level.

Factors Influencing Temperature
• When the door is open, warmer air from the room displaces the cold air in the refrigerator.

✓ *Never leave the refrigerator door open, for example when pouring milk into a cup of coffee or tea, always shut the door as soon as you have removed the food.*

• Warm and hot food placed in the refrigerator will increase the temperature of the surrounding air. Therefore always make sure food is cool before putting it in the refrigerator.

✓ *If leftover cooked meat or poultry is part cooled it should be placed in the refrigerator in preference to being left in a warm room for long periods. For example if you plan to go out for the rest of the day, then place leftovers of a warm lunch roast or casserole in the refrigerator. This should not be a regular practice. Increase the setting of the refrigerator.*

• Open the refrigerator door as little as possible. Think before you open the door – never stand in front of the refrigerator, looking at all the contents trying to decide what to cook or eat.

Signs of Food Decay

If you have any doubts about the quality of food, look for the following and throw suspect food away. Wash and dry your hands after handling suspect food.

• Any mould, however light.

• Brown, soft or discoloured patches.

• Discoloration, particularly on meat, poultry and its fat. Any signs of brown-beige patches, yellow or green tinging.

• Unpleasant or strong odours (when they are uncharacteristic of the food).

• A slimy texture, particularly on poultry and meat.

Do Not

• Store canned food in the refrigerator. Cans may be chilled before opening but not stored permanently.

• Leave food uncovered or in dishes that are too small.

• Allow food to drip.

• Allow pets to lean into the open refrigerator.

Reheating Food

Leftover food should not be wasted but it is important that it is handled properly to avoid possible food poisoning.

• Warm food is a suitable environment for bacteria to multiply or for their spores to germinate.

• Cool leftovers rapidly by transferring them to clean, cold covered containers, rather than leaving them in hot, thick serving dishes that keep them warm. Place the covered food in a cool place, such as a utility room, away from sources of heat.

• Chill leftovers as soon as they are cool.

• Use leftovers within 1–2 days, depending on the type of food.

• Reheat food thoroughly until every part has reached the original cooking temperature. Reheating should be slow enough to ensure that the food is hot through before the outside is overcooked.

• Never warm food slowly, then serve it before thoroughly heated. Keeping food warm for long periods can cause food poisoning.

• Never reheat food more than once. On each occasion, as the temperature of the food passes through warm to hot, the conditions are ideal for food poisoning bacteria to multiply.

• Serve reheated food promptly.

Religion and Food

Religion has played a major role in the development of different cuisines and styles of eating. Religious food laws relate not only to which foods may or may not be eaten but also to when they should be avoided, how the food should be prepared, the serving and combining of different foods. Many religions and cultures impose complicated rules while others follow traditions, including fasting and the preparation of certain celebration dishes.

Detailed study of individual cultures and diet may be made through specialist publications and by contacting relevant official organisations. Also, up to date information relating to convenience foods and contemporary practices should be obtained from such sources. The few notes included here are interesting in the context of meals eaten in foreign countries and what to expect of menus in ethnic restaurants. They may also be helpful when cooking for anyone complying with particular food laws, although some staunch followers avoid eating food that may be unsuitable.

Buddhists Generally follow a vegetarian diet as they are forbidden from killing animals for food, also from eating animals especially killed for them.

Christians Food laws relating to fasting (for example avoiding meat on Fridays) are no longer imposed but certain traditions are followed. Fasting during Lent, prior to Easter, and many speciality dishes relating to the religious calendar are common.

Hindus There are many areas of the religion and dietary laws vary according to the sect. The cow is sacred to Hindus and therefore beef is not eaten. Many may also be vegetarian or even vegan. Alcohol is forbidden.

Jews Including some of the most complicated and widely known food laws. The killing, preparing and combining of food is strictly governed.

The pig is considered unfit for consumption, therefore pork and all other products are not eaten. Shellfish is not eaten but fish is acceptable.

Kosher meat and poultry is butchered according to religious laws, with many bakery products and convenience foods produced to the necessary standards. Dairy products are never mixed with meat, neither in the preparation or in the cooking and serving. This calls for the use of separate cooking utensils and serving dishes.

Muslims Pork is not eaten. Rules relating to butchering ensure that all meat is properly prepared, when it is known as halal meat. Alcohol is not consumed.

Rhubarb

See Fruit*.
Available from January, early, or forced, rhubarb is blanched during growing (that is the light is excluded) so that the stalks are small and pink.

Buying

Look for firm stalks that are not too large. Avoid limp rhubarb or any with very thick, fibrous looking peel.

Storing

Use freshly picked or within a day of purchase or picking. The best way to keep it is to prepare the fruit and cut it up, then place it in a covered dish or polythene bag in the refrigerator. It will keep for 2–3 days but will not be at its best.

Preparation

Trim off the leaves and the root end (or crown end). Young rhubarb (slim and tender) should be washed well, sliced and used as required.

Larger, tougher stalks should be peeled of any stringy outer covering.

Cooking

Place the prepared rhubarb in a saucepan with sugar (about 100 g/4 oz to 450 g/1 lb fruit) and 30 ml/2 tablespoons water. Heat gently until the sugar dissolves, stirring occasionally. Put a lid on the pan and simmer the fruit gently for about 15–25 minutes, depending on the size of stalks and how tender they are. Allow 30 minutes, stirring often, if the fruit is to be puréed.

Microwave Cooking Place the fruit in a covered dish with sugar and water as above. Allow 6–8 minutes on High, stirring once or twice, for 450 g/1 lb fruit with 100 g/4 oz sugar. Allow to stand for 3 minutes.

Use

● Add grated orange rind and juice and some chopped preserved stem ginger to rhubarb to make a delicious compote for serving hot or cold.

● Purée cooked rhubarb in a food processor or liquidiser and use to make fool or mousse.

● Use in pies and crumbles or top with sponge mixture then bake.

● Use in jam and for chutney.

Freezing

Rhubarb freezes extremely well. Trim and slice it, then pack and freeze. It keeps well for up to a year, or longer, but its colour tends to diminish.

Rice

See Bacillus cereus*.

Buying

Buy according to use; however, if you do not want to bother with using different types for different dishes, the best advice is to buy good quality brown or white long-grain rice.

Since rice keeps well, it makes sense to experiment with different types and to make full use of them to achieve quite different results. For example, delicate steamed white rice complements light Chinese dishes, whereas nutty brown or wild rice is better with stews of vegetables and pulses.

Storing

Keep rice in the unopened packet or transfer it to an airtight container. Keep in a cool, dark cupboard where it will stay fresh for many months.

Types

Carolina and patna rice were once commonly used terms and patna was considered to be the best long-grain rice. Different types have different textures and flavours when cooked.

Brown rice has some of the outer seed covering left on the grain, whereas white grains have been polished. Some easy-cook types are processed by part cooking to seal the grain, preventing

---

SEE ALSO **Relish:** Chutney; **Render, Rennet:** Glossary; **Riboflavin:** Vitamins

MILANAISE RISOTTO

This is a classic saffron and cheese risotto. Use this recipe as a basic guide for making risotto. Remember that the result should be moist and creamy.

INGREDIENTS
50 g/2 oz butter
1 onion, finely chopped
225 g/8 oz risotto rice
450 ml/¾ pint hot chicken
    stock
salt and pepper
5 ml/1 teaspoon saffron
    strands
300 ml/½ pint dry white
    wine
100 g/4 oz grated Parmesan
    cheese

FOOD VALUES:
TOTAL • PER PORTION
kcals: 2262 • 566
kJ: 9487 • 2372
protein: 59 g • 15 g
fat: 113 g • 28 g
carbohydrate: 220 g • 55 g
fibre: 7 g • 2 g

Serves 4

Melt half the butter in a heavy-based saucepan, add the onion and cook, stirring occasionally, until soft but not browned. Add the rice and cook gently, stirring, until well coated in butter.

Pour in the stock, stir once, then add a little seasoning and bring to the boil. Reduce the heat, cover the pan tightly and cook for 10 minutes.

Meanwhile, pound the saffron to a powder in a pestle and mortar, then stir in a little hot cooking liquid from the rice. Add the wine and the saffron to the rice, re-cover and leave the risotto to cook gently for a further 20 minutes or until most of the liquid has been absorbed.

Add the remaining butter and stir in the Parmesan, then cover the pan tightly and leave to stand off the heat for 10 minutes before serving.

it from sticking. Easy-cook types have a distinct texture and they may be quite chewy; depending on quality they may taste bland.
Basmati This Indian rice has long grains. It has a distinct aroma and flavour, and it is dry and fluffy when cooked correctly. Use basmati for making pullao, biriani and as an accompaniment to spiced foods. Mainly white but also available as brown rice.
Brown Brown rice still retains some of the outer grain covering. It has a nutty flavour and a slightly chewy texture.
Canned This is virtually cooked. Follow the instructions for completing the cooking and heating, usually adding a little water.
Easy Cook This is available both white or brown. The grains are processed and part cooked so that they cook quickly, without sticking together.

Frozen Cooked and ready to thoroughly re-heat and serve. Follow the packet instructions. Cooked and cooled rice may be frozen but it tends to become soft and grainy, unlike the commercial product which is dry and firm (although somewhat tasteless).

A broad selection of rice mixtures are also available frozen.
Glutinous This is a long grain which is white and it becomes sticky on cooking. Available from Chinese supermarkets, glutinous rice is used for rice balls and other dishes in which the cooked grain has to be moulded.
Long-grain Ordinary long-grain rice is used for savoury and sweet cooking, boiled and served plain as an accompaniment, for stuffing, salads and so on. It usually has a slightly better flavour than easy-cook rice but

this depends on the quality and brand. Both Italian and American are usually superior to the anonymous types.
Pudding, Round-grain or Short-grain These are all terms for round-grain rice that becomes very soft and sticky when cooked. Used for milk pudding, the grains cook down to a creamy porridge.

Not all round-grain varieties become as soft during cooking.
Risotto Risotto rice is fairly round in shape and it becomes slightly sticky when cooked, but the grains still retain a firmness and bite. It is essential for making authentic, creamy risotto.
Wild Not from the same family as rice, the grains are long, thin and dark brown, almost black, in colour. Wild rice requires longer cooking, it does not swell as much as other rice and it is nutty with more bite.
Sushi Another speciality rice, obtainable from Japanese and other Oriental stores. The grains are shorter and, like glutinous rice, they become sticky on cooking and cooling, allowing them to be moulded and shaped.

Cooking

Washing Some types of rice should be washed before cooking, including basmati, ordinary long-grain, glutinous and wild. Place the rice in a bowl and pour in plenty of cold water. Swirl the grains very gently, then drain off most of the water. Repeat several times, until the water is clear not cloudy. Do not handle the grains roughly or they break and become starchy and soft during cooking. Drain the washed rice in a sieve.
Absorption Method Good quality rice is best cooked by a combination of boiling and steaming. Place the rice in a saucepan, then pour in water to cover the grains by about 2.5 cm/1 inch. As a guide, allow 600 ml/1 pint water for each 225 g/8 oz rice. Brown rice requires more water – 750 ml/1¼ pints.

Add a pinch of salt, then bring the water to the boil. Reduce the heat at once, give the grains one stir and put a tight-fitting lid on the pan. Leave the rice over the lowest setting for 15–30 minutes, depending on type.

Easy-cook types take about 15 minutes, basmati about 20, brown nearer 30 minutes.

Microwave Cooking Using the above quantities, place the rice and water in a large mixing bowl or casserole. Cover with a lid or neatly fitting plate. Cook on High for about 15 minutes, then leave to stand for 5 minutes before forking up the grains. Brown rice takes 20–25 minutes.

The advantage of microwave cooking is that the rice cooks well, without bursting the grains and without sticking. However, if the cooking dish is too small the water will froth over.

Boiling This should be used for wild rice and for the cheapest long-grain types that tend to become very stodgy.

Bring a large pan of water to the boil (add a pinch of salt if liked). Add the rice, then simmer steadily, covered, until the grains are tender. Ordinary white rice cooks in about 15–20 minutes. Wild rice requires 50–60 minutes.

Drain the rice at once by pouring it into a fine sieve.

Steaming This may be used for long-grain rice. It may be used to make fluffy, plain cooked white rice to accompany Chinese dishes.

Wash the rice well, then place it in a boilable dish. Add about 150 ml/¼ pint boiling water and stand the dish in a steamer over boiling water. Steam the rice for 30–40 minutes, until the grains are swollen and fluffy.

X *Never keep rice warm for long periods. If rice is cooked ahead and reheated, always make sure it is thoroughly reheated. Spores of food poisoning bacteria may be present in the rice (even when cooked) and these can germinate and multiply if the rice is kept warm for long periods or reheated on several occasions.*

RICE PUDDING

INGREDIENTS
40 g/1½ oz pudding rice
30 ml/2 tablespoons sugar
600 ml/1 pint milk
small piece of lemon rind
a little nutmeg
25 g/1 oz butter
Serves 4

FOOD VALUES:
TOTAL • PER PORTION
kcals: 843 • 211
kJ: 3534 • 884
protein: 23 g • 6 g
fat: 44 g • 11 g
carbohydrate: 95 g • 24 g
fibre: 1 g • 0 g

Set the oven at 160°C, 325°F, gas 3. Grease a 1.15 litre/2 pint ovenproof dish. Wash the rice, then place it in a saucepan and pour in enough cold water to cover. Bring to the boil, stir the rice, then remove from the heat and drain well.

Turn the rice into the dish. Add the sugar, then stir in the milk and lemon rind. Sprinkle with a little grated nutmeg and add the butter. Bake the pudding for 2¼ hours, then stir it well. Continue cooking for a further 30 minutes, or until the pudding is thick and creamy. The pudding may be allowed to brown on top or it may be stirred once or twice during the final 30 minutes. Stirring makes the pudding creamy.

Cooling: Cold Rice Dishes

Rice which is to be served cold, for example in salads, must be cooled quickly, then chilled. It should be kept chilled until used. Any cold rice dishes should be kept chilled, not allowed to stand at room temperature for long periods.

Reheating Rice

Rice must be heated quickly and thoroughly before serving. Once it is reheated it should be served promptly. Do not reheat rice more than once. There are several ways in which rice can be reheated.

Over Boiling Water One method is by standing a covered dish of rice over a saucepan of boiling water. This is only suitable for smaller quantities (up to four servings). A large pan and dish should be used so that the rice heats quickly and the water should be boiling. Never put large quantities of rice in a dish and leave over hot or warm water – the rice will not heat quickly enough.

Boilable Bags Placing the rice in boilable bags is a good way. The hot cooked rice may be placed in the bag, sealed, cooled and chilled. The bag, or bags, of chilled rice may be dropped into a pan of boiling water and heated rapidly.

Oven Large quantities are best heated in a couple of covered dishes placed in a hot oven. Sprinkle a little water over the rice before putting it in the oven.

Microwave The microwave is ideal for reheating rice as it does heat quickly. Always use the High setting and heat large quantities (over 4 servings) in 2 or more batches. Place the rice in a suitable covered dish and stir it thoroughly with a fork halfway through heating. Before serving, check that all the rice is thoroughly reheated.

Use and Flavouring

● Toss chopped fresh herbs (such as parsley, chives or basil) into cooked rice.

● Add chopped lemon or orange rind to cooked rice.

SEE ALSO **Ricotta:** Cheese; **Rissole, Rock Cake:** Glossary; **Rolls:** Bread; **Roly-Poly:** Suet Pastry; **Roquefort:** Cheese;

- Toss chopped walnuts and spring onion into cooked brown rice before serving.

- To make pullao, add a bay leaf, cinnamon stick, 4–6 green cardamoms and a finely sliced onion with the cooking water for basmati rice. Cook a second sliced onion in butter until brown, then stir in 15 ml/1 tablespoon cumin seeds and cook for 2 minutes. Pour this mixture over the cooked rice and fork it in, then serve.

Leftover Rice

- Make rice cakes with cooked rice, cooked chopped onion, cooked chicken or ham and an egg to bind the ingredients. Shape into cakes and shallow fry until golden and hot through.

- Mix chopped crystallised ginger, flaked almonds, raisins and chopped glacé cherries into leftover rice pudding. Chill well before serving.

- Fold a little whipped cream or fromage frais into leftover rice pudding, then serve in individual dishes. Top each portion with poached fruit – apricots, plums, cherries, pears and so on.

Roasting

This is a dry cooking method, suitable only for tender foods that are large enough to be sealed outside and to take time to cook through for succulent results.

Tough meat, small portions and delicate foods (small whole fish) are not suitable for roasting. Some large portions of fish (such as monkfish) may be roasted.

Technique

The food to be roasted should be placed on a spit or, more usually, on a rack over a roasting tin. It should be cooked uncovered for the majority of the time.

Food that is covered is baked, not roasted.

Preparing the Food The food should be trussed neatly, then seasoned outside. In some cases, the food may be marinated before roasting.

Dry meats should be larded or barded to keep them moist (see Glossary, page 275). For low-fat results, the minimum extra fat should be used.

Sealing Meat Although lower roasting temperatures are used, meat benefits from being cooked at a high temperature for a short period. This hardens the protein on the outside and seals the surface to keep in moisture for the main cooking time.

Meat may be sealed in a pan on the hob before roasting.

Basting During roasting, the food should be basted with fat to keep it moist. Food on a spit roast is, to a large extent, self-basting as less fat drips off.

Spit Roasting

Many ovens have a rotisserie which may be used to skewer whole joints, birds or kebabs. This consists of a spindle which is threaded through the skewered food and fitted into the rear of the oven. The rotisserie is operated and the food cooked as for normal roasting times. A large roasting tin should be placed under the food.

Split roasting promotes even browning and cooking. Because the cooking juices and fat are constantly coating the food as it turns, there is no need for basting and the results are moist.

Always follow the manufacturer's instructions for using the rotisserie attachment.

Rough Puff Pastry

See Flaky Pastry*, Pastry* and Puff Pastry*.

This is a cross between flaky and puff pastry. It has more layers than flaky pastry but it does not give as good a rise as puff pastry, and it is not quite as rich as puff pastry.

Quantities

Use the same quantities as for Flaky Pastry (page 129), with all butter.

Technique

1. Cut the fat into 1–2 cm/ ½–¾ inch chunks and chill thoroughly.

2. Place the flour in a bowl, then stir in the fat. Mix in the water to make a soft dough, then knead it very lightly into a ball.

3. Press the dough into an oblong shape on a well floured work surface. Roll and fold it as for flaky pastry, without any additional fat. Chill well.

4. Repeat the rolling and folding 3 times, chilling each time. The pastry is then ready for use.

Use

Use instead of flaky or puff pastry. Note that rough puff will not give as good a rise for making items such as vols-au-vents; however, it may be used for other puff pastry items.

Storing and Freezing

As for puff pastry.

Rough Puff Pastry
The lumps of fat are gradually incorporated during rolling and folding.

Rosemary: Herbs; **Rose Water:** Glossary; **Roux:** Sauces; **Royal Icing:** Icings; **Rusk:** Glossary; **Rye:** Flour

Sago

Sago is starch extracted from a tree, the sago palm, grown in the swamps of south-east Asia. Small grains of washed and sieved starch are known as pearl sago.

Sago Pudding

To make traditional sago pudding, gently simmer 50 g/2 oz pearl sago in 600 ml/1 pint milk for 15–20 minutes, or until the grains are swollen and most of the milk is absorbed. Add about 50 g/2 oz sugar to sweeten the pudding, which may be flavoured with grated nutmeg or lemon rind, and brown in the oven.

Salads and Salad Dressings

See Lettuce*, Mayonnaise*, Oil*, Sauces*, Vegetables* and Vinegar*. Salads are cold dishes of one or more foods, usually mixed with a dressing. Some salads include hot ingredients or a hot dressing may be used. Salads may be served as accompaniments, main dishes or as light meals.

A dressing is meant to moisten and season a salad, at the same time linking the different ingredients. Personal preference is important, so always taste a dressing before adding it to salad.

Salad Ingredients

Almost any food may be used to make a salad, from fish and meat to vegetables and fruit.

● Salad leaves, spring onions, celery, cucumber and other raw ingredients should be really fresh.

● Always trim, wash and dry salad ingredients before preparing them. Even if bought vegetables look trimmed and clean, they must be washed.

● Leafy vegetables should be tossed with dressing just before serving to avoid a limp result.

● Cooked foods, such as roast chicken, ham or hard-boiled eggs, should be freshly cooked, quickly cooled and chilled until used.

● Celery and spring onions can be crisped and curled by cutting them into fine strips, then soaking them in a bowl of iced water for about an hour.

● Either use one main ingredient or combine foods carefully to avoid a complete jumble – individual flavours and textures should be recognisable in the salad.

● Any dressing should bring out the flavour of the salad without drowning the ingredients.

Salad Leaves
See Watercress*

Chicory* Whole leaves may be used to hold small portions of dressed salad or the leaves may be shredded.
Cress Familiar, small tubs of cress shoots. Cress is easy to grow at home. To prepare it, take firm hold of a small handful, snip it off, then wash it under running water.
Endive or Frisée Rather like a round lettuce which has suffered from a bad perm, endive has crisp frilly edged leaves. Dark green at the base graduating to light green on top. Easy to grow, endive has more body than lettuce. Good with an oil-based dressing and hot crispy bacon.

Radicchio Small, round, tight heads of red chicory. This Italian chicory has a bitter taste. The leaves should be separated and washed, then mixed with other salad leaves. Good with a slightly sweetened dressing.
Rocket Usually sold in small packs, the leaves are about the same size as dandelion leaves. Rocket has a distinct smell and its flavour is slightly bitter, almost spicy. Trim off any stalks from the ends of the leaves, then roughly chop or shred the greenery and toss it into a salad. It gives a good savoury, herby flavour.
Bought Salad Mixtures Ready cut salad vegetables, sold mixed but not dressed, look jolly but they are more expensive than buying the fresh ingredients. Also, salad vegetables should be served fairly soon after they are washed and shredded or cut, so quality is forfeited to convenience with these packs.

☒ *Do not serve mixed salad packs without washing the ingredients first. Place them in a sieve under cold running water and rinse well, then drain before tossing with dressing.*

For Flavour and Texture

Bacon Crumble crisp, cooled, grilled bacon and toss it into plain salads. Use with either an oil dressing or a creamy dressing.
Alternatively, quickly cook diced bacon in a little oil (olive or sunflower), then remove from the heat and add a little lemon juice, chopped fresh parsley and freshly ground black pepper. This hot dressing is good with spinach or endive.
Croûtons Small cubes of bread, fried until golden, add flavour and crunch to all sorts of salads. Chopped fresh herbs or garlic may be tossed with the croûtons.
Nuts Chopped walnuts, roasted hazelnuts, toasted blanched almonds or pistachio nuts are all good in salad. Toasted flaked almonds are good with green salad and orange segments.

SEE ALSO **Saccharometer:** Glossary; **Saffron:** Spices; **Sage:** Herbs; **Saithe:** Fish; **Salame:** Sausages; **Salmis:** Glossary; **Salmon:** Fish;

Parsley Roughly chopped fresh parsley adds a fresh taste to green salad. Add a large bunch if you like the flavour.

Seeds Sunflower seeds or lightly toasted sesame seeds add a nutty flavour and a bit of crunch to tomatoes or cucumber.

Oil and Vinegar The basic ingredients for vinaigrette dressing. As a general rule, use one third vinegar to two thirds oil. The choice of oil is up to you – olive oil gives a strong flavour, sunflower is lighter, grapeseed oil is very light. Nut oils (walnut and hazelnut) are strong so they benefit from being used with another light oil. Sesame oil is too strong; however a few drops may be added if its flavour is required in a certain dish.

Wine vinegar (red or white) is the usual choice. Flavoured vinegars may be used, tarragon is typical. Balsamic vinegar is a dark, rich vinegar which gives the dressing a good flavour – look out for it in delicatessen shops or good supermarkets. Cider vinegar is not quite as harsh as other types and it makes a good dressing.

Salt, freshly ground pepper and a little sugar are essential; mustard (mixed or dried), garlic, chopped fresh herbs (for example, parsley, chives, thyme, tarragon or mint) and chopped capers are other basic flavourings. A little honey instead of sugar and grated lemon or orange rind are excellent additions when used sparingly.

Whisk the dressing in a basin or shake it up in a screw-topped jar. Once mixed the dressing will keep well in the refrigerator for up to 4 weeks. If any strong flavourings (garlic or citrus rind) are added, then do not keep the dressing for longer than 2 weeks unless you like the strong flavour that develops.

Salt and sugar will not dissolve in oil so always shake or mix them with the vinegar first, then add the oil and other flavourings. This produces a slightly thickened, well-flavoured dressing.

Soured Cream Soured cream, with snipped chives and a little seasoning, makes a delicious dressing. Try it with sliced cucumber, peeled sliced tomatoes or diced avocado with shredded lettuce.

Yogurt Natural yogurt makes a light dressing. The low-fat type gives a slightly tangy result and a little sugar or honey may be added to give a sweet-sour flavour. Greek-style yogurt makes a creamy, slightly richer dressing. Mix low-fat yogurt and mayonnaise, half and half for a delicious dressing that is not too rich.

Fromage Frais This makes excellent, low calorie, low-fat dressings. Add seasonings as for other dressings but remember that fromage frais is very light so add salt, pepper, sugar and mustard sparingly. Taste the dressing to check if more is needed.

Lemon Juice Lemon juice with a dash of soy sauce.

Peanut Butter Dressing This goes well with shredded white cabbage, chopped apple and onion. In a screw-topped jar, shake 30 ml/2 tablespoons crunchy peanut butter with 15 ml/1 tablespoon cider vinegar, 5 ml/1 teaspoon sugar, 1 crushed clove garlic and 90 ml/6 tablespoons oil until creamy. Add seasoning to taste.

Salmonella

See Bacteria*, Chicken*, Cross Contamination* and Hygiene*.
Salmonella bacteria are often present in uncooked poultry, such as chicken and turkey. The bacteria are killed at temperatures of 100°C/212°F or greater, therefore they are not a problem in food that is properly handled and cooked. In wet dishes the bacteria are killed at a lower temperature (about 68°C/154°F).

Prevent Food Poisoning

By Correct Storage Poultry should always be kept chilled after purchase and before cooking. It must be placed in a covered

container to avoid any chance of contaminating other foods in the refrigerator.

In Preparation When preparing raw poultry, it is essential to avoid transferring bacteria to other foods which may be eaten raw. For this reason, all utensils, knives, surfaces and dishes used for raw poultry should be washed in hot soapy water immediately after use. Wooden boards are not recommended for food preparation, particularly for cutting raw poultry, because they are absorbent and harbour bacteria. If a wooden board is used it should be thoroughly scrubbed in a mild bleach solution, well rinsed with hot water and dried after use.

Never to be tempted to wipe boards instead of washing them and do not put them away damp. Leave them to dry standing upright in the air.

In Cooking Make sure that chicken and turkey are cooked through before serving. Thaw frozen poultry (in a dish on a low shelf in the refrigerator to avoid 'drip' falling on other foods) before cooking, otherwise the meat near the bone may remain undercooked.

Salmonella and Eggs Due to the link between eggs, chicken and salmonella, it is important to follow the information given on buying, storing and using eggs (page 108). The same degree of risk of salmonella poisoning does not occur with eggs as with uncooked poultry but good hygiene practice should still be followed.

Salt and Seasoning

Salt is a natural mineral, sodium chloride, which is used in cooking to emphasise the flavour of foods; without salt many recipes are bland and uninteresting. Traditionally, salt is also a preservative, used for curing meat (as in bacon) as well as for preserving vegetables.

Salt is essential in the diet but it is obtained from a variety of sources. As well as sodium from table salt, it is eaten in many other foods, including fish, meat and some vegetables such as celery.

Concern over the high sodium content of many ready-prepared foods and other products used in cooking has made us aware that we can eat too much salt. Although some savoury packet snacks are very salty, many convenience foods are manufactured to meet the demand for less salty food. Check the labels on products for details.

On an everyday basis, avoiding sprinkling salt over food is a good rule. If the food is well prepared it should not need salting (with a few exceptions) and sprinkling salt over food destroys any subtle flavours.

Pepper

Pepper is equally as important in cooking. Buy peppercorns and grind them in a mill as you use them. This gives a flavour which is far superior to that found in pepper which is bought ready ground.

White peppercorns are not as common as black ones but they are usually obtainable from wholefood shops or alongside any good selection of spices. White pepper has a more 'peppery' taste and it should be used with more care than black pepper. Add white pepper to delicate sauces and to mashed potato.

Other Seasonings

Herbs and spices are the other main seasoning ingredients. Use them with other ingredients that have a distinct flavour (such as nuts and seeds) to complement the main food in a dish.

Adding Seasoning

Season food carefully, adding a little at a time and always taste before adding more.

Omit or add only a little seasoning to foods that are simmered for long periods. As liquid evaporates, the flavour and seasoning becomes more concentrated.

Balance salt and pepper with other flavouring ingredients. Too much salt will make the flavour of some foods seem overpowering and unpleasant. Remember to balance the seasoning in different dishes that are served together.

Seasoning with salt and pepper is a matter for personal taste. The more salt you use the more you become accustomed to it. When the palate has adjusted to eating foods and dishes that are only lightly salted, more delicate flavours may be appreciated.

Saucepans and Cooking Pans

The choice of cooking pans depends on the heat source, the type of cooking and the number of people for whom you normally cook. With proper use and care, good quality pans will last for many years; indeed they may outlive the cook. Cheap pans on the other hand are usually thin, they bend and buckle when exposed to high heat and burn easily. They cook unevenly and develop hot spots. Worst of all are thin pans with thin non-stick coatings that chip and peel.

Materials

Aluminium Avoid cheap, uncoated aluminium pans as there is some transfer of the metal to the food being cooked. Replace old aluminium pans. Most aluminium pans have a non-stick coating and some are good quality, depending on thickness and the type of coating.

Cast Iron Uncoated frying pans need a lot of attention to prevent rusting. They are cleaned by scouring with oil and salt.

Enamelled cast iron pans are good quality and ideal for solid fuel cookers. They are particularly good for long slow cooking as they conduct heat evenly but not quickly. These pans retain heat well, so casseroles and simmered foods continue to cook briefly after the heat is turned off.
Copper Copper conducts heat well, therefore it makes good saucepans that respond to changes in temperature. Apart from use in preserving pans, copper is usually coated on the inside, or tinned. Uncoated pans are not suitable for cooking other than sweet preserves and a stainless steel preserving pan is preferable.

Tinned copper has a thin coating on the inside. This can wear off with use and the pans may be retinned but this is an expensive exercise.

Copper pans look good but they are not particularly practical as they need regular cleaning and careful handling to avoid damage.
Enamel Enamelled pans vary enormously in quality. Lightweight pans are not a good buy as the coating chips easily and the pans heat unevenly, tending to burn.

Heavy pans with a good quality enamel coating can give long service; however, they must be stored carefully to avoid chipping or damaging the coating.
Glass Flameproof glassware does not conduct heat as well as some metals. These pans should be used only over medium to low heat to prevent burning. However, they retain heat well so foods continue to cook briefly after the heat source is switched off. They have the advantage of allowing the user to see what is happening in the pan.

They represent good value compared with other pans in the same price bracket but they do not compete with top quality saucepans.

SEE ALSO **Samphire:** Glossary; **Sandwich:** Glossary; **Sardine:** Fish

Stainless Steel Stainless steel does not conduct heat well so it is usually combined with copper or aluminium bases. It has good properties as a cooking surface and good stainless steel pans with a heavy base are the best choice.

Non-stick Finishes These vary enormously, from some that are thin, cheap and poor quality to others that are thick and durable. Price and brand are the best guide to quality; look for a reputable brand name with a good guarantee.

Bases

Copper A copper base conducts heat well and makes a pan responsive to changes in temperature. The copper base takes the form of a disc, brazed on the pan. This type of base is slightly concave (shaped inwards in the middle) to allow for expansion when heated. Not suitable for use on halogen, ceramic or solid hotplates as the concave bases are not flat enough for these heat sources.

Thermocore Base This thick sandwich base has a layer of aluminium between 2 layers of stainless steel. This type of base is only slightly curved, therefore suitable for all heat sources except an induction hob.

Thermocopper Base This heavy base has a top layer of stainless steel over aluminium and a copper bottom. The base is thick, stable and an excellent, even conductor of heat. It is responsive and efficient, suitable for all heat sources except induction. Thermocopper is one of the best bases available.

Pans for Induction Hobs

An induction hob relies on contact with a solid stainless steel base in order to produce heat. The contact between the metal and an induction coil in the hob creates a powerful magnetic field which creates heat (see cookers*). Follow the hob manufacturer's advice about saucepans.

Features

Whichever type of saucepan or cooking pan you intend buying, here are some features to expect.

Weight and Feel Look for heavy pans that feel comfortable to lift and well balanced.

Handles Strong handles, securely fitted, made of a material that will not overheat. They should be angled upwards away from the heat source. Look for a second, small, handle on large pans which are heavy to lift.

Lids Lids must fit well and have handles that are easy to grasp. Look for handles that do not conduct heat well otherwise they become very hot.

Good quality pans should have tight-fitting lids with steam vents that may be opened or closed. Some pans have lids that rattle if the heat is too high and the contents are about to boil over – a useful feature to prevent spillages. This feature is sometimes known as 'audible rattle'.

Shape and Depth Straight sided pans that slope outwards towards the rim do not have lids and are useful for reducing liquids (stocks, sauces or for brief poaching) but they are not suitable for boiling and simmering or long poaching and slow cooking where moisture retention is important.

Curved sides and a slightly curved edge around the base allows for even cooking and helps to avoid having food stuck in any corners around the base.

Storage Some pans have lids that may be reversed for easy stacking, others have a hole in the handle for hanging. Remember that stacking pans inside each other is the worst way to store them as it causes scratching and chipping.

Frying and Omelette Pans Look for pans of a suitable size. An omelette pan should have a curved base so that the omelette may be folded over and slid out easily. Ideally, keep an omelette pan for that purpose only, not for other shallow frying.

Individual Needs Buy to suit requirements. A gleaming set of attractive pans may not be the best purchase. Mix different materials, sizes and shapes according to what you cook. For example, a cheap, non-stick omelette pan, never used for any other purpose, will give years of service. Unless you cook omelettes frequently, this is a good option.

A heavy enamelled cast iron saucepan may double as a flameproof casserole or ovenproof pot, depending on handle type.

Look for a thermocopper base on an expensive stainless steel pan for sauces, plus years of service for boiling and simmering foods such as vegetables, rice and pasta.

Dishwasher Proof Check if the pans, lids and handles are dishwasher proof before purchase.

Steamers When buying a new pan, check whether there is a steamer attachment and if so make sure it fits neatly and has a tight-fitting lid.

Care of Cooking Pans

• Always follow manufacturer's instructions for use and cleaning.

• Use pans that are the right size for the hob: do not have gas flames licking the outside of the pan or a large area of uncovered hot electric hob surrounding the base of a pan. This is not economical and it damages the side of the pan as well as the handle.

• Avoid harsh abrasives; instead soak off any food that is stuck.

• Soak or simmer burnt or badly stuck pans with washing soda and water.

• Rinse, drain and dry pans immediately after washing. Store them in a dry place – do not stack pans inside each other.

Cook's Tip

Discard non-stick pans on which the coating has deteriorated and flaked.

Sauces

See Apples*, Arrowroot*, Béchamel Sauce*, Bread*, Chocolate*, Cranberries*, Cumberland Sauce*, Custard*, Fruit Sauces and Glazes*, Gravy*, Horseradish*, Mayonnaise*, Meat*, Mint* and Raspberries*.

Sauces are served to complement foods, by moistening them and enhancing their flavour. They are usually classified according to the way in which they are thickened.

Roux Sauces

A roux is a paste of fat and flour to which liquid is added.

Technique The fat is melted, then flour is stirred in and cooked briefly, stirring all the time. At this stage the fat may be cooked until it is brown to colour the sauce (as for gravy). The flour must be cooked to prevent the sauce from tasting raw; if it is not cooked with the fat, then the sauce must be simmered for at least 3 minutes after it has come to the boil.

With the pan over low heat, add the liquid slowly, stirring all the time. The mixture will thicken at first, then thin down when all the liquid has been added. Cook over medium or low heat until the sauce boils. Stir all the time to prevent lumps forming, then reduce the heat so that the sauce just simmers and continue to cook for a few minutes. If the fat and flour paste was cooked, then this simmering period can be kept to about a minute. However, it may be extended to thicken the sauce.

Use For gravy and savoury sauces using milk, wine or stock.

Cornflour or Arrowroot Sauces

Cornflour or arrowroot are mixed to a paste with cold liquid before being added to the bulk of hot liquid.

Cornflour has a slight flavour and it produces a sauce with a slightly gelatinous texture.

SAVOURY WHITE SAUCE

INGREDIENTS
40 g/1 ½ oz butter or margarine
40 g/1 ½ oz plain flour
600 ml/1 pint milk
salt and pepper

FOOD VALUES:
TOTAL • PER PORTION
kcals: 829 • 207
kJ: 3459 • 865
protein: 24 g • 6 g
fat: 56 g • 14 g
carbohydrate: 61 g • 15 g
fibre: 1 g • 0 g

Serves 4 Makes 600 ml/1 pint

Melt the butter in a saucepan. Stir in the flour, then cook the paste over low heat for 3 minutes, stirring often. Gradually pour in the milk, stirring all the time, and increase the heat to medium. Bring the sauce to the boil, still stirring to prevent lumps forming. Reduce the heat and simmer gently for 3–5 minutes. Add seasoning to taste and use as required.

VARIATIONS

Onion Sauce Cook a finely chopped large onion in the butter for about 20 minutes over low to medium heat. When the onion is soft but not browned, stir in the flour and continue as above. Serve with sausages, poultry or boiled ham.

Mushroom Sauce Finely slice 225 g/8 oz button mushrooms. Cook them in the butter, stirring often, until softened and juicy. Continue cooking until the liquid from the mushrooms evaporates – about 5 minutes over medium heat – to give the sauce a good flavour. Use a slotted spoon to remove the mushrooms from the pan and set them aside. Add the flour and continue as above. Replace the mushrooms at the end of cooking, stir well and serve with fish, poultry, vegetables or pasta.

The flour may be added to the mushrooms without setting them aside but the result is not as good as the flour tends to cling to the slices.

Parsley Sauce Make the sauce as above. Stir in 90 ml/6 tablespoons chopped fresh parsley at the end of cooking. Serve with poached fish or chicken.

Mustard Sauce Stir in 60 ml/4 tablespoons made Dijon or other mild mustard at the end of cooking. Serve with rabbit, ham or sausages.

Cheese Sauce Stir 75–100 g/3–4 oz grated Cheddar cheese into the sauce at the end of cooking. Stir over low heat until the cheese has melted. Season, if liked, with a little made mustard (about 5 ml/1 teaspoon), a pinch of cayenne pepper or paprika. Serve with vegetables, fish, eggs, stuffed pancakes or pasta.

Egg Sauce Hard boil, shell and chop 4 eggs. Add them to the cooked sauce. Serve with fish, boiled ham or vegetables.

Anchovy Sauce Drain and thoroughly mash a 50 g/2 oz can anchovies, then beat them into the sauce. Sharpen with a squeeze of lemon juice. Serve with eggs, vegetables or pasta.

Butter Sauce Cut 100 g/4 oz butter into small pieces, then whisk them into the sauce at the end of cooking. Serve with eggs, vegetables or fish.

Cream Sauce Use 450 ml/¾ pint milk and make the sauce as above, using just 25 g/1 oz butter. Simmer for 5 minutes. At the end of the cooking time, stir in 150 ml/¼ pint single cream and heat gently without boiling. Serve with fish, vegetables or eggs.

WINE SAUCE

INGREDIENTS
25 g/1 oz butter or margarine
1 small onion, finely chopped
40 g/1½ oz plain flour
300 ml/½ pint stock
300 ml/½ pint dry wine
1 bouquet garni
salt and pepper
Serves 4

FOOD VALUES:
TOTAL • PER PORTION
kcals: 863 • 216
kJ: 3612 • 903
protein: 11 g • 3 g
fat: 49 g • 12 g
carbohydrate: 51 g • 13 g
fibre: 2 g • 0.5 g

Melt the butter in a saucepan. Add the onion and cook for 10 minutes over medium heat, until softened. Continue as for Savoury White Sauce, adding the flour, stock and wine. Add the bouquet garni and cover the pan, then simmer the sauce gently for 15 minutes. Season the sauce to taste and remove the bouquet garni before serving.

SWEET CORNFLOUR SAUCE

INGREDIENTS
45 ml/3 tablespoons
    cornflour
30 ml/2 tablespoons sugar
600 ml/1 pint milk
25 g/1 oz unsalted butter
a little vanilla essence
Serves 4

FOOD VALUES:
TOTAL • PER PORTION
kcals: 853 • 213
kJ: 3575 • 894
protein: 20 g • 5 g
fat: 44 g • 11 g
carbohydrate: 101 g • 25 g
fibre: 1 g • 0 g

Blend the cornflour and sugar to a paste with a little of the milk in a bowl. The paste should be about the same consistency as double cream (unwhipped).

Pour the remaining milk into a saucepan and heat it until just about to boil. Pour a little of the hot milk into the cornflour paste, stirring as you do so. When the cornflour is well mixed, pour it into the pan with the rest of the milk, scraping any sugar into the sauce.

Bring the sauce to the boil over medium heat, stirring all the time to prevent lumps forming. Reduce the heat so the sauce simmers and leave to cook for 3–5 minutes.

Beat in the butter and add a little natural vanilla essence to taste before serving.

VARIATIONS
Brandy or Rum Sauce Stir in 45 ml/3 tablespoons brandy or rum at the end of cooking.

Chocolate Sauce Stir in 100–225 g/4–8 oz plain chocolate, broken into squares, at the end of cooking. Continue stirring until the chocolate has melted completely.

Orange and Honey Sauce Omit the sugar but add the grated rind of 1 orange to the cornflour. Sweeten the cooked sauce to taste with honey. Do not add orange juice as it curdles milk.

Arrowroot is flavourless and it produces a clear sauce.

Technique Blend the cornflour or arrowroot to a smooth paste with a little of the measured cold liquid – this is known as slaking. Heat the remaining liquid until just below boiling point. Pour some of the hot liquid on the paste, stirring, then pour the mixture back into the liquid. Place the sauce over medium heat and bring to the boil, stirring all the time.

Remove an arrowroot sauce from the heat immediately it boils as it becomes slightly thinner if it is allowed to simmer.

Simmer cornflour sauce for 3–5 minutes as the cornflour continues to thicken. If cornflour is not simmered it has a slightly raw taste.

Use Cornflour is used for thickening Chinese sauces. It is used for making sweet sauces either with milk or with fruit. Arrowroot is used for thickening fruit sauces and clear sauces.

Emulsified Sauces

Either hot or cold, these are a liaison of egg yolks and fat. For example Hollandaise and mayonnaise*.

Sauces Thickened with Egg

These are usually rich sauces and cream is often used as well as the egg yolks. They may be sweet (such as custard) or savoury.

Technique Blend the yolks with a little liquid – this may be hot or cold – then add them to the hot, not simmering, liquid off the heat. Return the sauce to a low heat or cook in a double boiler (or bowl over hot water) until it is just thickened. Do not allow the sauce to simmer or overheat as the eggs will cook completely and separate out. This is known as curdling.

Do not add egg yolks or cream to sauces before freezing.

Use To thicken cooking juices from fish, poultry or meat. To thicken and enrich wine sauces and casseroles.

Reduced Sauces

These are unthickened but boiled down until the flavours are concentrated. Used with roast or fried food as well as for braised or poached dishes.

Technique Cooking liquor from braising or poaching may be boiled rapidly in the open pan until it is reduced to a small quantity of sauce.

When roasting or frying meat, liquid, such as water, stock or wine, may be added to the pan (when the food has been removed) and brought to the boil, stirring all the time to loosen the cooking residue. The liquid is boiled until reduced and slightly syrupy, then strained (not always necessary) before being seasoned and served.

Use With roast meats or poultry, poached fish steaks, lightly cooked vegetables (such as glazed carrots). Reduced sauces may be enriched with cream, egg yolks or fromage frais.

Butter Sauces

These may be rich liaisons of butter with cooking liquor or a simple combination of butter heated with cooking juices. They are very rich and usually served in small quantities with plain poached food.

Technique Have a small amount of cooking liquor (from fish or poultry, or use a reduction of wine and water) not quite simmering over low heat, then gradually whisk in knobs of unsalted butter. The butter and liquor form a smooth, glossy liaison which must not be boiled.

The simpler butter sauces simply consist of butter in which food is cooked (fish or poultry breast fillets) or additional butter, cooked with pan juices, sometimes sharpened with lemon juice or flavoured with herbs. The butter may be cooked gently until it begins to brown (known as *beurre noir*).

Use With poached cod or other white fish, fried or sautéed foods.

HOLLANDAISE SAUCE

INGREDIENTS	FOOD VALUES:
2 egg yolks	TOTAL • PER PORTION
15 ml/1 tablespoon lemon juice	kcals: 1236 • 309
15 ml/1 tablespoon water	kJ: 5084 • 1271
150 g/5 oz unsalted butter	protein: 7 g • 2 g
salt and white pepper	fat: 134 g • 35 g
Serves 4	carbohydrate: 1 g • 0 g
	fibre: 0 g • 0 g

Place the egg yolks in a heatproof bowl. Pour the lemon juice and water into a small saucepan and heat until boiling. Boil the mixture until it is reduced by half – this takes 2–3 minutes. Remove the pan from the heat and allow the small amount of liquid to cool slightly, then whisk it into the egg yolks.

Set a saucepan of water to simmer on the hob, then reduce the heat so that it is not quite simmering. Cut the butter into small cubes or chunks. Stand the egg yolks over the pan of water and whisk in 4 cubes of butter. Continue whisking until all the butter has melted, then add the remaining cubes, one at a time, whisking well until each addition has melted.

When all the butter has been added, continue whisking the sauce until it is thickened, creamy and very shiny. This takes about 5–7 minutes. Season to taste. Transfer the sauce to a heated sauce boat or ladle it over the food.

VARIATION

Béarnaise Sauce Place 30 ml/2 tablespoons chopped onion, a sprig of tarragon, 4 black peppercorns and 100 ml/4 fluid oz dry white wine in a small saucepan. Bring to the boil, then boil until reduced to about 30 ml/2 tablespoons. Allow to cool slightly, then strain the liquid and add it to the yolks. Continue as above. Serve Béarnaise sauce with grilled steak.

MICROWAVE COOKING

Heat the lemon juice and water on High for 1–2 minutes, until boiling, then whisk the mixture into the yolks.

Cut the butter into pieces and melt them on High for 2–3 minutes, until very hot. Whisk the yolks all the time with an electric beater and slowly trickle in the hot butter. Return the sauce to the microwave and cook on High for 30 seconds. Stir well and the sauce should be thick and ready to serve. Taste and season.

LIQUIDISER OR FOOD PROCESSOR METHOD

Heat the lemon and water to boiling point, then process with the egg yolks. Heat the butter until very hot but not smoking. Trickle the butter on the eggs as they are being processed. The eggs combine with the butter to make a smooth, thick sauce. Serve at once.

SAVOURY SAUCES
A Quick Guide to Types and Uses

Type and Examples	Fish and Seafood	Poultry	Meat	Sausages and Offal	Game	Eggs	Vegetables	Pasta
Roux								
Béchamel	●					●	●	●
Savoury White	●					●	●	●
Cheese	●					●	●	●
Mushroom	●	●	●	●	●			●
Onion				●				●
Parsley	●	●				●	●	●
Wine Sauces	●	●	●	●	●			
Gravy		●	●	●	●			
Cornflour/ Arrowroot								
Oriental-style	●	●	●	●				
Sauces Thickened with Eggs								
Enriched Savoury (wine or cooking juices)	●	●	●		●			
Reduced Sauces								
Gravy		●	●		●			
Cooking Juices	●	●	●	●	●			
Emulsified Sauces								
Hollandaise	●					●	●	●
Béarnaise			●					
Mayonnaise	●	●				●	●	●
Tonnato (with tuna)		●	●			●	●	●
Aioli (with garlic)	●	●				●	●	
Sauces Thickened with Butter								
Beurre Blanc	●							
Other Sauces								
Bread		●			●			
Vegetable Purées	●	●	●		●	●		●

SWEET SAUCES A Quick Guide to Types and Uses			
Type and Examples	Steamed/Baked Puddings	Poached Fruit, Pancakes and Hot Puddings	Ices and Cold Desserts
Cornflour/ Arrowroot Sweet White Sauce	•	•	
Fruit Sauces and Glazes	•	•	•
Sauces Thickened with Eggs Custard	•	•	
Reduced Sauces Syrups	•	•	•
Other Sauces Fruit Purées	•	•	•
Jam Sauce (heated jam, thinned with a little water or dry sherry)	•	•	
Chocolate Sauce	•	•	•

TOAD-IN-THE-HOLE

INGREDIENTS
8 thick sausages
30 ml/2 tablespoons chopped fresh parsley
5 ml/1 teaspoon dried thyme or 10 ml/ 2 teaspoons chopped fresh thyme
1 quantity Thin Batter (page 28)

FOOD VALUES:
TOTAL • PER PORTION
kcals: 2221 • 555
kJ: 9266 • 232
protein: 96 g • 24 g
fat: 142 g • 35 g
carbohydrate: 149 g • 37 g
fibre: 7 g • 2 g

Serves 4

Set the oven at 200°C, 400°F, gas 6. Place the sausages in a shallow ovenproof dish or baking tin. A small roasting tin, gratin dish or large flan dish may be used. Cook the sausages in the oven for 20 minutes, then pour off any fat.

Beat the parsley and thyme into the batter, then pour it into the hot dish around the sausages. Bake for about 40 minutes, or until the batter is risen and crisp around the edges and the sausages are golden. The baking time may vary slightly according to the size of the dish – the narrower and deeper the batter the longer it will take. If a large shallow dish is used the batter may be cooked in about 30–35 minutes.

Serve at once. Good with onion gravy* and peas or with baked beans.

Sausages

These can be separated into 2 main groups: fresh or raw sausages and cured sausages.

British Sausages

There are laws governing the manufacture and labelling of sausages.

Pork sausages must contain a minimum of 65 per cent meat, 80 per cent of which must be pork. Any other type of sausage must contain at least 50 per cent meat and at least 50 per cent of this must be lean meat. This includes beef sausages.

Additional ingredients usually include rusk, herbs, spices, salt and water. Preservatives are added to ensure that the sausages are safe to eat by the time they are purchased.

Independent butchers often make excellent sausages to their own recipes but these must comply with the above minimum requirements. In many cases butcher's sausages have a higher percentage of meat. Some butchers make sausages without preservative and freeze them immediately.

Low-fat and skinless sausages are also sold fresh and frozen. Short, thin cocktail sausages are also available for cooking and serving cold.

Buying and Storing

Check the label on packs for details of the type, guide to cooking and storage time.

Use by the date suggested on the packet or within 2 days of purchase. Keep covered in the refrigerator as soon as possible after purchase until ready to cook.

Traditional Types

There are many types, including lamb, game and turkey sausages. Delicious combinations of herbs, vegetables such as leek, apples and herbs are used.

SEE ALSO **Sauté:** Frying; **Savarin:** Glossary; **Saveloy:** Sausages; **Savory:** Herbs; **Savoury:** Glossary; **Scallops:** Shellfish

Black Pudding A black ring sausage made from pig's blood. A spicy sausage which is sliced and fried.

Chipolatas These are thin, fine textured meaty sausages. Excellent served cold as well as hot.

Cotswold Flavoured with sage and thyme.

Cumberland A traditional long sausage with a spicy flavour and coarse texture, curled into a spiral. Cook curled, then cut into pieces to serve.

Lincolnshire Seasoned with sage.

London Mild pork sausage, lightly seasoned with ginger or nutmeg.

Oxford Made from veal, pork and beef.

Saveloy A red-skinned smoked sausage similar to the frankfurter.

Continental Sausages

The following are a few examples.

Bratwurst Smooth, with a delicate flavour. Best blanched in boiling water for 10 minutes before grilling. Most pre-packed types are cooked ready for grilling.

Boudin Blanc French white sausage which is cooked by poaching, then sliced.

Boudin Noir The French equivalent of black pudding.

Cervelat A cooked sausage with fine speckled texture.

Cotechino Coarse Italian sausage for boiling. Once boiled it may be grilled.

Chinese Sausages Dried spicy sausages made from pork, sometimes with offal and liver (the dark coloured ones have a high offal content, the pink ones are mainly pork). Poach or steam, then slice and stir fry or braise with other ingredients.

Chorizos Spicy red Spanish sausages. Cut them into chunks or cook them whole. Good in paella or with vegetable mixtures.

Frankfurters Cooked, fine textured sausages. The quality varies enormously. Poach in boiling water to serve hot.

Meguez or merguez Spicy, coarse red sausages of Algerian origins. Cook whole or cut up, allowing plenty of time for tenderising. Add in small quantities to casseroles and stews. Good with beans and pulses or with couscous.

Mortadella An Italian cooked sausage, rather like a luncheon meat. Speckled with fat, sometimes with pistachio nuts and/or green peppercorns.

Kabanos Slim, slightly wrinkled cooked Polish sausage. Good hot in stews or with cabbage.

Peperoni A spicy uncooked Italian sausage for slicing and cooking. Often served on pizza.

Salame The plural of salami; there are many types. Italian towns and villages produce their own and there are other types from other countries. Textures and tastes differ widely but salami should always be served very finely sliced.

Toulouse Coarse, meaty, French boiling ring. Used in casseroles and stews. Traditional ingredient for cassoulet (a stew of mixed meats and haricot beans).

Smoked Pork With or without added garlic. This ring of smoked sausage is similar to frankfurter but weighs about 350 g/12 oz. Serve raw or cooked. Boil or grill.

Weijska Large Polish boiling ring, sold by the piece, the whole ring may weigh about 1 kg/2 lb. Tough if not long cooked in moist mixture; then delicious and meaty.

Cooking Fresh Sausages

Do not prick the sausages. Preheat the grill. Place the sausages on a rack in the grill pan and cook them well away from the heat for about 15–20 minutes, turning often, until they are golden all over and cooked through.

Chipolata sausages take 10–15 minutes and they may be cooked slightly nearer the heat source.

Cumberland sausages should be cooked under a moderately hot grill for about 30 minutes, allowing time for the filling to become tender and succulent.

Freezing

Bought frozen sausages should be stored according to the packet instructions. Most sausages will keep for 3–4 months. Some remain fresh longer.

Nutritional Value

Sausages provide protein, iron, vitamin B12, nicotinic acid and calcium. The fat content depends on the sausage as does, to a large extent, the other values.

Scones

Scones are semi-sweet non-yeast breads. They may also be made savoury or enriched with fruit and nuts. As well as being cooked plain, the mixture can form the base for a variation on pizza or it may be divided and used as a topping for casseroles and stews, called cobblers.

Quantities

Use a quarter fat to flour, and bind the mixture with milk. To 225 g/8 oz plain flour, add 10 ml/2 teaspoons cream of tartar and 5 ml/1 teaspoon bicarbonate of soda. Alternatively use 15 ml/3 teaspoons baking powder. Use 50 g/2 oz butter, 25 g/1 oz sugar (if used) and a scant 150 ml/¼ pint milk.

FOOD VALUES: TOTAL • PER SCONE
kcals: 1368 • 137
kJ: 5769 • 577
protein: 28 g • 3 g
fat: 49 g • 5 g
carbohydrate: 219 g • 22 g
fibre: 8 g • 1 g

Makes 10

Technique

1. Set the oven at 230°C, 450°F, gas 8. Grease a baking tray.

2. Sift the flour and raising agent into a bowl. Add the butter, then cut it into the flour with a knife.

3. Wash and dry your hands, then rub the butter into the flour.

Stir in the sugar and mix in the milk to make a soft dough.

4. Turn out the dough on to a lightly floured surface and knead it very lightly into a smooth ball.

5. Use a lightly floured rolling pin to roll out the dough to about 1 cm/½ inch thick.

6. Use a 5–7.5 cm/2–3 inch cutter to stamp out 9–10 scones, re-rolling the trimmings as necessary.

7. Place the scones on the baking tray and brush with a little milk. Bake for 7–10 minutes, then cool the scones on a wire rack.

Variations

Fruit Scones Add 50 g/2 oz dried mixed fruit.
Wholemeal Scones Use wholemeal flour instead of plain flour, add a little extra milk.
Apricot and Walnut Scones Good with wholemeal flour. Add 50 g/2 oz chopped walnuts and 50 g/2 oz chopped ready-to-eat dried apricots.
Cheese Scones Omit the sugar and add 50 g/2 oz grated Cheddar cheese.

Using Scone Dough

• Press the scone dough out into a ring and cut it into wedges but do not separate them. Bake as above until risen and golden.

• Make a dough without sugar and roll out into a 25 cm/10 inch round. Use as a base for pizza, reducing the cooking temperature to 220°C, 425°F, gas 7. Cook for about 20 minutes.

• For cobbler, make a plain unsweetened dough, adding some herbs or grated cheese, if liked. Arrange the scones overlapping on top of an ovenproof dish of cooked casserole (beef or pork stew) or a basic Meat Sauce (page 176). Have the oven heated to 220°C, 425°F, gas 7. Glaze the scones with a little beaten egg. Bake the cobbler for 10–15 minutes, or until the scones are risen and golden.

Semolina

A coarse wheat product, semolina is used for milk pudding, couscous and gnocchi.

Storing

Semolina should be stored in an airtight container in a cool, dry cupboard, for several months.

Semolina Pudding

Bring 600 ml/1 pint milk and 50 g/2 oz sugar to the boil in a medium to large saucepan. Remove the pan from the heat and slowly pour in 50 g/2 oz semolina, stirring the mixture all the time. Return the pan to medium heat and bring the semolina to the boil, stirring. Reduce the heat and allow the semolina to simmer very gently for 5 minutes. Serve at once with cream or jam. Stewed fruit or chocolate sauce go well with semolina. **Chocolate Semolina** Stir 175 g/6 oz plain chocolate, broken into pieces, into the hot semolina. When the chocolate has melted, serve topped with cream or fromage frais or set in mould and serve cold.

Couscous

A semolina product, part cooked and ready to steam. Cover with cold water, leave 15 minutes, then steam in a metal sieve over simmering stew for 20 minutes. Alternatively, add boiling water, then fork grains after 15 minutes and toss in hot butter.
Microwave Cooking Soak in cold water; cook on High for about 5 minutes, depending on quantity. Serve with a spicy meat and vegetable stew.

Serving Food

See Hygiene* and Cross Contamination*.
The information on hygiene is equally important when serving food as when cooking it. There are a few common pitfalls to avoid to prevent contamination from bacteria which may cause food poisoning.

• Use clean utensils and dishes for handling and holding cooked food; never use the same utensils used to handle the raw food. A typical problem is using tongs to handle raw chicken, then using the same tongs to transfer it to the plate when cooked (particularly when grilling or barbecuing). The same goes for forks, knives and spoons.

• Use clean, dry oven gloves for handling hot serving dishes. Use a clean, dry tea-towel for plates.

• Serve food freshly cooked. Cover serving dishes to keep food clean as well as hot when it is transferred to the table.

• Food not served promptly should be kept hot, at the original serving temperature. Do this over a pan of just simmering water or in a moderate oven, depending on the type of food.

• Do not cool food until barely hot, then keep it warm. This encourages bacteria to grow.

Shellfish, Prawns and Shrimps*

See Crab*, Fish*, Lobster*, Prawns, Shrimps* and Squid*.
Shellfish includes mussels, cockles, scallops, oysters, clams, crab, winkles and whelks. Lobster, prawns and squid (also snails) are often grouped with shellfish.

Buying

Shellfish should look moist and fresh. The shells (mussels,

cockles and so on) should be shut. Mussels, oysters (native or Pacific oysters refers to species, not origins, the latter is more common) and scallops are in season from September to March (April for oysters). Frozen seafood is available all year.

Scallops, winkles and whelks are usually sold cleaned, without shells. Cockles, winkles and whelks are usually cooked and preserved in brine or vinegar.

Mussels, cockles and clams may be sold by the pint or by weight. About 600–900 ml/1–1½ pints or 350–450 g/12–16 oz are sufficient per person.

Preparation

Mussels, cockles and clams are all prepared and cooked by the same method.

Purging Most shellfish sold in fishmongers has been purified or purged. However any bought from seaside towns and markets may be sandy. Place the shellfish in a bucket of cold water, add a good sprinkling of salt and leave outside or in a cold utility room overnight. During this time any grit or sand is ejected from the shells.

Scrubbing Thoroughly scrub the shells, cleaning off all barnacles and dirt. Pull away the black hairy protrusion from mussel shells – this is known as the beard.

Discard any broken or open shells. If a shell is part open, tap it firmly and it should shut immediately. Any which do not shut are dead and they must be discarded as they can be a source of food poisoning.

Cooking

Finely chop a small onion. Melt 25 g/1 oz butter or heat a little oil in a large saucepan. Add the onion and cook it, stirring occasionally, for 5 minutes, until beginning to soften.

Pour in 150 ml/¼ pint dry white wine. Add a bay leaf, parsley sprig, thyme sprig and a couple of celery leaves. A little chopped carrot may also be added. Sprinkle a little salt and pepper into the liquid and bring it slowly to the boil.

Add up to 1.4 kg/3 lb mussels, clams or cockles. Turn the heat to high and put a tight-fitting lid on the pan. Cook, shaking the pan occasionally, for 5 minutes.

Check the shellfish – if the shells are opened they are cooked. If not, cook for another minute and check again. Shaking the pan ensures that the shellfish cook evenly.

Strain the liquid off then divide the shellfish between serving bowls. Discard any shells that have not opened and empty shell halves.

Pour the cooking liquid back into the pan, bring it to the boil and boil hard for 2 minutes. Taste and adjust the seasoning, then pour the liquid over the shellfish and serve.

Alternatively, the shellfish may be picked out of their shells and the shells discarded.

Scallops

Scallops consist of a nugget of white meat and a 'tongue' or coral. The coral should be bright orange-red in colour.

Queen scallops are a separate species.

Cooking Methods
● Poach very gently for 5 minutes, or until just firm.

● Wrap in bacon rashers and grill.

Serving Ideas
● In a Wine Sauce (page 235), made with white wine, served with pasta.

● In a Cream Sauce (page 234), served in a ring of piped mashed potatoes, topped with a little grated cheese and grilled.

Oysters

A short-bladed, heavy knife is used to open the shells. Protect your hand with a folded clean tea-towel. The cupped shell should be underneath. Insert the knife between the shell halves at the hinged end and twist it to prise them apart. Save the juice.

The fishmonger will open oysters for you, which is the safer way of dealing with them.

Oysters to be eaten raw must be absolutely fresh and kept chilled.

Shellfish Notes

● Always discard broken or open shells when handling mussels, clams or cockles.

● Always discard shells which remain shut after cooking.

● Never overcook shellfish – the result is rubbery.

● If the shells are to be used for serving scallops, they should be thoroughly scrubbed and cleaned in boiling water, then dried.

Shopping for Food

See Hygiene*, Labelling of Food* and Storing Food*.

Plan Ahead

Making a shopping list makes sense. List the essentials and check storecupboard and freezer for any necessary replacements. Think about the number of meals you have to shop for and the main food for each occasion. Add to these basic items.

A good list must be flexible, allowing the shopper to take advantage of fresh produce that is at its best, both in terms of quality and price. As well, the list should allow for any 'good buys' such as fresh foods that are reduced because they have reached their best before or use by date. A minor change to meal planning for later in the day means you can take advantage of special offers.

Be wary of buying special offers that are totally superfluous to your requirements.

Take advantage of bulk purchases or multi buys, when you

receive a discount. Buy small sizes of new items which you want to sample, or own brand goods which are less expensive. Try them out before buying in huge amounts to be sure you (and the family) approve.

The Organised List If you are familiar with the supermarket, list items in the order in which you shop for them, grouping them according to where they are in the shop and at what stage you want to select them.

Many large supermarkets have a welcoming display of fresh fruit and vegetables just inside the entrance, but these should not go into the trolley first as they will be thoroughly squashed under other goods. Plan supermarket purchases in the following order.

1. Heavy items (bottles, cleaning materials and so on), cans and goods that will not get crushed.

2. Packets and lighter items that may burst or be crushed in the bottom of the trolley, including bakery goods.

3. Fruit and vegetables: arrange the fragiles ones on top or to one side.

4. Dairy produce and other chilled products.

5. Fish, poultry and meat.

6. Frozen foods.

Pack different groups of foods into separate bags.

Specialist Shops

Although the supermarket may be a convenient one stop option, it is not necessarily the best place to buy all food. Independent traders often provide excellent quality food, in the amounts you find most convenient and at a very competitive price. The smaller specialist shopkeeper values customers and provides a specialist service on request, for no extra charge.

Assessing the Store

Whether you shop in a supermarket, small shop or local fish farm, there are certain standards to expect if the seller is handling food. The shop is offering a service for which you pay, not doing you a favour.

General Cleanliness Are the floors, walls, shelving, windows and displays clean, fresh and neat? Does the shop smell fresh and is it well ventilated but at the same time free from flies in summer? Take a look in the refrigerators and freezers to check that the stock is all properly chilled or frozen, correctly packed and fresh.

Hygiene Standards Staff handling fresh foods should wear protective clothing to prevent fluff and dirt from everyday clothes being transferred to the food. Hair should be neat and out of the way. Hands and nails should be clean. The staff should use tongs and utensils or polythene bags to handle food. Check that all utensils and equipment look clean and that all uncooked food (meat, fish, poultry) is handled quite separately from cooked foods (ham, cheese, salad vegetables or fruit). Staff who handle fresh unpacked food should not take money. For example, the butcher who bones a joint should have a cashier to take your money.

Be particularly aware of standards when raw and cooked unwrapped foods are being handled. For example, when buying fish, smoked fish such as mackerel or smoked trout should be kept separate from wet fish. Tongs or separate utensils should be used for the smoked fish which should be placed in a clean wrapper. The person who guts trout, then lifts smoked trout fillets by hand is likely to transfer bacteria from the innards of one fish to the ready-to-eat smoked food.

Advice, Assistance and Attitude

There are qualified staff behind the supermarket shelves as well as behind the counter of a small shop. So, ask for information or advice and expect to receive an answer. If the assistant does not have the answer, then the owner, manager or department supervisor should be able to help.

If you cannot find a product or food in a supermarket, then ask for it. Enquire why it is not available or whether it is out of season in the case of fresh foods. This way you are getting what you want, rather than simply accepting whatever is on offer. Most senior staff in larger supermarkets are most helpful; if they are not, then complain.

Transporting Food

Once you have bought the food it is important to transport it correctly to avoid contamination.

● Use a chiller bag for frozen and fresh foods that should be chilled.

● Take fresh food home promptly. Never leave food in a warm car while you finish other shopping.

● Unpack food promptly and place it in the refrigerator or freezer as appropriate.

Complaining

There are two situations in which a complaint should be made. If standards in a supermarket or shop are inadequate the problem should be brought to the attention of the manager or owner and the relevant local authority. If food is found to be unsatisfactory when unpacked, tasted or used within the recommended time period then it should be returned to the shop.

Short Crust Pastry

See Pastry*.
Short crust is easy to make and versatile. It may be bought ready made or as a packet mix but neither compare well with the homemade version.

Quantities

Use half fat to plain flour. Traditionally a combination of half lard and half margarine make the dough short and well flavoured but all margarine may be used. Block margarine is best; however tub margarine may be used although the very soft type makes the pastry difficult to handle.

With 225 g/8 oz plain flour, use 100 g/4 oz margarine or 50 g/2 oz margarine and 50 g/2 oz lard and about 45 ml/3 tablespoons cold water to bind the pastry.

FOOD VALUES: TOTAL
kcals: 1518
kJ: 6359
protein: 22 g
fat: 84 g
carbohydrate: 180 g
fibre: 8 g

Technique

1. The fat should be chilled and all utensils should be cold. Make sure the work surface is clean and dry. Measure the ingredients, then wash and dry your hands, rinsing them under cold water before drying.

2. Place the flour in a bowl. Add the fat and use a knife to cut it into the flour. When the fat is cut into small pieces, use your fingertips to rub it in.

3. Lift a little fat and some flour, then rub the mixture between your thumb and fingertips. Do this very lightly, then let the mixture drop back into the bowl.

4. Carry on rubbing the fat into the flour until the mixture resembles fine breadcrumbs.

5. Use a round-bladed knife or palette knife to lightly mix the water into the dough. It should form small clumps.

6. Draw the dough together into a ball with your fingertips, then press this lightly into a smooth, flattened round shape.

7. Place the dough in a polythene bag and chill for 30 minutes. This is not essential but it improves the texture of the finished dough.

8. Roll out the dough on a surface dusted very lightly with flour. Try to keep the dough in the shape required and lift it slightly occasionally, moving it around a little. Do not turn the dough over.

9. Keep the rolling pin lightly dusted with flour and sprinkle a little flour under the pastry if it sticks.

10. As you roll the dough, pinch the edges lightly to close up any cracks, then roll them evenly. Gently pinch or press together any breaks as they occur.

Makes about 350 g/12 oz

Use

For savoury or sweet flans*, pasties and turnovers*, pies* and tarts*.

This quantity provides enough dough to:

- line a 23–25 cm/9–10 inch flan tin or dish;
- cover a 1.1–1.7 litre/2–3 pint pie dish;
- make 20–24 open tartlets or 12 individual covered tartlets (mince pies);
- make 4 rounds for pasties (15 cm/6 inches each) or squares for turnovers (about 15 cm/6 inches each);
- make a 15–18 cm/6–7 inch plate tart (double crust).

Variations

Wholemeal Pastry Use 175 g/6 oz wholemeal flour and 50 g/2 oz plain flour. All wholemeal may be used but an extra 25 g/1 oz fat should be added: the texture is grainy. Add a little extra water to bind the dough.

Rich Short Crust Use 175 g/6 oz butter or margarine instead of the 100 g/4 oz fat. Use 1 egg yolk and 15 ml/1 tablespoon water to bind the dough.

Sweet Rich Short Crust As above, with 25 g/1 oz caster sugar stirred in before adding the egg yolk and water.

Cheese Pastry Add 50–100 g/2–4 oz finely grated Cheddar cheese to the rubbed in mixture. The smaller amount for savoury vegetable pasties and pies or whenever a light cheese flavour is required, the larger amount for cheese biscuits when a stronger taste is needed.

Additional Flavouring Ingredients

- Grated orange or lemon rind may be added to sweet pastry; lemon rind is also good with fish in savoury dishes.

- Chopped fresh or dried herbs may be added to savoury pastry. Try parsley, chives, thyme or marjoram.

- Finely chopped nuts, such as walnuts, almonds or hazelnuts, may be added to savoury and sweet. Add small amounts with some cheese for vegetable pies;

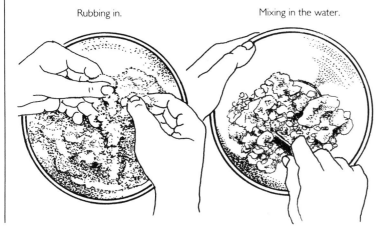

Rubbing in.

Mixing in the water.

more with grated orange rind and sugar for sweet pies.

- Ground almonds may be used with rich sweet pastry to make flans or biscuits.

Cooking

The cooking depends on the filling. As a rule, short crust is best started at 200°C, 400°F, gas 6 for 15–20 minutes, then the heat reduced to cook other ingredients. If the temperature is maintained, the pastry cooks in about 30 minutes.

Sorbet

A sorbet is based on a frozen syrup which is whisked part-way through freezing to break down the ice crystals. The result is smooth and creamy if properly whisked.

Basic Syrup

Some recipes use a very heavy syrup but this one works well. Place 175 g/6 oz sugar in a large saucepan and add 600 ml/1 pint water. Stir until the sugar dissolves, then bring the syrup to the boil. Reduce the heat so that the syrup does not boil over, then boil for 7 minutes. Remove from the heat and allow to cool.

Flavouring

The following all make 8 portions.

Lemon Sorbet

Add the grated rind and juice of 3 lemons to the sugar and water.

Using Fruit Juice

Use unsweetened fruit juice instead of the water. Try passion fruit, mango, pineapple, apple (add the grated rind of 1 lemon as well), grapefruit or any of the exotic juices. Boil for 5 minutes instead of 7 minutes.

Using Fresh Fruit

Purée soft fruit (raspberries or strawberries), peaches or apricots. Sieve the purée to remove seeds if necessary. Use 300 ml/½ pint purée. Reduce the volume of water to 450 ml/¾ pint.

Freezing

Chill the syrup if possible, then pour it into a rigid freezer container and freeze until the edges of the syrup are becoming hard – about 3 hours, depending on the freezer.

Whisk the mixture well using a rotary whisk or electric beater. The best way is to whiz the sorbet in a food processor. Chill utensils, including bowl and beaters or blades, beforehand.

Refreeze the mixture until it is hard around the edges again and the consistency of a sludge in the middle (this takes a few hours). Whisk until smooth, then freeze the sorbet until firm, usually overnight.

Place the sorbet in the refrigerator about 15 minutes before serving if very hard.

COLD LEMON SOUFFLE

INGREDIENTS
25 g/1 oz gelatine
60 ml/4 tablespoons water
4 eggs
100 g/4 oz caster sugar
3 lemons
450 ml/¾ pint fromage frais
50 g/2 oz blanched almonds, chopped and toasted

FOOD VALUES:
TOTAL • PER PORTION
kcals: 1684 • 211
kJ: 706 • 882
protein: 108 g • 13 g
fat: 81 g • 10 g
carbohydrate: 141 g • 18 g
fibre: 20 g • 2 g
Serves 8

Sprinkle the gelatine over the water in a small basin, then set aside for 15 minutes, or longer, until the gelatine has sponged. Set the basin over a pan of hot water and stir the gelatine occasionally until it has dissolved completely. Prepare an 18 cm/7 inch soufflé dish by wrapping a band of greaseproof around it.

Separate the eggs, placing the yolks and whites in 2 large, clean mixing bowls. Add the sugar to the yolks, then beat the mixture well until the yolks are very pale, thick and creamy. Doing this over a saucepan of hot (not simmering) water speeds up the process but it is not necessary.

Pare the rind from one of the lemons, then use a pair of kitchen scissors to cut it into long thin shreds. Place these in a small saucepan and cover with cold water. Bring to the boil, then reduce the heat and simmer the lemon rind for 5 minutes. Drain well, place in a small covered container and chill.

Grate the rind from the remaining lemons and add it to the yolk mixture. Squeeze the lemon juice. Gradually stir in the lemon juice. Stir in the gelatine, then fold in the fromage frais.

Use a clean whisk to whisk the egg whites until they stand in firm but not dry peaks. Use a large metal spoon to fold the whites into the mixture, then turn it into the prepared dish. Chill the soufflé until set – at least 4 hours, preferably overnight.

Remove the paper and press the nuts against the side of the soufflé. Decorate the top with the shreds of lemon rind.

SEE ALSO **Shortening, Shred:** Glossary; **Shrimps:** Prawns; **Shuck, Sieve, Sift:** Glossary; **Skate:** Fish;

Soufflés

These are neither difficult nor expensive to make.

Types

Both cold and hot soufflés may be either savoury or sweet.

Cold Soufflés These consist of a mixture lightened with egg white and set with gelatine. As well as the use of gelatine, 2 skills are involved: whisking egg whites and folding in. The mixture is set in a dish which has a band of paper around the outside. The paper stands above the rim of the dish to give the set soufflé the risen appearance.

Hot Soufflés A thick roux sauce, known as a panada, forms the base for most savoury cooked soufflés. Thick Confectioner's Custard (page 101) may be used for a sweet baked soufflé.

First the flavouring ingredient is added to the base, along with egg yolks. Then the egg whites are whisked and folded in just before the soufflé is baked.

Although a band of paper may be tied around the outside of the dish, this is not usually necessary when making a baked soufflé.

The soufflé may be baked in a hot oven so that it is risen, browned and firm outside but very creamy in the middle. This type of soufflé must be served swiftly as it tends to collapse.

Alternatively, the soufflé may be baked at a lower temperature for longer until it is lightly set in the middle. These soufflés do not collapse as quickly as the soft-centred ones.

Preparing a Soufflé Dish

A straight-sided dish must be used for making a soufflé. An ovenproof dish should be used for a baked soufflé. Individual soufflé dishes or ramekins (smaller but the same shape) may be used.

Cold Soufflé Cut a double-thick band of greaseproof paper 7.5 cm/3 inches wider than the depth of the dish. The band of paper must be long enough to wrap right around the dish and overlap by 2.5 cm/1 inch.

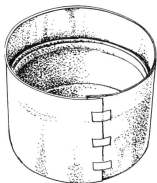

Prepared soufflé dish.

HOT CHEESE SOUFFLE

INGREDIENTS
25 g/1 oz butter
25 g/1 oz plain flour
150 ml/¼ pint milk
100 g/4 oz mature Cheddar cheese, grated
10 ml/2 teaspoons mild made mustard
salt and pepper
4 eggs

FOOD VALUES:
TOTAL • PER PORTION
kcals: 1118 • 280
kJ: 4649 • 1162
protein: 61 g • 15 g
fat: 85 g • 21 g
carbohydrate: 30 g • 7 g
fibre: 1 g • 0 g

Serves 4

Grease an 18 cm/7 inch ovenproof soufflé dish and dust it with a little flour. Set the oven at 190°C, 375°F, gas 5.

Melt the butter in a large saucepan. Add the flour and stir the mixture over low heat for 2 minutes. Gradually pour in the milk, stirring all the time, and bring the mixture to the boil. It will become very thick and should be beaten well to prevent lumps forming. Cook the mixture for 1 minute, then remove the pan from the heat and beat in the cheese.

Add the mustard and a little salt with plenty of pepper, then beat well again. Separate the eggs, then beat the yolks into the cheese mixture. Whisk the whites in a bowl until they stand in firm but not dry peaks.

Add a large spoonful of egg white to the cheese mixture and beat it in well. This softens the mixture and allows for the remaining whites to be folded in easily. Use a clean metal spoon to fold in the remaining whites, then turn the mixture into the prepared dish.

Bake the soufflé for 40–50 minutes, or until it is well risen, golden and just firm to the touch. To check if the soufflé is cooked, gently touch the top without removing it from the oven. If the mixture feels soft in the middle it should be cooked slightly longer; if it feels just firm, then serve the soufflé at once.

Wrap the paper around the outside of the dish and use a little sticky tape to keep it in place.

Grease the inside of the paper with a little light oil.

Hot Soufflé Grease the dish and dust it with a little caster sugar if making a sweet soufflé. For a savoury soufflé, dust the inside with a little flour or very fine, dry white breadcrumbs. The coating provides a surface for the mixture to cling to as it rises.

Finishing Cold Soufflés

1. Use a sharp knife to slit the tape holding the paper band in place. As you peel back the paper, slide a kitchen knife

Removing the paper.

between it and the side of the soufflé. This ensures that the soufflé does not break and gives the side an even surface.

2. Use a palette knife to press finely chopped nuts, biscuits crumbs or grated chocolate on the side of the soufflé.

3. A border of whipped cream may be piped around the top edge of the soufflé.

Soup

See Stock*.

Soup may be thick or thin, chunky or smooth, piping hot or chilled, even sweet as well as savoury. The easiest and most heart-warming of soups are the ones laden with vegetables, with some pearl barley added; these are meals in themselves. By way of contrast, avocado or cucumber may be puréed with chilled yogurt to make delicate soups for summer first courses.

Ingredients and Techniques

Stock Good stock is important for some plain soups (potato, leek, celery and so on), whereas other soups which contain plenty of different ingredients make their own stock. Homemade or good quality bought stock should be used for light soups, usually chicken. Canned beef consommé is excellent for making French onion soup.

Vegetables An onion is the basic vegetable used to flavour most savoury soups. Finely chop it, then cook in a little fat until soft before adding other ingredients.

Soups may be made from individual vegetables – potatoes, leeks, carrots (flavour with orange), parsnips (add some curry spices), beetroot*, peas (with ham stock), celery, spinach, lettuce (with a potato for body) and so on.

Mixed vegetable soups are delicious and filling. Dice carrots, swede, onion, potato and parsnip and cook these in a little butter or oil before adding stock or water. Canned tomatoes or tomato purée, cabbage, peas and French beans should be added when the other vegetables are two-thirds cooked.

Fish Fish and other seafood make chowders – milky soups that are chunky with vegetables such as leeks, carrots and potatoes.

Cook the vegetables in butter, then fish stock. Top up with milk and add skinned white fish or smoked haddock fillet (cut in chunks) towards the end of cooking. Simmer the fish for about 5 minutes, or until it is just cooked.

More adventurous fish soups – almost stews really – include famous bouillabaise which combines vegetables and many types of small whole fish with lobster, prawns and other shellfish. Spiced with garlic and saffron, bouillabaise is a seafood enthusiast's dream but not ideal for bone-shy diners.

Poultry The carcass remaining from chicken or turkey makes excellent stock and any diced leftover meat should be added to the soup.

However, to make delicious chicken soup, simmer a quarter portion in 1.1 litres/2 pints water with a chopped onion, diced carrot, bay leaf and parsley sprig for 1 hour. Remove the joint on a slotted spoon and discard all skin and bone, then dice the meat. Make the soup chunky by adding vegetables to the cooking liquid and simmering until tender, or

cook 2 potatoes until tender. Purée the soup until smooth, then thin it with a little milk. Replace the chicken meat, season the soup and heat it through.

Meat Ham is the most popular for making soup. Save the stock from boiling a joint of ham or bacon. Diced bacon may be fried with onion and other root vegetables in the first stages of soup preparation (excellent with potatoes and celery in a chunky soup). Beef stock makes good soup, either from bones or from boiling a joint of beef.

Beans, Pulses and Grains All go well in soup. Add rice, pearl barley or lentils to soup to thicken it slightly, to make it more filling and to add interest texturewise. Canned beans may be added to vegetable soups.

Pasta Soup pasta consists of very small shapes. Add them to thin soup about 5 minutes before the end of the cooking time. Be sparing as they swell.

Milk or Cream Both are added to enrich delicately flavoured soups (chicken, fish, asparagus and so on). Add milk towards the end of the cooking time and heat the soup until it is just below simmering point. Depending on the type of soup and the proportion of ingredients, the milk may curdle if it is boiled. Cream is always added just before the soup is served and usually in small quantities. If enough is added to cool the soup slightly, then reheat it very gently. Boiling curdles the cream.

Fromage Frais and Yogurt Both should be treated as for cream and barely heated as they curdle readily. Useful for cold soups.

Thickening Soup

Roux See Sauces*. Made at the beginning, when onion has been cooked. Useful for most soups.
Beurre Manié See Glossary, page 275. A good thickening for smooth soups that are not thick enough.
Potatoes and Other Vegetables Potatoes are cooked with delicate vegetables such as lettuce, spinach, asparagus, onions and

artichokes, then puréed until smooth. Carrots, parsnips and celeriac thicken puréed soups.

Eggs and Cream Added at the end of cooking to lightly flavoured soups. Must not be boiled and make a rich soup.

Cornflour Added to Oriental soups and fruit soups (or use arrowroot*).

Cold Soups

These may be cooked, then puréed (if necessary, or strained) and chilled or they may be made from puréed raw ingredients.

Vichyssoise

Cook 225 g/8 oz peeled and diced potatoes and 350 g/12 oz cleaned and sliced leeks first in 25 g/1 oz butter, then in 600 ml/1 pint chicken stock for 30 minutes in a covered pan. Purée until smooth, season to taste and chill. Stir in 300 ml/ ½ pint single cream or fromage frais and check the seasoning before serving.

Gazpacho

Purée 1 chopped onion with 450 g/1 lb ripe tomatoes, 2 cloves garlic, ½ peeled cucumber, 1 deseeded and diced red pepper, 15 ml/ 1 tablespoon sugar, 15 ml/ 1 tablespoon cider vinegar, 60 ml/4 tablespoons olive oil and 5 ml/1 teaspoon dried marjoram. Sieve the mixture to remove seeds and traces of skin, then stir in 300 ml/ ½ pint tomato juice and seasoning to taste. Chill well. Serve with diced cucumber, diced green pepper, chopped olives and croûtons.

Sweet Soups

Made by cooking fruit in water and fruit juice, sometimes with

wine or liqueur added, and sweetened with sugar. Extra cooked fruit is usually added to the puréed mixture which is enriched with soured cream and chilled. Plums, cherry and apricots may all be used to make fruit soups.

Spices

Spices were the culinary gold of medieval cooks, kept locked away in spice chests in the affluent households of the day. The history of spices is fascinating, from their Eastern origins to eventual introduction to northern Europe via the nomadic traders and great explorers. Even today certain spices are used with respect in cooking and savoured by the appreciative palate. Saffron, cardamom and vanilla are probably the most expensive.

Buying and Storing Spices

Buy packed spices displayed in dark glass jars or pots. If buying loose, make sure the spices are fresh. Buy often rather than hoarding large quantities that become stale as they lose their flavour.

Store spices in airtight containers in a dark, cool place. Clear bottles on open racks are not suitable for storing spices, even though they may look attractive.

Grinding Spices

A heavy pestle and mortar is best for grinding small quantities. A coffee grinder may be set aside especially for the purpose, or use a pepper mill for coriander, allspice and similar spices. Label the spice mills to avoid muddling them with the ones that hold pepper.

Glossary of Spices

Allspice Small dark berries about the size of peppercorns. Their

flavour is reminiscent of cloves, cinnamon and nutmeg. Used in sweet and savoury cooking. Also known as Jamaican pepper.

Aniseed Small dark seeds that have a strong, distinct flavour. Used in Chinese dishes and in some baking.

Star anise is a star-shaped seed pod. Although it has a very similar flavour to aniseed, it is a different spice.

Caraway Small slightly curved, striped seeds with a strong flavour. Used in cakes (a Madeira-style cake flavoured with caraway is known as seed cake), bread (Polish rye bread) and savoury cooking. Good with cabbage and pork.

Cardamom There are 3 types. White cardamom seeds are rare and expensive. They are bleached and reserved for use in sweet cooking. Green cardamoms are more common. Both white and green are pods about the size of the small nail, or slightly larger, oval and papery in texture. Black seeds nestle in the pod compartments.

Black cardamoms are quite different – large, brown in colour and hairy. All are aromatic and similar in flavour, the black ones being stronger. The flavour is citrus-like and zesty. All may be used whole, the green ones may be eaten. Green cardamoms are chewed as breath fresheners.

The tiny black seeds may be extracted and ground when they give off a wonderful aroma. The dark powder may be purchased from some specialist Indian grocers but it is very expensive.

Used with rice, in subtle curry mixtures, in Indian desserts (rice pudding or ice cream known as kulfi), in dried fruit compote or to spice coffee.

Cayenne One of the hottest of spices. Ground dried cayenne chilli peppers produce a dark red-brown powder that should be used sparingly. For seasoning cheese mixtures, sauces and other savouries.

Chillies* See separate entry.

Chilli Powder There are different types, some hotter than others. Chilli powder should be used with caution until you are familiar with its strength. It is not as hot as cayenne pepper.

Cinnamon Buy ground for baking; sticks (the rolled bark of a tree) for adding to pullao rice, curries, mulled wine and dried fruit compotes.

Cloves Strongly flavoured, tiny unopened buds. Cloves are used in curries, rice dishes, pickles and chutneys as well as in sweet cooking, including apple pies, and for making mulled wine. Ground cloves are very strong and should be used sparingly.

Coriander Pale seeds about the same size as peppercorns. Coriander has a distinctive, mild flavour and pleasant aroma. Used in curries and other savoury cooking as well as in pickles and chutneys. Coarsely crushed seeds are delicious baked with chunks of potato and onion in a covered dish in the oven.

Cumin Small long seeds, either white (beige, in fact) or black. Another spice that is widely used in Indian cooking to flavour breads as well as vegetables and rice dishes. Also used in North African recipes, this is a sweet spice which has a more prominent flavour than coriander. Also available ground.

Fennel Seeds Small, oval seeds with a mild caraway flavour. Used in savoury cooking with meat, poultry, vegetables or as a topping for breads.

Fenugreek The whole spice looks like tiny, very hard, mustard-beige stones. Difficult to grind (just about possible in a coffee grinder) but usually sold ready ground. The strong flavour is characteristic of curry powder.

Ginger, Crystallised Chunks of tender stem ginger coated in sugar. Used for desserts or as decoration when sliced.

Ginger, Fresh Root Fresh root ginger is knobbly, with a beige skin. The young root is pale and thin skinned with small shoots. Young roots are juicy, succulent and tender, available from Chinese supermarkets in the summer months when they are well

worth freezing. The flavour is tangy and just slightly hot, not to be compared with ground ginger.

Avoid old, dried or wrinkled roots as these are fibrous and lacking in flavour.

Wash and grate or thinly peel root ginger. When grating a piece, be prepared to discard the last, tough sliver of skin that remains.

Thinly slice or chop peeled roots. Cut slices into fine slivers if liked.

Prepared ginger freezes well for up to 6 months.

Ginger, Ground A powder used in baking and for making ginger beer. The powder has a hot taste.

Ginger, Pickled A Chinese product. Sliced young root ginger is pickled in sweetened vinegar for savoury cooking.

Ginger, Preserved Stem Chunks of preserved stem ginger bottled in syrup. Used in desserts.

Juniper Small, slightly soft, dark purple-black berries. They give gin its distinctive flavour. Used in small numbers in savoury cooking, particularly for marinating meat and game. Easy to crush in a pestle and mortar.

Mace The dull orange net-like covering from around the nutmeg. Sold ground or in pieces known as blades. Mace has a strong flavour and it is used in sweet and savoury cooking, notably pâtés and sausages.

Mustard Seeds There are many types, some hot others mild. Small dark crunchy mustard seeds are often fried with other spices to flavour diced potatoes and other vegetables cooked Indian style. They are sometimes used in the filling for samosas (triangular Indian pasties), to which they add pleasing crunch.

Nutmeg Small round dark nuts, slightly smaller than walnuts. Nutmeg is grated on a small coarse grater, although it is also available ground. Freshly grated has by far the best flavour. Used in savoury and sweet cooking; this is a pleasing seasoning for cheese, egg and vegetable dishes.

Paprika A sweet, mild, deep red pepper. Used to flavour Hungarian goulash. Some hot types are available but they are labelled 'hot paprika'. Most paprika is mild. Used with cheese, eggs, vegetables and in casseroles.

Saffron The stamens of a particular variety of crocus. Saffron is expensive but it is used in comparatively small quantities. It contributes a delicate, yet distinct, flavour and bright yellow colour.

Correct preparation is important to extract both flavour and colour. Place the strands in a pestle and mortar and pound them to a fine powder. Then add a little hot water (about 30 ml/ 2 tablespoons) to dissolve the powder and make a red liquid. Stir well, then add every drop to the dish. Powdered saffron is also available.

Saffron is added late in the cooking to rice (pullao or risotto) or used as a marinade for meat and poultry. Saffron is used in sweet cooking as well as savoury dishes.

Although some recipes suggest that turmeric may be substituted, the colour may be similar but the flavour is quite different.

Turmeric A bright yellow root with dark brown skin. Rarely available fresh (sometimes found in Chinese supermarkets), the dried root is ground to a powder which has a strong, vaguely musty taste and shocking yellow colour.

Used in curries and other savoury cooking.

Vanilla Long, black, wiry pods that have a strong flavour. They are very expensive and sold singly or in pairs. Split a pod, then infuse it with hot liquid (often milk) to extract the flavour.

Alternatively, place the pod in a jar of caster sugar, burying it well, then leave for at least 3 weeks. The vanilla imparts its flavour to the sugar which may be used in desserts or baking.

Natural vanilla essence has an excellent flavour; however the

SEE ALSO **Split Peas:** Beans and Pulses, Dried; **Sponge:** Glossary; **Spring Greens:** Cabbage

synthetic essence (or flavouring) is a strong, crude substitute. Natural vanilla essence is available from larger supermarkets, some chemists, wholefood shops or herbalists.

Spice Mixtures

These are just a few examples. Different cuisines have their own standard seasoning mixes.

Curry Powder See separate entry under curry*. A British invention to replace the combination of spices used in authentic curries. Some of the more expensive brands are good; many cheap, bright yellow and hot mixtures are inferior and poorly balanced in terms of flavour.

Five Spice Powder A Chinese seasoning, consisting of cloves, star anise, peppercorns, cinnamon and fennel.

Garam Masala Roasted or raw mixed cardamoms, coriander, cinnamon, cloves and cumin, sometimes with a bay leaf or curry leaves (small oval, dark green leaves found in Indian greengrocers). The spices are ground and may be sprinkled over dishes before serving.

Mixed Spice Familiar ground spice mixture used for baking.

Spinach

See Vegetables.*
Available all year, with home-grown spinach in season early and late summer.

Buying

Look for bright, fresh undamaged leaves that are not limp, broken or wilted. Small to medium leaves are best with thin stalks.

Spinach shrinks remarkably, so what looks a lot when weighed reduces to very little in the pan. Allow 175–225 g/6–8 oz raw spinach per portion.

When comparing weight, the cooked weight is about half that of the raw amount.

Storing

Use on the same day as buying or freshly picked. It will keep in a polythene bag in the refrigerator overnight.

Preparation

Wash the spinach in a sink full of water, then cut off the stalks and discard damaged leaves. Rinse again.

Cooking

Put the wet spinach in a large saucepan, putting in as many leaves as possible as they reduce when cooked. Put a lid on the pan and place over high heat, shaking the pan often, for about 5 minutes. Turn the heat down, check the spinach and stir it for another 2 minutes or so until limp and tender.

Drain the spinach in a sieve, squeezing out all the liquid.

Serving

Dot with butter and sprinkle with a little grated nutmeg or freshly ground black pepper.

Use

• Small tender leaves may be served raw in salads. Wash them really well, then shred them and serve with bits of hot crunchy bacon, chopped spring onion and an oil and vinegar dressing.

• Serve chopped cooked spinach topped with poached or boiled eggs and cheese sauce.

• Serve as a base for poached white fish coated in cheese sauce.

• Add chopped cooked spinach to cooked onion, garlic, a little ground coriander and cumin. Mix well and serve topped with a little yogurt as a side dish for curry.

• Stir chopped cooked spinach with cooked onion, a few pine nuts, some currants and a chopped eating apple.

• Add chopped cooked spinach to spicy red lentils*.

• Combine chopped cooked spinach with onion, garlic and ricotta cheese as a filling for pancakes or cannelloni.

Freezing

Cooked spinach freezes well for up to a year.

Bought frozen spinach, either chopped or leaf, is an excellent freezer standby.

Nutritional Value

Spinach contains some iron, calcium, folate and vitamin C; however, it also contains phytic acid which inhibits the absorption of minerals.

Squid

These are molluscs, with an internal shell which is known as the pen or quill.

Buying

They are often sold prepared, sliced into rings, as well as whole.

Preparing

1. The squid is made up of the tentacles with head and the sac which is covered in dark mottled skin. Hold the head and tentacles firmly in one hand and pull them out of the sac. The intestines of the squid will come out attached to the tentacle part.

2. Cut off the tentacles if they are to be used, then discard the head and remainder of the body except for the sac. The tentacles may be cut off just above the eyes if wished, in which case they then remain together all in one piece.

3. A transparent quill, rather like a fine backbone, runs inside the length of the sac: remove and discard this, it comes away easily.

Preparing Squid
(Numbers relate to text steps)

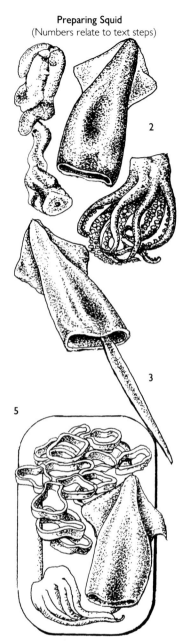

4. Rub the mottled skin off the sac under cold water, then rinse and drain it well.

5. The sac may be stuffed or sliced into rings. The tentacles may be left whole, cut into pieces or diced.

Cooking Methods

• Rings and tentacles may be coated in Light Batter (see page 29) and deep fried.

• Poach squid in casseroles or sauced dishes.

• Add to risottos or paella.

• Stuff with a Breadcrumb Stuffing (page 254), adding the chopped tentacles and brush with olive oil, then grill until golden or poach in a tomato sauce.

Staphylococcus

See Bacteria* and Hygiene*.
A type of toxin-producing bacteria found in the human body, particularly in the nose and in any cuts or spots. They may be passed to food when the cook coughs or sneezes, from handling used handkerchiefs and from scratching spots.

Although the bacteria themselves are not poisonous, the toxins which they leave behind cause food poisoning. *Staphylococci* are particularly resilient and they will survive in foods that have a high sugar concentration (preserves and sweet dishes such as puddings and cakes). The toxins are not destroyed by cooking so it is most essential that food is handled properly to prevent any contamination.

Meat and meat products, cheese and other highly nutritious protein foods are the ideal breeding ground for *Staphylococci*. For this reason, such food must always be fresh and a high standard of hygiene should be observed.

Steaming

Steaming is the process of cooking in water vapour, usually over boiling water. However, stock or moist dishes, such as stews, may serve as a base for cooking other ingredients in the steam which they produce.

Equipment

Saucepan and Steamer Set This consists of a large saucepan with one or more steamer compartments which fit neatly on top. The bases of the steamers are perforated to allow the vapour to rise through the layers. A close-fitting lid is placed on top of the steamer.

The steaming compartments may be deep, allowing enough height for cooking food in a large basin. Check the size of a steamer before buying it if you want to cook traditional puddings in deep basins. Also, make sure that the steamer fits well on the pan and that the lid fits tightly to prevent any loss of steam.

Graduated Steamer This type of steamer is designed to fit on pans of different sizes. The base of the steamer has a stepped arrangement so that it will fit on pans of different diameters. Two or more steamers of this type can be stacked on top of one pan.

Expanding Steamer These are small containers which are designed to stand in a saucepan. They are made up of a number of perforated metal plates in a circular fan arrangement, with feet underneath and a handle rising up through the centre.

This type of steamer is placed in a saucepan which contains a shallow depth of boiling water. The food is arranged around the handle and the lid is placed on the pan. This is only suitable for steaming small amounts of food and not for holding basins or other cooking containers.

Wok and Bamboo Steamer Steaming is widely used in Chinese cooking and special bamboo steamers are designed to fit on a wok. Several layers of bamboo steaming compartments can be stacked on one wok. The steamers come in a variety of diameters but they are usually fairly shallow.

These are ideal for steaming vegetables, rice in shallow bowls, fish, poultry and meat but they are not usually deep enough to hold a large basin. Also, the

---

SEE ALSO **Squash:** Vegetables – exotic; **Starch:** Carbohydrate; **Star Fruit:** Fruit – exotic; **Steak:** Meat

limited capacity of the wok makes long steaming a tedious task as the water has to be replenished frequently – so they are not recommended for long cooking of items such as Christmas pudding.

Plates on Pans One of the simplest methods of cooking fish is by indirect steaming. Two heatproof dinner plates which have a reasonable rim are used. One holds the food and this is placed over a pan of simmer water, the second is inverted on top to act as a lid. The food cooks in its own juice.

Colander or Sieve A metal colander or sieve may be used to steam certain foods instead of specialist equipment. Useful for vegetables, rice and couscous – a semolina product eaten in place of rice in Middle Eastern countries.

The colander or sieve is placed over a pan of boiling water, then the top is covered with foil to keep in the steam. Remember that the bottom of the container must be above the water level and that any plastic handles will melt.

Fish Kettle Fish kettles are expensive, quite specialist and usually used for poaching whole fish. These long, narrow cooking pans contain a metal trivet, or stand, which stands slightly above the base of the pan. This may be used for short term steaming only over the shallow depth of liquid below.

Steaming for Flavour

Forget the bland image associated with steaming and think in terms of international cooking styles to discover the full potential of this cooking method.

Fish This may be placed between plates on top of a saucepan or it may be wrapped in foil and placed in a steamer. A shallow dish with a foil cover also works well in a steamer.

The fish should be carefully seasoned before cooking, with a little salt and pepper, a squeeze of lemon juice and a sprinkling of chopped fresh herbs or herb sprigs – tarragon, parsley, thyme, bay, marjoram or basil are all suitable. A knob of butter or margarine may be added. The fish should be steamed until the flesh is just white and firm, not overcooked and falling apart.

For flavour and colour, finely cut vegetables, such as carrots and celery, may be cooked with the fish. Chinese-style steamed fish is full-flavoured and succulent, being sprinkled with a few drops of sesame oil and some soy sauce before cooking. Shredded spring onions and fresh root ginger are often sprinkled over the fish.

The cooking juices on the plate make a delicious sauce.

A selection of steamers.

Poultry Both chicken and turkey portions may be steamed successfully. The bland image is not a fair one. Fresh herbs (as Fish), grated lemon rind and finely cut vegetables all add flavour and help to make a delicious sauce.

Breast meat may be cut into single portion fillets, fine strips or across into rounds (known as medallions).

It is important to cover poultry during cooking to keep in flavour and to avoid diluting it with water condensed from the steam.

Meat Steamed meat is not to everyone's taste as it is bland unless marinated with strong ingredients and spices.

Vegetables Steaming is an excellent method of cooking vegetables, either over boiling water or over a simmering stew. This is ideal for floury potatoes that tend to fall apart during boiling. It is also ideal for carrots, green beans, turnips, celery and courgettes. As well as cooking vegetables very simply, they may be packed in foil with herb sprigs and a little butter or margarine. It is important not to overcook vegetables as they lose their flavour and become limp in texture.

Savoury Puddings Good winter food, traditional British steamed puddings made with suet pastry* and meat, vegetable or poultry fillings make hearty meals.

Dumplings As well as traditional British suet dumplings, Chinese dumplings, known as dim sum, are cooked by steaming. They are rather like small portions of fine pasta dough with a tasty meat or seafood filling. They are arranged in shallow dishes and placed uncovered in a steamer. The juices which collect in the dish make a flavoursome sauce. Most good Chinese cookbooks include at least one type of savoury dumpling.

Custards Simple sweet custard may be steamed in a covered dish or in ramekins. Savoury custards may sound strange but they can be delicious (page 102) and are ideal for a light meal.

Sweet Puddings A wide variety of puddings are cooked by steaming, from a light sponge pudding to rich Christmas pudding. Remember too, that rice pudding, 'stewed' fruit and dried fruits may all be steamed to give good results.

Benefits of Steaming

Nutritional Compared to boiling, steaming results in slightly less nutrient loss by seepage. This depends on the exact method used. For example, vegetables that are packed in foil and cooked, then eaten with their cooking juices contain more nutrients than others that are cooked in an expanding steamer directly over water. Some nutrients are obviously lost in seepage to the steam as it condenses on the food and drips back into the pan below. However, if vegetables are steamed over a casserole, the nutrients given up in seepage are caught in the sauce below.

One distinct benefit of steaming is that it does not require the addition of any form of fat. Of course, a knob of butter or margarine or a little oil may be used to flavour food which is covered in a steamer but this is not essential and a good flavour will result from using herbs and lemon juice alone.

Stewing

A long, slow, moist cooking method for tough meats or for bringing out the flavour in foods.

Technique

1. Trim excess fat and any gristle from meat, then cut it into chunks. Trim joint ends from poultry and remove the skin. Trim vegetables and cut them into large chunks.

2. Dust meat or poultry with a little seasoned flour. Heat a little fat in a flameproof casserole or frying pan.

3. Brown meat or poultry in small batches otherwise they cool the fat and give up their juice, making gravy which does not seal the outside of the ingredients. Transfer the pieces to a plate as they are browned.

4. Cook onion, garlic and other vegetables (such as peppers or carrots) in the fat remaining in the pan until the onion is just beginning to soften.

Typical Stews

The following serve 4. The ratatouille will serve 6 as a side dish or 4 on its own with bread, rice or pasta.

Beef Stew
Use 675 g/1½ lb stewing beef, 40 g/1½ oz seasoned flour, 1 sliced onion, 225 g/8 oz sliced carrots, 1 bouquet garni, 600 ml/1 pint water, salt and pepper. Add 225 g/8 oz thickly sliced mushrooms two-thirds of the way through cooking. Cook for 3 hours.

Coq au Vin
Use 4 chicken quarters and marinate them overnight in a bottle of red wine (in a covered dish in the refrigerator). Use 25 g/1 oz flour, 225 g/8 oz small whole pickling onions, 2 crushed cloves garlic and 1 bouquet garni. Add 100 g/4 oz small button mushrooms halfway through cooking. Cook for 1½ hours in the oven.

Ratatouille
Use 2 large cubed and salted aubergines, 150 ml/¼ pint olive oil, 2 crushed cloves garlic, 10 ml/2 teaspoons chopped fresh marjoram, 1 large chopped onion, 1 large diced green pepper, 225 g/ 8 oz thickly sliced courgettes and 1 kg/2 lb peeled and quartered tomatoes. Season the mixture lightly and cook on the hob for 45–60 minutes. Add plenty of chopped fresh parsley at the end of cooking.

5. Replace the main ingredients and mix well. Add the liquid and a little seasoning, with any herbs. Heat until only just simmering. Do not allow to boil rapidly as this toughens meat and poultry or reduces vegetable stews to a soft consistency.

6. Cover the pan and cook over the lowest heat or in the oven at 160°C, 325°F, gas 3. The time depends on the food: between 1½–3 hours for meat; 1–1½ hours for poultry; 45–60 minutes for vegetables.

7. Stir occasionally during cooking, then taste and adjust the seasoning before serving.

Stock

Homemade stock is superior to many of the bought alternatives because it has a light flavour. Stock is an ingredient, meant to complement other foods in a dish. For example, it is not the main item in a soup, stew or sauce. Strong-flavoured stock cubes can be over seasoned and dominate the dish. However, some cubes have a more delicate flavour and there are excellent chilled stocks available.

Making Stock

*See Fish**
Stock may be made from marrow bones which are sawn into manageable pieces by the butcher, chicken bones (preferably raw but cooked or portions may be used), fish trimmings or vegetables. Giblets, the neck and other edible offal from poultry, may also be used to make stock, particularly for gravy to accompany a roast bird.

Technique

1. Browning the bones in a roasting tin in the oven gives the best flavour. Place them in the oven at 190°C, 375°F, gas 5 and roast marrow bones for 1 hour, or longer for a brown stock.

SEE ALSO **Stilton:** Cheese; **Stir Frying:** Frying; **String:** Glossary

Chicken bones may also be treated in this way, although this will not give as light a stock.

2. Place the bones in a large saucepan. Add a thickly sliced onion, bouquet garni, quartered carrot and sliced celery stick. Pour in water to cover the bones.

3. Heat the water until it is just boiling, then cover the pan and allow the stock to simmer. Simmer marrow bones for 2–3 hours, topping up the water as necessary. Simmer poultry bones for 1½–2 hours.

4. Vegetable stock should have an extra carrot, 3 celery sticks and 1 onion added. Simmer vegetable stock for 1½ hours.

5. Strain the cooked stock through a fine sieve. At this stage the stock may be boiled hard to reduce and make it more concentrated in flavour. This is useful for freezing as the concentrated stock takes up less space and it may be diluted on thawing.

6. Transfer the stock to a clean container and cover it, then place in a cool place (utility room or cool room if possible) to cool. Either freeze or chill the stock as soon as it is cold.

7. Lift any fat off chilled or freshly frozen stock. Stock placed in the refrigerator should be used within 2 days.

Storing Food

See Freezing* and Refrigerator*.
Notes are given throughout on how best to store food and for how long. These are a few general reminders.

Storage Areas

Refrigerator This is usually the main and busiest storage area, therefore it must be large enough to cope with the requirements of the household. The refrigerator should be kept scrupulously clean and all food must be rotated regularly.

Keep perishable foods chilled and use by their best before date. Keep leftovers chilled and use promptly, preferably within 1 day, depending on the food.

Keep salad vegetables and highly perishable vegetables chilled.

✔️ *Check the temperature in the refrigerator and freezer occasionally, particularly in summer months when you may have to increase the setting to counteract warm weather.*

Freezer The freezer is a long-term larder. As well it makes sense to use it for storing foods for shorter periods (a few days or up to a couple of weeks) rather than risk keeping food chilled for too long, when it can pass its prime or, worse, become a health hazard. The same applies to leftovers: if you suspect that you cannot use them within 1–2 days, then freeze them at once.

Foods which have been chilled promptly following purchase and which are about to pass the 'use by' date may be frozen rather than wasting them or allowing them to deteriorate in quality in the refrigerator. Never freeze old food.

If the freezer is working properly, food will not become hazardous to health if it is stored for slightly longer than recommended. It may deteriorate in flavour and texture but it will not cause food poisoning if it is constantly frozen.

Cupboards For storing cans, packeted foods, preserves. These must be cool, dry, dark and clean. They should be easily accessible both to reach the food and check what is there and for cleaning. Rotate stocks. If you have well filled food cupboards, then turn them out occasionally to check the contents.

Shelves Only suitable for food storage when using dark storage jars or other airtight containers. Glass jars may be used for foods that are eaten quickly (rice, pasta and so on) but herbs and spices or foods kept for longer periods are better in the dark.

❌ *Never leave open packets on shelves or in the cupboards. Once the manufacturer's seal is broken, use a wire tie or clip to keep the packet shut or overwrap the packet in a polythene bag.*

Vegetable Racks Perishable vegetables should be kept in the refrigerator. Never leave salad stuff, carrots, cauliflower, broccoli and greens on a vegetable rack.

Other vegetables should be stored in a cool, dark place. If you do have a vegetable rack, keep it in a cool place but not tucked away where you forget about it. Use it only for potatoes, onions, swedes and parsnips (in brown bags). Carrots are best stored in the refrigerator.

Never leave vegetables on the rack until they deteriorate in quality. Empty the rack completely every week and wash and dry it often.

Other Storage Areas Containers such as bread bins, cake tins and containers should be emptied and washed regularly.

A pantry or other walk-in cupboard should be treated as a cupboard and not as a place to store fresh or perishable foods.

Strawberries

See Fruit*.
Available all year but very expensive during winter and early spring. Outdoor grown fruit sold from May to October.

Buying and Storing

Look for ripe but firm fruit. Very dark red, over-ripe strawberries lack flavour. Avoid any with bruising or brown patches. Check the bottom of punnets for juice stains which indicate that fruit in the bottom of the container is squashed.

Lay strawberries in a single layer on absorbent kitchen paper in a shallow covered container and chill. They are best eaten fresh but will keep for about 2 days if they are not too ripe.

Preparation

To hull a strawberry, hold the stalk firmly and twist it out of the fruit.

Rinse the fruit under cold water, then drain well.

Use

- Serve dusted with icing sugar, with cream or fromage frais.
- Use to fill flans or gâteaux.
- Add to red fruit salad or mix with melon to make a refreshing salad.
- Purée and use for ice creams, mousses or soufflés.
- Slice and combine with thinly sliced cucumber in a light side salad.
- Use to make conserve or jam. Strawberries do not have a good pectin content, so use commercial pectin, apple pulp, lemon juice or preserving sugar with pectin for a good set.

Freezing

It is best to open freeze the fruit, then pack it. Strawberries may also be packed with sugar or syrup. They keep for up to a year but are soft on thawing, not suitable for serving alone. Strawberry purée freezes well.

Stuffing

Stuffings are used with meat, poultry, fish or vegetables to complement the flavour of the food. In the case of vegetables, the stuffing often plays a more significant role to transform the vegetables into a main course.

Stuffings are typically based on breadcrumbs, rice or a minced meat mixture. Lentils or buckwheat may also be used. The choice and combination of flavouring ingredients is all important, they must enhance each other as well as the food to be stuffed.

BREADCRUMB STUFFING

INGREDIENTS	FOOD VALUES:
1 onion (100–150 g/4–5 oz), finely chopped	TOTAL
175 g/6 oz fresh breadcrumbs	kcals: 701
salt and pepper	kJ: 2977
herbs or flavourings as below	protein: 24 g
about 100 ml/4 fluid oz milk	fat: 7 g
	carbohydrate: 144 g
	fibre: 7 g

Makes enough to stuff a 1.8 kg/4 lb boneless joint, 1 chicken, 8 mushrooms or artichoke bottoms, 4 pepper halves, 4 onions

Place the onion and breadcrumbs in a mixing bowl. Use a mixing spoon and a cutting action to ensure that the onion and crumbs are evenly combined. Add seasoning and the herbs or other flavourings, then mix well again before moistening with the milk. Stir in enough milk to bind the bread. The quantity given makes a moist stuffing, ideal for slicing or scooping. For a crumbly result (perhaps to fill mushrooms or artichoke bottoms) use slightly less milk.

VARIATIONS

Sage and Onion Wash and finely chop the leaves from a large sprig of fresh sage or use 15 ml/1 tablespoon dried (rubbed) sage.
Use: chicken, turkey, pork, mushrooms, onions.

Parsley and Thyme Add 90 ml/6 tablespoons chopped fresh parsley and 15 ml/1 tablespoon chopped fresh thyme or 7.5 ml/1½ teaspoons dried thyme.
Use: fish, chicken, lamb, mushrooms, onions, aubergines.

Lemon Herb Add the grated rind of 1 lemon to the parsley and thyme above or use 30 ml/2 tablespoons chopped fresh dill instead.
Use: fish, chicken, artichoke bottoms.

Garlic and Parsley Cook 1–2 crushed large cloves garlic in 15 ml/1 tablespoon olive oil or a little butter for 1 minute over medium heat. Scrape all the fat and garlic into the stuffing. Add 60 ml/4 tablespoons chopped fresh parsley.
Use: fish, poultry, all meat, mushrooms, aubergines, artichoke bottoms.

Bacon and Herb Cook 100 g/4 oz chopped rindless bacon with 1 crushed clove garlic in 15 ml/1 tablespoon oil for 5 minutes, stirring over medium heat. Add 30 ml/2 tablespoons chopped fresh parsley and 5 ml/1 teaspoon dried thyme, rosemary or marjoram.
Use: poultry, lamb, beef olives, veal, game, vegetables and leaves.

Nut and Raisin Add 50 g/2 oz chopped walnuts, 25 g/1 oz raisins, 30 ml/2 tablespoons chopped fresh parsley and 5 ml/1 teaspoon dried thyme or chopped rosemary.
Use: poultry, all meat, game, vegetables.

Apricot and Orange Add 100 g/4 oz chopped ready-to-eat dried apricots, 30 ml/2 tablespoons chopped fresh parsley, 5 ml/1 teaspoon dried oregano, grated rind of 1 orange and orange juice instead of the 100 ml/4 fluid oz milk.
Use: all poultry, meat and game.

SEE ALSO **Strudel**: Filo Pastry

RICE STUFFING

INGREDIENTS
**100 g/4 oz long-grain
   rice**
1 bay leaf
300 ml/½ pint water
25 g/1 oz butter
1 clove garlic, crushed
1 onion, finely chopped
**30 ml/2 tablespoons chopped
   fresh parsley**
**5 ml/1 teaspoon dried
   marjoram**
salt and pepper

FOOD VALUES:
TOTAL
kcals: 415
kJ: 1729
protein: 10 g
fat: 22 g
carbohydrate: 47 g
fibre: 2 g

Makes enough to stuff 1 chicken, 1 shoulder of lamb, 8 cabbage leaves, 4 peppers, 8 large mushrooms, 8 tomatoes or 4 aubergines

Place the rice in a saucepan with the bay leaf and water. Bring to the boil, then reduce the heat and cover the pan tightly. Cook over low heat for 15 minutes, then remove from the heat and leave to stand for 15 minutes. Discard the bay leaf unless the stuffing is used in a joint or chicken, in which case discard the leaf when serving.

If the stuffing is used for vine leaves, then cook the rice for 10 minutes and drain it immediately.

Melt the butter in a small frying pan, then add the garlic and onion. Cook, stirring occasionally, over low heat for 10 minutes, or until the onion is softened slightly but not browned. Add the cooked onion and all fat to the rice. Add the parsley, marjoram and seasoning. Lightly fork the ingredients together, taking care not to overmix the rice and crush the grains.

VARIATIONS

Currant and Pine Nut Add 25 g/1 oz currants and 45 ml/3 tablespoons pine nuts. For lamb, vine leaves, aubergines or cabbage, add 15 ml/1 tablespoon chopped fresh mint too.
Use: lamb, vine leaves, aubergines, cabbage, chicken, pork or game.
Rich Prune Chop 6 stoned, ready-to-eat prunes and sprinkle 30 ml/2 tablespoons port over them. Leave to soak for 30 minutes, then add them to the rice at the end of the cooking time, before leaving it to stand. Do not stir them into the rice and re-cover the pan quickly. Crush 6 juniper berries and add them with the herbs.
Use: game, turkey, pork, lamb or aubergines.
Note The soaked prunes may also be added to forcemeat or breadcrumb stuffing (with sage and onion).
Spicy Apple Add 1 cinnamon stick and 6 green cardamoms to the rice with the bay leaf. Add 15 ml/1 tablespoon each of cumin and mustard seeds to the onion and garlic. Omit the marjoram. Add 15 ml/1 tablespoon ground coriander, 25 g/1 oz raisins and 1 peeled, cored and chopped eating apple with the parsley.
Use: chicken, turkey, pork, lamb or cabbage.

Basic Stuffings

Breadcrumb Stuffing This forms the base for herb stuffings, such as sage and onion or parsley and thyme. It goes well with all foods, depending on the flavouring.
Forcemeat This pork and breadcrumb mixture may be used to stuff chicken or turkey, slices of beef (to make rolls known as olives), vegetables and leaves (vine leaves or cabbage leaves). The cooking temperature and time must allow the forcemeat to cook through.
Sausagemeat Stuffing For poultry, lamb breast (it extends the meat and gives an excellent flavour), vegetables and leaves.
Rice Stuffing For all poultry, meat, fish, vegetables and leaves. Vary the flavouring ingredients according to the main food.
Lentil Stuffing Good with lamb, slices of pork (rolled into olives) or pork chops, vegetables and leaves.

Cook 175 g/6 oz lentils following the instructions on page 168. Add 4 chopped spring onions, 1 crushed clove garlic, 2 peeled and chopped tomatoes, 10 ml/2 teaspoons chopped fresh sage (or 5 ml/1 teaspoon dried sage) and 30 ml/2 tablespoons chopped fresh parsley.

Stuffing Techniques

1. Prepare the stuffing and allow it to cool (if necessary). Taste cooked stuffings for seasoning before using.

2. Prepare the food to be stuffed. The prepared food is usually completely edible, that is all cores, seeds, stalks, bones and other inedible parts are removed.

3. Some vegetables should be blanched or par-cooked before the stuffing is added. For example, onions should be par-cooked and peppers are better if blanched.

4. Use a metal spoon to put the stuffing into the main food. A teaspoon is suitable for small or fiddly portions, such as chops or mushrooms.

5. Secure the stuffing if necessary (by trussing, covering or packing food neatly in a cooking container), then cook the food promptly.

X *Do not stuff poultry and meat far in advance of cooking. Keep meat or poultry chilled until it is to be stuffed. Have cold stuffing, preferably chilled too. Cook the stuffed food immediately or place it in the refrigerator and cook meat within 2 hours of stuffing; poultry within 1 hour (although cooking straight away is preferable in the case of poultry).*

Stuffing Vegetables

Aubergines* Halve and remove flesh by cutting into it in a criss-cross pattern, then scoop it out. Salt, rinse and chop the flesh. Cook in a little olive oil for 5 minutes to soften, then mix with breadcrumb, meat, rice or lentil stuffing. Bake in a covered dish at 190°C, 375°F, gas 5 for 1 hour. Uncover and cook for a further 15 minutes.

Artichoke* Bottoms Prepared fresh or canned may be used. Place in an ovenproof dish. Fill with breadcrumb or meat stuffing. Bake at 200°C, 400°F, gas 6; 20 minutes for breadcrumb stuffing, 30–40 minutes for meat.

Cabbage Leaves Use large Savoy leaves (or those from another green cabbage). Trim off tough stalk end, then blanch in boiling water for 2 minutes. Drain well and dry on absorbent kitchen paper.

Use breadcrumb, rice, lentil or meat stuffing. Place a portion in the middle of the leaf, fold the stalk end over, then fold the sides over. Roll up from the stalk end. Place in greased ovenproof dish and moisten with canned tomatoes or a little stock. Cover and bake at 180°C, 350°F, gas 4 for 45–50 minutes. Serve with Tomato Sauce (page 263) or Cheese Sauce (page 234).

Mushrooms Use breadcrumb or meat stuffing. Select medium to large open or cup mushrooms. Remove and chop stalks, then toss in butter until soft. Add to stuffing. Dot filled mushrooms with butter or margarine or trickle a little olive oil over. Bake with breadcrumb stuffing at 200°C, 400°F, gas 6, for 20 minutes with meat at 190°C, 375°F, gas 5 for 30 minutes. Serve on rounds of toast or fried bread with cooking juices poured over.

Onions Select large Spanish onions. Peel, then boil whole until par-cooked, about 30 minutes. Cool, then remove and chop middle. Add to breadcrumb, rice, lentil or meat stuffing instead of onion in recipe. Place in ovenproof dish and dot generously with butter or margarine. Bake at 180°C, 350°F, gas 4 for meat stuffing, allowing about 1 hour. Bake at 200°C, 400°F, gas 6 for others, about 35 minutes.

Peppers Stuff deseeded whole or halved (a better option flavour-wise). Select rounded vegetables rather than long ones and make sure they stand neatly, trimming off slivers as necessary. Blanch in boiling water for 2 minutes, until soft but not collapsing. Drain well and place in ovenproof dish. Use meat, breadcrumb, rice or lentil stuffing. Cover dish and bake at 180°C, 350°F, gas 4 for about 50 minutes. May be uncovered and topped with cheese 10 minutes before end of cooking. Serve with Tomato Sauce (page 263), if liked.

Vine Leaves Buy preserved in packets. Drain, rinse and blanch in boiling water for 5 minutes. Use rice or meat stuffing made with minced lamb. Simmer rice for only half cooking time. Stuff

FORCEMEAT

INGREDIENTS
1 onion
450 g/1 lb minced pork
50 g/2 oz fresh breadcrumbs
30 ml/2 tablespoons chopped fresh parsley
10 ml/2 teaspoons chopped fresh thyme or 5 ml/1 teaspoon dried thyme
5 ml/1 teaspoon ground mace
grated nutmeg
salt and pepper
1 egg

FOOD VALUES:
TOTAL
kcals: 2146
kJ: 8902
protein: 114 g
fat: 165 g
carbohydrate: 55 g
fibre: 3 g

Makes enough for 4 peppers, onions or aubergines, 8 cabbage leaves, 2 pheasant, 1 turkey (with a second stuffing)

The onion may be minced or grated. Alternatively, process it in a food processor or liquidiser until almost smooth but not too sloppy. For a coarser texture, finely chop the onion.

Mix the onion, meat, breadcrumbs, parsley, thyme and mace together in a bowl. Add a good sprinkling of nutmeg and seasoning. Make sure all the ingredients are thoroughly combined, then mix in the egg.

VARIATION

Sausagemeat Stuffing Substitute sausagemeat for the pork in the above recipe and omit the mace.

leaves as for cabbage leaves, making small, tight packages. Overlap pairs of small or broken leaves. Pack into a heavy-based saucepan to fill base completely. Pour in 300 ml/½ pint good stock, the juice of 1 lemon, 60 ml/4 tablespoons olive oil (this may be omitted), then heat until just simmering. Cover pan and cook over lowest heat for 1 hour, checking that the liquid does not dry up. Serve hot or cold.

Freezing

Prepare stuffing in larger batches or in advance and freeze it raw. Freeze breadcrumb stuffing mix without the milk or moisture for about 4–6 weeks. Forcemeat may be frozen for up to 3 months. Rice stuffing should be no more than three-quarters cooked and stored for up to a month as the grains become floury.

Suet

See Fat*.

Suet is the fat from around beef kidneys. The fat surrounding lambs' kidneys may be used but it is inferior in flavour to beef suet. Suet is now sold shredded and floured in packets. It is difficult to obtain fresh suet in large chunks, mainly because all beef offal is processed quite separately from the main part of the carcass, also due to less demand.

Suet is used to make a pastry, in some traditional sweet steamed puddings, in Christmas pudding and mincemeat.

Vegetarian Suet A substitute for proper suet, this is solid white vegetable fat, shredded and coated in flour.

Suet Pastry

Unlike other pastries, this uses self-raising flour. It is easy to make and has a light, spongy texture when handled and cooked properly.

Quantities

Use half suet to self-raising flour. To 225 g/8 oz self-raising flour, use 100 g/4 oz shredded suet and add a pinch of salt. Use 175 ml/6 fluid oz cold water to mix the ingredients to a soft dough.

FOOD VALUES: TOTAL
kcals: 1589
kJ: 6649
protein: 20.9
fat: 89.4
carbohydrate: 186.5
fibre: 8.3

Technique

1. Place the flour and a pinch of salt in a bowl. Stir in the suet.

2. Sprinkle the cold water over the dry ingredients, then use a mixing spoon to mix them into a soft dough. Wash and dry your hands.

3. Lightly flour a clean work surface. Gather the dough together into a ball and turn it out on to the surface. Knead it lightly into a smooth ball. Use the dough promptly.

Makes about 450 g/1 lb

Use

Dumplings

Divide the dough into 8 portions and roll them into balls. Cook the dumplings in barely simmering soup for about 15 minutes, turning once, until they are light and risen. On top of a stew in a covered casserole, allow about 40 minutes.

Roly Poly

Roll the dough into a 20 × 25 cm/8 × 10 inch oblong. Spread the chosen filling over the middle of the pastry, leaving a 2.5 cm/1 inch margin around the edge. Fold the edge over the filling, then roll up the pastry and filling from the long side.

Wrap loosely in greased greaseproof paper and foil, then place on a baking tray. Bake at 190°C, 375°F, gas 5. The package may be opened after 30 minutes to brown the pastry.

Suggested Fillings

Bacon and Mushroom Lightly cook 225 g/8 oz diced rindless bacon with 1 chopped onion. Add 100 g/4 oz sliced mushrooms, plenty of chopped fresh parsley and 10 ml/2 teaspoons dried sage. Cooking time: 45 minutes.

Jam Spread thickly with jam. Cooking time: 45 minutes.

Apple and Sultana Peel, core and grate or chop 450 g/1 lb cooking apples. Spread over the pastry, then sprinkle with 50 g/2 oz sultanas, 60 ml/4 tablespoons caster sugar and 10 ml/2 teaspoons ground mixed spice. Cooking time: 1¼ hours.

Puddings

The dough will line and cover a 1.1 litre/2 pint pudding basin. Grease the basin.

Roll out the dough into a round about 10 cm/4 inches larger than the top of the basin. Cut a quarter segment out of the dough and set it aside.

Dust the top of the three-quarter section with a little flour, then fold it in half so that the cut edges lie on top of each other.

Lift the folded dough into the basin, then open it out and press it around the sides to line the basin completely.

Brush the cut in the dough with a little water and overlap the edges slightly to seal the join. Ease the pastry down or up the side of the basin, as necessary, so that its edge rests on the top rim.

Fill the pudding, then pat the reserved portion of dough into a round and roll it out large enough to cover the pudding. Place it over the filling, dampen the top all around the edge and fold the pastry rim over slightly, pressing it down to seal in the filling.

Cover the pudding with pleated greased greaseproof paper and foil. Depending on the filling the pudding may be steamed or baked.

Suggested Fillings

Steak and Kidney Combine 450 g/1 lb diced braising steak, 100 g/4 oz diced lamb's kidney, 1 chopped onion, 30 ml/2 tablespoons plain flour and plenty of seasoning. Stir in plenty of chopped fresh parsley and a sprig of thyme, then moisten the mixture with 300 ml/½ pint beef stock. Fill the pudding. Steam for 4½–5 hours.

Chicken and Mushroom Pudding Cut 450 g/1 lb uncooked skinned, boneless chicken breast into thin slices. Layer them in the pudding with 100 g/4 oz halved button mushrooms, adding plenty of seasoning and sprinkling each layer with chopped fresh parsley. Add 2 bay leaves between the layers, then moisten the filling with 150–300 ml/¼–½ pint milk. Steam the pudding for 2 hours.

Freezing

Do not freeze uncooked but it may be frozen cooked. Storage time depends on fillings. Dumplings keep well for 6 months and may be thawed and reheated in the microwave, on a casserole or in the oven.

Sugar

See Caramel*, Carbohydrates*, Spices (vanilla)* and Syrup*.

Sugar is extracted from the sugar beet plant or from sugar cane. It is refined to varying degrees to produce the types that are available. Black treacle and syrup are sugar products.

Types and Their Uses

Black Treacle Thick and black in colour, treacle is made from syrup with molasses added. Treacle has a rich, slightly bitter taste. Used in small quantities in baking, puddings and confectionery.

Brown Sugar There are several types, including soft dark or light brown and other terms used by individual manufacturers. Most are a combination of refined (granulated) sugar with added molasses for flavour and colour. Used in baking, for puddings and in other areas of cooking where the flavour and colour are important.

Caster Sugar This has fine crystals and it dissolves more easily than granulated sugar. Used in baking and desserts, also for sifting over pastries, cakes and biscuits to enhance their appearance.

Coffee Crystals Large brown or coloured crystals which dissolve slowly. Brown and gold crystals are coated in molasses which also flavours them. The idea is that the sugar dissolves slowly in the coffee, so that the drink becomes sweeter towards the end of the cup.

Cubes For serving with tea, these are made from granulated sugar bound with syrup.

Demerara Separate, large crystals of sugar with molasses. Used in baking, savoury cooking or puddings. It adds crunch to biscuits, crumble mixture and similar toppings.

Golden Syrup A syrup with caramel and flavouring. Used in baking, puddings or as a glaze. It is also served as an accompaniment to steamed sponge pudding, pancakes or waffles.

Granulated Sugar The most widely used and versatile of sugars. Refined white sugar with medium crystals that dissolve well. Used in all cooking, including cake making, although it requires more creaming or whisking in mixtures than caster sugar.

Icing Sugar Both traditional and golden types are available. The sugar is ground to a fine powder which dissolves rapidly in the minimum of liquid. The golden type has a small amount of molasses added which can give icing a slightly dirty appearance.

Used to make icing, butter cream and sifted as a decoration. Also for whipped cream, fruit purées or for sprinkling over soft fruit. Overwrap opened packets in a sealed polythene bag to prevent the sugar becoming lumpy.

Molasses Raw cane sugar. Thick, dark treacle-like and bitter. Has limited use in cooking as the flavour is strong. Used to enrich fruit cakes and puddings, or for adding to chutneys.

Muscovado Sugar Very moist, dark sugar with a high molasses content. Used in rich fruit cakes or Christmas pudding.

Preserving Sugar Large, refined crystals which dissolve more slowly and do not settle in a layer at the bottom of the saucepan when making jams. Preserving sugar requires less stirring and produces less scum.

Sugar with Pectin Also known as jam sugar, this has smaller crystals than preserving sugar, and it contains balanced proportions of fruit pectin and citric acid. It must be used according to the manufacturer's instructions; the boiling time is usually short.

Storing

Keep all types in an airtight container in a cool, dry place, where it will keep for many months.

Swedes

See Vegetables*.
A large root vegetable with thick skin and pale orange flesh.

Buying

Look for firm, fairly even-skinned vegetables without any deep cuts or crevices. The skin is shaded from a brown-aubergine colour down to beige at the base.

Storing

Store swedes as for potatoes, in a brown paper bag in a cool, dry place. In the right conditions in a dry outhouse or utility, swedes keep well for months. Indoors, they tend to dry out if stored for more than 2 weeks.

Preparation

Wash off the dirt, then cut the swede in half. Place it cut side down on the board and trim off both ends. Cut the peel off thickly, working down the side of the vegetable to the board.

Cut swede into thick slices, then into chunks. Rinse well under cold water.

Cooking

Place in a saucepan with cold water to cover. Add a pinch of salt, if liked, and bring to the boil. Cover the pan and reduce the heat, then simmer for about 20 minutes, or until the swede is tender.

Drain and mash with butter and pepper.

Use

• Add diced swede to vegetable soup, casseroles and stews.

• Served mashed swede with haggis*.

• Mash boiled swedes with carrots.

• Layer mashed swede with diced cooked ham, cooked onion and cheese in a baking dish, ending with a layer of swede. Top with breadcrumbs and cheese and bake until golden. Good for supper with baked potato.

• Use boiled and diced in vegetable pies, pasties or curries.

Freezing

Cooked mashed swede may be frozen for up to 6 months but the raw vegetable does not freeze well.

Nutritional Value

Swedes supply vitamin C, minerals and fibre.

Syrup

See Sugar*.

Syrup is made by dissolving sugar in water. Depending on the proportion of sugar to water used the syrup may be light, medium or heavy. By boiling a syrup, some of the water evaporates and the solution becomes more concentrated, at the same time developing different characteristics that are used in cooking and eventually browning to make caramel*.

Making Syrup

Place the sugar and water in a saucepan and heat gently, stirring, until the sugar has dissolved. Bring the syrup to the boil and boil for 1 minute, or until clear. Remove from the heat and allow to cool or use as required.

Quantities of Sugar

The following are all syrups for dessert use, such as for salads, soaking savarin, preserving fruit, making sorbet and so on.
Light Syrup 225 g/8 oz sugar to 600 ml/1 pint water.
Medium Syrup 350 g/12 oz sugar to 600 ml/1 pint water.
Heavy Syrup 450 g/1 lb sugar to 600 ml/1 pint water.

Boiling Syrup

If a concentrated syrup is required for boiling to one of the following stages, begin by using a higher proportion of sugar to water. About 350 g/12 oz sugar to 300 ml/½ pint water is suitable. The proportions used in the first instance are not crucial, except when following a specific recipe; if less sugar to water is used, then the syrup takes longer to boil down to a specific concentration and temperature.

Once the sugar has dissolved, the syrup should be brought to the boil. Do not stir the syrup once the sugar has dissolved as this causes some of the sugar to crystallise on the saucepan sides. Once the sugar begins to crystallise the rest will follow suit.
Preventing Crystallisation Adding a little liquid glucose* to the syrup helps to prevent it from crystallising as it boils and later when it is used.

Add a pinch of cream of tartar with the sugar as this also helps to prevent crystals forming.

Have a mug of cold water at hand and use a pastry brush to dampen the inside of the saucepan very slightly at the first signs of any white crystals.
Checking the Temperature Have a sugar thermometer in a jug of hot water. Shake off excess water before using it to check the temperature of the syrup.

Never leave the thermometer resting on the base of the pan as this gives a false reading. Do not transfer the thermometer from the extreme temperature of the syrup to cold water.

Stages in Boiling

To test for each of the following stages without using a thermometer, have a small basin of cold water and drop a little of the syrup into it. However, it must be stressed that using a thermometer is both safer and more accurate. The stages are not reached at one specific temperature, so information on thermometers or in recipes varies.

Remove the pan from the heat as soon as the syrup has boiled to the required temperature.
Long Thread 110°C/230°F. At this stage the syrup will form long thin threads as it cools and when pulled with a fork. Test by holding a small drop between thumb and index finger. Separate the fingers to see if the syrup forms threads.
Soft Ball 116°C/240°F. A drop of syrup should form a soft ball. Work the ball of syrup between 2 fingertips and it should form a soft paste-like ball.
Hard Ball 121°C/250°F. As above but the drop forms a hard ball.
Small Crack 130°C/266°F. The syrup forms a film when cooled. Dip the handle of a metal teaspoon quickly into the syrup, then into the cold water and a crisp coating should form. This may be peeled off the spoon and it will become pliable.
Hard Crack 150°C/300°F. As above, the syrup forms a hard film that cracks like glass.

Tea

There is an excellent range of teas available, including traditional blends and interesting scented, spiced and fruit beverages.

Making Tea

1. Use fresh water and a clean tea pot. Pour boiling water into the tea pot to warm it.

2. Add the required amount of tea to the pot. A rule of thumb is 5 ml/1 teaspoon for each cup, plus one for the pot but this depends on the size of pot, type of tea and personal taste.

3. Pour freshly boiled water on the tea, cover the pot, then allow the leaves to brew.

4. Brewing time is very important as this is when the flavour is infused from the leaves. Small leafed teas (such as Assam, Ceylon, Indian and English Breakfast) should be allowed to brew for 3 minutes. Large leafed tea (such as China, Earl Grey, Jasmine, Green Gunpowder and Lapsang Souchong) should be left for 6 minutes.

5. If milk is to be served with the tea, then pour the required amount into the cup. Use a tea strainer and pour the brewed tea on the milk in the cup.

6. Top up the pot with extra boiling water, not full but replace about a third to half of the volume which has been poured. Tea that has been allowed to stand for too long is known as stewed.

Teabread

Place 350 g/12 oz mixed dried fruit in a bowl. Pour in 250 ml/8 fluid oz freshly brewed, strained tea. Cover and leave to stand overnight.

Set the oven at 160°C, 325°F, gas 3 and base line and grease a 1 kg/2 lb loaf tin. Sift 250 g/9 oz plain flour into a bowl with 2.5 ml/½ teaspoon bicarbonate of soda. Stir in 100 g/4 oz light soft brown sugar and 100 g/4 oz walnut pieces. Make a well in the middle, then turn the soaked fruit and all juice into the middle. Add a beaten egg. Mix all the ingredients until thoroughly combined, then turn the mixture into the prepared tin. Bake the teabread for 1¼–1½ hours, or until risen, browned and firm.

Cool on a wire rack, then wrap in a polythene bag and mature for at least a day. Serve sliced and buttered.

Tea with Lemon Some teas are not suitable for serving with milk but a slice of lemon may be added instead. Delicate or scented teas, such as China or Earl Grey, may be served with lemon or milk. The lemon should be cut in very thin slices and one slice should be floated on the poured tea.

Use

Strained cold tea may be used in cooking. For example to soak dried fruit for making teabread, or instead of water in the syrup for making sorbet. Use a scented tea, such as Earl Grey or fruit tea, to make sorbet.

Temperatures and Thermometers

See Freezing*, Meat*, Refrigerator*, Frying* and Sugar*.

Storing food at the right temperature is important to keep it in good condition, both in the short or long term. Also, in certain cooking methods checking the temperature of the cooking medium or food is important for success. Kitchen thermometers are inexpensive and valuable.

Food Probe Indicator lights show when food has reached certain pre-selected temperatures, including 5°C/41°F for thawed food, 75°C/167°F for reheated food and 85°C/185°F when cooking.

Refrigerator and Freezer Thermometer Indicate temperatures from about −30°C/−22°F to 40°C/104°F. Freezers should operate at −18°C/0°F or lower and refrigerators should have an internal temperature of less than 5°C/41°F.

Types of Thermometers

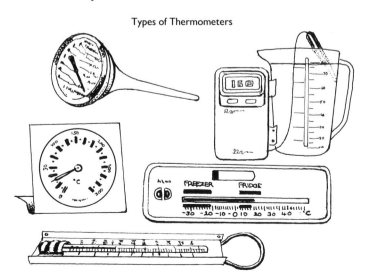

Meat Thermometer For use in a conventional oven, this is inserted into the thickest part of the joint and it registers temperatures up to 90°C/194°F.

Oven Thermometer To check the temperature of your conventional oven. Registers temperatures up to 300°C/572°F. Useful if you think the thermostat may not be working correctly.

Sugar Thermometer For checking the temperature of oil when deep frying as well as the temperature of boiling syrup. Registers temperatures up to 220°C/450°F.

Temperature Probe A digital, battery operated food probe. Do not place in the oven or microwave. Do not immerse in hot oil or boiling sugar. For checking the internal temperature of foods.

Thawing Food

See Freezing* and Hygiene*.

Frozen food must be treated according to its type. Freezing does not kill micro-organisms or enzymes that are present in fresh food before freezing; they remain dormant in the frozen state, so as the food thaws they again become active. As the temperature of the food reaches −10°C/14°F and above it becomes subject to very slow attack from enzymes and bacteria. By the time it reaches the temperature of chilled food it must be treated as perishable food and cooked or used.

The following are general guidelines:

● Always keep frozen food in cool conditions as it thaws to prevent any bacteria multiplying.

● Place unwrapped food in a covered dish to thaw.

● Never re-freeze food that has thawed once. Bacteria may multiply during the first thawing period; the second time may result in high levels of bacteria which may cause poisoning.

● Use or cook frozen food within 24 hours of thawing.

Fish Although fish may be cooked from frozen, and some convenience products are prepared for cooking straight from the freezer, it has a better texture and is more succulent if thawed first. Thin fillets thaw quickly at cool room temperature but they should not be left unattended in a warm room to become warm.

The best way is to leave the fish in a covered dish in the refrigerator for several hours or overnight.

X *Never rinse frozen fish under cold water to thaw it. This spoils both flavour and texture. It is better to cook from frozen than to rinse the fish.*

Poultry The vast majority of poultry must be thawed before cooking. The only exceptions are manufactured products intended for cooking from frozen and fine slivers of boneless meat (goujons) which may be stir fried or deep fried from frozen. Care must be taken to ensure the pieces are cooked through.

Portions should be thawed in a covered dish in the refrigerator overnight. Whole small poultry, such as chicken or duck, should be thawed in the refrigerator for up to 24 hours.

If time does not allow for overnight thawing, the poultry (portions or small birds only) may be left in a covered dish in a cool room. They should be cooked as soon as they are thawed but not allowed to become warm.

Whole turkey requires long thawing, see turkey*.

Always make sure that whole birds are thawed, removing giblets as soon as possible. Rinse well under cold water and dry on absorbent kitchen paper before cooking.

Meat With the exception of burgers and products prepared for cooking from frozen, meat should be thawed before cooking for best results.

Unwrap steaks, chops, mince or joints and place in a covered dish in the refrigerator. Ideally, a joint should be placed on a rack so that it does not sit in any drip. Leave until thawed, up to 24 hours, draining off drip occasionally.

Rinse and dry chops, steaks and joints before cooking.

Vegetables Most vegetables should be cooked from frozen. Add them to the minimum of boiling water and bring back to the boil over high heat. Reduce the heat, cover the pan and cook for slightly longer than for fresh vegetables. Some vegetables that have been blanched before freezing, and commercially frozen vegetables, cook in the same or slightly less time than fresh ones. Peas and Brussels sprouts are good examples.

Fruit The majority of fruit is best used from frozen, for example for poaching, filling pies, layering in trifle and so on. However, time must be allowed for the fruit to thaw either during cooking or before serving.

Allow pies to cook slightly longer at the cooler temperature (once the pastry has been cooked briefly in a hot oven), poach fruit for slightly longer and allow trifles with frozen fruit to chill overnight or for several hours.

The main reason for thawing fruit is when it is packed in blocks, for example a solid block of apples. Fruit purée has to be thawed to make it practical for use.

Baked Items Breads, cakes, pies and so on generally have to be thawed before use.

Sliced bread, crumpets and muffins may be toasted from frozen. Unwrap bread, plain cakes and buns, then cover loosely with absorbent kitchen paper and leave to thaw at room temperature.

Cream cakes should be thawed in the refrigerator. Pies should be treated according to content. Home-made meat and poultry pies should be thawed in the refrigerator for several hours or overnight. Bought pies should be cooked according to the manufacturer's instructions. Always

---

check the filling is thoroughly reheated before serving.

Dairy Produce Thaw in the refrigerator. This includes cheese, cream, eggs, butter and dairy desserts such as cheesecake.

Uncooked Pastry Thaw in the refrigerator for 3–4 hours, depending on thickness. Best to leave it overnight if possible.

Cooked Dishes Casseroles, lasagne, cottage pie and so on should be thawed before cooking or reheating. Leave them in the refrigerator overnight or at cool room temperature until they are just thawed.

Small portions of cooked dishes thaw quickly and these should be placed in a slightly cooler oven than normal. Cover loosely with foil until thawed, then uncover and reheat thoroughly, checking that the middle of the food is properly heated before serving.

Cooking From Frozen

● Follow manufacturer's instructions.

● Always check that food is properly cooked or reheated before serving.

● Pack cooked foods in small portions in boilable bags before freezing. Flattening them into thin shapes that will thaw and heat evenly and quickly.

● Make sure that the food is placed in dishes that will withstand the change in temperature from frozen to hot.

Toast and Toasting

See Melba Toast*.
Toast is made by browning a slice of bread near radiant heat. Complicated chemical reactions cause the surface of toast to become crisp, brown and quite different in flavour from the original slice of bread. The same is true of toasted crumpets, muffins, buns and other similar starchy products.

Electric toasters have a thermostat and timer control which automatically switches off the heat and ejects the bread when it has been cooked for a pre-selected period.

To toast bread under the grill, the grill should be preheated first, otherwise the bread tends to dry out before the surface browns. The bread must be near enough to the heat to brown quickly but far enough away, in some grills, to brown evenly.

☑ *Have softened butter or margarine to spread on the toast and warm the plates. If toast is placed on cold plates condensation forms underneath the toast, cooling it rapidly and making it soggy.*

Toasting Nuts and Seeds

These should be spread out on a piece of foil or a foil container (placing baking tins under the grill makes them buckle) under a moderately hot grill. If the grill is heated on the maximum setting, nuts brown quickly and unevenly, and they burn easily.

Toasting in a Pan The alternative method, also referred to as roasting, is to cook the nuts or seeds over low heat in a heavy-based pan without any additional fat.

Whichever method is used, never leave the nuts and seeds unattended and rearrange them often for even browning.

Tomatoes

See Fruit*.
British tomatoes are available from March (expensive and not at their best) through to October. However, imported fruit is available all year.

Buying

Look for tomatoes that are ripe or very slightly under-ripe. They should be firm, red and bright in appearance. Avoid any fruit that is very dark red, indicating that it is over-ripe, and soft.

Look at the stalk end (calyx) for an indication of freshness. This should be green and firm not grey and withered.

Storing

Keep ripe fruit in the refrigerator but allow it to come to room temperature for best flavour before using raw. Slightly under-ripe fruit should be kept in an open dish at room temperature.

Green tomatoes (home grown) may be ripened by placing them between a folded clean tea-towel in a cardboard box (in a single layer). Check them daily and remove ripe fruit.

Preparation

Remove the calyx and wash the fruit well under cold running water, then dry it on absorbent kitchen paper. The stalk end may be removed using the point of a sharp knife.

Slicing and Cutting Use a serrated knife to cut tomatoes. Place the stalk end down on a board, then cut the fruit downwards.

Peeling Place the tomatoes in a bowl and pour freshly boiling water over them to cover completely.

Leave to stand: ripe fruit should be left for 30–45 seconds, slightly less ripe fruit for 1 minute and very firm fruit for 1–2 minutes. Any longer and the flesh becomes soft.

Drain the tomatoes and slit the skin with the point of a knife, then slide it off – it should come off easily in about 2 pieces. Trim the skin off at the stalk end if necessary.

Deseeding Halve the fruit, then scoop out all the seeds with a teaspoon.

Types

Beef, Marmande or Mediterranean Tomatoes These are very large. When sun ripened on the plant they have a terrific flavour (they may be grown in a greenhouse) but most of the imported

SEE ALSO **Thyme:** Herbs; **Timbale:** Glossary; **Tofu:** Bean Curd; **Tomato Chutney:** Chutney; **Top and Tail:** Glossary;

TOMATO SAUCE

INGREDIENTS
20 ml/4 teaspoons olive oil
1 small onion, chopped
1 celery stick, sliced
1 small carrot, diced
1 clove garlic, crushed
1 bay leaf
1 parsley sprig
1 thyme sprig
450 g/1 lb ripe tomatoes,
  quartered
15 ml/1 tablespoon tomato
  purée
150 ml/¼ pint vegetable or
  chicken stock
salt and pepper
10 ml/2 teaspoons sugar

FOOD VALUES:
TOTAL • PER PORTION
kcals: 490 • 122
kJ: 2047 • 512
protein: 9 g • 2 g
fat: 36 g • 9 g
carbohydrate: 33 g • 8 g
fibre: 8 g • 2 g

**Makes about 600 ml/
1 pint (Serves 4)**

Heat the oil in a saucepan, then add the onion, celery, carrot and garlic and cook the vegetables gently until the onion is softened but not browned, 15–20 minutes. Add the bay leaf, parsley, thyme and tomatoes. Stir in the purée and stock, then bring the mixture to the boil. Reduce the heat, cover the pan and simmer the sauce gently for 45 minutes.

Allow the sauce to cool slightly, then purée in a liquidiser or food processor. Pass the sauce through a sieve to remove all seeds and skin.

Return the sauce to the rinsed-out saucepan and add seasoning to taste with the sugar. Bring the sauce back to the boil, then serve as required.

CANNED TOMATOES

Instead of fresh tomatoes, use two 400 g/14 oz cans chopped tomatoes. For a very quick tomato sauce, simply add the canned tomatoes to a finely chopped onion softened in olive oil. Heat through to boiling point and season the sauce to taste.

Cook's Tip
Tomato purée referred to in recipes is the bought, concentrated type, except when fresh tomato purée or puréed tomatoes are mentioned. Fresh tomato purée has a far weaker flavour and it is more liquid than the commercial type (known as paste in American cookbooks).

Freezing

Whole tomatoes collapse on freezing but tomato sauce or puréed and sieved tomatoes freeze well. Sauce keeps about 6 months, the purée for up to a year.

Nutritional Value

Fresh tomatoes are a good source of vitamin C. They also provide vitamins A and E, folate, potassium and calcium.

Turkey

See Chicken* and Poultry*.
All the information given on chicken and poultry applies to turkey.

Cuts

A wide variety of turkey cuts are now available, even down to sausages.
Breast Whole breasts from smaller birds, rolled breast as a roasting joint or fillets sliced off the breast. Whole breasts for roasting are often sold with skin on but other types are usually skinned.
Drumsticks These are large, will easily serve 2, and require long slow cooking otherwise they can be tough.

Portion Guide

Estimating the number of servings from a whole bird is not easy as it is usual to rely on the breast meat for the first serving and to

fruit sold in this country is miserably lacking in flavour, and is watery and woolly. A pale colour is a good indication that the flavour is equally pallid, and they are usually expensive.
Use: for stuffing. Deep red, full-flavoured fruit is delicious sliced or cut into chunks in salads.
Cherry Tomatoes Very small, bright red tomatoes with an excellent, sweet flavour. Sold in cartons, check that the fruit is not over-ripe and squashed.
Use: in salads or as crudités.
Plum Tomatoes These are deep red, very smooth and oval in shape. They tend to have thicker skins than the round fruit. They

are sweet and full-flavoured. Available from Italian grocers and some greengrocers.
Use: traditionally used for making sauces and cooking. Also delicious in salads or for serving on toast.
Yellow Tomatoes Cherry and ordinary types are available with yellow skins. Apart from their colour (and sometimes the price), they are not remarkable and tend to be a fashion food or gardener's novelty.
Use: their colour is attractive in salads, particularly combined with yellow peppers and courgettes, or for 'white' ratatouille (with white aubergines).

expect to have leftovers for serving cold. The following is a rough guide:

2.75 kg/6 lb – 6–8 servings
4.5 kg/10 lb – 12 servings
6.8 kg/15 lb – 20 servings

A breast roast is an excellent alternative to a whole bird for small families. It is also more economical for those who do not particularly enjoy the dark meat from the thighs and drumsticks.

Thawing

Turkey must be completely thawed before cooking. Unwrap the turkey and place it in a large covered dish. A casserole, roasting tin lined with foil or a mixing bowl may be used. Thaw the turkey in the refrigerator.

2.75 kg/6 lb – 2–2½ days
4.5 kg/10 lb – 2–3 days
6.8 kg/15 lb – 3–4 days

Drain off drip every day during thawing and check that the joints are flexible and that the body cavity is thawed before cooking. Remove the giblets as soon as possible and use at once to make stock.

Roasting Times

Calculate the roasting time according to the weight of the oven-ready bird, including stuffing.

Up to 4.5 kg/10 lb Allow 20 minutes per 450 g/1 lb plus an extra 20 minutes at 180°C, 350°F, gas 4.

Over 4.5 kg/10 lb Allow 15–18 minutes per 450 g/1 lb plus an extra 20 minutes for birds up to 6.8 kg/15 lb.

Roast the bird with the breast down for the first third to half of the cooking time (the longer period for large birds), then turn it over. Keep the turkey covered with foil until 30–60 minutes before the end of cooking, depending on how large the bird is and how well browned it is.

Baste the bird often during cooking once it has been turned breast meat uppermost. When cooking a large turkey, of 6.8 kg/15 lb or more, turn it

several times during cooking, resting it on both sides to promote even cooking and moist results.

During the final 30–60 minutes, the skin should become brown and crisp.

X *Never serve turkey until all the meat is thoroughly cooked through. Test by piercing the thick thigh meat (see chicken*). If the thick meat is not cooked, return the bird to the oven. Do not slice off breast meat to serve before the rest is cooked.*

Cook's Tip
To help speed up the cooking time in an 'emergency' slit the skin between the drumsticks and breast and push the joints away from the body, or cut them off completely, then return the bird to the oven. This exposes the thick area of meat, allowing it to cook faster.

Accompaniments for Turkey

● Sage and onion stuffing, chestnut stuffing, forcemeat or sausagemeat stuffing (see chestnuts* and stuffing*).

● Bacon rolls, chipolata sausages or roast pork.

● Bread sauce*, cranberry sauce and gravy. Also apple sauce.

● Roast potatoes and parsnips, Brussels sprouts.

Coping with Leftovers

● Cool rapidly and chill.

● Cut off meat then return to the refrigerator at once.

● Trim off all meat within 2 days and use or freeze leftovers.

● Freeze them in gravy or sauce, make rissoles or burgers, cut up for cottage pie base or pasties.

X *Do not take the whole bird to the table at every meal occasion as this warms the meat, allowing bacteria to multiply.*

Turnips

See Vegetables*.
Young turnips are available in spring and early summer; main crop vegetables are sold in winter.

Buying

Look for firm, bright vegetables with white and pale, bright green peel. Avoid soft or wrinkled turnips and bruised or damaged vegetables. As well as the green and white types, look for the slightly flatter, purple-white turnips.

Preparation

Trim off the ends and peel the turnips thinly, then wash them well. Small young turnips are best cooked whole – select very small ones for serving whole as a side vegetable.

Otherwise they may be cut into chunks, diced or cut in fine strips.

Cooking

Place in a saucepan and cover with cold water. Add a little salt, if liked, then bring to the boil. Reduce the heat and simmer the turnips for 10–15 minutes, or until just tender. Drain and serve tossed with butter and snipped chives.

Serving Ideas

● Top with soured cream. Mix some breadcrumbs, browned in a little butter, with a sprinkling of grated Parmesan cheese and sprinkle over the turnips.

● Coat small whole turnips with Béchamel Sauce (page 35), Cheese Sauce (page 234), Butter Sauce (page 234) or white Wine Sauce (page 235) and serve as a special vegetable. The top may be browned under the grill.

● Toss small whole turnips with baby carrots in butter, grated orange rind and snipped chives.

SEE ALSO **Turmeric:** Spices; **Tzatziki:** Cucumber; **Univalve, Unmould:** Glossary; **Vanilla:** Spices

Freezing

Turnips do not freeze well raw or cooked but they may be puréed or mashed and frozen for about 6–9 months.

Nutritional Value

Turnips provide some vitamin C, sodium, potassium and trace elements as well as fibre.

TVP

TVP stands for Textured Vegetable Protein, produced from soya beans. It is not a popular product, neither with meat eaters nor vegetarians.

Dehydrated chunks, minced pieces and other shapes have been produced and some wholefood shops sell unflavoured TVP. In this state, it usually has an unpleasant aftertaste of soya which is incredibly difficult to disguise. It is detectable even through rich sauces with herbs, spices and a proportion of meat or poultry. Flavoured types include beef or chicken chunks and bacon-flavoured bits. Rarely available as a consumer product, these are used in some commercial, made up dishes.

It is used in a more advanced form in burger mixes and various other vegetarian products, as well as in some meat pies and other meat products. Sometimes it may be detected in meat products by anyone who is familiar with the flavour or the slightly mushroom-like texture.

UHT

See Milk*.
UHT, meaning ultra heat treated, refers to a preservation process involving heating to and holding a high temperature for a controlled period. This destroys or inhibits the growth of microorganisms and increases the safety and shelf life of foods which are subsequently packed under sterile conditions.

Veal

See Beef* and Meat*.
Veal is the meat from calves. It is not popular in Britain.

Buying

Veal meat should be pale pink and moist in appearance. Veal is not a fatty meat but meat on the bone should have pale, creamy-white fat with shiny membranes covering the flesh. Avoid dry-looking or darkened meat.

Storing

Check the use by date on packed veal. Keep the veal wrapped and chilled. Veal bought loose or frozen should be transferred to a covered container and chilled. Use minced veal and stewing cuts within a day of purchase; others within 2 days.

Cuts and Cooking Methods

Neck, Clod and Shin From the front quarter of the carcass, the meat is usually diced for pies and casseroles or minced.
Shoulder, Oyster and Breast Boned joints with a little fat, all suitable for stuffing and roasting.
Best End of Neck and Loin Prime roasting joints. Also available as cutlets and chops for grilling and frying.
Rump and Top Rump Sliced for beating out into thin escalopes.
Leg and Knuckle Stewing cuts. Knuckle is chopped into pieces on the bone.

Cooking

Veal roasts should be barded with bacon or pork fat to keep them moist and covered for most of the cooking time. More correctly, this cooking method should be called baking.

Cook at 180°C, 350°F, gas 4, allowing 25 minutes per 450 g/ 1 lb, basting occasionally.

Stewing veal should be barely simmered or cooked at 180°C, 350°F, gas 4. Allow 1½–2 hours, the longer time for knuckle on the bone.

Whole joints, such as breast, may also be boiled or braised for 1½–2 hours, then served cold.

Accompaniments

● Serve thin gravy and boiled vegetables with roast veal.

● Tonnato sauce – puréed canned tuna fish with mayonnaise – is a classic accompaniment for cold boiled veal in the Italian dish of Vitelo Tonnato.

● Sage, ham and mozzarella cheese may be rolled with escalopes or used as a topping for cutlets and chops before baking.

Vegan Diet

This is a diet which excludes all animal products, including milk, eggs, butter and cheese. It is often linked with other theories on combining plant foods in the diet, and macrobiotic food laws.

It is not widely followed and should not be considered without serious attention to the type and mix of plant foods. There is a danger that the diet may be lacking in vitamin B12 and all foods must be eaten in sufficient bulk to provide adequate supplies of other essential nutrients.

Those who follow a vegan diet seriously pay close attention to the quality and type of food they eat as well as the cooking methods to use.

Vegetables

See separate entries for each type, for example, Artichokes*, Asparagus*, Aubergines* and so on.

Along with fruit, fresh and frozen vegetables provide a valuable source of essential nutrients, including vitamins, minerals, protein and fibre. They also contain a high percentage of water.

Vegetables also make animal protein and other carbohydrate foods more palatable, providing contrast in texture as well as in flavour. Their contribution to the appearance of meals and snacks is significant.

Since staleness and cooking destroy a certain amount of the nutrient content, especially vitamins, including a regular supply of fresh, raw fruit and vegetables in the diet is important. Good quality frozen vegetables retain valuable nutrients but attention should be paid to the preparation and cooking methods for all vegetables to minimise nutrient loss between buying or harvesting and serving. For this reason, the value of salads made with very fresh foods must be stressed.

Seasonal Produce

Apart from any nutritional benefit, there are 2 distinct advantages to buying British grown produce when it is in season, particularly when buying directly from local producers. Cost and flavour are both at their best.

Exotic Vegetables

Butternut Squash Gourd-shaped, peach-coloured skinned squash with bright orange flesh and a small central hollow with few seeds. Some are about the size of large potatoes and excellent for baking or boiling whole, others may be the size of small yellow melons. Halve and scoop out seeds, dot with butter and wrap in foil to bake or steam until tender. Excellent served with herb butter, soft cheese or soured cream and chives. Good stuffed and baked.

Cassava Also known as manioc, this is a large root vegetable which is used to manufacture tapioca. There are many varieties. They are not that common in supermarkets but are available from ethnic shops and markets.

Cassava has white flesh and thick, dark skin, rather like yam. It must be peeled, sliced and thoroughly soaked before cooking to remove a natural toxin. Boil or bake as for potatoes.

Sometimes served in Caribbean restaurants (plain boiled as an accompaniment), the starchy texture complements rich spicy main dishes very well.

Edoes Also known as eddo, taro or dasheen. Thick-skinned and hairy, these can be quite small (about the size of a small lemon). They are a member of the yam family and must be cooked before eating as they are also poisonous raw.

Taste very like potatoes and should be cooked by boiling for about 15 minutes until tender, or baking.

Okra Also known as ladies' fingers. Green, ridged pods which may be cooked whole or sliced. They are added to gumbo – a South American stew – as a thickening, since they contain a gum-like substance. Trim off stalks and wash well. Cook quickly in hot fat or stew slowly until tender. Small pods are most tender. Thinly sliced and cooked with spices in hot fat, okra can be crunchy; otherwise its texture is not to everyone's taste.

Spaghetti Squash A yellow squash that looks like a large melon. Cook the squash whole by steaming or boiling (about 45 minutes) or in the microwave (prick all over and place in a covered dish, turn twice, allowing about 20 minutes for a medium-size vegetable, on High). Large vegetables may be halved and placed in a roasting bag for cooking.

Cut the cooked squash in half and remove the seeds, then use a fork to scoop out the flesh which comes away from the shell in spaghetti-like shreds.

It has an excellent, delicate flavour and is delicious with a little butter, cheese and parsley. Good with a Béchamel Sauce (page 35) and a browned cheese and breadcrumb topping. A versatile vegetable that is also easy to grow.

Sweet Potatoes Red and white skinned. The red-skinned type has peach-coloured flesh. Scrub well and boil in their skins until tender (about 30 minutes or longer, depending on size). Peel and slice or cube, or bake until crisp, then halve and stuff. Texture like potato but with sweet flesh. Good with ordinary potatoes. Sweet spices such as cinnamon and coriander go well with flesh.

Yams Large, thick-skinned root vegetables with white flesh similar to potato but with a lighter texture and less flavour. There are many different varieties. Never eat yams raw as they contain a poisonous natural toxin. Cook as for sweet potatoes.

SEE ALSO **Venison:** Game; **Verbena:** Herbs; **Vichysoisse:** Soup; **Victoria Sandwich:** Cakes – Basic Creamed Mixture, Glossary

BRITISH VEGETABLE CALENDAR

JANUARY	FEBRUARY	MARCH	APRIL
Brussels sprouts, cabbage: winter, savoy, white and red; celeriac, Jerusalem artichokes, kohlrabi, leeks, spring greens, onions, parsnips, shallots, swedes and turnips.	Brussels sprouts, cabbage: as January; celeriac, Jerusalem artichokes, kohlrabi, leeks, onions, parsnips, shallots, swedes and turnips.	Cabbage: as January; leeks, onions, parsnips, spinach, sprouting broccoli, swedes, tomatoes and turnips.	Cabbage: winter, white, red and greens; cape broccoli, chicory, cucumber, leeks, spinach, sprouting broccoli, swedes, tomatoes and watercress.

MAY	JUNE	JULY	AUGUST
Asparagus, cape broccoli, chicory, Chinese leaves, cucumber, leeks, radishes, spinach, spring greens, sprouting broccoli, tomatoes and watercress.	Asparagus, beans: broad; beetroot, new carrots, chicory, Chinese leaves, courgettes, cucumber, endive, lettuce: cos and iceberg; new potatoes, peas, radishes, spinach, sprouting broccoli, tomatoes, turnips and watercress.	Beans: broad; beetroot, broccoli, peppers, carrots, celery, chicory, Chinese leaves, courgettes, cucumber, endive, fennel, globe artichokes, lettuce: as June; peas, new potatoes, radishes, tomatoes, turnips and watercress.	Beans: broad, French and runner; beetroot, broccoli, peppers, carrots, celery, chicory, Chinese leaves, courgettes, cucumber, endive, fennel, globe artichokes, kohlrabi, leeks, lettuce: as June; marrow, new potatoes, radishes, tomatoes and turnips.

SEPTEMBER	OCTOBER	NOVEMBER	DECEMBER
Beans: broad, French and runner; broccoli, peppers, celery, Chinese leaves, courgettes, cucumber, endive, fennel, kohlrabi, leeks, lettuce: as June; marrow, onions, parsnips, pumpkin, radishes, spinach, sweetcorn, tomatoes and turnips.	Broccoli, Brussels sprouts, cabbage: red, white and savoy; chicory, Chinese leaves, endive, fennel, kohlrabi, leeks, lettuce: as June; marrow (end of season), onions, parsnips, pumpkin, shallots, spinach, sweetcorn, tomatoes and turnips.	Brussels sprouts, cabbage: as October; Chinese leaves, fennel, Jerusalem artichokes, kohlrabi, leeks, onions, parsnips, shallots and turnips.	Brussels sprouts, cabbage: as October; celeriac, Jerusalem artichokes, kohlrabi, leeks, onions, parsnips, shallots, swedes and turnips.

Note: Potatoes, carrots, mushrooms, watercress and cauliflower are available all year. Other types of vegetables are cultivated in comparatively small amounts and new trends are continuously developing in the type and availability of crops.

Vegetarian Diet

Vegetarians do not eat fish, poultry or meat but they may eat animal products which are obtained without the necessity for killing. Ingredients to avoid include gelatine, suet and some margarine made with fish oil or cooking oils which include fish oil. Although most vegetarians eat cheese, some will only eat vegetarian cheese. Rennet, from calve's stomachs, is used to make ordinary cheese, whereas vegetarian cheese is made using a non-animal separating agent.

Nutrition

By combining a broad variety of vegetables, cereals and pulses with some animal products, the vegetarian diet can be well balanced. However, it tends to be rather bulky compared to diets in which protein is obtained mainly from animal foods.

Demi or Semi Vegetarians

A food fashion, some people do not eat poultry or meat but they will consume fish. This is not a true vegetarian diet but it is often mistakenly equated as such.

Ventilation

The kitchen should be well ventilated to allow cooking smells to escape and to prevent condensation from building up. A window which opens is fine in winter but during summer a fan or vent which prevents flies from entering is better.

Cooker hoods are designed for filtering cooking fumes by pumping them through 1–2 paper or charcoal filters. The air may be re-circulated into the room or ducted from the kitchen to the outside.

Vinegar

Vinegar is a fermented liquid, traditionally a product of wine production and literally sour wine. Wine which is fermented for a second time by micro-organisms that produce acetic acid becomes vinegar. The same process may be used to make malt vinegar from beer.

True vinegar must be distinguished from acetic acid with added flavouring. The former retains some of the flavour and character of the original liquid whereas the latter is a poor substitute. Check the labels for details – it is usually fairly easy to recognise good quality vinegar by price apart from anything else.

Vinegar Mother During the second fermentation a skin-like film forms in the vinegar, not on the surface but floating in the liquid. Hold an old bottle of vinegar up to the light and there may be a mother in it. Adding a mother to good wine will turn it into vinegar.

Types

Balsamic Vinegar Dark, aged wine vinegar produced in Modena in Italy, available from larger supermarkets, delicatessens and wine merchants. This is rich and strong, and it makes excellent, dark, thick salad dressings when combined with olive oil.

Cider Vinegar Made from apples, this is not as harsh as other types. It makes good salad dressings and it is useful for preserving. Used to sharpen sauces, drinks and other dishes.

Distilled Malt Vinegar Clear malt vinegar, useful for pickling and for making chutneys such as peach, apricot or mango, in which ordinary malt vinegar produces a dark preserve.

Malt Vinegar Dark and fermented from malted liquid. A traditional British vinegar for sprinkling over chips or for pickling. Malt vinegar is much too harsh to use for salad dressings and savoury dishes.

Rice Wine Vinegar Japanese vinegar, made from rice wine. Obtainable from wholefood shops as well as specialist stores. Used for adding to cooked rice to make sushi or for balancing sweet and sour flavours in savoury cooking.

Sherry Vinegar Made from sherry, this is quite tart but it has an unmistakable hint of sherry in its flavour. A dark vinegar for salad dressings.

Wine Vinegar Both red and white. Quality varies, some are quite harsh. For cooking and for making dressings.

Flavoured Vinegars

Herbs, spices and fruit may be used to flavour vinegar. Tarragon, rosemary and dill are all popular and some may be purchased.

They are easy to make. Place washed and dried fresh herb sprigs in clean bottles. Cover with white wine or cider vinegar, then leave for at least 3 weeks for the flavour of the herbs to infuse with the vinegar.

Spices such as chillies, coriander, cloves and cinnamon may be added to the vinegar, or a mixture of complementary spices may be used.

Fruit vinegars have been highlighted by food fashion. Raspberries, strawberries, lemon or orange may be used. The soft fruit should be covered with white wine or distilled malt vinegar and crushed over a period of a week before being strained. The vinegar may be sweetened. Strips of orange or lemon peel may be added to white wine vinegar to flavour it in the same way as herbs.

Flavoured vinegars are useful ingredients for salad dressings. The sweetened fruit vinegars may also be added to dessert sauces, mousses, ice creams or sprinkled over pancakes and waffles.

Vitamins

See Balanced Diet*
The diet must regularly supply adequate amounts of all vitamins. Deficiencies result in general poor health and retarded growth or development in children; however, specific problems result from a lack of individual nutrients.

To ensure an adequate supply of vitamins is obtained, the way in which food is stored, prepared and cooked is important.

It is equally important that a balanced diet does not provide an excess of some, mainly fat soluble, vitamins. Although this is unlikely to be the case for normal adults eating a broad variety of foods, specific groups of the population may be susceptible to vitamin overdose. Specifically, extreme care should be exercised in the use of supplements as these should not be necessary if the diet is well balanced and in normal health.

Vitamin Groups

Vitamins may be separated into 2 groups, those soluble in water and others soluble in fat.

Fat Soluble Vitamins

Vitamin A
Known as retinol which is found in animal foods. Vitamin A can be synthesised in the body from carotene, the yellow substance familiar from vegetables such as carrots.

Function and Deficiency Vitamin A is essential to prevent night blindness, or poor vision in the dark. It is also essential for the proper development of sight in children and for good skin condition in adults.

If excessive amounts of vitamin A are eaten, they are accumulated in the liver and may produce illness.

Sources Fish oils, liver, kidney, dairy produce and eggs. Carotene is found in vegetables such as carrots, swedes and green vegetables, including spinach and watercress (the darker the green the more carotene).

Stability Vitamin A is not affected by cooking, although it can be destroyed by high temperatures or prolonged cooking. Since it is stored in the body, there is little danger of deficiency.

Vitamin D
Function and Deficiency Vitamin D is essential for adequate calcium absorption and a childhood deficiency results in rickets. Osteomalacia (brittle bone disease) in older women can be the result of vitamin D

---

deficiency (combined with a lack of calcium in the diet and loss of the mineral during childbearing).

An excess of vitamin D can be the cause of calcium deposits causing damage to the kidneys. Therefore, it is important that the intake is not too high.

Sources Vitamin D is added to margarine by law and is present in milk, butter, oily fish and many animal products. However, it is manufactured by the body following exposure to sunlight which acts on a substance in the skin.

Vitamin E
Function and Deficiency Vitamin E may play a role in fertility but this is not proven. There is no scientific proof of the vitamin's specific role.
Sources Widely available in milk, wheatgerm, vegetable oils, cereals, fatty fish and eggs.

Vitamin K
Function and Deficiency Vitamin K is necessary for blood clotting. Deficiency is rare as the vitamin can be synthesised in the body.
Sources Readily available in vegetables and cereals.

Water Soluble Vitamins

Vitamin C
See Ascorbic Acid*.

Vitamin B1 – Thiamin
Function and Deficiency Thiamin enables the body to release energy from carbohydrate. Deficiency results in a disease known as beri-beri, found in populations with a very high carbohydrate diet and low thiamin intake.
Sources Milk, offal, eggs, vegetables and cereals.
Stability Thiamin is stable to boiling point of water but destroyed at higher temperatures, for example in frying. It is also destroyed by alkaline substances, for example when bicarbonate of soda is added to cooking water.

Vitamin B2 – Riboflavin
Function and Deficiency Plays a similar role to thiamin and deficiency is rare.
Sources Milk, meat, cereal products with added riboflavin and eggs.
Stability Riboflavin is destroyed by light, therefore milk should not be left to stand in sunlight.

Niacin
Nicotinic acid and nicotinamide are both forms of niacin, another of the B group of vitamins.
Function and Deficiency Important for obtaining energy supplies from food. Deficiency results in pellagra, a disease in which the skin becomes darkened and scaly.
Sources Meats, potatoes, bread and breakfast cereals with added vitamins.

Vitamin B6 – Pyridoxine
Function and Deficiency Used for haemoglobin production and for metabolism of amino acids (see protein*). Deficiency is rare and high intakes should be avoided.

Sources Readily available in all food, including fish, meat, eggs, milk, wholefood cereals, potatoes and vegetables.

Vitamin B12
As vitamin B12 is not found in vegetables, vegetarians, and specifically vegans, must ensure they receive a good supply. The vegan diet is most likely to be deficient and yeast extract can be a useful source.
Function and Deficiency Essential for the manufacture of blood and for the proper function of the nervous system. Deficiency results in pernicious anaemia and nervous disorders.
Sources Liver, meat, yeast, eggs, cheese, milk.

Folate
Function and Deficiency Important for blood manufacture and during pregnancy. Deficiency results in a form of anaemia. Certain gastric disorders and drugs used in the control of epilepsy can inhibit absorption.
Sources Offal, green vegetables and in small amounts in many foods, including fruit, meat and dairy foods.
Stability Folate is destroyed or made unavailable to the body by cooking and lost in cooking water, therefore regular supplies of raw vegetables and fruit are an important source.

Pantothenic Acid
Function and Deficiency Pantothenic acid plays a role in carbohydrate and fat metabolism. Deficiency is rare as the vitamin is widely available in all foods.
Sources Key sources include meat, poultry, fish, dairy produce, cereals, beans and pulses.

Biotin
Function and Deficiency Essential in small amounts for fat metabolism. It may be synthesised in the body.
Sources Offal, eggs, milk, fruit and vegetables. The body may manufacture all it needs.

A Guide to Vitamin Groups
Fat Soluble Vitamins
Vitamins A, D, E and K.
Water Soluble Vitamins
Vitamins C and B Group.
Vitamin B1 – Thiamin
Vitamin B2 – Riboflavin
Niacin
Vitamin B6 – Pyridoxine
Vitamin B12
Folate
Pantothenic Acid
Biotin

Washing up

Here are a few traditional and up-to-date points to remember.

• Never leave dirty dishes stacked in the kitchen for hours. Washing up promptly makes the task easier.

• Rinse saucepans and empty cooking or food preparation containers immediately after use.

• Place heavily soiled cooking dishes, tins and pans to soak in hot soapy water at once. This loosens baked or burnt on food.

• Wash dishes and utensils in hot soapy water as you are preparing food and cooking. Use fresh water for each batch: do not keep a sink full of warm, greasy water.

• Use fine, textured (for a good grip) rubber gloves and very hot water with plenty of washing up liquid.

• Wash glasses and cutlery first, then plates, cups and saucers.

• Wash serving dishes and any cooking dishes last.

• Change the water during washing up if it becomes cool or very dirty. Pre-rinsing dishes keeps the water clean.

• Rinse all items in clean hot water and place them to drain. Use a clean tea-towel to dry the dishes. As the tea-towel becomes damp, discard it (for washing) and use a fresh one.

• Remember to wash out the sink, draining board and surrounding areas after washing up. Use a disinfectant or bleach (in solution).

• Soak cloths and brushes in bleach or boil them regularly.

Watercress

See Vegetables*.

Buying

Look for bright, crisp watercress which is dark green and shiny. Really fresh bunches are far easier to use than bags filled with stalks and leaves all in a muddle.

Avoid limp, pale or yellowing watercress.

Storing

Place bags in the refrigerator. Snip the ends off a bundle of stalks, then stand the bunch, stalks down, in a jug of cold water.

Use within a day of purchase. In a jug the watercress will usually keep for 2 days.

Preparation

Trim off tough stalk ends, leaving the leaves attached in sprigs. Wash really well and drain.

Use

• Watercress adds a refreshing peppery taste to salads.

• Use to make a delicious sauce – follow the recipe for Cream Sauce (page 234) and purée the watercress with half the sauce. Good with fish, chicken or light vegetables such as Swiss chard stalks.

• Chop and add to Breadcrumb Stuffing (page 254).

Weighing and Measuring

See Using This Book (page 6).

Equipment

Kitchen Scales There are many types from which to choose, including electronic, spring scales, beam scales and balance scales. Most types include metric and Imperial weights, although some are metric only – which is fine if you do not have to convert back to old measures. Balance scales with a good set of weights and good quality electronic scales are the most accurate.

A good set of balance scales, with a large scoop on one side and platform for weights opposite, is the best option. There are no batteries to replace or components that are likely to malfunction. However, they do take up more work surface space than the streamlined modern types.

The scales to avoid are inexpensive spring scales which are not graduated to weigh less than 25 g/1 oz with any accuracy.

Measuring Spoons A set of measuring spoons is essential. Either metric, Imperial or with scoops for both.

All spoon measures in this book (and in most reputable cookbooks) refer to level measuring spoons not to kitchen or serving cutlery.

Measuring Jug Select a clear one which will give an accurate reading. Plastic jugs graduated on the inside are not as accurate and it is difficult to tell exactly how much liquid they contain.

Kitchen Ruler For cutting rolled out pastry or other doughs, measuring cake tins and so on.

SEE ALSO **Walnut:** Nuts; **Weijska:** Sausage; **Wensleydale:** Cheese; **Whisk:** Glossary; **Whitebait, Whiting:** Fish; **Woodcock:** Game;

Keep a washable plastic rule solely for kitchen use.

Cup Measures These are American measures (except for very old British measures, long since out of use). Sets of cup measures may be purchased from good cook shops, where they will be sold as standard American cup measures. Some notes on sizes and quantities are given at the front of the book.

The Importance of Accuracy

In some cooking, accurate measuring and weighing is all important. Cake making is the best example, as the exact balance of fat, sugar, flour and moisture are essential for achieving good results. Breads, biscuits, soufflés, custards and many other mixtures all require the right proportion of ingredients for success.

● Before weighing ingredients make sure that scales are registering a zero reading with the container for food in place.

● All spoon measures must be using standard measuring spoons and they should be level unless otherwise stated. Mismeasuring spoon amounts can ruin dishes – sauces and soups become too thick, flavourings are too weak or strong, raising agents, sweetening or crucial moistening can be wrong.

● Stand a measuring jug on a level surface to check the volume of liquid and bend down so that you look at the content at eye level for a correct reading.

Ordered Weighing and Measuring

Weighing and measuring ingredients in a sensible order makes the task easier and less messy.

● Read the ingredients list and have all the items ready.

● Weigh dry ingredients first – flour, sugar and so on. There is no need to wash the container before weighing the next item.

● Next weigh any fat, cheese or slightly sticky ingredients.

● Weigh any liquids last.

● Use a flexible plastic spatula to scrape out all the ingredients.

● To remove syrup or honey from a pot, heat a metal spoon in boiling water (or hold it in a gas flame for a few seconds), then use it to scoop the syrup which will slide off easily into the measuring container.

Throw-it-all-in Approach

Cooking is not just a necessity and there are many areas which lend themselves to individual interpretation. It must be emphasised that before the cook can begin to adapt or construct individual combinations of ingredients, he or she must have a good basic working knowledge of the taste and texture of different foods and seasonings, and the way in which ingredients react when heated. Bearing this in mind, there are lots of opportunities for the enthusiast to adopt a more casual approach to weighing and measuring.

Stews, soups, sauces, salads, savoury bakes, even bread making can be quite successful.

You can always add a little extra but once something is mixed in, it cannot be removed. This is especially true of seasonings and liquids. Taste as you add to sauces, soups and savoury dishes – it is the best way of learning about ingredients.

X *Although a flamboyant dip of the finger may look artistic, it is the wrong way to treat food. With every dip of the finger, unwanted micro-organisms are passed into the food, along with other particles, hairs or dirt from under the nails or surrounding surfaces and utensils that have been handled.*

The rules for testing are simple:
● *Tasting is vital for good cooking.*
● *Have 2–3 clean teaspoons ready and set them aside for washing up after each tasting.*
● *The same applies to mixing spoons. Never re-dip the same spoon.*

Whitecurrants

See Redcurrants* and Blackcurrants*.
These are an albino variety of redcurrants and are not widely available. They may be used as for redcurrants in desserts but not for making jelly.

Yeast

See Bread* and Fermentation*.
Yeast is available in different forms. Brewer's yeast is used for making beer or wine and baker's yeast is used for cooking; this information applies to baker's yeast.

Fresh Yeast

Available from hot bread shops in supermarkets or bakers who prepare their own bread.

Fresh yeast should be creamy-beige in colour, firm and of a texture that flakes easily. It should have a pleasant, fresh smell.

Avoid yeast that is darkened, runny or very broken with a strong odour.

Preparation

Cream fresh yeast with a little sugar, then add warm liquid and stir well. Leave the yeast in a warm place in a covered jug or basin until it becomes frothy and bubbly.

Alternatively, this yeast liquid may be poured into a well made in dry ingredients and a little of the flour mixture sprinkled over the surface of the liquid. The flour mixture prevents crusting and it may even be mixed to a thin batter to provide food for the yeast. This process is known as sponging.

Much fresh yeast used now is fast acting and it tends to ferment speedily; however, never underestimate the proving time required for doughs, particularly sweet or rich ones.

Dried Yeast

There are 2 types, the traditional granular type and the easy-blend, finer yeast. The easy-blend type is now most popular as it is easier and quicker to use. Read and follow the manufacturer's instructions for both.

Ordinary Dried Yeast Stir a little sugar (5 ml/1 teaspoon) into lukewarm liquid, then sprinkle the dried yeast over the top. Leave in a warm place and the granules of yeast absorb water, swell and ferment, forming a thick, soft foam on the surface of the liquid. Stir well before use.

Easy-blend Dried Yeast This should be mixed with the flour or dry ingredients according to the manufacturer's instructions. The resulting dough requires only one proving.

Storing

Fresh yeast will keep for 3–5 days in a polythene bag in the refrigerator.

Dried yeast should be stored in the sealed sachets or airtight container in a dry, cool cupboard and used before the date recommended by the manufacturer. The shelf life is long and most packets keep for many months.

Freezing

Fresh yeast may be frozen for up to 3 months.

Pack it in usable quantities, then add straight to hand-hot water and leave for longer to thaw and ferment.

Yeast Products

Yeast extract is used as a savoury spread or for flavouring stocks, sauces, soups and other cooked dishes. It is very salty.

Yeast pastes, available in tubes or small tubs from wholefood shops, may be plain or flavoured with vegetables. They are useful for sandwich fillings and spreading on crackers. Store in the refrigerator once opened.

Yogurt

See Milk*.

Yogurt is a milk product, produced by fermenting the milk with a culture consisting of 2 different bacteria, that work in tandem to set and sour the milk. Beforehand the milk is heat treated to destroy unwanted micro-organisms and most yogurt is heat treated after manufacture to prevent further fermentation.

However, some yogurts, labelled live yogurt, contain the active culture.

Storing

Keep yogurt in the refrigerator and use it by the date on the carton. Although most manufacturer's do not recommend freezing yogurt, the full fat types do freeze successfully and are not curdled after a good stir on thawing.

Yogurt Ice Cream

Mix equal quantities of natural yogurt with well sweetened fruit purée. Freeze until hardening around the edges, then whisk until smooth. Repeat once more before allowing to freeze until firm. Place in the refrigerator 15 minutes before use.

Strawberry, raspberry, banana, peach or mango purée are all suitable. Creamy Greek yogurt makes a delicious ice.

Use

● Use in desserts set with gelatine instead of cream.

● As a dessert topping instead of cream – remember that some of the richer yogurts have a high fat and calorie content.

● Beat with eggs and seasoning for topping moussaka.

● Add to sauces, soups or savoury dishes and warm

through very briefly. Yogurt curdles easily when heated in a sauce.

● Use to make tandoori paste, combining it with garlic and curry spices, then pour over meat or poultry and allow to marinate.

Yorkshire Pudding

See Batter*.

A savoury pudding served with roast beef. Traditionally, the pudding is served with gravy before the beef; the original intention being to fill up a hungry family before serving small portions of expensive meat.

Make a Thin Batter (see page 28). Set the oven at 190°C, 375°F, gas 5 or adjust the cooking time as necessary if the meat is roasted at a different temperature.

Pour a little oil or dripping from roasting a joint in a roasting tin or 4 individual Yorkshire pudding tins. Place the fat in the oven to heat for 2–3 minutes, then pour the batter into the tin or tins.

Bake a large pudding for about 40–50 minutes, until risen, crisp and golden. The exact cooking time depends on the size of the tin. It may be placed under meat which is roasted on a rotisserie or on a rack above. Small puddings take about 30 minutes.

Serve the pudding as soon as it is cooked, cutting a large one into portions.

Zinc

See Minerals*.

Zinc is important for the efficient function of the body's enzymes and the healing of wounds. It is found in a wide variety of foods but it is not readily absorbed. In particular, phytic acid present in unrefined cereals and legumes tends to inhibit zinc absorption.

Sources Meat, milk and its products, bread and cereals.

SEE ALSO **Zest:** Glossary; **Zucchini:** Courgettes

Useful Food Values

Note All figures quoted are per 100g.
**This symbol indicates that the flour is fortified with the nutrients.

Food	Energy (Kcal)	Protein (g)	Fat (g)	Carbo-hydrate (g)	Dietary Fibre (g)	Vitamin C (mg)	Vitamin A (μg)	Vitamin B1 thiamin	Vitamin B2 ribo-flavin (mg)	Calcium (mg)	Iron (mg)
Bacon: back, lean, grilled	292	30.5	18.9	0	0	0	Tr	0.6	0.2	13	1.6
Bread: white	235	8	2	49	4	0	0	0.2	0.06	110	1.6
wholemeal	215	9.2	2.5	41.6	7.4	0	0	0.3	0.09	54	2.7
Butter: salted	737	0.5	81.7	Tr	0	Tr	886.7	Tr	0.02	15	0.2
Cheese: cheddar	412	25.5	34.4	0.1	0	Tr	362.5	0.03	0.4	720	0.3
cottage	98	13.8	3.9	2.1	0	Tr	45.7	0.03	0.26	73	0.1
Cream: double	449	1.7	48	2.7	0	1	654.2	0.02	0.16	50	0.2
single	198	2.6	19.1	4.1	0	1	335.8	0.04	0.17	91	0.1
Eggs: whole, raw/boiled	147	12.5	10.8	Tr	0	0	190	0.07	0.35	57	1.9
yolk, raw	339	16.1	30.5	Tr	0	0	535	0.3	0.54	130	6.1
Fish: cod fillet, poached	94	20.9	1.1	0	0	Tr	Tr	0.08	0.08	29	0.3
haddock, smoked, steamed	101	23.3	0.9	0	0	Tr	Tr	0.1	0.11	58	1.0
mackerel, fried	188	21.5	11.3	0	0	Tr	52	0.09	0.38	28	1.2
trout, fried	135	23.5	4.5	0	0	Tr	Tr	0	0	36	1.0
tuna, canned in oil	289	22.8	22.0	0	0	Tr	Tr	0.04	0.11	7	1.1
Flour: plain, white	341	9.4	1.3	77.7	3.6	0	0	0.31**	0.03	140**	2.0**
wholemeal	310	12.7	2.2	63.9	8.6	0	0	0.47	0.09	38	3.9
Fromage frais: very low fat	58	7.7	0.2	6.8	0	Tr	3	0.03	0.37	87	0.1
Fruit: apple	46	0.3	Tr	11.9	2	3	5	0.04	0.02	4	0.3
banana	79	1.1	0.3	19.2	3.4	10	33	0.04	0.07	7	0.4
orange	35	0.8	Tr	8.5	2.0	50	8	0.10	0.03	41	0.3
pear	41	0.3	Tr	10.6	2.3	3	2	0.03	0.03	8	0.2
Ham, boiled: lean joint	191	26	9.7	0	0	0	Tr	0.37	0.3	15	1.9
Meat, roast, lean: beef, topside	156	29.2	4.4	0	0	0	Tr	0.08	0.35	6	2.8
lamb, leg	191	29.4	8.1	0	0	0	Tr	0.14	0.38	8	2.7
pork, leg	185	30.7	6.9	0	0	0	Tr	0.85	0.35	9	1.3
Milk: whole	66	3.2	3.9	4.8	0	1	56	0.03	0.17	115	0.06
semi-skimmed	46	3.3	1.6	5.0	0	1	23	0.04	0.18	120	0.05
skimmed	33	3.3	0.1	5.0	0	1	1	0.04	0.17	120	0.06

Food	Energy (Kcal)	Protein (g)	Fat (g)	Carbo-hydrate (g)	Dietary Fibre (g)	Vitamin C (mg)	Vitamin A (μg)	Vitamin B1 thiamin	Vitamin B2 ribo-flavin (mg)	Calcium (mg)	Iron (mg)
Nuts: peanuts	570	24.3	49	8.6	8.1	Tr	0	0.9	0.10	61	2
Offal, fried: kidney, lambs'	155	24.6	6.3	0	0	9	160	0.56	2.3	13	12.0
liver, lambs'	232	22.9	14	3.9	0	13	17,400	0.27	4.2	12	10
Poultry, roast: chicken breast	142	26.5	4.0	0	0	0	Tr	0.08	0.14	9	0.5
turkey, breast	132	29.8	1.4	0	0	0	Tr	0.07	0.14	7	0.5
duck, meat only	189	25.3	9.7	0	0	0	0	0.26	0.47	13	2.7
Pulses, boiled: lentils, brown/green	105	8.8	0.7	16.9	3.8	Tr	0	0.14	0.08	22	3.5
lentils, split red	100	7.6	0.4	17.5	1.9	Tr	0	0.11	0.04	16	2.4
red kidney beans, dried	103	8.4	0.5	17.4	9.0	1	0.6	0.17	0.05	37	2.5
Rice, boiled: white	123	2.2	0.3	29.6	0.8	0	0	0.01	0.01	1	0.2
brown	141	2.6	1.1	32.1	1.5	0	0	0.14	0.02	4	0.5
Spaghetti, boiled: white	104	3.6	0.7	22.2	1.8	0	0	0.01	0.01	7	0.5
wholemeal	113	4.7	0.9	23.2	4	0	0	0.21	0.02	11	1.4
Vegetables, boiled: broad beans	48	5.1	0.8	5.6	3.8	20	24.2	0.03	0.06	18	0.8
broccoli	24	3.1	0.8	1.1	2.3	44	79.2	0.05	0.05	40	1
Brussels sprouts	35	2.9	1.3	3.5	2.6	60	53.3	0.07	0.09	20	0.5
cabbage, average	16	1.0	0.4	2.2	2.3	20	35	0.08	0.01	33	0.3
carrots	24	0.6	0.4	4.9	2.8	2	1260	0.09	Tr	24	0.4
cauliflower	28	2.9	0.9	2.1	1.6	27	10	0.07	0.04	17	0.4
peas, frozen	69	6	0.9	9.7	7.3	12	67.5	0.26	0.09	35	1.6
potatoes, new	75	1.5	0.3	17.8	1.2	9	Tr	0.13	0.02	5	0.3
potatoes, old	72	1.8	0.1	17	1.4	6	Tr	0.18	0.01	5	0.4
spinach	19	2.2	0.8	0.8	3.1	8	640	0.06	0.05	160	1.6
Yogurt: natural low fat	56	5.1	0.8	7.5	0	1	8.8	0.05	0.25	190	0.1
Greek-style (cows')	115	6.4	9.1	2	0	Tr	121	0.03	0.36	150	0.3

The reference source is McCance and Widdowson's **The Composition of Foods**, 4th edition and 3rd, 4th and 5th supplements (see Bibliography, page 288).

Abbreviations Kcal – kilocalories; g – grammes; mg – milligrammes; μg – microgrammes; Tr – trace.

Vitamin A These quantities are expressed as retinol equivalents. Retinol is the chemical term for the vitamin; however our bodies also convert carotenes into vitamin A. The vitamin value of carotenes is calculated using a standard formula.

GLOSSARY

Many classic, contemporary and international terms are used in recipes, cookery books and other written information relating to food. The more important, basic and practical terms are explained within the main text; this glossary includes a selection of additional useful terms, some techniques and classic dishes.

Acidulated Water Water with a little lemon juice or vinegar added. Used to prevent discoloration of food during preparation, for example apples.

Almond Paste An alternative name for marzipan.

Al Dente To cook until tender but with bite. Italian term used to describe cooked pasta.

American Measures and Terms American recipes are written in cup measures. A set of measures may be purchased from better cookshops but do not confuse them with old-fashioned British cup measures. Basic guidelines on following American recipes, or on adapting the information in this book, are given in the display copy.

Angelica The candied stems of the plant of the same name. Angelica is easy to grow and young stems may be preserved. Used in cake making and for decorating cakes and desserts.

Au Bleu Refers to freshly caught and cooked fish, particularly trout. The natural coating on the skin forms a blue-ish tint when cooked.

Baba A small sweet bun made from a rich yeasted batter (as savarin), usually with raisins added. Soaked in rum-flavoured syrup to make rum baba. Babas may be filled with whipped cream.

Bain Marie Also referred to as a water bath. A container of hot water in which to stand dishes of food. This may be a roasting tin or ovenproof dish; a flameproof container may be used on the hob.

The dish of food is placed in the container and boiling water poured in to just below the rim of the outer container, depending on the depth of the cooking dish.

A bain marie prevents the outside of the cooking dish from overheating and the food inside from cooking too fast.

Bake Blind See Flans*. A method of cooking an empty pastry case by placing greaseproof paper and baking beans or dried peas in it during cooking to prevent the pastry from bubbling up in the middle.

Bakewell Tart A short crust pastry flan spread with jam, then topped with an almond sponge. The Basic Creamed Mixture (page 54) may be used with the addition of 50 g/ 2 oz ground almonds and a few drops of natural almond essence.

Baking Beans Small ceramic balls used instead of dried beans to weight down empty pastry cases when baking blind.

Bard To wrap fat, or fat bacon, around or over lean meat or poultry before cooking. This prevents the flesh from drying out. Rolled topside, turkey, pheasant and venison are barded before roasting. The technique may be used with large or small cuts. The barding fat is usually discarded from poultry and other birds; it may be sliced with meat.

Baste To spoon cooking juices, fat or marinade over food at intervals during cooking. This prevents drying and may promote even browning or cooking. For roasting, grilling, poaching in shallow liquid or shallow frying.

American Cup Measures

Cup measures are used in American recipes. Although they are not referred to in the recipes, these notes may be useful should you come across cup measures elsewhere or for American readers.

¼ cup – 50 ml – 2 fluid oz
⅓ cup – 60 ml – 2½ fluid oz
½ cup – 100 ml – 4 fluid oz
⅔ cup – 160 ml – 5 fluid oz
¾ cup – 175 ml – 6 fluid oz
1 cup – 250 ml – 8 fluid oz
The American pint equals 16 fluid oz (Imperial pint equals 20 fluid oz).

Measuring Solids in Cups

The following are sample equivalents for cups and weights of some dry ingredients.

Almonds, ground: 1 cup = 90 g/3 oz
Breadcrumbs, fresh:
 1 cup = 50 g/2 oz
Butter: 1 cup = 225 g/8 oz (also measured by sticks, marked by the manufacturer during production: 1 stick = 50 g/2 oz)
Cheese, grated (Cheddar type):
 1 cup = 100 g/4 oz

Cherries, glacé (whole):
 1 cup = 175 g/6 oz
Flour: 1 cup = 100 g/4 oz
Raisins: 1 cup = 150 g/5 oz
Rice, long-grain (uncooked): 1 cup = 175 g/6 oz
Sugar, granulated: 1 cup = 200 g/7 oz
 icing: 1 cup = 150 g/5 oz
American tablespoons are slightly smaller than British measures: 2 British tablespoons = 3 American tablespoons.

American Terms

As well as slight variations in spelling, American terms for ingredients, cooking techniques and equipment vary. For example, icing sugar is known as confectioner's or powdered sugar. Many examples are mentioned under relevant entries in the text.

When following American recipes, it is also worth remembering that the strength of flour varies. All-purpose flour is the term for plain flour and self-rising flour is the equivalent to self-raising flour. However the protein (gluten) content of the wheat used varies so results in baking can differ.

Baumé A measurement of sugar density. Degrees baumé are taken by floating a saccharometer or hydrometer in syrup. Named after the French scientist who invented the scale for measuring sugar and salt densities of liquids.

The boiling temperature of syrup is the more practical domestic indication of strength, tested using a thermometer.

Beat Technique used for mixing ingredients, also for eggs. A mixing spoon is used in a vigorous circular movement which incorporates air. The bowl must be large enough to prevent spills but small enough for a good depth of ingredients.

Beignet A choux pastry fritter, usually sweet and containing large pieces of fruit, or plain and dredged with icing sugar or served with a sweet sauce.

Beurre Manié Flour creamed to a smooth, thick paste with softened butter for use as a thickening. Small knobs of the mixture are whisked or stirred vigorously into simmering liquid (sauces, soups or stews). The flour combines with the liquid as the fat melts but it must be mixed in immediately.

Two or three parts butter to flour are average proportions: the paste should be pale and floury but soft enough to drop off a teaspoon when tapped firmly.

Bisque A shellfish soup, enriched by the addition of finely ground shell. Lobster, prawns or shrimps may be used and the simmered flesh is pounded to a paste to thicken the soup.

Bivalves Shellfish such as cockles, mussels, clams and oysters with a hinged shell.

Black Forest Gâteau
Chocolate-flavoured Whisked Sponge (page 58), sandwiched with whipped cream and black cherries. Covered in cream, topped with cherries and decorated with chocolate caraque. Kirsch (an almond-flavoured liqueur) may be sprinkled over the cake.

Blanquette A white stew or braise, usually of veal, chicken or rabbit or other white meat. Onions and button mushrooms may be added. White stock, milk or cream may be used.

Blend To mix well. The term is also used for ingredients that are processed in a liquidiser (or blender) or food processor.

Bombe Moulded ice cream, set in a domed mould. Layers of different prepared ice creams are built up in the mould, each one frozen until firm before the next is added, to give a layered effect when cut into wedges. Bombe moulds (basin-like but taller) may be made of tinned copper and they have lids.

Bourguignonne Usually *beouf* or beef Bourguignonne. A casserole of beef with small whole onions and mushrooms in red wine.

Bran Coat covering grain. It may be removed during milling or milled with the grain. White flour has the covering removed, wholemeal flour includes the covering.

Broil American term for grill: to broil, broiling or broiler.

Butterfly Cake Small cake made from Basic Creamed Mixture (page 54), with a slice cut off the top and halved. The halved top is secured back in reverse on a dab of buttercream to represent wings.

Buttermilk Traditionally the sour milk left when making butter. Now produced by adding a culture to milk to sour it. Use in some baking, where its acidity assists as a raising agent.

Candied Peel Orange, lemon and citron peel, preserved by soaking in sugar syrup. The best quality is expensive and purchased in slices or wedges of peel. Cut mixed peel is more economical and practical for baking.

Capers Small, unopened flower buds of a Mediterranean shrub. Pickled in brine and/or vinegar, they have a piquant flavour which complements a wide variety of foods. Good with fish, poultry and vegetables; add to sauces or salads; or use on pizza.

Carbonade Beef stewed in beer, cooked in the oven. Thick slices of bread, buttered side up, are laid over the stew to absorb the cooking juices. The top forms a crisp, golden crust.

Caul Fat Lace-like membrane and fat from around internal organs, traditionally used for wrapping pâtés and faggots. Reference to caul fat may be found but it is not readily available.

Chantilly Cream Or *Crème Chantilly*. Whipped cream slightly sweetened with icing sugar. A little vanilla may be added.

Charlotte A straight-sided moulded dessert, either hot or cold. The mould is lined with sponge fingers for cold set desserts. Buttered bread is used for lining the mould or baking dish when making a hot dessert, for example apple charlotte.

Savoury charlottes are based on the same principle and should include bread, with a savoury custard or sauce.

Chaudfroid A coating sauce which sets when cold. Béchamel Sauce (see page 35) may be used and aspic* should be added when the sauce has cooled. The cool sauce is poured over ingredients such as fish, poultry or eggs. Chaudfroid dishes are usually decorative, with garnishes of cucumber, herbs and blanched carrot set in the sauce. Chaudfroid dishes are excellent for buffets or as summer main courses. The food should be kept chilled until it is served.

Chocolate Caraque Long curls of chocolate, used to decorate desserts and cakes.

Chop To cut finely into small, fairly even pieces. Finely chopped indicates that the pieces must be very small. Roughly chopped suggests that the pieces do not have to be tiny and that their size may vary.

Chowder A thickened fish soup, usually well flavoured with vegetables, possibly with other seafood.

Chine The backbone in a joint of lamb or pork cutlets, ribs or loin. The technique of sawing through the bone (completed by the butcher) is known as 'chining'; the joint of meat is then 'chined'.

Compote Fruit in syrup. The fruit should be lightly poached and the syrup may be flavoured with spices, spirits or other liquor such as wine.

Condiment Seasoning or relish served as an accompaniment. Salt and pepper, mustard or horseradish sauce are examples. Condiments are usually highly flavoured and eaten in small amounts to complement the food.

Confectioner's Sugar American term for icing sugar.

Coulis A purée of cooked vegetables, fish, poultry or meat. Used to describe vegetable or fruit purées, seasoned and served as sauces but without additional fat or thickening.

Crêpe A very thin, large pancake. Crêpes Suzette are served with orange sauce and fresh orange segments and flamed with orange liqueur.

Croquette A small portion of food shaped into an oblong patty, wider at one end, then coated in egg and breadcrumbs. Puréed cooked fish, poultry, game, vegetables or cheese may be bound with Savoury White Sauce (page 234), then poured into a shallow container and chilled for several hours until set before coating.

When deep fried, the crisp breadcrumb crust covers a soft creamy middle.

Croustade A casing of bread made by hollowing out a thick chunk, whole loaf or roll. The bread case is brushed with melted butter or a mixture of olive oil and butter, then baked or grilled until golden. A hot sauce of fish and seafood, poultry, eggs or vegetables is spooned into the croustade just before serving.

Croûte A slice of bread baked or fried until crisp, then used as a base for serving cooked items or for garnishing sauced dishes. Small game birds, fillet steaks and large grilled mushrooms may be served on croûtes of bread. Neat triangular croûtes

are a classic garnish for stews such as *beouf bourguignonne*.

Crudités A selection of raw vegetables, cut into bite-sized pieces and served as an appetiser. Carrots, cucumber, peppers, cauliflower florets, radishes and celeriac may be included. Crudités are often served with a dip.

Crustaceans A term for creatures with limbs and a segmented shell covering, such as prawns and lobsters.

Crystallised With a coating of sugar crystals. Also applied when syrup separates into sugar crystals or when crystals form on sweet preserves or honey.

Dal Spelling variations include dhal. An Indian speciality, this is a thick purée of pulses cooked with spices. There are many recipes: one classic dish is topped with browned onion rings and spices in ghee. Red lentils may be cooked very successfully in this style.

Daube Meat stewed in red wine.

Decoration Ingredients added to sweet dishes to improve their appearance. Used on desserts, cakes and sweet baked goods.

Deglaze The term used for simmering the cooking juices and residue off a cooking pan. After the poultry, meat or other ingredients have been cooked, excess fat is poured away and a small amount of liquid added (stock, wine or water). The liquid is boiled while the cooking residue is scraped off the pan using a mixing spoon or spatula. Rapid boiling reduces the liquid to make a flavoursome sauce.

Degorge The process of salting, usually for short periods of 15–30 minutes, to extract excess water and/or bitter juices or strong flavours. Aubergines* are degorged to remove bitter juices, cucumber is degorged to remove excess liquid and sliced onions may be degorged before being used raw in salads.

Dice To cut into small even cubes. The size of dice may vary from tiny to small, any larger and the pieces are referred to as cubes or chunks.

First cut food into slices, then into fingers and lastly across into dice.

Dissolve To change from solid to liquid in the presence of a liquid. For example, sugar dissolves in water and salt dissolves in water.

Drain To pour away liquid from food. For example, cooked potatoes are drained. The liquid is discarded.

Dredge To sift thickly, as when applying a thick, even covering of icing sugar to the top of a soufflé or cake.

Dumpling British dumplings are made from a suet pastry* mixture, rolled into balls and steamed, boiled or braised in soups or stews.

Dumplings may also be made from potato mixtures (German, Polish and Italian dumplings of this type can be light and delicious), bread-based dough or pasta-like dough. Filled dumplings are a feature of many cuisines, including Polish and Chinese cooking. Fruit-filled dumplings make a tempting dessert when dredged with icing sugar and served with soured cream or fromage frais.

Duxelle Chopped mushrooms cooked with a little chopped onion or shallot in butter or oil. When all the liquid from the mushrooms has evaporated, chopped parsley is added. The mixture is used as a stuffing, particularly for rolled fish fillets, meat olives or pockets slit in chops.

Eccles Cake Individual pastry filled with currants, chopped mixed peel and sugar. Flaky pastry is used to enclose the fruit in a circular cake which is slashed across the top, glazed with egg white and sugar, then baked.

Eclair A finger of choux pastry, with a cream filling and coating. Whipped cream and chocolate coating is the classic combination. Savoury éclairs have a sauce-based filling.

Eggplant American term for aubergine.

En Croûte In a case of pastry. Lamb cutlets and other small cuts of meat or items of food may be wrapped in puff pastry. Whole pâtés or joints of meat may also be cooked en croûte, again in puff pastry or in a firmer crust of short pastry or hot water crust.

En Papillote Enclosed in paper. Fish, vegetables, fruit or other ingredients may be enclosed in a neat double covering of greaseproof paper or cooking parchment before baking. Foil may also be used, particularly for steaming.

Entrée A term traditionally used for a dish served after the starter and before the main course of the meal. However, it is generally used for the main course and should refer to the complete course, that is the meat served with all the necessary accompaniments and garnishes.

Escalope A thin slice of prime meat. The meat is sliced, then beaten out between two pieces of greaseproof paper until very thin. Veal, pork, lamb or poultry may be treated in this way.

Espagnole A brown sauce, made by browning vegetables and a roux of flour and fat, then adding good brown stock and tomatoes or tomato purée. The reduced sauce is strained and it may be enriched with sherry. Served with meats and game.

Flambé Refers to a flamed dish. Warmed spirit or other alcohol, such as brandy, rum or Grand Marnier, is poured over the food and ignited. The alcohol is burnt off, leaving an intense flavour of the liquor. Used part-way through the cooking process, as when frying steak for beef stroganoff, or when the food is served, for example when presenting Christmas pudding or crêpe Suzette.

Fleurons Small shapes (traditionally crescents) of egg-glazed and baked puff pastry used as a garnish for sauced dishes, particularly fish. They are also a suitable accompaniment or garnish for soup.

Florentine A dish which contains spinach. Typically, the spinach may be a base on which to pres-

ent eggs, poultry or fish and a coating sauce may be added.

Fondue There are three types. The classic Swiss cheese fondue is a pot of melted cheese (often enriched with kirsch) in which diners dip chunks of crusty bread. Celery and apples may also be dipped. The pot of cheese is kept hot over a spirit burner and the traditional treat is the crust of browned cheese which forms on the base of the pan.

A fondue bourguignonne consists of a pot of oil in which small pieces of prime steak are cooked at table. Accompanying sauces and condiments are served to each diner.

A Chinese-style fondue is based on fire-pot cooking. The authentic cooking pot includes a rack on which to burn coals, a chimney for smoke to escape and a moat-shaped cooking vessel in which a rich stock simmers. Various ingredients, including seafood, meats, offal and poultry are simmered in the soup and retrieved using small draining scoops. The cooking liquid is served at the end of the meal.

Fricassée A white braise or sauced dish, usually of chicken, veal or fish.

Fruit Butter A sweet preserve of thick fruit purée which spreads like butter.

Fruit Cheese As butter (above) but thicker and set in a straight-sided pot. The cheese is turned out and sliced for serving, hence its name.

Fumet A well-flavoured fish or seafood stock.

Galantine Stuffed boned poultry or a neatly-tied stuffed piece of meat which is roasted, poached or boiled, then cooled. A chaud-froid coating should be applied to finish the galantine.

The term is commonly used for boned stuffed chicken, turkey or duck whether it is served hot or cold as tradition dictates.

Garnish The term used for decoration added to savoury foods and dishes.

The garnish should complement the main ingredients in a

dish as well as enhance the appearance of the food. In some instances the garnish may be eaten with the main food, for example sautéed mushrooms or croûtons are excellent garnishes.

A garnish may be used to add colour to bland dishes or to add texture to soft foods. For example, salad ingredients, blanched carrots, parsley or crisp-fried bacon pieces may be used.

Citrus fruit wedges may serve a dual purpose, providing colour as well as juice to squeeze over the food.

A poor garnish can ruin a dish. A slightly limp mound of untrimmed watercress with sad wedges of tomato washed up to one side of meat or poultry coated in a good sauce is one example of bad garnishing: the garnish cannot be eaten with the sauce, the bits of leaf are irritating as they intrude upon the food and the combination of ingredients is absurd.

• All garnishes should be freshly prepared and complementary to the main food in every way.

• Garnishes not intended for eating (for example, herb sprigs) should be small and neat.

• Unnecessary or over-extravagant garnishes spoil the appearance and eating quality of food.

Gâteau A highly decorative, rich cake. Based on a light sponge or including pastry, gâteaux may be served as desserts.

Genoese Sponge A Whisked Sponge (page 56) enriched with butter which is melted and folded in last, just before the mixture is baked.

Giblets Edible organs of poultry, including gizzard, heart, liver and the neck. Sold with poultry, found in a small sealed pouch in the body cavity of many birds.

The giblets may be boiled to make stock.

Gingerbread A classic melted cake made by the same method as used for Date and Walnut Cake (page 56). It is best wrapped in a polythene bag and allowed to mature for 2 days before eating.

Making Gingerbread
A cake made by the melted method. Follow the recipe for Date and Walnut Loaf (page 56), omitting the dates and walnuts. Add 15 ml/1 tablespoon ground ginger and 5 ml/1 teaspoon ground cinnamon with the flour. Heat 75 g/3 oz black treacle with the syrup and substitute 75 ml/5 tablespoons milk for the orange juice if liked. Mix and bake following the recipe instructions.

Gingerbread is also the term used for ginger biscuits, baked to crisp and dark gold.

Eastern European gingerbread can be quite different, made with boiled honey and spices but not with ginger.

Glaze The term has two meanings. A glaze may be brushed over food before cooking to improve browning or texture: beaten egg, egg yolk beaten with a little salt and water, milk or water may be used. Egg glaze (also known as egg wash) is used on savoury pastries and pies, also on breads; milk is used on sweet pastries. Water is brushed over breads to give a crisp crust.

A glaze may also be applied to cooked food or fruit. A syrup glaze may be brushed over freshly baked sweet breads. A glaze of fruit juice thickened with arrowroot may be used for fresh fruit.

Apricot glaze is boiled and sieved apricot jam, brushed over fruit, cakes or nut toppings on cakes. Honey and other preserves such as fruit jellies or sieved marmalade may be used as a glaze.

Goulash A Hungarian meat stew, generously seasoned with paprika. Soured cream is often served with goulash.

Gratin or Au Gratin Describes a dish with a browned, crisped topping – usually of breadcrumbs and often combined with cheese. Food may be coated in sauce before the topping is added but this is not an essential feature of a gratin.

Grease To rub with fat or brush with oil.

Griddle Also known as a girdle or baking stone, this is a heavy, flat cooking plate, usually of cast iron. For cooking Drop Scones (page 106) and crumpets as well as specialities such as Welsh cakes, griddle scones and potato scones.

Honey May be set or runny. There is a wide variety of types, depending on the source of the pollen from which the honey is produced by the bees. There are distinct flavour variations between types, some are highly scented with the essence of flowers or other plants.

Hotpot A stew of meat or poultry and vegetables, making a complete meal in itself. Lancashire hotpot is a good example – lamb, onions and carrots are stewed under a topping of potatoes.

Hull To twist the stalk and calyx off a strawberry.

Jamaican Pepper Another name for allspice.

Julienne Fine, evenly cut strips about the size of matchsticks. A cutting technique often used for vegetables, particularly carrots.

Kebab Skewered food, cooked under the grill, on a barbecue or baked.

Langue de Chat A thin finger of whisked sponge, baked until golden and crisp outside. Sponge finger biscuits are a manufactured alternative. Served with desserts or set into charlottes.

Lard Clarified pork fat, used for pastry-making as well as for frying.

The term is also used for a technique involving threading strips of pork fat through lean meat. Thin strips of pork fat are cut. The lean meat is pierced with a skewer, then lardons are threaded through the holes. A larding needle, with a serrated gripper to hold the end of the strips of fat, is used.

Pieces of lean venison, beef or other lean meat are larded to keep them moist during cooking. The lardons may be seasoned with herbs or spices before they are threaded.

Larding Needle A large, strong needle with a serrated clip instead of an eye.

Lardon Strip of fat for larding.

Laver Bread A Welsh speciality, made from cooked seaweed, combined with oatmeal to make a thick purée. Fresh laver bread is far superior to canned types. Pats of the mixture are coated in oatmeal and fried until crisp on both sides. Excellent with bacon.

Liaison The term is used for an emulsion of ingredients which do not mix easily. Hollandaise sauce, mayonnaise and vinaigrette dressing are examples of liaisons.

Macédoine A mixture of diced or small vegetables, including carrots, potatoes, turnips, onion and peas or beans.

The term may also be used for a cocktail of mixed fruit, cut into small pieces.

Macerate The term used when soaking fruit. Fruit may be macerated in alcohol, cold tea or juice. Flavouring ingredients such as spices may be added.

Madeleine Basic Creamed Mixture (page 54), baked in dariole moulds, then coated in jam and desiccated coconut when cold. Glacé cherries and angelica leaves are added for decoration.

French madeleines are made from a whisked sponge mixture baked in individual, shell-shaped tins.

Maid of Honour Individual pastry tartlet, spread with jam and topped with Basic Creamed Mixture (page 54), then baked until golden and set.

Mandolin A flat implement with a wide blade for slicing food, such as vegetables.

Marinate To soak food in a marinade. The term is applied to savoury foods, such as meat, poultry or vegetables.

Marmelade A fruit pulp boiled with sugar until thick. Rather like a fruit cheese or butter.

Medallion Or *medaillon* (the French term) refers to food cut into neat rounds or oval shapes. Typically applied to slices of meat cut from the fillet.

Melt To change from solid to liquid on the application of heat. Butter and other solid fats melt, and chocolate melts. The term is also used for substances that become more liquid, for example honey or liquid glucose both become runny when warmed.

Meunière A method of cooking fish very simply in butter. Small whole fish, dusted with flour are cooked this way and the cooking butter is served poured over.

Mocha A variety of Arabic coffee. The term is also used for the combined flavours of coffee and chocolate. Cakes or desserts in which both coffee and chocolate are used often take the name.

Molluscs Class of shellfish including bivalves and univalves, such as whelks and snails. Molluscs do not have bones but they have an intestinal sac and most types have the typical, tough shell which can enclose them completely. However, there are exceptions: squid is a member of the mollusc family.

Mornay Béchamel Sauce (page 35) flavoured with cheese. Also used for dishes coated with a cheese sauce.

Mould A container in which to set, freeze or bake food to produce a decorative or distinct shape. The moulded food may also be referred to as a 'mould'.

Mutton Meat obtained from sheep rather than lamb. Tougher and usually with more fat than lamb, mutton is not readily available; however if long braised or well stewed mutton has a good flavour.

Nibbed Cut into small pieces, slightly larger than chopped. Used for nuts.

Niçoise The term is used for dishes using ingredients such as tomatoes, garlic, olive oil, olives and anchovies, all common to the French region of the same name.

Noodles Strips of pasta.

Nut Butter Ground nuts pounded to a paste with their own oil. Peanut, hazelnut and mixed nut butters are available.

Olives Black, green and stuffed olives are readily available, both small and large. Stuffed olives may have pimiento, pieces of almond or anchovy fillet in them.

Olives are salted for several days before being pickled in brine or preserved in olive oil.

Organic The term applied to food produced by natural methods, without the use of artificial agricultural aids, such as fertilizers and pesticides. Establishing an organic production system, whether for crops or animal rearing, takes several years in order to allow substances used previously to work their way out of the system.

Organic food products are clearly marked as such on the labels or packets. Look for symbols indicating that the suppliers are members of a recognised body of producers.

In terms of flavour and value within the diet, current assessments of organic produce does not indicate that it is superior, other than in the case of meat, notably pork, which does have an improved flavour.

Panada A very thick roux sauce used as a base for thickening or for certain dishes, particularly soufflés.

Parboil To part cook by boiling. The food should be half cooked.

Parcook To part cook.

Pâte The French term for pastries such as *pâte brisée*, an equivalent to short crust, and *pâte sucrée*, a rich, sweet short pastry.

Pâté A smooth or coarse paste of fish, meat, offal or vegetables.

Paupiette A rolled thin fish fillet or slice of poultry or meat, usually spread with a stuffing or flavouring ingredients such as herb butter.

Pestle and Mortar The pestle is a pounding implement and the mortar a container. Used for grinding spices. A heavy pestle and mortar are useful for crushing seeds and for grinding items such as blades of mace. Lightweight implements are a waste of time.

Petits Fours Tiny, decorative biscuits, cakes and pastries or stuffed fruits. Served with coffee at the end of a meal or with tea.

Pilaf A Middle Eastern rice dish, usually consisting of rice, onions, raisins or currants and sweet spices such as cinnamon. Pine nuts or almonds may be added and the dish may be served with meat (often lamb) or poultry.

Pilau Other spellings include pullaw. Basmati rice cooked with sweet spices (cinnamon, cardamom, cumin) and a bay leaf, then enriched with fried onions or other ingredients. Saffron may be added towards the end of cooking to further enrich the flavour of the rice.

Pimento Pimiento is also used. Red peppers, usually bottled or canned. Sweet not hot.

Pith The white soft area under the skin of citrus fruit. It is bitter and should not be grated with rind.

Purée A smooth mixture made by sieving, liquidising or processing one or more ingredients. The mixture must be sieved to remove fibres or seeds.

Queen Cake Individual cake made using Basic Creamed Mixture (page 54).

Queen of Puddings Fresh breadcrumbs are soaked in egg custard mixture, then baked. A thick layer of good jam is spread over the custard, then a meringue topping is added and browned. The pudding may be served hot or cold.

Quenelle A light mixture of puréed fish, poultry or meat with eggs. Spoonfuls of the mixture, shaped into ovals, are poached gently in stock or water until set, then served with a sauce.

Quiche A savoury flan with a pastry case and a custard-based filling.

Ragoût A rich stew.

Ramekin A small, straight-sided ovenproof dish resembling a miniature soufflé dish. Individual soufflé dishes are larger than ramekins.

Ratafia Biscuits Small almond macaroons. Traditionally used in, or as a decoration on, trifle.

Réchauffé A dish of reheated cooked meat or poultry.

Refresh To rinse under cold running water and drain quickly. Used for cooked vegetables or blanched food. Refreshing prevents further cooking by residual heat.

Render To melt down fat. The pieces of fat may be placed in a heavy-based pan over low heat or in the oven. Another method is to boil pieces of fat with water until it melts, then to cool and lift off the fat.

Rennet Obtained from the stomach of an animal, rennet is used to coagulate milk when making junket.

Residual Heat Heat remaining after the source has been switched off or after food has been removed from a heat source. For example, heat in an oven after cooking, heat retained in a heavy-based pan or heat retention in food.

Rissole A small patty made from minced cooked meat, finely chopped onion, herbs and some mashed potatoes or breadcrumbs for binding. Rissoles may be coated with egg and breadcrumbs or flour and fried or grilled; they may also be baked.

Rock Cake Small rubbed-in bun, so named because of its peaked shape rather than texture.

Rose Water An essence of scented rose petals, this is used to flavour sweet dishes. Orange flower water may also be used in the same way. Available from chemists and specialist food shops.

Rusk Bread roll, split and baked at a low temperature until pale golden, dry and crisp.

Saccharometer An instrument similar to a hydrometer but used to measure the density of sugar in a syrup. Used when preparing candied fruits but not essential.

Salmis A twice-cooked dish of poultry or game. The bird is part-roasted, then cut into portions and braised in sauce.

Salsify An autumn root vegetable, salsify is similar to a thin parsnip in appearance. Scorzonera is black-skinned salsify. Prepare salsify just before cooking it. Have a pan or bowl of cold water with the juice of 1 lemon added or add 30 ml/2 tablespoons white wine vinegar or cider vinegar instead. Wash the roots well, then cut off the tops and ends. Peel the roots, rinse well and place in the acidulated water.

Simmer salsify for 50–60 minutes, or until it is tender.

Drain and serve with butter or coat in a sauce, such as Hollandaise Sauce (page 236) or Béchamel Sauce (page 35).

Samphire A plant found on coastal cliffs and dunes, this has long, bright green fronds. It is sometimes packed with shellfish or sold by fishmongers. It may be pickled in brine or vinegar.

The raw vegetable may be blanched and served with seafood or puréed in sauces. It may also be added to salad.

Sandwich Food enclosed between two slices of bread. The bread should be fresh and spread with a little butter or other fat to prevent any soft filling from being absorbed by the bread. Low-fat soft cheese or peanut butter makes a good alternative to butter or margarine.

Different types of bread may be used and the fillings may be sweet or savoury.

Open sandwiches have a base slice of bread with a decoratively arranged topping and a salad garnish – they are eaten with a knife and fork.

Club sandwiches have two or more layers of bread and fillings.

Sauté To cook quickly in a little fat over high heat, turning and rearranging the food often. The food should be browned when sautéed.

Savarin A rich yeasted batter baked in a ring tin until golden, then soaked in rum-flavoured syrup while hot. When cold, savarin is filled with fresh fruit and served as a dessert.

Savoury A savoury is served at the end of a meal, after the dessert. Portions should be small and flavoursome. Fingers of Welsh rarebit or a piquant anchovy relish are suitable.

Scalloped Sauced food edged with piped mashed potato and baked or grilled.

Sear To seal the surface of meat or poultry by placing it on a very hot, greased frying pan or griddle. This browns the outside of the food and seals in juices.

Shellfish The term for seafood with shells, including cockles, mussels, whelks and so on.

Shortbread Traditional biscuit made with butter, sugar and flour. Use 175 g/6 oz butter creamed with 75 g/3 oz icing sugar, then mix in 250 g/9 oz plain flour. Press into 2 15 cm/6 inch, greased round sandwich tins and prick all over. Chill for 30 minutes. Mark the edge with a fork and cut into 6 wedges. Bake at 160°C, 325°F, gas 3 for 50–60 minutes. Cool in the tin for 15 minutes, then on a wire rack.

Shortening An American term for white fat used to make pastry.

Shred Cut into strands or long pieces. Shredding is coarser than grating; however the shreds may be fine or coarse.

Shuck The term used for opening oysters.

Sieve To press a mixture through a sieve, then discard any residue. For removing pips or fibres from purées.

Sift To shake dry ingredients through a fine sieve or through a sifter (a container with a perforated lid). Flour and other dry ingredients are sifted.

Skillet An American term for frying pan. Also used to denote a frying pan of about 5 cm/2 inches deep with a lid.

Slake To mix to a thin paste with cold or other liquid, as when combining cornflour with liquid.

Slice Thin pieces of food with a large area. Slices may be thick, thin or of medium thickness.

Slivered Cut into fine strips or shreds. Used for nuts, notably almonds.

Souffléed A lightened mixture, usually by the addition of whisked egg whites. The mixture may be baked and the term is often used for a topping.

Soused Cooked or marinated in lightly spiced acidulated water, usually with bay, onion and vinegar. Oily fish, such as mackerel and herring, are soused and they may be served hot or cold.

Spatula A flat implement which may be rigid or flexible, for mixing or turning food. A flexible spatula is useful for scraping mixture out of bowls.

Sponge As well as being the term used for a light cake, this denotes the technique of sprinkling gelatine over water and leaving it to soak until it absorbs water, expands and looks sponge-like in texture.

String To scrape currants off their stalks using a fork.

Summer Pudding A delicious cold dessert, made by lining a large basin with thick slices of white bread (with crusts removed). The slices must overlap well. A mixed fruit filling is prepared: redcurrants should be poached with sugar, then strawberries, raspberries or other soft fruit may be added. Peeled, stoned and diced peaches, blackberries or cooked fruit may be used. When the basin is filled, a thick layer of bread should be placed on top and any remaining fruit juice poured over. The pudding must be weighted and chilled overnight.

Next day, the pudding is turned out just before serving it with whipped cream, fromage frais or thick yogurt.

Sundae An elaborate ice cream dessert with fruit and sauce.

Suprême The boneless breast of poultry. Also used for food served with a cream sauce.

Tainted The term for flavour contamination. Butter, milk and other dairy produce easily picks up flavours from other ingredients, such as jellies, garlic and dishes or foods with a strong aroma. The smell of fresh paint in a house can taint delicate foods.

Tart A French tart is a pastry case with a fruit filling but without a lid. A British tart has a double crust (base and lid) and it is baked in a shallow dish, on an ovenproof deep plate or tart plate. A lattice tart has a pastry base and a covering of pastry strips, crossed in a lattice.

Tenderise To make more tender, usually referring to meat. There are various methods: the food may be marinated or it may be beaten with a mallet. Enzymes present in certain fresh fruit (pineapple and papaya) have the effect of tenderising meat.

Terrine A lidded cooking dish. A coarse pâté may be referred to as a terrine, primarily because it is traditionally cooked in such a container.

Timbale A moulded item, usually set in a ramekin, small pot or basin, or large container then turned out.

Top and Tail To pick off the ends of gooseberries.

Trifle A traditional British dessert. A layer of sponge cake should be placed in a bowl. Homemade cake is best. The cake may be spread with good quality jam. A little sherry may be sprinkled over the cake or fruit juice may be used.

Fresh or canned fruit may be added next, then a thick topping of Confectioner's Custard (page 101) or thick Pouring Custard (page 103), made with an extra 2 whole eggs, should be added. The trifle should be chilled for several hours, then topped with whipped cream and decorated with ratafia biscuits or toasted flaked almonds.

There are many variations on this theme.

Trivet A perforated plate which is placed in the base of a cooking container to keep the food or container of food off the base. Used in a pressure cooker and roasting tin. In the latter case it allows fat to drip away from meat being roasted and prevents spitting.

Univalve Single-shelled shellfish or creature, such as abalone, whelk or snail.

Unmould To turn food out of a mould.

Victoria Sandwich Layer cake made from Basic Creamed Mixture (page 54) and sandwiched together with jam, then sifted with caster sugar.

Vine Leaves Leaves of grape vine, sold canned or vacuum packed. Rinse, boil for 5 minutes, then drain and stuff. May also be used to wrap food before roasting or grilling. Fresh are sometimes available.

Whisk To vigorously beat using an implement of the same name. A whisk is made of looped wire so that it traps and incorporates air into the food.

Egg whites are whisked; whole eggs with sugar are whisked to a foam; whole eggs may be beaten if worked alone and until frothy rather than thick.

Whisking is more prolonged than beating and it incorporates more air in a foam-like structure.

Zest The oils that spit from the rind of fresh citrus fruit. The term is also used to indicate the thin rind itself, although this is a confusing reference to be avoided.

The zest may be extracted from citrus rind by rubbing a sugar cube over the washed and dried fruit.

INDEX

A–Z ENTRIES

GENERAL TEXT

ACKNOWLEDGEMENTS

The author would like to thank the following for providing information used in the preparation of this book.

Aga-Rayburn
British Chicken Information Service
British Egg Information Service
British Food Information Service
British Gas Plc
British Meat
Cherry Valley Farms
Cranberry Information Bureau

Electricity Council
International Supply Co. Limited*
Lakeland Plastics**
Lever Brothers Limited
Milk Marketing Board
Prestige Group UK Plc
Sea Fish Industry Authority
Van den Berghs

* For information on the IFC Food Dehydrator. Address: PO Box 189, Granary House, The Grange, St Peter Port, Guernsey, Channel Islands.

** For Kitchen equipment and freezing equipment. Address: Lakeland Plastics, Alexandra Buildings, Station Precinct, Windermere, Cumbria LA23 1BQ.

BIBLIOGRAPHY

Davies, Jill and Dickerson, John **Nutrient Content of Food Portions** Royal Society of Chemistry
Fair Deal (A guide to shoppers' rights and family budgeting) Office of Fair Trading HMSO
Food Safety Act 1990 HMSO
Holland, B., Unwin, I.D. and Buss, D.H.,
    Cereals and Cereal Products The Third Supplement to McCance and Widdowson's Royal Society of Chemistry
    Milk Products and Eggs The Fourth Supplement to McCance and Widdowson's Royal Society of Chemistry
    Vegetables, Herbs and Spices The Fifth Supplement to McCance and Widdowson's Royal Society of Chemistry
Home Preservation of Fruit and Vegetables AFRC Institute of Food Research HMSO
Manual of Nutrition Ministry of Agriculture, Fisheries and Food HMSO
McGee, Harold, **On Food and Cooking The Science and Lore of the Kitchen** Unwin Hyman
Paul, A.A. and Southgate, D.A.T., **McCance and Widdowson's The Composition of Foods** HMSO

Note: a variety of leaflets on Food Safety and Nutrition is available from libraries and consumer organisations as well as in larger supermarkets.

HMSO publications are available from:

HMSO Publications Centre
(Mail and telephone orders only)
PO Box 276, London, SW8 5DT
Telephone orders 071-873 9090
General enquiries 071-873 0011
(queuing system in operation for both numbers)

HMSO Bookshops
49 High Holborn, London, WC1V 6HB   071-873 0011 (Customer service only)
258 Broad Street, Birmingham, B1 2HE   021-643 3740
Southey House, 33 Wine Street, Bristol, BS1 2BQ   (0272) 264306
9–21 Princess Street, Manchester, M60 8AS   061-834 7201
80 Chichester Street, Belfast, BT1 4JY   (0232) 238451
71 Lothian Road, Edinburgh, EH3 9AZ   031-228 4181

HMSO's Accredited Agents
(see Yellow Pages)

and through good booksellers

Printed in the United Kingdom for HMSO Dd294385 10.91 C100 3937/2C 12521